Eighth Edition

Retail Merchandising

John W. Wingate

Professor of Marketing Emeritus
The City University of New York

Harland E. Samson

Professor, Distributive Education
University of Wisconsin-Madison

S26

Published by

SOUTH-WESTERN PUBLISHING CO.

CINCINNATI   WEST CHICAGO, ILL.   DALLAS   PELHAM MANOR, N.Y.
PALO ALTO, CALIF.   BRIGHTON, ENGLAND

ISBN: 0-538-19260-7
Library of Congress Catalog Card Number: 73-83507

2 3 4 5 6 7 K 1 0 9 8 7 6 5

Printed in the United States of America

Preface

This, the Eighth Edition of *Retail Merchandising,* continues the primary aim of previous editions: to present to the young person considering a career in retailing the opportunity to gain understanding and competence in the activities in retail distribution of merchandise. The major emphases of the text center on the basics of retailing in a free enterprise society, the various functions within the operation of a retail merchandising business, and the importance and value of the individual worker in the retail firm. Not long ago most successful retail executives started at the bottom, gaining their knowledge and expertise largely through personal experience on the job. Today retail management, as never before, is turning to schools and colleges to provide future employees with basic information about the retail field and the skills it requires. This book is designed to fill this need.

Many retail innovations have been incorporated in the discussions of the appropriate functions. The use of automatic and electronic data processing, introduced in the Seventh Edition, has been integrated more thoroughly with retail record processing in Chapter 16. Emphasis has been given to the increasing concern about merchandise shortages by devoting one part of Chapter 17 to this important topic. Most major retail jobs have been explained in the context of the work that an employee will be expected to perform. Examples of how individuals eventually may become retail store owners have been added to provide models for students who may wish to pursue independent business careers. As an aid for those who wish to use the book as a resource for career information a special index has been included on retail careers and job references made throughout the text.

Where the retail merchandising course is preceded by a general study of marketing and distribution, Unit 1, including Chapters 1 and 2, may be given a quick review; and in-depth instruction may begin at Chapter 3. Portions of Chapter 19, "Planning a Career in Retailing," may be used as an introductory unit if students have not had career studies prior to the retail merchandising course; or this chapter may be included at any other point where occupational planning and job application are appropriate.

This book is designed for use in a full year's course. However, by omission of the more advanced topics, such as Unit 5, "Controlling the Store," and limited use of the end-of-chapter activities, the text may be satisfactorily used for a one-semester course.

Each chapter of the Eighth Edition of *Retail Merchandising* continues to be divided into five parts. Each part is followed by the key vocabulary terms introduced in that part, review questions, and discussion questions. At the end of each chapter there are skill-building exercises in communications and arithmetic, including, for most chapters, a problem on the metric system. (A special appendix has been included to aid in conversion to metric measures.) Also, there are activities which provide for development of research and decision-making skills. To help the student apply what has been learned in the chapter, there is a chapter project as well as a continuing project of the book which is the development of a manual for organizing and operating a retail store. The number of discussion questions and the end-of-chapter activities have been increased significantly in this edition.

The authors gratefully acknowledge the assistance and generosity of many retail firms and individual retailers as well as the numerous teachers of retail merchandising upon whose experience they have drawn.

They also with to express their indebtedness to the many companies that have provided photographs, particularly Federated Department Stores, Inc.; *Penney News*, J. C. Penney Company, Inc., for copyrighted material; Sears, Roebuck and Co.; Montgomery Ward; Flah & Co.; Monarch Marking Systems, a Subsidiary of Pitney Bowes; Key-Rec Systems, Division of SCM Allied/Egry Business Systems; Dayton Hudson Corporation; and others.

John W. Wingate
Harland E. Samson

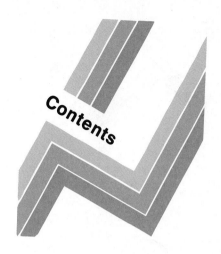

Contents

pg. 90 - lighting

v

UNIT 1
Retailing in America

The purpose of retailing is to provide a constant flow of goods and services to the consumer. Retailing is a servant: its function is to satisfy the merchandise and service needs and wants of each individual in a society. The retail merchant operates in a free competitive economy where individuals have freedom of decision. To an important degree the retail merchant contributes to the level of the standard of living enjoyed by Americans.

chapter 1

Production and Distribution

a. Freedom of choice, for both business and the consumer, is the basic ingredient of our American way of life.

b. Every person is an ultimate consumer. Consumer demand determines what the private enterprise system will provide.

c. Form utility is created by the producer; place, time, and possession utilities are created by other businesses.

d. The flow of a product from producer to consumer is called its channel of distribution.

e. The condition of the economy is judged by several economic measurements. Three major measures are (1) the gross national product, (2) the net national product, and (3) the national income.

Part a

The American Way—Freedom of Choice

The greatness of America rests with the freedom of the individual. Free people in a free economic system have the potential for a bountiful society. The individual has freedom to choose the type of work he will do and freedom to negotiate for the amount of money for which he will work. The individual has the freedom to choose how he will spend his money, where he will buy, what he will wear, the place where he will live, and even the person he will marry. These are decisions in which the individual has freedom of choice.

The traditional American emphasis on independence is expressed in the desire of many to own their own business. The possibility that any American with initiative, ability, and thrift can start a business and with hard work develop it into a successful enterprise spurs the imagination. The opportunity for business ownership is one of the characteristics of the American economic system.

ELEMENTS OF OUR PRIVATE ENTERPRISE SYSTEM

The economic system found in America is a *private,* or *free, enterprise system.* The theory behind this system is that, when businessmen are free to follow their own inclinations in business, those who serve their customers best and most efficiently will succeed and the inefficient will fail. Freedom of choice is the major element of the private enterprise system. Most Americans exercise their freedom of choice in what they will eat, wear, and use through purchases at retail stores. The activity of the retail stores is called *retailing,* which means the buying and selling of goods in small quantities to the individual consumers. The term *retail merchandising* tends to emphasize the planning aspects involved in the buying and selling activity. There are other elements besides freedom of choice, which set this economic system apart from all others. You will read about these elements in the following paragraphs.

Competition

Because freedom of choice exists for the buyer as well as for the seller, *competition*—the rivalry among businesses for buyers—is an important element of the private enterprise system. The force of competition has resulted in tremendous change and growth through the years and has improved living conditions for all of us. So long as there is competition, one person will struggle to do better than the next, and it is this struggle which results in progress.

Suppose a man opened a shoe store in a new community and enjoyed excellent demand for his line of shoes. Another man, seeing the store crowded, might decide to open a shoe store, too, and on that very same street. He has the freedom to do that. The demand for shoes in that community would now be divided between the two stores. In a little while, a third shoe store might open; but there probably would not be enough business for the three stores to operate successfully. One store might be forced to close its door. Competition decides which of these stores will succeed. The store that offers better quality and service, the same quality of goods and service at a lower price, or an assortment of goods well suited to an important segment of the market will usually succeed.

Competition serves as an invisible control of business. It forces stores to become efficient, to find and develop better products, to offer better services, to keep facilities up-to-date, and to lower prices. So keen is the struggle among stores for buyers that some stores offer everyday necessities at prices lower than those of rival businesses in an attempt to attract customers. This is called *price competition*. For discretionary goods (goods for which people make a choice), however, competition usually results in improved quality, better merchandise assortments, and more efficient service. This is called *nonprice competition*.

Adaptability to Change and Growth

Because people are free to compete with one another, there has been a continuous growth in our economy. This has meant a steady increase in incomes, better living conditions, and a constant expansion of the output of goods and services. Only in a free society can an individual profit by his ideas and by carrying them out. A free society grows on new ideas that may come from anyone. If a person gets an idea which he thinks will satisfy a human need or want, he is free to present it to a business firm. If the idea is rejected, he can approach another business firm or carry out his idea by going into business for himself. Changes in our economy are occurring all the time. Experimentation and development of new products and new processes are taking place all the time to meet the changes in the tastes of people.

Courtesy of Federated Department Stores, Inc.

Illus. 1-1   Some stores offer necessities at low prices in order to attract customers.

Ownership of Private Property

Individuals in our society may own property both for their personal use and for purposes of production and trade. Anything that persons can use, buy, or sell is called *personal property*. The right to buy and sell property and rights to property, such as patents and copyrights, means that individuals can personally gain on their business transactions.

Profit Motivation

The reasons for people engaging in the production and distribution of goods and services are mixed. The two main motivations of the businessperson are (1) to achieve the satisfaction of performing a useful service to others thus contributing to general prosperity and (2) to receive a monetary reward for his services equivalent to the effort, skill, and risk he has assumed. The excess of sales income above the costs and expenses of providing the goods and services is called *profit*.

Business can expand and keep abreast of the changes in customer demand only by reinvesting accumulated profits. The businessperson's own investment is called *capital*. He frequently adds to this investment by borrowing from others on *credit*—a promise to repay in the future. The total investment, while expressed in terms of money, is productive only when put into materials, merchandise, buildings, machinery and other equipment, and the payment of workers. Since our private enterprise system consists mainly of businesspeople investing in businesses, our economic system is often called *capitalism*. Under capitalism, the incentive of profit causes a businessperson to produce goods and services for public consumption in competition with other businesspeople. Since freedom of competitive action is limited by government regulation and by other social restraints, the system is also referred to as *modified capitalism.*

Many persons, much concerned with the great social needs of the population for better housing, medical care, public utilities, and transportation, have been critical of the profit motive. They argue that it leads to an unfair distribution of wealth and that businesspeople often put profit before community need, influencing people to buy gadgets and services which they don't really need. This leads to the neglect of expenditures in the "social sector" where many would benefit from better community facilities.

In answer, the defenders of our free system argue that people, not central planners, should decide the priorities for spending. If people are not spending their incomes wisely today, education must be relied upon to change their spending habits. It is true that some businesspeople push for quick gain regardless of social consequences, such as polluting the environment. However, the flexibility of our system and the opportunity for profit from supplying the changing needs of customers are major reasons for our country having the world's highest income.

BALANCE OF SUPPLY TO DEMAND

In a free and competitive economy producers and distributors are continuously attempting to balance supply with changing demand. If customers buy more ice cream, producers quickly increase the supply in order to meet the additional demand. If there is a decline in the demand for ice cream, production and retail inventories are promptly reduced.

A rise in demand may be accompanied by a rise in the price of the product to balance supply with demand. Likewise, an increase in supply often brings a cut in prices to encourage a demand equal to supply. Imbalance, however, does not necessarily mean price adjustments are needed. Producers are often able to increase the supply at no increase in unit cost and sometimes at a lower cost per unit. Nor does every drop in demand lead to lower prices. It may be wiser for the producer to make and sell fewer products at the old price than to try to stimulate demand by cutting prices.

Thus, in the free marketplace, supply is being continuously balanced to demand. Price changes are used as stimulants—they tend to reduce demand when prices are increased during periods of short supply, and they tend to increase the demand when prices are cut during periods of excessive supply.

COMPARISON WITH OTHER ECONOMIES

Free enterprise, with the profit motivation, is standard in the United States and many Western European countries. Many other countries, however, operate with other economic systems. In government-controlled economic systems, authorities of the state decide what and how much to produce. Customers are expected to purchase what is made available to them at prices set by the central administrators. There is very little freedom of choice. Of the over 800 million mainland Chinese, for example, 80 percent live in country communes. The Communist Party leadership directs enterprise in every commune, even controlling thought and intellectual life. Every peasant is assigned his task and shares in the basic foodstuffs produced by collective labor. He is also provided a small plot of land to grow vegetables for his own family. He pays a standardized rent out of his standardized wage. This system, void of the profit motive and of competition, depends upon the zealous loyalty to the goals of the leadership. While this system has brought stability and security to peasants, who had none in past generations, it has so far failed to result in a degree of productivity even close to that of the Western world.

CHECKING YOUR KNOWLEDGE

Vocabulary

The following terms were used in Part A. Learn their meanings and try to use them frequently in your conversation.

1. private, or free, enterprise system
2. retailing
3. retail merchandising
4. competition
5. price competition
6. nonprice competition
7. personal property
8. profit
9. capital
10. credit
11. capitalism
12. modified capitalism

Review Questions

1. What is the major element of the free enterprise system?
2. How does competition control business?
3. How does ownership of private property allow a person to make a profit?
4. In what ways is modified capitalism different from capitalism?
5. How is the supply of goods determined in a controlled economy?

Discussion Questions

1. Does individual freedom mean a person can do whatever he wants?
2. What obligations go along with ownership of private property?
3. How would the elimination of competition affect individual living standards?
4. Do you think that our long-established system of free enterprise needs a complete overhaul, as some economists argue, or do you think that the major change needed is an increase in the sense of responsibility for others?

Part b

The Consumers

Nancy wearing a new sweater, Tom eating a pizza, Mary getting on a bus, and Jim buying a dollar's worth of gas—all have something in common. They are all *consumers.* Any person who uses goods or services is a consumer. More precisely the final user of a product or service is the *ultimate consumer.* Nancy's sweater, Tom's pizza, Mary's bus ride, and Jim's gas were not purchased for resale. They were purchased for the individual's own use. Every person is an ultimate consumer, and it is the responsibility of retailing to provide the needed goods and services. A distinction should be made between a consumer and a customer. The former is the user, and the latter the one who makes the actual buying decision, who may or may not be the user. The businessman observes the activity of customers and assumes that they represent the needs and wants of consumers.

In addition to the ultimate consumer, *industrial, commercial,* and *institutional users* consume over half the dollar value of all manufactured goods. These users produce other consumer or industrial goods and services or operate institutions such as hospitals, schools, banks, and public buildings. All businesses in this country are set up to satisfy the needs and wants of these two classes of consumers—the ultimate consumer and the industrial, commercial, or institutional consumer.

In this book we shall center our attention on the ultimate consumer and on consumer goods. Because women play the dominant role in the purchase of consumer goods, we shall frequently speak of the ultimate consumer as *she* or as *her*.

FREEDOMS OF THE ULTIMATE CONSUMER

Today's American consumer has three relatively new freedoms which were not available to consumers of former generations. These three new freedoms are (1) the freedom to spend, (2) the freedom of time, (3) the freedom of action.

Freedom to Spend

Years ago most consumers had to limit their spending to necessities. They had very little surplus income to spend as they pleased. Today most families have considerable income that they may allot to any merchandise or service that appeals to them. It is this surplus income that provides our high standard of living and for which sellers actively compete by presenting to the consumer the special uses and benefits of their particular offerings.

Freedom of Time

The consumer today also has freedom of time. Working hours are usually 40 a week or less for the wage earner. And laborsaving equipment has provided the homemaker with more time for more varied pursuits, many of which demand spending for the appropriate merchandise and service.

Freedom of Action

Today's customer can also move about freely. In a few hours she can fly from New York to Los Angeles. She is now much more willing than in the past to move to a place distant in miles, provided that work opportunity or climate beckons. Such mobility has greatly increased the size and shape of our transportation industry and results in a more homogeneous population. This makes it possible for sellers to develop national markets for their brands and for stores to open additional outlets all over the country.

WHO IS THE CONSUMER?

Both manufacturers and retailers know that any sound marketing plan must begin with the consumer's interests and with the goal of satisfying her wants. It was her nod of approval that created main street, the great department stores, the giant supermarkets, the modern discount houses, the suburban shopping centers, the far-flung chains, and the famous brands.

The Average Consumer

Today's average consumer is an aggressive and critical customer who demands her money's worth and pays only for what she wants and gets. She is better educated, more sophisticated, and fonder of luxuries than her mother was. Her yearly family income exceeds $10,000. Formerly she did most of the shopping for all the family, but today male members of the family also participate in shopping trips. Today's average consumer is interested in fashion. She is more casual; more dependent on laborsaving devices; and more dependent on services, such as hair, beauty, and health care.

Other Important Consumers

It must not be assumed that all consumers are like the average just described. Even though the standard of living has risen generally over the past decade, there are still a great many consumers who live at a bare subsistence level. Many of these show very little interest in fashion and service and always seek bargains. At the other extreme are the well-to-do who commonly demand maximum personal attention and the latest fashions and expect to pay substantial prices.

The life span of the average American has increased to 70 years. About 10 percent of the population is over 65, and this proportion is increasing. In an attempt to appeal to this increasingly large number of senior citizens, businesspeople are studying the particular needs and wants of this group. At the other end of the range of consumer age groupings is a large segment of babies and small children. Their individual consuming habits must be studied by businesspeople who sell products for this age group. In between are the preteen age group, the teenager, the young man and young woman, and the middle-aged.

Teenagers have received more attention because their number has increased very rapidly in proportion to the total population. They have their own money to spend and exert a great deal of influence on family spending. Certain major industries today—the recording industry, for example—would be very minor ones were it not for the teenage market.

Nevertheless, the most rapidly growing segment of the consumer market today is the young adult. This group spends its income freely and even borrows in order to set up its households.

United States Population by Age Groups *			
Age	1970 Population	1985 Population	Increase
0-14	57.9 million	69.4 million	11.5 million
15-24	36.1	39.1	3.0
25-34	25.1	40.4	15.3
35-44	23.1	31.4	8.3
45-54	23.2	22.0	− 1.2
55-64	18.6	21.4	2.8
65 plus	20.1	25.5	5.4

* U.S. Department of Commerce, Bureau of the Census, Statistical Abstract of the United States (Washington: U.S. Government Printing Office, 1971) p. 8.

Illus. 1-2   Note that the young adult is the fastest growing segment of the population. How will the shifts in population by age group probably affect retail sales in total and by type of merchandise during the decade ahead?

INFORMING AND PROTECTING THE CONSUMER

When money was scarce in the early 1930's, consumers became more and more concerned with ways and means of getting as much as possible for their money. Advertisers frequently made unjustifiable claims, and customers were often disappointed with their purchases. They resolved to do something about it. At first, the consumer's struggle for more knowledge and protection was unorganized, but eventually it evolved into what was known as the *consumer movement*. It attracted the support of government and business organizations, with the result that today both government agencies and private groups help the consumer to become a wise buyer.

Independent Advisory Services

Independent groups that provide merchandise advisory services for the consumer are Consumers' Research, Inc., and the Consumers' Union of the United States, Inc. These evaluate and recommend specific brands. Others are the consumer institutes of *Good Housekeeping* and *Parents' Magazine* and the Better Business Bureaus, financed by businessmen, that offer aid to consumers subjected to unethical selling practices. In addition, companies, such as Sears, Roebuck and Co., General Motors, and General Electric, operate testing laboratories to assure satisfactory products that will meet the changing and exacting demands of today's consumer.

Major Consumer Population Changes

Growth of the Population

Following a sharp increase in births right after World War II, the rate of growth of the population has been slowing and is now about 1.2 percent a year. The rate of growth varies in different parts of the country.

Urbanization

The population is concentrated in cities and suburbs. The farm population now accounts for less than 7 percent of the total population.

Age Distribution

The age group that is currently showing the largest increase in number is the group comprising the young adults. In the late 1960's it was the teenage group that was enjoying the greatest increase, accounting in part for the great emphasis on youth.

Size of Family

The size of the average family, nearly four in the mid-60's, has been declining.

Incomes

The median family income today is about $10,000, compared with only $3,000 in 1947. By 1980, the figure is expected to reach $15,000.

Distribution of Income

The middle class is the great consumer market for the majority of retailers. Families earning $5,000 to $15,000 a year receive about 60 percent of total consumer income, compared with only 40 percent in 1955.

Source of Family Income

Over a third of the families in the country have two or more bread-winners, and the ability to buy on credit augments purchasing power considerably.

Techniques of Communication

Television is now tending to surpass the printed media as the consumer's major means of obtaining knowledge. The telephone is replacing correspondance and personal visits in two-way com-munications with others.

Illus. 1-3   The retailer should know a great deal about the cus-tomer he serves. These characteristics are always changing, and if the retailer is to meet customer needs he must know what they are.

Major Changes in the Life-Style of Consumers

Mobility

Consumers have more freedom than ever before to move about; they have more free time and have never had more money to spend as they wish.

Leisure Time

The work week has been sharply shortened, in some instances to only four days a week. Many laborsaving devices are now available to the homemaker, greatly reducing the amount of time that must be devoted to household care.

Physical Well-Being and Security

Good health and a healthy appearance are highly prized by most; and there is a sharp demand for personal security—social security, national health care, pensions, unemployment insurance, and public housing.

Education

More young men and women are entering college, and many are working for advanced degrees. College enrollment has doubled in the last ten years, with many adults taking noncredit courses in continuing education. Increased education has developed a more sophisticated customer with better judgment about merchandise values and with less dependence upon national brands as the symbol of quality.

Demand for Services

Consumers are alloting an increasing portion of disposable income to services—currently about 40 percent. Family budgets for travel and health, beauty care, and entertainment are growing. There is even a trend towards leasing goods, such as cars and appliances, rather than buying them.

Insistence upon Meaningful Work

People are rebelling against the tedious performance of many routine and repetitive tasks. Jobs that require only mechanical skill and provide no opportunity to make decisions nor to apply imagination or creativity are held in low esteem. Workers want to become involved in the broader dimensions of a project or product and contribute to more than a single segment.

Illus. 1-4   The life-style of consumers means their behavior or activities as they work and play. Such life-styles are important indicators of what people want. As people change their daily behavior, new products and services for new ways of living are needed.

Consumer Legislation

The public concern over the rights and safety of the consumer has resulted in local, state, and federal legislation. Significant legislation affecting the retail phase of distribution is presented in Chapter 18.

Since consumer problems are encountered locally, not nationally, it is not surprising that most activity for consumer protection and education has been at state and local levels. Perhaps the toughest program is that of the Consumer Affairs Department of New York City. It polices truth-in-lending practices, unfair collection procedures, and misleading advertising and sales techniques. The Health Department in the same city reports publicly restaurants and markets that fail to meet strict standards of sanitation.

Trends in Consumerism

Even with the considerable consumer-educating and consumer-protecting services, buyers will purchase by trial and error. It has been determined that purchasers often buy on "emotion" rather than use their knowledge of quality, price, and dependability of an item. So long as emotional buying motives exist, knowledge about items will not fully determine the buyer's selection. This fact, however, should not stop government and other agencies from giving the consumer more adequate aid.

Continued concern for the consumer's welfare will produce very practical gains for both the consumer and the retailer. First, consumerism will increase the amount and quality of product information. Second, misleading and ineffective promotional expenditures will be reduced or eliminated. Third, unsafe or unhealthful products will be more quickly identified and corrected. Fourth, consumerism will demand that manufacturers be socially and environmentally responsible.

CHECKING YOUR KNOWLEDGE

Vocabulary

1. consumer
2. ultimate consumer
3. industrial user
4. commercial user
5. institutional user
6. consumer movement

Review Questions

1. How do industrial consumers differ from ultimate consumers?
2. What three freedoms are enjoyed by the modern ultimate consumer?
3. What are some of the characteristics of the average consumer?
4. What information sources are available to the consumer who wants to know more about goods?
5. List four gains that will result from continued consumerism.

Discussion Questions

1. How do changes in consumer life-styles affect the nature of consumer goods?
2. Which of the changes in consumer characteristics would be of greatest interest to an owner of a clothing store?
3. For what kinds of consumer goods do you believe governmental protection would be most important?
4. Congress recently set up a Consumer Product Safety Commission to protect the public against unsafe goods. Hazards found in a product are to be reported to the Commission that will set standards of composition, construction, performance, etc., to reduce unreasonable risk of injury. Which types of products are likely to require special attention? Do you think this Commission can assure the safety of all consumer products?

Part **C**

The Producers

That wonderful musical instrument of swinging sound, the trumpet, contains two and one-half pounds of brass. To obtain enough brass for one trumpet, 250 pounds of copper and zinc ore must be extracted from the earth, smelted, and refined. A ladder-back chair contains less than six board feet of lumber. Yet it takes the better part of several hundred board feet to get the right grain and match for a piece of fine furniture. All consumer goods have their origin in our natural resources. The way that nature's products are changed into valuable consumer goods represents man's response to challenge. Every retailer should be familiar with how his merchandise was created from nature.

PRODUCTION AND UTILITY

Production in the broadest sense means the creation of utility. *Utility* is an economic value in goods that makes them useful to consumers. Any person or organization which produces or creates useful goods and services to sell is said to be "in business." Businesses supply form, place, time, and possession utilities to the raw materials that they produce or process.

Under the broad definition of production given here, all our farms, manufacturing industries, mines, construction firms, hotels, restaurants, theaters, personal service industries, business service industries, banks, transportation businesses, and retail and wholesale places of business are producers. All these businesses must produce something of value in order to succeed. In a narrower and more customary sense, the producer is the creator of form utility—he is either the extractor of raw materials or the manufacturer.

The Extractor

The production of some of nature's products can be controlled by man, while the supply of other natural products is fixed by nature. The farmer can control the production of such crops as fibers, fruits and vegetables, grains, tobacco and rubber, animals raised on a farm and the products obtained from them. His work is of utmost importance to the consumer, for some of his agricultural products need no processing and are used by the consumer just as they come from his farm.

The fisherman who takes animal life from the sea can control only his "catch," not the supply of seafood. Like the farmer, the fisherman is an *extractor* and supplies raw materials to industry for drying, canning, or freezing, and fresh seafood for the consumer.

Forest products are supplied by the lumberman. A small portion of his raw material is used by the consumer as firewood, but most goes to industrial users to be converted into consumer products.

Copper, iron ore, coal, petroleum, and other minerals are extracted from the earth by the miner. The supply of these raw materials is fixed by nature, and companies engaged in their extraction and in the manufacture of products coming from them are continuously searching for new sources of supply. Consumers seldom use minerals as they come from the earth. Minerals, like most other raw materials, must go through one or more changes before they can be used by the consumer.

The Convertor or Manufacturer

The conversion of extracted raw materials to materials and products useful to the consumer is the major activity of manufacturing. Materials are brought in at one end of the factory and moved from one point to another where they are subjected to various treatments by means of labor and machines. This is called *assembly-line production* and is found in nearly all our modern manufacturing plants.

If a pencil had to be made by hand, it could never be sold for a nickel. Thousands, or even millions, of pencils have to be produced in order to bring the cost of production down. The use of machinery to manufacture great numbers of the same kind of an article in our modern factories is called *mass*, or *large-scale*, *production*. In addition to the use of costly machinery, a large-scale producer buys his materials in large quantities and ships to his customers in large quantities.

The builder is a major form of convertor. Until recently most of the construction process took place at the building site, but the builder is now employing factory techniques. He prefabricates parts of the structure in a factory setting or constructs *modular homes*. These homes are then moved to the building site, virtually ready for occupancy.

Producers today manufacture items scientifically. Many have established engineering and research divisions which find new items to manufacture and discover how to improve old ones. New equipment and new methods of production, which tend to lower costs, are also being studied and discovered by engineers. Furthermore, today's modern large-scale manufacturer has scientifically trained personnel to manage labor and capital. Only when there is a proper balance among orders, labor, power, and machinery can a large-scale producer make money. Properly trained executives maintain this balance.

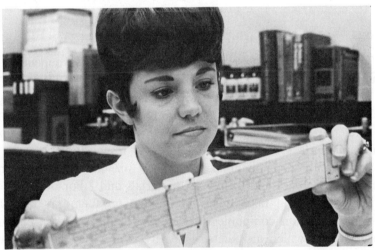

Courtesy of Eli Lilly and Company

Illus. 1-5   Today products are manufactured scientifically. Research divisions develop new items and improve existing ones.

CREATION OF THE FOUR UTILITIES

Consumers use goods because they need or want them. For instance, suppose a boy is ordered by his doctor to eat a hot cereal every day for breakfast. He now has a need for the wheat, corn, or oats that a farmer raises. But he has no use for the grain in its raw state. He must have it in the form of a breakfast cereal. So he looks to the manufacturer to give it a new form, to refine it, to clean it, to make it edible, and to package it. On the farm the wheat or corn is of little value to the boy. The manufacturer, by means of labor and machinery, changes the raw grain to a breakfast food and gives it *form utility*. But the boy cannot yet use it, since the finished box of breakfast cereal is still in the manufacturer's plant. The cereal has to be transported to a place where the customer can readily procure it. Thus, the manufacturer ships it in large lots to a wholesaler who delivers it in small lots to the retailer. The box of breakfast cereal now has *place utility*.

It is not enough to have goods available at the right place—they must also be available at the time the boy decides to procure the cereal for his needs. Thus, we say that the goods must possess *time utility*. Even though the cereal is available on the grocer's shelf at the right time, the boy still has no right to use it. He or his mother has to purchase it from the retailer. At that moment—the sale of the cereal—*possession (ownership) utility* is created. Thus, before it is ready for consumption, the cereal has acquired four utilities.

SUPPORTING AGENCIES

The producer, whether extractor or convertor, is dependent upon a number of specialized agencies in the creation of utilities.

Transportation companies move materials and supplies by rail, truck, boat, air, and pipeline. They are creating place utility by moving raw materials from the extractor to the manufacturer and finished goods and parts from the manufacturer to his customers.

Banks and other financial institutions provide funds to construct plants and machines and to pay for materials and labor during the conversion process that takes place before the product may be sold.

Communication companies provide the media to carry informative messages upon which all business activity is now dependent. The telephone, the telegraph, the newspaper, the magazine, the direct-mail piece, the television, the radio, and the newer audiovisual devices allow the producer to talk with his sources of supply and with the markets for his product.

The distributors, whom we shall discuss in the next part, also make use of these agencies in the conduct of their business affairs and could not function without them.

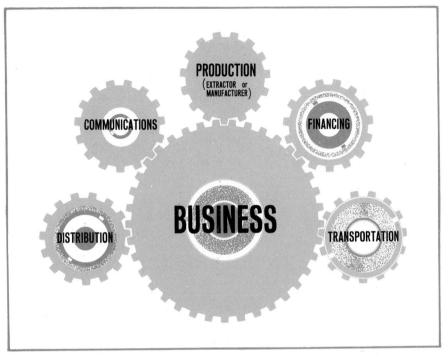

Illus. 1-6   No business can exist without other businesses. The interdependence of businesses engaged in production, distribution, transportation, financing, and communication is pictured above.

MODERN PRODUCTION TECHNOLOGY

The techniques and processes of industry, manufacturing, and construction are the results of important discoveries in science and technology. The electronic transistor, polyester fibers, laser beam, and hosts of similar developments have meant improved production procedures, more effective equipment, and ultimately more and better consumer goods. The computer controlled machine, the robot welder, inspection by closed circuit television—each are examples of technology used in the production of consumer goods. Application of technology to mass production of goods allows producers to deliver a continuous supply of new and better merchandise for personal consumption. Modern production technology is not limited to big business. Many of the ideas are developed and used in smaller independent productive businesses.

The miracle of modern production permits much of what the consumer uses today to come from far places and often unexpected sources. The curtains in a home may come from a chemical combination of alcohol and acids. Furniture may be made from South American fruitwood laminated over Georgia pine. The main ingredients of a frozen dinner may be chicken from Iowa, rolls from North Dakota wheat, Idaho potatoes, and California berries for the tart. All these products came originally from nature, and through processing they are converted into consumer goods.

CHECKING YOUR KNOWLEDGE

Vocabulary

1. production
2. utility
3. extractor
4. assembly-line production
5. mass, or large-scale, production

6. modular homes
7. form utility
8. place utility
9. time utility
10. possession, or ownership, utility

Review Questions

1. List four different kinds of extractors.
2. What is a major advantage of mass production?
3. What is the difference between *place* utility and *time* utility?
4. How does the creation of the four utilities help the consumer?
5. How does modern technology assist the convertor?

Discussion Questions

1. What kinds of goods can the consumer use directly from the extractors?
2. What might happen if no new technological changes were made in the production of consumer goods?
3. What problems would the consumer have were is not for *place* utility?

Part d

The Distributors

A major manufacturer produces 12 million men's shirts annually. The production and packaging of 12 million shirts is not enough. These shirts must reach the people who will buy and wear them. The shirts must be *distributed* to ultimate consumers. A whole group of businesses has therefore developed which is chiefly concerned with the task of marketing or distributing the goods produced. These businesses are called *distributive businesses,* and they serve as the connecting link between the producers and the consumers.

THE FLOW OF MERCHANDISE

The path that an item takes on its way from the producer or manufacturer to the consumer is called its *channel of distribution*. At one end of the road is the producer, and at the other end of the road is the consumer. There may be stops, detours, forks in the road, and even bottlenecks, all of which make the distribution of goods to the consumer a long and costly affair. Yet there is a need for new methods of distribution. The economies of large-scale production have surpassed the savings realized in our methods of distribution. Looking at the total cost of an item, the proportionate cost of producing the item has decreased while the proportionate cost of distributing the item has increased. This does not mean that our methods of distribution are inefficient. It merely means that the technological improvements of production have not lowered costs in the field of distribution. Newer ways of getting the goods from the producer to the consumer for less cost is a problem which is a challenge to the knowledge and imagination of students of distribution.

From Producer Directly to Consumer

At first glance it would seem that moving goods directly from the producer—whether he be manufacturer, grower, or extractor—to the consumer is the simplest channel of distribution. This method is used infrequently, however. In the case of tailor-made men's clothing and some farm products, this path is the means by which the producer gets his goods to the consumer. A simple example of this route is the consumer's purchase of garden products direct from the farmer.

While this method of distribution is excellent for some perishable goods or for goods manufactured to the specifications of an individual consumer, for most merchandise it is more expensive than it seems. For a large manufacturer to attempt to make sales contacts with thousands or even millions of consumers would cost much more than it would to move goods through more involved channels.

However, some manufacturers, notably the Fuller Brush Company and the Avon Company, have quite successfully used this method of distribution. When a firm employs salespeople to contact customers and demonstrate merchandise from door to door, the *direct-selling* method of distribution is being used; but it is seldom the most economical.

Channels with One Middleman

When a producer finds that consumers cannot get to him in large numbers or that he cannot get to them, he may choose to distribute his goods through a retail store. The retail store can give him wide distribution at a lower cost. Thus, one middleman is introduced into the channel of distribution. A *middleman* is any dealer who is responsible for the distribution of goods from producer to ultimate consumer.

Distribution through a retail store gives the consumer an opportunity to choose from a larger assortment than one manufacturer produces and permits the consumer to make selections locally rather than traveling to the manufacturers' showrooms. When the retailer buys merchandise directly from the manufacturer it is called *buying direct.*

The retailer who buys direct gains the advantage of newer fashions, lower prices in many instances, and often receives the benefit of manufacturers' *sales aids,* such as advertising and display material. On the other hand, the retailer may have to forego some of the services given him by the service wholesaler, such as immediate delivery, easy ordering of many kinds of goods together, and liberal credit.

Channels with Two Middlemen

If a store does not need to buy goods in large quantities, it may be easier to buy from a wholesale middleman than it is to buy direct. The goods then make two stops on their way to the consumer. The first stop is at the wholesaler's, and the second is at the retailer's.

Wholesalers are dealers who buy from producers or other wholesale dealers and sell to retailers or to institutional, industrial, or commercial users. Thus, some specialize in selling goods to such institutions as hotels, hospitals, and schools. Others sell materials, supplies, and parts to producers. Wholesalers that sell primarily to retailers are sometimes called *wholesale merchants.* They buy goods outright and generally store them and then resell them through salesmen. Ordinarily they grant credit to their retail customers, and they make deliveries.

The wholesaler is the retailer's usual source of supply for convenience and staple items. Food, drugs, and stationery, for example, are sold in many small stores all over the country and are produced by thousands of manufacturers and packers. For each producer to make direct contact with each retailer would involve a costly and cumbersome selling process. Thus, if 1,000 retailers each bought direct from 100 producers a month, they would have to make 100,000 sales contacts. But if a wholesaler acts as an agent between the retailers and the producers, only 1,100 contacts are required. Each of the 1,000 retailers can order all products at once from the wholesaler, who can consolidate the orders and replace his stock by means of 100 orders with the producers. Such a reduction in the necessary number of contacts needed to move a specific quantity of goods greatly reduces the selling costs for manufacturers and the buying costs for buyers. Transportation costs are likewise decreased. It costs much less to ship a large lot a long distance from producer to wholesaler and then to break it up into several small lots and ship them a short distance than to ship each of many lots a long distance.

The small retailer may find it advantageous to purchase from a wholesaler for one or more of the following reasons:

1. The wholesaler will sell in small quantities.
2. There may be no saving in buying from the manufacturer direct.
3. Transportation charges from the manufacturer to retailer may consume any saving in direct buying.
4. The wholesaler provides quick delivery and may offer better credit and other services than the manufacturer.
5. Time and effort are saved by placing one large order with the wholesaler rather than by dealing with many manufacturers.
6. It is unnecessary for the retailer to foresee his requirements far ahead. He can procure goods promptly from the wholesaler as needed.

Large retail concerns, of course, purchase in sufficient quantity to deal economically direct with many manufacturers. Chains of retail stores also set up their own wholesale warehouses to service their own stores. Thus, they perform the wholesale function even though they do not buy from wholesale merchants. Even the largest department and chain stores, however, handle some items in such small quantities that it pays them to purchase from wholesale merchants.

Channels with Three Middlemen

The paths of some goods pass three middlemen before they eventually reach the consumer. The goods pass first through agent middlemen, then wholesalers, and finally retailers on their way to the ultimate consumer. The *agent middlemen* assist in the sale of goods but do not own the goods in which they deal. There are two main types of agents: commission merchants and brokers. *Commission merchants* handle the physical goods in which they deal. *Brokers* do not handle the goods, but simply help sellers find buyers or buyers find sellers.

From the viewpoint of the retailer, the commission merchant is very similar to a wholesaler. Since he does not own the goods in his possession, however, he may not be free to set the price or the terms of sale. If he is given this authority, he is then a *sales agent*.

Commission merchants are often exclusive agents for the distribution of certain manufacturers' products in territorial regions. These

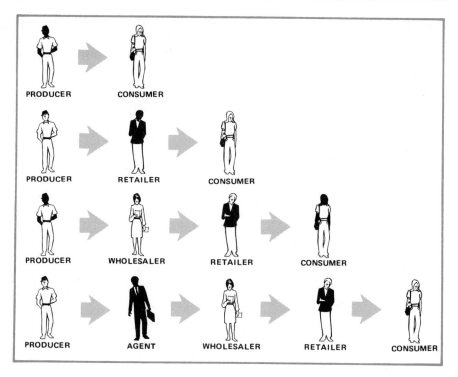

PRODUCER   CONSUMER

PRODUCER   RETAILER   CONSUMER

PRODUCER   WHOLESALER   RETAILER   CONSUMER

PRODUCER   AGENT   WHOLESALER   RETAILER   CONSUMER

Illus. 1-7   A channel of distribution with no middlemen is commonly used for door-to-door selling. Women's clothes may be distributed through one middleman, while products such as drugs may travel through two middlemen. Some food lines are even distributed through three middlemen.

are called *manufacturers' agents*. They sell to wholesalers, large department stores, and chains. The retailer who buys from such commission merchants is virtually buying direct from manufacturers, for these merchants function as the manufacturers' sales departments.

Although each middleman adds his expenses and a little profit before he passes the goods on to the next middleman, the services he performs in buying, selling, storing, and perhaps grading the goods usually justify the cost. In the past, producers and retailers have tried to bypass the wholesale middleman so that the cost of goods would be lower for the consumer, but up to the present time no other more efficient system has evolved for the marketing of many staples.

Combination of the Channels of Distribution

While it is possible to buy goods that pass through only one channel of distribution, most stores use two or more channels. For instance, a drugstore may buy soap, toothpaste, and certain creams direct from the manufacturer if these items are handled in quantity. Yet that drugstore may buy combs, rubber bands, stationery, bathing caps, sunglasses, and many other items from a drug and sundry wholesaler, since it does not handle enough of one item to permit it to buy economically from the many different manufacturers involved.

PHYSICAL DISTRIBUTION

A distinction is made between the physical distribution of merchandise and the channels of distribution. *Physical distribution* consists of transporting goods and storing them. The responsibility for finding a market for the goods may pass through the hands of numerous middlemen.

For example, a manufacturer may store his goods in a public warehouse and arrange with a commission agent to find a wholesale distributor. A wholesaler may agree to buy the goods but continue to store them in the warehouse. The wholesaler may provide his retail customers with samples to show their customers. When a sale is made to the ultimate consumer, the retailer may order the wholesaler to ship the goods directly to the consumer and not to the retail store. When shipped, the goods will be billed by the wholesaler to the retailer. Thus, the physical distribution may be limited to transportation to the warehouse, storage there, and finally shipment to the consumer. The marketing channel would, however, consist of the commission agent, the wholesaler, and the retailer. None of these middlemen have handled the physical goods. However, all have assumed either ownership or selling responsibility or both.

THE COST OF DISTRIBUTION

The cost of distributing goods is shared by the producers and the middlemen involved. For consumer goods, the costs of distribution frequently exceed the costs of production. In fact, the typical consumer goods manufacturer spends about half his sales dollar on his marketing activities. These include planning, advertising, sales promotion, marketing research, personal selling, field services, and pricing. Companies with the highest relative marketing costs include producers of drugs and beauty aids. Somewhat lower is the cost of marketing foods. Lower still are gasoline and home appliances. Increased sales volume tends to reduce relative marketing costs, provided the amount of service required is not increased.

CHECKING YOUR KNOWLEDGE

Vocabulary

1. distributed
2. distributive businesses
3. channel of distribution
4. direct selling
5. middleman
6. buying direct
7. sales aids
8. wholesaler
9. wholesale merchant
10. agent middlemen
11. commission merchant
12. broker
13. sales agent
14. manufacturers' agents
15. physical distribution

Review Questions

1. For what types of goods is the producer direct to consumer channel most appropriate?
2. What is meant by a middleman?
3. What special purpose does the wholesaler perform in a channel of distribution?
4. Why do some large retailers deal directly with the manufacturer?
5. What is the difference between the channel of physical distribution and the channel of distribution as generally understood?

Discussion Questions

1. What factors must a producer consider in deciding which channel of distribution to use?
2. What value is added to goods handled by middlemen between the producer and consumer?
3. In what ways do the communications industry and the transportation industry assist in distribution of consumer goods?

Part e

Measurement of Our Economic Growth

The word *economy* has many meanings. When used in a business sense it means "a system of producing, distributing, and consuming wealth." If someone asks, "How is the economy?" he is referring to the condition of the system. The ways in which we measure the condition of production, distribution, and consumption of the nation's wealth should be understood by every student of retailing. Terms, such as *gross national product, personal income,* or *discretionary fund,* contain concepts essential for analyzing the economy.

MEASUREMENT OF THE ECONOMY AS A WHOLE

It is important that economic measurements be given for both the economy as a whole and for segments of the economy. The most meaningful measures of the economy as a whole are (1) the gross national product, (2) the net national product, and (3) the national income.

Gross National Product

The *gross national product* is the market value of this country's total output of goods and services during a given period of time. It is usually expressed in terms of a year. The gross national product, commonly abbreviated as the GNP, has four major components: (1) personal consumption expenditures, (2) gross private domestic investment, (3) net exports of goods and services, and (4) government purchases of goods and services.

Changes in the GNP, as reported by the Department of Commerce, are watched closely by all businessmen and government officials. These changes reveal how the country is progressing economically. Since World War II the GNP has grown an average of about 4 percent a year. Currently the annual GNP is over a trillion dollars. Increased spending and investing by major segments of our economy are signals to businessmen, including retailers, that sales opportunities may be expanding.

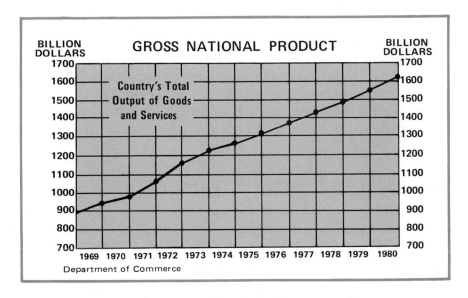

Illus. 1-8   1973 to 1980 figures are estimated on a basis of 4¼ percent annual long-range growth of GNP.

The growth of the GNP depends primarily upon three things: (1) the growth of the population, (2) the growth of the labor force, and (3) the productivity of each worker. Population is currently growing at the rate of about 1¼ percent each year. The labor force is growing at a somewhat lower rate because of the growing proportion of children and retired persons not included in the working force. Productivity per man hour of work is increasing at about 2½ percent a year. Taking all these statistics into consideration, experts predict that the present trend of the GNP will continue.

Net National Product

Each year some machinery, equipment, and buildings are used up in the production of goods. They receive wear (depreciate) or become out of date (obsolete). The amount of money lost because of depreciation or obsolescence is deducted from the GNP to give a more realistic measure of our economy's production. The figure which results after these deductions are made is known as the *net national product*.

National Income

Another concept that all students of retailing should understand is the nature of national income. *National income* is the total earnings of labor and business owners resulting from the production of the GNP. The amount of national income may be calculated by deducting from the net national product certain indirect business taxes—such as sales taxes—and some other minor items.

The national income figure may be broken down into the following categories: (1) compensation for employees, (2) proprietors' (owners) incomes, (3) rental income of persons, (4) corporate profits, and (5) net interest. Employees receive over 70 percent of the national income, and proprietors receive about 10 percent. Less than 20 percent goes to the owners of real property and capital.

MEASUREMENT OF CONSUMER INCOME AND EXPENDITURES

The economy of our country cannot show growth without an increase in consumption. By buying or not buying, the consumer influences what is produced, how much is produced, and for whom it is produced. And the consumer thus influences all the measures of our economy as a whole.

There are certain kinds of information which are regularly collected about the consumer and with which the retailer should be familiar. The consumer information in which retailers are most interested concerns personal income, disposable personal income, and consumer expenditures.

Personal Income

Personal income, as expressed for all persons in the country, is the total income of all persons from all sources. (Personal income may also be expressed as the total income of one individual from all sources.) The personal income for all persons in the country may be figured by deducting from the national income taxable corporate income and undistributed profits, social security payments, government and business transfer payments (payments of money for which no current goods or services are produced), and a few other minor items. Total personal income in 1973 was more than one trillion dollars. Illus. 1-9 shows the growth of the average family income and how it is shared by each fifth of the families, arranged by income size.

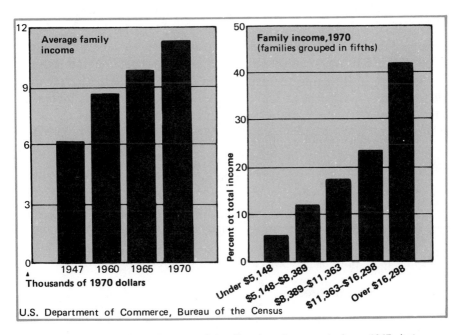

U.S. Department of Commerce, Bureau of the Census

Illus. 1-9   Real income of families has increased since 1947, but income shares in 1970 show large variations.

Disposable Personal Income

Retailers across the country are most interested in the disposable personal income that consumers have. *Disposable personal income* is the amount of money consumers actually have to spend. It is calculated by deducting from the personal income figure all state, local, and federal taxes that consumers must pay.

Discretionary Income. Until a generation ago, disposable personal income provided for most people only enough for basic living requirements, enough to maintain a minimum standard of living. For the average family, the cost of such a minimum standard of living has been estimated at about $5,300. The difference between a person's total disposable income and the cost of his minimum standard of living is known as *discretionary income*. It is income that may be spent on any good or service which appeals to the individual.

Discretionary income today is about 40 percent of total disposable income, and this percentage is likely to increase. Many of the merchandise items and services presently offered to the public are not needed for physical well-being. Rather, they fulfill personal wants and provide psychic satisfaction. What people buy to satisfy their wants depends upon their appraisal of the choices presented to them by retailers and manufacturers. Sellers are competing for the consumer's discretionary income; in fact, most advertising is aimed at attracting this business rather than at attracting the expenditures for necessities. If a company fails to increase its sales as rapidly as discretionary income is increasing, the company is falling behind in the competitive race.

Discretionary Fund. Sellers of durable goods and luxury products are interested not only in discretionary income but also in the discretionary fund. The *discretionary fund* consists of the amount of discretionary income plus the amount that is purchased on installment credit. Together these figures give a sound estimate of the total money available for discretionary spending. Installment buying increases discretionary income by about one third, and more and more people are increasing their purchasing power by buying on credit.

Consumer Expenditures

Personal consumption expenditures account for about 65 percent of the gross national product. Consumers spend their money in three major areas: (1) for durable goods, such as cars and furniture; (2) for nondurable goods, such as food, clothing, and gasoline; and (3) for services, such as rent, medical care, recreation, and education.

It is interesting to observe that consumers are spending almost as much today on services as they are spending upon nondurable goods. Retailers recognize this fact, and many merchants now offer services in addition to their other products. Modern department stores may contain—besides the usual departments—insurance agencies, car rental agencies, beauty salons, interior decorating services, travel and entertainment agencies, cleaning services, and furniture repair shops.

Since so much of the personal income today can be spent at the discretion of the family, it is not surprising that expenditures in some areas are becoming more important than those in others. For example, studies show that during the last 20 years, expenditures for food and footwear have increased much less rapidly than have expenditures for appliances, furniture, recreation, travel, and gasoline.

The retailer should not assume that consumer expenditures can be expected to vary directly with changes in personal income or in discretionary income. Discretionary spending depends upon both *ability* and *willingness* to spend. Willingness depends not only on one's current income and savings but also on his outlook toward the trend in the general economy. If he is worried about the future he saves rather than spends. The economic recession of 1970 was attributed partly at least to a tendency of consumers to "hang on to their money."

CHECKING YOUR KNOWLEDGE

Vocabulary

1. economy
2. gross national product
3. net national product
4. national income
5. personal income
6. disposable personal income
7. discretionary income
8. discretionary fund

Review Questions

1. What are the four major components of the gross national product?
2. How may the national income figure be subdivided?
3. How does personal income differ from disposable personal income?
4. What is the difference between discretionary income and discretionary fund?
5. In what major areas are consumer expenditures made?

Discussion Questions

1. Which of the factors influencing changes in the gross national product are likely to be especially favorable for economic growth during the next ten years?
2. Since consumers must pay for what they buy—at least over a period of years—how can credit buying increase their purchasing power?
3. Is it more important for the seller to watch changes in the national income or in the personal income?

4. Is the uneven distribution of family income revealed in the chart in Illus. 1-9 something that can be defended from the social point of view? Should any steps be taken to avoid the large differences in family income?

BUILDING YOUR SKILLS

Improving Communication Skills

Each of the following sentences contains two verbs in parentheses. Only one of the verbs may be used correctly in the sentence. On a separate sheet of paper, write the number of each sentence and the correct verb to be used in that sentence.

1. I (saw, seen) Mary Jo waiting for the bus at Vine Street and First Avenue.
2. Mabel and Bill (was, were) working in the produce department this morning.
3. Jim (done, did) all the copy for yesterday's advertisement.
4. After Peggy had (went, gone) to lunch, Jerry was the only salesperson in the department.
5. At the store meeting we (sang, sung) "America, the Beautiful."
6. If Bob White (was, were) here, we could start the sales meeting.
7. John (lay, laid) aside the order book and helped the customer.
8. Faye has (broke, broken) five pieces of glassware this week.
9. The men from the display department have (hanged, hung) a new sign.
10. Don't (sit, set) on the counter when serving a customer.

Improving Arithmetic Skills

Perform the arithmetic exercises given below. On a separate sheet of paper, write the number of each exercise and your answer(s). Frequently problems will be in metric system terms. Refer to the Appendix for the conversion chart.

1. A store's floor space is 30.5 meters long and 10 meters wide. What are its dimensions in feet?
2. You have a can that contains 6 liters of punch and a jug that contains 2 liters. How many quarts do you have?
3. Ten salespeople at Allen's Shoe Store earned the following commissions during the first week of September. Find the total commissions paid. $17.80, $24.70, $6.90, $21.50, $24.30, $15.10, $11.20, $29.00, $19.60 and $14.40.
4. The Purple Fox had a week long sale on sport coats and slacks. The sales for the week were as follows:

	M	T	W	Th	F	S
Sportcoats	$340	$408	$306	$510	$578	$544
Slacks	$105	$168	$147	$126	$231	$420

(a) What was the total dollar value of sales for the week?
(b) What was the total dollar value of sales for Sportcoats?
(c) What was the total dollar value of sales for Slacks?
(d) On which day did The Purple Fox have the greatest amount of sales?

(e) On which day did The Purple Fox have the smallest amount of sales?

5. A customer stopped at a farmer's roadside market and selected the following items at the prices indicated. How much was her total purchase if no sales tax was involved?

12 ears of sweet corn at 55 cents a dozen
3 pounds of tomatoes at 12 cents a pound
3 pounds of green beans at 15 cents a pound
3 squash at 35 cents a squash

Improving Research Skills

1. Using library references and local resources such as the Chamber of Commerce or city offices, determine the following facts about your community:

(a) Total population
(b) Number of men and number of women
(c) Number of persons below age 18
(d) Number of persons who are 65 or older
(e) Number of families
(f) Number of homeowners
(g) Number of new persons who have moved into the community during the past year

Based upon this information, what kinds of new retail stores do you think would be successful in your community? Explain your answer.

2. Make a list of the last five items that you or your family have purchased. Select two of these items and draw for each a chart showing the channels of distribution used to get the item to you, the ultimate consumer.

3. Select one of the topics below as the subject for a debate. Take your stand, pro or con, research the position you have taken, and defend your point of view.

(a) The elimination of the middleman would lower prices for the consumer.
(b) Additional federal legislation should be passed to protect the consumer.
(c) The private enterprise system is the most effective way to balance supply and demand of consumer goods.
(d) Is the businessperson's search for profits compatible with public interest?
(e) Consumers are not really free to choose what to buy; for they are brainwashed by advertising, disc jockeys, and entertainers to buy what sellers want to sell.

Improving Decision-Making Skills

1. Some food researchers have developed a process whereby seaweed from the Pacific Ocean can be converted to delicious and inexpensive food. The processing plants must be located next to the ocean. Prepare a report on the channels of distribution to the consumer that might be used and recommend that which you think is best.

2. In order to operate a business in the city of Dawson, the business firm must first get a permit from the City Council. For the past year all requests

for business permits have been refused. The City Council believes that there are enough businesses in Dawson. You want to start a business in Dawson. Prepare a paper containing the reasons why the City Council should change its policy and permit new business firms to operate.

APPLYING YOUR KNOWLEDGE

Chapter Project

Locate in the library the most recent issue of the *Survey of Current Business*. Find the current figures for each of the following items:

1. Gross national product
2. National income
3. Personal income
4. Disposable personal income
5. Consumer expenditures

Continuing Project

The opportunity for individual enterprise and independent businesses continues in the field of retailing. As a project, which will continue with the study of each chapter in this book, you will prepare a retail merchandising manual. At the end of the course, you will have a manual—*Organizing and Operating a Retail Business*—which will contain your notes and research on a business of your choice. From the facts that you have learned in this chapter and in your research, start your manual by writing about each of the following topics:

1. The kinds of consumer goods that you would like to handle. Explain why you would like to handle these kinds of goods.
2. The manner of producing or manufacturing the goods.
3. The usual channel of distribution for the goods.
4. The consumers you plan to serve.
5. The prospect of demand for the consumer goods that you have chosen.

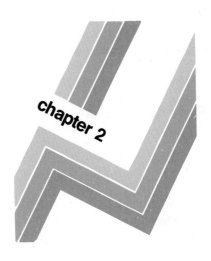

chapter 2

The Last Step in Marketing

CHAPTER PREVIEW

a. Retailing exists in an economy because it serves as an essential last step in the distribution process.

b. The small retailer has learned to adapt merchandising policies and procedures to meet the needs of changing consumer demand.

c. The chief types of large-scale retailing establishments are the department store, discount store, variety store, supermarket, and mail-order firm.

d. The independent type of store operation is found in about 90 percent of all retail stores.

e. Proprietorship, partnership, and corporation are the three major forms of store ownership.

Part a

Retailing in the Economy

Retailing is one of the oldest trades of the business community. Retailing emerged from the early concept of trade. *Trade,* meaning the exchange of goods, is undoubtedly the oldest form of business activity. To trade meant that two people, each possessing some property, would make an exchange. Each would give up something that he had for something that he wanted. A *trader* was a person who acquired and exchanged goods. Over the centuries money became the medium of exchange so that merchandise could be bought or sold for currency. The development of credit, banks, and other financial services made modern business possible. The development of the trader, peddler, shopkeeper, storekeeper into the modern retail business represents several chapters of fascinating business history.

CONTRIBUTIONS OF RETAILING

Retailing involves the sale of goods to the final consumer. Retailing, the final step in distribution, serves as the collector or assembler of products from all over the country and the world. These goods are then sold to those persons who will use them. The contributions of retailing include the following: specialization, place utility, time utility, possession utility, information, interpretation, and supportive services.

Specialization

The division of labor so that individual workers may concentrate on one specialized area is a well-known means of increasing overall productivity. The same is true in business. Through specialization in one aspect of distribution—the one in direct contact with the consumer—retailers can conduct that part of the work most effectively.

Place Utility

Place utility was introduced in Chapter 1. The role of the retailer in assembling goods at a source readily available to customers is certainly one of the major economic justifications of retailing.

Courtesy of Union Camp Corporation

Illus. 2-1   Whether you buy a book, a birthday card, or a poster, you normally buy it from the retailer not the producer.

Time Utility

Time utility was also introduced in Chapter 1. The collection of goods in a convenient location is necessary, but they must also be carried in sufficient quantity and at the time people want them. Having the right goods at the right time is part of the retailer's responsibility.

Possession Utility

Possession utility is the use or value one receives from actually having goods or services. In helping the customer buy and in arranging for the transfer of ownership, the retailer provides possession utility.

Information

With a constantly changing array of products available, the customer is faced with the need for buying information. He can get information from manufacturers, friends, or the retailer. Because the customer deals with the retailer, he expects the retailer to provide complete and accurate answers to his questions about the merchandise. Well-informed customers receive the greatest use and satisfaction from their purchases.

Interpretation

The retailer serves as a prime source of information to manufacturers and producers regarding customer needs, wants, and individual preferences. The retailer, because of his contact with the buying public, can interpret trends in demand for various goods to the suppliers.

Supportive Services

The retailer provides many supporting services to customers. Many of these are necessary if the buyer is to procure and enjoy the merchandise. Such services include credit, delivery, installation, and maintenance. By making these services available, the retailer assures potential customers the greatest opportunity to gain satisfaction from their purchases.

Without the retailer in our economy, the cost of merchandise to consumers would be higher, the choice of goods would be less extensive, and the opportunity to enjoy merchandise would be reduced.

SERVICE ESTABLISHMENTS

While not usually classified as retailers, establishments that provide services rather than merchandise are growing in importance. Many of these are small independent establishments such as dry cleaners; beauty and hair styling salons; picture framing studios; and shoe, furniture, and auto repair shops. Many large stores have in recent years added service departments and are now expanding them. Sears, Roebuck and Co., for example, operates an insurance company, a savings and loan association, a mutual investment firm, and a car rental service. Some stores offer lessons of various kinds, such as sewing and driving. They provide home cleaning and garden services and income tax assistance.

COMPETITION IN RETAILING

The very nature of retailing is competitive. Each retailer is striving to do a better job of serving a segment of the consuming public. The success or failure of his business depends on having people buy the merchandise and services he offers. In addition to the task of estimating the amount and nature of consumer demand, the retailer must make sure his goods, prices, and services are favored by a substantial segment of the consuming public over those of his competitors. However, a retailer who has established a successful business cannot stand still. He may find that some innovative retailer is entering his market with ideas and actions that challenge existing operations.

Hundreds of firms enter and exit retailing every month. Those retailers who are successful receive big dividends. Those who fail may lose their own investment as well as funds provided by others. The causes of failure in retailing rest primarily with the retailer himself. The basic causes are (1) lack of training, (2) lack of perserverance, (3) lack of capital, (4) lack of experience, and (5) lack of personal qualities needed in retailing. Lack of any one or more of these may make a retailer a prospect for failure. The opportunity to enter and try one's skill at retailing is a freedom that exists in this country. Thus, even though there is a high rate of failure (most within the first two years), new retail stores continue to open.

RETAILING METHODS

One of the largest retail firms in the United States, Sears, Roebuck and Co., did not have a retail store during the first forty years of its existence (1886-1925). It was initially in the mail-order business exclusively. Most persons think of a retail business as being a store where people can go to buy goods. The "store" is only one of four distinct forms of retailing.

Over-the-Counter Retailing

Over-the-counter retailing is the most common form of retailing. It involves having a store where the customer may come personally to examine, select, and purchase what she wants from the retailer's stock. There are about two million retail stores operating in the United States.

Mail-Order Retailing

In this form of retailing, the customer examines a catalog or advertisement for merchandise she wants to purchase. Her order is mailed or telephoned to the retailer's business place. The retailer receives the order and then sends the merchandise to the customer by mail or other delivery. For the busy American consumer, *mail-order* retailing provides a quick and convenient way to get much of the merchandise she wants.

Direct Retailing

In *direct retailing* the salesman comes to the home of the consumer with merchandise or samples. Door-to-door selling is one common form of direct retailing. Generally orders are taken and the goods delivered later, although some salesmen carry a supply of goods and make delivery at once. The necessity of making many calls to sell to a few customers increases distribution expenses, but for many customers this is a welcome service and provides an extra inducement to buy.

Automatic Retailing

In this type of retailing the customer deposits money in a machine and receives the goods immediately. This is called *automatic retailing*. Introduced originally to sell penny goods such as gum and peanuts, vending machines are now used to sell many small articles. Merchandise sold in this manner is usually of the convenience type such as stamps, soft drinks, hosiery, personal grooming items, foodstuffs, or reading material. In some cases vending machines are designed to serve as a cafeteria and contain a wide range of hot and cold, prepared and semi-prepared foods.

NEW VARIETIES OF RETAILING

The concept of retailing is taking on new dimensions today. Premium centers are a relatively new type of retail store doing an annual volume exceeding a billion dollars. Here customers "pay" for a wide variety of general merchandise by means of trading stamps that they have accumulated in purchasing other goods.

Many savings banks, during campaigns for new depositors, turn temporarily into retail establishments. They offer depositors a wide variety of gifts. For example, a $500 deposit qualifies the depositor for an article that retails for about $10 and costs the bank about $5.

SOME DEVELOPMENTS IN RETAIL DISTRIBUTION

Changes in retailing have followed the changes demanded by the consumer in the past, and this pattern will continue. As new consumer demands evolve so new types of retailing will emerge. Retailing cannot change customers, but customers can change retailing. A major attraction of retailing is the constant challenge of change. Great retail stores come about through constant adjustment to changing demands of customers. The retailer introduces new devices, ideas, merchandise, and fashions to favor and please a considerable segment of the public.

This is a period of great opportunity for the retailer who has the consumer foremost in mind. Consumers are critically looking at retail institutions, products, and practices. Their response will be continued patronage of the retailer who is constantly looking for better products and services to offer at competitive prices.

GROWTH IN RETAILING

As Illus. 2-2 shows, dollar sales of retailing are exhibiting a sharp upward trend. But when the dollar figures are adjusted for inflation, the increase in the actual volume of merchandise sold has been much more moderate. Also, the number of retail establishments is increasing slowly, since the trend is toward large stores rather than small ones.

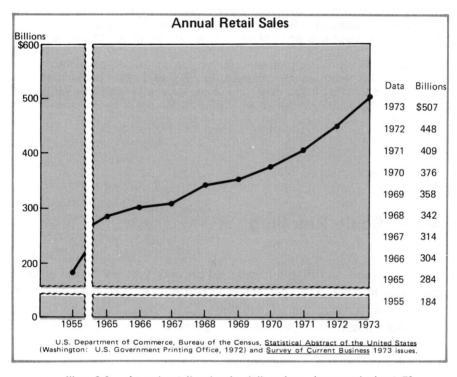

Annual Retail Sales

Data	Billions
1973	$507
1972	448
1971	409
1970	376
1969	358
1968	342
1967	314
1966	304
1965	284
1955	184

U.S. Department of Commerce, Bureau of the Census, Statistical Abstract of the United States (Washington: U.S. Government Printing Office, 1972) and Survey of Current Business 1973 issues.

Illus. 2-2   Annual retail sales in dollars have increased about 78 percent from 1965 to 1973 and have tripled in the past 20 years.

CHECKING YOUR KNOWLEDGE

Vocabulary

1. trade
2. trader
3. retailing
4. over-the-counter retailing

5. mail-order retailing
6. direct retailing
7. automatic retailing

1. What are the contributions made by retailing?
2. What services are provided by retail service establishments?
3. What are the basic causes of failure in retailing?
4. List four basic retailing methods.
5. Describe two new varieties of retailing.

1. What could be done to reduce the amount of failure in retailing without seriously interfering with the right of individuals to start a business?
2. From the consumer's point of view, what are the limitations of automatic retailing?
3. In 1965 the purchasing of services by the consumer consumed about 34% of his total dollar expenditures. By 1972 this percentage had increased to 38%. If you operate a large store with merchandise departments only, what actions would you consider seriously in view of this trend?

Part b

Small-Scale Retailing

Ken invited two of his friends, Brian and Van, to his three-room apartment to listen to a new stereo he had bought. Brian, who lived in one-room apartment, considered Ken's place large. Van, who lived in a six-room house, thought that Ken's home was small. Brian and Van were, of course, looking at Ken's apartment from different points of view. The same thing may happen when you are considering retail businesses. What may seem large to you may seem small to someone else. Nevertheless, size is one useful method of classifying retail stores.

A DESCRIPTION OF SMALL-SCALE RETAILING

When a person thinks of going into business for himself, he generally has in mind the operation of a small-scale retailing outlet. This kind of store is usually owned and operated as a single unit, has little or no specialization in management, is not departmentalized, and is operated by an owner-manager who also performs the activities of salesperson, buyer, stock clerk, and bookkeeper. About four fifths of all retail stores are of this type, but they account for less than one fourth of the total retail business.

In the large store a number of specialists divide the work. There are usually persons who buy the goods for resale, persons who supervise the store's general operations, persons who advertise the store's products, and persons who keep records. For our purposes, we shall think of the small store as one which employs fewer than 15 persons and which does less than $500,000 business yearly.

KINDS OF SMALL-SCALE RETAILERS

The chief types of small-scale retailing establishments are the general store, single-line store, roadside establishment, itinerant (traveling) store, and personal service store. It should be remembered that some of these types also exist as large-scale retailing establishments.

General Stores

General stores have served the American public for over 200 years. They are still found, although they are declining in number and in volume of sales. The general store may handle the mail for the community as well as supply townspeople with a variety of merchandise. It provides a gathering place where farmers and tradesmen can swap news and discuss politics. The owner of the store depends upon wholesaler salesmen to keep him informed about new merchandise and to keep up his stock. Occasionally the merchant visits wholesale centers to buy new merchandise. His store carries groceries, low-priced clothing, house furnishings, simple drugs, and numerous other articles; but it is not organized into separate departments.

Single-Line Stores

As the population of towns and cities increases, a demand arises for a greater variety of goods than a general store can carry. Moreover, the general-store proprietor does not buy in sufficient quantities to get the lowest prices. As a result, stores that specialize in one line or in a few related lines are opened. For example, a small mill town had one general store. As the population increased, a store that dealt only in groceries was set up. Across the street a store that specialized in dry goods was opened. Later there appeared a shoe store, a drugstore, and a stationery store. As the town grew, a bakery and a store specializing in ready-made clothing were opened. Thus, a number of specialized stores, called *single-line stores,* developed. They came in answer to the demand of the public for better merchandise assortments than the general store provided.

Neighborhood and Convenience-Goods Stores. Single-line stores which are located conveniently to residential neighborhoods and which specialize in *convenience goods* (goods which must be bought frequently and for which people do not want to make special shopping trips) are called *neighborhood stores*. Examples are food, drug, stationery, houseware stores, and quick-lunch establishments.

Many convenience-goods stores are located in business districts and cater to office workers going to and returning from work. Such stores may include coffee shops, bakery shops, candy stores, and magazine and newspaper stands. Another good location for the small convenience-goods store is a bus, rail, or air terminal. Gift shops, record shops, and clothing accessory stores are also found in transportation terminals.

Shopping-Goods Stores or Specialty Shops. Many single-line stores are found in the central shopping district rather than in neighborhood locations and feature shopping goods rather than convenience goods. *Shopping goods* are goods, such as fine jewelry, which a customer wishes to examine and compare in several stores before buying. Shopping goods are usually more expensive than convenience goods.

The shopping-goods stores which specialize in clothing are usually called *specialty shops*. Specialty shops are generally ahead of other stores in offering fashion merchandise to the customer. Specialty shops give department stores keen competition because the specialty shop can offer complete assortments in the one line of goods it handles, and it can offer customers many specialized services which the busy department store cannot offer. Many specialty-shop merchants know their customers very well and select goods that appeal to individual tastes.

Roadside Stores

Our dependence upon the automobile for transportation has led to the development of many stores and service establishments along major traffic arteries. There are five distinct types of *roadside businesses*:

1. Gasoline service stations which often sell automotive accessories, snacks, and soft drinks in addition to gasoline and oil
2. Open stores or roadside markets which sell fruit, vegetables, garden supplies, and lawn decorations
3. Eating and drinking places which sell hamburgers, soft drinks, and other standardized ready-to-serve foods
4. Motels which offer clean and well-appointed rooms, air conditioning, television, swimming pools, and dining rooms
5. Enclosed stores which feature such merchandise lines as furniture, building materials, paint, and shoes

As you will learn later, large stores handling general merchandise are also found today along major highways or within easy access of them. These stores are often located in planned shopping centers.

Itinerant Stores

The *itinerant*, or *rolling*, *store* is a familiar sight in rural districts, where people do not have ready access to ordinary stores. Groceries, meats, bakery products, tea and coffee, and ice cream are sold by itinerant stores. Notions, shoes, and dry goods are sometimes distributed by the store on wheels. This is in reality a combination of the portable store and direct selling.

Courtesy of New York Convention and Visitors Bureau

Illus. 2-3   A store on wheels. This kind of itinerant store carries a minimum assortment of items of interest to a large number of customers who live, work near, or pass by the places where it stops.

Personal Service Stores

In Part A, we referred to service establishments. Most of them are small but are necessary in number and variety. While beauty shops, shoe repair shops, and dry-cleaning shops have long been established, new kinds of service stores are constantly appearing. The services offered by these new types include window washing, rug cleaning, baby-sitting, a variety of repair services, car washing, pet boarding, appliance and car rental, packing of household goods, and travel services. As consumers become more wealthy and have a larger amount of discretionary income, they tend to spend relatively more of it for services as compared with merchandise. Retailers have become aware of this trend and are now introducing service selling departments in order to cater to the changing demand.

SUCCESS IN SMALL-SCALE RETAILING

It has been gloomily predicted that the small retailer will eventually be knocked out of the marketplace by his large and strong adversaries—the department store, the huge national chain-store groups, the giant supermarkets, and the mushrooming suburban branch stores and discount stores. However, successful small retailers have learned to adapt their merchandising policies and procedures to meet the needs of the consumer and the developments in the retailing field. They use their weapons of competition—specialization, personal service, and convenience of location—very skillfully. They have the ability to enter a market and to move out more quickly, and to adjust more easily to specialized consumer needs and wants, than the large-scale retailer.

In addition to his flexibility and convenient location, the small, alert retailer may make use of a specialist. He may engage a retail consultant to give his business a periodic checkup, to answer the question "How am I doing?" and to give him a fresh viewpoint based on wide experience. Probably the most important move that the small-scale merchant has made has been to associate himself with other noncompeting merchants to gain buying power and promotional aids. Such cooperation will be discussed in Part D of this chapter.

Many small retailers can survive and prosper because of a location which is convenient either to householders, workers, or travelers. But most small retail establishments must attract people who are looking for specific merchandise or service features. The store must establish a unique image in the minds of its customers. It must not try to outdo the large-scale retailers in the breadth of its merchandise assortments or in the offering of rockbottom prices. Rather, the small store must develop a character of its own. The small retailer must be sure that his store fills a definite need for a considerable number of customers. Quality merchandise selected with his clientele in mind—plus reasonable prices, efficient service, and a friendly attitude—is his insurance for remaining in business. It must also be observed that most of our great retail establishments have sprung from small beginnings. If a merchant has the ability to organize and supervise other people, rather than to do the job himself, he can aspire to a large-store operation.

CHECKING YOUR KNOWLEDGE

Vocabulary

1. general store
2. single-line store
3. convenience goods
4. neighborhood store
5. shopping goods

6. specialty shop
7. roadside business
8. itinerant, or rolling, store
9. personal service stores

Review Questions

1. What is the definition of a small store?
2. What are the chief types of small-scale retail establishments?
3. What is the difference between shopping goods and convenience goods?
4. List four examples of roadside retail businesses.
5. What competitive advantages do small retailers have?

Discussion Questions

1. What would be the advantages of owning or working in a small retail business?
2. Under what circumstances would it be desirable to run a general store?
3. With more and more large retail businesses being formed will most small-scale retailing be eliminated?

Part C

Large-Scale Retailing

Successful small-scale retailers frequently expand their operations into large-scale retailing establishments. A small grocery store, for instance, may grow into a huge supermarket or move into a large building, rent space to other merchants, and operate as a type of discount outlet. The owner of this small grocery store might also decide to open more grocery stores of his first type and operate a chain of grocery stores. Or he might decide to open in his store other departments such as housewares, cosmetics, records, or clothing. Ultimately he might be operating a department store. The grocer might even decide to sell by mail; and if he has specialty products, mail-order selling might become his main business. These are some of the ways in which a small-scale retail business may grow into a large-scale retail business.

The chief types of large-scale retailing establishments are the department store, discount store, variety store, supermarket, and mail-order firm. While these large retailers have numerous advantages there are certain shortcomings. Many customers like to be greeted by the owner or manager of a store, to be called by name, and to be assured that their patronage is appreciated. In large-scale retailing this friendly personal relationship between customer and merchant is missing. Even though the store staff is trained in customer relations, the impersonality of the large store is difficult to overcome.

DEPARTMENT STORES

If specialty shops handling such lines as women's ready-to-wear clothes, dry goods, shoes, men's clothing, home furnishings, cosmetics, jewelry, and stationery, were put under one roof and coordinated by a central management, we would have a *department store*. The variety of clothing and home furnishing goods carried in the typical department store is called *general-merchandise*. The term would exclude such lines as foods and automotive goods. The department store offers the people of the community an opportunity to do their shopping in one place. Some department stores even have a food department. Most department stores permit customers to have their purchases charged and delivered. Other services, such as ordering by mail and telephone, are enjoyed by the patrons of many department stores. Because department stores are large (employing at least 25 persons according to the United States Bureau of the Census classification) and because they enjoy a large volume of sales, they are able to employ specialists in buying, advertising, displaying, store planning, and controlling finances. Also their size enables them to obtain merchandise at advantageous prices.

Department stores have won the distinction of being the best known large-scale retailers because they have successfully pioneered in many retailing operations, have been alert to current developments in retailing, and have been able to maintain their image and vitality.

Problems of Downtown Department Stores

Department stores were initially developed in central city or downtown locations. There are three crucial problems facing these stores today. First, is the problem of adjusting the store to crowded shopping conditions that exist in most cities. Parking space, public transportation limitations, traffic congestion, distant store deliveries, and outmoded store buildings are most common. The second problem is the continuing shift of population to suburban areas of large cities. This outward movement has placed potential customers farther and farther from the central stores. The growth of excellent specialty stores and shopping centers in the suburbs further reduces the number of potential downtown department store customers. Third, the success of the low-margin retailer—the discount store—has forced major changes in central city department-store operations.

Combating Downtown Problems

Department-store managers are working hard to overcome the problems facing them. They are pressing for urban renewal to handle the problems of parking, transportation, and traffic congestion. Where possible, they are building stores which have parking lots or are starting "park-shop" or "ride-shop" programs. Another possible solution lies in the building of malls which eliminate all cars from the downtown streets and force cars to park on side streets, on store roofs, or on parking lots provided by the stores or by the city.

To meet the problem of dwindling customers because of population movement to the suburbs, department stores have opened *branch stores* and *twig stores* (small branches carrying only a few specialized lines such as shoes) in the suburbs or in shopping areas. These branches are generally not replicas of their downtown stores but handle mainly women's and children's soft goods or other merchandise necessary to take advantage of the local situation and to meet competition. In some cases these stores have established full-fledged suburban department stores. Often these new operations are larger than the parent store. Many big department stores have discovered opportunities for new branches, not in the suburbs, but in the growing areas of the city itself.

VARIETY STORES

Like the department store, the *variety store* handles a large assortment of general merchandise. Unlike the department store, the variety store specializes in low-priced goods and gives little attention to furniture, major appliances, or carpeting. Variety-store merchandise includes women's accessories, infants' clothing, toys, notions, tableware, light hardware, costume jewelry, cosmetics, and candies. Many of these stores offer luncheonette service.

Variety stores operate mainly on a cash basis and most have shifted to self-service. Some small-scale independent variety stores are found in small towns and in neighborhood areas. Most of those in the city and in shopping centers are large chain-store types such as Woolworth, Kresge, Murphy, Newberry, Kress, and McCrory. Some are approaching department stores in their assortments.

SUPERMARKETS

The *supermarket* is a large departmentalized store which features foodstuffs, is characterized by self-service in the grocery and other departments, and operates generally on a cash-and-carry basis. Its chief appeal is low prices on standard goods. Customers assemble their merchandise in carts or baskets and take it to a checkout counter where it is packaged and payment is made. The supermarket has had a phenomenal growth since it was first introduced in the 1930's. Organization on a self-service basis in low-rent locations permitted operation at an expense rate one-third lower than that of grocery stores that provided salespeople.

Characteristics of Successful Supermarket Operation

Self-service
Low prices in high-turnover food lines
Use of experts in buying, advertising, display, and store management
Dynamic, consistent advertising and promotional methods
Use of electronic tabulating equipment
Wide variety of food and other merchandise

Illus. 2-4   All successful supermarkets have certain characteristics of operation. The most important are given above.

Trends in Supermarket Operation

Competition has led to the installation of more expensive fixtures and equipment, the employment of experts in buying and display, the application of scientific, large-scale retailing methods, and the selection of more convenient locations. Today some supermarkets have public address systems, conveyors for package delivery to cars, doors opening automatically through electric eye devices, rest rooms, and piped-in music. One supermarket has increased business by using an electronic "truckster" which shutttles customers with groceries to their parked cars.

Supermarkets are expanding, or mixing, their lines. While they remain primarily food stores, many of them have added other lines, such as house furnishings, hardware, drugs, and soft goods. They are commonly departmentalized as follows: self-service grocery, meat, produce, dairy, frozen food, bakery, drug, and general merchandise.

Superettes

Many grocery store owners have gone only part way in the direction of self-service. They operate stores that are called *superettes*. Goods are arranged and displayed as in self-service stores, and customers may wait on themselves. Counter service is also available for those who want it. These stores can operate at a lower expense than full-service grocery stores yet still maintain the atmosphere of personal service.

Quick-Service Stores

With the increased size and frequent checkout delays in the regular supermarket, customers who want just a few items are being served through *quick-service*, or *convenience*, stores. These stores are small in size, carry limited stocks of the most common grocery items, and are open extended hours. These stores need parking for only a few cars, since turnover is rapid.

MAIL-ORDER FIRMS

If a customer is too far from a town store, if she is not satisfied with the goods or prices of the local store, or if she does not like to shop in crowds, she may select goods from a catalog sent by a *mail-order firm*, send payment for the goods with her order, and receive the goods by mail. Increasingly the customer is telephoning her order to a local office of the mail-order firm rather than mailing in the order. Installment terms are available at an additional charge, and more and more mail-order customers are taking advantage of the credit privilege. Formerly most mail-order business came from rural districts, but many city residents now patronize mail-order firms. Many people prefer to shop at home from a catalog rather than visit a crowded store. The "salesperson" for the mail-order firm is a beautifully illustrated catalog that is usually sent free to those who ask for it.

The *general merchandise mail-order firm* and the *specialty mail-order firm* are the two chief kinds of retail firms doing business by catalog in this country. The former is departmentalized along department store lines; the latter is more like a specialty shop. The general merchandise mail-order firm does over 75 percent of the mail-order business and is dominated by four major firms—Sears, Montgomery Ward, Spiegel, and Penney. The specialty firms, such as Sunset House, Auto World, Gurney's, and Guilford Forge, deal in rather specific merchandise lines, many of a novelty nature.

In order to help customers inspect samples and place orders, a number of the general merchandise mail-order houses have set up *order offices* in towns and smaller cities. The clerks who handle the mechanics of ordering goods see that the merchandise is delivered from the nearest warehouse to the order office at a minimum charge. Like the department stores, the larger mail-order firms employ specialists for buying, advertising, and control. They also maintain testing laboratories which assure high standards of quality at low prices.

DISCOUNT STORES

Even before World War II, discounters set up shop with a telephone and a catalog. They featured radios and appliances at less than the list price. They had low overhead expenses, cheap locations, and offered

Courtesy of K Mart

Illus. 2-5 Discount retailing provides the opportunity to save because of large volume and self-service. Location of store in suburban area and provision of parking have made this type of store operation attractive to many customers.

Features of Discount-Store Operation

Lowest possible prices

Good quality but not high fashion or exclusive merchandise

Large stocks of selected merchandise

Amount sold to each customer high because customers buy several items

Customer services and sales gimmicks reduced

A liberal adjustment policy, with ready refunds to encourage rebuying

Buying and selling planned by experts who use modern equipment and techniques

Located in low-rent areas with adequate parking space available

A number of store outlets clustered in a single trading territory so that central newspaper and radio advertising benefits all stores in the area

Maximum use of facilities—long hours often from 10 a.m. to 10 p.m.; open on Sundays where laws permit

---

Ilus. 2-6   Certain characteristics and methods of operation set the discount store apart. Some of these are given above.

no services. Their cash-and-carry practices enabled them to give customers substantial discounts. There were hundreds of items on which the customer had been totally sold before she went out to purchase, and she merely wanted to own them as cheaply and quickly as possible. The idea of getting a discount was attractive and caught on.

Underselling the competitor is an old story. When, in 1859, the A & P purchased tea directly from the Orient and sold it below the price of competitors, underselling became a tool of competition. Then, in 1912, the "Economy Store" was born; and, after World War I, "Cut-Price" and "Cut-Rate" stores dominated the retailing price scene. In fact, many department stores started as price-cutting institutions.

In the women's clothing field, discounting started with canny, independent merchants who bought "overruns" (production in excess of orders) from top manufacturers for cash. Some of these merchants have expanded their operations into large chains. They both buy and sell for cash and make no deliveries or alterations. After the designers' labels have been removed, the garments are sold for about 40 percent less than the same garments offered by exclusive shops.

Kinds of Discount Stores

Basically there are two kinds of discount stores—the *open-door*, which sells to all persons, and the closed door. The *closed-door discount* store sells only to persons who are members. Government employees, members of the armed forces, teachers, and similar groups are the types of customers this discount store attracts. Monthly mailings to its members constitute its advertising. It seldom has a sale. It is constantly upgrading the quality of its merchandise with emphasis on well-known clothing items. It tries to create a feeling of belonging in its customers and uses a low-key approach.

There has recently emerged a partially closed-door discounter that has aspects of the mail-order firm. Potential customers are mailed catalogs of offerings, but neither mail nor phone orders are accepted. Rather, they visit the catalog firm's retail store, ask to inspect certain items featured in the current catalog, pay cash for their selections, and carry the goods home with them.

An example of the open-door discounter is the retail gasoline discounter whose prices average about four cents a gallon less than those charged for the standard brands that carry heavy advertising. The discounters typically concentrate on pumping gas, eliminating costly service operations associated with the gasoline service station. Some depend on self-service pumps operated by the motorist himself.

Discount Units of Conventional Stores

Department stores have faced up to the challenge by establishing discount subsidiaries of their own. Among others, Federated Department Stores has set up its Gold Circle discount stores, May Department Stores its Venture Stores, and Penney its Treasure Island stores.

Variety stores have followed suit. Kresge has opened about 400 K Mart stores that now do much more business than its conventional stores and have made Kresge the third largest retailer of general merchandise, surpassed only by Sears and Penney. Woolworth, the fourth largest, has set up its Woolco discount division.

Discounting had been thought of as impractical in the case of furniture, but that is now a fast-growing segment of that business. Customers shop in giant warehouse-showroom outlets located where land is cheap and adjacent to rail sidings.

Even supermarkets have been forced into discounting in order to maintain their market share of potential business. One of the largest, the A & P, has converted its regular stores into WEO (Where Economy Originates) stores. The same facilities are used as before, but slow-sellers have been dropped; and gimmicks, such as trading stamps and some other services, have also been eliminated.

CHECKING YOUR KNOWLEDGE

Vocabulary

1. department store
2. general merchandise
3. branch store
4. twig store
5. variety store
6. supermarket
7. superette
8. quick-service, or convenience, store

9. mail-order firm
10. general merchandise mail-order firm
11. specialty mail-order firm
12. order office
13. open-door discount store
14. closed-door discount store

Review Questions

1. What are the chief types of large-scale retailing?
2. What are the chief problems facing the conventional department store?
3. How does a variety store differ from a department store?
4. What are the characteristics of a supermarket operation?
5. How are conventional stores meeting discount competition?

Discussion Questions

1. Because every consumer desires lower prices, all department stores should change to discount operations. Why do you agree or disagree with this statement?
2. What problems will continue to face downtown retailers even with extensive urban renewal and central city modernization?
3. What are the advantages of one company having a mail-order operation as well as regular retail stores?
4. Why do most motorists still buy a national brand of gasoline even though the discounter often sells the same gas under his own brand?

Part d

Types of Store Operations

If you were to go to several retail stores in a business district and ask who owned the store, you would get some interesting information. You would find that some stores are owned by the people who operate them. Other stores are part of a group of stores that are centrally owned. Some stores are owned by their customers. Other stores are owned by companies which have retailing as only part of their business interests.

A retail outlet—whether small-scale or large-scale—may be operated as (1) an independent store, (2) a unit of a contractual group of stores, (3) a part of a corporate chain of stores, (4) a branch store, (5) a cooperative, (6) a sideline store, or (7) a conglomerate [widely diversified company] group. In the paragraphs that follow, you will learn more about these types of store operations.

INDEPENDENT STORES

A store that is owned and operated by the same person or persons is known as an *independent store.* Most small stores, and a few large stores, fall into this category. As already reported, about 90 percent of the country's retail businesses are independent stores, and they account for about three fourths of the total retail trade. When an owner operates two or three stores which are generally close enough together for him to spend some time in each daily, the group is known as a *multi-independent.*

Most independents—except those which limit their operation to the sale of convenience goods to local customers—find it necessary to associate themselves with others to gain in buying power and to obtain promotional aid from experts. Only those independent stores which offer highly personalized service, goods from a certain locality, or tailor-made goods, can safely get along today without some sort of affiliation. Those carrying a wide variety of goods and who are in daily competition with other stores for consumer patronage must affiliate if they hope to grow with the population and the rapidly increasing personal incomes of consumers.

CONTRACTUAL GROUPS

Associations of independent stores that contract with other stores or organizations may take one of several forms. These forms are discussed below. It should be pointed out that, no matter which form of association is followed, ownership of the independent store is not relinquished.

Voluntary Chain

When independent stores form a *voluntary chain,* a wholesaler makes a contract with them to provide special merchandise values and supervisory aid in return for a substantial portion of their business. The stores usually operate under a common name with a standardized store front and perhaps with a standardized layout. Examples of voluntary chains are the IGA (Independent Grocers' Alliance) supermarkets, the Red and White Supermarkets, the Rexall stores, and the Super Valu stores.

Some corporate chains have also organized what they call *agency stores.* These are independent stores with whom they affiliate in localities where it is not feasible for the chains to open their own stores.

Franchise Store

When an independent retailer contracts to handle a single manufacturer's or wholesale supplier's line of merchandise the retailer is said to have a *franchise.* A franchise exists when the owner of a business or a product extends to others the right to conduct a similar business or sell the product. A franchise agreement spells out the conditions of the franchise, fees to be paid, and services to be provided. The *franchisor* (the person or firm that owns the idea or product) authorizes the *franchisee* (the retailer) to operate under his corporate name and to take advantage of his advertising. The franchisor may finance the merchant at the start, even erecting the store building and providing the initial stock of goods. In return, the merchant agrees to follow standardized operating procedures, to use a standardized store layout, and to promote the franchisor's products effectively. He also pays a substantial fee for his right to represent the line. Two forms of franchising are commonly found in retailing.

Manufacturer-Retailer Franchise. In this type of franchise the retailer agrees to handle only the manufacturer's product line, except for fringe items. The retailer is identified by customers as being part of the manufacturer's distribution structure. Automobile dealers, service stations, and shoe stores are examples of this form of franchising.

Sometimes the manufacturer contracts with a wholesaler, not a retailer. This type of franchise operation assures a controlled distribution system for the manufacturer. The franchise gives the wholesaler the right to distribute a product in an area. Examples are beverage bottlers (Pepsi-Cola, Seven-Up, and others) and building materials.

Supplier-Retailer Franchise. This form of franchise operation is most visible to the consumer. In this arrangement a supplier prepares a package of products and services which are franchised to a local retailer. The supplier may manufacture part of the components or buy them from other sources. The supplier works with each retailer and helps the retailer to operate along franchise guidelines. Examples are quick lunch food businesses (McDonald's, Dairy Queen); motels (Holiday Inn, Howard Johnson's); and car rentals (National, Avis).

Franchising by retailers has grown tremendously in recent years. There are currently over a half-million retail outlets. One of the reasons for the success is that, through the help of the franchisor, the franchisee can become established with a rather small investment. Furthermore, the franchisee receives considerable assistance in the operation and management of the business. Through franchising, economies can be shared among many small independent firms.

On the other hand, many franchisees have become disillusioned. The opportunity for sales and profits have sometimes been overstated. The franchisor sometimes has made demands that the franchisee could not meet if he, too, was to prosper; and, in case of discontinuance of the arrangement, the disposition of stocks in the retailer's possession has not been spelled out. Before entering into any franchise arrangement, the independent retailer needs the advice of an expert who has no connection with the franchisor under consideration.

Retailer-Owned Cooperative Wholesale Warehouses

Sometimes a group of independents may establish a jointly owned subsidiary wholesale establishment, called a *cooperative wholesale warehouse*. By obtaining merchandise through this wholesale unit, each store can obtain lower prices than it could if it were to purchase the goods itself. Large department stores frequently set up cooperative wholesale warehouses.

Resident Buying Offices

Most independents in the clothing and home furnishings fields find it desirable to affiliate themselves with a *resident buying office* to which similar but noncompeting stores belong. The resident buying office assists its members in keeping abreast of the changing market for fashion and nonstandardized goods and assists in all matters having to do with obtaining merchandise. Most of the resident buyers are independent and sell their services for a fee, but some are owned by stores or by groups of stores.

CORPORATE CHAINS

Four or more stores of a similar type, centrally owned and with central control of operations, are generally considered a *chain*. Thus, there can be a chain of grocery stores, a chain of variety stores, a chain of department stores, a chain of shoe stores, a chain of drugstores. Most of the well-known discount houses are now chains. While many started as independents, they have found it easier to expand by opening additional outlets than by developing large central stores. In fact, there can be a chain of any type of store, but chains predominate in the above-mentioned fields. Sometimes, a chain finds it more economical to expand by franchising independents or setting up voluntary units than to set up more stores of its own.

Advantages of the Chain Store

The chain organization has certain advantages. First, the relative cost of buying is very small because all units handle almost identical goods. Second, the many sales outlets make it possible to buy in large quantities and to obtain low prices. Third, it is possible for chains to deal direct with manufacturers, whereas the independent generally buys from wholesalers at a considerable addition to cost. Fourth, the chain generally specializes in fast-selling goods and does not carry items for which there is only an occasional demand. Fifth, the chain saves in managerial expenses. Mistakes made in one store need not be repeated in another; and efficient methods of display, selling, and record keeping, once devised, can be readily applied to all units.

Disadvantages of the Chain Store

Chains have some disadvantages, too. They have been charged with tending toward monopoly; consequently, special legislation has been passed against them, and they have been highly taxed. Their chief disadvantage, however, lies in their difficulty in adjusting their buying and selling practices to local conditions as readily as independents. Also, local chain-store managers may not be as strongly motived as are independents who are members of a contractural group.

Chains of Leased Departments

Both department and discount stores frequently want to expand their variety of goods and merchandise lines. Often the easiest way is to rent space to a company specializing in the merchandise desired. These specialized companies lease space in the retail store and operate just like other departments. Any department in which specialized knowledge of goods or the market is necessary is a potential *leased-department* operation.

Such departments as beauty shops, optical, millinery, women's shoes, paints, and wallpaper are commonly leased departments in department stores. Discount firms rent to a much broader field of merchandisers, including ready-to-wear operators, soda fountain, and appliance dealers. Some successful discount operations are entirely

Courtesy of Flah & Co.

Illus. 2-7   The women's shoe department in a department store may be a leased-department operation.

leased. The owners of the discount firm coordinate the services and the promotions and determine merchandising policies, but every line is merchandised by a lessee.

Rent for the department is usually paid as a percentage of sales, ranging from 8 percent in discount stores to 15 percent in department stores. The lessee pays for his own salespeople, manager, and advertising. Recently, as chains of discount stores have become more firmly established, they have tended to replace leased departments with those they own outright. This gives management better control and the opportunity to earn profits formerly retained by lessees.

BRANCH STORES

Branch stores began as extensions of downtown department or specialty stores. As new shopping areas opened, many downtown stores found it necessary to have a store near their customers. Branch stores were opened in suburban shopping centers; some have been established in cities other than that in which the main store is located; and a few have been started in growing secondary shopping districts in the same city as the parent store.

The branch store differs from the typical chain store unit in that it has more freedom. It is usually responsible for its own stock assortments and selling methods, even though new additions to the merchandise lines are purchased centrally and newspaper advertising covers the main store and branches throughout the trading area. Some branch store systems now regard the main store as simply one of the branches, with central buyers no more responsible for it than they are for any of the other branches. These stores are thus getting very close to chainstore operation, but they have more variations in merchandise assortments than do the chains of food, drug, and variety stores.

CONSUMER COOPERATIVES

Consumers interested in forming a *cooperative store* invest small sums, such as $5 each, in the enterprise and hire a manager. Prices are ordinarily set at the market level rather than below. Records of members' purchases are kept; and net earnings are distributed to members on the basis of the amount of their purchases, rather than on the basis of their investments. Each member has one vote, regardless of the number of shares of stock he owns. Cooperatives are most important in agricultural areas for the sale of gasoline, oil, and farm implements and supplies. These are technically producers' cooperatives since they provide goods used in production rather than in consumption. True consumer cooperatives are found in grocery, dry goods, apparel, meat, fuel, and general merchandise lines.

SIDELINE STORES

A *sideline store* is one that is owned and operated by groups or by individuals who have other major interests. Thus, we have manufacturers' and wholesalers' stores operated by those whose major activity is production or wholesaling; company stores operated by industrial plants for the benefit of their employees (particularly in regions where independent and chain stores have not been established); utility stores operated by utility companies to further the sale of equipment using electricity and gas; and post exchanges run by the armed services for the benefit of soldiers, airmen, and sailors.

CONGLOMERATE GROUPS

Today there is an increasing growth of retail companies that do more than operate corporate units of chains, leased departments, and branch stores. They have subsidiaries that operate a wide variety of retail and service businesses. This collection of a number of unrelated and diversified companies under one corporate ownership is called a *conglomerate*.

For example, the J. C. Penney Company, Inc., once a chain specializing in apparel, now operates the following distinct divisions in order not to be dependent on the success of one type of operation:

1. Full-line department store
2. Limited-line general merchandise stores (largely in small towns)
3. Auto service shops
4. Discount stores (Treasure Island Stores)
5. Drug chain (Thrift Stores)
6. Catalog mail-order unit
7. Life insurance company
8. European chain
9. Subsidiary to finance its credit sales

Some conglomerates consist of both manufacturing firms and chains of retail stores as in the case of Spartan Industries. Starting as a manufacturer of soft goods, it acquired and operated the Korvettes' chain of promotional discount stores. Now an affiliated realty company that develops shopping centers has assumed control of Korvettes.

CHECKING YOUR KNOWLEDGE

Vocabulary

1. independent store
2. multi-independent
3. contractual group
4. voluntary chain
5. agency store
6. franchise
7. franchisor
8. franchisee
9. cooperative wholesaler warehouse
10. resident buying office
11. chain
12. leased department
13. cooperative store
14. sideline store
15. conglomerate

Review Questions

1. List seven types of retail store operation.
2. Describe two forms of retail franchising.
3. What are the advantages of a chain store organization?
4. How do branch stores differ from typical chain stores?
5. What are the characteristics of a cooperative store?

Discussion Questions

1. Under what circumstances would the formation of consumer cooperatives be most apt to take place?

2. Under what conditions can small independent stores be successful without affiliating with other stores?
3. Why do some chain stores confine their operation to a certain region rather than spread to all parts of the country?
4. A franchisor has been accused by the government of an unfair trade practice and restraint of trade because it insists that its 38 franchised quick-lunch restaurants sell food at identical prices and that they buy all their bakery products, salads, coffee, meats, orange juice, and paper products from the company. The company also owns outright 50 other restaurants where its right to control is recognized. Do you think it unfair for the company that provides the name and reputation for a high standard of quality but a limited menu to demand that the restaurants it franchises observe the rules indicated above? Do you think that these rules restrain trade in any practical way?

Part **e**

Types of Store Ownership

One or more persons may own a store or a chain of stores. When one person is the sole owner, the form of ownership is known as an *individual proprietorship*. Two or more persons may join together to own a store. This type of ownership is called a *partnership*. When several people want to own a store, they can choose either the partnership form or the *corporation* form, in which ownership is evidenced by shares of stock. Since each one of these types of ownership has its advantages and disadvantages, the type of ownership must be carefully selected. Such factors as capital needed, experience of each person, type of store, goods to be handled, tax laws, and the financial risk each person is willing to take should be considered. Of course, a store may be started as an individual proprietorship and later be changed to a partnership or a corporation; or it may be begun as a partnership or a corporation and later be changed to any one of the other forms.

Nearly two thirds of all retail establishments are the individual proprietorship form of ownership, about one eighth are partnerships, and only one fifth are corporations. But the first two groups consist mostly of small stores with sales of $80,000 a year or less and are decreasing in number. The number of retailers using the corporate form of ownership is increasing; it seems best suited for large-scale operations, and that is the direction in which retailing is moving.

INDIVIDUAL PROPRIETORSHIP

Since graduating from high school eight years ago Gene Sanchez has worked in a hardware store. During the eight years he has performed just about every job required including that of acting manager during his boss's vacation. Mr. Sanchez has decided that he would like to go into the hardware business for himself. He has accumulated some savings and can borrow some money from some close friends. During the last few years he has become acquainted with several hardware wholesalers. He has found a suitable location, has received a license to operate a store, and has invested in merchandise. He is now in business. Going into business for oneself is much more than this, of course; but for our purposes of illustrating store ownership, this will be sufficient.

Mr. Sanchez is the sole owner. He acquired all the money necessary to get started. He makes his own decisions as to buying and pricing. He decides whom to employ, when to open, and when to close. He is free to do as he pleases within the restrictions of law. If Mr. Sanchez's business prospers, he is entitled to keep all the profits remaining after paying expenses and taxes.

Let us say that the hardware business which Gene Sanchez established was successful and prospered. He found that the new business demands were too much for him, and his capital was inadequate for needed expansion. He considered the possibility of adding a partner who could invest additional capital and assist in the work. Mr. Sanchez knew that he could best handle the buying, inventory control, and promotional activities. His partner would have to be someone who could

---

Advantages and Disadvantages of Individual Proprietorships

Advantages   Easy to start
              Complete control in one individual
              Taxation and supervision relatively light

Disadvantages Difficult to obtain capital for expansion purposes
              Lack of permanence
              Heavy inheritance taxes
              Lack of exchange of opinion before decisions are
                made, leading at times to poor management

Illus. 2-8   The individual proprietorship has some advantages and some disadvantages. Before adopting this form of store ownership, the retailer should consider carefully whether the advantages outweigh the disadvantages for his particular business.

keep accounting records and manage the selling phase of the business. Mr. Sanchez also knew that his present individual proprietorship had disadvantages. The lack of certain abilities, the lack of funds for expansion, the assumption of all losses, and the discontinuance of the business in case of death are some of the disadvantages of an individual proprietorship.

PARTNERSHIP

The more Mr. Sanchez thought about a partnership the more he liked the idea. He inquired among his business associates and friends. He put an advertisement in the wholesalers' trade paper. Mike Cohen, who had worked as a hardware department manager for a department store and taken accounting courses in evening school, contacted Mr. Sanchez. It was decided that Mr. Cohen would supply as much money as was already invested in the business and take over as operations manager and bookkeeper. He would come in as an equal partner in the already established business. With the extra money the two men decided to modernize the hardware store and add a paint and wall-covering section. They put the principal points of their agreement into writing and, with the aid of a lawyer, drew up the *articles of copartnership*. This contract stated the important points of the partnership agreement between Sanchez and Cohen, even as to what should happen to the partnership in the event of death of either partner.

The partnership of Gene Sanchez and Mike Cohen had a number of advantages. First, their combined skills resulted in a more efficient operation. Second, the increased capital enabled them to stock more merchandise, to use better equipment, to improve their credit position in the market, and to expand the services of their store. Third, each person assumed the financial responsibility of the partnership, dividing the losses, if any.

Mr. Sanchez and Mr. Cohen found the partnership had some disadvantages. The law about partnerships makes each partner responsible not only for his share of the debts of the business but also for the share of any other partner who cannot pay. To pay the partnership liabilities, each partner may have to contribute not only the portion he owns in the business but also other private property. Furthermore, each partner is bound by the contracts of the other partners. For example, if Mr. Sanchez buys merchandise which Mr. Cohen does not want, Mr. Cohen still must allow the partnership to pay for it. This can be a cause of friction and disagreement between the partners. Another difficulty is that one partner may think he is not getting a satisfactory share of the

Advantages and Disadvantages of Partnerships

Advantages   Two heads better than one
               More capital obtainable (compared with individual
                  proprietorship)
               Partners have direct voice in management (compared
                  with corporation)
               Less regulation and taxation than is true of a corpora-
                  tion

Disadvantages Disagreement among partners
               Each partner liable for acts of others
               Liability not limited to investment
               Lack of permanence, since death of a partner or addi-
                  tion of a new partner dissolves the old partnership
               Difficult for a partner to withdraw

Illus. 2-9   For such businesses as restaurants, appliance stores with
both sales and repair departments, and camera stores with film developing and printing services, the partnership form of ownership is efficient
and effective. No form of store ownership, however, is without disadvantages.

profits according to the amount of time and effort he expends. He may
have difficulty withdrawing from the partnership if he should be
dissatisfied. Furthermore, the life of a partnership is always uncertain.
Death causes a complete liquidation, even if the agreement of the
partnership runs for a certain length of time.

It should be noted, however, that it is possible to organize a *limited
partnership*, in which the limited partners have no voice in the management of the business and are liable only for the amount of their investment. The business is directed by a few general partners.

CORPORATION

The hardware store of Mr. Sanchez and Mr. Cohen prospered under
their hard work and direction. Soon the partners considered opening
a much larger store in a new shopping center about to open nearby.
They consulted a lawyer and found that the best way they could raise
more capital was to form a corporation. The ownership of the new
store would be held by a group of individuals who would buy shares
of stock in the corporation. Each share of stock was to have a *par value*
(stated value at time of issuance) of $1. Shares would be sold in 100
share lots. Mr. Sanchez and Mr. Cohen talked to their friends and
customers and found that many were willing to invest. The partners

---

Advantages and Disadvantages of Corporations

Advantages   Limited liability—each stockholder liable only for amount of his investment

Long life—does not dissolve with the death of owners

Much capital can be raised, making possible large-scale operation

Easy for a shareholder to withdraw by selling stock

Disadvantages   Ownership and management separated—danger of irregularities and fraud because of impersonal management

Subject to many laws, regulations, and taxes

More difficult to form

Illus. 2-10   When a business grows from a small-scale to a large-scale operation, it generally turns to the corporation form of ownership. Large retail stores, such as Marshall Field in Chicago, are operated as corporations.

told the lawyer to apply to the state for permission, in the form of a *charter*, to incorporate their hardware business. When the charter was granted, the corporation—a legal person—was created. The corporation could make contracts, own property, borrow money, and perform other activities necessary to operate a business.

The new corporation was to have a beginning *capitalization* (authorized value of stock to be issued) of $250,000. Mr. Sanchez and Mr. Cohen bought 35,000 shares each with the money they received from the sale of their old hardware store. They then sold 60,000 additional shares to five other persons who were willing to invest. One person bought 10,000 shares, three persons bought 15,000 shares each, and one person bought 5,000 shares. The remaining 120,000 shares remained unissued but could be sold if the hardware store later needed extra money for expansion. The seven principal stockholders held a meeting and elected directors. These directors could be the principal stockholders themselves or any other persons they thought would provide guidance and prestige to the business. The directors have the responsibility of outlining the general plans and policies for the store and of appointing officers to manage the business.

The corporation is the most common form of ownership for large stores. In case of financial difficulties, stockholders are responsible for losses only to the extent of the stock they own. If a stockholder dies, the corporation need not be liquidated but can continue indefinitely.

It is easy for a stockholder to withdraw by selling his stock to someone else. If needed, more capital for the corporation can be raised by the sale of authorized stocks and bonds, thus making large-scale operation possible.

The corporation, however, has some disadvantages. It is subject to many laws, regulations, and taxes. It is much more difficult to form a corporation than an individual proprietorship or partnership. Also, where ownership and management are separated, there is a possibility of irregularities and fraud and of laxity on the part of both owners and managers.

SUMMARY OF CHANGES IN TYPES OF STORES

The retail store has undergone major changes since the era of the small independent store over one hundred years ago. Every student of distribution should be aware of the trend toward large-scale operation and suburban outreach.

General Stores and Specialty Shops

Until the time of the Civil War, retailing in the United States was conducted largely in small stores with individual proprietorships. In the cities, there were specialty shops, some making and selling their wares. Shoe shops are an example. In the rural development westward, general stores at the crossroads handled the goods not produced on the farm.

Department Stores

Shortly after the Civil War, a new type of retail institution was born—the department store. It stressed wide assortments of general merchandise, grouped into distinct selling departments. Foodstuffs and other convenience goods, however, were handled largely by grocery and other neighborhood stores. Many of the department stores were partnerships.

Chains

Late in the 1800's the chain store appeared, first in the variety store field as five- and ten-cent stores in the urban centers. The success achieved, because of central buying and standardized methods of store operation, led to the spread of this concept. Grocery stores and drugstores particularly were quick to join the movement. Department stores and specialty stores in the apparel and home-furnishings fields were slower to join the chain movement because of variations in customer requirements in different localities. But since World War II they, too, have adopted the chain concept, and most are corporations.

Mail-Order Firms

In the rural areas, where most people lived until about 60 years ago, something had to replace the local general store. This was done by national mail-order firms that brought broad assortments and reasonable prices to isolated homes with their poor access to cities. These mail-order firms later developed chains of their own, selling merchandise in towns all over the country. These are now readily reached by the rural community thanks to improved roads and the automobile.

Suburban Stores

Shortly after World War II, the great shift away from the farm and the downtown cities to the suburbs got underway. Sears, Roebuck was one of the first to recognize the trend and the need for parking lots, since most customers were acquiring cars. Sears set up big department stores in virtually unpopulated areas but close to major highways. The success of these stores led to the great suburban shopping centers discussed in the next chapter.

Self-Service and Discount Stores

During much of the development sketched above, most retailers assumed that each customer needed personal attention in making buying decisions. But it was becoming apparent that self-service, along with centralized mass buying, would lower prices sharply. Corporate chains of grocery stores were among the first to adopt the new idea in the form of supermarkets. These could be thought of as discount stores, but the term was first applied to stores selling appliances on a self-service basis. The concept spread to home furnishings stores and also to departmentalized stores specializing in clothing and household goods. Many of the old-line variety store chains, such as Woolworth and Kresge, now place their major emphasis on their discount self-service subsidiaries. Leading department store chains have followed suit. Even the supermarket chains are entering the discount field by streamlining operations and concentrating on items of greatest importance to the customer.

Today we find the same customers buying much of their everyday convenience goods and standard appliances in discount stores, and yet patronizing high-class department stores and specialty shops (many of them units of chains) for outer clothing and decorative home furnishings. These are areas in which they express their own individuality.

CHECKING YOUR KNOWLEDGE

Vocabulary

1. individual proprietorship
2. partnership
3. corporation
4. articles of copartnership
5. limited partnership
6. par value
7. charter
8. capitalization

Review Questions

1. Name three types of retail store ownership.
2. List the advantages and disadvantages of an individual proprietorship.
3. List four disadvantages of a partnership.
4. Describe the rights of a corporation.
5. Which type of ownership is most common for large stores? Why?

Discussion Questions

1. Is the unlimited liability of proprietors and partnerships fair to those who want to run their own business?
2. Since Mr. Sanchez's store was prosperous at the time of partnership with Mr. Cohen, was it fair that Mr. Cohen became an equal partner investing only an amount of money equal to Mr. Sanchez?
3. How specific should the articles of copartnership be?

BUILDING YOUR SKILLS

Improving Communication Skills

Only one of the three principal parts of each irregular verb is given below. On a separate sheet of paper, copy the form below and write in the correct verb forms.

	Present	Past	Past Participle
1.			burst
2.		chose	
3.	come		
4.		ate	
5.	go		
6.			lent
7.		rang	

On a separate sheet of paper, complete each of the following sentences by writing in the blank the correct tense of the irregular verb given in parentheses after each sentence.

8. The personnel from the housewares department _____ four songs at the Christmas party. (sing)

9. Mr. Lambrecht _____ to arrange the garden center yesterday. (begin)
10. For the past five years the women's sportswear department has _____ in sales during the Easter season. (lead)
11. Marilyn Merrill has _____ more orders than anyone else for the new custom designed glassware. (write)
12. The section manager reprimanded the stock boy because he carelessly _____ the fragile items on the ground. (throw)
13. The credit personnel have _____ at 11:30 a.m. during the past month. (eat)
14. The new sales people were told that the store would open five minutes after the first bell had _____. (ring)
15. The supermarket concept _____ in the middle 1930's. (begin)

Improving Arithmetic Skills

Perform the exercises given below.

1. The Briggston Company incorporated with a beginning capitalization of 300,000 shares of stock. The following number of shares were bought by stockholders: 4,000, 11,000, 7,000, 15,000, 3,500, 5,500, 9,000, 14,000, 20,000, 30,000. How many shares were sold? How many shares remain unissued?
2. Mr. Cohen made the following bank deposits during the month of September: $310.44, $378.54, $429.94, $546.73, $274.00, and $310.70. The amounts withdrawn during September were: $198.70, $174.44, $192.58, $293.20, $149.80, $49.37, and $169.57. How much was deposited? How much was withdrawn? If Mr. Cohen had a bank balance of $916.36 at the end of August what was the new bank balance at the end of September?
3. If a customer needs carpeting for a hallway measuring 10 square meters how many square yards of carpet should she buy?
4. A garden store offered the items listed below at reduced prices. What was the amount of savings to a customer on each item?

Item	Regular Price	Sales Price	Savings
Mixed Dutch tulips	$ .08 ea.	12 for $ .89	$......
Mixed hyacinths	.35 ea.	3 for 1.00	......
Crocuses	.03 ea.	50 for 1.19	......
Rose bushes	3.69 ea.	2.98	......
Ornamental shrubs	2.49 ea.	1.95	......

5. Shown below is a partial list of an inventory sheet giving the number of items on hand as ascertained by a physical inventory and the number of items on hand according to the stock control records. Determine the amount of shortage or overage for each item.

Stock Card No.	Stock Control Records	Inventory Count	Overage (+) or Shortage (−)
4032	1,943	1,943	......
4033	827	839	......
4034	409	418	......
4035	2,768	2,647	......
4036	4,990	4,623	......

Improving Research Skills

1. Listed below are several store characteristics. For each, name two stores in your community which possess this characteristic.

   (a) Sells shopping goods primarily
   (b) Sells convenience goods primarily
   (c) Offers a great number of customer services
   (d) Offers few or no customer services
   (e) Small-scale retailer

2. All types of retail outlets are today changing their sales methods—moving into new lines, planning new locations, and offering new kinds of services. Prepare a report about a store in your community which has recently changed in one or more of these ways.

3. Draw a map of the area around your home or school encompassing three to five blocks in all directions. Enter on the map all the service establishments in this area assigning a number to each. Attach a legend that names the type of establishment in each numbered area. Are there any types of needed service establishments that are not present in the area? Do there seem to be too many of one kind?

4. Determine requirements for a business to incorporate in your state. Are there any additional city or county regulations that must be met?

Improving Decision-Making Skills

1. If you had been in Mr. Sanchez's position with a successful retail hardware store, would you have entered into a partnership with Mr. Cohen? What factors would you consider before agreeing to a copartnership with a person you did not know very well?

2. You have obtained a good business location for a fast-food type store. There is a great deal of traffic during the noon and evening hours. There is an opportunity to acquire a well-known franchise, or you can open an independent restaurant. What are some factors that would have to be considered before making the decision on a franchise? What would you do? Why?

APPLYING YOUR KNOWLEDGE

Chapter Project

Go to your school or public library and locate the current edition of the *Statistical Abstract of the United States.* Look in the index for retail trade. Find the number of establishments by type and sales. Prepare a chart showing the figures for each type of store as a percentage of the total retail industry. What conclusions can you draw from this data?

Continuing Project

In the next section of your manual, *Organizing and Operating a Retail Business,* discuss the following topics:

1. The kind of retail store you will open
2. The form of ownership you plan to have
3. The kinds of stores which will be your major competition

Collect pictures of stores similar to the kind you plan to organize.

UNIT 2

Starting a Retail Business

The merchant who intends to start a new store does a great deal of planning. He must first determine the needs of the community and how he can satisfy a need with a store that he has the ability to operate. Following this come the selection of a location, the planning of the building, decisions about equipment, and then the actual layout of the store. Much of what a merchant can do is dependent, of course, on the money he has or can get for developing his store. He must also organize the functions to be performed in the store and establish policies in regard to merchandise, customers, and employees.

chapter 3

Establishing the Retail Store

CHAPTER PREVIEW

a. The location of a retail store involves three distinct steps—choosing the community, choosing the shopping district, and choosing the site.

b. In addition to checking the characteristics of a building, questions of leasing or buying must be examined.

c. Equipment includes everything that is necessary to perform the selling and nonselling functions, except the building and the merchandise.

d. The arrangement of a store's selling area should be made from the customer's viewpoint.

e. The store image is the result of careful planning in all aspects of the store. Image is created through store design, features of merchandise carried, and services to customers.

Part a

Selecting a Location

Have you ever wondered why a drugstore or a bakery is located where it is? Have you ever seen a new retail store being built and wondered why the owners are having it built in that particular place? Most existing businesses and especially new stores are located where they are for good reasons. The merchant recognizes that the location of his business is one very important factor in his success.

The determination of a business location usually involves three steps. The first is to determine in what city or general geographic area the store is to be located. Second, there must be a determination of the specific district within the city or area. Third, the actual site within a shopping center or on a street must be selected.

CHOOSING THE COMMUNITY

The person who intends to become a merchant will probably open a store in the community in which he lives. Since he knows the community, he is more likely to be successful in adjusting his merchandise and his services to customer demand. On the other hand, there may be no need for another store of the type the would-be merchant plans to operate. In this case he may consider nearby towns with which he is already familiar.

Large-scale retailers, however, are less dependent on personal preference. They employ specialists who scientifically study the various factors connected with selecting a location and recommend to the retailer towns or cities where there is an opportunity to do a large volume of business at a relatively low expense. The ages, incomes, and life styles of the residents are determined, as well as the prices they usually pay for various classes of merchandise.

A number of factors should be considered in choosing a community for a store location. If the community seems to have an assured future with a growing population and a rising standard of living, it is usually a desirable one. In general, a community with several different industries is likely to provide greater stability for the future than one that is dependent on one industry, such as steel manufacturing or cotton growing.

 With the decided movement of population to areas in and around large cities, many small towns are finding it difficult to maintain prosperous shopping centers. With the decline in the farm population that formerly supported these towns and with the attraction of young people to the cities, many once thriving towns are stagnating. Efforts are now being made to attract industry to these localities in order to provide jobs. With low rents and a potential labor force of willing workers, such locations often prove to be attractive for many manufacturing plants. This success in turn brings a need for more retail stores.

Factors to Consider in Choosing the Community	
People of the Community	Population
	Income groups
	Differences in race, nationality, age, and family size
	Standard of living and buying habits
	Employment conditions and kinds of occupations and wage levels
Community Services	Banking and credit facilities
	Insurance rates
	Advertising media available
	Parking facilities
	Transportation facilities
	Local legislation, including taxes
	Protection facilities
Business Growth and Development	Present and future industries
	Kinds of stores and competition facing new store
	Rental costs
	Accessibility to market resources

 Illus. 3-1   This illustration presents the factors that should be considered when choosing a community for a store location. Merchants may weigh the factors differently according to their type of business, but the factors taken together will tell the businessman whether the community is a desirable one.

CHOOSING THE SHOPPING DISTRICT

 When the businessman has found the community in which he wishes to place his business, he must then select the appropriate kind of shopping district. He may choose from a central shopping district, fringes of the central shopping district, a secondary shopping district, a planned shopping center, string streets, or a neighborhood district.

Central Shopping District

The *central shopping district* is commonly called "downtown." People living in all parts of the city and even in the suburbs go there to shop, especially when they want wide assortments from which to choose.

Department stores are generally located in central shopping districts, and specialty shops are crowded close by. One of the chief problems in such districts today is to provide adequate parking space. Even though parking lots and parking buildings are provided for store customers and all-day parking is generally prohibited, it is still difficult for customers to find parking space; thus, public transportation has to be depended upon. Since rental costs in the downtown location are high and since the number of downtown shoppers is increasing much more slowly than it is in the suburbs, this type of location is not so desirable as formerly—at least for a new store.

Fringes of Central Shopping District

Stores that do not depend primarily on women shoppers often prefer side streets and similar locations within easy walking distance of the central district. Here the rents are considerably lower than in the center of downtown, and there is more space available for goods that require quite a bit of display room. Examples of stores locating on the fringes of the central shopping district are appliance stores, auto accessory stores, men's stores, and discount houses.

Secondary Shopping District

In all cities and many large towns there are *secondary shopping districts.* Many residential communities have a business street on which stores are located. The people of the area go to these secondary shopping districts because they find it more convenient than going downtown.

Planned Shopping Centers

A *planned shopping center* is a facility designed to accommodate several retail and service businesses. Such centers, usually with *malls* (pedestrian walks surrounded by stores), are developed by a single individual or firm for a predetermined number and type of stores appropriate to the expected needs of a shopping public. Most such centers have been developed in suburban areas where no businesses previously existed.

Courtesy of Winkelman's

Illus. 3-2   This planned shopping center, with a large mall, is designed to accommodate retail and service businesses. Most such centers are located in suburban areas.

There are three basic types of shopping centers. The *neighborhood shopping center* serves a residential area within a radius of about twenty blocks. It may have four or five stores and a few service businesses. The *community shopping center* is planned to serve customers in an area three to five miles from the center. It provides easy access, adequate parking, and a mix of retail businesses. A *regional shopping center* is designed to meet the needs of customers of a much larger geographic area. It has a greater number of stores, and most are larger in terms of size and merchandise offerings. Three of the largest regional shopping centers are Roosevelt Field, Long Island, New York (2.1 million square feet); Woodfield, near Chicago, (2 million square feet); and East Ridge, San Jose, California (1.75 million square feet).

Shopping centers, which started around 1950, are becoming an increasingly important factor in retailing. Currently they account for over a third of total retail trade of the country. These centers have attracted many related businesses such as banks, law and medical offices, travel agencies, and auto service centers. Large retailers find the planned shopping centers ideal locations for their mass selling activities.

String Streets

Stores are often located for miles along a main artery of traffic leading to a business center. Service stations, refreshment stands, res-

Store Sites within a Community

Downtown or Central Shopping District	Department stores Women's specialty stores Variety stores Women's shoe stores Drugstores (with large novelty and luncheonette sections)
Fringes of Central Shopping District	Specialty groceries Men's specialty stores Home furnishings stores Automobile agencies Auto accessory stores Appliance stores Discount houses
Secondary Shopping District	Same as downtown shopping district, but department stores may be absent and specialty stores may be smaller
Planned Shopping Center	Commonly built around the branches of large department stores with branches of specialty stores, units of chain stores, discount houses, and some independents
String Street	Supermarkets Fruit and vegetable stores Garden supplies Furniture and shoe stores Service stations Lunchrooms Discount houses
Neighborhood Shopping District	Unit stores such as grocery stores, drugstores, stationery stores, shoe repair shops, hardware stores, and bakeries

Illus. 3-3   Different stores locate in different shopping districts for different reasons. Consumers soon become familiar with their community's shopping districts, and they know which district to go to for a particular item. Listed above are the stores usually located in the various kinds of shopping districts.

taurants, vegetable markets, garden supply stores, and even large home furnishings stores are examples of stores found on *string streets*. With some suburban shopping centers becoming crowded, such stores have a splendid future if they provide good parking facilities.

Neighborhood Shopping District

Stores may also be located on residential streets, frequently at intersections. The neighborhood pharmacist, the neighborhood grocer, the baker, the stationer, and the shoe repairer—all find these locations well suited for their businesses because they deal principally with the people who live in the neighborhood.

CHOOSING THE SITE

Once the merchant has decided on the general location for his store, the next decision is that of selecting the exact site he will occupy. In small business districts there may be only one or two possible sites available. In large shopping districts there may be several potential sites from which the merchant may choose. The site should be near successful businesses on an active street as opposed to being near vacant buildings or empty lots. The buildings that adjoin a site under consideration should be in good condition; for a store, like a person, is judged by the company it keeps.

The side of the street on which to locate is often important, too—especially in downtown, secondary, and string street locations. Sometimes customers shop on one side simply because of habit, sometimes because it is the shady side. Successful stores have often built up one side of the street, while the other side has a reputation for stores that fail or for "cheap" stores. The direction of traffic on a street is sometimes the reason for one side being better than the other. Most customers, rather than cross traffic, want to get to the nearest sidewalk after getting off a bus.

Corner and Inside Locations

Drugstores, even in the central shopping districts, are well suited to corner locations. Such a location allows the store to attract passersby on two streets. It also provides additional window space, more light, and easy entrances. If the store has a corner entrance, customers may have to pass the entire length of the store to reach the entrance; and they thus get a chance to see the window displays.

Customer Traffic

One of the most important factors in determining a location, in other than a planned shopping center, is to know the number of people who pass by. The best method of determining the number of potential customers is to count them. A traffic count is taken by means of a clock that registers each time a little button is pressed. To get an accurate count, the shoppers coming from both directions must be counted throughout the day.

The mere fact that a large number of people pass the proposed store site, however, does not mean that the store will be successful. The retailer must determine why these people are passing. Large crowds may pass the store on their way to a bus, train, theater, post office, or bank. Such traffic is called *lane traffic*. The people involved are almost always in a hurry and would not be customers for stores carrying goods that require careful shopping. Stores selling novelties, gifts, and other pick-up articles locate where there is lane traffic.

The people passing may be going to business or to work. They represent what is known as *structural traffic*. Stands selling cigarettes, newspapers, magazines, and candies nearly always are successful in locations enjoying structural traffic.

Stores selling goods for which a great deal of thought or a large outlay of money is needed should locate where people pass in a shopping mood, that is, where there is *shopping traffic*.

Competition

The retailer who has a service to offer his community should not be afraid of competition. If he has goods that his competitors do not have, or sells at a lower price, or offers a distinctive service, he should succeed. He should, however, be aware of his competitors. He should know what they are doing, how they are operating, and what they are selling, so as to maintain at least equal standards.

Where traffic is heavy, two stores handling similar lines of merchandise may locate close together and both may be successful. Variety stores usually locate near other successful variety stores and near department stores. Shoe stores are generally found in the same block as department stores. One merchant who sells novelties, gifts, and greeting cards opened his store as near as possible to variety stores. He knew that the agents of the big variety chains were excellent location spotters and that they were required to find suitable locations through scientific analyses. Hence, the merchant who located nearby profited by the investigations of the chains.

CHECKING YOUR KNOWLEDGE

Vocabulary

1. central shopping district
2. secondary shopping district
3. mall
4. planned shopping center
5. neighborhood shopping center
6. community shopping center

7. regional shopping center
8. string street
9. lane traffic
10. structural traffic
11. shopping traffic

Review Questions

1. What three steps are taken in the process of selecting a business location?
2. Describe factors that a merchant must consider in choosing a community in which to establish a retail business.
3. Name the three types of planned shopping centers.
4. Which factors should be considered when deciding upon the specific site to locate a store?
5. What is the best method of determining the number of customers who pass a certain location? How is this done?

Discussion Questions

1. If suburban shopping centers expand into miniature cities, what will be the effect on present downtown locations?
2. Should the developers of shopping centers have the right to keep out stores, such as discounters, which they deem undesirable?
3. What types of retail stores benefit most from locating near competition?
4. Many old central shopping districts are modernizing business buildings and limiting certain streets to walking traffic. What advantages do such changes have to retail stores?

Part b

The Building

Very often there will already be a building at the site on which the merchant would like to locate. The quality and characteristics of the building will be of importance in deciding if the retailer will start a business there. Some sites, of course, will not have a building, and one will have to be constructed.

If the selected site is in a proposed shopping center, the retailer can work with the center developer in designing the proposed store. The new retailer, however, usually is more concerned with the suitability of an existing building than with the planning of a new one.

The store which is modern and up to date, both outside and inside, will win customers for the retail merchant. The store's exterior design must fit pleasantly into the entire business community, yet must be sufficiently different to attract customers.

EVALUATING A BUILDING

While homes, garages, factories, and warehouses have been used as places to start clothing stores, supermarkets, and discount stores, it is generally best to locate a store in a building that has been designed for retail selling. Modern retail buildings have features that may not be found in buildings originally planned for other purposes. Retail stores need wide entrances, display windows, unobstructed interiors, air conditioning, and escalator access from one level to another.

Using a Checklist

Successful merchants prepare checklists to be used when judging the suitability of buildings for their businesses. Such a list enables the merchant to compare the suitability of one building with another on such important features as exterior, interior, basement, heating, lighting, ventilating, plumbing, and sprinkler systems. Given below are some of the questions which might be included on a merchant's checklist:

1. Is the building large enough to accommodate the amount of business the merchant hopes to do in a few years?
2. Is the construction soundproof and fireproof? Can additional floors be added if needed?
3. Does it have a good heating system?
4. Are the windows suitable for displaying the types of merchandise for sale?
5. Do posts block the floor?
6. Are there facilities for receiving incoming goods without blocking the main thoroughfare?
7. Are there enough exits in the proper places?
8. Is the lighting system modern and in good condition?
9. Are the plumbing facilities adequate?
10. Is the building air conditioned?

Planning the Exterior

The exterior of a store building indicates to the public the nature of the store and the activity within. The *face* of a store helps give the store a personality. An attractive front is to a store what an attractive appearance is to a person. Many chain stores use the same exterior design for all their stores in order to make them easy to identify.

Courtesy of Home Fair

Illus. 3-4   The exterior of a building indicates the nature of the store and the activity within.

Display Windows. Exterior display windows should be of a size and shape suitable to the kind of merchandise that will be displayed. Furniture displays need deep windows; housewares and small appliances need wide, shallow windows; jewelry should be displayed in narrow, shallow windows.

Window backgrounds are of three kinds:

1. The *closed background* found in the majority of department stores.
2. The *semiclosed background,* with a partition, often found in hardware stores, drugstores, and laundry service shops.
3. The *open background,* called a "see-through" window, that shows the entire interior of the store. Such backgrounds are often found in grocery stores, florists' shops, and some clothing stores.

Entrances. Entrances should be wide enough and numerous enough to enable customers to enter without effort after looking at a window display. Steps should be avoided. To prevent drafts that endanger the health of employees and customers, some stores have installed infrared lamps in the store entrances. These not only warm the customers as they come indoors but also melt snow, dry puddles, and provide light. Often revolving doors or swinging doors that close themselves are used to reduce drafts and conserve heat. Many supermarkets and discount stores have installed automatic doors controlled by electric beams or pressure pads. Customers can easily enter and leave even if carrying packages.

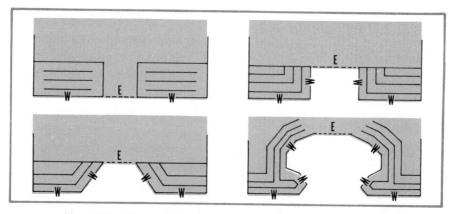

Illus. 3-5   Shown above are four common plans for store fronts. *E* in the illustration means *Entrance*, and *W* means *Window*. Which stores in your community use each of these plans?

LEASING A BUILDING

After a suitable and available building is found, the prospective merchant is ready to arrange an agreement with the owner of the property. An agreement for the use of property is called a *lease*. It is made for a certain length of time, often from three to ten years, and usually has an option to renew. This is necessary because it takes time to build up a business, and a merchant does not want the lease to expire or the rent to be increased for a reasonable length of time.

Many minor agreements between the owner and the user of the property should be written into the lease. It is important to obtain the assistance of a lawyer in drawing up the lease because there are many provisions that should be covered in the agreement.

The rent agreed upon in the lease is generally an annual sum, payable in monthly installments. Sometimes rent is set as a percentage of store sales, often with a stated minimum. The *lessee* (tenant) should always think of the rent as a percentage of his sales. The percentage of sales that can economically be paid as rent varies with the type of business and may be from 1 percent to 10 percent. In general, a beginning merchant should try to avoid paying a rent that exceeds 5 percent of his lowest estimated sales. Thus, if the merchant expects to sell $60,000 worth of goods, his annual rent should not exceed $3,000 or $250 a month. It is usually better not to go into business at all than to agree to pay a rent so high that it absorbs most of the profits.

The rentals for leased departments of modern discount houses generally average about 8 percent of sales. In department stores, real estate costs average under 3 percent of sales. In cases where the building is owned, this figure includes real estate taxes, interests on the investment in land and building, and depreciation on the building. The expenses of heating and lighting are not included. In the case of leased departments, the landlord usually provides these services in his rental charge. Other typical rents paid by retail stores (by percentage of sales) are: hardware stores, 2.4; shoe stores, 3.4; supermarkets, 1.4; and variety stores, 5.05.

Precautions in Leasing

Examine the property thoroughly to make sure that it meets the purposes for which it is to be used.

Examine the lease thoroughly to make sure that it contains:

1. No narrow restrictions on merchandise that may be sold or on services that may be provided
2. Statements of the duration of the lease, the amount of rent, the date on which the rent is to be paid, and the conditions in case of nonpayment
3. Arrangements for subleasing, subletting, and assignment to another merchant
4. Provisions in case of fire or other hazards
5. Mutual obligations concerning major and minor repairs
6. Options and renewal arrangements

Make sure that the signatures are properly witnessed.

Illus. 3-6   Since a lease is a legal document, it is important that certain precautions be observed before the lease is signed. Some of the most important precautions are listed above.

BUYING AN EXISTING BUSINESS

In some cases the search for a site and a building will result in finding an existing business of the type the retailer would like to operate. The considerations in buying an existing business include those previously discussed. In addition, the following major questions should also be answered before deciding to buy a business already in operation.

1. Why does the present owner want to sell?
2. How successful has the business been in the past?
3. What are the strengths and weaknesses of the business?
4. Is it necessary to take over the existing inventory and fixtures?
5. Are the business records complete and accurate?
6. Does an audit of the business records reveal potential for the desired level of sales?

7. If accounts receivable (amounts due on credit sales) are to be included in the purchase, do they represent a good investment?

8. How much improvement and repair will be necessary to modernize the store?

9. Does the price asked cover only the physical assets involved, or does it include an estimate of the present value of the potential earning power of the business?

10. What recommendations are made by a lawyer and accountant after their examination of the condition of the business?

The new retailer should enter into the purchase of an existing business with extreme care to avoid taking over someone else's problems and mistakes.

CHECKING YOUR KNOWLEDGE

Vocabulary

1. closed background window
2. semiclosed background window
3. open background window
4. lease
5. lessee

Review Questions

1. Why is it best to locate a business in a building that has been designed for retail selling?
2. List ten factors that should be considered in evaluating a building.
3. Describe the three different kinds of window backgrounds.
4. Name six features that should be contained in a lease.
5. What are the major considerations in buying an existing business?

Discussion Questions

1. Generally new retail stores should be on good streets, in attractive buildings, and near other stores. What type of retail businesses might be successful in remote locations and away from other stores?
2. Store space in some shopping centers is leased for a modest fixed rent plus a percentage of the monthly sales. What are the advantages of this to the retail store? to the shopping center owners?
3. Chain stores and large-scale retailers may build a store, then sell it to a commercial real estate investor, then lease it from the new owner for a long period of time. Why would this be done, and what are the advantages of this practice?

Part C

The Equipment

Merchants are keenly interested in the equipment used in their store because using proper equipment can reduce labor costs, speed and control the movement of merchandise, and add to the attractiveness of the store. The term *equipment* includes everything—except the building, people, and merchandise—which is necessary to perform the selling and nonselling functions. Articles of equipment may be classified as (1) *selling equipment,* such as shelves, counters, display racks, sales registers, and lighting; (2) *building equipment,* such as escalators, conveyor systems, floor coverings, and sprinkler systems; or (3) *nonselling equipment,* such as delivery trucks, data processing equipment, ticket marking machines, and hand trucks. In this part you will learn about some of the more important equipment with which the customer comes in contact.

SELLING FIXTURES

Those items of selling equipment which make it easy for the customer to find, examine, and buy the merchandise the store has for sale are called *selling fixtures.* Fixtures that help the customer find and examine merchandise are referred to as *merchandise hardware* and include wall shelving, showcases, counters, garment racks, display accessories, turntables, and interior signs. Fixtures that help the customer buy are those necessary to measure or fit merchandise and process sales transactions. These include measuring devices, scales, cash registers, wrapping counters, credit authorizing machines, and service desks.

Today there are wide varieties of selling fixtures available. Modern selling fixtures are simple, not elaborate; they are designed to make it easy for the customer to approach, handle, and select merchandise, and to permit easy restocking. Self-selection fixtures serve in place of salespeople and are carefully placed to present merchandise with appeal, clarity, and force. One such fixture holds 8,400 pairs of hosiery. Another type of fixture holds 400 pairs of men's slacks.

FLOOR COVERING

Regardless of the kind of store, a handsome floor covering is a definite sales asset. The floor covering should be chosen with care in

Courtesy of Gross & Associates/
Public Relations, Inc.

Illus. 3-7 This selling fixture features over 300 pantyhose of various sizes and colors. One unit such as this may yield a profit of about $1,300 a year.

order to insure easy cleaning, long wear, an attractive appearance and to minimize fatigue. Expensive floor coverings are not necessary in stores in which emphasis is placed on low prices, but even low-priced floor coverings can be durable and attractive in appearance.

An exclusive women's specialty shop may have expensive carpeting, while a service business may use flooring such as asphalt or vinyl tile. Many supermarkets and hardware stores are now carpeting their floors with the new man-made fibers such as olefin. Other floor coverings from which retailers can choose are marble, terrazzo, linoleum, rubber, cork, and several varieties of wood. Building material companies are very helpful to the retailer who needs advice on the kind of floor that would be appropriate for his store.

AIR CONDITIONING

A type of equipment that has become of major importance is the air-conditioning system. Although some air-conditioning systems cool, circulate, and filter the air, others add or remove moisture to provide the most healthful humidity. Also available on the market are combination heating and cooling systems that will keep the inside temperature of the store at any point desired. Both large and small stores find that a cool store draws customers in summer.

LIGHTING

Good store lighting doesn't just happen. It comes about through careful planning and coordination with the store's interior design. In many old stores and even in some new ones lighting is viewed as a mere necessity. In such stores merchandise tends to look less attractive. Frequently customers return purchases saying, "It didn't look the same at home." Proper store lighting can add glamour and elegance to the overall store *decor* (decorative scheme) and increase the appeal of merchandise.

Three basic categories of lighting may be considered for retail store use. First, general lighting or the lighting of large store areas. General lighting is almost always installed in the ceiling and provides the light for most store purposes. Second, wall lighting, which provides light for the interior surfaces and the walls, is usually individually designed for stores. This type of lighting makes a store seem larger and all parts equally inviting. Third, display lighting which supplements general and wall lighting and serves to highlight special displays and merchandise.

Courtesy of Federated Department Stores, Inc.

Illus. 3-8   Proper display lighting is very important—whether the product is appetizing food or expensive wearing apparel.

Types of Lamps

Either fluorescent or incandescent lamps or both in combination are used for store lighting. *Fluorescent* lamps create light by having the electricity jump from one electrode to another in a vacuum or vapor. *Incandescent* lamps or bulbs have the electricity pass through a filament which gives the light. Fluorescent lamps are more widely used, for they give more illumination per watt and are inexpensive to operate. Fluorescent lamps are designed for cool or warm lighting needs, and certain types (such as quartz or mercury vapor lamps) can give color rendition very close to natural light. Incandescent lamps, however, give the broadest range of natural light color rendition.

Types of Lighting Systems

The chief factors to be considered in planning a lighting system are: (1) the type of fixtures, (2) the number and types of lamps used for fixtures, (3) the length and width of the room, (4) the height of the room, (5) the color of the walls and ceilings, and (6) the nature of the merchandise. There are five types of lighting systems:

1. *Direct.* Virtually all the light comes downward directly from the lighting units.
2. *Semidirect.* Most of the lighting is direct, but some is reflected from the ceiling.
3. *Semi-indirect.* Some of the light is transmitted directly downward, but over one half is reflected from the ceiling.
4. *Indirect.* Practically all the light is reflected from wide ceiling or wall areas.
5. *Panel.* A glass panel is so treated that when an electric current is passed over it, the entire panel glows. There are no filaments.

Advantages of Good Lighting

Increases the selling power of displays

Makes the store look pleasant and up to date

Permits customers to inspect merchandise carefully and to buy with less likelihood of merchandise being returned

Lessens salespeople's fatigue

Allows complete utilization of selling area

Creates a shopping atmosphere

Illus. 3-9   A few of the many advantages resulting from good lighting are listed above.

Semidirect lighting is usually used for store interiors, because it is inexpensive and fixtures are easy to keep clean. Fixtures should be at least 12 feet from the floor to avoid glare. Three-hundred-watt lamps are commonly used, and they are usually placed 10 to 15 feet apart.

Semi-indirect and indirect fixtures are very popular in high-class stores because of the well-diffused, soft light; but they consume more electricity than semidirect fixtures.

To get the most out of a good lighting system, it is necessary to have light walls and ceilings. Good colors are cream, white, and greenish gray, with the ceilings lighter than the walls. A cream color never creates glare. The effectiveness of a lighting system may be reduced as much as 40 percent by dirty or dingy ceilings and walls; hence, they should be kept clean.

Illus. 3-10   In the illustration on the left the ceiling light strikes the showcase, and the light reflection is directed away from the customer. In the illustration on the right the ceiling light strikes the showcase directly, and the customer receives a glare and finds it hard to see merchandise. This points out that the moving of a selling fixture even a few inches can make a big difference in the effect of lighting on customers and merchandise.

TRENDS IN RETAILING EQUIPMENT

Changes and modifications in retail equipment are constantly being made. Computerized merchandising systems are being adopted in stores with accompanying changes in selling fixtures. Computer-type sales registers speed sales, credit, and inventory records to the point that each is updated within seconds of a sale. In some cases the equipment automatically reorders needed merchandise. Electronic credit control devices which check the validity and buying limits of a credit card are becoming commonplace in stores.

The use of closed-circuit video tape recording has been used in store security and personnel training. Video tapes are becoming more widely used in merchandising presentations such as interior decorating, landscaping, and similar areas where in-store visualization of products is limited.

CHECKING YOUR KNOWLEDGE

Vocabulary

1. equipment
2. selling equipment
3. building equipment
4. nonselling equipment
5. selling fixtures
6. merchandise hardware
7. decor

8. fluorescent
9. incandescent
10. direct lighting system
11. semidirect lighting system
12. semi-indirect lighting system
13. indirect lighting system
14. panel lighting system

Review Questions

1. What are ten examples of retail store selling fixtures?
2. What are the characteristics of a good floor covering?
3. What are the three categories of lighting used in retail stores?
4. Describe the five kinds of lighting systems.
5. What are some of the new types of equipment used in stores?

Discussion Questions

1. It is generally believed by merchants that fixtures should not be gaudy or excessively elaborate. Are there stores or circumstances when such fixtures might be appropriate?
2. Customers associate expensive store fixtures and floor coverings with high prices. Do you agree with this statement? Explain.
3. Some stores attempt to create moods or atmosphere through various lighting and musical sound techniques. Do you think that such efforts are successful? Are customers influenced by these efforts?

Part d

The Layout

Surveys show that customers tend to stay longer, buy more, and return frequently to the store that they find warm, attractive, and comfortable. Modern store design strives to provide the atmosphere and convenience desired by customers. The physical arrangement of a store for selling, displaying, storing, receiving, and delivering goods is called the *store layout*. Many large-scale retailers have special planning departments that analyze and plan layouts for various departments and stores. Any merchant who fails to realize the importance of good store layout may be getting only a small part of his potential business.

MERCHANDISE ARRANGEMENT

In almost any store the space nearest the customer entrance has the potential for the greatest amount of sales. As you move away from the store entrance, the space has less potential for generating sales. Store owners recognize this fact and select the location for merchandise accordingly. The back of a store or the upper floors are given over to nonselling activities such as receiving, marking, and store offices.

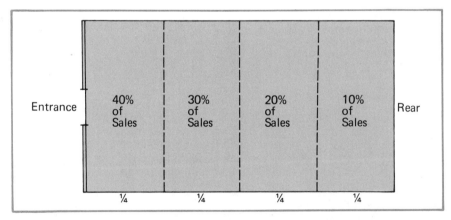

Illus. 3-11   The selling space closest to the store entrance will generate the greatest amount of sales. The value of selling space thus decreases as it is farther from the customer entrance. The traditional illustration above indicates that 40 percent of the sales will be in the first one fourth of the store, 30 percent in the second one fourth, 20 percent in the third fourth, and only 10 percent in the fourth part that is farthest from the entrance. The merchant who understands this makes merchandising adjustments that will counteract the illustrated results.

Placing Goods for Customer Convenience

Store layout is considered from the customer's viewpoint as well as from the expense angle. In the case of a drugstore, for example, where would a customer expect to find toothpaste, soap, or sun-tan lotion? Will the customer go to any part of the store for a certain cough medicine that he wants? Are skin creams called for frequently? If not, would it be wise to place them in the front of the store? Nose drops and cold remedies are moved a little nearer to the front of a drugstore in the wintertime. Items for which a customer makes a special trip to the store are often placed in the back or on an upper floor.

Department stores place furniture, rugs, and outer clothing above the main floor because customers make special trips to see them. Near the front of the main floor, department stores generally carry hosiery, neckwear, costume jewelry, handbags, and umbrellas. Silverware is often placed in this location because an effective display can be made in a small space. The men's furnishings department must be easily accessible to women, since women do much of the shopping in this department and frequently buy ties and shirts for male members of their families.

Related Merchandise Lines

Related articles should be grouped together. If a customer comes into a store for one article, other merchandise closely related to the first article should be displayed nearby. Handbags and gloves may be sold close to the neckwear department. In drugstores, shaving creams, after-shave lotions, shaving talc, razors, and blades should be close together.

Placing similar lines of goods together saves the customer both time and energy by calling to her attention goods that she will need later but can buy now. The grouping of related merchandise also makes it convenient for the salesperson to serve the customer quickly and makes it easy to offer suggestions.

The merchant who divides his store into departments soon can tell which lines move quickly and which are slow sellers. A departmentalized store, regardless of size, is usually a better managed store— stock turnover is better; sales increase because one item suggests another; and a tighter check on inventory is possible.

Attraction of Different Merchandise Types

For purposes of proper arrangement, goods may be classified as feature goods, impulse goods, and staple goods.

Feature goods are those that are advertised or displayed in the outside store windows. They have a special, timely appeal such as fashion, novelty, or low price. Since they will be sought by customers, they need not be located on major traffic aisles but rather in parts of the store that customers may not otherwise visit.

Impulse goods are those purchased without prior intent. They are usually placed near entrances and in major traffic areas. With the shopping trip now becoming a family affair, sales of impulse goods such as candy, gourmet foods, household extras, and novelties have increased. Where goods are only of seasonal interest, they should not be left long in the preferred location.

Staple goods are basic items unaffected by fashion change. They tend to form the framework around which other merchandise is arranged. Because they are repeatedly purchased by customers, they need not be located where passing traffic is heavy; but they should be assigned a permanent place since customers expect to find staples where they bought them before.

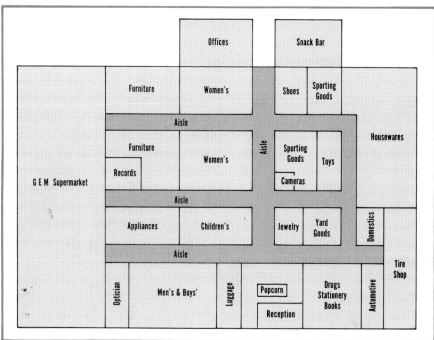

Courtesy of GEM International

Illus. 3-12   This is the layout of a large discount store. Study the layout now and study it again after you have finished reading Part D. Then see if you can explain the reasoning behind the placement of the various departments. Would you make any changes in the layout?

ARRANGEMENT OF SELLING AREA

The following points should be considered when planning the general arrangement of aisles, counters, and other selling fixtures.

1. Major aisles should run without interruption from entrances to elevators, escalators, and stairways.
2. Major aisles should be wide enough to permit three or more people to walk abreast. Minor aisles should be at least wide enough to permit two people to walk abreast.
3. Fixtures at store entrances should guide customers away from the door area so as not to interfere with incoming traffic.
4. Counters, cases, and shelving, except wall fixtures, should be low enough to permit customers to view the entire selling floor.
5. Arrangement of store fixtures should make all merchandise readily visible to customers and easy for them to examine goods.
6. Counters should be positioned so that customers examining goods are not jostled by passing traffic.
7. Checkout counters should be arranged so that the traffic flow of outgoing customers does not cross or interfere with incoming customers.
8. Service desks should be well marked and centrally located in the areas they serve.
9. Dressing rooms for trying on clothing should be spacious and well lighted and located where the staff can provide maximum service and control.
10. Identity of departments and merchandise areas should be provided by a combination of signs, decor, and merchandise arrangement.

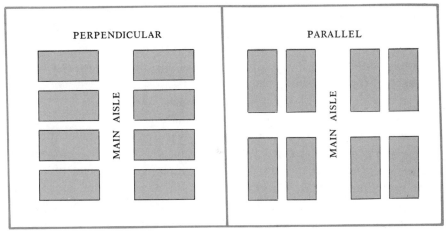

Illus. 3-13   Placing counters perpendicular to the main aisle is preferable to placing counters parallel to the aisle. In some new stores, however, architects are using fewer rectangular floor layouts and instead are using aisles with gentle curves which provide for better distribution of customer traffic.

Standard selling fixtures, manufactured in large quantities, meet the requirements for most store fixturing. Four arrangements, however, frequently require special fixtures. These are feature units, merchandise islands, ends, and self-service.

Feature Units

For variety stores, department stores, grocery stores, and specialty stores, the use of *feature units* to display "specials" has many advantages. Feature units may be used to call attention to marked-down goods or special items of an impulse nature that many people would miss if the goods were carried only in the regular department. By using an aisle table, portable cart, or by stacking, a great deal of merchandise can be placed at a favorable spot to gain the attention of a large number of people, For example, a man who has no intention of visiting the men's department may buy a shirt if he sees a special value on a "feature" on his way to an escalator. Or bargain hunters, who will not buy regular merchandise, may be attracted and purchase a special.

Feature units do have certain disadvantages. Their inclusion in an aisle can add to traffic congestion and require service of salespeople from an adjoining department. The danger of theft and damage to merchandise is also increased.

Merchandise Islands

The *merchandise island* is similar to the aisle table but has an open space in the middle where a salesperson is stationed to serve customers on all sides. It allows for effective display and protection of the goods and for very rapid handling of sales. It is excellent for the sale of one or two commodities, frequently of a seasonal nature, that sell rapidly enough to keep one salesperson busy.

Ends

Supermarkets move the location of advertised items about the store by means of *ends*. These are displays of specials which the management features for the week. These "ends" are placed at the end of a merchandise aisle regardless of their normal location in the store. For example, canned peas would generally be found in the canned vegetable section. But when an "end" of peas is scheduled, an additional display of these canned peas is erected at the end of a merchandise aisle containing paper, or baking needs, or fruit juices. The "end" attracts the customer's attention just because it is out of place from the usual location.

Courtesy of Federated Department Stores, Inc.

Illus. 3-14   This cosmetic department uses merchandise islands
and feature units effectively. Displays are oriented to feminine tastes.

Self-Service Fixtures

With the increase in self-service and semiself-service stores, layouts
have been planned to make it possible to display all the stock and to
make it all accessible to the customer. When there is complete self-
service, however, it is necessary to install wrapping stations and change-
making stations in locations that control all the exits.

Courtesy of Federated Department Stores, Inc.

Illus. 3-15   Stacked cookies at the end of the canned goods aisle
feature this supermarket special of the week.

Modern discount stores, which have improved on the self-service layouts of the supermarkets, have rows of traffic aisles that give the customer easy access to all merchandise. Usually the main aisles are at least seven feet wide to allow for free movement during the busy periods.

FLEXIBILITY IN STORE LAYOUT

Flexibility in store layout determines how easily a merchant can rearrange the fixtures of a department or section of his store. Such flexibility is becoming increasingly important in modern merchandising. Adjustments for seasonal goods, fast- or slow-selling items, customer traffic, and simply a fresh look require that a store layout have considerable flexibility.

If sales of certain goods have been unsatisfactory, the retailer may change the store layout to direct more traffic to that department. Often customer habit, such as that of going to the right upon entering the store, will influence layout. Department stores have endeavored to distribute customer traffic evenly by placing attractive displays on the left side of the store in sections away from entrances and escalators. Store layout may have to be changed because of the type of customer attracted. An effort to attract customers interested in fashion and quality may mean that the store layout should be more elegant and comfortable. An effort to attract customers interested in the price of goods may call for a less elaborate layout.

CHECKING YOUR KNOWLEDGE

Vocabulary

1. store layout
2. feature goods
3. impulse goods
4. staple goods

5. feature unit
6. merchandise island
7. ends

Review Questions

1. Which location in the store has the greatest potential for sales?
2. What advantages does grouping related items have for the customer? for the store?
3. How does the type of merchandise affect its location?
4. Name three disadvantages of feature units such as aisle tables.
5. What are some of the reasons for changing a store layout?

Discussion Questions

1. Some downtown stores and even some shopping center stores are used as "shortcuts" by people who are going to some other store or place. How does such traffic affect the store layout? Is such traffic an advantage to a store?
2. In a self-service store, such as a supermarket, what devices can you suggest to make it easy for the customer to locate a specific item that she is looking for without having to ask for help?
3. How can a merchant tell if he has too much merchandise in one selling area?

Part e

Creating a Store Image

If we could listen to a conversation of people getting ready to go shopping, we might hear such things as these: "Let's go to Barker's; that is such a nice store." "Lord's would be a good place to go for that dress material we need." Each of these comments expresses the shopper's feelings about a store. The impression people have of a store is called the *store image*.

The retailer will locate his business, plan his store layout and policies, and select merchandise in order to create a certain image in the minds of customers. If a department store wants to be known as a good place to shop for exceptional values and good service, it attempts to create that image. It does so through selection of fixtures, store layout, store decoration, choice of merchandise, and customer services, all of which develop the desired image in the minds of customers. The advertising of the store and the performance of salespeople are planned to strengthen the desired image.

A low-margin store may create an image of bargains and low prices by working toward an exciting, carnival-type atmosphere. Banners, giveaways, and personal appearances of disc jockeys and recording stars are used for attractions.

STORE QUALITIES IMPORTANT TO CUSTOMERS

Every customer is looking for different characteristics in a retail store. Overall, however, studies show that the most important characteristic of a retail store is its merchandise—its quantity, attractive price, assortment, and ready availability. This is followed by a series of factors related to store appearance—neatness, cleanliness, and spaciousness. The store's image or personality comes largely from the visual impression it leaves with a customer. Store characteristics can be classified in three categories—physical qualities, character qualities, and skill qualities. The physical qualities depend heavily on topics discussed in this chapter. Character qualities and skill qualities will be presented in more detail in later chapters.

Physical Qualities

The store building, the front and display windows, as well as the entrances, make up the outside *physical qualities* of a store. Inside, both the interior building material and the building equipment, including elevators, escalators, heating, lighting, air conditioning, and aisle space also are among the physical qualities. In fact, everything that makes up the physical appearance inside and outside is included in the store's physical qualities.

Character Qualities

In discussing the *character qualities* of a store, we should consider what kind of store it is, what it sells, the type of ownership, the services it offers, and how it attracts its customers. Included, too, in the character qualities are the reputation and goodwill that it has achieved throughout its business life. Do people trust the store's values, find its ads wholly believable, depend upon its buyers, have faith in its integrity? The kind of customer the store attracts is another indication of the character of the store.

Skill Qualities

A store's *skill qualities* are based upon its "know-how" of doing business. The number of experts a store employs will be an indication of its skill qualities. Skills of a store depend upon the amount of study the store has given to the various merchandising activities. Buying, receiving, checking, marking, storing, displaying, advertising, selling, and delivery are some of the skills in which a store can excel.

STORE DESIGN

The most obvious of the physical qualities of a store is the store design. The types of fixtures, arrangement of fixtures and equipment, and store decoration are all carefully planned to enhance a particular image. Good store design should present the merchandise in the best manner possible, as well as provide an inviting and comfortable setting for the customer to shop. A design should never be so unusual that it detracts from the merchandise or offends customers.

Some stores are designed around a theme. A men's store may want to stress a manly and athletic image. By use of solid wood fixtures, natural wood colors, a few autographed photos of local and national sports personalities, the store has the basis for the desired image. A children's store uses light colors, balloons, clowns painted on the walls, and perhaps storybook characters to create a desired image. A furniture store uses model rooms of furniture to give customers an idea of how living room, bedroom, or dining room furniture will look in their homes. In recent years store designers have started using wide varieties of materials for store interiors. Interesting, new developments in store design include:

1. Increased use of bold and bright colors
2. Increased use of store walls for displays
3. Few storage cabinets and drawers on the selling floor
4. New lighting fixtures (more use of quartz vapor lamps)
5. Extensive use of carpeting
6. Increased use of lightweight fixtures (plastic and metal) that can be easily relocated or changed
7. New forms of self-service fixtures
8. Layouts and equipment aiding in control of shoplifting
9. Creation of little shops (ministores) within departments of a store.

Courtesy of Federated Department Stores, Inc.

Illus. 3-16   A furniture store uses model rooms to give customers ιn idea of how a room will look.

Illus. 3-17   An attractive display of dinnerware features current patterns of one manufacturer's china in an eye-catching manner.

MAINTAINING THE PHYSICAL IMAGE

Once a retailer has developed a design which provides the desired image he cannot sit back and relax. Unless the merchant constantly checks and updates his store, he may soon find that his customers are going to other stores that are maintaining the images they want. Some merchants try to redo their stores each season. Others attempt to make annual improvements. The merchant who realizes that he has not kept pace with change is faced with a catching-up problem. A smart retailer has a regular plan for keeping his store attractive. This is less costly than periodic major remodeling.

The following questions will serve as a checklist to determine where a store image might be in need of attention. You can also use this checklist to make your own evaluation of a store.

1. How old are the selling fixtures?
2. In what condition is the finish of the fixtures?
3. Are the fixtures flexible and easily changed for different purposes?
4. How old is the lighting system?
5. Are all parts of the store equally well lighted and can variations in lighting be easily made?

6. Do the lamps give good color rendition?
7. When were the walls last painted or cleaned?
8. Are floor coverings in good condition and easy to maintain?
9. Do colors used in the store reflect current tastes?
10. Are all departments clearly marked by signs and/or decor?
11. Are aisles wide enough to permit good traffic flow?
12. Have feature units or aisle tables become permanently located?
13. How long has it been since the store front was redone?
14. Has there been any significant change in the nature of store customers in the past five years?

A key point to keep in mind when reviewing the previous questions is not whether fixtures, floor, and lights were new six or eight years ago, but rather what impression do customers get now when they walk into the store?

CHECKING YOUR KNOWLEDGE

Vocabulary

1. store image
2. physical qualities
3. character qualities
4. skill qualities

Review Questions

1. What factors enter into a store's image?
2. Name the three quality categories into which store characteristics are classified.
3. List at least six recent developments in store design.
4. Why should retailers have a continous program of updating their stores?
5. List at least ten questions to include in a checklist of the physical elements in the store's image.

Discussion Questions

1. During the past few years many stores, particularly department stores, have created theme shops and ministores in several of their main merchandise divisions. What are some of the reasons for doing this, and why have such stores often been successful? What drawbacks exist from the customer's point of view?
2. Pilferage and shoplifting continue as serious problems for most retailers. The free flow layouts and self-service fixtures seem subject to unusually high levels of loss. What layout and fixture designs would serve to best control customer pilferage?
3. Although the overall trend is toward bold colors and simple modern fixtures, are there certain types of retail stores or merchandise lines where heavy and elaborate fixturing would be appropriate?

BUILDING YOUR SKILLS

Improving Communication Skills

Each of the following sentences contains two verbs in parentheses. Only one of the verbs can be used correctly in the sentence. On a separate sheet of paper, write the number of each sentence and the correct verb to be used in that sentence.

1. Of the three locations the one on Johnson street (comes, come) closest to our requirements.
2. The problem with the wall lights (was, were) a faulty switch.
3. All six entrances (are, is) equipped with forced-air heating.
4. There (were, was) many customers crowded into the Yarn Yard Shop.
5. Bold colors and simple design (is, are) features of modern fixtures.
6. Custodians (work, works) at night in the shopping center.
7. The store image (depend, depends) upon a variety of factors.
8. There (is, are) many different types of stores in a regional shopping center.
9. Only a few of the stores (was, were) planning to remodel next year.
10. Everyone (is, are) ready for the movie on store lighting.

Improving Arithmetic Skills

Perform the following multiplication exercises on a separate sheet of paper.

1. A customer buys 4 pairs of socks at 99 cents a pair and 2 knit shirts at $2.90 each. If there is a 4% sales tax, how much change will you give the customer if he pays with at $20 bill?
2. An acetate fabric is priced at $4.97 a yard. A customer buys 3½ yards of the material and must also pay a 3% sales tax. What is the amount of the sale?
3. A set of socket wrenches comes in the following sizes: 1 inch, ¾ inch, ⅝ inch, ½ inch, and ⅜ inch. What are the approximate sizes of these 5 sockets in millimeters? (Conversion of inches to millimeters can be approximated by multiplying inches by 25.)
4. Burke Hardware received a shipment of paint consisting of 16 gallons, 58 quarts, and 24 pints. Gallons of paint cost $2.90, quarts cost 80 cents, and pints cost 45 cents. What was the total cost of this shipment of paint?
5. A drugstore chain reported that the average annual sales volume for each of its 36 stores was $196,450. What was the total sales volume for this chain?

Improving Research Skills

1. You make a series of traffic counts in front of a building you are considering renting. You learn that on a typical day 4,000 shoppers pass during the hours you will stay open. Experience indicates that 25% of the passersby will enter the kind of store you have in mind and that 50% of those who enter will buy. The average unit of sale

of the kind of merchandise to be carried is $6. Assuming that you plan to be open 310 days a year, what annual sales volume can you reasonably expect? What is the most you should pay for rent?
2. Visit a large-scale retail firm such as a department store or variety store. Identify examples of the three categories of store lighting—general, wall, and display. Identify, if possible, the five types of store-lighting systems (direct, semidirect, semi-indirect, indirect, and panel). What merchandise area is associated with each type?
3. Make a list of selling equipment found in either a grocery store or variety store at which your family shops.
4. Check with local supermarkets to determine the items placed at checkout points to stimulate impulse buying. Can you suggest any improvements in the merchandise selection? What seasonal changes would you recommend?
5. Ask five of your friends their opinions (images) of a local retail store. Why do you think they gave the answers they did? On what did they agree? On what did they disagree?

Improving Decision-Making Skills

1. The Schreveport Department Store is remodeling its downtown store. The main-floor selling area will be 120 feet by 200 feet. The main entrance will be in the center of a 120-foot side, with a minor entrance on one of the 200-foot sides. The following departments are to be on the main floor: (1) books and stationery, (2) costume jewelry, (3) cosmetics, (4) handbags, (5) junior misses' dresses, (6) women's lingerie and sleep wear, (7) luggage, (8) men's accessories, and (9) women's sportswear. How would you arrange these departments in the space available?
2. Mr. Carson has the necessary capital to start a retail hardware store. In his city there are two possible sites for the store. The first is a corner location in the downtown business district; it has a 35-foot frontage on the main street and extends for 90 feet down a side street. The second possible site is also in the downtown area on the main street, but it is located in the middle of the block and has a 50-foot frontage. The corner location rents for 25% more than the inside location. What factors should Mr. Carson consider in deciding on a location? Which location would you suggest? Why?
3. In this chapter there is a statement that two stores handling similar lines of merchandise may locate close together and both may be successful. Do you think this applies in the following case?
   On a residential street within easy walking distance of a secondary shopping center in a large city, a shop called Pampered Kitchens, carrying gifts for informal dining and kitchen use, has been operating successfully for six years. The proprietor has only one part-time assistant. A similar shop has just been opened in the same block, on the same side of the street, about 120 feet away. It is about the same size.
   The proprietor of the established shop is uneasy, even though the merchandise of the two stores is somewhat different. The new store emphasizes novelty rather than practical items.
   What advice would you give the established proprietor? Will the competition help or hurt her? Should she take any defensive action?

APPLYING YOUR KNOWLEDGE

Chapter Project

The class may do this project as a group or subdivide into committees, each committee completing a portion of the project. The explanation is directed to a committee.

A committee from the class is to select a vacant building on a shopping street that is well known to the entire class. The committee is to determine from the real estate agent the size of the store (frontage and depth, basement and upper floor), structural details, rent asked, and the types of businesses which formerly occupied the building. The committee also is to make an estimate of the number of people that pass the site on a normal day between 9 a.m. and 6 p.m. and during any evening hours that stores on the street are open.

The information gathered by the committee will be presented to the class for a discussion of the following: (1) the type of store which should be most successful in the location, (2) how much merchandise or service the store should be able to sell in a year, (3) whether the rent asked is reasonable, and (4) what structural changes are necessary and their cost.

Continuing Project

In your manual, prepare a report on the considerations and specifications in selecting your store location, building, equipment, and layout. Illustrate the report with pictures, sketches, and drawings. Describe the store image that you want to establish in the community.

Financing and Organizing a Store

CHAPTER PREVIEW

a. A person can become the owner of a business by buying into an existing business, by purchasing an existing business, or by starting a new business.

b. The amount of money needed to start a retail business will vary depending upon the nature of the store. The beginning merchant usually must provide most of the money, but help can be obtained from other sources.

c. The capital of a business is divided into three categories—fixed capital, working capital, and cash reserves. The working capital should be emphasized because this money buys the merchandise that will be resold.

d. Business risks are classified as insurable or non-insurable. Good merchants protect their businesses against possible loss by carrying appropriate insurance.

e. Good store organization assures that all necessary functions will be performed by those who are best able to carry them out. Large and small retail stores must have good organizational structures.

Part **a**

Acquiring a Business

To own a business, to try out ideas, to be the boss—these are frequent thoughts of many who plan to go into retailing. The independence and security that are expected from business ownership do not come automatically. Success results from careful planning; long, hard hours of work; and a willingness to accept the life and responsibilities of being a business owner. Every day new businesses are launched. Some will be successful, some will get by, but soon a great number will only be history.

There are three common ways by which a person can become an owner of a retail business. First, he can buy into an existing business by becoming an active partner or by buying substantial shares of stock. Second, he can buy an existing business from someone else. Third, he can establish a new store.

BUYING INTO AN EXISTING BUSINESS

Dennis Scholl worked for seven years at Burke's Hardware store. Mr. Burke, the owner and manager, planned on retiring in a few years; and none of his children was interested in taking over the business. Dennis knew this and talked with Mr. Burke about "buying into the business." Mr. Burke thought this would be a good arrangement. He agreed to have Dennis as a junior partner until he retired. Then Dennis would have the option to buy the store.

Becoming a partner in an existing business is relatively easy compared with buying a business or establishing a new store. A retail business looking for a partner is generally on the way toward expansion. Partnership opportunities can be found by contacting manufacturers and wholesalers and by talking with salesmen. Store owners looking for partners may advertise in newspapers and trade journals, or they may list the opportunity with a business broker. The soundness of the business may be established by having an accountant check the records and by inspecting the merchandise inventory to be sure that it consists of readily salable goods. The reader should refer to Chapter 2 to review the advantages and disadvantages of ownership either by means of a partnership or by purchasing stock in a corporation. The latter method does not normally provide participation in the management of the business, but simply the right to share in any profits that may be made available for distribution.

BUYING AN EXISTING BUSINESS

The Adobe Shop and the New Cargo are two men's stores in the college shopping district of the city of Winfield. Pat Baxter is a salesman and, recently, also a buyer for New Cargo. He thoroughly enjoys merchandising men's clothes and is eager to have his own store. He analyzed the local market and learned that it would be difficult to start a third men's store in the college area. Unexpectedly the owner of the Adobe Shop announced that he was interested in selling his business. Based on the results of his analysis, Pat Baxter knew that this was an opportunity he couldn't pass up; and he began to negotiate for the purchase of the Adobe Shop.

The seller of a going business will have an asking price. The buyer must test the reasonableness of that price by determining the condition of the premises and the stock and by checking the records to see if the business has been making a profit. A good business may be worth 10 to 20 times its current annual profits. The advantages and disadvantages of buying an existing business are difficult to weigh. On the plus side, the advantage of getting started immediately is a big factor. The store is known and accepted in its location, and the new owner can get underway almost immediately after purchase. Another advantage of buying an existing business is that the records of the business are available. The new merchant has a concrete picture of sales, purchases, resources, percentage of expenses, and other necessary figures not available when establishing a new store. The physical stock is also available for study, making it possible to trim from the seller's valuation obsolescent and even worthless stock.

The chief disadvantage of buying a going business is that more capital is generally required than would be necessary to establish a new store of similar kind since the owner wants to be paid for goodwill as well as for tangible assets. *Goodwill* is that value which is in excess of the owner's total investment. Goodwill arises from the reputation of the business and its relations with its customers. Stores which are offered for sale may not have enough of an assured following to justify paying extra money for goodwill. However, well-established stores that are sought after and eventually purchased may include goodwill as a part of the selling price.

Buying an Existing Business

Advantages   Buyer can start operation immediately.

Past business records are available to guide future operations.

Capital requirements are easy to determine.

Problems of location, equipment, layout, and merchandise assembly are already solved.

Disadvantages   The reasons for selling may be hidden.

It generally requires more capital to buy an existing business than to start a new store of a similar type.

It is difficult to evaluate assets.

The buyer may have to pay for goodwill.

Illus. 4-1   There are both advantages and disadvantages involved in buying an existing business. The prospective owner should evaluate the business carefully, considering these advantages and disadvantages, before he makes an offer to buy.

Sometimes there are legitimate reasons why an owner would want to sell his business. The old age of the owner, his ill health, or his change in location or occupation are possible reasons. Also, an owner may sometimes be unsuited to business ownership and may wish to liquidate his investment, although there is nothing wrong with the business that careful management could not correct.

ESTABLISHING A NEW BUSINESS

Marilyn Marsh has been working for the past five years in the china, glass, and giftware department of a large downtown department store. She has been buying for the giftware area for the last two years. The city has grown rapidly during the past ten years, and a new community shopping center is being built to serve an area of better than average income families. Marilyn checked with the center developer and found that she could get space in the new center for a card, book, and gift store. It would be five months before the center would be ready for opening, and Marilyn decided she would lease the space and get ready to open her own store.

The mistaken idea that retailing is an easy road to riches is the lure which attracts so many incompetents to open stores of their own. The inability of people to judge themselves objectively and to recognize their shortcomings for a retailing career will always be a major

Courtesy of Flah & Co.

Illus. 4-2   A demand for the merchandise should exist if a business is to be successful. A thorough market analysis should be conducted before a retail store is opened.

cause of retailing failure. Those who venture to start a business of their own must be ready to assume great risk and must have perseverance and personal capacity for sacrifice. Studies show that there is generally more than one cause for failure, but the principal one is within the person himself.

Personal Qualifications

The person planning to operate a retail business obviously should have some prior experience in retailing. A few years' work in a business similar or closely related to the one planned will give the new business owner insights and a basis for making effective decisions. Work in small retail firms usually provides experience in many tasks and problems of retailing. Work in large firms may mean an opportunity to go through a company training program and to work with highly successful retailers. The prospective business owner should have had some experience at the supervisory or managerial level.

In addition to the practical experience, the aspiring retailer should obtain some formal retail education in high school or college. More and more schools are providing full-time courses as well as part-time evening classes. Such formal training provides a good background for retail ownership. A study of economics, government, and distribution, for example, will provide the beginning retailer with a broad viewpoint of business and the place of retailing in the overall picture. The study of more specific subjects such as retail merchandising, advertising, display, and salesmanship permits the person to develop practical competencies which are needed. Such formal training enables a retailer to meet and to understand problems—an ability that experience alone cannot provide.

If a prospective retailer has both experience and training in the kind of store he wants to establish, plus a background of formal training, he has largely eliminated the two major causes of retail failure—inexperience and lack of training.

Management Aids

There are many resources available to the person planning to open his own store. Many of these aids are free, and many more require only a small expenditure in terms of the value of the help received. The United States Department of Commerce and the Small Business Administration provide literature as well as referral to helpful personal resources. The Small Business Administration has prepared a series of booklets covering most of the operating problems of the small retailer, as well as some booklets specifically directed to certain types of retail businesses. One of the most useful is called *Management Audit for Small Retailers*. The retailer dealing with food and fiber products will find a great deal of literature available from the United States Department of Agriculture. Other sources not to be overlooked are the commerce departments of the various states, public libraries, and the publications of trade associations of merchants who deal in the types of merchandise that the new owner plans to handle.

Individual aid for the new retailer is available from the suppliers of merchandise. Leading wholesalers maintain service departments that specialize in helping new merchants get started. Equipment supply houses help merchants plan layouts and modern systems of inventory and sales control.

CHECKING YOUR KNOWLEDGE

Vocabulary

goodwill

Review Questions

1. What are the three common ways by which one becomes an owner of a retail business?
2. What are the advantages and disadvantages of buying an existing business?
3. Outline the educational background that a prospective retailer should have.
4. Name the two major causes of retail failure.
5. What sources of information about management and operation of retail stores are available to the new retailer?

Discussion Questions

1. In many occupations, such as plumbing, barbering, and real estate, the individual must show evidence of ability before he is given a license to work. Should prospective retail store owners be required to show evidence of qualifications before they are given permission to run a business? Be sure to consider carefully objections to such licensing.
2. In what circumstances would it probably be more desirable to start a new business rather than buy an existing one?
3. Would it be ethical to go to work for a large chain retailer just to get the training and experience you need to open your own business which may be in competition with one of the chain's stores?

Part b

Raising Capital

In order for Dennis Scholl to become a part owner of Burke's Hardware store, he had to invest a certain amount of money even though the business was already operating. He was fortunate in that Mr. Burke was willing to let him share in the business for a modest beginning investment. For the person just starting in business, the matter of finances can be rather critical. Money is required to purchase equipment and merchandise, and money is needed to pay expenses. The inflow and outflow of money in a business must be carefully regulated, or the business will soon be in financial difficulties. The balance of the investment between equipment and merchandise must be such that adequate sales and profits can be made.

DETERMINING CAPITAL NEEDS

The amount of *capital* (the money needed to run a business) that a person needs to start a business will vary. The capital needed will vary with the type of store, the volume of business expected, the cost of necessary equipment, and the kinds of goods to be sold.

The roadside stand offering farm produce or light refreshments requires much less money to start than a modern grocery or restaurant. The type of service that will be given also affects the amount of beginning capital needed. If the store is to be a cash-and-carry business, the capital requirement will be less than that needed for a store planning to extend credit.

For help in determining how much money is needed to open and operate a store, the beginning retailer should obtain operating data for the type of store he has in mind. He should also consult his banker, accountant, and lawyer, who will have information about the amount of money other people have needed to enter similar businesses. The typical investment for a small retail business ranges from an average low of about $10,000 to an average high of about $50,000. When fixtures are expensive, or when the merchandise assortment must be quite large, the amount is much more.

SOURCES OF CAPITAL

To finance the business, several sources of capital are available to the retailer. These sources are (1) individual savings, (2) buying on credit, (3) personal loans, (4) partners, (5) corporate financing, and (6) small business investment companies. Most of these sources are available to the beginner in business.

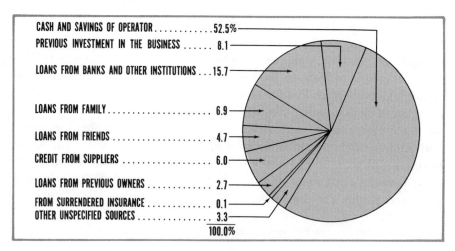

CASH AND SAVINGS OF OPERATOR	52.5%
PREVIOUS INVESTMENT IN THE BUSINESS	8.1
LOANS FROM BANKS AND OTHER INSTITUTIONS	15.7
LOANS FROM FAMILY	6.9
LOANS FROM FRIENDS	4.7
CREDIT FROM SUPPLIERS	6.0
LOANS FROM PREVIOUS OWNERS	2.7
FROM SURRENDERED INSURANCE	0.1
OTHER UNSPECIFIED SOURCES	3.3
	100.0%

Small Business Administration

Illus. 4-3   A prospective business owner may call upon a number of sources of capital to finance his business. The graph above shows how much of the total capital needed to finance a business is usually contributed by each source.

Individual Savings

Most small retailers start their businesses by using their own savings. If the amount of the savings is not enough for the initial investment, they may call upon relatives and friends for loans. Sometimes personal savings and small loans are not enough, and the retailer must turn to other sources of capital.

Buying on Credit

Arrangements may sometimes be made to purchase furniture and fixtures on credit. Such arrangements reduce the amount of ready cash needed to open the store. One large seller of store fixtures will sell fixtures on these terms: 25 percent down before the fixtures are shipped, 8 percent paid upon installation, and the balance covered by notes bearing 6 percent interest and payable over a period of one year. Stock for resale may also be bought on credit if the new store has a reasonable cash reserve. Many sellers will grant a store 30 to 90 days' credit if the store cannot pay more promptly.

Personal Loans

Borrowing money as a means of raising needed capital for a business should normally be limited to emergency needs. The necessity of paying interest rates on the amount borrowed and the possibility of losing one's property if the loan cannot be repaid are reasons why retailers often prefer to use other methods of financing.

Commercial banks will usually lend money only on *negotiable collateral* (something of value which the bank can sell if the buyer fails to repay). However, if a merchant has an established good reputation, collateral may not be required on small loans that are to be repaid within a short period of time.

A retailer can also obtain money from personal loan companies. Such firms will lend money on collateral, as a bank does. They will also lend money if the prospective borrower gets a responsible person or persons to sign the note as a guarantee that the loan will be repaid. Such a person is called a *comaker*.

Banks and personal loan companies are probably the main sources for personal loans, but retailers sometimes borrow on life insurance policies or on their automobiles. They may also obtain money from a cooperative credit union if they are members of the union.

The landlord, if the premises are leased, is sometimes an excellent source of needed capital. He has an interest in the success of the store,

Courtesy of New York Life Insurance Company

Illus. 4-4   How much capital is needed and where it can be raised
is a challenge to the young person determined to start his own business.

particularly if the rent is set as a percentage of sales. A loan from him
may be incorporated in the rental contract so that it may be repaid as
rent is paid.

If an existing business is being purchased, still another source of
capital is the former owner. The seller may agree to receive his payments over an extended period of time, or he may even invest in the
business as a silent partner.

Partners

One of the best sources of capital is the taking of partners, either
active or silent, into the business. An *active partner* furnishes money
for the business in return for an interest in the business. He also helps
in the management of the business. *Silent partners* invest money for a
pledged interest in the business but take no part in the management of it.
Under certain conditions, the silent partners can assume control of the
business.

Corporate Financing

Corporate financing is generally not used by the small retailer, but
large companies raise most of their capital by this means. Corporate
financing may be done through the sale of stock or the sale of bonds.

Stock represents shares of ownership in the corporation. Owners of stock are entitled to a share of the profits if any profits are earned and dividends declared.

A *bond* is a written promise by the corporation to repay a definite sum of money at a specified time and to pay interest at regular intervals. Persons who buy bonds do not actually have a share of ownership in the corporation; the bond is simply evidence that the corporation owes them money. Persons who own bonds must be paid interest before stockholders can receive any dividends.

Pitfalls in Raising Capital

Loan sharks who charge excessive interest rates

Fees to promoters to raise capital

"Partner Wanted" opportunities in newspaper ads

Deals or propositions which involve relinquishing ownership in the business

---

Illus. 4-5   When an individual is in dire need of money, he is likely to act hastily and do something which will make his business situation even worse. Listed above are four of the most common pitfalls in raising capital; every merchant should beware of them.

Small Business Investment Companies

Congress, realizing the financial difficulties of many small-scale businessmen, passed the Small Business Investment Act in 1958. This Act licensed the Small Business Administration to set up local investment and development companies to lend money to small businessmen who have exhausted their funds or have been turned down by private sources. Under some circumstances these companies can also provide *equity capital* (capital that makes the lending company a part owner of the business).

CHECKING YOUR KNOWLEDGE

Vocabulary

1. capital
2. negotiable collateral
3. comaker
4. active partner
5. silent partner
6. stock
7. bond
8. equity capital

Review Questions

1. For what sorts of things is money needed when opening a retail business?
2. List the sources of capital available to the new retailer.
3. Name the sources of capital that usually contribute the most to the investment in a new business.
4. List at least three dangers a merchant should beware of when raising capital.
5. What is the function of small business investment companies?

Discussion Questions

1. What are some of the advantages and disadvantages of raising capital through personal loans from family and friends?
2. When a merchant borrows money does he lose control of his business?
3. Should a merchant be limited as to how much he can borrow, such as a specified percentage of net worth of the business?

Part C

Distribution of Capital

When Pat Baxter began his negotiations to buy the Adobe Shop, he recognized that he was going to have to arrange for a lot more money than just the cost of the business building. He knew from his experience at the New Cargo Store that the total capital of a business is generally divided into three categories—fixed capital, working capital, and a cash reserve.

Fixed capital is the money invested in land buildings, fixtures, and equipment. These funds are used to provide the merchant a place in which to do business. *Working capital* is the money that is invested in merchandise and—as goods are sold and paid for—used to pay operating expenses and reinvested in additional merchandise. A *cash reserve* is the amount of money held for emergency or unexpected situations. Funds invested in saving certificates or easily cashed government securities are usually treated as cash.

FIXED CAPITAL

A portion of the money needed to start a business must be spent for equipment and fixtures. Certain types of retail stores will need more fixtures than others. Furniture stores, for example, need fewer fixtures than grocery stores, and shoe stores need fewer than automobile service stations. On the other hand, retail establishments that handle bulk goods, such as lumber, need extensive buildings for ware-housing and storage. The cost of altering or repairing a building must also be considered in deciding upon the total amount of fixed capital that will be needed.

As a general rule, it is a good policy to keep the fixed capital, as a percentage of the total capital, as low as possible—consistent with getting the maximum results. This may be accomplished by renting a building instead of buying, by leasing or buying fixtures on the install-ment plan, or by considering secondhand equipment wherever possible. Once again, however, the beginning merchant should be cautioned about attempting to operate with insufficient or obsolete fixtures and equipment. To lose sales because merchandise cannot be properly dis-played or controlled is poor management.

WORKING CAPITAL

The major portion of the funds needed to begin a retail business is invested in merchandise for resale. If some goods are sold on credit, this investment includes goods sold but not yet paid for. As the merchandise is sold and paid for, the receipts are used to buy more merchandise and to pay expenses. Thus, the funds are used over and over again.

How much money to invest in merchandise is a difficult question to answer. The answer depends upon the size of the assortment needed.

A conservative estimate of sales is first necessary. This must come from the retailer's past experience in his type of business and from an estimate of the customer traffic, the number of sales transactions, and the value of the average sale.

It is next necessary for the retailer to determine the customary *stock turn* (number of times the average stock is sold during the year) in his kind of business. For example, suppose a man going into the grocery business expects to sell $96,000 of goods a year. He knows that the yearly stock turn of a retail grocery store is about 12. This means that approximately $8,000 of stock at retail value should pro-duce those sales. If the wholesale price of this merchandise is about 4/5 of the retail value, he will need $6,400 to buy goods that will retail at $8,000.

As money flows in from sales, it is spent for merchandise and expenses. These expenses include salaries, rent, heat, light, supplies, taxes, insurance, advertising, as well as many minor expenses which are sometimes unforeseen. There must be sufficient working capital to cover the cost of goods that produce sales.

It is necessary to study the published financial reports from other similar businesses to determine the normal percentage of working capital to total capital. One must plan far in advance for merchandise requirements and allow a substantial margin for slow-selling periods and unforeseen developments. A new merchant should not expect to do quite as well as "normal" or "typical" until his business is well established. This means he should allow for relatively more working capital during the beginning years than most established stores seem to require.

CASH RESERVES

After a location has been selected, the building altered or repaired, suitable fixtures and equipment installed, and stock purchased, the merchant often finds that he does not have enough cash reserves to meet expenses that arise before he receives any income from sales. Many merchants hope that sales will take care of salaries and bills as they come due, but it takes time to establish a business. Then, too, sales may fail to meet expectations, and unforeseen expenses may arise. For example, a merchant may have invested his working capital in a stock of goods for the winter season expecting enough sales in November to provide funds for November expenses. If, because of various reasons, such as weather or economic conditions, November sales were low, he may not have earned enough on sales to pay for November expenses. He would have to draw upon his cash reserves. If December sales were then higher than expected, he would be able to build his cash reserves back up to the planned level. If the merchant does not have a cash reserve to use in such situations he may get a poor reputation for not

---

Pointers for Handling Cash (Reserves)

Bond all employees who handle cash.

Have all mail opened and a record of enclosed checks prepared by someone other than the bookkeeper.

Deposit all cash receipts daily.

Pay for all merchandise and regular expenses by check. Make only small disbursements from a petty cash fund.

Never sign blank checks in advance or make out checks to Cash.

Use only prenumbered checks.

Illus. 4-6   What are the reasons for each of the above suggestions?

meeting his operating obligations promptly. Another use of the cash reserve is to have funds with which to take advantage of unusual buying opportunities.

Even if a store is making a profit, there is no assurance that there will be plenty of cash on hand. As the profit comes in, an unwise merchant may buy a piece of expensive equipment outright or buy merchandise in quantities entirely out of line with sales. Profit should not be confused with cash available. Sometimes a store may have a good deal of cash on hand and yet not make a profit. If merchandise is sold at cost or below cost, the goods can be turned into cash readily, but no profit is made on the sale. A merchant must keep enough cash on hand to meet bills as they come due and expenses as they arise.

CAPITAL RATIOS

A *ratio* is simply a fraction showing a comparison of one quantity to another. Comparisons of a merchant's capital to various aspects of his business operation provide him a basis for judging whether he is successful in meeting his goals.

Courtesy of Armstrong Cork Company

Photo by the makers of Armstrong flooring

Illus. 4-7   A gift, book, and card shop is an example of a store that requires a fair amount of working capital invested in merchandise for resale.

Fixed Capital to Working Capital

For most types of retail stores, a sound rule to follow is to invest in merchandise two to four times the amount invested in fixtures and equipment. This is a desirable ratio for most stores, but there are exceptions. For example, the costly equipment for a supermarket, plus the rapid stock turn that can be realized on food products, makes it often necessary to invest more in equipment and fixtures than in merchandise. A hardware store, however, which needs a wide assortment of goods, may have several times as much money in merchandise as in equipment and fixtures.

Current Assets to Accounts Receivable

Current assets are items of value that can be converted into cash in a short period of time or are already in cash form. The current assets of a business include not only the merchandise inventory but also cash and accounts receivable. *Accounts receivable* is the amount owed the store by customers who have purchased merchandise on credit. Care must be taken not to tie up any more money than is necessary in accounts receivable. The importance of controlling accounts receivable through good credit policies is discussed in the next chapter.

Current Assets to Current Liabilities

Current liabilities represent the amount that a merchant currently owes other people and firms. The merchant must be careful not to owe too much to wholesalers, banks, and equipment dealers. Ordinarily, his current assets should be three to five times the amount he currently owes. The store should have on hand enough cash to pay its current debts.

Store profits, assets, and liabilities are shown in two important financial reports which the merchant prepares. One is the income statement, or profit and loss statement, and the other is the balance sheet. More will be told about these in a later chapter.

CHECKING YOUR KNOWLEDGE

Vocabulary

1. fixed capital
2. working capital
3. cash reserve
4. stock turn

5. ratio
6. current assets
7. accounts receivable
8. current liabilities

Review Questions

1. For what three purposes is the total capital of a business used?
2. Why is working capital the "heart" of the business?
3. Why should a merchant be sure he has sufficient cash reserves?
4. As the yearly stock turn increases, what is the effect on the amount of working capital invested in merchandise?
5. How would the fixed capital to working capital ratio differ between a furniture store and a flower shop?

Discussion Questions

1. Should the new merchant expect the relationship among fixed and working capital and cash reserves to change as he becomes established in business? If so, in what ways?
2. What precautions should a merchant take when allocating his funds among the three kinds of capital needs?
3. Some people might say that specific details on capital distribution are really of concern only to the large-scale retailer. Small-scale retailers need not bother with such comparisons. Is this statement true? Defend your position.

Part d

Protecting against Risk

As Marilyn Marsh developed her plans for the book, card, and gift shop she was to open in the new shopping center, she became aware of the number of risks that face businesspeople. Marilyn expected to have to run the store alone and to put to work every penny of her savings. So she investigated the ways that she could protect herself against *risk*—the possibility of loss. She knew that some retailers—usually those who are just starting in business or those who own small businesses—are apt to view insurance as a needless expenditure. They operate without any insurance or with inadequate coverage. In doing so, they face a strong possibility of having all their years of hard work destroyed by a single fire, accident, or robbery.

KINDS OF RISKS

Businesspeople can protect themselves against some risks by buying insurance; other risks cannot be covered by insurance. No store owner should attempt to assume serious risks when it is possible to obtain insurance protection at a reasonable cost.

Noninsurable Risks

The largest element of risk in retailing grows out of change. People change in their needs and wants, their tastes in fashion, and their modes of living. There is always a risk that goods purchased will fail to sell as expected. Prices change because of changes in supply and demand, in competition, in population, and in the government's spending and taxing policies. Rainy weather can cause a carefully planned sale to result in a complete loss, or a mild winter can ruin the sale of overcoats. These outside changes are examples of normally *noninsurable risks*. If such risks are not recognized and adjustments made, they can cause serious injury to the retailer. Noninsurable risks are minimized by careful forecasts, by setting up working capital reserves against such perils, and by constant study of trends. Skillful management is the only defense against noninsurable risks.

Insurable Risks

There are many possibilities of danger, however, which the retailer can guard against by means of insurance. Such common hazards as loss through fire, windstorm, theft of cash, death, and accident to customers and employees are easily insurable. Insurance does not eliminate the risk; it merely transfers the burden of the loss from the merchant to a business firm better able to assume that burden by "spreading the risk." The retailer—called the *insured*—enters into a contract—called the *insurance policy*—with an *insurer,* the insurance company. For a fee—called the *premium*—a retailer protects himself against the possibilities of suffering a large, serious loss.

There are four principal kinds of *insurable risks*: (1) loss or damage to the property; (2) injury to customers, the public, and employees; (3) loss to the business from the death of key employees; and (4) loss to employees caused by disability, illness, unemployment, and old age.

KINDS OF INSURANCE

There is no complete agreement among retailers as to which kinds of insurance are necessary. It is generally believed that the kinds of insurance which constitute minimum coverage and which every business should have are property insurance, liability insurance, business life insurance, and employee insurance.

Business Protector Policy

Great American Insurance COMPANIES
99 JOHN STREET, NEW YORK, N.Y. 10038

A CAPITAL STOCK CORPORATION

Insurance is afforded by Company initialed:

☒ G = GREAT AMERICAN INSURANCE COMPANY
☐ A = AMERICAN NATIONAL FIRE INSURANCE COMPANY

SUMMARY

Item	DECLARATIONS	POLICY NUMBER **BP** 258-19-05	PREVIOUS POLICY NO. OR INSURER
1.	*Named Insured* and P. O. Address (Number, Street, Town, County, State & Zip No.) The Named Insured is: ☒ Individual ☐ Corporation ☐ Partnership ☐ Joint Venture ☐ Other:	Herbert Longnecker 1868 Buffalo Street Olean, New York 14760	2516879
2.	Policy Period: NOON STANDARD TIME AT LOCATION OF DESCRIBED PROPERTY From: To:	12/12/75 To: 12/12/78	
	PRODUCER: Agent or Broker	The Biren Agency 444 State Street Portville, New York 14770	CODE
	Sub-Producer		
3.	Location of Premises (ENTER "SAME" IF SAME LOCATION AS ABOVE)	Same	
	Occupancy of Premises		

4. Insurance is provided with respect to those premises described above and with respect to those coverages and kinds of property for which a specific limit of liability is shown, subject to all of the terms of this policy including forms and endorsements made a part hereof:

SECTION I PROPERTY COVERAGE

	Coinsurance Percentage Applicable	LIMIT OF LIABILITY Loc. No.	Bldg. No.	Loc. No.	Bldg. No.	Loc. No.	Bldg. No.	Applicable Form(s)
Cov. A—Building(s)	%	$27,500.	$		$			1679
Cov. B—Personal Property	%	$ 6,800.	$		$			1969A
Addl. Cov. (Specify)								
		$	$		$			

Loss Deductible Clause No. 1 is Not applicable.   Loss Deductible Clause No. 2 is Not applicable.

SECTION II LIABILITY COVERAGE

DUAL LIMITS	LIMIT OF LIABILITY		Applicable Form(s)
Cov. C—Bodily Injury Liability	$	each person	
	$	each occurrence	
	$	aggregate	
Cov. C—Property Damage Liability	$	each occurrence	
	$	aggregate	
Cov. D—Premises Medical Payments	$	each person	
	$	each accident	

SINGLE LIMIT	LIMIT OF LIABILITY			
Cov. C—Bodily Injury & Property Damage Liability	$50,000.	each occurrence	$	aggregate
Cov. D—Premises Medical Payments	$ NIL	each person	$	each accident

SECTION III SUPPLEMENTAL COVERAGE(S)

	LIMIT OF LIABILITY	Applicable Form(s)
B.F. Money & Securities	$ Per Form 1608A	1608A
Plate Glass	$ Per Schedule	1701A
Neon Sign	$ 120.(Value)	
	$	
	$	
	$	

5.	Additional Forms and Endorsements made part of this Policy at time of issue: (Insert No. and Edition Date)	1608A, 1665A, 1670A, 1661A, 1679, 1698, 1969A, 1697, 1701A, 1731, 1760, 1761, 1812, 5215D
6.	Mortgagee: (Name and Address)	
7.	The Total Provisional Premium is $1,794.00 and is payable $598.00 at inception, and $598.00 at each anniversary.	

FOR STATE EXCEPTIONS SEE PAGE 2

F.22900

Countersigned by _Paul A. Biren_   Authorized Representative

Illus. 4-8   Here is an example of an insurance policy which might be held by a retail business. Notice the kinds of coverage that the policy provides, the amounts of coverage, and the premium.

Property Insurance

Many things can happen to a retailer's property. His stock, fixtures, and store may be ruined by fire or by water damage in putting out a fire. Merchandise which he purchased may be lost, stolen, or damaged on its way to the store. A windstorm can cause damage both to his store building and to his merchandise. These possible losses could be serious and should be covered by adequate insurance.

Property insurance includes fire, theft, windstorm, and loss of shipment insurance, marine insurance, plate-glass insurance, automobile insurance, and burglary insurance. It does not include insurance on shortage of merchandise inventory caused by shoplifting and pilferage.

With the heavy losses from floods along rivers and lowlands in recent years, flood insurance is also important in many localities. Such insurance is available only in communities that meet criteria set by the federal government. Insurance agents can determine if criteria are met in each locality.

Liability Insurance

It is possible for a retailer to suffer as great a loss from a liability suit as from a fire. A customer may accidentally fall in the store, or he may be injured by the ill effects of a product purchased in the store and sue the retailer for a substantial amount of money. A store's delivery truck may cause personal or property damage. To cover such risks, the retailer purchases *liability insurance*.

Business Life Insurance

Business life insurance that will protect a business, or the family of a businessman, from the financial loss which results from the death of an owner or a key executive of a store is being widely purchased today by small- and large-scale retailers. Billions of dollars worth of this protection is now in force, giving assurance of business continuity to the store and full value of the business equity to the family of the deceased. Plans are tailored to fit individual stores. Sole proprietorship life insurance, partnership life insurance, and corporation life insurance are available for each type of store ownership.

Employee Insurance

The kinds of insurance discussed so far are optional for the retailer. He could take a chance on any of the risks described. No retailer, however, who employs four or more persons can operate without paying a tax—a certain percentage of his payroll—to state governments for a system of *unemployment compensation insurance.* This provides for a type of insurance that pays benefits to the unemployed. All states have federally approved unemployment compensation plans. The retailer's tax is based on his employee turnover. Retailers who have very few employee separations pay a smaller tax than firms that frequently lay off workers.

All states have compulsory laws which require employers to provide for insurance for an employee's sickness, injury, or death arising from his work on the job. Such insurance is called *workmen's compensation insurance.*

Another type of compulsory employee insurance is Old Age, Survivors, and Disability Insurance (OASDI, or Social Security). A tax is levied on wages up to a specified amount each year. An equal amount of tax is paid by employee and employer. Benefits are payable to qualified retired workers, dependents of workers, and disabled employees.

Many stores carry *group health insurance* covering disability, hospitalization, and medical care for employees; and in some localities such insurance is required.

Other Kinds of Insurance

Several other kinds of insurance are available to the retailer and probably should be carried, particularly by large-scale retailers:

1. *Use and occupancy insurance,* covering loss of earnings in case of suspension of business due to fire or other catastrophe
2. *Fidelity bond,* covering theft or embezzlement by an employee
3. *Fraud insurance,* covering counterfeit money, bad checks, larceny, and some robberies

The trend today is for insurance companies to write single insurance contracts that cover all the insurance needs of the merchant except for employee and life insurance. This package costs less and is more convenient than buying separate insurance policies. The *package policy* covers building and personal property and includes coverage for every type of hazard to property and coverage for legal liability for bodily injury to others.

ADJUSTING INSURANCE COVERAGE

With inflation likely to continue, many merchants will find that the coverage they now carry will become inadequate to cover risks from fire, theft, and public liability. The adequacy of insurance coverage should be reviewed annually.

On the other hand, to keep insurance costs in check, it is often wise to ask for *deductibles* for small risks. Thus, theft insurance may be written with a $100 deductible, with the insurance company liable for only established claims in excess of this amount.

INSURANCE COMPANIES

The insurance company should be carefully selected. The insurer should be strong and reliable and able to provide expert advice to the retailer on his needs and costs. A low premium is often a poor investment if the insurance company does not make prompt and fair settlements. In practice the small merchant generally consults an insurance broker rather than the companies that actually provide the protection. The broker helps the merchant determine his insurance needs and recommends the appropriate insurers.

Major Kinds of Insurance for a Store

Fire insurance, covering loss by fire

Public liability insurance, covering injury to the public

Workmen's compensation insurance, covering injury to employees

Other employee welfare insurance, including social security, unemployment, and health insurance

Plate-glass insurance, covering window breakage

Product liability insurance, covering injury to customers arising from the use of goods bought in the store

Use and occupancy insurance, covering loss of earnings in case of suspension of business due to fire or other catastrophe

Automobile insurance, covering fire, theft, and public liability

Burglary insurance, covering forcible entry and theft of merchandise and cash

Fidelity bond, covering theft by an employee

Fraud insurance, covering counterfeit money, bad checks, larceny, and some robberies

---

Illus. 4-9   Large-scale retailers should carry each of these kinds of insurance. The small retailer is wise to carry as many kinds as he can reasonably afford.

CHECKING YOUR KNOWLEDGE

Vocabulary

1. risk
2. noninsurable risk
3. insured
4. insurance policy
5. insurer
6. premium
7. insurable risk
8. property insurance
9. liability insurance
10. business life insurance
11. unemployment compensation insurance
12. workmen's compensation insurance
13. group health insurance
14. use and occupancy insurance
15. fidelity bond
16. fraud insurance
17. package policy
18. deductibles

Review Questions

1. What can the retailer do to control noninsurable risks?
2. Name four retail risks for which insurance may be purchased.
3. What business risks are covered by liability insurance?
4. List four types of employee insurance.
5. Name and describe the purpose of at least six major kinds of insurance for a store.

Discussion Questions

1. Should retailers who install safety devices such as handrails, sprinkler systems, and nonskid treads get lower liability insurance rates than stores without such features?
2. A small-scale retailer should carry the same kinds of insurance as a large-scale retailer since he functions in the same way and has the same risks. Do you agree?
3. A retailer has quotations on insurance from two insurance companies. One quotation is much lower than the other. What things should he check before making a decision as to which company to buy from?
4. If you purchase insurance policies with deductibles, should you make any plans to recover the cost of minor losses as they occur?

Part e

Store Organization

Organization is found everywhere. It is found in the home, where the work of running the household is divided among the members of the family. If the parents assign jobs to the children and to themselves in accordance with the ability of each and if they check to see that everyone does what is assigned to him, the home will run smoothly.

There is also organization in the school. From the principal to the custodian each person has a distinct and important place in the organization.

Every store must have good organization. When the retailing activities are divided and arranged so that they can be performed efficiently by the available manpower, good organization is achieved.

BASIC RETAILING ACTIVITIES

Regardless of the size, type, and ownership of a store, the basic retailing activities can be divided into four major groups: (1) *buying*—purchasing goods for resale; (2) *selling*—selling goods to customers; (3) *operating*—facilitating the transactions by providing personnel and storage space for goods and by performing the necessary physical movement of merchandise into and out of the store; and (4) *controlling*—keeping records and budgeting as guides to operations and profits.

Buying

A retailer assembles a line or assortment of goods for resale. In small stores, this important activity is sometimes conducted haphazardly. Because the independent retailer has so many other things to do, he cannot devote the necessary time to plan his buying and to contact the wholesale market. The small merchant often merely uses a sheet of paper on which he jots down items that are out of stock when customers ask for them. At the end of the week, he writes out an order after first glancing at his shelves. This "eye-control" of stock is a common cause of inadequate stock and lost sales. On the other hand, a small retailer may depend upon the wholesaler's salesman too much. He may allow himself to become overstocked because of the salesman's "deals" and his rosy prediction of profits.

In large-scale retailing, buying is given the attention it deserves. The activity is broken down into its major parts, and experts determine what is needed after first studying the needs and wants of customers. Locating sources of supply, after careful comparison of the advantages and disadvantages of each resource, is a continuous operation. Finally, the actual negotiation, the bargaining, and the placing of the order are all features of this retailing function of buying.

How well this function is performed determines, in many instances, the profit or loss of the business. The old saying, Goods well bought are half sold, applies equally to small and large stores. A good buy makes selling easier, increases stock turn, and produces profit.

Selling

The selling process actually begins before the buying of merchandise. Before he selects goods for resale, the merchant should be convinced

Courtesy of <u>Penney News</u>, J. C. Penney Company, Inc.

Illus. 4-10   An interested salesperson can do much to help a customer select merchandise that he will enjoy.

that customer demand exists or can be stimulated. When we speak of selling, we generally have in mind the work of a salesperson. *Selling,* in the true sense of the word, means identification of a customer's need, helping the customer arrive at a decision to buy goods which will satisfy the need, suggestion of additional goods that might be needed, and information to increase the customer's satisfaction from the goods purchased. In the modern store, however, we find that customers are assisted and persuaded to buy through a number of nonpersonal selling media as well as through the efforts of salespeople. Advertising may bring a product to the attention of a potential customer. A beautiful store display may cause a customer to buy goods without a word being spoken by a salesperson. Vending machines have eliminated personal selling in some instances. In large self-service stores a minimum of personal selling is used.

Selling may be broken down into (1) *personal selling* and (2) *nonpersonal selling.* The coordination of the two kinds of selling to give the best results is called *sales promotion.* Both personal and

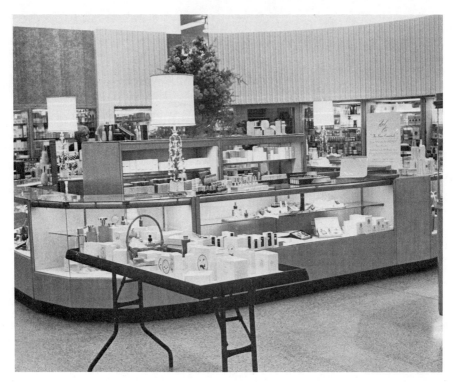

Courtesy of Flah & Co.

Illus. 4-11   Goods displayed effectively may cause a customer
to buy without a word being spoken by a salesperson.

nonpersonal selling may be divided into (a) selling outside the store,
or *external selling,* and (b) selling inside the store, or *internal selling.*
Every merchant tries to use the particular combination of personal and
nonpersonal selling media that will sell his merchandise most effectively and yet most economically.

Operating

Not only must goods be bought and sold in retailing, but the
customer must be assured good service, particularly fair and prompt
handling of complaints. Protection must be provided for the building,
the merchandise, customers, and employees. Necessary supplies must
be obtained. Merchandise must be moved into the store, placed in
storage, and moved out when sold. Store personnel must be hired,
trained, paid, promoted, discharged on occasion, and sometimes negotiations with labor unions undertaken. All these duties fall into a general
classification called *store operations.*

In small stores, the owner-manager handles these duties, sandwiched among others, to the best of his ability. In large stores, they are performed by experts and are continuously studied for improvement. Responsibility for the overall operating activity generally goes to a person called the operating superintendent or store manager. He has under him a group of specialists such as a service manager, a building and protection manager, a traffic manager, and a personnel director.

Controlling

If the man who must keep records of the store's business transactions must also pay attention to the buying, selling, and operating, very little can be expected in the way of organized control. Most small-store owners do their bookkeeping at night after a busy and tiring day. They concern themselves chiefly with the amount of sales, the amount paid for merchandise received, and, perhaps, with the cash balance in the bank. They have neither the time nor the training to study expenditures, budgets, inventories, and sales.

Many small-store owners employ part-time bookkeepers to do the necessary record keeping. These merchants find it advantageous to turn over the preparation of tax forms, business statements, and employee records to public accountants. It is thus possible for even small-store owners to get specialized service for the control function of their businesses.

Large-scale retailers pay a great deal of close attention to the control phase of retailing. Chain stores, department stores, discount houses, and mail-order houses have controllers in charge of financial records and budgeting.

SMALL-STORE ORGANIZATION

Because one man supervises all the activities of a small store, he may think that it is unnecessary to bother with an organization plan. In fact, few small retailers give much thought to the principles of organization. Nevertheless, a small store should be carefully organized, thereby saving time, energy, and money.

A store may use a chart to show how the work is divided. An *organization chart* gives a graphic picture of the division of work in the store, indicates the flow of authority, and shows the people to whom employees are responsible. A simple organization chart may resemble Illus. 4-12 which shows how the work of a small store may be divided among the owner and four employees.

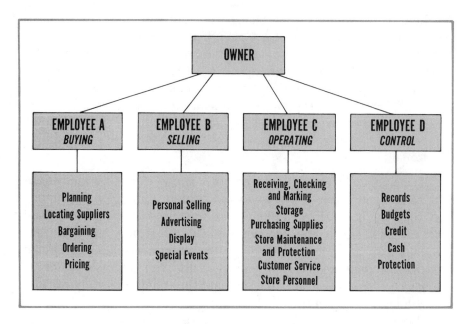

Illus. 4-12   This organization chart shows how the four basic retailing activities could be divided among the employees in a small retail business. Each employee has responsibility for one of the retailing activities, in addition to selling when needed, and the owner-manager provides general supervision.

LARGE-STORE ORGANIZATION

As more and more employees are added, the proprietor places certain individuals in charge of special divisions of work. The proprietor retains control over his business by requiring these executives to submit to him reports about the workings of their respective divisions. Thus, in a condensed form, he knows what is going on, supervises wherever necessary, and has his orders carried out through these executives.

With the growth of the store, the proprietor must do the following things:

1. Group and arrange the retailing activities into large separate divisions
2. Find the person best suited to supervise the functions of each division
3. Provide adequate checks and balances so that the duties of the various divisions will not overlap and so that all divisions will be in agreement and act in accord on activities that involve all of them
4. Establish authority and responsibility so that each employee knows where he fits into the organization
5. Secure the cooperation of employees
6. Produce an efficient set of rules and regulations to govern employees in transacting business

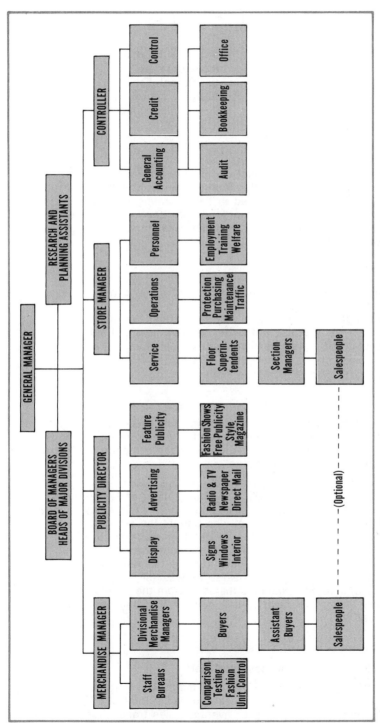

Illus. 4-13   As a store becomes larger and its operations more complex, its organization chart also becomes more complicated. Above is a typical organization chart for a large department store. No large store could operate efficiently without such an organization chart.

CHECKING YOUR KNOWLEDGE

Vocabulary

1. buying
2. selling
3. operating
4. controlling
5. personal selling
6. nonpersonal selling

7. sales promotion
8. external selling
9. internal selling
10. store operations
11. organization chart

Review Questions

1. Name the activities that are included in the buying function.
2. How does personal selling differ from nonpersonal selling?
3. What specific duties are included in the operating activity?
4. What are the advantages of an organization chart to the small retailer?
5. Describe the six organizational activities that must be performed as a store grows larger.

Discussion Questions

1. Why would a small retailer assign some activities to his employees and perform others himself?
2. Why must organizational charts vary for different retail stores?
3. In large-scale retail firms, is it better to have personal selling under the store manager or under the merchandise manager?

BUILDING YOUR SKILLS

Improving Communication Skills

Each of the following sentences contains two pronouns in parentheses. Only one of the two pronouns may be used correctly in the sentence. On a separate sheet of paper, write the number of each sentence and the correct pronoun to be used in that sentence.

1. He is as good a salesperson as (we, us).
2. Bill, Judy, and (me, I) will work Friday night and Saturday.
3. It was (she, her) who sold the blouse from the display window.
4. I am sure it was (they, them) who bought the red grill.
5. It is up to you and (I, me) to get this stock on display.
6. The job of bagging and marking produce was given to (I, me).
7. Either you or (he, him) will have to move this rack to the department.
8. The customer said, "That salesgirl was (she, her)."
9. (Us, We) students examined the store from the basement to the roof.
10. (They, Them) will have to sell more if the stock turn is to be increased.

Improving Arithmetic Skills

Perform the division exercises given below:

1. If 3 picture frames cost $5.10 how much will 5 frames cost?
2. If you made 174 sales last week and had a total of $755.16 in sales, what was the amount of your average sales transaction?

3. If a container holds 5.7 liters about how many quarts does it hold? (1 quart equals about .95 liters)
4. At a price of $4.08 for a 24-can case of peas what is the cost per can?
5. During one week, 5 saleswomen sold $1,930 worth of sweaters. What were the average dollar sales for each saleswoman?

Improving Research Skills

1. Visit two businessmen in your community and determine whether their stores opened as new stores or whether they purchased existing businesses. Also, ask these businessmen what seems to be the customary way in which stores are opened in the community and which types of businesses seem to change ownership most frequently.
2. Make a list of the kinds of insurance which should be carried by the owner of a small drugstore with an annual sales volume of $70,000. What additional types of insurance would be carried by a chain of six drugstores with an annual sales volume of about $200,000 for each store?
3. Find out what insurance must be carried in your state to protect employees against costs growing out of their loss of health. How is the insurance cost divided between the employee and the employer?

Improving Decision-Making Skills

1. In the process of developing the partnership agreement between Dennis Scholl and Mr. Burke, the question of insurable risks came up. Mr. Burke had maintained only the insurance required for his employees. If you were Dennis Scholl what points would you make to convince Mr. Burke that protection on business interruption, product liability, employee dishonesty, and partnership life insurance should be purchased?
2. The present owner of the Adobe Shop was asking $35,000 for the building and fixtures, $18,000 for the merchandise in the store, $8,000 for the accounts receivable, and $6,000 for goodwill. Yearly sales had averaged $79,000 for the past five years. Pat Baxter examined the goods on hand and found that at least 40% of the stock was old or obsolete. The fixtures were about 15 years old, and the building needed a new air-conditioning system as well as a general redecorating. A fifth of the accounts receivable were over a year old. An accountant who examined the records advised Pat Baxter that the total current market value of the business was about $42,000. If you were Pat Baxter how would you go about negotiating for a purchase price of $42,000? What distribution of capital would you plan for the first year of operation?

APPLYING YOUR KNOWLEDGE

Chapter Project

This project asks that you do three things. First, obtain information on the organizational structure of five different retail establishments. Second, from the information obtained draw the organization charts of each firm. Use the basic retailing activities—buying, selling, operating, and controlling—as guides unless the firm clearly has some other breakdown of functions.

Third, analyze the similarities and differences of the five organizational patterns and prepare explanations of why they are organized as they are. Also, prepare a set of changes you would recommend for each of the five.

Continuing Project

In your manual you should prepare a section on financing and a section on organizing your business. Some items which you will want to consider are:

1. How much money will be needed to start your store
2. How the total amount of money needed will be divided among the various capital needs of your store
3. Where you will get the necessary capital and how much you will get from each source
4. The kinds of insurance you will purchase to cover your retailing risks
5. The organization chart for your store showing the major retailing activities and the specific work to be done in each activity

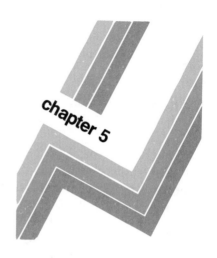

Developing Store Policies

CHAPTER PREVIEW

a. General policies for the retail store provide a systematic and consistent means by which questions about merchandise assortments, customer services, and employee relations can be answered.

b. Store services—those provided at no cost and those for which a charge is made—are developed to keep the customer satisfied before, during, and after the sale, and, in some instances, to provide additional sales.

c. To be able to buy on credit is expected by most customers and necessary for some in order to buy at all. The retailer can operate his own credit system or affiliate with credit card granting organizations.

d. No sale is complete until the merchant has collected the money owed. Effective collection procedures are necessary if the retailer is to continue in business.

e. The success of a retail business depends greatly on the people involved. Good personnel policies help make sure that worker morale and efficiency are high.

Part **a**

General and Merchandising Policies

During the typical business day of a retail store a great number of decisions must be made. To the casual observer these decisions may go unnoticed, but each is important to the success of the business. Questions such as the following must be answered: Should we buy the entire assortment in a manufacturer's line or concentrate on a few best-selling items? Can we give credit to Mrs. Alworth; and, if we do, how much and what kind? Should we charge for the delivery of a couch and chair to a customer who lives outside the city?

Questions about what a store will do are not limited to its internal operations or customer contacts. Questions will also arise about the store's relationships with employees, suppliers, community groups, and governmental agencies. In order to have a systematic and consistent means by which such questions can be answered, the firm must have guidelines to follow. These carefully planned courses of action relating to all phases of retailing activity are called *policies*. Policies must be clearly worded and made known to all concerned.

MAJOR STORE POLICIES

The development of the policies for an enterprise is the responsibility of top management. The effect of the policies set by a store results (1) in customers associating a store with certain kinds of goods and types of services and (2) in employees and potential employees associating it with a pleasant working environment.

The retail store can build its policies around a number of different features. Merchandise and promotion policies will be discussed in this part. Service policies will be presented in Part B. Credit and collection policies will be found in Parts C and D. Part E discusses personnel policies.

Selection of Policies

A store cannot be all things to all people. The store management must develop policies around those features that contribute best to the merchandising and operating philosophy of the store.

A combination of features is entirely possible for a consistent store personality. For instance, an independent grocer may decide to build his store's policies around, first, excellent customer service; second, convenience of location; and third, a wide assortment. A chain grocer may place first emphasis on low prices; second, on complete stocks of best-selling items; and third, on recognized quality of standard brands. To achieve his low-price policy, he may decide on a self-service and cash-and-carry operation. A service station may emphasize convenience of location, customer service, and high quality of product, in the order named. A department store may give first attention to wide assortments; second, to low prices; and third, to customer service. An exclusive specialty shop may plan for fashion leadership first, customer service next, and high quality third.

Implementation of Policies

In order to have effective policies, they must be communicated to the store staff, to customers, and to others who might be affected. Small-scale retailers seldom give much attention to the question of store policy and generally improvise policies as situations arise. All too frequently, however, the next time a similar situation occurs, a different policy is likely to be adopted. This inconsistency is confusing to suppliers, customers, and employees.

A policy should be altered as changing conditions warrant. For example, in years past most stores attempted to give each customer the individual attention of a salesperson. However, in order to keep prices low, many stores have replaced this policy with one of self-service and minimum customer help. New procedures, necessitated by policy changes, should be explained to employees and to customers in order to get their cooperation.

Steps in Developing Store Policy

1. Establish or reaffirm the long-range goals of the store.
2. Determine needed objectives in order to reach store goals.
3. Determine the various means of reaching these objectives.
4. Write out tentative policy statements for the most appropriate means.
5. Have these statements reviewed by store staff and others.
6. Modify and rephrase policy statements to assure complete understanding.
7. Issue the statements as official store policy explaining them carefully to both employees and customers.

Illus. 5-1   A well-planned store policy should result in successful store-customer relationships.

ESTABLISHING MERCHANDISE POLICIES

Probably the most important of all store policies are the policies involving merchandise. Merchandise offered by a store, except in the case of a service business, usually has more power to attract customers than does any other single feature of the store's operation. What kinds and how much merchandise to stock, the quality to be offered, and the prices at which the merchandise should be sold are only some of the elements to be considered.

Merchandise Mix

The merchandise policies of a store depend primarily upon the decision made concerning the merchandise mix. *Merchandise mix* refers to the variety of merchandise lines carried and the depth and breadth in which these lines are stocked. The merchandise mix may vary considerably from store to store depending upon the store's customers, the store's financial resources, the location, and the owner's ability and experience. For example, one men's store may carry all classes of men's clothing. Another may carry only a few selected lines of sportswear.

Courtesy of Hart, Schaffner and Marx

Illus. 5-2   A quality men's apparel store will carry men's clothing, accessories, and other male personal items.

The small merchant has a better chance of success if he carries one or a few merchandise lines in depth rather than many lines with shallow assortments. For example, if the owner of a women's clothing store has limited financial resources, it might be better for the store to specialize in junior-size daytime dresses with wide and deep assortments than to carry misses' sizes, half sizes, and evening wear as well. A safe rule for the small merchant is to add no new line until there is appropriate space, capital, and merchandise talent.

Quality of Merchandise

A *quality product* is merchandise that is made of excellent material and constructed with good workmanship, so that it will wear or perform well. In essence, quality merchandise is merchandise that will serve customers so well that they will have little question about price and will purchase the item again if needed.

Quality appeal varies with the store's clientele. Obviously a store that specializes in discount merchandise does not attempt to carry the finest merchandise the market offers. Stores are becoming more concerned about testing the quality of new items they purchase rather than waiting for customers to complain. The largest retailers—Sears and Macy's, for example—have their own testing laboratories and test all goods sold under their labels. Small stores cannot afford such testing, even by an outside laboratory, and are wise to concentrate their buying with the leading manufacturers who adhere to high quality standards and are always checking their own output.

Stocking Fashion Merchandise

For stores that want to attract a fashion-conscious clientele, broad and deep assortments of good quality merchandise are not enough. It is important to develop a reputation for stocking new styles that are achieving fashion acceptance. Such fashion leadership requires close contacts with manufacturers in New York and other fashion centers.

Pricing the Merchandise

Pricing considerations are a major phase of merchandise policies. Most stores attempt to keep their retail prices competitive, and some stores have a definite policy not to be undersold. They watch their competitors' prices carefully and meet all prices that are lower than their own. Some specialty stores pay little attention to competitors' prices. Such stores stock a great deal of exclusive merchandise that their competitors do not carry, and they can justify somewhat higher prices on goods because of their extra services.

Price Competition. The question underlying all price competition is "Who is my competitor?" For example, a large department store or discount house may regard all stores in the same city as its competitors. Many department stores, however, rule out discount stores on the assumption that, because of their different service policies, they are not competing for the same trade.

Few small stores, unless they are affiliated with other independent stores, have the buying power to compete on a low-price basis with large department or discount stores. They are better off depending upon service and upon well-chosen stocks tailored to customer requirements.

Other Price Policies. Almost every reputable store today has a *one-price policy*. This means that on any given day all customers will be charged the same amount for a particular article. It is still possible, of course, to lower the price so long as the goods are made available at that price to everyone.

Many stores have a *price-line policy*. This practice involves selling goods at a few predetermined prices or lines rather than at many different prices. Stores also have policies about price endings. Some

Courtesy of American Electric Power Corporation

Illus. 5-3   For stores that want to attract a fashion-conscious clientele, it is important to have a reputation for stocking new styles that are achieving fashion acceptance.

merchants mark their goods with odd prices, such as $3.79, because they think that the odd price implies the article is a bargain. Other retailers use even prices, such as $5.00, because they believe that the even price conveys the impression of quality.

PROMOTION POLICIES

Customers are influenced by what the store tells the public about itself. Stores that stress special sales, bargains, price reductions, and claim to undersell competitors are called *promotional stores.* Stores that advertise their assortments of goods, leadership, and customer services are called *nonpromotional stores.* Stores which generally advertise their regular assortment of merchandise but periodically hold special sales with bargain appeals may be called *semipromotional stores.*

CHECKING YOUR KNOWLEDGE

Vocabulary

1. policies
2. merchandise mix
3. quality product
4. one-price policy

5. price-line policy
6. promotional stores
7. nonpromotional stores
8. semipromotional stores

Review Questions

1. What are two results of having store policies?
2. List at least six steps that should be taken in developing store policy.
3. What influences a store's merchandise mix?
4. When should the small merchant add a merchandise line?
5. Define a promotional store, a nonpromotional store, and a semipromotional store.

Discussion Questions

1. How frequently should a store make changes in its store policy? What are the results of too frequent changes in policy?
2. In what ways would you expect the merchandising policies of a specialty store to differ from those of a large department store? a rural general store from a suburban supermarket?
3. The use of odd prices on merchandise is supposed to create an impression of a good buy or a bargain. Is this always true? In what kind of store would this price policy be most effective?
4. What types of customers are most attracted to promotional stores? to nonpromotional stores? Does the degree of attraction depend on the types of goods handled?

Part **b**

Service Policies

The service policies of the retail store are intended to create a certain image in the minds of customers before, during, and after the sale. All the services a store provides aid in creating the personality of the store. There are four different types of services that a store may provide: selling and shopping services, convenience services, profit services, and community services. Most customers are influenced by the store's *selling and shopping services*. These services are associated with the actual merchandise carried by the store. *Convenience services*, the second type, are the numerous nonproduct services provided customers. The third type of service in the retail store is known as *profit services*. There is a charge for these services, and the store expects to make a profit from them. *Community services*, the fourth type, reflect the activities undertaken by the store on behalf of the community. It should be noted that the classification of services into one of these four types will vary depending upon the image that the store is attempting to project.

SELLING AND SHOPPING SERVICES

The services associated with merchandise are probably the most frequently used by the customer. The presence or lack of a selling or shopping service may influence the customer's decision to buy.

Personal Selling and Self-Service

Every retailer is confronted with the question of how much personal salesmanship is required in his store. Some customers look upon the salesperson as an obstacle and would rather wait on themselves, particularly when they think they are getting a low price by so doing. Others prefer personal attention and assistance, especially when buying clothing or home furnishings. For some clothing items customers expect the services of a tailor to provide needed alterations.

If a store decides not to depend on personal selling, is it better to adopt self-service or self-selection? Under the former, the customer selects the particular item she wants from open display and then takes it to the checkout point where she pays for it and has it packed. Under

Store Services

Selling and Shopping Services	Convenience Services
Personal selling	Doormen
Mail-order selling	Lounges and playrooms
Telephone selling	Information desk
Personal shopping service	Lost-and-found desk
Fashion shows	Parcel checking
Gift wrapping	Parking space
Returns and adjustments	Telephones
Delivery	First-aid station
Credit	Convenient store hours
Layaway Plans	

Profit Services	Communicty Services
Installation and repair	Entertainment
Restaurants	Exhibits
Snack counters	Demonstrations
Travel and ticket bureaus	Lectures
Insurance	Sponsorship
Rentals	Contributions

Illus. 5-4   The inclusion of a service in one of these four categories indicates the attitude of the store toward its customers. Gift wrapping is considered a selling service by some stores, while other stores charge for gift wrapping and classify it as a profit service.

self-selection, she makes decision as to what she wants by examining samples that are carefully labeled. She then asks a salesperson to get the wanted article from stock in order to complete the sales transaction.

Many department stores make use of a combination of methods depending on the nature of the goods. For men's clothing, fashion ready-to-wear, and major home furnishings, personal selling is used. Toiletries, beauty aids, small toys, and foods are sold on a self-service basis. For other merchandise, such as hosiery, women's accessories, or housewares, goods are sold from self-selection counters with salespeople completing the transaction.

Shopping Services

A policy for shopping services should include decisions on providing mail orders, telephone orders, personal shopping, and similar services to help customers buy from the store. Mail-order and telephone shopping are becoming increasingly popular, but they demand a specialized type of store personnel to handle them satisfactorily. The merchant must decide whether he will obtain enough added sales to cover the additional expenses of catalogs, larger reserve stocks, extra employees, credit, and delivery.

Personal shopping service is usually found in prestige stores. Some large department stores promote their personal shopping services, particularly at Christmas. Personal shoppers assemble articles in advance of store visits; accompany customers to various departments; select items for gifts; and, where the store has many boutiques, help the customer decide which to shop.

The fashion show, conducted in the store or at out-of-store locations, is another form of shopping service, which is also a selling device. Gift wrapping and mailing are common shopping services at better stores.

Courtesy of Federated Department Stores, Inc.

Illus. 5-5   Luncheon fashion shows for career girls are both a popular shopping service and a selling device, particularly in downtown stores.

Returns and Adjustments

Many stores have adopted a liberal return goods policy. This means that the customer who wishes to return an item or believes that an adjustment should be made is given prompt and often generous treatment. Many adjustments are made in cash, or, if an item was purchased on credit, by an account credit. Merchants know that a cash adjustment is less costly because it eliminates record keeping and the red tape of a rigid return policy. Some stores, however, will not give cash when an item is returned. Instead they give a credit slip which can be applied on other purchases. Store policy may require that a return and adjustment be made only if the customer has the sales slip and price tag and only within a definite number of days after purchase.

Delivery Services

A store may adopt one of five delivery policies:

1. It may deliver all purchases free of extra charge, at least in the immediate neighborhood.
2. It may deliver in case of emergency only.
3. It may make a charge for all deliveries.
4. It may refuse to deliver or may charge for the delivery of small packages or those that cost less than a stated amount, such as $5, and it may deliver costly and bulky articles free.
5. It may provide no delivery service.

Courtesy of Montgomery Ward

Illus. 5-6   Some stores own and operate their own delivery service.
They also pick up and return appliances that must be serviced.

The delivery policy chosen depends upon the type of store and upon its other store policies. For example, supermarkets that make low price a major appeal may offer no delivery service. Downtown department stores usually make deliveries because it may be inconvenient for the customer to carry even small packages, but they usually insist that the value of the purchase be greater than a prescribed amount.

Until fairly recently stores that provided delivery service usually made no charge, except for out-of-town delivery involving mail or express. The delivery costs were absorbed in the total operating expense figure. In effect, then, all customers were sharing the cost of delivery even though many did not avail themselves of the service. Today many stores as a standard practice charge for delivery, pricing the goods at a "take-with" price.

The major kinds of delivery service are:

1. *Independent delivery service,* where the store owns and operates its own service and where deliverymen act as store representatives.

2. *Consolidated delivery service,* where a private agency, such as the United Parcel Service, contracts for the delivery service of a group of stores for a fee based on number and type of parcels.

3. *Cooperative delivery service,* where a group of stores in the same community contracts to provide joint delivery service.

4. *Express company or messenger company,* where an outside company provides delivery service for a store as a sideline.

5. *Parcel-post service,* where delivery is made by means of fourth-class mail. While slow for local delivery, it is commonly used for out-of-town delivery.

CONVENIENCE SERVICES

Many retail stores provide services that are designed to make shopping a pleasure. These services need not relate to any product or merchandise the store may sell. In many cases, stores may join in a cooperative effort to provide some of these services. For example, several stores located in a shopping area may share the cost of developing a parking lot for customers.

In-Store Services

The use of doormen and the provision of lounges may be services of prestigious stores. Information desks, lost-and-found departments, rest rooms, and first-aid stations are provided by large stores and planned shopping centers. Playrooms where preschool-age children can play under supervision while parents shop are provided by some stores. Pay

Courtesy of Dayton Hudson Corporation

Illus. 5-7   Rooms where preschool-age children can play under supervision while parents shop are provided by some stores.

phones and parcel-checking lockers are also conveniences which many shoppers appreciate. Store-attached garage parking is, of course, one of the important convenience services.

Store Hours

Years ago most stores, except neighborhood and convenience-goods stores, had a policy of being open from 9 a.m. to 6 p.m. six days a week. Changes in customer living styles have led to marked adjustments. Many stores now stay open from one to six evenings a week, and the opening hour in many cities is now 10 a.m.

In many states and localities where *blue laws*—laws that prohibit most business activity on Sunday—do not prevent their doing so, hundreds of department stores, particularly in the suburbs, now are open on Sunday, usually from noon to 6 p.m. Evening, Sunday, and holiday store hours depend partly on the policies of competing stores in the shopping area. The added cost of extended hours has to be measured against the added sales. Most merchants have found that the extra business and customer goodwill gained justify the extra hours.

PROFIT SERVICES

Profit services provided by retail stores are of two kinds. One relates directly to the merchandise carried by the store. For example, the installation of carpeting sold by the store is provided to customers for a charge. Furniture reupholstering is another. The other kind of profit service relates to customer convenience and is illustrated by food service which makes it easy for the customer to get a snack at a store luncheon counter or a complete meal in a store restaurant. The intent of profit services is that they return to the store sufficient income to cover all expenses and also provide a profit.

Courtesy of Federated Department Stores, Inc.

Illus. 5-8   Most stores provide food service which makes it easy for the customer to eat a snack at a luncheon counter or a complete meal in a store restaurant.

The number of profit services being adopted by retail stores is rapidly increasing. Some stores provide travel and ticket bureaus where customers buy tickets for sporting events, theater events, and travel tours. Examples of other profit services include hair-dressing salons, eyeglass fitting, key cutting, insurance, and car or equipment rentals. Some of these services may not always produce significant revenue, but they do have immense value in getting and keeping customers in the store.

COMMUNITY SERVICES

Stores are often asked to sponsor softball and bowling teams, beauty contestants, and holiday baskets for the needy. To attract community

interest stores may set up exhibits of art, sports cars, or historical arti-
facts. They may also provide live entertainment or informative lectures
by well-known persons. The store manager and other store staff may
be members of Lions, Rotary, Kiwanis, or other civic groups engaged
in community projects. More and more stores include in their budgets
financial contributions for community betterment. Some stores make
space available for community activities. The use of meeting rooms,
parking lots, and malls by various community groups brings additional
people into the store. The purpose of store involvement with community
activities is to tie the people of the community more closely to the store
as a center for community development.

CHECKING YOUR KNOWLEDGE

Vocabulary

1. selling and shopping services
2. convenience services
3. profit services
4. community services
5. independent delivery service
6. consolidated delivery service
7. cooperative delivery service
8. express company, or messenger company
9. parcel post service
10. blue laws

Review Questions

1. What are the four types of services that a retail store may provide?
2. List five kinds of delivery services that stores may use.
3. Describe at least seven convenience services.
4. Name two kinds of profit services and give an example of each.
5. Of what value is store participation in community activities?

Discussion Questions

1. The shopping services of a store are often used as an indicator of the
   store's policy of pleasing customers. Would you agree that stores that
   have the greatest number of shopping services are also the most eager
   to please customers? Why?
2. Delivery services should be charged to the customers who use them, and
   the costs should not be buried in the markup taken on all merchandise.
   Is this a statement of good retailing policy?
3. One retail executive stated that the inclusion of profit services in a store
   was in no way different from adding another line of merchandise. Is this
   a fair comparison? Is there any difference between service merchandising
   and product merchandising?
4. Compare the various kinds of delivery service, the advantages and disadvantages of each, and the suitability of each to different types of stores.

Part **C**

Credit Policies

Today's shopper frequently wishes to use credit and expects to find it readily available. In most segments of American society there is little if any stigma attached to buying goods on credit or to debt financing. The retailer who wishes to make shopping easy and convenient for the customer is, therefore, faced with the question of providing credit.

Whenever possible the beginning small store is wise to operate on a cash basis so as to conserve capital. Where merchandise has low unit value and the total customer purchase is fairly small, a cash-only basis is advisable. For example, most food stores sell on a cash-only basis because the goods are promptly consumed and because customers do not have to spend large amounts all at once. Other stores handling more expensive merchandise, such as major appliances or furs, must grant credit. Well-to-do customers expect credit as a convenience. Low-income customers must be granted credit if they are to buy at all. The nature of our economic system makes both cash and credit selling necessary.

THE THREE C's OF CREDIT

There are three basic factors for the merchant or outside lender to consider in granting credit to an applicant: (1) character, (2) capacity, and (3) capital.

Character

Character, as it relates to granting credit, concerns the customer's honesty. This is indicated by his habits of living, by his reputation in the community, by his associates, by his stability of employment, and by his payment habits in the past.

Information about character is obtained largely from a *retail credit bureau* to which merchants subscribe. The bureau accumulates from each merchant complete information about his experience with each of his credit customers. The local credit bureaus are generally members of a national association, which makes it possible for any member merchant to obtain information about the payment habits of almost any customer in the United States.

Capacity

Capacity, as a factor in granting credit, means the ability to earn. The merchant must decide whether the applicant's skill and intelligence are such that he will retain steady employment with sufficient income to warrant the granting of credit.

The credit granter must develop the ability to forecast an applicant's probable earnings in the future. When credit is extended to low-income groups, capacity is the chief consideration. The credit manager who is best able to forecast earning power is the most successful in increasing his store's business without incurring undue loss.

Capital

Capital consists of the tangible assets that are owned by the applicant and that can be seized in case of default. The ownership of a home or the possession of a bank account are indications of an ability to pay that will influence the merchant in granting credit.

The capital of an applicant can be determined from his bank and from his references and, if he owns a business, from a trade credit bureau. In the past, capital was given more weight by the retail credit evaluator than it is today. Ability and willingness to pay in the future, rather than present assets, are what really count.

CREDIT SCORING

A formal rating plan may be developed to evaluate applications for credit. An analysis is made of the characteristics of both good and bad credit customers—those who consistently and regularly pay their bills and those who default. One careful study revealed that the critical customer characteristics determining credit performance are:

> Marital status
> Existence of a home phone
> Time at present address
> Residence (owned, rented, board)
> Occupation
> Length of time with present employer
> Other charge accounts
> Salary bracket

Point values are determined for each of the above factors and a total minimum score set, below which an applicant will not be accepted. Customers who score well above the minimum are given a more liberal credit line. The point values and minimum acceptable scores have to be developed by each store.

RETAIL CREDIT PLANS

There are three basic types of credit plans that a store may offer a customer: (1) open, or regular, account; (2) deferred, or revolving, account; and (3) installment plan. The layaway plan may be regarded as a fourth type.

Open, or Regular, Account

Under the first and most common credit plan—the *open, or regular, account*—a customer is billed each month for purchases made during the previous month. He is expected to pay promptly. Limits as to the amount each customer may purchase and owe at one time are set, but the store may frequently allow the customer to exceed these limits. The store does not have the right to *repossess* (take back) the goods bought on open account and not paid for, but it can sue for the amount owed.

Deferred, or Revolving, Account

In recent years retail stores have introduced modified open accounts, called *deferred, or revolving, accounts*. For buyers of nondurable goods who want to pay a small sum each month rather than the full amount of their monthly purchases, a *service charge*—generally about 1 to 1½ percent of the balance due—is added to the monthly account balance. As consumers make their monthly payments, they are allowed to buy more so long as their account balances do not exceed the established credit limits at any one time.

Installment Plan

For those customers who wish to make major purchases of expensive durable goods—such as washing machines, television sets, refrigerators, automobiles, furniture, and jewelry—and pay for them over a long period of time, the *installment plan* of credit is available. Under this plan, the buyer is required to sign a contract whereby he agrees to make a series of stated payments on the merchandise purchased.

Usually a finance charge is added to the purchase price of the item, a down payment is made, and the balance due is spread over a series of monthly payments, such as 12, 24, 30, or 36. If the buyer defaults on his payments, the seller has the right of repossession. However, this does not free the buyer from the remainder of the obligation. If the seller does not get enough to cover the amount due him when he resells the merchandise, he can sue the buyer for the difference.

Charge Account Agreement

I agree that the following terms will govern any charge account you may establish for my use.

1. I will pay the time sale price of items charged to my account. The time sale price shall consist of the cash sale price, including applicable sales taxes and delivery charges, if any, plus any **FINANCE CHARGE** that may accrue.

2. Each **FINANCE CHARGE** will be computed on the "Adjusted Balance" of my account at the close of any billing period; that is, the balance at the beginning of the period, including any unpaid **FINANCE CHARGE**, less payments and credits received during that period but not including purchases made during that period. I can avoid incurring a **FINANCE CHARGE** for any billing period by paying my account balance ("New Balance") in full before the next billing date as set forth in the monthly billing statement.

3. Each **FINANCE CHARGE** will be determined by applying a monthly periodic rate of 1% (**ANNUAL PERCENTAGE RATE** 12%) to the Adjusted Balance, subject to a minimum monthly charge of 50¢ on Adjusted Balances less than $50, except there is no minimum monthly charge in Wisconsin. There is no **FINANCE CHARGE** on any Adjusted Balances under $5.

4. Whenever there is a debit balance in my account at the end of a billing period, I will make a payment on my account before the next billing date. That payment may be any amount up to and including the "New Balance", but not less than the minimum monthly payments, as follows:

Unpaid Balance	$11.00 or less	$11.01 -200	$200.01 -250	$250.01 -300	$300.01 -350	$350.01 -400	$401.01 -450	$450.01 -500	Over $500
Minimum Monthly Payment	Balance	$10	$15	$20	$25	$30	$35	$40	1/10 of Balance

5. You have the right to amend this Agreement as to purchases made thereafter, by advising me of your intention to do so in the manner and to the extent required by applicable law.

6. My charge privileges shall be subject to your right to limit or terminate them as to future purchases without prior notice. Every account identification you may issue to me shall remain your property, which I will return or surrender to you upon request.

7. If I default in the performance of any obligation to you under this Agreement, my entire balance may, at your option, become due and payable. Your waiver of any default shall not operate as a waiver of any other default.

8. In the event my account is referred for collection to an attorney, not your salaried employee, I will pay reasonable attorney fees and court costs incurred, to the extent permitted by law.

9. I hereby authorize you, in connection with the establishment and maintenance of the account to investigate my credit-worthiness and capacity and to furnish information concerning my account to credit reporting agencies and others who may lawfully receive such information.

10. The local law of the state where I reside shall govern this Agreement. If my state of residence changes, I will immediately notify you. If your charge account terms then applicable in my new state of residence differ from those herein, I will sign a new charge account agreement made available by you, and, until I do so, this Agreement shall be deemed amended to conform to that new agreement as to any purchase made after my change of residence and you may act accordingly.

11. Should any provision hereof be finally determined inconsistent with or contrary to applicable law, such provision shall be deemed amended or omitted to conform therewith without affecting any other provision or the validity of this Agreement.

NOTICE TO THE BUYER: DO NOT SIGN THIS AGREEMENT BEFORE YOU READ IT OR IF IT CONTAINS ANY BLANK SPACES. YOU ARE ENTITLED TO AN EXACT COPY OF THE AGREEMENT YOU SIGN AT THE TIME YOU SIGN IT. KEEP IT TO PROTECT YOUR LEGAL RIGHTS. YOU MAY AT ANY TIME PAY OFF THE FULL UNPAID BALANCE UNDER THIS AGREEMENT.

RECEIPT OF COPY IS ACKNOWLEDGED.

Buyer's Signature_____ Date_____

Address_____

City_____ State_____ Zip_____

Illus. 5-9   Retailers must be sure that charge account agreements are clearly written and fully explained to the customer. This agreement is carefully worded to accommodate state-to-state differences in credit requirements. This is basically a contract for a revolving credit account that may be treated as an open account.

Layaway Plans

To accommodate customers who may not qualify for credit privileges, many stores provide *layaway plans.* If the customer selects an item which costs more than she can afford to pay in cash, the store will agree to hold the item for her in a layaway or holding room. The customer agrees to make regular payments until the full purchase price of the item has been paid. The goods are then delivered to her.

Courtesy of Penney News, J. C. Penney Company, Inc.

Illus. 5-10   Various credit plans make credit purchasing available to almost everyone. Many department stores offer time payment plans to enable customers to purchase regularly as long as their account balances do not exceed the established credit limits at any one time.

OUTSIDE FINANCING OF RETAIL CREDIT

For many retailers the cost of operating their own credit system is more than the cost of using an outside system. They may continue their own system, however, because they can use it to attract and hold customers. Retailers who prefer using an outside credit system may choose among several that are available in our credit-oriented society.

Bank Credit

One outside type of retail credit plan is known as the *instant money,* or *bank credit,* plan. Under this plan, a bank grants a customer a certain amount of credit and asks a 1 to 1½ percent monthly service charge on the unpaid balance. The customer decides how much she is able to pay the bank each month, multiplies this amount by 12, and determines the amount of her maximum credit figure. For instance, suppose a customer decides she can pay the bank $40 each month. Her credit maximum will be $480. She now can write checks up to $480 if her credit application is approved by the bank. As she repays what she spends, the money becomes available for her to use again. She pays a carrying charge only on what she owes.

Factoring

Retailers who, for the most part, sell on installment often lack the capital to carry a great number of contracts for long periods of time. In such situations the retailer may resort to *factoring.* Factoring is the practice of selling installment contracts or accounts receivable to a finance company at a discount. The customer's responsibility for payment is then no longer to the retailer but to the firm that has bought his contract.

Commercial Bank Credit Card Plans

Commercial bank credit cards are being used by more consumers in their purchasing than ever before. The two major bank credit cards—Master Charge and BankAmericard—are issued by over 6,000 banks to a total of more than 40 million holders and are honored in fully a million stores. This widespread use of bank credit cards represents a major market of established credit users for retail purchases. These cards are recognized in all stores with which the bank has made arrangements. Each subscribing store sells on credit to customers presenting a card. The charge slips are given to the bank which credits the store's account for the amount, less an agreed percentage which is usually 3 to 5 percent. The bank bills the customers.

Other Credit Card Plans

Carte Blanche, Diners Club, American Express, and a few similar organizations specialize in granting credit to affiliated restaurants, motels, and other retail establishments, such as gasoline stations, airlines, exclusive clothing stores, and other specialty shops. Credit cards are issued by these organizations to firms and individuals who are recognized as

Total Annual Family Income	Type of Credit Card	Percentage of Families Who Use Credit Cards	Median Amount Charged by Credit Card Users in a Typical Month	Credit Card Users Who Charge $1 to $49 a Month	Credit Card Users Who Charge $50 to $99 a Month	Credit Card Users Who Charge $100 or More a Month
$5,000-$7,499	Store	23%	$30-49	32%	12%	6%
	Gas	29%	$15-29	66%	9%	1%
	Bank	11%	$50-74	22%	20%	6%
	Travel & Entertainment	5%	$15-29	26%	0%	0%
$7,500-$9,999	Store	36%	$30-49	33%	10%	9%
	Gas	34%	$15-29	60%	15%	3%
	Bank	14%	$30-49	25%	6%	14%
	Travel & Entertainment	8%	$15-29	24%	6%	0%
$10,000-$14,999	Store	50%	$30-49	33%	14%	13%
	Gas	47%	$15-29	64%	13%	4%
	Bank	22%	$30-49	22%	9%	7%
	Travel & Entertainment	10%	$30-49	20%	8%	3%
$15,000-$19,999	Store	56%	$30-49	34%	10%	14%
	Gas	57%	$30-49	65%	14%	4%
	Bank	30%	$50-74	16%	13%	10%
	Travel & Entertainment	14%	$50-74	21%	11%	7%
$20,000-$24,999	Store	66%	$50-74	23%	11%	26%
	Gas	67%	$30-49	56%	29%	5%
	Bank	40%	$50-74	22%	8%	17%
	Travel & Entertainment	30%	$50-74	21%	14%	8%
$25,000 and over	Store	61%	$ 75-99	24%	17%	36%
	Gas	70%	$ 30-49	61%	23%	7%
	Bank	37%	$100-149	17%	5%	30%
	Travel & Entertainment	40%	$100-149	13%	18%	34%

Illus. 5-11   Credit Card Spending.

excellent credit risks, typically for an annual fee of $15. Merchants and other granters of credit are reimbursed for the amount of customers' charges less the amount charged by the credit organization for assuming the collection cost and the risk.

Abuse of Credit Cards

The tremendous increase in the use of credit cards has been accompanied by a corresponding increase in the use of stolen cards. To counteract this, merchants are provided lists of outstanding cards that are in default or reported as lost or stolen. In addition to refusing to honor such cards, the merchant may be required to phone a central bureau for clearance of all charges above a certain amount. Under federal law the credit card holder is responsible for only $50 of charges against his account made by an unauthorized user. The credit card holder has no liability if he reported the loss of his card immediately.

REGULATION OF CREDIT

Both federal and state governments have legislation affecting retail credit. The federal Truth-in-Lending Law was intended to assure that consumers know exactly the credit charges made by a lender. The law gives customers the opportunity to get better information about two of the most important things about the cost of credit. One is the *finance charge*, the amount of money to be paid to obtain the credit. The other is the *annual percentage rate,* the annual cost in percent of the average amount owed. This provides a way of comparing credit costs regardless of the dollar amount of those costs or the length of time over which payments are made. State governments set maximum permissible charges, generally in terms of the annual rate.

The federal Fair Credit Reporting Act requires every creditor, or credit bureau service providing credit information on individuals, to meet certain requirements relative to verification and investigation procedures. The files of credit information and the reporting must also meet specified requirements. An individual may obtain information about his file and include his own statements to explain or challenge existing reports about his credit history.

CHECKING YOUR KNOWLEDGE

Vocabulary

1. character
2. retail credit bureau
3. capital
4. capacity
5. open, or regular, account
6. repossess
7. deferred, or revolving, account
8. service charge
9. installment plan
10. layaway plans
11. instant money, or bank credit
12. factoring
13. commercial bank credit cards
14. finance charge
15. annual percentage rate

Review Questions

1. Why is it necessary for many retail stores to sell on credit?
2. What are the three factors a merchant considers in granting credit to an applicant?
3. Name at least three types of credit plans a store might offer its customers.
4. How does an open charge account differ from a revolving charge account?
5. What information must be provided by a lender to a customer as specified in the federal Truth-in-Lending Law?

Discussion Questions

1. In comparing the three basic types of credit plans, does any one plan have greater merit for most retailers than the other plans?
2. Is it possible to determine for sure if a customer will pay if credit is extended? Why?
3. What sort of credit plan would be good for a small neighborhood store such as a grocery or hardware store? for a large discount house?
4. Should a large store that has its own established credit plan also honor bank credit cards? Why or why not?

Part **d**

Collection Policies

Merchandise which has been sold on credit does not represent a complete sale until the customer has paid the bill. Inexperienced merchants assume that the transaction is completed when the credit sale is made; this assumption leads to problems with debtors. The merchant who does a large volume of business on credit and who does not insist upon prompt payment will soon find himself short of capital with which to purchase more goods and pay expenses. The merchant needs sound policies and procedures in his collection activities to make sure that he does not have too much money tied up in accounts receivable.

FACILITATING PROMPT PAYMENT

The term *collection* does not refer to the normal receipt of payments at the time agreed upon by merchant and customer. Rather, it refers to those efforts to obtain the amount of a debt that is owed. Perhaps the most important part of establishing a good collection procedure is to do everything possible to facilitate prompt payments on accounts. Every successful merchant who extends credit himself rather than extending it through an outside institution has learned that he can facilitate prompt payment by (1) choosing carefully the customers to whom he will extend credit, (2) emphasizing to new customers that they have an obligation to make their payments promptly, (3) sending out bills at exactly the time agreed upon, and (4) following up accounts immediately with reminders if there is any delay in payment.

COLLECTION PROCEDURES

With good credit management and effective collection procedures, most department and specialty stores—which account for most of the retail credit that is granted—have been able to keep their losses on uncollectible accounts to a fraction of one percent of their total credit sales. In the paragraphs that follow, you will learn about the various aspects of a good collection procedure.

Follow-up Plans

In most stores that grant credit, an orderly follow-up plan for credit accounts must be established. One plan is to review the accounts receivable records at regular intervals to spot those accounts which are *delinquent* (past due). The store then decides how to handle each separate account, and notes are made of the steps taken to collect the amount due. This method, called the *ledger plan,* is quite time-consuming; and most stores prefer to use the *tickler system.* When this system is used, a card for each delinquent account is prepared and placed in a file under the date when the next collection effort is to be made. When the date is reached, the appropriate follow-up notice is sent to the delinquent customer.

In modern store operation the computer makes it possible to determine automatically those accounts which are past due. The computer records all charges to each customer's account and all payments made. It can even report charges beyond a set limit and failures to pay at established times.

Classifying Delinquent Customers

The same collection methods should not be applied to all delinquent customers. Stores classify their delinquent customers as good risks, fair risks, and poor risks.

A *good risk* is a customer who in the past has exhibited character, capacity, and capital but who is temporarily negligent. Such a customer should be treated leniently in the retailer's collection process.

A *fair risk* is a customer who can be relied upon to pay but who tends to put off his payments. Most delinquent customers can be classified as fair risks. If a fair-risk customer has an open or revolving account, he should not be pushed too hard with stern collection measures. However, if he is buying an expensive item on an installment plan, a quick and positive collection action is warranted.

Poor risks are customers whose credit ratings are barely good enough to be granted credit and who have a low credit limit. Some of these customers will prove unwilling to pay unless collection pressure is applied, and a small percentage are deadbeats who have no intention of meeting their obligations. Collection measures for poor risks should start promptly after the account becomes past due.

Communicating with Delinquent Customers

A customer is not considered delinquent until he has failed to respond to the regular statement mailed by the store at the end of the billing period. To give the customer every opportunity to make payment, the store generally allows some time to elapse between the time the statement is sent and the time a collection sequence begins.

A number of means are used to communicate with delinquent customers. The one usually used first is a duplicate of the regular statement which is mailed without any additional comment. The second step may be to send a similar statement which contains a notice—called a *collection sticker*—calling the customer's attention to the fact that the account is past due. If the second statement brings no results, a series of letters is likely to follow. Each letter becomes more urgent in its demands for payment. Some merchants prefer to call the customer on the telephone rather than communicate by mail, and in some cases a telegram may be sent. The telephone call, however, gives the customer a chance to air his grievances which often leads to a quick settlement.

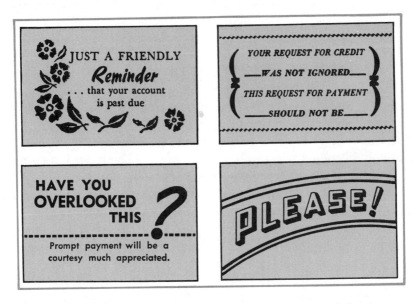

Illus. 5-12   Collection stickers are a simple means of flagging a customer's attention and alerting him to the fact that his account is overdue. Merchants like collection stickers because they are easy to use, inexpensive, and usually not offensive to customers.

No matter what means of communication the merchant uses, he should be careful of what is said. If the merchant seems to harass the customer or if the communications are allowed to fall into the hands of a third party and become public, the customer may file a libel suit.

If all communications with delinquent customers fail to bring payment, the account may be turned over to an outside collection agency. The agency will then try to collect the amount owed and will charge a certain percentage of the collections for its services.

Legal Action

The nature of the collection effort takes into consideration the degree of delinquency, the amount of the debt outstanding, and past experience with the customer. If other means of collection fail, the merchant can sometimes collect the money owed him by taking legal action against the customer.

Repossession of Property. When goods are sold on an open or revolving account, the merchant can recover the amount owed only by suing in court for the amount of the debt. This action should be considered carefully before it is undertaken, because the cost of a law suit can sometimes exceed what might be recovered from the debtor.

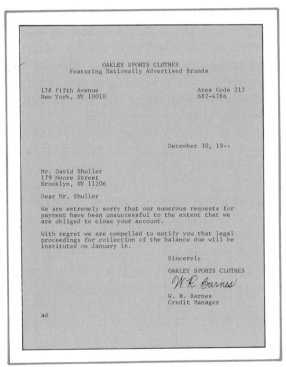

OAKLEY SPORTS CLOTHES
Featuring Nationally Advertised Brands

178 Fifth Avenue   Area Code 212
New York, NY 10010   682-4786

December 30, 19--

Mr. David Shuller
179 Moore Street
Brooklyn, NY 11206

Dear Mr. Shuller

We are extremely sorry that our numerous requests for payment have been unsuccessful to the extent that we are obliged to close your account.

With regret we are compelled to notify you that legal proceedings for collection of the balance due will be instituted on January 16.

Sincerely

OAKLEY SPORTS CLOTHES

W. R. Barnes

W. R. Barnes
Credit Manager

ad

Illus. 5-13   If the letters in a collection sequence—each of which becomes harsher in its demands for payment—fail to bring results, merchants may resort to legal action to collect the money owed them.

If, however, the merchandise is sold on installment with the seller retaining title, the merchant has the right to repossess the property and resell it. Theoretically if the amount received from the resale is less than the amount still owed, the customer can be held responsible for the balance. As a practical matter, stores set the monthly installments high enough to cover estimated depreciation on the merchandise so that the market value at the time of repossession and resale cannot be less than the amount still owed.

When merchandise sold on installment is repossessed, an officer of the law contacts the debtor, informs him of what is transpiring, and seizes the merchandise.

A questionable credit practice has to do with *add-ons*. As a customer makes periodic payments on his debt, he is permitted, even urged, to make additional purchases and to extend the length of the period over which his payments are to be made. Should he default in paying for this additional merchandise, even though he has completed payment on his original purchase, the seller repossesses not only the add ons, but also the original purchase which may now be fully paid for. The installment contract, often in fine print, gives the merchant this right.

The laws governing installment selling were originally written to protect the seller, but they are now being revised to protect the customer as well. Even if legally permissible, it is a poor policy to attempt to make a profit by repossessing merchandise.

Garnishment. Sometimes legal action brought by a merchant against a debtor results in a court order which requires the debtor's employer to pay to the merchant a certain percentage of the debtor's wages until the amount of the debt has been paid. This procedure is called *garnishment*. State laws vary, but there is usually an established minimum salary below which wages cannot be garnisheed. A merchant is well advised to demand garnishment only as a last resort. It causes resentment and hardship to the debtor. He is not likely ever to buy from that merchant again, even when his economic circumstances improve.

MEASURING EFFECTIVENESS OF COLLECTION POLICIES

To determine whether collection policies and procedures are functioning effectively, various measures of performance have been devised. Those measures on which a store most often relies are the bad debt loss index, the collection percentage, the accounts receivable turnover rate, and the age analysis of accounts.

The *bad debt loss index* is figured by dividing the bad debts incurred during a given period by the total credit sales for that period. Separate indexes for open accounts, revolving accounts, and installment sales are commonly figured. The bad debt loss index is generally lowest for open accounts and highest for installment sales.

To determine the *collection percentage,* the merchant divides the payments made by credit customers during a certain time period by the accounts receivable outstanding at the beginning of that period. Thus, if customers owed $50,000 at the beginning of the month and paid $10,000 on account, the collection percentage would be 20 percent.

The annual *accounts receivable turnover rate* is computed by dividing the total yearly credit sales by the average amount owed each month. Thus, if credit sales for the year were $50,000 and the average amount owed each month was $10,000, the turnover would be 5. The higher the turnover, the more efficient are the store's collection procedures.

The analysis of accounts receivable in regard to length of time the accounts are past due is an important indication of how effectively the collection procedures are functioning. This analysis is called *aging of accounts.* A store may set up five classes into which past-due accounts may fall: (1) accounts 30 to 60 days past due; (2) accounts 60 days to 6 months past due; (3) accounts 6 months to 1 year past due; (4) accounts 1 to 2 years past due; and (5) accounts more than 2 years past due. Periodically the store reviews and classifies accounts receivable. If there are many accounts in Classes 3, 4, and 5, it is an indication that the collection procedures are not effective.

Many analyses of bad debt losses have been made to determine what percentage of past-due accounts are likely to prove collectible. One such analysis showed that for a retail account which is less than three months overdue, about 90 percent of the account's face value will be collectible. Accounts which are one year past due are likely to be collectible at only 30 percent of their face value; and those which are more than two years overdue usually are collectible at no more than a few cents for every dollar owed. These figures emphasize the importance of establishing an effective collection procedure which will initiate collection steps promptly after an account has become past due.

CHECKING YOUR KNOWLEDGE

Vocabulary

1. collection
2. delinquent
3. ledger plan
4. tickler system
5. good risk
6. fair risk
7. poor risk
8. collection sticker
9. add-on
10. garnishment
11. bad debt loss index
12. collection percentage
13. accounts receivable turnover rate
14. aging of accounts

Review Questions

1. What are four ways of facilitating prompt payments on a credit account?
2. Describe two methods of following up accounts for collection purposes.
3. Comment on various ways of communicating with delinquent customers.
4. Under what condition may a store repossess merchandise?
5. What is the value of aging accounts?

Discussion Questions

1. Is there any relationship between a store's credit policies and its collection policies?
2. Suppose that one of your customers failed to make a payment on time. What successive steps would you take, assuming that the customer fails to respond to each step you take?
3. What response would you make to a customer's request for credit on a sizable purchase when he is already 90 days behind in paying for goods previously purchased on open account?
4. Is it possible to use the collection process to build goodwill and yet keep the patronage of delinquent customers? Explain.

Part e

Personnel Policies

The success of a retail business depends greatly on the human factor. Retailers have learned that a satisfied employee will devote his best efforts to the store's success and to the needs of customers. A dissatisfied worker will reduce sales volume, increase expenses, and create a poor store image in the customer's mind. Good personnel policies help to insure that an employee is loyal and productive. These policies are formulated and carried out in a large store by a separate department, called the personnel department, which is headed by the personnel manager. The persons working in the personnel department may be divided into groups to handle specific areas such as selection of employees, training of employees, promotion and transfer of employees, determination of wages and benefits, maintenance of health and safety programs, and union negotiations. In a small store all personnel policies are formulated and put into effect by the owner-manager. Some of the more important personnel policies that a retailer must decide upon are those concerning employment, compensation, fringe benefits, working conditions, job relocation, communication, and labor relations.

SELECTING AND TRAINING EMPLOYEES

Many small retailers depend on relatives and acquaintances to fill positions in their stores. As a store grows, however, it should adopt a policy of hiring and training the right person for each job to assure an effective and efficient store operation. To get an adequate staff requires four major steps.

The first step is to determine just what abilities a worker in each position must have. To do this the retailer prepares a written description of the job and lists the skills needed by the worker to perform that job.

The second step is to locate sources of potential employees. Some retailers put signs in their store windows or let present employees know of a position to be filled. Some merchants depend on advertising through the want ads of a newspaper. Other merchants may use the state employment service, private employment agencies, or work with high school or community college distributive education departments. Whatever source of supply is used, it should be able to provide qualified people.

The third important step is to make the correct selection from among the applicants for a position. Usually an application form is used followed by an interview. Some stores use one or more tests to check the individual's ability to perform and to determine his or her interest in retailing. Those who pass the initial screening and testing may then have additional interviews with the personnel director and the department head. In the selection process, stores have adopted a policy of avoiding discrimination against minority groups.

The fourth step is to provide the new employee with an orientation to the company and to the work to be done. The training program should be tailored to the new worker's needs and should be continued until he has acquired all necessary information and skill.

COMPENSATION POLICIES

If a store is to attract competent people, it must have a policy of offering salaries and wages that are competitive with other opportunities that are open to potential employees. It must also conform to the federal and state minimum wage laws. There should also be a policy to set wage ranges for each job classification, with annual increases within each range. Straight commission plans may be an exception. Thus, the range for a stock clerk may be set at $85 to $125 a week, with annual increases of $5 a week.

To be sure that increases are deserved and to identify promotable people, an annual or semiannual rating plan should be used to evaluate performance and personality traits. Wage scales must not discriminate against women employees or members of minority groups. The federal Equal Pay Act requires that women be paid as much as men for jobs requiring substantially equal skill, effort, and responsibility.

WAGE AND SALARY PLANS

Several types of wage and salary plans are used to compensate retailing personnel for their efforts. It is not unusual for one store to use all these plans, one for each different kind of employee. The most common plans are the straight salary plan, salary and commission plan, quota plan, and straight commission plan.

Straight Salary Plan

Many stores pay both selling and nonselling employees a definite amount of money per hour, week, or month. A flat sum is paid the employee for the time he works; no direct attempt may be made to measure his productivity. This is the *straight salary plan*. For example, a cashier who receives $2.10 an hour and works a 40-hour week will receive a gross wage of $84. Management personnel are almost always paid under the straight salary plan but have the possibility of year-end bonuses based on the increases in sales or profits.

Salary and Commission Plan

Another widely used means of compensating salespeople is the *salary and commission plan*. Under this plan, the salesperson receives a base salary plus an additional amount of money depending upon his sales. This additional amount is usually figured as a percentage of his sales. Thus, a salesperson whose sales for one week amount to $1,500 and who receives a commission of one percent would be paid $15 over his base salary. If his base salary were $95, his total pay would be $110.

Quota Plan

A variation of the salary and commission plan is the *quota plan*. Under this plan, the person in charge sets a definite amount that a salesperson must sell in a given time period. This amount is called the *quota*. If the salesperson sells more than his quota, a certain percentage of all his sales above the quota is paid to him in addition to his base pay.

Straight Commission Plan

The *straight commission plan* is preferred by retail salespeople who want to earn in accordance with their individual abilities. A flat commission, such as 6 percent of sales, is agreed upon. The salesperson would then receive $6 for every $100 in sales. The amount he can earn is limited only by the amount he can sell. To insure that the salesperson earns a reasonable wage even during the slowest selling seasons, stores often establish *drawing accounts*. Salespeople are paid from their accounts at regular intervals, and the payments are charged against commissions later earned.

Supplementary Incentive Plans

Stores often establish special compensation plans which supplement the wage payment plans. One financial incentive plan is the *P.M.*, (*premium money*). It is a reward for selling a certain article. For example, a 50-cent P.M. may be placed on a style of shoe that has not sold well in order to move it out of stock. There is some danger, however, of the salesperson using high-pressure selling to get the P.M.

Profit-sharing and bonus plans are becoming increasingly common as supplementary incentive plans. In some stores profit-sharing plans represent a sizable part of the annual earnings of all employees including management personnel.

FRINGE BENEFIT POLICIES

Fringe benefits are the extra benefits that retail personnel receive in addition to a regular salary. Some fringe benefits, such as unemployment compensation and social security, are required by federal law. Other fringe benefits are provided voluntarily by employers to keep their employees contented and to attract new employees. Various fringe benefits in retailing add 15 percent or more to the direct cost of salaries and wages.

One of the most important fringe benefits today is health insurance. The store pays all or part of the premiums for hospital and medical care. Group rates are available at a savings even if employees must pay part of the cost.

Most stores also give employee discounts ranging from 10 to 33 percent on purchases in the store. This practice builds goodwill and, in a clothing or department store, gives the employee an opportunity to buy better clothing and thus make a better appearance. Since the employee usually shops during slow hours of the selling day and usually takes his purchases with him, most stores can well afford to offer substantial discounts for employee business.

Large stores also maintain employee cafeterias where well-balanced meals are sold at less than restaurant prices. Stores may also provide medical, dental, and occasionally legal aid at a nominal cost. Some stores have a vacation camp that employees can attend free or for a modest fee. Pension and annuity plans are being used in an increasing number of leading stores, and others are planning to introduce them.

POLICIES GOVERNING WORKING CONDITIONS

One of the potential employee's major concerns is how many hours a week he will have to work. In spite of the long hours a store must remain open, the workweek of employees is shortening. In many localities, full-time employees are required to work only 7 hours a day for 5 days a week. By using staggered hours and more part-timers, the store can be open as many as 70 hours a week with each employee working only 35 to 40 hours. In order to be competitive with other jobs, stores are becoming more flexible in the choice of hours they can offer.

Working conditions satisfactory to employees also involve pleasant physical surroundings—air conditioning, freedom from drafts and excessive noise, stools for salespersons behind counters, and comfortable rest rooms. Coffee breaks are routine in most localities.

RELOCATION POLICIES

Relatively few employees who remain with a retail establishment for any length of time stay in the same job or department. New jobs may be created as the store grows, and some jobs may be vacated due to illness or death. It is sometimes necessary for retailing employees to be relocated within a store or within a chain or branch store system, and policies governing promotions and transfers must be established.

A *promotion* moves an employee into a new job in which he has more responsibility and authority. An employee's ability and seniority are the two most important factors in determining whether he should receive a promotion. Most retailers prefer to fill new or vacant jobs by promoting from within their organization rather than hiring a new employee. Promoting from within means that the store can avoid the costs of hiring and most of the costs of training a new worker. Also, this policy usually increases goodwill on the part of the employee. If employees know that their store has a fair promotion policy and that there are good opportunities for advancement, they are more likely to be loyal and enthusiastic workers.

A *transfer* involves the moving of an employee to another job at about the same level of responsibility. Sometimes an employee is placed in a job for which he is not suited. His supervisor may realize that he would be more productive if he were transferred to another job. Managerial personnel are commonly transferred from department to department as part of their training programs so that they can learn all aspects of the store's operation. In some cases, too, an employee is transferred to reduce friction among employees who do not get along.

COMMUNICATION POLICIES

A major problem in large stores is communication among employees and between employees and management. The owner of a small store usually has no such problem. He knows his employees by name, and it is easy for them to talk to him if they have complaints or if they have suggestions for improving the store's operation. The large discount or department store has hundreds of employees, and it is necessary to set up definite means of communication.

Much communication between employees and management is handled through department supervisors. Employees discuss their problems with the supervisor, and the supervisor relays the information to management. When any action on a problem is taken, the information is given first to the supervisor so that he may relay it to the employee. Communication among members of management is usually done through reports and memorandums or committee meetings and conferences.

If the store is unionized, there will be a union representative to whom an employee can turn for help. Store executives should never take action on a complaint until the supervisor also has been given an opportunity to present his case.

Employee manuals which contain general information about company rules and regulations are quite beneficial to new employees. Bulletin boards placed in prominent spots, such as near the time clock or in the employees' lounges, are useful tools for transmitting information about such things as weekly performance records and social events of interest to employees. Some of the large department stores publish a *house organ* for their employees. Such a publication may take the form of a weekly newspaper or a monthly magazine and contains personal stories about the employees and articles of general interest to everyone in the store.

LABOR RELATIONS POLICIES

The National Labor Relations Act—passed in 1935—prohibits employers from interfering with unions, from discriminating against union members, and from refusing to bargain with their representatives. Unions bargain most often for direct pay increases; but they also negotiate for holiday pay, vacation length and pay, insurance and health programs, provision of educational incentives, and seniority rules. Both sides—retail management and labor—should seek to avoid all-out strikes. If a store loses customers because of labor problems, both management and store employees will suffer.

Retailing has not been a fertile field for unions. The bulk of retailing consists of small establishments, retail labor turnover is high, and many workers strive toward management level jobs. On the other hand, enlightened union leaders now recognize the need for a profitable store operation if jobs are to be secure and if increases in employee benefits are to be assured. Bargaining with a union may reveal to a retailer the need for a more liberal employee policy, and he may learn to see his workers in a different light.

CHECKING YOUR KNOWLEDGE

Vocabulary

1. straight salary plan
2. salary and commission plan
3. quota plan
4. quota
5. straight commission plan
6. drawing accounts
7. premium money
8. fringe benefits
9. promotion
10. transfer
11. house organ

Review Questions

1. Describe the four steps that are necessary to obtain appropriate personnel for the retail store.
2. Why do many salespeople prefer the straight commission plan of compensation?
3. What are some of the fringe benefits offered in retail employment?
4. Why would a retail store transfer a worker to several different jobs?
5. How is communication achieved in large retail stores?

Discussion Questions

1. What are the advantages to both the retailer and the prospective employee of a well-organized system of selection and training?
2. The nature of fringe benefits is becoming increasingly important to both the new and experienced worker. Why is this so? Which benefits are most important to the young worker?
3. Do typical retail hours of employment make it difficult for stores to obtain satisfactory employees?

4. Under what circumstances would retail store workers be most likely to join a union? Should retailers try to avoid unionism?

BUILDING YOUR SKILLS

Improving Communication Skills

On a separate sheet of paper, write the missing forms for each of the adjectives listed.

	Positive	Comparative	Superlative
1.	little	. . . . . .	. . . . . .
2.	. . . . . .	busier	. . . . . .
3.	big	. . . . . .	. . . . . .
4.	. . . . . .	. . . . . .	most brilliant
5.	. . . . . .	smaller	. . . . . .
6.	. . . . . .	. . . . . .	largest
7.	bright	. . . . . .	. . . . . .
8.	. . . . . .	better	. . . . . .
9.	careful	. . . . . .	. . . . . .
10.	. . . . . .	. . . . . .	fastest

Improving Arithmetic Skills

Perform the exercises given below:

1. During inventory a stock clerk found the following partial rolls of floor covering:

   Vinyl—3 yards; 7 1/2 yards; 5 1/2 yards; 4 1/4 yards
   Vinyl asbestos—9 5/6 yards; 6 3/4 yards; 5 3/4 yards; 4 2/3 yards
   Linoleum—7 yards; 8 1/3 yards; 1 2/3 yards; 4 3/4 yards; 1 1/2 yards

   How many yards of each type were in partial rolls? How many yards of all types were in partial rolls?

2. One day Kay Long sold 6 3/8 yards of dacron polyester, 5 1/2 yards of acetate taffeta, 3 1/2 yards of shantung, 6 1/4 yards of percale, 2 yards and 30 inches of brocade, and 1 5/6 yards of broadcloth. How many yards of fabric did she sell during the day?

3. From one roll of window screening, the following pieces were cut during one day: 4 feet, 8 inches; 30 inches; 5 1/2 feet, 18 inches; 11 1/4 yards; and 3 feet. What was the total number of feet of window screening cut from the roll? total yards?

4. A 100-yard dash is equal to a dash of how many meters?

5. Paul Mann opened his service station at 7 a.m. and sold the following amounts of gasoline before 8 a.m.: 13.4 gals., 8.5 gals., 17.9 gals., 5.0 gals., 12.7 gals., and 9.6 gals. How many gallons did he sell in the hour? If he continues to sell gasoline at that rate, how many gallons will he sell by the time he closes at 9 p.m.?

6. During the year, your credit sales were $100,000; you had bad debts for the year of $2,000; the average amount owed by customers each month was $25,000; and the average amount paid by customers on account each month was $10,000. Compute (1) the bad debt percentages, (2) the average monthly collection percentage for the year, and (3) the accounts receivable turnover rate.

1. Determine what it would cost for a retailer in your city to deliver 100 four-pound packages to various homes within a 20-mile radius by each of the following methods:
   (a) parcel post
   (b) independent delivery service
   (c) consolidated delivery service

2. As a member of a team from class, visit one of the largest department stores in your community and by means of the analysis form on page 179 determine which of the customer services listed are provided. Add to the list any other services that may be offered, such as profit services. Then, based on the experiences of some members of the group or of their families, rate the quality of each service provided as *Excellent, Good, Fair,* or *Poor.*

   Prepare a group report including the services offered; those offered that are well performed; those offered that are poorly performed, and how they could be improved; those that should be eliminated and why; other services that should be added; and a general evaluation of the quality of the store's services. Compare the classifications of services here with those in Illus. 5-4.

3. Talk to workers or managers of three different stores about the fringe benefits provided. Compare the benefits of the three stores for similarities and differences.

Improving Decision-Making Skills

1. As the owner of a small variety store, you operate with a cash-only policy. Occasionally you do extend credit for a short period of time to a person you know. A woman who recently moved into your neighborhood wants to buy $40 worth of assorted housewares and children's clothing. She wants to pay $15 at this time and the rest at the end of next week when her husband who is on road construction work comes home. Would you extend her credit? Would you do any checking first? If so, what questions would you ask?

2. You are the buyer for women's ready-to-wear for a junior department store. Store policy has been that the quality of merchandise comes before price. In one line of dresses prices have been $10.99, $15.99, and $19.99. Your merchandise manager wants you to add another line of dresses of questionable quality at a price of $8.59 to meet chain-store competition. What effect might this have on your customers? What arguments, if any, will you present to the merchandise manager?

APPLYING YOUR KNOWLEDGE

Chapter Project

The matter of store services is a continuing concern to most retailers. In this project you may find information that will be of interest to retailers in your community.

ANALYSIS OF CUSTOMER SERVICES

	Evaluation	
Classifications	*Offering*	*Quality*

I. CUSTOMER SHOPPING CONVENIENCES

A. Customer service desk—amusement tickets, information, check, cashing, utilities' payments, money orders, travelers' checks, gift certificates _____ _____

B. Food services, rest rooms, nursery _____ _____

C. Extended store hours _____ _____

D. Parking _____ _____

E. Vending machines—cigarettes, coffee, candy _____ _____

F. Store atmosphere and arrangement—layout, fixtures, noise, temperature, etc. _____ _____

G. Community services—Boy Scouts, charity festivals, scholarships, free concerts, etc. _____ _____

II. CREDIT SERVICES

A. Regular 30-day charge accounts _____ _____

B. Revolving accounts _____ _____

C. Installment accounts _____ _____

III. MERCHANDISE HANDLING SERVICES

A. Mail and telephone orders _____ _____

B. Delivery and shipping _____ _____

C. Wrapping and packing _____ _____

D. Layaway _____ _____

E. Catalog sales _____ _____

IV. CUSTOMER ACCOMMODATION SERVICES

A. Adjustments, refunds, and exchanges _____ _____

B. Guarantees _____ _____

C. Special orders and custom services _____ _____

D. Installations _____ _____

E. Repairs and alterations _____ _____

F. Approval sales _____ _____

G. COD's _____ _____

V. INFORMATION AND ADVISORY SERVICES

A. Personal shopping _____ _____

B. Fashion consultation _____ _____

C. Wedding arrangements—bridal consultant, register, etc. _____ _____

D. Interior decorating _____ _____

E. Landscaping _____ _____

F. Educational services—classes in cooking, sewing, knitting, painting, sports, hobbies _____ _____

G. Printed instructions—do-it-yourself materials _____ _____

H. Sales assistance and technical merchandise information _____ _____

I. Point-of-sale display information _____ _____

J. Testing and analyzing _____ _____

You, along with your classmates, if your instructor so wishes, are to interview several individuals and obtain their views about store services in other than food and neighborhood stores. The more interviews you are able to get the more valid the results will be. Ask each person interviewed the following two questions:

1. What store services are most important to you when you are shopping?
2. What store services are least important to you when you are shopping?

Keep a record of the following characteristics of each person interviewed: male or female, approximate age, married or single, and occupation.

When you have completed your interviews, tabulate the data you have collected and arrange your findings and interpretations in a report form.

Continuing Project

Add to your manual, sections which illustrate and explain your store's policies in regard to:

1. Merchandise—merchandise mix, pricing, quality, stocking of fashion merchandise
2. Services—selling aids, shopping conveniences, installation and repair services, delivery service, group presentations, community services
3. Credit—evaluating applicants, credit plans
4. Collections—follow-up plans, means of communicating with delinquent customers, measuring effectiveness of collection policies
5. Personnel—selection and training, compensation, fringe benefits, labor relations

UNIT 3
Buying for Resale

Buying of merchandise for resale is a glamourous part of retailing. Goods purchased, however, are expected to sell quickly and at a price that will provide a profit on the investment. The buying process starts with an analysis of customer demand. This leads to determining what to buy, how to buy, where to buy, how much to buy. Through all these considerations runs the question of the retail prices to place on purchases. While each purchase need not contribute to profits directly, the overall pricing operation must yield a profit if the store is to grow and prosper.

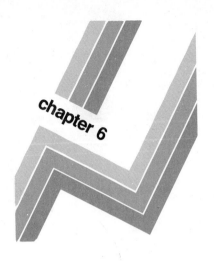

chapter 6

Buying

a. The merchant who listens to his customers, observes their shopping habits, and is sensitive to changes in customer demands is able to buy merchandise that is well suited to customer needs and wants.

b. The buyer obtains information about merchandise in the market by reading journals and trade reports and through direct contact with manufacturers and whole-salers.

c. Fashion buyers must know the language of fashion and recognize the cycles of the various fashion articles they handle.

d. Product or brand names are used nationally by manu-facturers to promote their goods. Large retailers often develop private brands that compete with national brands.

e. The buying plan should provide for an assortment of goods balanced to customer demand in terms of price, size, color, type, and material.

Part **a**

Studying the Customer

Successful buying for resale is an outgrowth of the image that the store management wishes to project. In Chapter 5 we discussed the various merchandise policies from which the merchant may select those best suited to the life styles of the customer groups that he hopes to attract. His selection is also influenced by his own skill and resources in implementing a particular policy.

BUYING AND THE STORE IMAGE

Since no store can hope to attract everyone, good judgment in selecting the right merchandise policies is essential. For example, a large city department store recently doubled its sales volume and made itself the city's fashion leader by selecting exclusive (not available elsewhere) merchandise as its major characteristic. To accomplish this, the store sends more buyers to Europe than any other competing store; it is constantly in search of little-known manufacturers who produce distinctive merchandise that will appeal to sophisticated people. Buyers are constantly challenged by management to search for the unusual and the exclusive. They are aided by expert fashion coordinators and by the members of a fashion "research and development" department. They are given great freedom in controlling their advertising expenditures and the size of their sales force. In this store, little attempt is made to meet price competition, even in the relatively few items that are available elsewhere. Unprofitable, highly competitive lines, such as major appliances and cheap furniture, have been dropped entirely.

This store's remarkable success provides an excellent example of the importance of a clear-cut merchandise policy. In this case it is *exclusiveness,* expressed in the merchandise selections in all departments of the store. Not many stores, of course, have both the proper kind of customer and the skill to make exclusiveness the central policy. Every store, however, must build its assortments around certain features, be they quality, fashion, wide assortments, deep stocks of best sellers, consistently low prices, or special sales featuring bargains. Each merchant must try to select those few merchandise features that will build for his store a clear-cut and attractive image, rather than attempt to be all things to all people.

Even in the highly competitive supermarket field, where low price is often the most important merchandise feature, it is possible to attract customers by means of characteristics other than price. For example, one great chain stores' prices on national brands are often higher than those of their competitors. Nevertheless, they attract a large segment of the public because their stores are clean, the quality of their meats and produce outstanding, and the stock so arranged as to make selection easy. And for those customers who do demand the lowest prices, the stores offer their own private brands that account for about a fourth of their sales volume.

DETERMINING CUSTOMER WANTS

In order to determine the items to select for resale within the confines of a particular merchandise policy, the retailer must study his customers. He must come to know their tastes and preferences and the current changes taking place in their styles of living. So important is this study that merchants have developed various methods to find out what their customers need and want, how they want it, and why. One merchant invites several typical customers to sit in with his executive staff to discuss buying, advertising, and services provided. Such groups are called *customer panels*. These typical customers can provide helpful opinions on merchandise as well as store procedures and services. Some stores use groups of selected high school or college students, called *teen boards*, to advise on youth activities and fashion trends. Another merchant requests the opinions of his customers by sending them letters asking them to comment freely on the goods and services of his store. One fashion store tests and checks customer preference with regard to styles, colors, sizes, and price ranges. This is done by placing small initial orders for a rather large variety of garments. Customer reaction to each garment is carefully observed, and the favored items are reordered in depth. A large department store has a "What's New?" corner where new fashions are displayed to get customer reaction. Some merchants conduct surveys and polls which reveal customer preferences and use the results of such polls as guides in buying. Suggestion boxes, where customers may indicate their opinions upon every phase of retailing, are found in many stores.

If a retailer could read customers' thoughts and discover their preferences, their price limits, their ideas of style, beauty, and comfort, he would have the answer to the question of "what to buy." People often reveal what they are thinking, and the retailer must learn to read and interpret the outward signs. He must watch the facial expressions of

Illus. 6-1   Some retail stores that specialize in teenage fashions employ the talents of carefully chosen teenagers who act as consultants and models in promoting teen clothing.

customers when they see something they like or something they particularly dislike; he must listen to what they say; and he must notice their eyes and their hands as they handle goods.

A study of the customer—including his education, interests, financial status, and buying habits—is the basis of successful retailing. If customers do not want an item, the merchant should not buy it; it does not matter how good a bargain an item might be or how attractive it might be. This does not mean that a buyer should never take a chance on an item, but an intelligent guess as to whether the item will sell should be based on past experience and on knowledge of the customers to whom the store caters.

How can a retailer tell what customers will want? Actually they tell him. Some of the ways to get them to tell have already been mentioned. The retailer who takes the time and trouble to study customers, to listen to them, and to analyze what they have bought in the past, has taken the first step toward successful buying.

Analysis of Past Records

A careful analysis of past sales records tells much about what customers want and are likely to buy again. Sales records can provide information as to the kinds, quantities, colors, sizes, and prices of merchandise that has been sold. A variety store owner knows that each week a certain amount of candy, envelopes, yarn, zippers, and picture frames probably will be sold in his store. Past sales records, therefore, give a fairly reliable indication of recurring customer demand.

Every good buyer keeps records of his past purchases and sales. He refers to these before deciding what to buy. These records give him a clear picture of his best-selling items and his slow sellers. For instance, the grocery buyer of a large food chain has at his fingertips the *rate of movement* of every item. He knows that 100 cases of a brand-name baking chocolate are moved from the warehouse into the stores each month and that he should reorder when the stock in the warehouse gets down to 150 cases. When the warehouse stock reaches the low point, the buyer is "flagged" through a system of colored tabs on stock cards or by means of a computer printout. He then places an order for the chocolate.

Want Slips

One way to find out what customers want that the store does not carry is to talk to customers and to require salespeople to report on merchandise asked for by customers but not carried by the store. Since salespeople often forget the details regarding such merchandise, they may be supplied with forms called *want slips* on which to jot down everything asked for that is not in stock. When a salesperson succeeds in selling an article other than that asked for, the substitution is also reported on the want slip. By studying these reports every day, a store

Date *March 11, 19--*	WANT SLIP				Dept. No. *42*	
					Employee No. *14*	
Keep this slip in your salesbook, or not, record that fact at once.	Whenever an item is called for that is not in stock, whether carried regularly or not. Make certain that you record every call.					
ITEMS CALLED FOR	WANTED				WHAT WAS SUBSTITUTED	BUYER'S DISPOSITION
	Style	Color	Size	Price		
Blouse	*shirt-waist*	*White*	*34*	*5.98*	———	*On order*
Sweater	*turtle-neck*	*Grey*	*36*	*9.98*	*V-neck*	*On order*
Flannel pajamas	*Coat style*	*Blue*	*10*	*7.98*	*Lounger*	*Discontinued*
Coat	*Car coat*	*Red*	*14*	*25.98*	———	*In reserve*
Gloves	*leather*	*White*	*6*	*6.95*	———	*On order*

Illus. 6-2   A want slip may be provided each salesperson daily. On it are entered items that are called for but which are not in stock.

buyer may find that there is a definite demand for certain articles. For example, a men's store that has not sold men's hats may have so many calls for hats that the management may decide to open a hat department.

The report of substitution sales on want slips indicates which goods in stock can readily be substituted for articles asked for but not carried. This knowledge may make it unnecessary to buy some articles in which customers show only a passing interest.

Comparison Shopping

An indirect way of determining customer demand is to study the activities of competitors. Merchants watch the advertisements and the windows of competitors and occasionally have their salespeople visit competing stores as though they were customers. Large stores have special comparison bureaus for this purpose and are thus able to determine whether competitors are selling the same articles at a lower price. Such *comparison shopping* may also show that a competitor is doing a good business with a type of merchandise that the merchant does not even carry in stock. Comparison shopping thus supplements the want-slip system in keeping up assortments of popular goods and provides the merchant many good ideas for display and personal salesmanship.

Merchants find it desirable to watch the advertisements of stores in nearby towns and in metropolitan centers. Local customers may make occasional buying trips to these places, and they may demand articles of merchandise being sold in large cities. By watching the demand in these places, stores find out what goods may become popular at home. Some articles sell well in a metropolis just a few weeks before the small-town stores experience a demand for the same articles. However, the time lag today is very short.

PREDICTING CONSUMER DEMAND

Stores cannot progress by buying only what has been sold in the past. They must move with the times and provide new goods for the customer's selection. In some cases the store buyer selects goods which he senses will be wanted by customers. In other cases the store depends on information from customers to guide the kind and amount of goods purchased for future resale.

New Items

The buyer must spend a good deal of time creating or seeking new items that incorporate features which will attract customers and make a profit for the store. For instance, what does the youth of the community want and like? What is the trend in the life style of the suburbanite, and what goods does this suggest? Since more and more wives are employed and now shop with their husbands in the evening, will impulse merchandise sell better than formerly? What new merchandise will make life easier or more pleasant for the customers who come to the store? With such questions in mind, the buyer is constantly on the lookout for merchandise not presently carried by the store.

Customer Surveys

While the average small store is not in a position to conduct consumer research on a sophisticated basis, it often has access to such surveys conducted by the manufacturers whose products it carries. For example, manufacturers of appliances, such as radios, sometime employ research agencies to obtain customer opinion as to the shape, color, and finish preferred. This information is actually used in setting the specifications and design for the product. The predicted sales by color and finish can guide the retailer in placing his order. Large stores may have trained personnel who plan and conduct studies about customer preferences and their intentions to buy.

CHECKING YOUR KNOWLEDGE

Vocabulary

1. exclusiveness
2. customer panels
3. teen boards
4. rate of movement
5. want slips
6. comparison shopping

Review Questions

1. How does merchandise policy control the selection of merchandise for resale?
2. Describe some of the ways a retailer may study his customer.
3. What information can the retailer get by studying past records?
4. What information is collected on a want slip?
5. How does comparison shopping differ from customer surveys?

Discussion Questions

1. For what types of retail stores would analyses of past records be most helpful in deciding what to buy?
2. What advantages do customer panels or teen boards provide the retailer?
3. Is the need for a want-slip system the same for small-scale retailers as for large-scale retailers?

Part **b**

Obtaining Market Information

The successful merchant continuously studies the products manufacturers and wholesalers are making available. The retailer must decide which new items or new models of existing items have a potential for acceptance by his customers. To do this the store buyer must keep in close touch with manufacturers and wholesalers and also keep up to date on product improvements and price quotations.

Marilyn Marsh, who was opening a card, book, and gift store, was very much interested in learning about new products that she might stock in her store. She knew that her potential customers would expect a variety to choose from in each of the three main product areas as well as a selection of unique and very new items. Although Marilyn had developed some good market contacts while working in the department store, she knew that more information would be needed. Also, as a beginning store owner, Marilyn realized that she could not personally visit the market as frequently as she might like. She would have to depend on a combination of personal examination of goods and reports on merchandise by others.

PERSONAL EXAMINATION

Undoubtedly most retail store buyers, like customers, want to be able to see and touch the merchandise in which they are interested. Firsthand observation of an item gives the examiner a far better understanding of its qualities and features than a picture or written description.

Visiting Sales Representatives

It is true that a merchant who sells only convenience goods can buy without ever leaving his place of business. He can rely on the salespeople employed by wholesalers and manufacturers who call on his store. The salespeople report what is new on the market, show the retailer samples, and indicate what is selling well in other stores. However, the merchant who depends wholly on the salespeople of suppliers is often taking a great risk. Those salespeople who call may not represent the merchandise lines incorporating the most important innovations, and they may not offer the most reasonable prices.

Nevertheless, personal acquaintance with product salespeople and supplier representatives can prove helpful in many ways. Information about products being developed and the needs of the retailer can be exchanged. If the retailer wants to clarify an order or needs a special aid, knowing someone in the supplying firm is very helpful.

Visits to Market Centers

It is important that a retailer keep in touch with the entire wholesaling and manufacturing market. Ideally periodic trips should be made to the great centers, such as New York City, Chicago, San Francisco, St. Louis, Philadelphia, and Los Angeles. In the market, the retailer can inspect merchandise that would otherwise not be seen, and he can become acquainted with personnel of the supplier firms.

Trade Shows

Often exhibits or shows of products from many suppliers will be organized by manufacturers' associations, wholesalers, or groups of retail stores. These are known as *trade shows*. They may feature either specific product lines or consist of several related merchandise areas. Such shows or conventions are held on a regional basis, serving retail stores in one or more states, or on a national level serving retailers from all over the country.

The scope of a national trade show can be illustrated by the National Housewares show. Under one roof there are approximately 1,500 manufacturer exhibitors. For the retailer looking for new and improved merchandise in the housewares area, this annual show represents the ultimate in opportunity. Similar shows are held for almost all other consumer merchandise.

Frequently wholesale firms will organize product shows for retailers in their area. The wholesaler will sponsor exhibits by manufacturers. Retail merchants who buy through that wholesaler will be invited to attend and look at new merchandise. In some cases permanent displays are maintained, such as the Chicago American Furniture Mart and the Merchandise Mart of Chicago.

PRODUCT REPORTS

Even with regular calls from salesmen and a few annual visits to market centers the retailer will need additional market information. He will need regular information about style changes, price changes, product improvements, and other data in order to buy intelligently for his customers. Such information can be obtained through trade papers, trade services, and market representation.

Trade Papers

If the merchant cannot afford to make trips to the wholesale markets, he should at least write for catalogs and price lists from the leading distributors in each line. He should also subscribe to the leading trade papers in his field.

Almost every line of staple and fashion merchandise has its trade publication. A *trade paper* or *journal* is a publication containing information that is of value and interest to people in a particular field or line. For instance, *Women's Wear Daily* carries information on what is new, which items the stores are selling, and what is enjoying popular appeal in women's apparel. *Drug Topics,* a trade publication in the drug field, keeps buyers advised on merchandise of interest to pharmacists.

Trade Services

The merchant can also subscribe to trade services in his field. Special market-reporting organizations report on the latest developments in the manufacture and sale of specific articles. Since the articles described may later be requested by a store's customers, a study of the market reports will enable the store to have goods in stock when they are in demand.

Some of the services specialize in reporting on items that are finding ready acceptance in various cities throughout the country. These are called *action item reports.* For example, the Retail News Bureau sends shoppers to report customer response to the feature advertisements of the leading stores in New York, Chicago, and Los Angeles. Detailed reports on each promotion are prepared and distributed to this organization's clients. Thus, a buyer knowing the degree of success of a specific item in a certain store, can come to an intelligent decision as to whether he should buy and promote the item himself. The service is generally able to locate the wholesale sources of the advertised articles so that a subscriber to the service can readily get in touch with the manufacturer or distributor if he is interested.

Market Representation

Many merchants are recognizing that the best way to keep in touch with market offerings is to join other stores in supporting an agency that specializes in locating the most suitable merchandise for its member stores. For the convenience-goods store, the best plan usually is to join a voluntary chain led by a wholesaler who maintains a wide selection of market offerings. This wholesaler should devote himself to providing his independent member stores with the

WEEK ENDING: 8/26/ — #1

Block 1

DEPT: LADIES COAT

S. Allan
K. B. BUYER

Fur-Trimmed Coat:
Broadcloth fitted coat. Ranch Mink colar. 5 button.
8/16. Black

STYLE: 3710
COST: 85.50
TERMS: 8/10 eom
DELIVERY: 2–3 weeks

MFR. Price & Sloan
225 West 37th Street
New York City

TYPICAL ACTION BY STORE IN	INITIAL ORDER	REORDERED TO DATE	COMMENT
Minneapolis, Minn.	50	40	
Richmond, Va.	6	12	
New York, N.Y.	16	36	
Charleston, W. Va.	8	14	
Warren, Ohio	3	6	
Duluth, Minn.	6	14	
New Orleans, La.	10	25	

ACTION TAKEN
STORE BUYER REPORT TO MDSE. MGR.

☐ WILL ORDER _____ QUAN.
☐ ON ORDER _____ QUAN.
☐ IN STOCK _____ SOLD TO DATE
☐ NOT INTERESTED BECAUSE:

BUYER: _____

Block 2

DEPT: LADIES COAT

S. Allan
K. B. BUYER

Double Breasted Coat:
Cashmere wool blend. shawl collar. three quarter sleeve.
10/18. Black. Blue. Nude. Red. Mink.

(Sidley)

STYLE: 111
COST: 85.50
TERMS: 8/10 eom
DELIVERY: 2 weeks

MFR. Levy–Goldman
241 West 37th Street
New York City

TYPICAL ACTION BY STORE IN	INITIAL ORDER	REORDERED TO DATE	COMMENT
Detroit, Mich.	24	136	3 wks.
Boston, Mass.	12	52	2 wks.
Cincinnati, Ohio	10	22	3 wks.
Atlanta, Ga.	8	18	1 wk.
Columbus, Ohio	16	24	10 days
Cleveland, Ohio	9	31	2 wks.
Pittsburgh, Pa.	10	19	3 wks.
Milwaukee, Wis.	8	42	3 wks.

ACTION TAKEN
STORE BUYER REPORT TO MDSE. MGR.

☐ WILL ORDER _____ QUAN.
☐ ON ORDER _____ QUAN.
☐ IN STOCK _____ SOLD TO DATE
☐ NOT INTERESTED BECAUSE:

BUYER: _____

Block 3

DEPT: LADIES COAT

S. Allan
K. B. BUYER

100% Camel Hair Casual Coat:
100% Camel hair slim coat. small notch collar. 3 button.
8/16 Natural color.

STYLE: 213
COST: 79.50
TERMS: 8/10 eom
DELIVERY: 2–3 weeks

MFR. Arista Fashions, Inc.
244 West 39th Street
New York City

TYPICAL ACTION BY STORE IN	INITIAL ORDER	REORDERED TO DATE	COMMENT
Boston, Mass.	8	23	
Portland, Oreg.	6	16	
St. Louis, Mo.	4	18	
Albany, N.Y.	2	11	
St. Louis, Mo.	4	16	
Kansas City, Mo.	4	16	

ACTION TAKEN
STORE BUYER REPORT TO MDSE. MGR.

☐ WILL ORDER _____ QUAN.
☐ ON ORDER _____ QUAN.
☐ IN STOCK _____ SOLD TO DATE
☐ NOT INTERESTED BECAUSE:

BUYER: _____

Illus. 6-3   This page, from a weekly action item report subscribed to by stores, lists the best-selling items in the whole-sale market, as indicated by orders and reorders placed by leading stores in key cities.

most suitable combination of assortments and to helping them in their merchandising and promotion efforts. For the shopping-goods store, the best plan for market representation is to join a resident buying office. Its operation is discussed in the next chapter.

CHECKING YOUR KNOWLEDGE

Vocabulary

1. trade show
2. trade paper or journal
3. action item report
4. market representation

Review Questions

1. What are the advantages of personal visits to market centers and trade shows?
2. List three main sources of information on product changes and improvements.
3. How to trade papers help the retailer keep up to date on market information?
4. What information is provided by a trade reporting service?
5. How can a merchant have continuous representation in the market?

Discussion Questions

1. Why should a retailer become personally acquainted with representatives of wholesaling and manufacturing firms?
2. If a small-scale retailer plans to buy primarily from suppliers' salespeople, is there any reason to also subscribe to trade journals? Why?
3. Is it of value for the retail merchant to follow manufacturers' television and newspaper advertising that is directed to consumers? Discuss fully.

Part C

Studying Fashion

The desire to be different, the desire for something new, the desire to identify with prevailing cultural or social ideas—these are the forces which create fashion. *Fashion* may be defined as a style in merchandise, art, or activity that is generally accepted or practiced by a sizable group of people.

Through the ages fashion has played an increasingly important role in the lives of all of us. Today, no retailers' convention program is complete if it does not include a speaker on fashion. What's new? has become one of the most common questions in retailing.

SCOPE OF FASHION

Fashion is most often thought of in connection with clothing. Further, fashion in apparel has traditionally been associated with women's attire. In recent years, however, the men's apparel field has experienced a great increase of fashion interest. Young people—teenagers and young adults—have also created fashion demands relevant to their own apparel tastes.

The American clothing industry is an important and interesting dimension of fashion. With the advent of mass production of clothing about one hundred years ago, the potential for providing fashion to the masses of people was realized. The ready-made clothing field is characterized by many small companies with no single firm exercising dominance. Because of this nature of the industry, a wide variety of items are introduced each season. The consumer's acceptance of a style can bring quick success to the fortunate firm.

While fashion is paramount in the apparel industry, fashion is found in nearly all other areas of consumer goods. There are fashions in home furnishings, in automobiles, in sports equipment, in art, and in books. In fact, there is fashion in almost everything we buy. Fashion is simply one part of modern life. We want comfort and convenience, we want health, we want beauty, we want to engage in sports, we want to escape from a humdrum existence. All these things make up our desire for variety; and if a new style contributes to one or more of these fundamental wants, it has a good chance to become the fashion.

LANGUAGE OF FASHION

If we are to understand fashion, we should be familiar with the exact meaning of three common terms—style, fashion, and fad.

Style

Everything has style. By *style* we mean the lines and characteristics of an article or activity that make it different from other articles or activities of the same general kind. One refrigerator may have square corners, one door, and a horizontal handle; another may have rounded edges, two doors, and vertical handles. Each has its own style, and the style of one will appeal to a customer more than the style of another.

Fashion

When a certain style has appeal for a large number of people and many want that particular style, the style becomes a *fashion*.

The style that is in fashion today may not be in fashion a month from today. Once the fashion has changed, a particular article still has its style, but it is not in fashion. We would then say that the item had an "old-fashioned style." Something new has appealed to a large number of people, and the new article has in turn become the fashion. This ever-changing element that people want in merchandise is good for business. When a new style comes into fashion, the wheels of industry and business keep on turning, and thousands of people are employed to produce and sell the new fashion.

Fad

When a style catches the fancy of a sizable group of people, has a brief popularity, and dies out quickly, it is called a *fad*. Generally fads are confined to minor apparel accessories, but sometimes they may be found in other areas. Fads are probably more common among teenagers than among any other consumer groups.

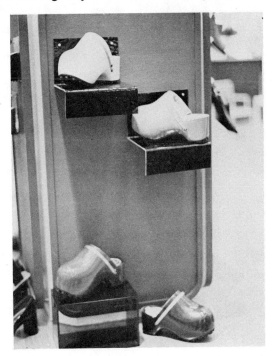

Courtesy of Federated Department Stores, Inc.

Illus. 6-4   These fad shoes come in four colors. They are placed in large boxes containing instructions in four languages for placing the foot in them.

Courtesy of Federated Department Stores, Inc.

Illus. 6-5 There is fashion in music as well as in clothes. Retailers are quick to supply the demands of large groups—whether for records, tapes, stereo or quadraphonic equipment.

FASHION CYCLE

A style which meets with sufficient acceptance to be called a fashion passes through rather definite steps in its rise to popular demand and in its decline from popularity. These steps—the rise, the acceptance, and the decline of a style—are called the *fashion cycle.*

The rapidity with which the style passes through the cycle varies greatly. Some styles are abandoned shortly after creation or adaptation without ever becoming popular. Normally styles in home furnishings and automobiles have a long cycle of years. Styles in clothing have a short cycle of years. Styles in accessories, such as jewelry and handbags, have a very short cycle—often only a few months. The length of a cycle also varies with different features of a style. For example, the basic lines, or silhouette, of a dress will have a much longer cycle than the color, material, or details of its design. Thus, the wise buyer is always looking for a garment that has basic lines that are popular but that contains new details that are enjoying an upswing in the fashion cycle.

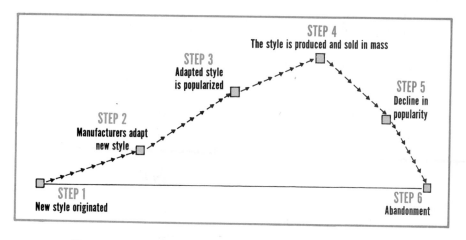

Illus. 6-6   The buyer of fashion goods must understand and study the fashion cycle for his line of merchandise so that he will know when to stock a new style and when to dispose of it. The steps of the fashion cycle are illustrated above.

PRINCIPLES OF FASHION MERCHANDISING

From the viewpoint of the retailer, fashion presents dangerous pitfalls as well as brilliant sales opportunities. When changes in fashion occur, sharp price reductions must be made on waning fashions or they will not sell, and resultant losses may eat away profits. Merchants are able to reduce the losses that arise in fashion merchandising only by keeping stocks low in relation to sales and by making prompt adjustments to changing conditions.

Since fashion is such an important buying motive in the lives of consumers, the retailer of fashion goods must consider fashion as a primary factor in the selection of goods for resale. In addition to the study of the customer and the study of sales results, he must also study the fashion picture. He must have a thorough knowledge of the fashion cycle, but he must also understand what current events do to fashion.

How long people will like a certain style is always a guess. Even though every effort is made to apply scientific principles to the buying of shopping goods, it must be admitted that public tastes are often unpredictable. However, certain principles are always adhered to by the wise retailer of fashion merchandise:

1. He will attempt to buy merchandise that is going up in the fashion cycle but has not yet reached the peak of popularity of the cycle.
2. He carefully avoids styles which are being sold in bargain basements or on reduction racks. He knows these styles are losing their appeal.

3. He will plan approximately how long he should keep a certain style in stock and what he will do if he has to get rid of it quickly.

4. He will discuss his buying plan and the styles he plans to buy with his salespeople, giving them information on the current styles and getting their opinions as to the wisdom of his buying.

5. He will make sure that his system for keeping an accurate record of his fashion goods is kept up to date so that he will know the sales trend at all times.

CHECKING YOUR KNOWLEDGE

Vocabulary

1. style

2. fashion

3. fad

4. fashion cycle

Review Questions

1. List three consumer desires that give rise to fashion.
2. What is the difference between a fad and a fashion?
3. Name the types of merchandise that tend to have a short fashion cycle; a long fashion cycle.
4. Describe the six steps in the fashion cycle.
5. Outline the principles that should be followed by the retailer of fashion merchandise.

Discussion Questions

1. What effect does rapid fashion change have on the retailer of fashion merchandise?
2. What are some ways that a fashion merchandiser can tell where a style is on the fashion cycle?
3. Name some current fashions and some current fads. Can you tell why each is so popular? Estimate how long the items you consider fads will last.

Part d

Buying Staples

From a buyer's viewpoint, merchandise can be divided into two groups: (1) goods that should always be in stock—called *staple goods* —and (2) new goods which have a relatively short life but are of interest temporarily to many people—called *fashion goods*.

The buyer also looks upon his stock as consisting of convenience goods and shopping goods. Convenience goods, as we have already seen, are items frequently purchased by customers with little advance planning. Shopping goods are articles requiring comparisons before a purchase is made. Most convenience goods are staples, and most shopping goods are fashion goods; but customers often shop for staples, and sometimes they buy shopping goods as a convenience.

STAPLE LISTS

The buying of staple goods is relatively simple, for what has been sold in the past will probably be sold again in the future. The quantities demanded are not likely to vary greatly from the quantities demanded by customers in the past. Staples enjoy a long period of active demand, generally many years, although certain details may change. A store can easily compile a *staple list* by analyzing records of previous purchases and sales and records of customer wants as reported on want slips. Even a man starting in business for himself will probably have had experience as an employee in another store and will have a fairly accurate knowledge of the staple articles he should carry. All wholesalers and many manufacturers will assist stores in working out correct lists of the staple items that should always be in stock. In chain-store operations much attention is given to working out separate lists of staples for small, medium, and large units; and store managers are instructed to keep their staple lists up to date at all times.

The staple list, however, should never be regarded as unchanging. By observing both customer wants and developments in the wholesale markets, the merchant will come across new items that should be added to his list. Many articles that were originally novelties become staples with continued customer acceptance. On the other hand, the sale of some staples may decline to the point where it is no longer profitable to carry them.

The ordering of staples may be entrusted to an assistant or a salesperson trained to make sure that staple items are always in stock. The buyer will thus be free to spend his time seeking new merchandise that earns additional profit for his store.

CONTROL OF QUANTITY

In the case of staples, the problem of how much to buy is often more difficult than the problem of what to buy. Well-operated stores control quantities of both staple and fashion goods by means of dollar purchase plans developed for each major merchandise line. On the basis of past experience, sales for each line are forecast; and a decision is made as to how much stock to carry at the beginning and end of control periods, which are usually a month. From the plans it is easy to decide how much to buy in each control period. The figures below show how a merchant can calculate how much merchandise to buy during a particular month.

Planned sales for month	$10,000
Planned stock (at retail) at end of month	25,000
Total stock required during month	$35,000
Stock (at retail) at beginning of month	8,000
Stock to be provided during month	$27,000
Stock (at retail) already on order for delivery during month	15,000
Open-to-buy (at retail)	$12,000

This plan tells the merchant that, in order to achieve his sales and stock goals, he should procure an additional $27,000 worth of stock during the month. Since he already has on order $15,000 of this requirement, he should order only $12,000 worth of goods for delivery before the end of the month. This is called the *open-to-buy*; that is, the planned order limit for delivery during a particular period.

To provide a tighter control over the quantity purchased, dollar controls are sometimes made for the subdivisions of each department. For goods of high unit value, unit control plans are developed. Unit plans are based on the same principle as are dollar plans, but unit control plans replace dollars with pieces of merchandise. Thus, in the example the planned sales may be 100 units rather than $10,000; the planned stock, 250 units; and the open-to-buy, 120 units.

For staples that are reordered at regular intervals, a common way to calculate the reorder quantity is to set a *minimum* and a *maximum* for each item. At the inventory counting date an order is placed up to the maximum. For example, the minimum (the normal reorder point) may be set at 18 units. This is believed to be adequate to take care of sales until a reorder can be placed in stock. If the item is to be reordered every 4 weeks, the sales for this period are estimated and added to the minimum quantity to give the maximum. If the sales estimate is 32, the maximum in the example is 50. If the actual count of the goods shows 18 on hand, 32 are ordered. If only 14 are on hand 36 are ordered (50 — 14). If 26 are on hand, 24 are due for reorder.

Staple stock lists are used to reorder individual items as just explained, but the open-to-buy figures in dollars for each major classification act as a guide to keep the amount received in each period in line with sales and stock plans. Thus, inventory investment is balanced to sales. Of course, the plan must be flexible to provide for unexpected increases or decreases in sales and for special purchase opportunities that could not be anticipated.

BRAND NAME MERCHANDISE

Brand—or the legal term, *trademark*—is used by manufacturers and others to indicate the origin or source of a product. A brand may be a word, mark, symbol, device, or a combination of these, used to identify a product or service. The brand may appear directly on the product, on the product container, attached by a tag, or on a label. The use of a registered trademark or brand name is limited to the firm that owns the name. The laws pertaining to trademarks are complicated and the services of a lawyer are necessary when creating a product trademark.

Brands used by manufacturers or producers of products are frequently called *national brands*. This is because such products usually have national distribution. When a product is brand named by a middleman, such as a wholesaler or retailer, it is referred to as a *private brand*. The private brand is made possible when a middleman has a producer make and identify a product with the middleman's trademark. In some instances the middleman produces or packs the private brand himself.

A brand name may be used for only one specific product, or it may be a blanket name used for a family of related products. An individual brand would be *Cougar* because it applies to only one type of automobile. A blanket brand would be *Maybelline* because it is used for several eye cosmetic products.

One of the difficult problems in the buying of staples is to decide how many brands to carry. In most lines there are many competing brands, and there is a temptation to carry many of these. This practice, however, leads to heavy stock assortments, since increasing the number of brands seldom increases sales in proportion to the additional stock that must be carried. The wisest policy seems to be to carry a few outstanding brands that will give satisfaction to the majority of customers. Some sales will be lost, of course, because a few customers insist on other brands; but if the brands carried are good ones, most customers can be prevailed upon to buy them.

National Brands

The producer of a consumer product may invest a great deal in building customer acceptance and preference for that product. If the producer can show features and qualities in his product that make it better and different from others, more customers will probably buy his brand. Furthermore, as the customer shops she will tend to buy brand products in which she has confidence as opposed to unknown products which may prove disappointing.

The retailer will want to choose carefully the brands for his staple merchandise lines. By carrying a line of national brand merchandise the retailer will enjoy several benefits. He has goods which have been carefully developed and are of consistent quality. The goods are heavily promoted through national media, and many customers are presold in favor of the merchandise. National brands often carry a standard price. This means that the manufacturer has entered into a contract, legal in many states, that prohibits retailers from selling the brand below a certain minimum price. This practice protects the retailer, particularly the small one, from price cutting and thus assures him an adequate markup.

Private Brands

While in the past, the public has tended to regard private brands as inferior to national ones (and many still do), the former are growing rapidly in acceptance. The well-known private brands are sponsored by great chains of stores which insist on quality standards and design excellent packaging. The products are often made by the producers of national brands, varying little if any from the national brand specifications. Whether they are bought from the national brand producer or from a company that specializes in making up private brands for retailers, the price is often 20 to 30 percent less, largely because the producer does not have to include heavy advertising in his cost. This lower cost may be reflected in a lower retail price. By developing his own brands, the merchant is not at the mercy of changes that the national brand producer may make in price and markup. Nor can the manufacturer set a minimum resale price below which private brand goods are not to be resold.

It is estimated that private labels now account for over half the annual volume of department stores. Sears does about 90 percent of its volume on its own brands, and it is estimated that about 30 percent of the grocery items carried by A&P are privately branded.

In spite of the fact that private brands may give a store a certain distinction, may free it from direct competition, and may allow it to buy for less, they are not always desirable. It costs more to sell and promote new private brands than to sell well-known brands. There may be considerable customer resistance to new private brands, and sales may be lost by not carrying nationally advertised brands.

Courtesy of Federated Department Stores, Inc.

Illus. 6-7   National brand and private brand food is usually placed side by side in supermarkets in order to give the customer a choice.

Department stores and supermarket and drug chain stores often carry their own private brands and also several leading national brands. The advantages of both national and private brands are thus realized. In general, small retailers—unless they are affiliated with a buying group— have difficulty developing accepted private brands. It is better for them

Advantages and Disadvantages of Private Brands	
Advantages	Generally cost the retailer less
	May be sold for less than competing national brands
	May allow higher markups to be realized, even with lower retail prices
	May build repeat sales
	Avoid direct price competition with other stores
	Allow goods to be made to specifications of the retailer
	Permit store to carry exclusive merchandise
Disadvantages	Bring about higher selling and advertising costs
	Encounter customer resistance, which may lead to markdowns and ill will for the store
	Involve packaging, labeling, and the making of commitments for large amounts of merchandise

Illus. 6-8   Before stocking private brands the retailer should consider carefully their advantages and disadvantages.

to feature well-known national brands and to depend on personal service to attract repeat patronage.

Product Specifications

It is often impossible for even an expert buyer to tell how well a new product will stand up in use or what its ingredients are. The buyer, therefore, should insist that manufacturers provide him with specifications, with results of performance tests, or with evidence that recognized standards have been followed in the production process.

Large chain organizations, such as Sears, Roebuck and Co. and J. C. Penney Co., Inc., do much of their buying on the basis of specifications they themselves set. This means that samples of competing articles are procured and tested in a laboratory and by consumers who put them to use. On the basis of these tests, specifications are drawn up for an article that will incorporate the desirable features and yet be economical to produce. One or more manufacturers are then chosen to produce the goods in quantity according to the specifications agreed upon. Thus, buying is not limited by what a manufacturer has to sell, but includes goods made to the retailer's specifications, based on a study of customer demand.

CHECKING YOUR KNOWLEDGE

Vocabulary

1. staple goods
2. fashion goods
3. staple list
4. open-to-buy
5. minimum

6. maximum
7. brand
8. trademark
9. national brands
10. private brand

Review Questions

1. Name the two ways of classifying merchandise from a retailer buyer's viewpoint.
2. List three reasons that make buying staple goods a relatively simple task.
3. What information is needed in order to calculate an open-to-buy? How does this help control purchases?
4. What are three advantages to the retailer who carries a national brand?
5. What are three advantages to the retailer who carries a private brand?

Discussion Questions

1. List five staple articles for which demand will probably remain the same from year to year.

2. (a) Name five private brands. What articles are sold under each of these brands? Which kinds of stores (independent, chain, department, specialty, or other) sell these brands? (b) Are there certain grocery items that give you a sense of safety by purchasing a national brand rather than a private brand? Why?
3. What are some of the problems faced by the low-margin retailer who wants the prestige of selling national brands but also wants to sell goods at the lowest possible price?
4. Why are many manufacturers who promote their own national brands willing to sell virtually the same products to retailers to be sold under the retailers' brands at lower prices?

Part **e**

Buying Shopping Goods

A young woman, Debbie Reed, planned to open a dress shop in the fall of the year. She found that her acquaintance with many fashion-conscious women in her community helped her in determining what to buy. By observing and by questioning her acquaintances and friends, she discovered many facts about their wants and needs. She found out much about sizes; about the relative demand for daytime, evening, and sports dresses; about the amount generally spent for dresses; about the types of dresses liked best and the colors preferred; and about preferences for synthetics, wool, and cotton.

Debbie did not want to invest all her working capital until after she had some experience in selling the first lot of dresses she selected. She, therefore, decided to make an initial investment of $3,500. With an average cost of $14 a dress, this would allow for 250 garments. At first thought, 250 dresses might seem a large number, but the dresses had to be of various sizes and suitable for various uses.

In view of the facts she had observed about possible customers, she decided to distribute the dresses she bought by classification, price, size, and color, in accordance with the plan shown in Illustration 6-9. Except for the very small sizes, she planned to have at least ten dresses in each size, at each price, so that the customer would have a good assortment of styles and colors from which to choose. She made no separate plan for different fabrics, but she knew that in the selection process she would need mostly polyesters for fall wear. She realized, however, that in the actual selection of styles a considerable proportion of wool dresses would also be necessary. She also realized that her plan might have to be changed when she actually began selecting dresses.

Debbie Reed's Fall Opening Plan

250 Dresses—Misses' Sizes Only

Types of Dresses:

Street Dresses .... 220 ⎰ 75 at $17.95 retail
⎱ 95 at $19.95 retail
50 at $23.95 retail

Evening Dresses .... 30 $29.95 retail

Total Dresses 250

Colors of Street Dresses—All Prices:

Basic Fall Colors .... 150 ⎰ Best basic color 75
⎱ Second best basic color 45
Third best basic color 30

Seasonal Colors .... 70 ⎰ Best seasonal color 35
⎱ Second best seasonal color .. 25
Third best seasonal color 10

Total Street Dresses 220

Illus. 6-9   Here is the buying plan followed by Debbie Reed. Do you think her plan is a wise one? Do you think she will be successful in selling her merchandise?

PLANNING THE ASSORTMENT

In planning the assortment of fashion goods which should be purchased, buyers usually begin by subdividing the general merchandise line. In the example which began this part, Debbie Reed divided her general line of women's clothing into the two classifications of street dresses and evening dresses. A buyer for a women's sportswear department in a large store might divide the merchandise line into slacks, sweaters, skirts, and so on.

Planning by Price

Within each subdivision of the general merchandise line, it is usually necessary to have an assortment at various prices. It is true that some men's hat stores and tie stores use a single retail price; but most of these stores are units in chains located in large cities and can attract many people by a single popular price. In most stores it is necessary to cater to people whose purchasing power and quality demands vary.

A good plan is to establish three main prices, all of which are within the range of prices paid by the group that the store desires as customers. Such planning makes it possible to cater to those who generally pay more and to those who generally pay less than the average price. It also suits the needs of the customer who occasionally wants a better or a less expensive article than she usually buys.

A limitation in the number of prices makes selling easier and quicker. The prices are far enough apart so that, near the start of a sales transaction, the customer can decide on the price she is interested in and then limit her attention to getting the best fit, style, and color at that price.

From the standpoint of buying ease, a limitation in the number of price lines is beneficial. It is very difficult to plan an assortment when there are many price lines. To put on paper a plan with many different price lines is difficult and time-consuming. Stores that have only a few price lines find buying greatly simplified, since they can concentrate on looking for the most attractive articles at those prices. They make better selections than do those stores that buy first and decide on retail prices later.

Courtesy of Target Stores

Illus. 6-10   Before an assortment of merchandise reaches a retail store, planning, record keeping, projecting of sales, and selecting of fashion goods go on behind the scenes.

Planning by Size

Size is an important factor in planning the assortment of fashion goods. This is true not only of clothing but also of many home furnishings as well. Hence, it is necessary to determine the customer demand for each size and to buy accordingly.

Manufacturers and wholesalers can provide information on the percentage of sales expected in each size of a merchandise line. The retailer, however, needs more than this general information to plan his buying. Past sales records must be examined periodically to determine which items can be reduced considerably in size assortment but still meet the requirements of most customers. The introduction of stretch fabrics, for example, has eliminated the necessity of stocking many sizes in such items as pantyhose and furniture slipcovers.

Planning by Color

Color has become a major consideration in selecting fashion goods. In the case of women's shoes, for example, color is more important to

---

Sources of Fashion Information

Manufacturers' preseason shows. At these shows new styles that will be offered to buyers are presented.

Color charts. Authoritative trade groups prepare these fashion information aids to suggest the colors and shades on which manufacturers and retailers should concentrate.

Publications. Consumer magazines and trade papers that report both new styles and trends in the market are important sources of fashion information.

Marketing services. Buyers receive regular bulletins from agencies that analyze and report fashion trends.

Manufacturers' salespeople. Visiting salespeople report on the merchandise of their own companies and on fashion acceptance of merchandise in other stores they have visited.

Retail salespeople. Salespeople can gather firsthand observations regarding customers' reactions to styles.

Customer preference clinics. At these clinics customers are asked to state the details of their last purchase and the details of what they plan to buy next.

Illus. 6-11   The difficult job of buying fashion merchandise can be made easier if the buyer will study carefully the sources of information available to him.

most women than is the material from which the shoes are made. Hence, we may say that with women's shoes, color becomes a major merchandise classification.

Standard and conventional colors always account for the majority of sales; but the new seasonal colors, called *high shades,* have great attraction and display value and hence are often stocked in large quantities. Because they are new and interesting, however, there is a danger of overstocking them and of failing to carry enough of the staple colors.

BUYING PLANS

Buying plans for fashion goods are developed along the same lines as are buying plans for staple goods. First, the total merchandise investment is controlled by the open-to-buy. Planning by price, size, and color is generally done in units rather than dollars. For example, the dollar open-to-buy for women's sweaters may be $800. If the average price of the sweaters is $10, the open-to-buy would be 80 units.

Suppose that there are three retail price lines—$17, $14, and $9. Considering the actual number of units on hand and currently on order for each price line and considering the planned assortment desired, the 80 units are divided among the three price lines. A possible division is:

20 at $17   35 at $14   25 at $9

Then, by noting the planned size and color distribution, the open-to-buy for each price line is divided into sizes and colors. For example, the 20 sweaters to be ordered for the $17 price line might be comprised of sizes 34-42, with the most sweaters in the heart sizes—36 and 38—where the demand is greatest and with fewer sweaters in the fringe sizes. Similar plans will be made to distribute the 20 units over the important colors, carrying the most sweaters in the basic colors and fewer sweaters in the seasonal shades.

Advance plans for the buying of fashion goods are not broken down by individual style or lot numbers; these are determined as the buying is done. Some of the best-selling styles are reordered within the framework of the plan, and new items are also included.

Perhaps the most difficult part of buying fashion goods is the need to anticipate customer demand. For example, orders for men's clothing must be placed in November for delivery in February and March. Manufacturers of some clothing do not order materials until they receive orders from retailers, and then they must wait for delivery from the textile mills. Moreover, the manufacturing of the clothing takes considerable time. The retailers who place their orders early have a greater assurance of getting the best materials and workmanship. Late-comers may have to be satisfied with the materials that are left and with the output of hard-pressed workmen.

The degree to which buying is done ahead depends to a considerable extent on the trend in prices. When prices are rising, retailers order the goods far in advance so as to take advantage of the current low prices. When prices are falling, however, retailers tend to buy from *hand-to-mouth*; that is, they buy in small quantities as the merchandise is needed. When prices are falling, retailers must sell quickly the merchandise they have in stock before it has to be marked down. Some buyers have a policy of buying small quantities of nearly everything new in their line and letting the public decide. Offhand, this seems to be an easy way of solving the problem and of assuring that the store will not miss out on something that may become popular. Such a policy, however, is dangerous. The store may accumulate so many odds and ends that it may eventually look like a junk store. Many of the items turn out to be failures and have to be sold at a loss. Since a merchant's investment and his selling space are definitely limited, he should select only those items that will probably sell in reasonable quantities and that will supplement, not compete with, the goods he already carries.

The subject of selecting the right item is so important that a part of the next chapter will be devoted to its discussion.

CHECKING YOUR KNOWLEDGE

Vocabulary

1. high shades
2. hand-to-mouth buying

Review Questions

1. With what considerations in mind did Debbie Reed plan the assortment of dresses that she was going to buy?
2. What are the reasons for carrying three major price lines?
3. Name at least five sources of fashion information that are helpful in determining the fashion merchandise to buy.
4. How are buying plans for fashion goods made?
5. List some of the problems in buying fashion goods.

Discussion Questions

1. What are the factors that should be considered when trying to decide whether to buy heavy early and be assured of merchandise or to buy light and take a chance on not getting quantities of merchandise desired?
2. Which factors (such as size) are most important when developing a buying plan for men's clothing?
3. What are the advantages and disadvantages for a store that establishes a few price lines with a complete assortment in each line?
4. Items, such as clothing, that come in various sizes, may be a problem to buyers. What can buyers do to make sure that they order the right quantities in each size?

BUILDING YOUR SKILLS

Improving Communication Skills

Only one of the two adverbs or adjectives given in parentheses may be used to make the sentence correct. On a separate sheet of paper, write the number of the sentence and the word you would use for each sentence.

1. Susan, the buyer, spoke (quiet, quietly) while bargaining with the manufacturer.
2. Jeffery handles the goods (rough, roughly) and causes many markdowns.
3. Jo Ann has sold sweaters particularly (well, good) in the short time she has been with us.
4. This leather feels (soft, softly) to the touch.
5. The new cashier dresses (plain, plainly).
6. Accessories move (quick, quickly) through the fashion cycle.
7. Some salespeople are (real, really) clever in originating sales ideas.
8. From past records, it is (easily, easy) to determine which sizes to buy.
9. Information about new goods may be obtained (ready, readily) from trade publications.
10. After one month's training, Ralph controls his merchandise very (good, well).

Improving Arithmetic Skills

Perform the subtraction exercises that follow and write your answer for each on a separate sheet of paper.

1. A salesperson sold 9 2/3 yards of cloth from a bolt that contained 28 1/5 yards. How many yards were left on the bolt?
2. A customer wants 5 gallons of linseed oil, but the merchant has only 9.5 liters. The merchant is how many gallons short? How many liters is the merchant short?
3. Fran purchased 3 3/8 yards of material for a dress. The pattern she will use requires 3 1/3 yards. How much material will be left over?
4. Bill Powell, owner of a hardware store, kept the following record of amounts of nails sold from a 60-pound nail keg during one week: 3 1/4 pounds, 1 1/2 pounds, 4 2/3 pounds, 5 1/8 pounds, 4 3/4 pounds, 3 1/3 pounds, 2 1/2 pounds, 6 7/8 pounds, 4 1/2 pounds,

and 5 1/4 pounds. At the end of the week how many pounds of nails should remain in the keg? If Mr. Powell finds only 17 pounds left, how would he account for the discrepancy?

5. Mark put the following amounts of milk in the supermarket dairy case: 17 one-gallon containers of milk, 25 half-gallon containers of milk, 14 quarts of milk, 9 quarts of chocolate milk, 7 pints of milk, 17 pints of chocolate milk, and 11 one-half pints of coffee cream. If, at the end of the day, 10 gallons of milk and cream in various sized containers are left in the case, how many gallons have been sold?

Improving Research Skills

1. Visit a leading store in your community and find some examples of goods the store carries under its own brand name or under the brand name of a store group to which it belongs. The brand name may be the same as the store's name, or it may be a coined name that the store or group has chosen. Do these items seem to be in direct competition with national brands? If so, are the private brands lower in price? Do they seem to have any advantages over the competing national brands?

2. Select a staple merchandise item and then visit three stores that carry the item. Observe exactly which brands, colors, sizes, and price lines of the item are carried in each store. Prepare a report of your observations. Indicate why each store handles the type and assortment of the item that it does. The class may be divided into groups of two or three, and several different items may be investigated and reported.

3. Assume that several of the clothing stores in your community have asked for your help in identifying the emerging fashions for the youth market. List the information that you would provide and the sources of information that you would use.

Improving Decision-Making Skills

1. Rick Harper is at the market selecting men's accessories for the coming season. He has already ordered $3,700 worth of merchandise for the period when he finds some top-quality lightweight leather vests. The cost to him would be $9 each. He checks his figures (all at cost) and finds: planned sales for the period, $4,100; planned stock at end of period, $8,400; stock at beginning of period, $8,550. Does Rick have any open-to-buy for additional purchases? If so, how many vests could he order?

2. Staple X in your stock sells at the rate of 25 a week and requires one week to obtain the delivery of a reorder. You have set a minimum (normal reorder point for this item) of 40 which is more than one week's expected sales in order to provide a reserve for possible increase in sales. You also decide to check the stock and reorder the item once every two weeks. (a) Set the maximum. (b) If you have on hand at present only 30 units, how many must you reorder?

3. A drugstore sells perfume in addition to its other cosmetics. The owner of the drugstore knows that his customers will not pay much more than $5 for a bottle of perfume. He can obtain nationally known brands of perfume to sell at $5 a bottle, but the bottles are very tiny. The drugstore owner has an opportunity to buy unbranded perfume which is equal in quality to the nationally known brands but which is packaged—to retail within the $5 price limit—in a bottle holding more perfume than the bottle of the nationally known brands.

The merchant could buy the unbranded perfume for considerably less than the nationally known brands, retail it within his $5 price limit, and realize a substantial profit. If he buys this unbranded perfume, he must buy it in gross lots. The minimum quantity he could buy would last nearly two months in his store, whereas he has been reordering the nationally known brands every three weeks. Should the druggist continue buying the nationally known brands, or should he try the unbranded perfume?

APPLYING YOUR KNOWLEDGE

Chapter Project

Obtain from 25 of your classmates the following information: (1) the five items of clothing that they are most likely to buy next and (2) the sizes, colors, styles, and brands of the items they intend to buy.

Assume that you are a merchant selling the five items which your classmates indicate they are most likely to buy soon. Develop a buying plan to cover the merchandise needed.

Continuing Project

Prepare in your manual a section in which you do the following things:

1. List ten characteristics—such as interests, incomes, and backgrounds—of the customers you will be serving.
2. Decide upon the major goods your store will carry and divide these into two major classifications—staple goods and fashion goods.
3. Describe the buying procedure you will follow in obtaining staple goods.
4. Prepare a buying plan for at least two important items of fashion goods that you will carry.

chapter 7

Resources

a. Small retailers make market contacts through sales representatives who call at their stores and through cooperative buying arrangements.

b. Large-store buyers use the services of resident, or central, buying offices which help them find the best resources and items available.

c. A store buyer should determine which services he needs most from his resources and then patronize those suppliers who are best qualified to perform these services.

d. Buyers have developed certain rules that greatly assist them in selecting a relatively few items from the many offered to the store.

e. Good business practices must be followed by both the vendor and the buyer. Only if both maintain high standards of ethical conduct will they be respected in the marketplace.

Part a

Establishing Market Contacts— Small and Convenience-Goods Stores

Deciding what to buy is only one phase of obtaining merchandise. Decisions on where to buy can be equally important. In Chapter 6 you learned that merchants study market offerings by visiting wholesale centers, studying trade papers, subscribing to **trade** services, and participating in market representation plans. The trade papers and trade services are especially important to the merchant because—in addition to telling him which products are being offered for sale in the market—they tell him which manufacturers and wholesalers are offering the products and where these suppliers are located.

The study of trade papers and trade reports begins the process of establishing market contacts to procure goods for resale. Each trade paper in a particular merchandise field carries many advertisements of manufacturers and wholesalers as well as news stories about manufacturers who are introducing a new product or who are using newsworthy promotional devices. There are also *trade directories* in each field that every merchant should keep on hand for quick reference. These directories list the names, addresses, and phone numbers of most of the manufacturers and wholesalers in the field. Examples of such directories are *Accessories and Small Wares, Fabrics, Millinery,* and *Menswear.* The classified section of a telephone directory provides similar information and is useful when a buyer is seeking to make contact with new resources.

Once a buyer has studied the market offerings, planned what he wishes to buy, and located the resources from which he will buy, the next step is to make contact with the resource. For the small independent store or the store handling convenience goods, the two most important means of making contact with the market are through sales representatives who call at the store and through a cooperative buying arrangement.

VISITING SALES REPRESENTATIVES

Wholesalers and manufacturers whose lines contain a wide variety of items can afford to send sales representatives to call on small stores. Depending on the merchandise lines, sales representatives may visit stores on a weekly, a monthly, or even a semiannual basis. Some manufacturers supplement or even replace sales representatives with direct-mail advertising. The merchant should read this direct mail carefully and follow up on it if he is interested. The merchant may either order samples without a visit from a representative, or he may ask the manufacturer to send a sales representative to show and explain the product.

Sales representatives who call on the retailer are divided into two groups. The first group provides information on a line of products and perhaps consults with the merchant on merchandising strategy. The second group provides more comprehensive merchandising service which may even include the display and rotation of stock.

Merchandising Service

Sales representatives of staple goods who call on the retailer may ask for a certain amount of shelf or display space. If the retailer agrees, the sales representative may assume the responsibility for arrangement, display, inventory, and reordering of the merchandise. With some merchandise, such as perishable goods or items with high turnover, the sales representative may call daily. In lines such as baked goods and produce, selling and delivery operations are combined. The supplier's delivery-salesmen check the stores' stocks and replace and replenish as needed.

Many supermarkets often buy their nonfood items from *rack jobbers*. These are wholesalers who agree to merchandise a rack or counter of their line—cosmetics, for example—in the supermarket. The rack jobber visits the store every few days, replenishes the items on the rack, removes slow-selling items and replaces them with other items, and makes sure the displays are in order. The supermarket manager can devote all his time to handling food items, yet can obtain considerably greater sales volume from nonfood items. There is more price competition in food items and the merchant must keep food prices as low as possible, but he can set a higher retail price on nonfood items and can make a greater profit.

Specialized Stockkeeping Representatives

Some manufacturers are concluding that the time of their sales representatives is too valuable to be devoted to stockkeeping in the supermarkets and discount stores that carry their lines. But they recognize that they cannot depend upon store managers to keep their stocks in the stores complete and properly arranged. With thousands of stockkeeping units to handle, many in direct competition with one another, the manager may feel that there is little loss to the store if it is out of stock of a particular manufacturer's goods. But the loss is very important to the latter.

Accordingly, some distributors now hire *route personnel,* often young women, who make the rounds in a limited trading area of all the stores that handle their employer's goods. They make sure that the space assigned to their products is full and that the goods are properly arranged. If the stock is depleted, they check on orders and requisitions for replacements. The sales representatives for the distributor are thus relieved of a routine function and can devote their time to presenting new products and special deals and arranging for adequate shelf and display space.

In a few instances these stockkeeping personnel are hired and trained not by the manufacturer himself but by a specialized organization that sells the service to manufacturers. One of these employs 400 young women to call on stores that handle the lines of the group of manufacturers it represents. Thus, each store visit becomes more productive, since they check many lines of goods in one visit.

Courtesy of Gross & Associates
Public Relations, Inc.

Illus. 7-1   Keeping up stock and displays of nonfood items in supermarkets and drug chains is often handled by route girls or route men. This route girl replaces stock and removes colors and sizes that fail to sell.

Scheduling Sales Representatives

In order to find time to see sales representatives who have new merchandise to present or who are other than route personnel, it is wise for the merchant to set aside regular days and hours. Otherwise, the merchant may find that he is constantly interrupted in the performance of other duties. Exceptions may have to be made for out-of-town salespeople who have travel schedules to meet. Merchants should request out-of-town salespeople to make advance appointments by phone or letter.

Burke's Hardware store, in which Dennis Scholl is a partner, has reserved Tuesday mornings each week for sales representatives to call. The weekly schedule for the store has Monday morning reserved for inventory taking and charge account billing, Tuesday morning for seeing sales representatives, Wednesday morning for getting weekly newspaper advertisements ready, Thursday morning for receiving and checking new merchandise. On Friday and Saturday store traffic is heavy; so no activity other than customer service is scheduled. Sales representatives are seen at other times by appointment. Mr. Burke believes it is important that both he and Dennis be available whenever a sales representative makes a call.

The retailer must be selective in granting visiting salespeople part of his valuable time. If the small retailer gives these people all the time they want, he will lose several hours each week. The retailer should screen those salesmen representing merchandise areas in which he has no interest. Repeat calls should be reserved only for those sales representatives who represent appropriate merchandise lines, who have new information to provide, and who are truly interested in the retailer's business.

By planning for each visit by a sales representative, the retailer can get the most from the contact. In addition to information on merchandise, the sales representative should provide promotional ideas, ways of displaying products, information on colors and styles that are moving well, and a variety of other merchandising ideas that will be helpful to the retailer.

COOPERATIVE BUYING ARRANGEMENTS

For many small and convenience goods stores, the most practical method of making market contacts is through a cooperative buying arrangement. You have already learned that this may be an arrangement with a wholesaler, with a chain-store organization as an agency store, or even with the manufacturer of a line in which the store has decided to specialize. In the food and drug field, a small store may also invest in a wholesale warehouse which is owned cooperatively by a group of non-competing stores and which acts as the buying agent for these stores.

Probably the most widely used of the cooperative buying arrangements is the voluntary chain where a contract wholesaler agrees to act as the buying and servicing agent for a group of stores. By serving a number of stores at one time, the contract wholesaler can reduce his selling expense; and, because he knows the needs of his member stores with considerable depth and precision, he is able to buy large quantities of goods for which he has an assured market. Thus, he can provide goods to the independent members at as low a price as the chains can provide goods to their units. The contract wholesaler also provides his member stores with managerial and promotional assistance, just as the chains do.

CHECKING YOUR KNOWLEDGE

Vocabulary

1. trade directories
2. rack jobbers

3. route personnel

Review Questions

1. Name the two most important means of making market contact for the small independent store.
2. What two things may a merchant do who wants more information on a product found in trade advertising?
3. List the advantages to the small retailer of using a rack jobber.
4. Why should a retailer set aside a regular time for seeing sales representatives?
5. What are the advantages of the voluntary chain for cooperative buying?

Discussion Questions

1. If a retailer agrees to allow a sales representative 12 running feet of shelf space for his products and subsequently finds that the representative is spreading his line on more shelf space, what should the retailer do?
2. Suppose a customer asks the owner of a men's clothing store for a style of sport jacket the customer has seen in New York City but is not carried in local stores. The merchant has not seen it among the offerings of his suppliers. How could he locate the merchandise for his customer?
3. Should a retailer continue to see at regular intervals a salesperson who represents a firm whose products he does not wish to handle? Why or why not? What should a retailer say to a sales representative who continues calling at times when the retailer does not want to talk with him?

Part **b**

Establishing Market Contacts—
Large and Shopping-Goods Stores

Large retail stores tend to make their contacts with the market directly rather than through middlemen. They, of course, do interview sales representatives and may buy some merchandise through them; but general merchandise, clothing, and furniture stores do not depend heavily on such calls nor on membership in voluntary chains. The large stores concentrate on other means of making market contact. These means are (1) market trips, (2) resident buying offices, (3) group buying, and (4) central buying.

MARKET TRIPS

Many retailers take the initiative of going to vendors instead of waiting for vendors to call on them. Wholesale markets are usually concentrated in small areas within a city. Practically every good-sized city has a local wholesale fruit and vegetable market where local growers bring their produce for sale. Retailers of these products go to these markets to inspect the offerings and to buy the goods. Philadelphia food wholesalers, for instance, have established a location in the city where food retailers may buy anything in food from the four corners of the earth.

In addition to local markets, certain cities become known as central markets for certain items. For instance, New York City is well known as the largest single market in the whole world for women's wear and many other types of merchandise. Los Angeles and San Francisco are giving New York some competition as a central market for fashion goods. For shoes, Boston, St. Louis, and Chicago may be considered as central markets, in addition to New York. Some of the central markets for furniture are High Point, North Carolina; Chicago; Dallas; Los Angeles; and San Francisco.

When a buyer visits these central markets, he goes to the individual showrooms or stalls of the vendors whose lines he wants to inspect. Usually these showrooms are located close together so that he can visit several in a short space of time. One advantage of going to the market is that the buyer can see the offerings of many manufacturers before placing his order.

Frequency of Trips

How often a buyer visits the central market depends upon the type of merchandise, the size of the retail store, and the distance of the store from the central market. Buyers of fashion goods for department or specialty stores, who do not use the services of resident buyers, may find it necessary to visit the central market as frequently as two or three times each week. One retailer of women's dresses in Philadelphia advertised that his buyer visited the New York central market daily and that new dresses were received from New York daily.

While many buyers will visit the market as frequently as possible, others may visit the central market once a year or only during seasonal market openings. Some people do not like the rush and excitement of a market trip. They believe that they can make better decisions without the pressure of the market and the presence of suppliers' representatives. By not going to the market these buyers may be missing some of the best sources of merchandise, since not all vendors can or will send sales representatives to the stores.

Meeting Other Buyers

A great deal of information is shared by buyers when they informally meet at the market. They compare notes on resources and merchandise that they have found profitable (or not so profitable). Such exchanges are likely to be between noncompeting buyers who are from stores in different cities. The sharing of ideas and details of merchandise, pricing, and promotion by buyers from similar stores can be helpful in many ways.

For example, three buyers of men's clothing were visiting over coffee about their needs and what they had seen in the market. One buyer commented on a style of men's jacket he had seen in a supplier's showroom that morning. The jacket was not a featured item but was available in a popular fabric and at a good price. Thus, this bit of information from a buyer friend helped another buyer get what he wanted to complete his buying plan.

RESIDENT BUYING OFFICES

For merchants of fashion goods whose stores are some distance away from the wholesale markets and who make few market trips, the resident buying office is essential. Even the buyers who make many trips to the central markets find that visiting the resident buying office is an excellent way to begin the study of the merchandise offerings and of the suppliers in the market.

Services of Resident Buying Offices

A resident buying office helps stores find the best sources for goods in the following ways:

1. It gives advice as to the best sources for goods of every classification, price, and style. These sources are secured from its up-to-date file of all manufacturers.
2. It keeps the store in touch with all developments in the wholesale market, including new styles, price changes, and bargains.
3. It buys goods for the store whenever the store buyer is unable to go to the market himself. The buying is based on a description of what is needed by the store.
4. It follows up on store orders to see that goods are shipped on time.
5. It handles adjustments involving returns or cancellations of orders.
6. It may consolidate into one large shipment purchases made from different manufacturers, thus saving transportation charges.
7. It provides a store buyer with office space, a stenographer, and personal service when he visits the market; and it notifies manufacturers when the store buyer will be in town.
8. It provides one of its own buyers to help the store buyer make selections.
9. It is occasionally able to get price concessions and exclusive styles for the store because of its association with other stores that buy the same styles.
10. It gives advice on problems of storekeeping with which a merchant or a buyer may experience difficulty.
11. It may arrange for group and central buying, as explained later in this chapter.

Kinds of Resident Buying Offices

There are two distinct kinds of resident buying offices: (1) the *independent office* that contracts with stores to provide them with market services and (2) the *store-owned office* that is owned by one or more stores.

There are, in turn, two classes of independent offices: (a) those that charge a service fee to the stores they represent and (b) those that collect a commission from the manufacturers on the orders they obtain from their store customers. The former are called *salaried, paid,* or *fee buying offices;* and the latter are called *merchandise brokers.* Since the salaried buying offices receive their compensation from their store clients, they are free to buy from any segment of the wholesale market and to negotiate for lower prices. Merchandise brokers are less likely to seek concessions that might reduce their own commissions. Nevertheless, to provide good service to store customers, a merchandise broker may place orders with firms that pay him no commission. Many small specialty stores are well satisfied with merchandise brokers partly because the stores pay nothing extra for the service.

The owners of most store-owned offices are chains of department stores. Such a chain maintains buyers in each of its stores to cater to the local demand in each community, and the resident buying office serves the buyers for the various units. This is known as a *syndicate buying office*.

Some independent stores have banded together to form jointly owned resident buying offices. These are called *associated buying offices*. A few independent stores still have their own private offices in the New York market.

GROUP BUYING

Resident buying offices sometimes arrange *group buying* for their member stores. Under this plan the buyers of a group of stores meet and select styles that all can sell. The usual procedure is for the resident buyer to assemble styles newly designed by different manufacturers. These are inspected at a meeting, each buyer voting on his preference. Usually every buyer agrees to take at least a minimum number of all styles approved by the majority. Occasionally, when the buyers are located in stores all over the country, the styles selected are advertised nationally. More commonly, however, advertising artwork and copy for the selected styles are prepared for the entire group but are run in local newspapers by each individual store. Group buying is now being supplanted to some extent by another method known as central buying.

CENTRAL BUYING

Chains separate their buying from their selling. In the chains, central buyers specialize in the selection of merchandise and store managers specialize in selling. Groups of independent stores are also experimenting with this plan, generally through the agency of their resident buying offices. The individual store buyers are replaced with sales supervisors, and buying is concentrated in a central office.

There are three main kinds of central buying: (1) central merchandising, (2) listing system, and (3) central warehousing and requisitioning.

Central Merchandising

The *central merchandising* plan is used extensively with fashion merchandise. The sales supervisor sends to the central office a daily

Illus. 7-2   The central buyer (sitting in the center and facing forward) is reviewing her selection of women's skirts from the New York City market with her associates and representatives of the stores that will present her selections to customers.

report of (1) the styles he received into stock and (2) the styles he sold. Once a week he writes a letter telling about local demand and sends in a list of the goods in stock, called an *inventory report.*

On a basis of the knowledge thus obtained from all stores, the central office decides what merchandise to buy for the group of stores as a whole, what to send to each store, and even when goods in the various stores should be marked down. The central buyers keep informed about peculiarities of demand in different stores and try to avoid sending styles that will not sell.

Listing System

Under the plan known as the *listing system,* the central buyers decide on the items that stores may carry, and also on their prices, and then send each store a list or catalog of these items. The store manager or sales supervisor decides which of these items to stock and orders them in the quantities and at the time needed. Special permission has to be obtained to buy items not listed. Thus, the buying function is split: the central office sets specifications, selects styles, determines prices, and makes shipping arrangements; the stores decide when and how much to buy and then order from the listed sources.

This plan is used for shopping goods that do not change so rapidly in style as do dresses and certain other items of women apparel.

Central Warehousing and Requisitioning

When central buying is applied to such products as groceries and drugs, the plan commonly used is called *central warehousing and requisitioning*. The central buyer purchases and warehouses the staple goods, and the stores order what they need by means of requisitions to the warehouse. Thus, the central buyers actually buy—they do not simply make buying arrangements—but the stores decide when and how much to requisition from the warehouse.

CHECKING YOUR KNOWLEDGE

Vocabulary

1. independent resident buying office
2. store-owned resident buying office
3. salaried, paid, or fee buying office
4. merchandise broker
5. syndicate buying office
6. associated buying office
7. group buying
8. central merchandising
9. inventory report
10. listing system
11. central warehousing and requisitioning

Review Questions

1. List the four primary means by which large stores establish contact with the market.
2. What factors influence the frequency of market trips?
3. In what ways does a resident buying office help retail stores?
4. How does a central merchandising plan operate?
5. Explain the listing system and the central warehousing and requisitioning plan.

Discussion Questions

1. Which of the services of a resident buying office would be most helpful to a large store setting up a new line of merchandise? Which services would be most helpful to a store with well-established lines of merchandise?
2. If you were to open a men's clothing store, how would you go about finding a suitable resident buying office? Where would you get the names of good offices, and which factors would you consider in making a selection of which to use?
3. If a central buyer selects all new clothing styles on his own responsibility and has them shipped to the various stores in his group, how can the wholehearted cooperation of the store and department managers be assured?

Part C

Selecting Preferred Resources

The number of manufacturers or sources of supply for a single consumer good is sometimes amazing. For example, in a current housewares directory there are 46 manufacturers listed for carpet and rug cleaners. Regardless of how the retailer locates resources, there remains the problem of making choices among them. With the consumer's growing insistence on sound values and suitable goods, the problem of selecting the right resources is particularly important.

There are many factors the buyer must consider before deciding from whom he will buy. He is constantly urged by sales representatives, manufacturers, wholesalers, and others who want his business to place his orders with them. Unless he is aware of some of the important factors in selecting a resource, the buyer is apt to make costly mistakes.

FACTORS TO CONSIDER IN CHOOSING THE RESOURCE

There are two broad classes of resources that a retailer can utilize in his buying practices: (1) manufacturers and producers and (2) wholesale middlemen. His goal in selecting from among the suppliers of merchandise is to find sources that will supply merchandise which will satisfy the wants of his store's customers at a price that will enable him to realize a profit on its resale. Specifically, the following factors must be considered.

Suitability of Supplier's Line to Store Customers

What a buyer purchases depends upon the type of customers who deal at a store. A supplier who specializes in high-grade, expensive merchandise must be passed up by a buyer who sells chiefly to low-income workers and their families. The buyer purchases only because he thinks he can resell the goods. He inspects the vendor's line or reads a description of it in a catalog. If the goods are similar to what his customers have been buying or if his customers could easily be persuaded to buy the goods, he classifies the resource as suitable.

The quality of the merchandise in a particular price line is an important consideration in determining the suitability of the goods for the store. There should be evidence that the vendor maintains a consistent standard of quality.

Completeness of Line

A vendor may have desirable merchandise, but his line of goods may be so narrow or incomplete that the buyer cannot depend upon him as a resource. The small store usually finds it desirable to buy from resources which carry broad assortments of many items that the store may need. This saves time in buying, reduces transportation charges, and provides discounts. The large store, on the other hand, can buy from more specialized resources but requires that these be equipped to handle very large reorders.

Ability to Manufacture to Store's Specifications

The ability to manufacture to a store's specifications is important to central buyers who develop exclusive merchandise for their stores by giving manufacturers detailed specifications in regard to materials, workmanship, and measurements.

How Much Vendor Can or Will Ship

A buyer who needs only a few items at a time cannot buy from a vendor who sells only in gross lots. The reverse is also true. A buyer who needs large quantities often cannot buy from excellent, but small, resources that cannot or will not ship the amounts needed.

Favorable Prices

Every buyer looks for reasonable prices. The buyer must exercise great care, however, so as not to buy inferior merchandise in an attempt to secure lower prices. In many lines prices are standardized. For instance, in stationery, an item priced to retail at 10 cents usually costs 72 cents to 75 cents a dozen. Should the wholesaler quote prices far below (60 cents) or a good deal more (85 cents), the buyer should make certain that the reason for the difference in price is justified.

Up-to-Dateness of Line

Every buyer likes a vendor who has up-to-date merchandise in his line. Particularly in fashion goods, it is important that the vendor have merchandise which is enjoying an upswing in the fashion cycle. A vendor who keeps abreast of the new features and items is one who can help the retailer make a profit.

Creativity

The buyer who aims at a reputation for unusual and exciting merchandise will give preference to the manufacturer—often a small one—who has a flair for developing new ideas in merchandise.

Speed of Delivery

When a retailer cannot estimate his requirements far in advance, he wants a vendor who can send goods to him quickly. In one case an unusual demand for caps because of a coming football game had caught a retailer short. However, the retailer had a supplier of caps who was able to deliver his order within a few days; thus, the retailer was able to take advantage of the opportunity to increase sales.

Credit Terms

How much time the vendor allows for paying bills is important to the buyer. If a vendor will not sell except for cash and if a retailer is operating on limited capital, it is doubtful whether the vendor will enjoy much of this retailer's business. On the other hand, a retailer with a poor credit rating will not be able to buy, except for cash, from many of the better resources.

Dealer Aids

The vendor who helps the retailer sell his goods is of especial interest to the merchant. The small store particularly likes to buy from vendors who will provide displays, advertising materials, and other sales aids. The buyer should ask about dealer aids before deciding upon a resource.

Courtesy of Federated Department Stores, Inc.

Illus. 7-3   Vendors who provide displays, advertising materials, and other sales aids are helpful to retailers. Buyers should ask about dealer aids before deciding upon a resource.

Pricing and Brand Policy

It is wise for the retail buyer to learn something about the vendor's pricing and brand policy. The vendor may insist on setting the retail price of the merchandise he sells to the retailer so that his merchandise will not be sold at many different prices in many stores. If a store wants the protection of a definite markup for its merchandise and does not want to see it sold for less in discount houses, such a pricing policy may be advantageous. On the other hand, the retailer may want to use the merchandise as a leader or may want to promote it in quantity at less than the retail price set by the manufacturer.

The buyer should learn also whether the supplier carries national brands or is equipped to sell goods that will carry the store's private brand. This information can guide him in determining the resource that best fits his promotional needs.

Fairness in Handling Complaints

Goodwill is an important factor in business. Buyers tend to select resources with whom they expect to have fair and pleasant relationships. A vendor who acquires a reputation of refusing to make adjustments when he ships the wrong merchandise or delivers late will be avoided by buyers. A vendor's merchandise guarantees and his reliability are worthwhile qualities that a buyer should investigate before selecting resources. Generally the length of time a vendor has been in business is a good measure of his ability to serve his customers, because an incompetent vendor cannot stay in business long.

Facilities for Repairing Its Products

A frequent consumer complaint today is that is difficult to have merchandise such as appliances repaired promptly. The buyer should determine if the manufacturer or distributor of electronic/mechanical products has made any arrangement to provide repair services. A product that has factory-authorized repairs centers throughout the country probably would be favored by customers.

PREPARING A RESOURCE FILE

For every one of the manufacturers and the wholesalers contacted, the buyer should make out a resource card, giving the name and the address of the seller, the terms allowed, the kinds of goods carried, the prices in which the seller specializes, the name of the salesman met, and the general impression of the firm. In the event that he makes a purchase, he should record on the card the promptness of delivery and the care exercised in filling the order. These cards should be arranged by classification and by price line. If this is done, the buyer will have an excellent resource file to refer to when in need of new stock.

KEY RESOURCES

Retailers find it advantageous to concentrate most of their business among a carefully selected group of vendors that have been found satisfactory in view of the factors just discussed. Each member of this group is called a *key resource* of a store or buyer. The vendors who supply goods on which the retailer enjoys a large sales volume with a substantial markup are generally found on his list of key resources.

The small retailer of convenience goods usually chooses a service wholesaler as his key resource; the large retailer of fashion merchandise will generally buy directly from manufacturers. There are other special resources, however, apart from the manufacturers and wholesale middlemen discussed. Retailers will call upon these resources for special merchandise or in special buying situations.

Private Resources

Large-scale retailers wishing to avoid the uncertainties of quality, delivery, prices, volume, and unsatisfactory relationships with independent vendors, often do some processing or even the complete manufacturing of some items they sell. This is particularly true in the case of large supermarket chains and large mail-order houses. They may purchase the entire output of an independent manufacturer or set up processing plants themselves. The retailer can thus control a satisfactory product and provide it in sufficient quantity to permit a low retail price.

Auction Resources

Retailers of specialized merchandise lines—such as Oriental rugs, objets d'art, valuable jewelry, and antiques—may buy goods at auction. Since such merchandise is mostly one-of-a-kind merchandise, there is not a going market price; and owners find it difficult to set a definite resale price on their goods.

At an auction, bids are solicited by an auctioneer and the goods are sold to the highest bidder. Many items of merchandise can be sold in a short period of time. The prices obtained might not be as high as those that could be obtained in private negotiations extending over a long period of time, but many owners are anxious to liquidate at once to raise needed cash. Most auctioneers act as selling agents for owners of the goods and are paid a commission of from 5 percent to 25 percent of the total auction sales receipts for their services. Usually, the larger the merchandise lot, the lower is the commission rate.

Foreign Resources

The consumption of goods manufactured in foreign countries has continued to increase. The development or expansion of trade relations with other countries has permitted more consumer goods to enter the retail channels of the United States. Many retailers have added import shops as well as individual items in many departments to give their store a certain prestige and exclusiveness.

Merchandise from foreign countries has always had a place on the shelves of our stores. Everyone knows about Belgian linen, Swiss watches, English woolens, and Japanese electronics. In addition to these items, new goods for household use or decoration are being imported from Uganda, Thailand, Brazil, Nigeria, China, and many other nations, which previously had few, if any, goods on the export market.

To obtain imported goods of the type and quality desired the retailer must be extra careful in his search for resources. Federal laws on merchandise, especially fabrics and toys, must be observed on all imports. The retailer may contact foreign resources using one or more of the following procedures: (1) sending a store buyer abroad regularly to comb the markets for the merchandise wanted, (2) using resident buyers who establish foreign offices, (3) buying from an American importer who has his own foreign supply lines, or (4) buying from a foreign exporter who has set up offices in American market centers.

CHECKING YOUR KNOWLEDGE

Vocabulary

key resource

Review Questions

1. List at least ten factors that the buyer should consider in selecting resources.
2. Why would a vendor's completeness of line be important to a small retailer?
3. What information should the retail store buyer keep in his resource file?
4. What are the reasons for developing a private resource?
5. What are the different ways that a buyer can gain access to sources of foreign goods?

1. Would the importance of the various factors in choosing a resource be different for staple goods and fashion goods? Which factors are especially important for a supermarket? a popular priced department store? a fashion leader?
2. Why should a store consider the variety of a wholesaler's stock before using the wholesaler as a source of merchandise?
3. Which wholesaler services should be considered by a retailer before the wholesaler is selected as a source of merchandise?

Part d

Selecting Specific Goods

Much buying involves simply the reordering of merchandise that has sold satisfactorily and that is now depleted in stock. In a drugstore, for example, items needed are jotted down on an order or want pad. The druggist calls his wholesale distributor, generally a local middleman, and gives him the order. Deliveries are made promptly, sometimes on the same day the order is placed. In this way the druggist keeps needed drug and prescription items on hand at all times. Other individual items sold in a drugstore—such as toothpaste, brushes, perfumes, face powders, and hair care needs—are reordered when the supplier's salesperson calls or at the end of definite periods such as a week or a month.

The real problem in buying is selecting new items for purchase. The sources of supply available to retailers offer many more items than even the largest store can afford to stock; and the number of new products appearing on the market each year far exceeds the number of new items with which a store can safely experiment. A typical supermarket, for example, can stock only about a sixth of all the market offerings in grocery products. Obviously, then, great selectivity is necessary in choosing the specific items to purchase for resale.

MAKING A BUYING PLAN

The first step in choosing the specific merchandise to buy is to make a buying plan of the classifications, price lines, and other important characteristics of merchandise needed to meet expected customer demand. In Chapter 6 you learned about buying plans for both convenience goods and fashion goods. Past sales for a particular merchandise classification are analyzed, and a forecast of sales is made. A decision is made as to how much stock to carry at the beginning and end of the control periods. The open-to-buy is then calculated and amount to be purchased is broken down into color, size, style, material, price, and other essential features. The procedure is as follows:

1. Planned sales for the period PLUS
2. Planned stock at end of period EQUALS
3. Total stock required during period MINUS
4. Stock at beginning of period EQUALS
5. Stock to be provided during period MINUS
6. Stock already on order for delivery during period EQUALS
7. Open-to-buy for period

The amount of the open-to-buy for a classification must be further broken down by *selection factors* such as price, material, and size. This breakdown of how much money will be invested in specific items or styles can be quite detailed for staple and convenience goods. For fashion goods the breakdown of an open-to-buy figure will be less detailed because the buyer will want to see what is available before making specific choices. The buyer takes this buying plan with him as he makes market trips or talks with sales representatives. As he looks over a manufacturer's line, he selects only those items that fit into his plan. As he selects an item, he checks it off on his buying plan. Careful checking with the buying plan assures a good stock assortment.

VIEWING MERCHANDISE OFFERINGS

As you know, buyers may view a manufacturer's line in person at a trade show or on a market trip, or they may view the line through the medium of a sales representative who calls at the store. Wherever the buyer actually views the manufacturer's products, he should not make a decision to buy on the basis of his first impression of the line. Most buyers like to jot down the number of an item as it attracts their attention, then inspect the item again later. The buyer usually makes this second inspection after he has had a chance to view other manufacturers' lines. The resident buying office may help a buyer by giving him a list of items in his merchandise field which other stores are buying and perhaps reordering.

Most buyers like to get the opinions of other retailing personnel when they are viewing a new item. A resident buyer may accompany the buyer on a market trip and may give the latter assistance in deciding on an item. If sales representatives are demonstrating the line in the store, the buyer may ask the opinions of his assistant and of his salespeople. This is a wise practice because if the salespeople feel they had a part in the selection of an item, they will usually feel a responsibility toward selling it and will present it more enthusiastically to customers.

Courtesy of Penney News, J. C. Penney Company, Inc

Illus. 7-4   This buyer of men's slacks is conferring with his assistants to get their opinion as to whether a new item offered to the store should be purchased.

A controversial question is whether a buyer should select a few individual items from among many shown in a manufacturer's line or whether he should select a line from among competing lines and then purchase all the items in that best line. Usually the manufacturer makes up a greater variety of items than any one store needs; so most buyers would be well advised to select items from lines. There are exceptions, as in the case of nationally advertised lines, where the store would lose business if it failed to carry in stock all the items that the manufacturer had advertised as being in his line.

EVALUATING MERCHANDISE OFFERINGS

A *buying checklist* is most helpful in evaluating merchandise offerings. This checklist may be written out, or it may simply be carried in the buyer's mind. The checklist contains questions which a buyer should ask about the merchandise item that he is considering for purchase. Here are some of the questions he might ask:

1. Is the item of a type suitable for my department or my store?
2. Does the item have appeal for a specific customer group?
3. Does it have some distinguishing feature that makes it of special interest to this group?
4. Will it stand up well in use?
5. Is it clearly not a duplication of goods already in my present stock or which I already have on order?
6. Will my customers be able and willing to buy it within the retail price range I would have to set?
7. Is it a good value at its price?
8. Will it provide a satisfactory profit margin in view of volume opportunities?
9. Is it properly packaged?
10. Is promotional support from the manufacturer desirable and, if so, is it being provided?

If a buyer can answer these questions—or most of them—in the affirmative, he will probably buy the item. Whenever possible, however, he should take the extra precaution of not ordering in advance the entire quantity he may need during the season. He should buy enough to test the item and depend as much as he can on reorders. Of course, there are cases in which a buyer must take a chance and order his estimated season's requirement in advance.

In evaluating a merchandise item, it is important that the buyer consider how he will sell the item if he does decide to buy it. As a general rule, a buyer should not just put an item in stock and hope it will sell; he should promote it enthusiastically. If the item is not worth promoting, it is not worth buying. Many potentially good items fail because they are not brought dramatically to the attention of customers. Most new items must be helped along by special attention until they catch on with the public or until it is clear that they definitely are not going to be accepted. Buying and selling are closely related; therefore, a selling plan should be formulated before a final decision is made to buy a new item offered by a manufacturer.

There is an exception to this suggestion. The new items that deserve special promotional emphasis should be items that have the potential for increasing total sales and not simply for switching demand temporarily from one item to another. For example, supermarkets sometimes give preferred display space and advertising attention to a new brand of a staple grocery product that is in competition with established brands. This special promotion is likely to result in a sharp increase in the sales of the new brand, but all the other brands in stock will suffer a decrease in sales. When the new brand is later assigned a regular position in stock, it may stand up very poorly in competition with established brands.

CHECKING YOUR KNOWLEDGE

Vocabulary

1. selection factors

2. buying checklist

Review Questions

1. What is the first step in selecting specific goods for resale?
2. Why do buyers sometimes ask the advice of other persons before purchasing merchandise?
3. What is the difference between buying an item and buying a line?
4. Name five questions that a buyer might ask when evaluating merchandise offerings.
5. Is it important that a selling plan be considered before an item is purchased for resale? Why or why not?

Discussion Questions

1. How would a buyer get an accurate sales forecast on merchandise which has not been carried in his store?
2. Should a buyer of children's clothing buy individual items or a manufacturer's line? What procedure should a hardware buyer follow?
3. If a buyer is rushed during his market trip, can he dispense with the practice of making second inspections of items in which he is interested? Explain your answer.

Part e

Ethics in Buying

The retailer and his suppliers should strive for a business relationship which is based on honesty and a spirit of fair play. Enlightened buyers and sellers know that it is to their advantage to work together to sell as much as they can to the ultimate consumer. Any misunderstandings that are created in the process of buying merchandise for the retail store should be settled privately and without public fanfare. If both parties adhere to good principles of business conduct and to established trade practices, most of the common trade abuses can be avoided.

LEGAL ASPECTS OF BUYING

An order properly filled out, signed, and accepted by the vendor, is a *legal contract*. This means that the order is an agreement containing a promise enforceable at law. The order has a lawful purpose (sale of goods); is made by competent parties (over 21 years of age, or now in some states 18 years of age, sane, and not alien enemies); contains an offer and acceptance (buyer offers a price for goods and offer is accepted by vendor); shows consideration (buyer promises to give up money, seller to give up goods, or a payment is actually made); and there is a meeting of the minds (both buyer and seller understand and agree on every condition in the order).

Trade practices and customs followed by the buyer and the seller will affect legal decisions regarding the validity of an order. The merchant or buyer should understand his legal rights and know what recourse can be taken in case of a breach of contract. Once aware of his rights, the buyer should be governed, however, by principles of good business conduct and fair dealing.

CONDUCT OF THE BUYER

Good business practices are those which consider the other fellow but do not allow sympathy for him to sway sound judgment. When a vendor makes a mistake and wants to rectify it, the buyer should remember that he himself is not perfect and allow the seller to do so. To stand "hard and fast" on legal rights, to take every advantage within the law, and to work under a tough vendor policy is not good retailing. It has been proven often in retailing that an easy customer adjustment policy is beneficial in the long run; a similar attitude toward vendors is also a good policy. This does not mean that the retailer should be a pushover, but it does mean that differences of opinion should be tempered with a give-and-take attitude and an appreciation of the opposite viewpoint.

The Buyer-Agent

Most retail buyers do not work for themselves; rather, they are employees of a store or a retail buying group. As agents for their principals, they have these responsibilities:

1. To be loyal and act in good faith in the best interests of their employers
2. To exercise reasonable care, diligence, and skill
3. To act in person and not to delegate authority unless expressly permitted to do so
4. To follow all lawful instructions given them
5. To render an accounting of their business acts
6. To turn over all concessions received to their employers and to make no personal profit

The merchant-employer has an ethical obligation to provide the buyer every assistance in making a success of his job, to remunerate him fairly, and to provide him reasonable security.

Sellers are sometimes guilty of entering into arrangements designed to induce buyers who work for large stores to concentrate most of their continuing orders with certain unethical manufacturers. Private gifts have been given to buyers with the hope that they will favor the giver's line of merchandise. These gifts are sometimes money bribes but more often take the form of expensive Christmas presents. To accept such gifts costs the buyer even more than it costs the seller, since the buyer is tempted to buy not the best merchandise at the best price, but rather the lines for which he is privately rewarded. Well-managed stores have rigid rules prohibiting their buyers from accepting gifts from suppliers and will dismiss any buyer caught doing so. Some will go even further and prosecute the offenders.

Relationships with Vendors

The buyer should not expect unreasonable concessions from the seller. Often a seller has to deal with a buyer who wants concessions in price, terms (discounts and datings), transportation, deliveries, allowances, guarantees, and return privileges. Such a buyer only incurs the ill will of the vendor and may be ignored by the vendor when *special-buy* opportunities become available.

Stores that take advantage of a vendor by returning merchandise when they have no legal right to do so are engaging in an unethical practice and soon become known in the market. When prices decline or changes in fashion cause an order for merchandise to become a poor buy, some retailers try to pass the loss on to the vendor by quickly canceling the order. The vendor should not suffer because of a retailer's poor judgment in buying nor assume the risks that the retailer should bear. Once the buyer has placed the order and taken title, he should not return merchandise unless:

1. The goods are not as described or fail to meet sample specifications.
2. The goods arrive after, or far in advance of, the date promised.
3. Quantities, colors, or styles are not as ordered.
4. The terms of sale on the invoice differ from those agreed upon.

If goods must be returned, send a letter of explanation and dispatch the goods promptly. To avoid a possible tendency on the part of individual buyers to take advantage of sellers, many large stores often require that cancellations of orders and returns of merchandise be approved by the merchandise manager.

In negotiating with sellers, some buyers try to bluff about their knowledge of the merchandise, its value, costs of production, and prices.

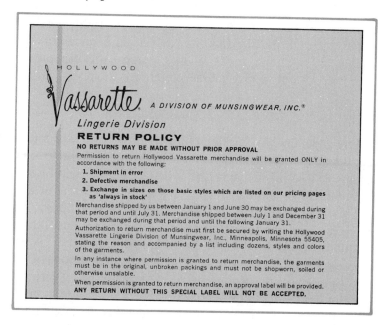

Illus. 7-5   Buyers should not cancel or return orders unfairly. Many suppliers have explicit policies on returns; here is such a policy. Is it adequate from the buyer's point of view?

They try to give the impression that they "know it all," with the hope that the seller will give them lower prices. On the contrary, such an approach usually works in reverse. The seller knows his merchandise, his costs, and his market conditions; and it takes him only a little while to distinguish between a phony buyer and one who really knows. The former buyer often finds his shelves stocked with exactly the merchandise he should not have bought. On the other hand, if a buyer knows that a vendor is granting concessions to others buying in the same quantity and under the same conditions as he, he should insist on receiving the same concessions.

While some store buyers tend to treat vendors from whom they purchase as antagonists, there are others who feel more friendly towards these vendors than towards their own employers. They are given such red carpet treatment by their key resources that they feel an obligation to handle and promote these sellers' lines. Buyers should view all vendors impartially as they search for the merchandise and service that best meets the requirements of their stores and their retail customers.

A good rule of ethical conduct for buyers is to try to appreciate the vendor's position and imagine yourself in his place, negotiating with a buyer such as you. Remember that getting the right merchandise is more important than playing favorites or getting a price concession on questionable or unsalable goods. It is important to keep the goodwill of the vendor, but not to give undue preference to certain favorites.

CONDUCT OF THE SELLER

Vendors or sellers have certain obligations to buyers for retail stores. Sometimes a vendor will make unreasonable concessions to one buyer in order not to lose his account and will then ignore or refuse to grant similar privileges to another. Vendors should be fair in dealing with buyers. This does not mean that they cannot offer different prices to different buyers, but the lower prices and concessions must be based on specific quantities ordered and conditions of purchase. Any buyer placing orders for those quantities and under such conditions of purchase is entitled to similar concessions on proportionally equal terms.

A vendor may *ship short* (not send the entire order) or make a style substitution with the hope that the merchandise will not be accurately checked by the store; or he may include unordered items, expecting the retailer to accept and pay for the goods rather than return them. If a seller engages in these practices or breaks his contractual obligations repeatedly, buyers soon learn about it from their buying offices or other central agencies and bring collective pressure on the seller to mend his ways.

The seller should appreciate the position of the buyer and do everything in his power to further the interests of the store the buyer represents. It is only by such an attitude that sellers can hope to retain, and grow with, their retail accounts.

CHECKING YOUR KNOWLEDGE

Vocabulary

1. legal contract
2. special buy

3. ship short

Review Questions

1. What conditions must an order meet to be considered a legal contract?
2. List the responsibilities of buyers as agents for their employers.
3. What obligations does the merchant-employer have to his buyers?
4. Under what circumstances may a buyer return merchandise after he has placed the order and taken title to the goods?

5. Name some principles of good business conduct which sellers should adopt.

Discussion Questions

1. While at the market a buyer places an order for knit vests. Upon returning to her store she finds that a low-margin store in the city is promoting the same knit vests at a price far below the retail price she has planned. What action can the buyer take?
2. A buyer ordered three dozen pairs of natural finish rough-out men's leather boots. Before the shipment arrived the price for such boots dropped, and the buyer knew he would have to take a loss. When the goods arrived, 30 pairs of the boots were as ordered, but 6 pairs were black smooth finish boots in the same style. The buyer returned the whole shipment. Was he ethical?
3. Do you believe there is anything wrong in a buyer employed by a store accepting a small personal gift from his supplier? What do you consider small?

BUILDING YOUR SKILLS

Improving Communication Skills

Only one of the two prepositions given in parentheses in each sentence may be used to make the sentence correct. On a separate sheet of paper, write the number of the sentence and the correct preposition for each of the sentences.

1. When viewing new merchandise in your own store, you can talk (with, to) salespeople about the new items.
2. New variations (of, on) a familiar theme can set a fashion trend.
3. Have you ever been accused (of, with) buying goods without planning?
4. New colors have to be acceptable (with, to) the customer's taste.
5. Her sources for ready-to-wear were identical (with, to) mine.
6. It is wise to select style numbers independently (of, from) the salesman's influence.
7. The buyer's assortment attracted favorable attention (of, from) customers.
8. His orders were written in accordance (with, to) the law.
9. The alert buyer is forever in search (of, for) new products.
10. We made a substantial profit (with, on) the increased volume.

Improving Arithmetic Skills

Perform the multiplication exercises given in the following five problems. Write your answers on a separate sheet of paper.

1. If a decorative chain sells for 17½ cents a foot, how much should a salesperson charge for a purchase of 11¼ feet?
2. If watermelons are priced at 5½ cents a pound, find the prices of melons with the following weights: (a) 12 pounds, 8 ounces; (b) 15 pounds, 4 ounces; (c) 9 pounds, 12 ounces; (d) 16 pounds, 8 ounces.

3. If a customer wants 2 kilograms of finish nails which sell for 45 cents a pound, how much should the salesperson charge for the purchase? (See Appendix.)

4. During a weekend promotion the following number of cases of motor oil were sold. What was the total value of the motor oil sold during the promotion?

Cases Sold	Price per Case
11 1/2	$ 7.20
8 1/4	$ 9.60
6 2/3	$14.40
4 1/2	$19.20

5. The record department of a store classified records into four price groups. Group A sold for $6.95, Group B sold for $5.95, Group C sold for $3.95, and Group D sold for $1.95. The number of records in each group sold each day for a week are shown below. What is the dollar value of the records sold during the week?

Record Group	Number Sold					
	M	T	W	Th	F	S
A	5	7	8	11	9	14
B	4	7	12	10	13	17
C	2	6	4	16	21	9
D	3	1	4	1	7	5

Improving Research Skills

1. Prepare a checklist of questions which each of the following buyers might ask before purchasing new merchandise:
   (a) A buyer of women's dresses
   (b) A buyer of housewares
   (c) A buyer of builder's hardware
   (d) A consumer buying clothing for his wardrobe

2. Visit a local merchant, interview him, and report on the following:
   (a) The extent of his buying from sales representatives who call at his store
   (b) His use of trade journals and market publications as aids in buying merchandise
   (c) The kinds of information provided by his suppliers and the degree to which he uses this service
   (d) The extent of his buying by means of market trips

3. Determine for your state what the legal requirements are for a person to be considered a competent party to a contract.

Improving Decision-Making Skills

1. Mike Merill was the men's and boys' clothing buyer for a small department store. The best resources were in three markets all about the same distance away. Mike was permitted to make two market trips a year. What would be some of the major factors in your decision, if you were Mike, as to which of the markets you should visit over the next two years?

2. A buyer of men's furnishings must make a special purchase of 50 dozen shirts for a storewide sale. His instructions are that he must purchase shirts of a quality identical to those shirts the store regularly purchases for $48 a dozen but that he must not pay more than $44 a dozen. The buyer has also been instructed not to buy discontinued styles, seconds, poor colors, or odd sizes. It is the height of the selling season, and the buyer is not certain which merchandise resource he should approach. Here are the possibilities.

Resource A—A manufacturer from whom the buyer has made occasional purchases at regular prices

Resource B—A manufacturer with whom the buyer has not been doing business but whose sales representative has been calling on the store for the past year and who is most eager to obtain an order

Resource C—A manufacturer who has obtained over a period of years a good share of the buyer's regular business

Resource D—A wholesaler who frequently has specials on merchandise but from whom the buyer has bought only rarely

Which resource is most likely to provide the buyer with the merchandise and price he wants? Which resource is most desirable from the buyer's viewpoint? Which is the next one to approach if the most desirable resource refuses? Write out reasons for your opinions.

APPLYING YOUR KNOWLEDGE

Chapter Project

Select a product or line of merchandise that you would like to buy for a retail store. Identify the primary central market city in which vendors for your merchandise would be located. Estimate the number of days you would need to spend in the market to make purchases necessary for one selling season. Prepare a complete estimated expense budget for the buying trip. Include travel, meals, hotel, taxis, and all other expenses you are likely to incur from the time you leave your city until you again return. Compare your estimate with those of other students who have selected different products and central market cities.

Continuing Project

In your manual you should now prepare a list of your key resources. You can find the names of suppliers of your merchandise lines by looking in trade directories. Determine the kind of merchandise you will buy from each supplier. You may want to visit a store of the same type as your store and talk with a buyer about his merchandise sources. Also, list ten rules of ethical buying conduct which you as a retailer will observe in your dealings with suppliers.

chapter 8

Negotiation of Price and Terms

CHAPTER PREVIEW

a. A thorough knowledge of prices is needed by the retail buyer. He may estimate prices, memorize prices, or estimate the cost elements of an item to arrive at a price.

b. Discounts from listed prices can often be obtained by the buyer. The usual discounts are quantity, seasonal, trade, cash, and anticipation.

c. Billing and shipping terms vary from one supplier to another; so the buyer must understand what they mean and how they affect the purchase he is planning.

d. There is a variety of special services from manufacturers and suppliers. These services most often are promotional aids in the form of advertising, display material, or demonstrators, but may be packaging, ticketing, or merchandise deals.

e. The buyer's order, when properly completed, becomes a legal document and, accordingly, must be filled out with care.

Part a

Deciding on Price

The focus of this chapter is on the understanding and negotiation of prices and terms that are quoted the retailer by his suppliers. Even after the buyer has selected the most appropriate resources, he is still faced with obtaining goods which can be sold at favorable prices to customers and provide a profit to the retail store. This means that the buyer must shop among key resources and others to become familiar with price quotations on various merchandise. The value of each offering by a vendor in comparison with price requires that the buyer have considerable knowledge of both the price and the quality of merchandise.

KNOWLEDGE OF PRICES

A capable buyer is one who can estimate from a close inspection of the merchandise the approximate cost price and probable retail price of merchandise in his line. He learns this valuable skill through the following techniques.

Estimating Prices

When the buyer examines goods, either at the market or in other stores, he practices *estimating the prices* before looking at the price tags. He takes every opportunity to exercise this skill until it becomes natural for him to place prices upon merchandise wherever he sees it—in other stores, in manufacturers' showrooms, or in his own store. The basis for making estimates is usually pricing experience with similar goods plus knowing the general condition of the market. Customers also often guess at prices of merchandise in somewhat the same manner that buyers do. Even though their reasons for estimating prices are not identical to those of a buyer, customers become quite good at judging merchandise prices.

Rather than attempt to estimate the cost price directly, some buyers find it better to do what the customer does—estimate the retail price first and then determine what an appropriate cost price would be. For example, the buyer may be examining a decorative steel drapery rod and estimate that his customers will buy it if priced at his $16.95 price line. If his cost price is customarily two thirds of his retail price, he expects to buy it for somewhere around $11.30, perhaps in the range of $10.90 to $11.75.

Memorizing Prices

Once the cost and the retail price are established in the mind of the buyer at a certain time, he seldom forgets them. Price changes as reported in trade publications or new quotations from manufacturers or sales representatives are quickly registered and stored away in his mind. The buyer collects and concentrates on all price information affecting items in his line in order to build up his storehouse of memorized prices. People are often amazed at the vast knowledge of prices that some buyers possess. How the buyer can know, without looking at price tags, the cost or retail value of hundreds of items in the store seems to be a remarkable feat. Yet this storehouse of prices has been gathered through repetition, close concentration on price information, and close attention to price changes.

Building Up Prices

The method of *building up prices* is used by buyers who know the cost of materials and labor and who are able to estimate accurately the manufacturer's overhead expenses. For example, upon being shown a selection of decorative steel drapery rods, a buyer might quickly build up the price of each rod as follows:

Basic manufactured materials—rod, rings, and brackets for 90-inch rod	$ 7.75
Labor for partial assembly and packaging	1.25
Overhead, transportation, and profit margin	2.75
Rod quotation to buyer (approximately)	$11.75
Retail price to customer (approximately)	$16.95

With this estimate the buyer is in an excellent position to judge the reasonableness of the price that is quoted him. At a retail price of $16.95 his markup would be somewhat below normal expectations, but the quality and attractiveness of the rod may make it an excellent seller and build goodwill for his department. If the price of the rod is quoted at $13.75 instead of the buyer's estimated $11.75, the buyer must assume there is some hidden value in the rod that he did not notice or that the manufacturer wants an unduly large profit. If the price of the rod is quoted at $9.75 instead of $11.75, the buyer must beware of the possibility that the materials may be inferior, that the workmanship may be poor, or that the item may be a poor seller that the manufacturer is anxious to move.

KNOWLEDGE OF FASHION STAGES

The concept of the fashion cycle was presented in Chapter 6. Buyers of fashion goods are particularly concerned that they buy merchandise in quantities and prices that are appropriate for a given stage of the fashion cycle. To check on where certain styles are in the fashion cycle, the buyer can follow a simple procedure. A fashion buyer usually visits first the manufacturers of the high-priced merchandise that he carries. He notes the details of the lines very carefully but does not purchase immediately. Next, he visits the vendors of the goods he sells at low prices and notes the styles they have copied. Then—having made a mental comparison between the most expensive and least expensive goods on the market—he visits his major resources, which make goods to sell in his medium-price range, and confidently places his orders. He then returns to the expensive resources and chooses the styles that are different from those available at low prices. Finally, a visit to the manufacturers of the low-priced merchandise allows him to select less expensive goods that are still in fashion. Following the procedure just described the buyer will (1) be assured complete coverage of available merchandise at the price levels important to him and (2) have current information on styles, models, values, and quality.

NEGOTIATION

While most store buying is done at the prices quoted by key resources, every buyer finds it necessary to shop for bargains occasionally. *Negotiation* is an attempt to get goods for less than the quoted price. Shopping around may reveal that someone is underselling a preferred resource; it is then desirable to bring the situation to the latter's attention. If the buyer is in the market for an unusually large quantity or is willing to relieve the seller of a normal expense—such as providing transportation, accepting less expensive packaging, or paying *spot cash*— he is justified in asking for a concession. Occasionally the buyer may suggest the detailed design for a fashion item and thus relieve the seller of the designing cost, or he may request simplifications in the merchandise specifications. In such cases a special price may be justified.

Sometimes a group of stores band together and place group orders. The manufacturer is then able to quote a quantity price to the group even though the portion to be taken by each member is small. The manufacturer saves in production costs by turning out a large quantity of identical articles at one time. He saves in selling costs by selling the lot as a unit rather than negotiating separately with each store.

Many bargains come in the form of a *job lot,* which is an assortment of articles that a manufacturer or a wholesaler has been unable to sell at a regular price and subsequently offers at a reduced price. The goods may be going out of style or may be shopworn. Generally the lot contains goods of different qualities, all offered at a flat price per item. Since job-lot merchandise becomes less valuable every day it remains unsold, the manufacturer may hesitate to refuse a price that is somewhat below the price he had asked. For the seller to refuse a low offer of the buyer may mean that the next buyer will pay even less. Many discount houses invite manufacturers to offer them such job lots or *distress merchandise* whenever it is available. The negotiated price is generally so low that the store buyers can easily sell the merchandise at discount prices to their customers and still obtain their normal markup.

As a general rule, it is much more important to buy the right goods than to save a few cents on the purchase price. Nevertheless, it is true that successful buyers are shrewd traders. They make no effort to bargain when the seller's price is right; but if they believe that the cost of production, the value of their purchases, the unusual conditions of sale, or the time of the season warrants a lower price, they do not hesitate to attempt to get concessions.

CHECKING YOUR KNOWLEDGE

Vocabulary

1. estimating prices
2. building up prices
3. negotiation
4. spot cash
5. job lot
6. distress merchandise

Review Questions

1. Why must a buyer continue to shop for merchandise even after he has selected his resources?
2. How can a buyer acquire skill in estimating prices?
3. What must a buyer know in order to build up to a price?
4. Outline the steps that a fashion buyer takes to determine where a certain style is on the fashion cycle.
5. Describe three circumstances that justify bargaining.

Discussion Questions

1. What would be some of the results of manufacturers and wholesalers having a one-price policy and refusing to bargain or make concessions?

2. When is it ethical for a buyer to try to get a price lower than that quoted by a supplier?
3. Should retail customers have the same right to negotiate price with salespeople as retail buyers have with suppliers?

Part b

Discounts

Retail store management, particularly large-store management, places a great deal of importance on the discounts arranged by the retail buyer. It is not unusual for some store managers to insist on certain percentage discounts when purchases are made from vendors and refuse to confirm orders that do not carry expected discounts. Other stores set a specific discount rate which buyers are to obtain or have the difference charged against their department or merchandise lines.

Discount, when used in connection with buying goods for resale, has a different meaning from that usually implied in day-to-day use. For buyers purchasing merchandise from their various suppliers, a *discount* may be defined as a percentage deduction from the *list price* (basic price of an item as published in a catalog) granted to the buyer when he meets certain conditions. The most commonly offered discounts are the quantity discount, seasonal discount, trade discount, cash discount, and anticipation discount.

QUANTITY DISCOUNT

A buyer may qualify for a *quantity discount* by buying in unusually large quantities. For example, an order for 1,000 items at $1 each instead of a usual order of 100 items may qualify a buyer for a 5 percent quantity discount, which would make the price $950 rather than $1,000. A quantity discount does not involve unfair discrimination and is thus permitted by law so long as it is limited to the savings the seller enjoys in manufacturing, selling, and delivery costs growing out of the unusually large quantity sold. However, a quantity discount is unlawful if it exceeds these savings. The federal law that governs the question of price discrimination among business customers is known as the Robinson-Patman Act.

Since discounts for buying in larger quantities are so attractive, they may lead to overbuying. Thus, a merchant who buys and sells

1,000 articles a month at $1 each may be offered a 5 percent discount if he will buy 3,000 articles, or a three-month supply, at one time. The saving of 5 cents an article seems very attractive. But the retailer should ask himself the following questions:

1. Have I $1,850 to spare for the extra quantity? Will this investment keep me from buying other goods I need? Or can I borrow the necessary money at favorable interest rates?
2. Have I enough storage space for this quantity?
3. Is there danger of the goods deteriorating during the three-month period before they can all be sold?
4. Is there danger that the goods will go out of style during the period and have to be sold at a loss?
5. Is there a possibility that the wholesale price may drop during the coming three months? If there should be a drop in the price, it is possible that normal requirements in future months might be purchased at less than the quantity price of 95 cents that was obtained at the beginning of the period.

If all of these questions cannot be answered favorably, the larger purchase should not be made unless the lower cost price permits a lower selling price that will stimulate sales. For example, goods that cost $1 may have been sold at $1.50 in quantities of 1,000 a month. If the manufacturer charges only 95 cents for larger quantities, the retailer may reduce his price proportionately to $1.43. At this price the merchant might be able to sell 1,500 a month instead of 1,000. Thus, the quantity of 3,000 would represent only a two months' supply, and the extra sales would probably more than offset the risk.

SEASONAL DISCOUNT

Vendors sometimes grant buyers a *seasonal discount,* or an outright reduction from the list price, if the purchases are made in the off-season. In many lines consumer purchasing is highly seasonal, and store buyers tend to concentrate their buying with manufacturers within a few months. As a result, during certain months the vendors are swamped with orders while at other times they find their plants nearly idle. Yet certain overhead expenses continue, and skilled workmen cannot be laid off since they will be urgently needed later. So the vendor finds it good business to offer a concession to the buyer who will anticipate his requirements further ahead than is customarily done and who will place an early order that will tend to stabilize the manufacturing activity. Not only may the buyer gain a price advantage for his foresight, but he is also likely to find that his goods are more carefully made, checked, and packed.

TRADE DISCOUNT

A *trade discount* is not usually a form of price concession but rather a method of quoting prices based on list prices. For example, in the hardware trade it is customary for a manufacturer to quote list prices which are approximate retail prices. Retailers are then granted a stated trade discount, perhaps 40 percent, off list prices. The percentage is set high enough to cover the average dealer's necessary markup for expenses, depreciation, and profit.

Wholesalers are generally granted larger trade discounts than are retailers. These are sometimes called *functional discounts* rather than trade discounts. Wholesalers generally buy in larger quantities than do retailers, and they perform a service for the manufacturer by extending his market. Thus, a local manufacturer may have been selling direct to stores in his city, but he may wish to obtain customers elsewhere. It may prove more economical to offer a wholesaler a price 10 percent below a retailer's price than to hire additional salesmen and to pay for additional advertising in order to get more customers.

A functional discount to the wholesaler may be quoted as "less 40, less 10." Thus, if the list price is $1, this amount is computed as follows:

$$
\begin{array}{lr}
\text{List price} \dotfill & \$1.00 \\
\text{Less } 40\% \dotfill & .40 \\
\hline
& .60 \\
\text{Less } 10\% \dotfill & .06 \\
\hline
& \$ \ .54 \\
\end{array}
$$

It should be noted that where there is a series of discounts, each is treated as a percentage of the previous balance, not of the original amount. In the example above, the 10 percent is a percentage of 60 cents, not of $1. If a manufacturer sells an article to be used by another manufacturer, he may grant him a functional discount in addition to that which the wholesaler obtains. Thus, the manufacturer may grant a discount of 40, 10, and 5 percent. A series of discounts like this is often called a *chain discount*.

The manufacturer often uses the trade discount as a device to change easily the prices of all goods in his line. For example, he may have a catalog with 1,000 items listed. He may decide to reduce the prices of all his goods 10 percent. It is costly to print and distribute a new catalog, but it is easy to send a notice to the retail trade to the effect that, whereas the former trade discount was 40 percent, it is now 40 percent and 10 percent. If prices have to be raised, it is also easy to change the discount or to remove the last percentage.

Ordinarily the trade discount to all retailers is the same, but occasionally retailers qualify for a wholesaler's functional discount by organizing buying offices with other retailers and sometimes by setting up a warehouse for a group of stores.

CASH DISCOUNT

A *cash discount* is given if a buyer pays promptly within a specified period, which is generally expressed as a certain number of days after the date of the invoice. Most sellers offer a cash discount as an inducement to the buyer to pay in advance of the final due date. Sellers do this in order to avoid borrowing and also to avoid the collection costs and bad debts that so often result when no special inducement to pay promptly is offered customers.

To obtain a cash discount, it is seldom necessary for a retailer to pay as soon as goods are shipped or even as soon as they are received. The common practice is to allow the retailer 10 days from the date of the invoice, which usually corresponds to the date the goods are shipped. The 10-day period generally provides ample time for the goods to arrive, for the buyer to inspect them, and to process the invoice for payment. Thus, if goods are shipped on July 5 with terms of 2/10, net 30, the invoice must be paid by July 15 to earn a discount of 2 percent. The full amount is due August 4.

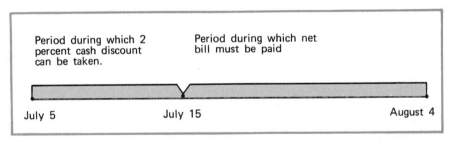

Illus. 8-1   The above scale shows the time during which the retailer may take advantage of a cash discount as compared with the time he is allowed for paying the net invoice.

Every retailer should take advantage of cash discounts. These discounts lower the cost of the goods to the store; and by paying within the discount period, the retailer also builds up a good credit rating in the market. Some retailers borrow the necessary funds in order to take advantage of cash discounts, for the interest they pay on borrowed funds is nearly always less than the discounts they earn.

ANTICIPATION DISCOUNT

Buyers with plenty of ready cash sometimes pay a bill before the date set for earning the cash discount. They deduct interest, often at the rate of 6 percent a year, for the number of days of prepayment. The amount deducted is called an *anticipation discount*. For example, suppose that for goods billed at $100, a buyer may deduct a discount of 3 percent if payment is made by April 10. The buyer, however, decides to pay the bill on March 10—one month before the discounted amount is due. Figuring interest at the rate of 6 percent for 12 months, the rate for one month is ½ of 1 percent. The buyer is entitled to an extra ½ of 1 percent of $100, or 50 cents, for paying one month ahead of time. Thus, he pays $96.50, deducting a total of 3½ percent.

Practice in regard to anticipation discounts varies with different companies and trades. Although some manufacturers will not allow such extra discounts to be taken, most of them do not object as long as the customary rate *per annum* (annually) is not exceeded.

CHECKING YOUR KNOWLEDGE

Vocabulary

1. discount
2. list price
3. quantity discount
4. seasonal discount
5. trade discount
6. functional discount
7. chain discount
8. cash discount
9. anticipation discount
10. per annum

Review Questions

1. List the five kinds of discounts usually available to the retailer.
2. What are some questions a retailer should answer before buying in large quantities in order to get a quantity discount?
3. Why are manufacturers willing to give additional discounts if buyers place orders during certain times of the year?
4. Explain how the series of trade discounts "less 20, less 10, less 5" should be computed.
5. What is the main purpose of a cash discount?

Discussion Questions

1. Is it proper for retail management to insist that buyers obtain certain discounts on all purchases?
2. Are quantity discounts a fair practice from the small store owner's point of view? Why or why not?
3. Is it proper for a wholesaler to receive an additional trade discount even though he may buy less than a large retailer?

Part C

Billing and Shipping Merchandise

Every manufacturer has his own billing and shipping terms, but the terms are standard in many industries. For example, the typical terms for ready-to-wear dresses are 8/10 EOM, FOB factory. Buyers generally accept the manufacturers' terms without question; but sometimes they ask for a larger discount, longer dating, or other shipping arrangements. They are probably not too successful in securing such concessions, because manufacturers have learned from experience that changing terms for one customer opens the door to the granting of additional concessions that may eventually absorb the manufacturers' legitimate profits.

DATING

The most important aspect in the billing of retailers for merchandise which they have purchased is *dating,* that is, the time that the retailer is given to pay his bill.

COD

Goods may be sold for cash or *COD* (*cash on delivery*), but almost all successful stores have achieved a credit rating that permits them to pay for goods after delivery has been made. The most common dating is 30 days, which means that payment is to be made within 30 days of the date of the invoice. Sometimes 60 or 90 days, rather than 30 days, are allowed.

EOM

In the case of clothing, dating is usually figured from the end of the month. Thus, if suits are shipped on April 5, they do not have to be paid for until a specified number of days after April 30. These terms are called *EOM* (*end of month*).

ROG

Retailers who are some distance from the market may be granted *ROG* (*receipt of goods*) terms. ROG means that the date of payment may be computed from the date the goods are received by the store rather than from the date of invoice (shipment). Thus, the usual net 30 terms in connection with a shipment made June 22 mean that the goods must be paid for on July 21. But if the goods are bought ROG, net 30, and arrive on July 2, they do not have to be paid for until August 1.

Extra Dating

In some trades buyers are given much longer datings than those just described. These may take the form of *extra dating.* In this case, the buyer is given a specified number of extra days in which to pay. Instead of 30 days, he may be granted 60 extra, giving him 90 days, or 120 extra, giving him 150 days within which to pay.

Postdating

Much the same result is achieved by *postdating,* also called *advance dating,* as is achieved by the extra dating. With postdating, invoices are dated after the date of shipment. For example, the invoice covering a shipment of hats made on April 15 may be dated June 1 with a regular 30-day dating, giving the buyer until July 1 to pay the bill. Postdating is often done to induce the buyer to purchase in a dull season rather than to wait until the rush period. Both extra dating and postdating are also used to obtain business from poorly financed stores that want time to sell the goods before they have to pay for them.

SHIPPING MERCHANDISE

After the billing terms are understood and agreed upon, the buyer must still decide upon shipping arrangements. There are several important points to be considered:

1. Who is to pay for the cost of transportation?
2. Who is to own the goods and to be responsible for them while they are on their way?
3. What will be the method of shipment?
4. How are the goods to be packed?
5. How will the transfer of title be handled?

The answers given by the buyer and manufacturer to these questions will determine the shipping arrangements that are made.

Shipping Terms

If the buyer is to pay all transportation costs and is to own the goods from the moment they are shipped, the shipping terms are *FOB* (*free on board*) *factory* (or mill). At the other extreme, if the seller is to pay all transportation costs and is to own the goods until they arrive at the store, the terms are *FOB destination.* In between are many variations. For example, *FOB shipping point* means that the seller pays any cartage necessary to the place at which the goods are to be turned over to a transportation company. *FOB destination, charges reversed,* means that the seller will own the goods until they get to the store but that the buyer agrees to pay the transportation charges. *FOB factory, freight prepaid,* means that the goods are to become the buyer's as soon as they are shipped but that the seller will pay freight charges.

As in the case of dating terms, FOB terms have become standardized in different trades; and the buyer generally accepts the terms offered. A manufacturer or a wholesaler may, however, make a concession on shipping terms instead of giving a quantity or a seasonal discount. Even if the seller is unwilling to pay transportation charges, he may be willing to have ownership pass to the buyer at the time of receipt rather than at the time of shipment. Such terms as FOB destination, charges reversed, may bring an important advantage to the buyer: if the goods are delayed or lost on the way, the buyer is not responsible for payment or follow-up, since the goods are not his.

Method of Shipment

In addition to determining the FOB point, a decision must be made in regard to the method of shipment. The main methods are by railroad freight, railway express, motor freight, fourth-class mail, air express, and air freight. An increasing amount of merchandise is being shipped by a truck-rail service known as *piggyback.* Goods are loaded at the factory or other assembly point into trailers and hauled by truck to a railroad siding where the entire trailer is hoisted onto a flatcar. At the city of destination, the trailer is removed and transported by truck to store or warehouse. This shipping method is now being used also in connection with ocean marine shipments, where it is called *fishyback.* An adaptation of the piggyback and fishyback services is called *containerization.* At the factory, goods are packed into large containers resembling boxcars which can be carried on railroad flatcars, on trucks, on ships, and on cargo planes. These containers are not as heavy and bulky as are trailers, and they can be transferred easily from one carrier to another.

When selecting the method of shipment, the buyer has two major factors to consider: time and cost. When a buyer can estimate his needs well in advance, the slower but less expensive freight shipments should be chosen. If goods are needed quickly, express or parcel post is generally used, but the parcel-post rates should be carefully compared

Courtesy of Martin J. Cooney Studio

Illus. 8-2   Here a containerized shipment is being hoisted onto a Japanese oceangoing vessel where it will travel to its destination.

with express rates. Air freight is becoming more popular for some perishables and high fashion merchandise and for emergency shipments of much-needed merchandise.

Stores sometimes designate not only the general method of shipment but the specific route as well. For example, the service of one truck line may have been found superior to that of another. Slower freight shipment by water may be justified by the saving in cost. Combination boat and railroad routing is used by some stores on the Pacific coast when they buy in New York.

While direct shipment from manufacturer to store is the most efficient and economical means of shipping staple and standard goods, some apparel chains prefer to have fashion goods delivered to their own central distribution points where the goods are checked to determine whether they agree with the buyer's specifications and are then marked and sorted for distribution to their stores. The extra cost of handling is more than offset by the reduction in returns from the stores to the manufacturers and from customers to the stores.

An efficient system of transportation, called *consolidation,* has evolved for retailers because of a large number of small shipments and a large daily movement out of major wholesale centers such as New York City, Chicago, and Los Angeles. Under this plan, each retailer names a *consolidator* as its shipper from these major centers. The vendors send their merchandise for this store to its consolidator, who then prepares a *manifest*—a listing of all the shipments from vendors in a given city on a given day. A progressive or consecutive number is assigned to each shipment, and this number is shown on each carton of the shipment. The consolidator then turns this merchandise over to the store's chosen carrier, and the merchandise moves as a group shipment rather than as hundreds of individual shipments on individual transportation bills.

Consolidation has proved to be a great time- and money-saving idea for stores, and the services of consolidators are available to stores at a modest per-carton charge which usually costs the store less than paying minimum charges on individual shipments.

Packing Arrangements

A few large stores specify the manner in which the goods should be packed for shipment. They have determined methods of reducing the weight of packing materials and of minimizing risk of damage in transit.

If it is possible for a buyer to reduce costs through special packing arrangements, every effort should be made to do so. For instance, bookcases packed *knocked down* are classified by the express company at one rate, while the same item *set up* is classified as furniture and shipped at a rate two times that of the knocked-down rate. Invalid wheelchairs—packed, boxed, or crated—are billed at a lower rate than chairs not boxed or crated. Wheeled goods, such as bicycles and children's vehicles, have several rate classifications according to the manner in which they are packed for shipment.

The buyer in a small store is somewhat handicapped in the matter of packing arrangements and transportation rates. He avoids the problem by buying largely from local wholesalers who may deliver by their own trucks at no extra charge. The large store can afford to employ a traffic manager whose duties include advising buyers of correct packing instructions which they give to vendors when placing orders. When the retailer buys in a central market, he should seek the services of a consolidator that will not only consolidate his shipments but also advise him on transportation problems.

Transfer of Title

Under the terms FOB destination and FOB destination, charges reversed, the seller retains title to the goods until the goods reach the buyer. Under the terms FOB factory and FOB factory, freight pre-paid, the buyer owns the goods from the moment they are shipped. These are the most common ways in which ownership of merchandise is transferred from the buyer to the seller. There are, however, two special shipping arrangements in which the buyer may not assume title to merchandise even though the merchandise is in his hands.

Vendors often sell goods *on memorandum*. This means that the retailer may return unsold goods to the vendor up to a certain date. (The goods sold on memorandum generally remain the seller's property, but the intention of the buyer and seller or the trade practices can determine the ownership.) Thus, goods shipped June 5 "on memorandum until July 15" may be returned to the seller on July 15 if any of the goods remain unsold. The offering of goods on memorandum is equivalent to a price concession in that the buyer assumes no risk of loss on goods that do not sell at a profit. Expensive jewelry is frequently bought "on memo."

Although buyers often seek memorandum terms, the terms are not always desirable. The goods offered on memorandum are sometimes out of style or of poor quality. Even if the goods are satisfactory, they often can be obtained at a lower price if they are bought outright in the usual ways.

Merchandise is also sometimes sold *on consignment*. This usually means that the merchandise does not become the buyer's property when it is shipped to him. It remains the property of the seller, but the retailer assumes the responsibility of protecting it physically and of trying to sell it at the retail price set by the seller. Unsold goods are returnable. Some manufacturers prefer to sell this way so that they can set the retail price.

CHECKING YOUR KNOWLEDGE

Vocabulary

1. dating
2. COD (cash on delivery)
3. EOM (end of month)
4. ROG (receipt of goods)
5. extra dating
6. postdating, or advance dating
7. FOB factory
8. FOB destination

Vocabulary (Continued)

9. FOB shipping point
10. FOB destination, charges reversed
11. FOB factory, freight prepaid
12. piggyback
13. fishyback
14. containerization

15. consolidation
16. consolidator
17. manifest
18. knocked down
19. set up
20. on memorandum
21. on consignment

Review Questions

1. What is the difference between extra dating and postdating?
2. What are some of the important points to be considered by the retailer when deciding upon shipping arrangements?
3. What is the difference between FOB factory and FOB destination?
4. List six methods of shipping merchandise from vendors to retailers.
5. Who holds the title to goods that are on consignment until sold?

Discussion Questions

1. What advantages does the retailer gain from specifying the shipping terms and type of shipment on the goods that he buys?
2. If you were a small retailer some distance from the market, would you prefer an EOM or an ROG dating on your purchases? Why?
3. Why would some retailers not want to take title to goods until the goods are actually received at their stores?

Part d

Special Services

When the retail buyer has two reputable resources and each offers products of equal quality and price, other factors affect the decision to buy from one or the other. More favorable discounts or preferred shipping arrangements by one manufacturer could be determining factors in the buyer's decision to purchase. There are other special services which may accompany a merchandise purchase which can also influence a buyer. These services generally involve an allowance by the seller for a particular service performed by the buyer or the provision of a special service by the seller. The offering of such allowances or services is lawful, if they are available on proportionally equal terms to all competing buyers.

PROMOTIONAL AIDS

An important service offered by manufacturers is the provision of promotional aids. Such a service may take the form of allowances for cooperative advertising, display space, free display material, and demonstrators.

Cooperative Advertising Allowances

Cooperative advertising is an arrangement by which the manufacturer agrees to pay part of the cost incurred by the retailer in advertising the manufacturer's product to the consumer. The manufacturer's justification for doing this is that he can obtain extra business at a lower advertising cost than if he were to advertise the goods himself.

The manufacturer's cooperative advertising allowance may be given to the retailer in one of two ways. The manufacturer may agree to pay a flat sum and will allow the retailer to deduct this amount on the merchandise invoice, somewhat as follows:

```
1,000 style #76 @ $1 ...........  $1,000
Less advertising allowance .........      25
Amount due ...................  $  975
```

Instead of using this procedure, the manufacturer may agree to pay a stated proportion of the retailer's advertising expense. The allowance does not then appear on the merchandise invoice; but when the advertising is run, the store bills the manufacturer for his share of the cost.

Cooperative advertising allowances have been abused by some buyers who have failed to spend for advertising the allowance obtained. In some instances an advertising allowance has become merely a disguised price concession similar to the quantity discount.

Display Space

A service that the buyer may provide the seller is to assign the merchandise to preferred selling locations in the store and perhaps to give it special window treatment. In chain stores, where the value of each display area in the store has been charted, an agreement to give preferred space to a certain manufacturer's product is an assurance of increased volume. The seller may be willing to pay for such increased sales by granting the buyer an allowance from the regular price. The store buyer who provides the special space may feel that the allowance received warrants the concession.

Display Material

Material for window and counter displays, often costing the seller a considerable amount of money, are frequently provided the buyer.

Vendors believe that the extra sales produced by this material are well worth the expense. Buyers, however, should use this material and service with a good deal of restraint. To have the store or windows cluttered with vendors' materials decreases the buyer's initiative and robs the store of display space that should be used for the store's benefit and not for a particular vendor.

Courtesy of Federated Department Stores, Inc.

Illus. 8-3   Display materials are often provided by vendors because they believe that the extra sales produced are well worth the expense.

Demonstrators

Perhaps the best-known example of the performance of a service by the seller is the provision of demonstrators. In many cosmetic, food, and home-furnishings lines, the manufacturer provides demonstrators at his own expense to work in the stores handling his line. These people are generally salespeople who concentrate on the sale of the manufacturer's product, although they may also be allowed to sell other goods. They are often trained by the manufacturer before being sent to stores.

Most stores are glad to use demonstrators because they reduce selling expenses and provide expert service. They have their disadvantages, however, for they tend to push their sponsor's brand rather than help the customer obtain the most appropriate choice from among competing brands. Moreover, they are sometimes difficult to manage, for they are not regular store employees and thus not subject to store rules.

Courtesy of Sears, Roebuck and Co.

Illus. 8-4   Some cosmetic firms provide trained personnel to demonstrate the features of their products.

UNIT PACKING

Another obligation that a seller may assume through special arrangement with the buyer is that of unit packing. In the home-furnishings and appliance fields especially, various articles are commonly packed by the seller in units suitable for retail selling. In fact, competition among manufacturers centers on more exciting, more convenient packaging. The seller who utilizes materials such as aluminum and plastics and uses bolder graphics, new sizes, and new opening and closing devices is most likely to stay ahead of his competitors. If the buyer can obtain this special unit packing service at no extra cost, he will eliminate the packing expenses at the store and avoid the risk of loss through unpacking, breakage, and repacking.

Other packaging arrangements may be made with manufacturers that will make the handling and displaying of goods easier. The use of *tray packs* makes a portion of the shipping carton removable leaving the contents exposed but still on a tray that can be shelved or stacked. This tray of goods can be stacked or shelved quickly, neatly, and with less labor than handling each item. Spots for pricing may be located on the top of each item so that automated pricing may be done without removing each item from the tray.

PRETICKETING

A service that some suppliers provide retailers is that of placing the retail price on merchandise before it is shipped to the retailer. *Preticketing* simply means that the retail price of the item to be sold is attached to or marked on the item by the vendor. In the case of packaged food products some stores also require that the unit price per pound, ounce, or other unit of measure be preprinted as well as the package price. This type of marking will be discussed in the next chapter.

If the buyer can negotiate preticketing of merchandise by the seller, it means both a savings to the retail store and faster movement of goods from the time they are received until they can be placed on the selling floor. Rapid movement through the receiving, checking, and marking process is particularly important for fashion goods. The vendor may supply the tickets, but more often the retailer supplies the type of ticket that is desired on the merchandise. The supplier then attaches the tickets as the goods are checked or prepared for shipment.

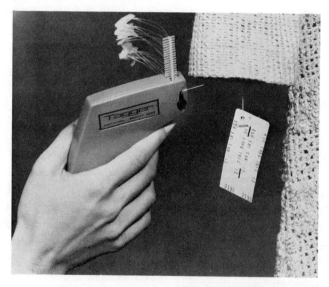

Courtesy of Monarch Marking Systems
A Subsidiary of Pitney Bowes

Illus. 8-5 This form of preticketing frequently is used on wearing apparel and other soft goods. This price tag must be cut to be removed.

The price included in the preticketing process may be the price
that the retailer specifies or a price suggested by the manufacturer.
Premarking of a suggested retail price by a manufacturer often shows
the optimum price for the goods. Retailers frequently remark the goods
with their own lower price. Premarking at an unusually high price so
that the retailer's price will make the item appear an exceptional buy
is considered an unfair business practice.

GUARANTEES AGAINST PRICE DECLINES

It is sometimes possible to obtain special guarantees against price
declines, particularly when seasonal requirements are ordered well in
advance. Suppose a buyer is encouraged in December to place an
order for goods that seasonally begin to sell in March. If the price
should drop during the interval from December to March, the vendor
may agree to credit or refund the store the difference between the
contract price and the market price on March 1. For instance, if a
buyer agrees in December to pay $5 for an article and the price on
March 1 is $4.90, the vendor will credit or refund the store 10
cents for each of the items the buyer has on hand on March 1. The
vendor may agree to this arrangement in order to secure orders during
the off-season so that he can keep his plant in operation.

Even though no guarantee exists, sometimes a vendor will grant
a refund to a store for unsold goods if the prices have been reduced.
It is well for the buyer to understand the policy of the vendor in regard
to guarantees and price reductions.

MERCHANDISE DEALS

The retail buyer is often offered a *merchandise deal* in which
goods are given free by the seller if the buyer orders in quantity or
performs some promotional service. For instance, a grocer may be
offered "a dozen free" if he orders ten dozen boxes of XYZ tea bags.
This may reduce the cost of XYZ tea bags to an attractive price and
may catch an unwary store buyer. The same deal, according to the federal Robinson-Patman Act, must be offered to all buyers; and it is likely
that all grocers in the area will have XYZ tea bags at the lower price.
Besides, if the consumer stocks up on XYZ tea bags because of the
low price, it is reasonable to expect a slump in the sale of tea bags for
a period after the special sale.

Nevertheless, some merchandise deals have attractive appeal. These
deals are usually originated by the seller to get the buyer to put special

effort into promoting the manufacturer's merchandise. Such deals are most commonly found in the grocery and drug trades where they are used to introduce new items. The free goods need not necessarily be the goods being purchased. They may consist of related goods or of another item made by the same manufacturer. For instance, if a druggist orders five gross of a certain razor, he may also receive three gross of double-edged blades.

CHECKING YOUR KNOWLEDGE

Vocabulary

1. cooperative advertising
2. tray packs

3. preticketing
4. merchandise deal

Review Questions

1. Describe two ways by which a manufacturer may provide an advertising allowance to the retailer.
2. Of what value is it to the seller to be given preferred selling locations in the retail store? What is the value to the buyer?
3. What are some of the ways that packaging can be of help to the retailer?
4. Why do some vendors provide guarantees against price declines?
5. What are the possible disadvantages of a merchandise deal from the viewpoint of the retail buyer?

Discussion Questions

1. What policies or practices could the manufacturer adopt that would prevent misuse of advertising allowances granted retailers?
2. For what reasons would a retailer want preticketing done with tickets from his store rather than those provided by the supplier?
3. Why may a manufacturer prefer to offer a merchandise deal instead of a discount of equivalent value?

Part e

The Buyer's Order

When the buyer has made all the necessary decisions for a purchase, he is then ready to place an order for goods. The preparation of the order must be done carefully, for when it is properly completed and signed it is a legal contract. Any errors or omissions on the document are the responsibility of the buyer who signs the order.

The buyer may use a form provided by the manufacturer or vendor, a form printed by his own store, or a form from his resident buying office. It is preferred that the buyer use his own store form. He will be familiar with it, and by using it he will be sure every necessary detail is included. Many large stores insist that their buyers use the store's order form. Each buyer can then be held responsible for every numbered order form issued to him, and an accurate record of all orders placed can be kept.

PREPARING THE ORDER

Buyers are sometimes careless in filling out orders and, as a result, later get into arguments with sellers or suffer direct loss. For example, credit terms and discounts are sometimes omitted, and the seller bills the

---

Information Contained in an Order

Names and addresses of both buyer and seller
Department for which goods are being purchased
Date of order
Quantity
Description of the goods
Unit cost
Extension
Total cost of order
Credit terms
Discounts
Transportation instructions
Delivery date
Terms and agreements that cover all orders placed
Signatures

Illus. 8-6   Buyers should make certain that the correct information is included on their orders; because, once an order is accepted by the seller, it is a legal document.

goods with shorter dating or lower discounts than the buyer assumed he was to be granted. An even more common error is to omit transportation instructions and date of shipment. Thus, the goods may be shipped by a slow route or by an unduly expensive carrier, such as air express, and the buyer may have to pay the cost. There is a tendency to state delivery terms as "at once" or "rush" which have no exact meaning, and a buyer may have to accept a shipment even though it arrived after the time the goods were needed for resale. To eliminate any misunderstanding, buyers should make it a practice to fill out their purchase orders completely.

Store's Standard Terms and Conditions

In addition to the terms that apply to the particular order, many stores print on their order forms (usually on the back) the conditions that govern all their orders. These include a statement that the seller must comply with all laws governing such matters as food and fiber identification on labels, product flammability, adulteration, and child labor. The conditions are also likely to include a statement that the seller carries adequate product liability insurance and that the buyer is not bound to accept substitutions in regard to such details as sizes and colors. A statement of conditions is shown in Illus. 8-7.

TERMS AND CONDITIONS OF PURCHASE

This purchase is given subject to the terms and conditions stated below and by accepting this order or by delivering merchandise pursuant thereto Seller agrees to be bound thereby.

1. Compliance with the delivery date is essential and guaranteed by Seller. The right is reserved to cancel all or any part of this order if merchandise is not delivered on dates specified herein or merchandise is delivered in any other way in violation of the terms and conditions of this order.

2. The right is reserved to return at Seller's expense all merchandise sent which fails to comply with any of the terms and conditions of this order, including colors, sizes, fabrics, etc. Acceptance of merchandise shall in no way bind Purchaser to accept future deliveries on any order or constitute a waiver of any rights Purchaser might have with respect to Seller's failure to deliver goods on time or otherwise in breach of the terms and conditions of this order.

3. Seller warrants compliance and conformity to all applicable Federal, State and Local Laws including, but not limited to, Pure Food and Drug Laws, Child Labor Laws, Wool Labeling Acts, Robinson-Patman Price Discrimination Act, Federal Textile Fiber Products Identification Act, Fire and Flammability Laws and Regulations, and Federal Trade Commission Rulings affecting sales of material, including rayon, wool, silk and other fabrics. In accepting this order Seller also agrees to provide a written guarantee that the goods meet the requirements of the Federal Flammable Fabrics Act, and the Federal Textile Fiber Products Identification Act.

4. Seller will carry insurance protecting itself and its vendees against a product liability in an amount commensurate with the risk and will upon request furnish Purchaser with proof of such insurance.

Courtesy of Kirby Block Marketing Services

Illus. 8-7   The terms and conditions under which the purchase is made are clearly stated on the order form. Why would the buyer want the seller to meet the terms and conditions given in this example?

Writing Up the Order

Buyers should write out their own orders even though the manufacturer's sales representative may be glad to do it for them. A manufacturer's sales representative may omit one of the essentials or may record a delivery date, style number, price, or quantity that is different from what the buyer intended. Writing the order also gives the buyer an additional opportunity to reconsider his order.

Making Copies of Orders

Every order should be made out in duplicate—the original copy for the seller and the duplicate for the buyer. In large stores four copies are often required so that different divisions of the store may have a record of all orders placed.

Store copies are tallied to determine the total amount of orders that have been placed for delivery each month. Totals of items that

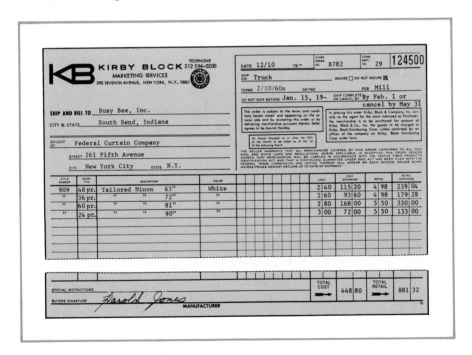

Courtesy of Kirby Block Marketing Services

Illus. 8-8   This illustration differs from the typical store order form only in that it is filled in by the store's resident buying office (discussed in Chapter 7) acting as agent for a store buyer. The retail price and extensions appear only on the duplicate copy not on the original sent to the vendor.

have been ordered are necessary to determine how much more may be ordered without exceeding planned purchases.

The same or another copy of the order should be used for a follow-up. This means that the manufacturer should be checked a few days before the delivery date of each order to be sure that he will ship the goods on time. Stores have to follow up orders continually in order to get goods when needed. If they do not do so, there may be delays in shipments that may lead to lost sales and to the receipt of goods after the seasonal demand for certain styles has passed.

The management of one department store insists that orders be written for all merchandise and that a copy of each order be sent to the receiving department in order to protect the store against *no order shipments*. This particular store exercises tight control over its buying and returns all merchandise for which there is no order, without notice to buyers. A problem arises, however, when a buyer is on a buying trip and orders merchandise. Frequently the merchandise arrives at the store before the buyer returns to give the receiving department copies of the orders he has placed.

More and more buying is being done by central buyers who buy for a group of stores. While the order may call for all the goods to be shipped to a central warehouse, the order is often broken down to show what is to be shipped directly to each store in the group. Copies of the orders are given to each store so that it can check the quantity received against the amount ordered by the central buyer.

CONFIRMING THE ORDER

The careful vendor will make sure that an order is confirmed by an authorized person connected with the store before making delivery of goods. Some stores may require the merchandise manager to sign all orders to vendors. The purpose of the *order confirmation* is to exercise a check on the buyer and to prevent any order of goods that the merchandise manager believes is unwise. On the other hand, stores not favoring this practice may permit their buyers to use their own judgment in placing orders for merchandise, provided that the buyers do not exceed their purchase limits. Other stores require the merchandise manager's signature on all orders over a certain set dollar amount.

CHECKING YOUR KNOWLEDGE

Vocabulary

1. no order shipment   **2.** order confirmation

Review Questions

1. List three common errors that are made when writing orders.
2. What information is usually found on an order?
3. Why should buyers write their own orders?
4. Explain how multiple copies of an order may be used.
5. What is meant by order confirmation?

Discussion Questions

1. If merchandise shipments arrived at your store before the buyer returned from market with copies of the orders he had placed, what would you as receiving manager do?
2. A good deal of ordering is done over the telephone. Since this practice may lead to error and misunderstanding, should it be eliminated? Explain.
3. If a buyer submitted a handwritten purchase order to a vendor and because of poor handwriting the vendor misread the amount of goods to be shipped, whose fault would it be?

BUILDING YOUR SKILLS

Improving Communication Skills

A conjunction is a word that joins sentences, clauses, phrases, or words. The conjunctions *and, but, for, or, neither,* and *nor* coordinate two ideas. The conjunctions *although, though, so, if, as,* and *since* subordinate two ideas. In the following sentences two conjunctions are given. Select the most appropriate conjunction and write it, with the number of the sentence, on a separate sheet of paper.

1. The lamps were a bargain (and, so) he took them.
2. Give the refund to the customer (or, as) she will be angry.
3. She enjoys going to the market (but, for) she says nothing about it.
4. The order did not state a delivery date (but, so) he wrote it in.
5. The demonstrator sold merchandise (and, as) she gave expert advice.
6. The buyer wanted an advertising allowance (but, so) he asked for five percent.
7. The buyer could get the goods on memorandum (but, or) consignment would be better.
8. The buyer wanted extra dating (or, as) a seasonal dating.
9. Resource A is good (and, although) Resource B might be better.
10. The goods will be shipped by both truck (and, or) rail.

Improving Arithmetic Skills

Calculate the discounts in the exercises on page 272. On a separate sheet of paper, write the number of each exercise and your answer.

1. Figure the amount of discount and the net amount of an invoice for $925 if the discount rate is 2%.
2. Find the discount and net amount of an invoice for $2,500 if there are discount terms of less 20%, less 10%.
3. A sportcoat is listed at $65 with a trade discount of 40%. If the terms of the sale to the retailer are 8/10, net 30, and the invoice is paid within the discount period, what is the net cost of the sportcoat?
4. A chair is listed at $95 with a trade discount of 30% and 10%. If the terms of the sale to a retailer are 2/10, net 30, and the invoice is paid within the discount period, what is the net cost of the chair?
5. It costs a manufacturer $810 to make and sell a trail bike. He wants to make a profit of $80 on each cycle. If he offers a trade discount of 10% and 5% and offers a cash discount of 2%, what should be the manufacturer's list price of the trail bike?
6. If 15 gallons of gasoline cost $7.50 what is the cost per liter? (See Appendix on page 622.)

Improving Research Skills

1. Under the direction of your instructor, members of your class should be organized into research teams. Each team should obtain the following information from a buyer or merchant representing a certain type of retail operation. Be prepared to report your findings to the class.
   (a) What datings, discounts, and shipping terms are common for his line? What exceptions are there?
   (b) Does he receive any cooperative advertising allowances, demonstrator service, or other promotional aid from his sources of supply?
   (c) Does he have much opportunity to bargain for better prices or terms? Under what conditions?
2. Again, utilizing the research team approach, with each team going to a particular transportation company handling shipments to retailers, determine the following about transportation services in your community.
   (a) Which types of merchandise are handled by this company?
   (b) Which types of services does this company provide retailers?
   (c) What are the transportation rates for various types of shipments, frequency of deliveries, and most commonly used terms of shipment?
3. Collect samples of purchase order forms from a variety of retailers. Compare the forms and identify similarities and differences. What are the most common features of the purchase orders that you have collected? What unique features did you find on some of the forms?

Improving Decision-Making Skills

1. A buyer has narrowed his search for merchandise to two suppliers. The merchandise of each supplier is similar; and the price of a unit is the same—$8 each. Company A provides the following: 2% cash discount, net 60 days; a 5% quantity discount for over 115 units; shipment FOB destination; $50 cooperative advertising allowance;

and free display materials valued at $35. Company B provides the following: 2% cash discount, net 30 days; a 6% quantity discount for an order of 100 units or more; shipment FOB factory; 1% advertising allowance; and display material valued at $10. The buyer knows that freight costs are about $65. If the buyer wants 100 units, from which company is it best to buy? If he wants 125 units, from which company is it best to buy? Why?

2. While a buyer was looking over a manufacturer's line of dresses ranging in price from $12 to $18, the manufacturer showed him a job lot of 30 dresses for the flat sum of $350. The lot contained about 8 dresses in the $18 price line, and the rest of the dresses came from the $15 price line. Three of the dresses were so shopworn that they could not be sold at all, and 5 were in such condition that they could not be offered for more than $10.95 each in the store. The buyer thought that the rest of the dresses might be sold at his regular price of $25.00. Should the buyer purchase the job lot? Why or why not? Do you agree that $25.00 is the proper retail price for these dresses?

APPLYING YOUR KNOWLEDGE

Chapter Project

Obtain a copy of a recent newspaper. Study carefully the advertising it contains. Locate ten advertisements which involve a price-saving offer for customers. Then answer the following questions:

1. For each product advertised, what discounts might the buyer have received to enable him to pass the savings on to the customer?
2. Which products might be accompanied by special dealer services?
3. If the customer could take advantage of all the price-saving offers, how much money would she save?

Continuing Project

Design an order form to be used for your retail store in the purchase of merchandise. Using the form that you have designed, prepare five orders for merchandise. Each order should be prepared to cover the purchase of at least five different items and should be for quantities and prices that you would expect for your store. Place these sample orders in your manual.

chapter 9

Handling Incoming Merchandise

a. The first series of steps in handling incoming merchandise are to examine the packages or other containers in each shipment, to assign identifying numbers to each, and to enter pertinent information about each shipment in a receiving record.

b. Incoming shipments must be checked for condition, and contents must be examined to see if quantity and quality agree with what was ordered.

c. Merchandise is marked to help both the customer and the store. Price tickets can indicate the date of purchase, cost of item in code, name of vendor, style number, size, color, and, of course, the retail price.

d. The proper arrangement of merchandise in the store increases sales, helps a new salesperson to learn the stock locations quickly, and makes it easier to maintain merchandise control.

e. Efficiency in receiving, checking, marking, storage, and stocking of merchandise is aided by modern mechanical and electronic devices.

Part a

Receiving Merchandise

One of Dennis Scholl's responsibilities at Burke's Hardware Store is to manage incoming merchandise. Shipments are received almost every day from the United States Postal Service, United Parcel Service, or REA. It is expected that all merchandise will be either on the selling floor or in reserve stock one day after it is received. Dennis must be constantly on the alert for any problem that will prevent merchandise from moving quickly from the receiving area to the selling floor.

Merchandise coming into Burke's Hardware Store goes through a series of steps which prepare it for sale: receiving the goods from the shipper, checking the merchandise, marking or tagging the individual items with a price and other identifying information, placing the goods in reserve stock, or moving the goods to their appropriate places on the selling floor. The proprietor of a small store may perform all the steps himself and use little special equipment in getting his goods prepared for selling. Large stores, however, may employ many people and elaborate machinery to handle the movement of merchandise.

EFFICIENCY IN HANDLING INCOMING MERCHANDISE

A major problem confronting retailers today is increased expenses. Successful retailers are cutting expenses by more efficient handling of incoming merchandise. Here are several ways in which they have achieved this:

1. They have largely eliminated reserve stockroom space.
2. They have eliminated or reduced costly duplication in handling goods in the checking and marking processes.
3. Whenever possible, they place the goods on the selling floor immediately after removal from the delivery truck.

An important way to achieve efficiency in handling incoming merchandise is to place in the hands of one responsible employee all the activities involved in getting incoming goods ready for resale. This employee should have charge of the goods from the time the order is written by the buyer until the goods are placed in stock. In a large store this man may be called the *receiving manager* or *traffic manager,* and he may have a number of assistants to carry out the various functions involved. High school boys and girls often qualify as receiving clerks, checkers, and markers. These are good beginning retailing jobs for young persons, because they offer excellent opportunities to learn about merchandise and sources of supply.

THE RECEIVING POINT

Receiving—the activities involved in actually taking physical possession of the goods in the store—must be carried out quickly and smoothly. Every store or leased department should have a definite place where all merchandise is received, unpacked, checked, marked, and distributed. In some cases, merchandise needs no unpacking. Some efficiency-minded retailers ask manufacturers to leave ready-to-wear garments on racks instead of placing them in boxes or cartons. Certain transportation companies will then take charge of the merchandise at the point of origin, premark it, and deliver it directly to the retail selling floor on racks. No additional pressing or marking is necessary. Most goods, however, will be shipped in some kind of container and must be received at a definite location for unpacking and for the performance of the other activities involved in getting them onto the selling floor.

In many large stores the receiving point is a platform built as high as the tailgates of trucks. This arrangement facilitates the receiving process and prevents damage to merchandise in handling. Receiving platforms are equipped with bright lights, elevators, scales, forklift trucks, and hand trucks. Such platforms are usually situated near the area where the goods are to be checked and marked.

Sidewalk receiving points should be avoided if at all possible, and back doors should be properly protected. Packages should be moved inside the store quickly so that they will be safe from theft. Much merchandise shortage has been traced to loss at the receiving point, thus careful physical control is necessary. The fewer the number of points which a store authorizes as official receiving points, the more control the store has over its incoming merchandise.

Many stores receive at one or more warehouses or service buildings in addition to receiving at the store. Where there are several units of a chain or branch system in a community, a warehouse may be used as the central receiving point for all units. Merchandise is received, checked, marked and then distributed to each of the several stores. Merchandise received at a warehouse may be held there until sold and then shipped directly to customers. Customers may select a model or style of appliance, furniture, or lawn equipment from a display at the retail store. Delivery is then made from reserve stock at the warehouse.

RECEIVING RECORDS AND IDENTIFICATION

When goods arrive at the receiving point, the receiving process begins. A receiving clerk first examines the unopened boxes, packages, cartons, or containers very carefully. He should count the packages, inspect the condition of each, and note the number and condition of the packages on the deliveryman's receipt or book. After the delivery receipt has been signed by the proper individual, a copy should be kept in case of need to submit a claim for loss or damage. If the transportation charges have not been prepaid, they may be paid to the deliveryman by means of a voucher that can be cashed at the office, or they may be noted for future payment.

The receiving manager, or a subordinate, should check and audit transportation bills and make claims against transportation companies for overcharges on incoming collect shipments.

A record of the number of packages received, the date, the vendor's name, the method of shipment, the transportation charges, and other facts about the receipt of the goods should be entered in a *receiving book* or *receiving record*. This first record of an incoming shipment is very valuable. It is useful in determining whether goods have been received or not. It also serves as a check against the payment of invoices for which no merchandise has been received. The receiving record should be filled out by the same person who signs the deliveryman's receipt and should be filled out immediately so that the goods may be moved promptly to the checking area.

The receiving record used in many stores today is shown in Illus. 9-1. Sets of forms having three or four copies each are so arranged that only the top line of each set appears on a writing board. The line at the top is filled out, and the copies are then removed from the board and attached to one of the cartons comprising the shipment. Beneath these forms is a receiving sheet which remains on the board until some 25 receiving entries have been made. Of the sheets removed, the first is called the *apron* and is the one on which checkers may make additional notations and which is then attached to the invoice; the second is the *marker's record*; and the third is the *buyer's record*.

As soon as the shipment has been marked on the receiving record, it must be *identified*. This means that the receiving clerk must assign an official receiving number to the entire shipment and must then mark each package in the shipment. The set of three sheets discussed above is attached to one of the packages in the shipment. These copies accompany the shipment to the checking area where they are checked and completed. The clerk also writes on each carton with crayon or marking

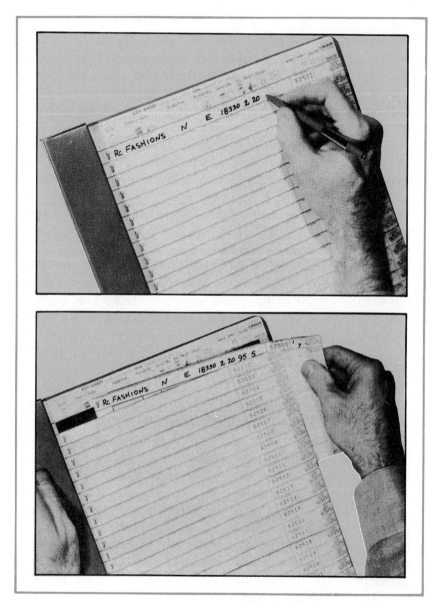

Courtesy of Key-Rec Systems, Division of
SCM Allied/Egry Business Systems

Illus. 9-1   Facts about the incoming shipment are recorded at the
receiving point—name of the shipper or vendor, shipping point, carrier's
name, carrier's number, number of cartons or packages received, weight
of the shipment, shipping charges, department number, and date of
receipt. The initials of the receiving clerk must also be included. The
form is then separated from the total assembly system and is attached
to one carton in the shipment.

Rec By	Shipper or Vendor	Shipped From	Received Via	Carrier's No	Pcs Rec	Weight	Charges		KEY-REC	Date Rec / Check-Out
Bc	FASHIONS	N	X	20017	3	92	1.62	5	26	1/18
Bc	SMITH BROS	N	X	13201	2	60	99	6	27	1/18
Bc	JONES INC	B	PRR	16-04	6	91	1.06	10	28	1/18
Bc	BROADWAY	N	E	36210	18	63	2.20	4	29	1/18
Bc	DOE DRESS	S	LTK	6102	8	161	2.03	5	30	1/18
Bc	SULTAN SHOE	S	MTK	5100	20	393	5.90	33	31	1/18
Bc	WHITE SHIRT	P	BO	51632	1	50	*1 carton SHORT*		32	1/18
Bc	NEW BLOUSE	N	NIT	2108	1/2	90	2.63	1	33	1/18
Bc	DAINTY DR	N	OP	31-626	1	53	1.46	5	34	1/18
Bc	KIDDYWEAR	LA	X	612-330	3	80	4.13	2	35	1/18
Bc	METRO	N	P		1	.62	5		36	1/18
Bc	REED INC	Smithtown	P		1	1.31	1		37	1/19
Bc	A+B	Tol	P		1	*shipment DAMAGED upon receipt*			38	1/19
Bc	REEVES	Hammond	P		1	1.21	1		39	1/19
Bc	VOGEL	N	X	321-190	2	70	2.15	9	40	1/19
Bc	BROWN HDW	CITY			1		DISPLAY		41	1/19
Bc	APEX COAL	CITY					EXP B		42	1/19
Bc	TALBOT STATY	CITY		1201	5		SUP 5		43	1/19
Bc	TYPE SERV	CITY			1		ADV 5		44	1/19
Bc	NRMA	N	X	162-103	1	10	PD	MR.VIP	45	1/19
Bc	UNITED MUS	SALEM O.	U+T	6101	5	156	PD	17	46	1/19
Bc	BRANCH SALE	SEATTLE	NO	4162	3	*carton SHORT from #51033 received the next day*			47	1/19
Bc	NEW BLOUSE	N	NIT	F/A2108	1/2	45	—	1	48	1/19
Bc	ALLIED/EGRY	DAYTON	Co	1250	10	200	3.20	REC 8	49	1/19
Bc	CANNON	KANN	PX	831056	19	800	10.51	21	51050	1/19

Courtesy of Key-Rec Systems, Division of
SCM Allied/Egry Business Systems

Illus. 9-2   This is a completed receiving sheet. Each line is identical to the top line of each of the 25 separate forms in the forms assembly on page 278. Diagonal lines have been drawn through the receiving numbers to flag shipments that were short or damaged on receipt and which must be followed up for claim filing.

pencil the receiving number assigned to the shipment, the number of the department for which the goods are intended, and the number of packages in the shipment. The numbering procedure helps get the shipment to the correct checking station and insures that all packages are on hand before the checking operation starts.

CHECKING YOUR KNOWLEDGE

Vocabulary

1. receiving manager, or traffic manager
2. receiving
3. receiving book, or receiving record
4. apron
5. marker's record
6. buyer's record
7. identified

Review Questions

1. Describe four steps that must be taken in order to prepare merchandise for sale to customers.
2. List three ways in which retailers have increased efficiency in handling incoming merchandise.
3. What is the first step to be taken when goods arrive at the receiving point?
4. List four items of information that must be placed in the receiving record.
5. What information should the receiving clerk write on each carton of a shipment?

Discussion Questions

1. What are the advantages of a centralized receiving system for a single store operation? What are the advantages for a multiple store operation?
2. What are the pros and cons of receiving merchandise centrally and then sending it to individual selling departments for checking and marking?
3. Why is it important to record where a shipment originated, the carrier, and the number of pieces in the shipment?

Part b

Checking Merchandise

The checking activity may be broken down into five steps: (1) matching the purchase order against the invoice; (2) opening the containers in which the goods have been shipped; (3) removing and sorting the merchandise; (4) checking the quantity of goods received against the amounts specified on the invoice; and (5) inspecting the goods for quality. These steps are carried out in different ways in different stores, but the basic aims of the checking activity are the same in all stores. The retailer must make certain that he is getting the goods in the quantity and quality he ordered; he must move the goods to the selling floor as quickly as possible; and he must keep the expenses of handling as low as possible.

What a Checker May Find Wrong in a Shipment

Breakage. Fragile merchandise which has been incorrectly wrapped may be found to be broken when the container is opened.

Damage. Rough handling in transportation may have caused damage to contents.

Shortage. Invoice or packing slip may call for a larger number than that received.

Overage. Invoice or packing slip may call for a smaller number than that received.

Substitution. Invoice or packing slip may call for a different style number, color, material, or size than that received.

Illus. 9-3   There may be something wrong with a merchandise shipment; therefore, each carton must be carefully checked.

LAYOUT OF RECEIVING AREA

The *receiving area* of a store is not the place at which the goods are received but rather the place in which the shipments are opened, checked, and marked. The size and arrangement of the receiving area will necessarily vary with the type of store, design of building, volume of goods to be handled, and the receiving system being used. The receiving area for many old stores has typically been one large room with stationary tables on which space is assigned to the different kinds of goods carried. Goods are laid out on the tables, counted, and marked with price tickets. They are then loaded on trucks and transported to the stockroom or the selling floor.

Today many large stores use two rooms, one for checking and one for marking. Portable double- and triple-decked tables are stationed first in the checking room. The goods are placed on the tables and counted, then the tables are wheeled to the marking room. After the price labels have been attached, the goods are wheeled either to the stockroom or to the selling floor. Although stationary tables require less space, portable tables eliminate the need to place goods on trucks after they have been marked in order to move them where they are needed. With portable tables, marking is done in a space free from the litter and dust of the checking room. The newest receiving room layouts have designs similar to assembly lines, and goods are moved by conveyors.

QUANTITY CHECK

Standard merchandise received in cartons containing a dozen, a half dozen, or a gross need not be opened for checking. There is usually enough information on the carton to make checking by number of cartons sufficient. If a shortage or a damaged item is found in a carton later when it is opened for marking, the manufacturer can usually be relied upon to make satisfactory adjustment. For most merchandise in which there are size, color, and style variations, it is necessary to open all containers and count the items. Every such shipment should be opened carefully so that the contents will not be damaged. The merchandise should be laid on the checking table in a systematic manner. All similar merchandise should be placed together in accordance with some classification such as size, color, or brand. This will help in counting the merchandise.

Direct-Check Method

With the neat stacks of merchandise before him, the checker is ready to count the quantities received. He may check the quantities against the invoice that was sent by the vendor of the goods or against a copy of the order. Checking goods against the invoice is more common than checking them against a copy of the order; but the use of the order copy makes it possible to check merchandise as soon as it is received, even though the invoice has not yet arrived. Checking goods against either the invoice or the order copy is called the *direct check*. When this method is used, the checker counts the quantity of each item received, lists these quantities on the *apron*—the first of the three copies sent with the shipment by the receiving clerk—then looks at the invoice or order to see if the amounts agree. If they do, the checker places a small check mark alongside the item on the invoice or order. If all the quantities, colors, sizes, and items are correct, the invoice or order is signed by the checker, or his signature may be placed on the apron, which is then attached to the invoice.

Blind-Check Method

The direct-check method is quick and inexpensive, but it is not always as accurate as it should be. After direct checking many shipments and finding them to be correct, the checker may come to believe that the goods received will always agree with the vendor's count or the order quantity; and he may therefore check the items without counting them carefully. To avoid this difficulty, a method known as the *blind check* is sometimes used. With this plan neither the invoice nor the order is given to the checker, but the checker is required to prepare a list of the contents of a shipment to be checked against the original invoice. The checker's list of what the shipment contains is

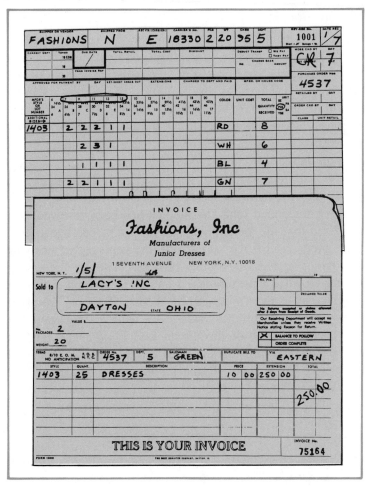

Illus. 9-4   The merchandise shipment—with the apron attached—
is opened in the checking section of the receiving room. The contents of
the shipment are then entered on the apron by the checker and are
checked against the invoice.

known as the *dummy invoice*. In some large stores the checker is provided with a copy of the invoice that is complete except for the quantities. It is then necessary for him to record only the quantities after his count is completed. The blind-check method provides an excellent invoice control because the original invoices are not scattered about the receiving room but are all kept in the office. This method is particularly useful for expensive items where a small error in checking would involve the loss of a large sum.

Choosing the Checking Method

The checking method which a store chooses usually depends upon whether the invoices arrive with the corresponding shipments, before the shipments have arrived, or after the shipments have arrived. When a store's shipments originate locally, invoices commonly accompany the goods; and the goods can be checked directly against them. If the invoice arrives before the shipment, it should be held in the receiving room office so that it is immediately available for a direct check when the corresponding shipment arrives.

If the invoice does not arrive with the goods or by mail before the shipment is received, there is always a question of whether the shipment should remain unopened until the invoice has been received. It should be remembered that the merchandise order was placed because the store needed the goods; and if the merchandise is kept in the receiving room until the invoice arrives, sales may be lost. Also, the receiving room may become crowded with unopened merchandise; and if the merchandise is perishable, the store may suffer a loss. To move goods through the receiving room and onto the sales floor as quickly as possible, some stores use a combination of the direct- and blind-check methods. All shipments are opened immediately after arrival and are checked against the invoice if it has arrived. If the invoice has not arrived, the clerk prepares a dummy invoice which takes the place of the regular invoice and is held in the office until the regular invoice arrives.

QUALITY CHECK

Many consumer goods must be checked for quality as they come into the store. Usually the buyer who ordered the goods or his trained assistant should examine the merchandise to see if it is of the quality expected. It is the duty of the person doing the quality check to verify that the styles and material are those selected, that the workmanship is satisfactory, and that the goods meet any other store standards that are to be maintained. Inspection of new styles of shopping goods is particularly important. Some stores have experts in fabrics who inspect all textile materials for quality and correctness of description.

Brand name and packaged goods such as shaving cream or canned goods usually need not be checked for quality. Periodic quality checking of privately branded goods from suppliers is, of course, important.

RETURNS AND CLAIMS AGAINST VENDORS

It is during the checking process that breakage, damage, shortage, overage, and substitution are discovered and adjusted. The checker must be alert to discover any irregularity in the shipment. If an irregularity is found, it should be noted on a *discrepancy report*. This report may then be used as the basis for a merchandise return or possibly for a claim against the shipper or transportation company.

The person who handles discrepancy reports and who packs and ships out returns must be skilled and very meticulous. A packing list, which is a copy of the return form, should be enclosed with the shipment; and an invoice should be sent separately by mail. Goods which have already been purchased by customers and which are being sent back for repair should be handled in much the same way; but these shipments should have special labels attached to them.

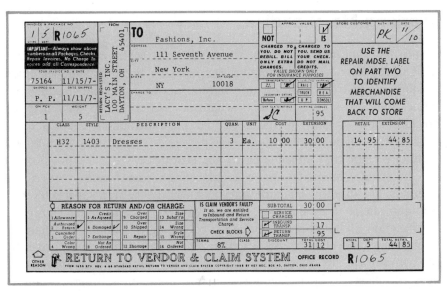

Courtesy of Key-Rec Systems, Division of
SCM Allied/Egry Business Systems

Illus. 9-5   Discrepancy report. When an error is found in an incoming shipment, a form like this is needed to communicate with the vendor. Try to determine the significance of each entry.

CHECKING YOUR KNOWLEDGE

Vocabulary

1. receiving area
2. direct check
3. blind check

4. dummy invoice
5. discrepancy report

Review Questions

1. List the five steps in the checking activity.
2. What activities take place in the receiving area of a store?
3. Explain the differences between a direct check and a blind check.
4. Describe the factors that influence the choice of checking method.
5. Who should be responsible for making the quality check of merchandise?

Discussion Questions

1. In what ways would the receiving area layout affect the efficiency of the checking process?
2. Is a quality check ever necessary for staple goods? Why or why not?
3. What qualifications should a person have in order to be a good merchandise checker?

Part C

Marking Merchandise

In planning her card, gift, and book shop Marilyn Marsh realized that there were two main reasons for marking her merchandise. First, customers must have certain information about each item, particularly price, but also size, color, and whatever else will help the customer decide to buy it. Second, she needs certain information to analyze her sales, such as merchandise classification, vendor's number, style number, date of receipt, and, in some cases, the cost price.

In some stores only price is placed on merchandise or on the merchandise display. Examples are packaged goods in a supermarket or shotgun shells in a sporting goods store. More and more, however, information in addition to price is becoming essential. Merchandise department and classification numbers make it possible to record sales and inventories by these store divisions and to determine profit and loss for each division. Vendor numbers assist in reordering and in periodically reviewing the desirability of repeat buying from various sources of supply. Style, color, and size data make unit control possible, and dates of purchase help in studying inventories so as to avoid an accumulation of old goods.

The process of stamping packaged goods or attaching tickets that contain such important information is called *marking*. This should not be confused with pricing the merchandise. Marking is merely a physical process that can be handled by junior workers—called markers—or by salespeople. Determining the retail prices to be placed on goods is a complex process that is based on many factors.

MARKING PROCEDURES

While the buyer is in the receiving room inspecting the merchandise shipment for quality, he may record on the invoice or attached apron the retail price of the goods. He may also indicate other information that he wants on the price tickets. Sometimes the retail price is placed on the duplicate of the purchase order by the buyer even before the goods are received. The goods can then be marked accordingly as soon as they are checked. Such advance marking from the purchase order is called *preretailing*. Preretailing saves time and speeds merchandise through the receiving and checking processes. Preretailing may even be done before the goods are shipped to the store. Some manufacturers receive tickets or price information from store buyers and attach tickets in advance of the shipment of goods, as you have already learned.

In a small store, marking the goods is a very simple process. The price is often written on the merchandise, or the merchandise is placed on a shelf or in a bin that has the price prominently displayed. This practice saves time and money but may not be helpful to customers unless carefully done.

In supermarkets and discount and other self-service stores, each individual item is usually marked. This is done so that neither the customer nor the cashier performing the checkout process will have doubts as to price.

PRICE TICKETS

Individual price tickets should be placed on most shopping goods, because the ticket is a direct aid to selling. It acts as a silent salesman and eliminates the possibility of misquoting prices. Customers like to see a price tag attached to articles because it gives them the assurance that the price is the same to everyone and that they are paying a price determined by the store owner or a store executive. Price tickets also can be the basis for a store's merchandise control procedures. The increasing use of computerized control systems encourages the use of price tickets on each item.

In large stores price tickets are often prepared in a central marking room separate from that in which the attaching of the tickets is done. The ticket markers are experts in preparing neat tickets with complete information and in the exact quantities called for on the marker's copy of the apron or on the invoice. When the attachers apply these tickets, they must be sure the quantities match. If they have too many tickets, it is clear that some of the shipment has failed to reach them. This procedure also acts as a check on the accuracy of the merchandise checkers.

Information Which May Be Found on a Price Ticket

Retail price

Unit price and quantity (on packaged goods)

Cost price in code

Season letter or date goods were received into stock

Date on which goods, if perishable, are to be removed from sale

Size and color

Kind of material

Style number

Manufacturer or vendor number

Department and classification

Illus. 9-6   A price ticket provides a great deal of information, but seldom is all the information given above placed on a single price ticket.

Kinds of Price Tickets

Many kinds of price tickets are used for marking merchandise. These tickets may be prepared by hand or by machine. Gummed labels and pin tickets are the most popular types because they are inexpensive and easy to attach. Gummed labels are usually used for items with a hard surface, such as books and appliances; pin tickets are usually used on merchandise which will not be damaged by pinholes, such as socks and underwear. String tags are commonly used for dresses and large articles. Another kind of price ticket is fastened onto items—particularly yard goods—by looping part of the goods into a slot on the ticket. Some tickets are punched with holes which can be read automatically by electronic equipment. Others have color bands that are also read electronically. For packaged goods, price tickets are often eliminated. Necessary data are stamped on the package.

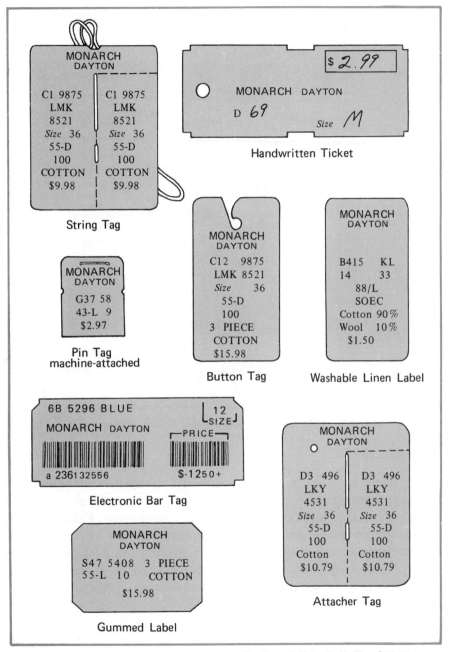

String Tag

MONARCH
DAYTON

Cl 9875   Cl 9875
LMK   LMK
8521   8521
Size 36   *Size* 36
55-D   55-D
100   100
COTTON   COTTON
$9.98 $9.98

Handwritten Ticket

MONARCH DAYTON

D 69   *Size* M

$2.99

Pin Tag
machine-attached

MONARCH
DAYTON

G37 58
43-L 9
$2.97

Button Tag

MONARCH
DAYTON

C12 9875
LMK 8521
Size   36
55-D
100
3 PIECE
COTTON
$15.98

Washable Linen Label

MONARCH
DAYTON

B415   KL
14   33
88/L
SOEC
Cotton 90%
Wool 10%
$1.50

Electronic Bar Tag

6B 5296 BLUE

MONARCH DAYTON

┌12
└SIZE┘

┌PRICE┐

a 236132556 $-1250+

Gummed Label

MONARCH
DAYTON

S47 5408 3 PIECE
55-L 10   COTTON
$15.98

Attacher Tag

MONARCH
DAYTON

D3 496   D3 496
LKY   LKY
4531   4531
Size 36   *Size* 36
55-D   55-D
100   100
Cotton   Cotton
$10.79 $10.79

Courtesy of Monarch Marking Systems
A Subsidiary of Pitney Bowes

Illus. 9-7   These are the most frequently used price tickets. For each type of ticket, name as many different merchandise items as you can on which you have seen that ticket.

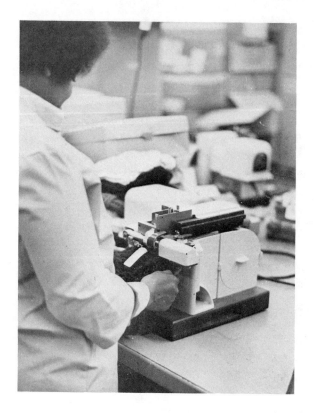

Courtesy of Federated Department Stores, Inc.

Illus. 9-8   This marker is applying pin tickets to winter caps.

Unit Pricing

In many localities packaged goods such as fresh meats, groceries, and detergents must be marked with the price of a pound, ounce, or other unit of measure, as well as with the selling price of the package. This is known as *unit pricing* and is required in order to make it easy for the customer to make valid price comparisons. For example, a small roast of chuck beef may contain 2.11 pounds and be priced at $2.43. It is important for the customer to know also the price of a pound. With unit pricing, this is shown as $1.15.

Cost Codes

If the store counts its stock at inventory time at cost rather than at retail price, it is necessary to show the cost of the article on the price tag. This cost price is almost always indicated in code. The average customer does not realize the retailer's heavy expenses of operation and will assume that the difference between the cost and the retail price is the retailer's profit. Some retailers use a word or phrase of ten letters, each of which represents a consecutive digit. For example:

$$\begin{array}{cccccccccc} M & A & K & E & & P & R & O & F & I & T \\ 1 & 2 & 3 & 4 & & 5 & 6 & 7 & 8 & 9 & 0 \end{array}$$

An article that costs $19.50 would be written **MIPT**. Other examples of word or phrase codes are: **MONEY TALKS** and **REPUBLICAN**. Another type of code is composed of symbols, one for each digit. Here is one:

$$\begin{array}{|c|c|c|} \hline 1 & 2 & 3 \\ \hline 4 & 5 & 6 \\ \hline 7 & 8 & 9 \\ \hline \end{array} \quad X = 0$$

The cost $19.50 is written ⌋⌈☐X . Another simple plan for coding is to place two meaningless figures or two digits of the year in front of the cost amount. Another figure, perhaps the month of the year, is placed after the cost amount. Omitting the decimal, a cost figure of $19.50 might be written 7419509.

Merchandise Dating

In addition to the cost and retail prices, stores often add the date when merchandise was received into stock or the last date on which it may be sold at the original price. *Code dating* is a system whereby a code letter or mark is used to indicate when the goods were processed or were brought into the store. *Open dating* is the system whereby the actual date is shown and made known to customers. For nonperishable goods a common code plan is to designate a six-month season by a letter and the month in the season by a number. Thus, *A* represents the spring and summer season of a specific year, such as 1974 (February through July). A *3* represents April. An item marked *A3* is one received in April, 1974.

For perishable goods the dating, commonly stamped by the supplier, may be the date of production or the last date that the goods should be sold to customers. The freshness period for milk, for example, might be set at seven days. Thus, milk cartons filled on November 2 would be marked *NOV 9*. This would indicate to the retailer and customer that the product should not be sold after November 9. Open-date marking for fresh meats and dairy products is mandatory today in many localities.

HAND AND MACHINE MARKING

An old practice, still in use in some small stores, is to write out all price tickets by hand. The practice often results in untidy price tickets and makes price changing easy. Some exclusive shops, however, adhere to the old handwritten tickets to avoid the impression that they have a number of identical articles.

Many stores use a machine in price marking, which aids in quantity control, since the marker cannot be one tag short or over. The information on the tag is the same for the entire quantity that is printed at one time. No item is forgotten and every line on the price tag is legible.

In supermarkets a rubber stamper is generally used for grocery items. The National Cash Register Company has developed a rubber price stamping set which requires inking only after several hundred impressions have been made.

RE-MARKING

All goods are not sold at the original price at which they were marked. Goods depreciate, mistakes are made in buying, goods go out of fashion, and it becomes necessary to mark them down. Occasionally goods increase in value while in stock and have to be marked up to a higher price than originally set. Re-marking may be done by making out a new ticket, or the price may be changed on the old one. In order

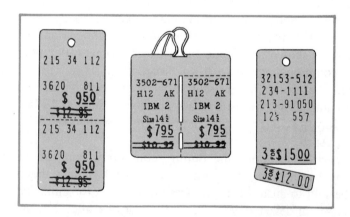

Courtesy of Monarch Marking Systems
A Subsidiary of Pitney Bowes

Illus. 9-9   A machine is available that cuts off old prices and prints new prices in matching type when merchandise is upgraded or the price reduced.

to get an accurate inventory, careful records of the price changes should be kept. Large stores have realized the importance of price re-marking and have established elaborate control systems for it.

CHECKING YOUR KNOWLEDGE

Vocabulary

1. marking
2. preretailing
3. unit pricing

4. code dating
5. open dating

Review Questions

1. What information may be found on a price ticket?
2. Why should every item of merchandise in self-service type stores be marked with a price?
3. Identify various kinds of price tickets and indicate the kinds of merchandise on which each is used.
4. Give an example of a letter cost code and a symbolic cost code.
5. Give three reasons why it may be necessary to re-mark goods.

Discussion Questions

1. Should producers of perishable goods such as bread and milk be required to place date of production or last date of sale on each container or package?
2. When goods are being re-marked, is it best to (a) cross off the original price on the tag and write in the new price, (b) attach a new tag bearing the new price, or (c) put up a sign indicating the reduced price and keep a count of the number of articles sold at the reduced price? Defend your answer.
3. Would a retailer from a variety store have different views on what information should appear on price tickets than say a retailer from a furniture store? If so, why?

Part d

Storing and Arranging Merchandise

Goods which customers cannot see are goods they cannot buy and *all space in a store costs money*—these two points were foremost in Pat Baxter's mind as he examined the procedures used in handling incoming merchandise at the Adobe Shop. Prior to his ownership, 10 percent of the main floor space was used for storage of *reserve stock* (merchandise held or stored off the selling floor and used to replace goods that are sold from the selling floor). Pat believed that much of this area could be remodeled into selling space. The Adobe Shop situation would, of course, not be true for all stores.

When it is possible to reorder at frequent intervals and in small quantities for immediate sale, there is no need for a reserve stockroom. However, in many lines it is economical to buy at one time more merchandise than can be stored in expensive selling space; and a reserve stockroom becomes necessary. It is also necessary where merchandise that is infrequently sold must be available. The small retailer may use a basement or back room as his reserve stockroom and operate satisfactorily with minimum storage space by reordering frequently and in small lots from a local wholesaler. On the other hand, the large store which handles bulky merchandise often requires a separate storage warehouse. Only samples are kept in the store, and customer orders are filled directly from the warehouse. Arrangements are sometimes made with manufacturers so that the manufacturer will fill orders for the store's customers and ship the goods directly to the customers. This procedure is called *drop-shipping* and eliminates the need for a store to maintain a reserve stock.

LAYOUT OF RESERVE STOCK

The layout of merchandise in the reserve stock should be similar to the way the goods are arranged on the selling floor. Thus, if goods on the selling floor are arranged by size and color in each classification, the reserve stock should be arranged in the same manner. Access from the receiving area to the reserve stock area should be achieved without passing through much of the selling area. One store in New York City, Lord & Taylor, has solved the storage problem by an unusual arrangement: The main floor reserves for each department are located under the selling departments. There is a space between the floors, with a short flight of eight steps connecting the two floors.

Because of the high value of space in the selling departments, it may be necessary to have reserves located on upper floors or in basements. Quick access to reserves may be assured by chutes or small service elevators. Telephone or intercom connections between selling floors and remote reserve areas are important so that a salesperson can get in touch with a stockroom clerk while a customer is waiting for information.

Usually the *forward stock* (stock in selling area) space should be adequate to house at least a few days' supply. Once each day, however, the forward stock should be checked carefully to determine which items need replenishing. A list of needed items may be made and sent to the reserve area so that the forward stock can be replenished by the next morning. The reserve requisition lists may also be used to maintain inventory control records for analysis purposes, since goods are ordered from the reserve only because sales have depleted forward stock. A record of the reserve requisitions thus gives a close approximation of actual sales.

Some supermarkets have reserve stockrooms in which merchandise received from the warehouse is stored before it is taken to the selling shelves. The reserve is usually arranged on the same plan as that used for forward stock. For example, if canned fruits are displayed on shelves next to canned vegetables in the store, the same arrangement is used in the reserve. Thus, in reordering it is easy for the grocery department manager to check his stock both in the store and in the reserve.

Supermarkets and discount stores attempt to reduce their storage space by stocking large amounts of merchandise directly on the selling floor and in the drawers of display fixtures. Certain sections of the

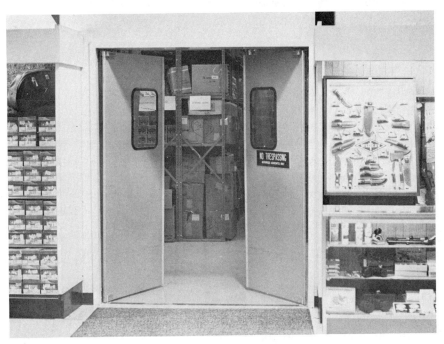

Courtesy of Federated Department Stores, Inc.

Illus. 9-10   This reserve stockroom is equipped with wide double doors that provide easy access to the selling area.

selling area are assigned to cashiers and wrappers or to selling personnel who have the responsibility of keeping their assigned sections bursting with merchandise for the peak selling periods. At slow times during the day and before or after business hours, they are at work restocking, marking, attaching price tags, and setting up merchandise displays.

Some retailers claim that eliminating the reserve stockroom helps in taking inventory, speeds the flow of goods to the selling shelves, reduces expenses, increases selling space, and permits visual control of stock. These merchants often ask the vendor to premark or preticket the merchandise.

ARRANGING GOODS IN STOCK

After goods arrive on the selling floor—whether directly from the carrier, from the central marking room, or from the reserve stockroom —they must be carefully arranged in stock. Proper arrangement of stock accomplishes three things: (1) it aids in the sale of the goods; (2) it allows the new salesperson, and also the customer, to learn the location of stock and to obtain the required goods quickly; and (3) it facilitates the control of stock. Merchandise should be arranged with these three goals in mind.

Arranging Goods to Aid in Selling

All items that a customer may want to inspect should be displayed close together. These items should be placed where the customer can easily see them and handle them if desired. They should be attractively arranged and well lighted. Fast-selling goods, in continued demand and not bought on impulse, should be placed so as to draw the customer's attention to other merchandise. Impulse goods should be placed along the main lines of traffic. Profitable goods—those on which the markup is high—should generally be displayed in a conspicuous place. From time to time the stock arrangement of fashion merchandise should be shifted so that the department may give new interest to regular customers.

In order to have fresh goods for the customer, it is necessary that old goods be sold first. This is brought about by placing new goods behind or beneath old goods on the shelf. If new goods are placed directly in front of or on top of the goods already there, the danger of accumulating old, shopworn, spoiled, or otherwise unsalable merchandise is greatly increased. So important is this principle—particularly for food, drug, and fashion items—that supervisors of chain stores in these lines almost always check the rotation of stock when visiting their stores. In fact, some manufacturers of such items as cookies, candies, cigarettes, spaghetti, and baby foods instruct their sales representatives to check the rotation of their goods when they visit the stores. As already explained, these manufacturers have placed a code on their goods so that the person checking the rotation can tell at a glance when the goods were shipped from the factory. The representatives are instructed to remove from display any merchandise which has remained unsold for a certain length of time and to replace it with fresh stock.

Arranging Goods to Aid New Salespeople

The arrangement of stock should be logical and simple so that a new salesperson may learn it in a minimum of time. In a shoe store, for instance, one wall may be devoted to women's shoes; the opposite wall to men's shoes; and the back wall to children's shoes. Each wall is then divided into three sections: the first for black shoes, the second for brown, and the third section for high colors.

This arrangement can easily be explained to a new salesperson so that if he is asked for a man's brown calf shoe, he can go immediately to the proper section of the store and there look for a suitable style in the correct size. From the salesperson's viewpoint, this arrangement is logical and simple for him to learn. If the stock within each section is arranged in such a manner that it is convenient for the salesperson to handle and keep it in order, the arrangement will have met all the requirements necessary for the salesperson's need.

Arranging Goods to Facilitate Stock Control

Stock should be arranged so that it can be easily replenished and counted. Visible dividers should be used where possible. Dark bins and corners where goods may be overlooked should be avoided. The arrangement should be flexible enough to allow for the introduction of new style numbers easily. If an item shows an increasing rate of sale, a good arrangement should make it easy to expand the space given to it in proportion to its rate of sale.

Every item that the store has for sale should normally have a place set aside for it in forward stock. If the space in forward stock is limited, fast-selling goods should be given priority on selling space. Slow-selling items may have only a single item displayed, but there should be a clearly visible sign that additional items are available in reserve stock.

INVOICE CONTROL

Paralleling the flow of merchandise from the receiving point to the selling floor is the flow of the vendor's invoice from the point of receipt—either the receiving point or the mail room—to the office for payment. Just as the merchandise must be controlled to avoid loss or delay, so must the invoice be controlled to insure accuracy and speed in order that cash discounts may be obtained and the correct charges made on the purchase records of the various departments. The procedure followed by a store to keep track of the invoice in process is called *invoice control.*

Invoice control begins by checking the invoice against the buyer's purchase order. The invoice is next checked against the appropriate receiving record, and the apron is attached to the invoice. Then the invoice is checked against the actual goods in the shipment. After these checks have been made, the buyer enters on the invoice the retail price of each item and approves the invoice for payment. If markers use the invoice to prepare price tickets they should, when finished, send the invoice on to the office for payment.

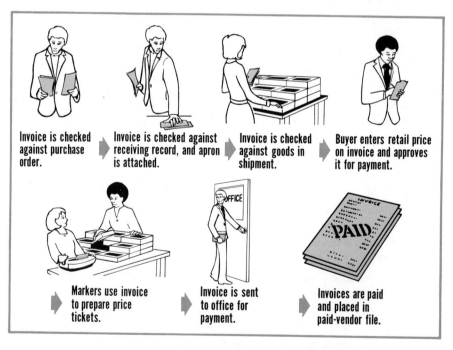

Invoice is checked against purchase order.

Invoice is checked against receiving record, and apron is attached.

Invoice is checked against goods in shipment.

Buyer enters retail price on invoice and approves it for payment.

Markers use invoice to prepare price tickets.

Invoice is sent to office for payment.

Invoices are paid and placed in paid-vendor file.

Illus. 9-11 The flow of the invoice from the receiving point to the office is carefully controlled. Persons involved in the receiving, checking, and marking procedures should be able to account for the invoice at all times.

In the office, payment vouchers are prepared, invoices are charged against the departmental purchase records, and the invoices are filed in a paid-vendor file. An important part of the invoice control process is that every person who handles the invoice—order clerk, checker, buyer, marker, receiving manager—is required to initial it. Thus, the office knows whether or not an invoice has passed through every necessary step.

Although the invoice must go through the same steps in a small store as it goes through in a large one, the small store's procedures seem much simpler because one man usually performs all the steps. When the invoice is received, it is checked against the purchase order and the goods. The retail price may or may not be placed on the invoice, depending upon the size of the store, the size of the order, and the store's procedures in pricing and marking goods. Finally, the invoice is placed in a file for payment.

CHECKING YOUR KNOWLEDGE

Vocabulary

1. reserve stock
2. drop-shipping
3. forward stock
4. invoice control

Review Questions

1. What are some of the different approaches to arrangement of reserve stock?
2. List three things that are accomplished by proper arrangement of stock on the selling floor.
3. Why is it necessary to stock goods so old merchandise will be sold first?
4. How does good stock arrangement aid in merchandise control?
5. Outline the steps in the invoice flow from receipt to payment.

Discussion Questions

1. Under what types of stores, merchandise, or conditions might it be possible to eliminate reserve stock?
2. Where reserve stock is necessary, what can be done to assure that salespeople and customers are aware of additional items?
3. Many customers are aware that the most recently received lot of reordered merchandise is stocked to the rear of a shelf or at the bottom of a display. Should salespeople insist that customers take merchandise only from the front or top of an arrangement?

Part **e**

Mechanization

The volume of merchandise to be moved in the modern retail store means that efficiency and speed in handling are essential. Supermarkets receiving tons of goods every week and department stores obtaining several hundred thousands of dollars worth of goods weekly need efficiency in handling goods or they will be unable to operate properly. Efficiency in the process of getting goods from the receiving point or warehouse to the proper selling areas is necessary for a profitable retail operation. Modern mechanized material handling systems, either in the store or in the warehouse, are frequently found in retailing today.

MECHANIZING THE RECEIVING PROCESS

Some large retail chains have equipped the receiving points in their warehouses with facilities for accommodating freight cars as well as trucks. Goods are removed from these carriers and into and out of stock by *forklift trucks*. Forklift trucks have lifts designed to slip under merchandise and then raise it, often as much as two tons, to heights of nine feet or more. The trucks can carry merchandise from the receiv-

Courtesy of Copps

Illus. 9-12   Forklift trucks have lifts designed to slip under merchandise and then raise it to heights of nine feet or more.

ing point to wherever it should be stored. The merchandise is then placed on boxed or flat wooden pallets for removal to the checking and marking areas. If the incoming merchandise is soft goods or if the shipment consists of only a few cartons, the forklift truck may be unnecessary. Merchandise may be moved by a roller conveyor system. *Roller conveyors* have small rollers or wheels built into a ladder type frame. These conveyors may be portable or permanently built into the receiving area. Boxes can be placed on the conveyor and, because of the rollers or wheels, easily pushed along to a desired location. A portable conveyor may be placed on the tailgate or side door of a truck and connected to a permanent roller conveyor system that extends into the checking and marking area.

In the newest stores the entire process of handling incoming merchandise is mechanized and is similar in operation to factory assembly lines. Packages move from the receiving point to checking stations on mechanical conveyors. The goods are unpacked and placed in large wooden trays, checked, and then moved along the conveyor to a separate marking section. Switches off the main track make it possible to move the goods to any desired point in the marking section. Conveyors also carry the goods to storage areas located as closely as possible to the selling floor. Overhead conveyors can carry hanging items—garments not stored in boxes—from the receiving point through checking and marking to storage or the selling floor.

MECHANIZING THE CHECKING AND MARKING PROCESSES

The use of conveyor belts and chutes to transport merchandise from the receiving point to the checking and marking areas was discussed earlier in the chapter. The efficiency of this operation depends largely upon the layout of the checking and marking rooms. Portable tables used in the checking and marking operations have been greatly improved. They are made of lightweight aluminum so that more merchandise can be moved in one trip. Improved machines for printing, counting, and attaching price tickets are also in general use.

To facilitate the checking of goods into supermarkets, a mechanical counter or tabulator is sometimes attached to the roller conveyor. As the cartons roll down this conveyor from the carrier, they trip a hammer which counts the number of cartons. At the same time a clerk checks off the kind of merchandise in the cartons. The total indicated on the tabulator must agree with the number charged to the store by the warehouse, or the shipment will be either short or over. The clerk also provides a check on this number since he has counted the cartons by the

Courtesy of Federated Department Stores, Inc.

Illus. 9-13   Conveyors may be portable or permanently built into the receiving areas. Boxes can be placed on the conveyor and be easily pushed to a desired location.

kind of merchandise in each carton. It is important that warehouse requisitions or purchase orders be on hand, or the system may not work properly.

MECHANIZING STORAGE

To lower storage costs and to keep merchandise protected from losses due to deterioration, spoilage, and breakage, many retailers have mechanized and modernized their storing processes. In grocery warehouses, for instance, each item is stored in its own individual space in a metal or wooden bin or on a pallet that can be moved by forklift trucks. In the large bins the small items are segregated by means of movable dividers. Further improvements that have reduced losses in certain departments are air conditioning, dehumidification, refrigeration, and automatic temperature control.

In some retailing storerooms the ready-to-wear items are stored in boxes according to the code and serial number of the goods. For the items that require hanging while in storage, there is a mechanical hanger dispenser which supplies hangers to the person storing the garments.

Courtesy of Federated Department Stores, Inc.

Illus. 9-14   Hanging garments—items not stored in boxes—are stored on overhead racks in the receiving area until they are needed on the selling floor.

ELECTRONIC EQUIPMENT

With the continued refinement of electronic methods to handle numerous aspects of the merchandise flow, more and more retailers are establishing push button systems. In operation is a warehouse where a customer's order is assembled automatically from the storage shelves, packed and wrapped, ready for delivery to the customer's car or truck. Other stores, which are part of a chain, are using electronic locators. When a customer asks for an item not in stock in one store, the electronic locators find the requested merchandise in another store and direct the shipment to the customer.

Retailing has clearly entered the era of applied electronics. Much of the processing of merchandise from suppliers to ultimate consumer is done by automated electronically controlled equipment. As procedures can be standardized the ordering, invoicing, receiving, and movement of goods to customers becomes more efficient. Machines can do much of the repetitive jobs more cheaply than can people. People can be freed for supervision and more complex or varied tasks.

MATERIAL HANDLING SAFETY

With the increased use of mechanical equipment in handling merchandise there is increased need for safety awareness on the part of all workers. Accidental injuries in the material handling process usually occur when persons are careless or are exposed to mechanical or physical hazards. Most stores have safety guides for their receiving and marking operations. The new employee should be sure to study these guides carefully.

Workers who receive and open merchandise containers may find it beneficial to wear gloves and protective aprons. Particular care should be taken when using carton-opening knives, removing metal-restraining bands from boxes, and in handling boxes with opened staples. When cartons containing glass items are emptied each item must be unwrapped with care in case of breakage. Proper techniques must be used in lifting and carrying heavy boxes to avoid back strain or injury.

CHECKING YOUR KNOWLEDGE

Vocabulary

1. forklift trucks   **2.** roller conveyors

Review Questions

1. In what ways has the receiving process in retail stores been mechanized?
2. How is the mechanical counter used in receiving by supermarkets?
3. What have some retailers done to protect merchandise while it is in storage?
4. How may electronic equipment help in the movement of goods in stores?
5. What is the purpose of an electronic locator?

Discussion Questions

1. What effect should the use of mechanical and electronic merchandise handling systems have on retail costs?
2. What aspects of handling incoming merchandise have the greatest potential for mechanization? Explain your answer.
3. With continued advancement in electronic materials handling, it may be possible to operate a store with only sample items on the selling floor. What might be customer reaction to this type of merchandising?

BUILDING YOUR SKILLS

Improving Communication Skills

In each of the following sentences there is a word or group of words that is frequently carelessly pronounced. On a separate sheet of paper, write each sentence with the correct words that should be used.

1. Wanna go to lunch now?
2. Gimme the tickets fur this box.
3. Doncha know where da gloves go?
4. Hey Bill, commere will ya?
5. We hafta get this cart to fourth floor.
6. I coulduv marked that shipment in an hour.
7. Woncha go to the game wid us?
8. I dunno what happened to that cart.
9. Tell Marge I'm gonna leave at noon.
10. Hooja say called?

Improving Arithmetic Skills

Calculate the percentages in the exercises that follow.

1. Merle opened and checked a shipment of china figurines. The shipment contained 6 dozen items. Merle found that 8 figurines had been damaged in transit. What percentage of the total shipment had been damaged?
2. During the month of April, Bloom's Style Shop received 450 dresses from suppliers. Of this number 17 dresses were returned because of wrong sizes, and 16 were returned because of faulty construction. Of the total number of dresses received what percentage was returned?
3. If a pin ticket machine operator can attach 270 tickets an hour, what percentage of a shipment of 90 dozen pairs of men's socks can she do in an hour?
4. Kent marked and put in stock 7 cases of breakfast cereal. Each case had 48 boxes. Kent found 5 boxes that had been damaged. What percentage of the total had been damaged?
5. How many square meters of carpeting would be needed to cover the floor of a room measuring 9 by 12 feet? (See Appendix on page 622.)

Improving Research Skills

1. Prepare a cost code made of a word or slogan of ten letters. Show how each of the following prices should be written with your code: $7.95, $15.00, $.60, $8.50, $40.00.
2. Each committee from your class should obtain price tickets or tags for the following items: man's suit or sportcoat, woman's dress, blanket or bed sheets, pair of gloves or hosiery, an appliance or furniture. Each committee will report to the class on the information contained on the various price tags collected or observed.
3. (a) The following types of price tickets, illustrated in Part C, are frequently used in retail stores: gummed label, string ticket, pin ticket, and machine readable ticket. Determine which stores in

your community use each type of ticket and on which kinds of merchandise.

(b) For what packaged goods are prices and related information stamped directly on the package? Compare with the use of gummed labels.

Improving Decision-Making Skills

1. A variety store has one main selling floor with a full basement for checking, marking, and storage. Receiving is done at a dock at the rear of the building. The store has nine employees—the owner, four cashiers, three stock-salespeople, and an office worker. Incoming goods are received and prepared for selling in a haphazard fashion. The owner cannot afford to hire more help, but he wishes to organize the handling of incoming merchandise into a more efficient operation. Outline the duties that he should assign to the different members of the staff.

2. Babinski's is a department-store operation consisting of the parent store and three branch stores in the city of Oaktown. Two of the branch stores are nearly as large as the parent store and together exceed the downtown store's sales volume. All receiving for these stores is done in a basement area of the parent store. Goods are then sent to the branches. Buyers operate out of the parent store but have no responsibility for supervision of the selling departments for which they buy. A problem has emerged as the four-store operation has grown. Merchandise that is received takes as long as five or six days to reach the selling area of the parent store, and branch stores may not get goods for ten days after arrival in the main store. What additional facts would you need in order to assess the merchandise flow problems of this department-store operation?

APPLYING YOUR KNOWLEDGE

Chapter Project

Organize your class into several committees. Have at least one committee visit a large retail store, a medium-size retail store, and a small retail store in your community. Each committee should observe the receiving, checking, and marking operations of the store. Each committee should then report back to the entire class on where receiving points and receiving areas are located, how they are laid out, and the procedures used by the store.

Continuing Project

Perform the following activities in the next section of your manual:

1. Outline the procedures for receiving, checking, marking, storing, and arranging stock that you will use in your store.

2. List the steps of invoice control from receipt of the invoice to payment.

3. Explain at least five policies that you will follow in preparing goods for selling.

chapter 10

Pricing Decisions

CHAPTER PREVIEW

a. Markup, the difference between retail and cost, may be expressed in actual dollars or as a percentage of retail price or as a percentage of cost price. Most merchants think of markup in terms of the percentage of the retail selling price.

b. Markdowns are the most common form of price reductions. Markdowns are taken in order to offer goods that are not selling adequately at prices that will encourage customers to buy.

c. The retailer must adopt a pricing policy that overall will provide a markup that will cover expenses and return a profit. The nature of a store's customers and of its competition has an important influence on pricing.

d. Items are sometimes priced below their most profitable point in order to attract customers to the store. Leaders, loss leaders, and premiums are all means to making a price appeal to customers.

e. The buying and pricing functions must be carefully organized in stores of every size. In large stores, these functions are performed by specialists.

Part a

Markup

The establishment of an appropriate retail price on merchandise is necessary if the retailer is to cover his expenses and earn a profit. The retail price must also be one that is attractive to customers and one at which they will buy the merchandise readily. The amount that a merchant adds to the cost price of merchandise in arriving at the retail price is called *markup*. Suppose a retailer buys a belt for $3.50 and sells it for $5.00. The $1.50 that the retailer adds to the cost price is the markup on the belt.

THE MARKUP EQUATION

Most merchants think of markup in terms of a percentage rather than a dollar-and-cents figure. With a percentage, it is easy to make a comparison of markups even though the prices on various items may be different. Once the dollar amount of markup is known, it is simple to convert this figure to a percentage. Markup may be expressed either as a percentage of retail price or as a percentage of cost price. If markup is to be expressed as a percentage of retail, it may be calculated by using this formula:

$$\text{Markup Percentage} = \frac{\text{Markup in Dollars}}{\text{Retail Price}}$$

Suppose that a merchant buys a pair of shoes for $9 and plans to sell them for $15. His markup is $6, and the markup percentage is 40 percent.

If markup is to be expressed as a percentage of cost, it may be calculated by using this formula:

$$\text{Markup Percentage} = \frac{\text{Markup in Dollars}}{\text{Cost Price}}$$

In the above example, the markup on the shoes—expressed as a percentage of cost—is 66⅔ percent. Note that although the percentages differ, the amount of markup in dollars and cents is the same. For any particular item, the *amount* of markup stated on a cost basis is the same as the *amount* of markup stated on a retail basis. Most merchants prefer to treat markups as a percentage of retail, and in this book markup percentages are always expressed on the retail basis.

The Markup Equation

Cost + Markup = Retail   Also,   C = R − M and

C   +   M   =   R   M = R − C

Illus. 10-1   These equations express the relationship of cost price, amount of markup, and retail price.

INITIAL AND MAINTAINED MARKUPS

Two kinds of markups are commonly used in retailing—the initial markup and the maintained markup. Let us suppose that a woman's scarf costs a retailer $3 and is priced to sell at $5. The $5 price is called the *original retail selling price*. Later the scarf may be reduced in price to $3.95, and finally sold at that price. The $3.95 price is called the *final sales price*. The difference between the cost price and the original retail price is called the *initial markup*; sometimes it is also called *markon*. The difference between the cost price and final sales price is the *maintained markup*. Some stores use the terms *maintained markup* and *gross margin* interchangeably. In the preceeding example, if the scarf had been sold at the original sales price of $5, the initial markup and the maintained markup on this scarf would have been the same. The maintained markup must be high enough to pay expenses and to provide a profit. The initial markup must be higher to provide also for any necessary price reductions.

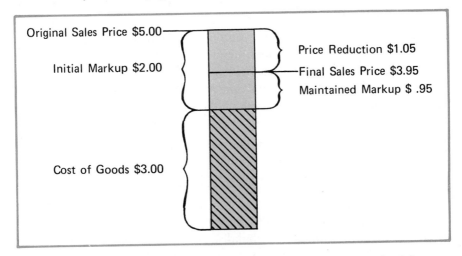

Illus. 10-2   The structure of initial markup is shown on the left. On the right is the structure of maintained markup.

Initial markups vary with the nature of the merchandise stocked and the type of store. Specialty goods often have initial markups of 50 percent or more. This is necessary because some goods in an assortment must usually be marked down to sell. With appliances, which are standardized goods, initial markups may be as low as 25 percent. A grocer may be able to realize little more than a 20 percent initial markup on canned goods because of the keen competition on such items. With meats, which involve greater handling and selling expense, he may set an initial markup of 25 percent. When there is a chance of spoilage in addition to high handling and selling costs—such as with fresh produce—the initial markup might be closer to 35 percent. And on gourmet items the initial markup might exceed 50 percent.

Stores that depend primarily on low prices to attract customers must set lower initial markups than stores that attract customers with emphasis on convenience, service, or exclusiveness. The hardware store in a shopping center might have a markup of only 25 percent on electrical fuses; but the neighborhood hardware store, because it offers convenience to the customer with an immediate need, will be able to sell fuses at an initial markup of 35 or 40 percent.

USING MARKUP IN BUYING FOR RESALE

If a retailer knows the markup percentage that he wishes to achieve, he can use this knowledge in buying merchandise for resale. He can use it, for example, in determining whether he is being offered a reasonable price for an item. A buyer may know that he wants to sell a pair of shoes for $20 and knows that he must have a 40 percent markup to meet expenses and have a reasonable profit. To calculate the price that he should pay for each pair of shoes, he first establishes that the retail price is the base upon which all other figures are reckoned and thus represents 100 percent. The cost price equals the retail price minus markup. In this case, the cost price is 60 percent of the retail price. So, the most the buyer can afford to pay for a pair of the shoes is 60 percent of the retail price, or $12. The formula for calculating the cost price when the retail price and desired markup are known is:

$$\text{Cost Price} = \text{Retail Price} \times (100\% - \text{Markup \%})$$

Since a supplier quotes prices on a wholesale basis, the buyer must translate these prices into retail prices to know whether he is getting a good buy and whether the merchandise will fit into his price lines. Suppose that a buyer is offered an article for $2.40 and he knows that he must have a 40 percent markup. As you have already learned, the retail price is 100 percent; and the cost price represents the retail price minus the markup percentage. If 60 percent multiplied by the retail price is $2.40, it follows that the retail price is equal to $2.40 divided by 60 percent. The retail price of the article should be $4.00. The formula for calculating the retail price when the cost price and desired markup are known is:

$$\text{Retail Price} = \frac{\text{Cost Price}}{100\% - \text{Markup } \%}$$

PLANNING MARKUPS

To plan markup, the retailer must estimate the following figures:

1. Total sales for the coming year or season
2. Expenses for that period
3. Price reductions (markdowns, shortages, employee discounts, etc.)
4. Profit goal for the period

He can calculate the correct initial markup by inserting the estimated figures into this formula:

$$\text{Initial Markup} = \frac{\text{Expenses} + \text{Profits} + \text{Price Reductions}}{\text{Sales} + \text{Price Reductions}}.$$

Suppose that a retailer estimates annual sales at $100,000, expenses at $30,000, and price reductions at $10,000, and he wishes a profit goal of $5,000. The formula would then read:

$$\text{Initial Markup} = \frac{\$30,000 + \$5,000 + \$10,000}{\$100,000 + \$10,000} = \frac{\$45,000}{\$110,000} = 40.9\%$$

The dollar markup the retailer must have is the total of the expenses, profits, and reductions—$45,000. The estimated sales of $100,000 is the expected result after the reductions have been made. Thus, the estimated reductions of $10,000 must be added to the sales ($100,000) to find the total retail at which the goods must first be put into stock ($110,000). Finally, $45,000 is divided by $110,000 to determine the markup as a percentage of the retail price. This retailer must have an initial markup of 40.9 percent.

This formula helps a merchant to determine what percentage of markup he must realize if he is to cover all expenses and price reductions and still make a profit. It does not follow, however, that he will always aim at this markup for his store or that he will attempt to realize this markup on each purchase. In practice, it is seldom that the formula for finding the initial markup percentage determines the price at which any specific item will be sold; but the formula does provide a useful guide in showing—on the average—what markup is necessary to realize a predetermined profit goal.

There are many national name brand articles over which the retailer has virtually no control of the retail price. These are *fair-traded* items where, by contract, the manufacturer or wholesaler sets the minimum price at which the goods may be resold to consumers. The minimum price tends to become the established price. Accordingly, the retailer must manipulate the prices of nonprice fixed goods in order to achieve a desired markup.

CHECKING YOUR KNOWLEDGE

Volcabulary

1. markup
2. original retail selling price
3. final sales price
4. initial markup

5. markon
6. maintained markup
7. gross margin
8. fair trade

Review Questions

1. What considerations enter into the establishment of a retail price?
2. Why do most merchants think of markup in terms of percentage rather than in actual dollars?
3. Give the formula for finding (a) markup expressed as a percentage of retail, (b) markup expressed as a percentage of cost, (c) cost price when the retail price and desired markup percentage are known, (d) retail price when the cost price and desired markup percentage are known, (e) initial markup percentage.
4. What is the difference between initial markup and maintained markup?
5. What four figures must be estimated before the retailer can plan a satisfactory markup?

Discussion Questions

1. If two merchants located in the same shopping center were selling identical articles, would it be reasonable to assume that they also were using the same percentage markup? Why or why not?
2. What are the advantages and disadvantages of calculating markup as a percentage of retail? What would be the advantages of calculating markup as a percentage of cost?
3. Should a store have a policy of taking approximately the same markup percentage on all kinds of merchandise? What would be the advantages and disadvantages of such a practice?

Part b

Markdowns

"Yost's Annual Half-Price Sale," "Buy Three and Get the Fourth One Free," "Fifteen Percent Off for Employees," "Ten Percent Off for Students," "One Fourth Off for Three Days Only"—these are all examples of reductions from the original selling price. *Price reductions* generally include markdowns, employee and customer discounts, and inventory shortages. Markdowns typically account for the greater part of price reductions. A price reduction of an item of merchandise from a former retail price to a lower asking price, except for discounts on special goods, is called a *markdown*. Properly taken, markdowns are an effective means of adjusting stocks to customer demand, competition, and market conditions.

CALCULATION OF MARKDOWNS

When retailers advertise markdowns to customers, the reductions are stated most often as a percentage off the original retail price. For their own use, however, merchants express markdowns as a percentage of the final sales price of all goods sold during a period—a month, a quarter, or a year.

The markdown percentage is calculated by using this formula:

$$\text{Markdown Percentage} = \frac{\text{Dollar Markdowns}}{\text{Total Sales}}$$

For example, if 10 items originally priced at $5 each are marked down to $3.95 each, the markdown is $10.50. If the total sales during the period are $100, including the sales of the marked-down goods, the markdown is 10.5 percent of the total sales.

REASONS FOR MARKDOWNS

The reasons for markdowns may be classified under two major heads: first, to reduce prices on merchandise that the customers are not buying at the expected quantity or rate of sale; and, second, to stimulate the sale of the item reduced or of other regularly priced goods during the special sale. Probably most markdowns are caused by errors made in merchandise selection (buying), in initial pricing, and in selling techniques. But many markdowns are taken for policy reasons, such as a sales promotion device.

Mathematics of Pricing		
GIVEN	TO FIND	PROCEDURE
Cost price, retail price	Markup in dollars	Subtract cost from retail
Markup in dollars, retail price	Cost price	Subtract markup from retail
Markup in dollars, cost price	Retail price	Add cost and markup
Retail price, markup in dollars	Markup percentage (retail)	Divide markup by retail
Cost price, markup in dollars	Markup percentage (cost)	Divide markup by cost
Cost price, original retail selling price	Initial markup	Subtract cost price from orginal retail selling price
Cost price, final sales price	Maintained markup	Subtract cost price from final sales price
Retail price, markup percentage	Cost price	Multiply retail price by (100% − M%)
Cost price, markup percentage	Retail price	Divide cost by (100% − M%)
Estimated expenses, profits, price reductions, sales	Initial markup	Add expenses, profits, price reductions; divide this figure by (Sales + Reductions)
Original retail selling price, final sales price	Markdown	Subtract final sales price from original retail price
Dollar markdown, total sales	Markdown percentage	Divide dollar markdown by total sales

Illus. 10-3   Given above are the various formulas used in pricing.
Every retailer should memorize these formulas.

Buying Errors

If the merchant fails to time his purchases correctly, buys too much too late, or fails to spot the best sellers in a line, he will probably be forced to take a markdown on his purchases. The buyer should carefully plan his purchases by class and price line; and, if possible, he should experiment with the sale of small quantities before placing large orders. Often goods are not examined carefully; and merchandise which is defective in workmanship, color, and fit is put into stock and must be marked down later. Goods bought right, styled right, and priced right will usually sell without markdown.

Pricing Errors

A buyer may be highly optimistic and price his goods too high even though he has bought the right quantities in the right styles at the right time. For example, one buyer purchased dresses at a cost of $12 each and priced them into stock at $24.95 each. The dresses did not sell well; but when they were marked down to $19.95 each, they sold in large quantities. If the dresses had originally been priced at $19.95, no markdown would have been necessary. Some merchants deliberately overprice the merchandise originally to make it seem more attractive later at a reduced price.

Selling Errors

The training and attitude of salespeople are important influences on markdowns. Salespeople may encourage customers to take merchandise which is wrong in color, style, fit, or quantity and hope that they will not return it. At the insistence of the salesperson, the customer may take home two or three dresses, keep them for a time, and then return all of them. Generally when goods are returned by customers, the goods must be marked down. Sometimes salespeople show only the style that they personally like, and some merchandise may stay in the store a long time because of a salesperson's failure to show it to customers who might have bought it. Other salespeople tend to show what is new and neglect to show old stock.

Poor control of the goods in stock may also be regarded as a selling error. Often goods that are in the process of aging are not noticed and are permitted to remain in stock with no attempt made to sell them before they become subject to drastic markdowns.

As the list of Reasons for Taking Markdowns indicates, many are the result of store policy and are not caused by error on anyone's part. These are discussed in the parts of this chapter that follow.

Reasons for Taking Markdowns

Buying errors—wrong styles, sizes, colors, patterns, prices, quantities

Selling errors—careless and high-pressure salesmanship, neglect of old stock

Pricing errors—marking goods too high at first

Poor control—failure to spot slow sellers promptly

Policy reasons—maintaining assortments until late in the season; deliberately taking a high markup quickly followed by a large markdown to cater to bargain seekers; meeting competition; stocking expensive goods for prestige purposes, which have to be later marked down to sell; leftovers from special-purchase sales; temporary markdowns on regular stock to stimulate business

---

Illus. 10-4   Retailers may be forced to take markdowns to insure making even a small profit on merchandise, and they may take markdowns voluntarily for policy reasons. Listed above are some of the reasons for taking markdowns.

MARKDOWN POLICIES

When to take a markdown and the amount of markdown to take will depend on the merchandise being sold and on the particular selling situation. It is essential, however, that there be an organized system of follow-up on every piece of merchandise to see that it does not remain in stock too long and ultimately require a drastic price cut.

Timing of Markdowns

Stores follow two general plans in timing their markdowns: (1) markdowns may be taken at several times within the selling season—as soon as an item's rate of sale begins to drop or it has remained in stock for a fixed length of time—or (2) they may be taken late in the selling season in the form of a clearance sale.

With fashion merchandise, it is generally best to mark the items down as soon as customer demand begins to drop. Daily sales records can indicate the state of customer demand. With staple merchandise, the markdown should be taken as soon as there is a danger of the goods becoming shopworn if they remain in the store any longer. Some stores set a definite limit on the amount of time merchandise can remain in stock at the original price and mark it down after that time limit has been reached. A two-, four-, or six-week limit is common for fashion merchandise.

There are advantages to either plan of timing markdowns. If a store takes markdowns several times within a selling season rather than having a large clearance sale at the end of the season, it can generally achieve a smaller markdown per item. The goods are marked down while there is still some active demand for them, and a small price reduction is generally enough to sell them. Early markdowns generally reduce the selling expense for a particular item; selling the goods eliminates excess storage expenses; and special salespeople do not have to be hired for a clearance sale. Also, reducing retail stock early in the season means that the store can buy more goods for resale and perhaps increase its profits.

On the other hand, clearance sales held late in the season are favored by many stores. Such clearance sales do not interfere with the sale of regularly priced merchandise as do markdowns offered several times within a selling season. A late markdown means that the goods are given every chance to be sold. Also, the quantity of stock accumulated for markdown during a season means that the clearance sale can become an important selling event. It can be promoted by advertising and is looked forward to by bargain seekers.

Amount of Markdown

There are no definite rules on the amount of markdown to be taken; the merchant must determine the markdown for each particular item in each particular selling situation. Some stores, however, do have fixed markdown percentages and mark their goods down a certain percentage, such as 25 percent, after the goods have been in stock for a certain period of time. This practice is called *automatic markdown.*

The first markdown which is taken should be large enough to sell most of the items which are being reduced in price. The retailer seldom comes out ahead if he takes a series of small markdowns instead of one large markdown; and obviously, the longer merchandise remains in stock, the more shopworn it becomes and the lesser are its chances of being sold. It is also important to have the markdown large enough to make the goods seem a bargain to customers at the new price and to make customers want to buy.

CHECKING YOUR KNOWLEDGE

Vocabulary

1. price reduction
2. markdown

3. automatic markdown

1. Which factors are usually included in price reductions?
2. Name two things that a retailer must know in order to calculate the markdown percentage.
3. What are the two major reasons for markdowns?
4. Why are markdowns sometimes necessary to change an unsatisfactory price?
5. What plans are generally followed with regard to the timing of markdowns? Give the advantages of each plan.

Discussion Questions

1. Are there any circumstances that justify a merchant placing goods in stock at a higher than normal markup with the intention of taking a markdown in order to present the goods as a bargain? Explain.
2. Why is it important for a merchant to know whether markdowns are due primarily to buying errors, selling errors, or pricing errors?
3. What can salespeople do to prevent markdowns?

Part C

Pricing Policies

The discussion of markup shows how a retailer can compute the retail price necessary to realize a desired markup. The discussion does not indicate whether it is wise to price individual items at the calculated price. In practice merchants tend to vary considerably in the pricing of individual items. Overall, however, they attempt to achieve an average planned markup on the total of their purchases.

Every retailer aims at growth through obtaining adequate markup over the long run. It does not follow, however, that he seeks maximum profit on every item sold or even on the gross amount of his current sales. The opportunities to grow and achieve goodwill have to be considered along with the profit opportunity.

COST AND EXPENSE FACTORS IN PRICING

The largest single factor in establishing a retail price is, of course, the cost of the merchandise to be sold. In addition, there is the expense of handling the merchandise in terms of getting it ready for sale. Then there are expenses in selling the goods and expenses which are necessary just to keep the store open for business. The terms *cost* and *expense* are frequently used interchangeably and may sound synonomous. There is, however, a technical difference that will be made more obvious in the unit on "Controlling the Store." The term *cost* is used to identify expenditures made to pay for the goods purchased, to transport them to the store, and to alter them, if necessary. The term *expense* is used to identify all the expenditures required to operate the store: for building, for merchandise handling, for buying, for selling, and for administration.

Expenditures for buildings and equipment, except for repairs, are not included in expense, but the annual depreciation on these assets is.

In determining the actual price that will be set on goods there are three kinds of expenses to be considered. *Flat expenses* are expenses that are about the same for every article regardless of its cost or retail price. Classified as flat expenses are most handling expenses such as receiving, marking, storage, wrapping, packing, and delivery. *Variable expenses* are different for each item but bear approximately the same percentage relationship to the retail price. Variable expenses include salespersons' salaries (especially if these are paid on a commission basis), advertising expenses, insurance, and interest on the investment in the goods. Markdowns and shortages, while technically not expenses, may be included, if they are significantly large. The third kind of expense is *overhead*—the joint costs of operating the store or department that do not vary with the number or value of the specific items being sold. Overhead includes expenses of rent and store maintenance, record-keeping expenses, and supervisory and administrative expenses.

Let us see how knowledge of costs and expenses can influence the setting of a retail price. Suppose that a television set costs a buyer $80. Flat expenses have been found to be about $10 a set, and variable expenses have been found to be about 10 percent of sales. Let us compare the results of three possible prices.

Retail Price	Cost	Flat Expenses	Variable Expenses	Estimated Sales Each Week	Overhead and Profit
$100	$80	$10	$10	10	$ 0
$110	80	10	11	8	72
$120	80	10	12	5	90

At a price of $100 there would be no contribution to overhead or profit regardless of the number sold. Of the three possible prices, the $120 price would contribute the most to overhead and profits and would thus be the best price—at least over the short run.

Another example of price adjustments justified by expense differences is the *multiple price*. An item may be retailed at 35 cents a unit or three for a dollar. The flat expenses of handling three as a unit may be no more than handling one, and the overhead may not be increased by the larger transaction. Thus, the profit margin at the multiple price may be even larger than that on three separate sales at the unit price.

DEMAND FACTORS IN PRICING

The initial markup must be set at a point at which the goods will readily sell. Thus, the nature of a store's customers and of its competition has an important influence on markup.

Knowing the Customer

In a well-to-do community, a high markup may be acceptable. This does not necessarily mean a large profit, however, since the customers may demand a great deal of service and wide assortments of fashionable goods. This increases a store's expenses and its losses from reductions. On the other hand, in a price-conscious community, low markups may be demanded. These may be offset by low expenses and small markdowns, obtainable by concentrating on fast-selling items and by giving minimum service.

Some retail merchants establish several price lines. It is possible that Retailer Y has found through experience that his customers like to buy shoes in three price lines—perhaps $15, $20, and $25. He may buy shoes at different wholesale prices but always retail them at those three prices. Retailer Z, however, may have many price lines. He may retail shoes at the price that he believes will move that style quickly. He may price his shoes at $8.50, $12.50, $15, $17.50, $20, and perhaps at still other prices.

Goods originally priced too low may cause customers to suspect that something is wrong with the quality. If a customer generally pays $8.50 for a dress shirt, he will probably not buy a shirt of the same quality for $4.95, even if the merchant has made an advantageous buy and can make a profit at the low price. Thus, shirts valued at $8.50 but marked at $4.95 may sell poorly because the customers are suspicious of their quality. The customer may be more interested if the original retail price is set at $6.95.

Studying the Competition

One of the major considerations in setting the price of individual items is the price that competitors are receiving for the same items. A supermarket, for instance, sets the major portion of its individual prices so that they agree with the prices that its competitors are charging. It will then try to undersell its competitors on certain featured items. Although most stores try to meet competition in prices, many compete in the offering of services. Thus, it is possible for a store to succeed and yet not meet a competitor's price—provided that the store offers additional services, such as credit and personal service.

One retailer explains that, when competition threatens to reduce his profit on an item, he searches for a method to free that item from direct price competition. He may repackage it more attractively, or he may add a detail that will make the product different from that of his competitors. When the manufacturer will give him the exclusive right to such product variation or when the retailer can put his private brand on it, he can assure himself of repeat patronage for his product at an adequate markup.

VARIATIONS IN MARKUPS

In the same store and even in the same department, the markups on items vary greatly. This is due partly to the varying expenses encountered on certain items. For example, a large table requires a great deal of display and storage space and will surely have to be delivered to the customer. Thus, it will normally require a higher markup than a lamp sold in the same department. The lamp occupies little space, and the customer will probably take the lamp with her at the time of sale.

Another reason for differences in markup lies in the amount of markdown and shortage risk. For instance, both basic styles and high-fashion styles are commonly carried in the same department. The likelihood of having to mark down a classic dress style is much less than in the case of a new style. Thus, the classic dress warrants a lower markup than the high-fahion dress. Similarly, the markup on basic shoe styles is generally less than that on the latest fads in footwear.

A higher-than-average markup is generally justified under the following conditions:

1. When the risk of price reduction is great
2. When the expenses of handling and storage are likely to be abnormally great
3. When the goods are exclusive and not subject to direct competition
4. When customers expect a great deal of service

A lower-than-average markup is generally justified under the following conditions:

1. When staple merchandise, which is carried by most similar retailers, is stocked

2. When no packaging or delivery is needed
3. When customers expect little personal service
4. When the stock turn is high, resulting in low space cost
5. When the volume opportunities at a lower-than-average markup will yield a larger dollar profit than could be obtained with an average markup

Every merchant should be constantly aware of the prices on his merchandise and should know which items are being sold at satisfactory margins. He should be willing to experiment with different prices on merchandise to assure competitiveness and adequate markup. The alert merchant is constantly searching to find the prices for his goods at which markup and volume combine to provide a desired profit. He must remember that these prices must also encourage repeat trade and maintain the goodwill of his customers by keeping a favorable store image in their minds.

SPECIAL SALES AND PRICING

Special sales policy has a good deal to do with pricing. Some stores attempt to make use of the same merchandise to cater to two

Courtesy of Rodale Press, Inc.

Illus. 10-5   Today's consumer goes to great lengths to compare prices and brands and to base her selection on both quality and quantity.

groups of customers: (1) those searching for the new or who buy when they feel the need and (2) those looking for bargains. New styles are put into stock early in the season at markups considerably above normal. Later in the season they are marked down sharply to appeal to the price-conscious group. The goal is to achieve a normal markup on the entire operation over the season.

Some stores hold frequent special sales. If regular goods are used for this purpose, it is hoped that the extra volume realized during the sale, even at a low markup, will yield a profit, since overhead expense will not be increased. After the sale the goods will be restored to their regular prices.

Often the special sale consists of specially bought goods, not regularly carried, on which the store can obtain a substantial markup and still offer a bargain price. But the management knows that there will be remainders of unsold sizes and colors which will have to be closed out at sharp markdowns.

CHECKING YOUR KNOWLEDGE

Vocabulary

1. cost
2. expense
3. flat expense
4. variable expense
5. overhead
6. multiple price

Review Questions

1. Describe the technical difference between the term *cost* and the term *expense.*
2. Name four examples of specific items included in flat expenses, variable expenses, and overhead.
3. What can a retailer do to avoid price competition with competitors?
4. Under what situations would a higher-than-average markup be justified?
5. Under what situations would a lower-than-average markup be justified?

Discussion Questions

1. Should merchandise ever be priced so low that the markup does not cover flat and variable expenses? Why?
2. What is meant by the expression *what the traffic will bear* in relation to pricing policy?
3. What are the advantages of odd cent price endings such as 79, 89, or 99? Are there any disadvantages?

Part d

Leaders and Premiums

Retail pricing is frequently done to assist in the promotional efforts of the store. The price itself may be the central feature, or the price in connection with a gift may be used. In either case, whatever is decided by the retailer should be a planned part of his pricing policies.

LEADER MERCHANDISING

Items are sometimes priced below their most profitable point or below the average markup in order to attract customers to the store. Whenever a store sells an article at a cut price—not to make a profit on the item sold but to attract customers who will buy other goods at regular markups—it is using the item as a *leader*. For example, an article costing 60 cents may be customarily retailed at $1. A store may cut the price to 79 cents, not in the hope of making money from increased volume, but to attract to the store customers who will buy other goods. The leader is thus a kind of advertising device.

When a store sells an article at less than cost, including direct handling expenses, the item becomes a *loss leader*. If the item in the preceding example were sold for 59 cents, the merchant would be losing at least one cent on every sale. In fact, he would probably be losing several cents more when flat and variable expenses and overhead are considered.

Disadvantages of Leaders

The leader policy has caused much criticism of retail stores. The advertising of leaders tends to mislead customers in that it gives the impression that all the store's prices are low. The leader is simply a device to get the customer to the store where she may be prevailed upon to buy other goods in addition to, or instead of, the leader. Some stores urge salespeople to hold back on leaders so as to keep unprofitable sales as low as possible.

The leader policy also works a hardship on competitors and on manufacturers. The cutting of a price may force competitors to meet the price change in order to maintain their reputations for reasonable prices and in order to get a share of the business. Major national brands and staple items that are frequently purchased are often used as leaders because the usual price is so well known to the consumer that the cut price is attractive. Such leaders become "footballs" in the trade—unprofitable to all retailers and sometimes leading to price wars. Manufacturers are injured because retailers attempt to switch customers away from the unprofitable leaders to profitable substitutes.

Advantages of Leaders

On the other hand, when leaders are not held back but are readily sold to those who ask for them, there are sound reasons for their use. For a new product they provide wide distribution leading to repeat patronage if the product proves successful, and it is often less expensive than advertising to produce additional volume. For established products it helps the store meet competition. It also benefits the customer.

False Leaders

A prevalent practice under attack by both the Better Business Bureaus and the Federal Trade Commission (the federal agency empowered to restrain unfair practices in interstate commerce) is to pretend that an advertised article is a leader by attributing to it a fictitious list price above the selling price. For example, a mattress listed at $79.50 is retailed at $39.50 as a great bargain. However, the mattress may have cost no more than $25. It is both unethical and illegal to advertise a list price that is other than the customary current retail price in the community in which the store is offering a lower price.

Some stores advertise leaders with the deliberate intention of selling a profitable substitute instead. This is done in various ways: the leader is "talked down" when the customer asks for it; something else, which is claimed to be much better, is shown to her; the store may claim that it is all sold out; or the store may actually refuse to deliver the advertised leader. Better Business Bureaus in various cities are frequently called upon to stamp out such practices which are clearly unethical.

PREMIUM MERCHANDISING

A *premium* is something of value given free or at a reduced price in order to induce a customer to purchase.

Coupons

For many years retail pricing policies have been influenced by manufacturers' marketing strategies, which include giving customers a reward for buying a product. The manufacturer's objective is to grant an indirect price cut that will make the merchandise the leading product

Illus. 10-6   Different kinds of coupons may be used in promoting the sale of goods.

in its particular field. This goal may be accomplished by the use of coupons. The consumer receives a coupon through house-to-house distribution or by mail, or perhaps she cuts one out of the manufacturer's advertisement appearing in the newspaper. The coupon may also be inserted in the package of a current purchase made at the regular price. In some instances, coupons are available to interested customers right in the store. Then, at the time of purchasing the item at the retail store, she surrenders the coupon which entitles her to a reduction in the price of the item purchased.

Gifts

Another type of reward is a gift that can be obtained after the consumer purchases the advertised item. The consumer is required to tear off the box top or the label and send it to the manufacturer with a small sum of money—25 cents to $1. In return, she may receive a pair of hose, a kitchen gadget, or another package of the item. An inexpensive premium is often enclosed in the package containing the product. This is a common practice in connection with packages of cereal that are frequently bought at the insistence of children. A variation of the gift offer is sometimes found in supermarkets where a pound of coffee or a pound of butter is given free, provided the customer buys a certain amount of other goods.

Illus. 10-7   Cereal companies often offer gifts at a small charge in an effort to sell their products by attracting the interest and desire of children to acquire both the product and the gift. (KELLOGG'S and RICE KRISPIES are trademarks of Kellogg Company.)

Trading Stamps

A widespread form of premium merchandising is the *trading stamp*. With each purchase of merchandise, the customer is given trading stamps—usually bought by the store from an outside company—which can be pasted in a blank book. Filled books can be redeemed for merchandise of the customer's choice, such as linens, lamps, tools, or even expensive items such as refrigerators or vacation trips. Some states require that stamps be redeemable in cash. Since the retail value of merchandise received by the customer is about $3 for every filled book and since the usual filled book requires the purchase of $120 to $150 worth of goods, the premium amounts to a discount of about 2 percent.

Present Status of Premiums

Like leader merchandising, the various premium devices have generally been successful in attracting customers; but many merchants question the further extension of their use. Many merchants believe that a product should be sold primarily on the basis of its merits, not because of gifts and extras. The handling of coupons and the giving of stamps slow down the checkout procedure and consume valuable selling time. Manufacturers who wish to use coupons attempt to overcome retailer resistance by refunding the face value of the coupons collected, plus a little more (usually 2½ to 3 cents a coupon) to compensate the retailer for expenses in collecting and turning in the coupons.

Certain consumer groups—pressing for lower prices and increased retail efficiency—have discouraged merchants from using premium-type promotions; yet many customers respond to them favorably.

Unfortunately, there has been considerable abuse in the handling of coupons. Dishonest dealers collect and accept quantities of coupons without requiring the purchase of the items they are intended to help sell. These are then turned in for the full cash value plus handling allowance. Thus, the manufacturer is saddled with heavy expense that brings no return in sales.

CHECKING YOUR KNOWLEDGE

Vocabulary

1. leader
2. loss leader

3. premiums
4. trading stamp

Review Questions

1. What is the difference between a leader and a premium?
2. What impact would a strong leader policy have on competitors and manufacturers?
3. What arguments may be advanced in defense of leader merchandising?
4. Give four examples of unethical practices in leader merchandise.
5. What kind of premium would be most effective in influencing children to urge their parents to buy a product?

Discussion Questions

1. What are the advantages and disadvantages of leader merchandising from the viewpoint of the retailer? the manufacturer? the consumer?
2. Is the prevalence of premium merchandising likely to increase or decrease in the near future? Upon what do you base your opinion?
3. Would food customers be better off with 2 percent lower prices than with the premiums they receive by accumulating trading stamps? If a supermarket eliminates stamps, which is more likely to happen—that it will reduce prices or that it will be forced to introduce another form of sales promotion device that will cost nearly as much as the stamps?

Part e

Organizing the Buying and Pricing Functions

If you were the owner of a retail business, you would want to be sure that the selection of merchandise and setting of retail prices were carried out effectively and promptly. The way in which a retail store owner organizes these two functions has much to do with how well they are performed. The procedures for the selection of merchandise and setting of retail prices, along with the supporting activities of order writing, receiving, checking, marking, and stocking, vary with the type and size of the retail firm.

BUYING AND PRICING IN SMALL STORES

The buying function in small stores is often not well organized. The merchant is so busy selling, handling deliveries, stocking, or keeping records that he must make buying decisions quickly and often without adequate thought regarding type or quality of merchandise. He relies heavily on wholesalers and other suppliers for suggestions regarding merchandise selection and the proper retail price to set. The retail price recommended by suppliers is nearly always used, and changes are made only when suppliers' prices change or when overstocking becomes noticeable.

If the store has two or more employees, the buying and pricing functions can be better organized. All workers in a small store can have selling responsibilities, and each can be assigned specific responsibilities for some sales-supporting duties. The manager, for instance, could be responsible for deciding what to buy, where to buy, how much to buy, and for setting the retail price. One employee might be responsible for receiving, checking, and marking all merchandise. Another employee might be responsible for putting the goods into stock, maintaining stock records, and keeping the manager informed of fast- or slow-moving items.

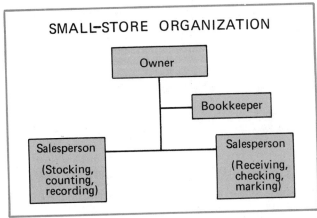

Illus. 10-8　　The small retail firm can be organized so that each person is responsible for certain functions but shares common duties.

BUYING AND PRICING IN CHAIN STORES

In most chain-store organizations, the buying function is set up as a division complete within itself. Since the store units of a chain are similar, it is more economical for one buyer to buy goods for all of them, rather than to have separate buyers for each store. Thus, the buyers are specialists, concentrating upon every change in the market, taking advantage of quantity and off-season buys, and working out advantageous merchandise deals with wholesalers and producers. Where more than one buyer is employed, the lines to be bought are divided among them so that each can further concentrate upon his items. As an example, in a grocery chain organization one buyer is responsible for all groceries, another for all fruits and vegetables, and still another for meats. The buyers usually set the retail prices of the merchandise they buy, but in some chains the unit managers may adjust the prices to meet local competition.

While the separation of buying from other retailing functions—such as selling—is successful for chain stores, it does have certain disadvantages. Buyers find it difficult to adjust their buying to the needs of each community in which there is a store unit. Too, unit managers sometimes feel no sense of responsibility to "push" the goods sent to them by the buyer. In order to overcome these disadvantages, buyers are often asked to visit individual stores to see how the goods they purchased are selling. Some chain stores allow unit managers to order a

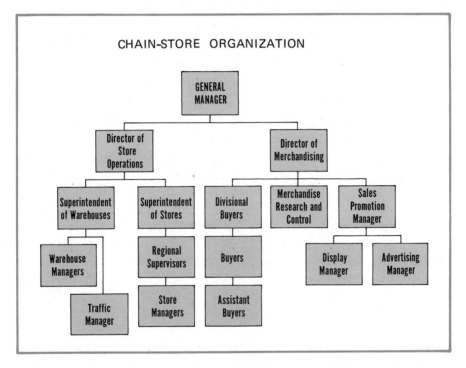

Illus. 10-9   Chain stores often have structures similar to the above.

limited amount of goods if the central buyer is not fully familiar with community needs.

The goods bought by the buyer are usually received in the chain's warehouse and then distributed to each store in the chain. This distribution is sometimes based on requisitions from the stores and sometimes upon plans made by the central staff. Sometimes the buyers instruct manufacturers to ship directly to the store units rather than to a central warehouse and may authorize the stores to reorder goods direct.

When a chain has a separate merchandising division, its organizational plan may be similar to that shown in Illus. 10-9. The general manager may be a vice president and may have other functions under his control that are not shown in this plan (such as real estate and personnel management). The director of store operations is responsible for the storage, movement, and selling of merchandise. The director of merchandising is responsible for the buying, promotion, and pricing of the merchandise.

BUYING AND PRICING IN DEPARTMENT STORES

Many departmentalized stores—whether specialty shops or general merchandise stores—adjust their buying to customer demand by combining buying and selling into one division called the *merchandising division*. The lineup of executives and personnel in the merchandising division is not uniform, and merchandising activities are not the same for all stores. The man usually found at the head of the merchandising division is called the *merchandise manager*. He may have under him a number of divisional merchandise managers who are specialists in their particular lines of merchandise. The latter supervise the activities of the buyers of the different selling departments of the store. Each buyer confers with his divisional merchandise manager as to the amount of merchandise to buy, the prices to set, the best methods of promoting sales, business trends, and plans for future activities. In many stores buyers' orders for merchandise must be approved by the divisional merchandise manager.

Under this plan of organization, the buyers, with their headquarters in each store, are also responsible for selling. They plan the size of the sales force, they supervise salespeople, and they take responsibility for departmental displays. Since the buyer has to be in the market and off the selling floor a good deal of the time, his assistant buyer supervises selling in his absence. The head of stock—if there is one—is responsible for putting new merchandise into stock, for maintaining an orderly arrangement, and for suggesting reorders.

Department Store Trend toward Chain Organization

The plan of combining in one division both buying and selling does have disadvantages. While supervising selling, buyers may fail to keep in close touch with changes in the wholesale markets; and while buying, they may neglect sales supervision. They may waste time traveling back and forth from markets. They may find it difficult to plan with other noncompeting stores to buy together and thus get lower prices or exclusive merchandise. With the trend toward branch-store operations, it is

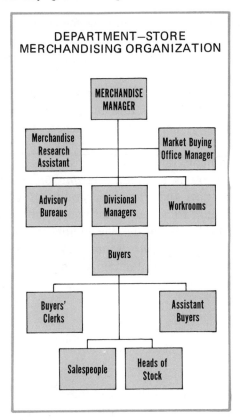

Illus. 10-10   The merchandising division is a major division of a department store. The merchandise manager directs the buying and pricing of goods for the store and its branches.

becoming impossible for buyers to supervise the selling activities in all the branches. Thus, buyers for many department stores perform just the buying and pricing functions; and department managers are responsible for carrying out the selling and sales supervision. This arrangement approaches the chain-store type of organization for buying and pricing. There is a growing tendency, however, to give department managers in each branch considerable authority in reordering merchandise and in deciding upon the assortment best suited to each branch. Branches cannot function satisfactorily if they are standardized to the extent that units of food chains and drug chains are.

Specialized Bureaus

Bureaus that provide specialized advice on phases of merchandising may be included in the merchandising division. Resident or market buying offices to assist buyers in making selections are also sometimes part of the organization. Workrooms to assemble or finish goods are sometimes in the merchandising division but are often placed in the store management division.

The merchandise manager often has a research assistant who makes analyses of sales and stocks, studies outside economic data, and presents summaries to the merchandise manager. There may also be a number of advisory bureaus. The *comparison bureau* compares the merchandise assortments and prices in the store with those elsewhere. Sometimes there is a separate *testing bureau* or laboratory to analyze the composition and the serviceability of goods. The *fashion bureau* forecasts fashion trends and coordinates the merchandise carried in different departments from the viewpoint of color, material, and design. The *unit-control bureau* records and analyzes sales of each article sold as a basis for maintaining balanced stocks.

CHECKING YOUR KNOWLEDGE

Vocabulary

1. merchandising division
2. merchandise manager
3. comparison bureau
4. testing bureau
5. fashion bureau
6. unit-control bureau

Review Questions

1. On whom does the small retailer rely for setting his retail prices?
2. How can buying and pricing be organized in the small store?
3. How is retail pricing usually handled in chain stores?
4. How are buying and pricing organized in department stores?
5. What are the disadvantages of having both buying and selling responsibilities in one division of a store?

Discussion Questions

1. Can the buying and selling functions be effectively separated in small stores? Explain.
2. For what reasons is the merchandising division often regarded as the most important division in departmentalized stores?
3. The person who buys merchandise is the best qualified to set the retail price on that merchandise. Do you agree with this statement? Why or why not?

BUILDING YOUR SKILLS

Improving Communication Skills

Each of the following sentences contains two conjunctions in parentheses. On a separate sheet of paper, write the number of each sentence and the correct conjunction to be used in each sentence.

1. Jack calculates markup just (like, as) the buyer taught him.
2. The small store can promote leaders just (like, as) the chain stores do.
3. Make up the price tickets (like, as) I told you.
4. Murphy's Shop sells the same merchandise lines (like, as) the Ace Stores.
5. Markdowns are taken automatically or (like, as) they are needed.

On a separate sheet of paper, write the number of each sentence and the correct plural form of the word given in parentheses at the end of each sentence.

1. Five of the new buyers for the department store were _____. (woman)
2. Two young buyers were promoted to _____ of store divisions. (chairman)
3. The markdowns were greatest in _____ suits and accessories. (man)
4. The markup on the shipment of _____ was 35% of retail. (goose)
5. The leader for the store was _____ sweaters. (child)

Improving Arithmetic Skills

Calculate the markups, markdowns, or prices in each of the exercises below. On a separate sheet of paper, write the exercise number and your answers for each.

1. Cost, $4; markup, $2. Find (a) retail price and (b) markup percentage.
2. Retail, $17; markup, $7. Find (a) cost and (b) markup percentage.
3. Cost, $3.50; retail, $5. Find (a) markup in dollars and (b) markup percentage.
4. Cost, $6; original retail, $10; sale price, $8.50. Find (a) initial markup, (b) maintained markup, and (c) markdown percentage (assuming no other sales).
5. Grapefruit costs $2.40 for 10 kilograms. If a 40% markup is taken what would be the retail price for 5 pounds of grapefruit? (See Appendix on page 622.)

Improving Research Skills

1. Obtain newspaper advertisements or other printed advertisements from several stores of the same type (supermarkets, variety, or other). Compare the advertised items, and for each store try to identify the leader if one is used. Also, which items are used as leaders by several stores. Try to list several ways of determining whether an item is a leader just from the advertisement.
2. As a class or in committees develop a questionnaire to determine how adult customers feel about trading stamps. Include such ques-

tions as: Do you prefer to buy at stores that give trading stamps? What types of merchandise do you get with your stamp books? Would you prefer stamps or a 2% discount on purchases? After obtaining responses from a sampling of adult customers prepare a report summarizing your findings and indicate what you believe the attitude of people in your community is toward trading stamps.

3. Visit several retail stores and observe the price endings used. Try to determine if the stores have a certain pattern to their price endings, such as 99 or 95 cents, rather than even amounts, such as $1, 75 cents or 50 cents. If there is a pattern, try to find the reason.

Improving Decision-Making Skills

1. Assume that you are a salesperson in a store in which the policy is to apply the same markup percentage to all merchandise. Some goods move very rapidly, while other items sell slowly and must be marked down rather drastically to be sold. Flat and variable costs also differ considerably in different merchandise lines. How would you go about analyzing the pricing problems in the store? Explain how you would present a better policy to your employer.

2. A merchant estimates that if he retails a certain article at $15 (a markup of 40%), he can sell 20 a week, that at $17.50 he can sell 12 a week, that at $20 he can sell 6 a week, that at $14 he can sell 30, and that at $12 he can sell 40. His flat expenses are $2 for each item, and his variable costs are 8%. At what price will the merchant make the largest contribution to overhead and profit? What objections are there to pricing at this point? Write out your computations and explanation of the possible objections to pricing the article at the so-called optimum price.

3. A survey of drug stores in a borough of New York City revealed that the price of a certain antibiotic drug, available only by prescription, varied from $2.25 to $7.75. The highest prices were found in low-income areas.
   What solution to this problem do you suggest? Should customers be trained to shop in a number of stores before leaving their prescriptions to be filled, or should government set the retail prices at which standard drugs available on prescription must be sold? What are the dangers in the second approach? Are there other possibilities?

APPLYING YOUR KNOWLEDGE

Chapter Project

Select an item of merchandise that is sold in several stores in your community. Visit each of these stores, and note the different prices asked for this item. In a written report state any reasons that justify the price differences.

Continuing Project

In your manual, indicate what your store policy will be for (a) markups (b) markdowns, and (c) leaders. Use several examples to explain your policies.

UNIT 4
Selling and Sales Promotion

The goal of the retail enterprise is to satisfy the wants of consumers for goods and certain services, while it maintains its own prosperity and growth. This means selling merchandise profitably. A business prospers because it sells its products and services in such volume and at such prices that the business grows and returns to the owners a profit for their investment. The retailer's most difficult problems are to select goods that will sell and to present them effectively to prospective customers. Presenting goods to the buying public involves the activities of selling and sales promotion.

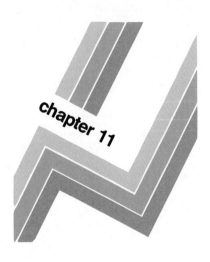

chapter 11

Selling

CHAPTER PREVIEW

a. Selling involves assisting or persuading customers to buy. It may be done through personal or nonpersonal means, inside or outside the store.

b. Most salespeople must perform duties in addition to personal selling. These duties include stockkeeping, preparing displays, merchandise control, directing customers, and handling complaints.

c. A successful sale is composed of eight distinct steps, each of which requires the application of proven techniques.

d. Merchandise presentation, the heart of a sale, is best accomplished when the customer is actively drawn into the demonstration and discussion.

e. Every sales contact cannot result in an immediate sale, but every contact can build goodwill for the salesperson and his store.

Part a

Kinds of Selling

On any shopping trip Mrs. Consumer may experience several different kinds of selling. She may seek advice from a salesperson on color, style, construction, and several other technical factors. For some goods the consumer may want only general information such as size or weight. In other cases the consumer may examine an assortment of merchandise and select an item without any assistance. In some cases the consumer will look at goods in a store as a result of advertising.

The concept of selling has varied over the years. For many hundreds of years selling meant the completion of a transaction in which goods or services were exchanged for a price. As the nature of goods became more complex and the variety more extensive, demonstration, information, and advice became essential to selling. Today in retailing, *selling* may be defined as the process of informing potential customers about an appropriate product and assisting and sometimes persuading them to buy. Selling may be done through personal contact between salesperson and customer, through publicity or mechanical means, or through a combination of personal and nonpersonal methods.

PERSONAL SELLING

There are two kinds of selling—personal selling and nonpersonal selling. In *personal selling* a salesperson makes direct contact with a customer. Realizing the need for speedier, simpler selling services, many stores are removing all unnecessary obstacles between the customer and the merchandise. In many cases this includes the salesperson. However, in situations where someone is needed to help customers solve their buying problems, personal selling continues to be essential. The qualified salesperson can be indispensable to the store by giving personal attention and worthwhile advice to all customers who wish service.

The coordination of personal selling and nonpersonal selling to give best results is called *sales promotion.* Both personal and nonpersonal selling may be divided into (a) selling outside the store, or *external selling,* and (b) selling inside the store, or *internal selling.* Every merchant tries to use the particular combination of personal and nonpersonal selling media that will sell his merchandise most effectively and most economically.

Courtesy of Sears, Roebuck and Co.

Illus. 11-1   A knowledgeable salesperson can be of great assistance in helping customers make decisions regarding major purchases.

External Personal Selling

Although most people are familiar with house-to-house selling, many people do not know that some stores hire outside salespeople. Such salespeople are frequently employed to sell household appliances, food plans, house renovations, upholstery, storm windows, and other goods. Since they can invite customers to come to the store to see a wide assortment, they have an advantage over the house-to-house salesperson who must carry all his samples with him.

Stores may also employ the mail and the telephone for outside selling. A store advertises that mail and telephone orders will be taken and employs special clerks to handle the orders. If the store builds up a reputation for quick and accurate filling of orders, it may soon enjoy a sizable mail and telephone business. In specialty shops it is not unusual for salespeople to call customers to tell them about special values.

Some retail distributors use their selling force to give demonstrations of merchandise, such as cooking utensils or sewing machines, at customers' homes and at clubs. Many stores send out interior decorators who make suggestions for beautifying the home and for arranging furniture and draperies. These decorators may increase sales by suggesting the purchase of additional furnishings.

Internal Personal Selling

Inside the store much selling still is personal. When the customer visits the store and is helped to reach a purchase decision on goods that will satisfy her needs and wants, it is called *over-the-counter selling*. This type of selling must not be confused with retail order taking, where the person behind the counter does nothing to aid the customer in reaching a decision. Retail order takers are being replaced by self-service wherever possible, for store owners have found that it is costly to employ someone merely to locate goods and handle the mechanics of closing. The true retail salesperson is secure in his position, because his services are needed as much today as ever. In fact, because of today's better-informed customer, his help in distributing goods is a key job in our economy.

Retail salespeople are found in every type of store from the small independent store to the large corporate chain; and in the minds of many customers, the store is the person behind the counter. The attitude with which the salesperson approaches the customer and the information, help, and courtesy shown leave a long-lasting impact upon the customer and determine her attitude toward the store itself.

NONPERSONAL SELLING

Selling through publicity and by mechanical methods, such as vending machines, is referred to as *nonpersonal selling. Publicity,* as retailers use the term, is the presentation of goods or services in a nonpersonal way both outside and inside the store. Publicity includes external and internal advertising, display, and special-purpose promotions, external sampling, and internal use of merchandise labels. Most publicity is paid for by the store, but some is free. Examples of free publicity are news items in periodicals and radio or television announcements for which no direct payment is made.

External Nonpersonal Selling

Advertising and window display are a store's chief means of external nonpersonal selling. *Advertising* is any paid form of nonpersonal presentation of information about merchandise or services. The newspaper is the retailer's chief medium for outside advertising; but direct mail, television, radio, and package inserts are also important media. The use of the newspaper and other advertising media will be discussed in Chapter 13.

Windows should show the store's best merchandise values and most outstanding goods. Stores occasionally set up displays of goods in hotel or theater lobbies in order to attract customers. Occasionally stores have displays at fairs or show merchandise arranged in model homes for potential buyers.

External special-purpose publicity is any exhibit or promotional event outside the store. A well-known form of special-purpose publicity is the Thanksgiving Day parade held by several of the country's largest department stores. As a result of watching the parade, both children and parents are eager to visit the stores to see the many toys that have been stocked for Christmas.

A store may also use outside sampling as a sales stimulus. It may employ people to go from door to door or to stand on a corner and offer samples of the article being promoted. This means of publicity is especially effective for food products and cosmetics.

Internal Nonpersonal Selling

While formerly most of a store's nonpersonal selling efforts were of an external nature, now a great deal of effort is devoted to internal promotion.

Advertising. A store must back up its outside advertising with internal advertising if it is to maintain the customer's interest. Such inside advertising is also called *point-of-sale advertising*. The internal advertising may consist of reproductions and enlargements of advertisements printed in newspapers. These are frequently placed on bulletin boards near the elevators or escalators. Manufacturers' advertisements are also used for internal advertising purposes.

A number of stores use the *handout* as one of their point-of-sale devices for increasing sales. When a customer enters a store, she is given a handbill on which is listed the merchandise and the prices that the store is featuring that day. All sorts of signs (counter, hanging, elevator, animated, and stationary) are used by stores for internal advertising. A few stores use closed circuit television, allowing customers to view events such as demonstrations of merchandise and style shows being carried on in another part of the store.

Merchandise Labels. A nonpersonal selling medium of growing importance is the informative label which both stores and manufacturers attach to their products. Organized consumers have demanded factual information to help them in buying, and the federal government has developed trade-practice regulations requiring that labels show the material content of many products. Labels have two functions: (1) they act as nonpersonal selling media and provide salespeople with specific facts needed for an intelligent presentation of goods and (2) they aid the customer in making a wise choice, especially if the store carries more than one grade of a product.

Interior Arrangement and Display. The knowledgeable merchant not only uses open and closed counters to display merchandise throughout the store, but he also uses walls, ledges, fixtures, and various kinds of equipment for display purposes. Occasionally interior windows are also available for displays.

Special-Purpose Publicity. Various devices for special purposes are used within the store to spur the sale of goods. Among these are dramatized merchandise presentations, such as fashion shows, classes for sewing and cooking, lectures, musical concerts and exhibits, and contests open to customers.

Courtesy of Montgomery Ward

Illus. 11-2   Interior decorators may increase sales as a result of in-store interior decorating classes.

Automatic Merchandising

One of the rapidly growing selling media is the automatic vending machine. It has been found to be a useful device for both internal and external selling. The rising costs of labor in personal selling activities make the use of vending machines an attractive alternative for selling many products. Vending machines can operate virtually anywhere at any time. They may be used for the sale of hot and cold drinks and foods and a wide variety of prepackaged merchandise. They may be located at various spots within the store, and can be placed in front of stores to dispense merchandise after hours.

Perhaps the brightest future for automatic vending is not in or near stores but at points where it is not economical to maintain a personal sales force over long hours. Examples of such locations are airports and bus and train depots. In some manufacturing concerns, cafeterias are operated almost entirely by means of vending machine units. Milk, fruit juices, pop, coffee, ice cream, candy, sweet rolls, hot and cold sandwiches, soup, and other prepared meals can be obtained during the lunch period or during rest periods.

RETAIL SELLING AT AUCTION

There is a type of retail selling that combines personal and non-personal selling methods. This is selling at auction. Goods are displayed to the audience item by item, and individuals bid on the merchandise. Two kinds of auctions are open to consumers: (1) the quick-sale business auction open to dealers and consumers and (2) the resort auction.

A quick-sale business auction may be held in a home to dispose of household effects or in an auction gallery where goods from different estates have been assembled. Sometimes dealers consign some of their stock to an auction gallery for quick sale. The selling presentation of each article at this type of auction is usually very brief. It is assumed that persons in the audience have had a chance to inspect the goods in advance of the sale and that they have a pretty good knowledge of what items are worth.

The resort auction specializes in objets d'art, linens, silver, jewelry, rugs, and small specialty items designed to catch the interest of the audience. Used household goods are seldom presented. Resort auctioneers are among the most skillful of retail salespeople. They are experts in building value in the customer's mind, in giving a great deal of factual information about each article, and in conveying enthusiasm about the merchandise. Every retail salesperson is well advised to attend a few resort auctions, for he will pick up valuable pointers on how to improve his selling techniques.

CHECKING YOUR KNOWLEDGE

Vocabulary

1. selling
2. personal selling
3. sales promotion
4. external selling
5. internal selling
6. over-the-counter selling

7. nonpersonal selling
8. publicity
9. advertising
10. point-of-sale advertising
11. handout

Review Questions

1. Name two kinds of selling that are coordinated by sales promotion.
2. What kinds of consumer merchandise can best be sold through house-to-house selling?
3. Why is retail order taking being replaced by self-service?
4. What are the chief methods of external nonpersonal selling?
5. What are the chief methods of internal nonpersonal selling?

Discussion Questions

1. For what kinds of merchandise will salespeople continue to be necessary, in spite of the trend toward greater self-service?
2. Is there a difference in the types of external nonpersonal selling that are suitable for small stores as distinct from large stores?
3. Can the use of automatic merchandising machines reduce store expenses? Give reasons for your answer.
4. A catch slogan sometimes used by sales training personnel in stores to define retail salesmanship is: The Power to Persuade Plenty of People to Purchase Our Products at a Profit. Is this a satisfactory definition around which to build a sales training program? Discuss.

Part b

Duties of the Salesperson

When customers enter a store or a department of a store, that is not a self-service operation, they expect to be greeted and served by salespeople. Selling goods to customers is the most important duty of the salesperson, and the greater part of his time will be devoted to this work. A salesperson does, however, have other duties and responsibilites. The most important nonselling tasks will be presented in this part.

MERCHANDISE KNOWLEDGE

Retail stores are seeking salespeople of integrity who are competent in *product knowledge* and trained in selling procedures. The salesperson must know his merchandise thoroughly before he can present it confidently and intelligently. One of his tasks is to acquire this knowledge. The average customer is a well-informed individual. Radio, television, motion pictures, magazines, and newspapers bring her the latest information about merchandise. There are books and magazines that tell her how to get the most for her money. Competition among stores is very keen, and every merchant is seeking the customer's patronage. The customer who has a buying problem needs a professional salesperson who is a merchandise specialist and who is also concerned about the customer's welfare. It is the responsibility of every salesperson to develop and maintain merchandise expertise.

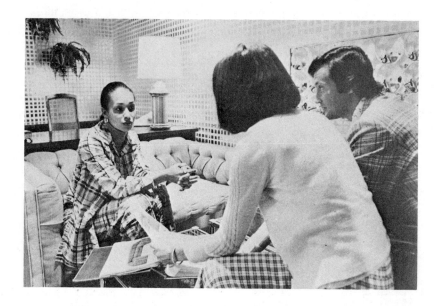

Courtesy of Sears, Roebuck and Co.

Illus. 11-3   Many customers depend on the merchandise knowledge of the salesperson to help them select quality goods that reflect their good taste.

STOCKKEEPING

In nearly every store *stockkeeping* is an important duty of salespeople. Each morning before customers enter the store, salespeople are often required to remove the cloths that cover the stock, fold them, and put them away until the end of the day, when they are replaced to keep dust off the goods. Next, salespeople arrange small fixtures, price stands, and displays. They put into current stock the merchandise received from the reserve warehouse or from an outside supplier, first checking the merchandise and then carefully placing it behind or below the stock already on hand. This is done so that the older goods will be sold before the new.

The salesperson must also look after the housekeeping of the department, for good housekeeping is essential to a good sales volume. Dirty, smudged displays downgrade both merchandise and the store image, while a clean, crisp look encourages business. Containers are provided for all trash, newspapers, boxes, wrapping paper, and string. Sales books, pencils, and forms should be kept in definite places. This housekeeping work is usually done in the morning and during the last few minutes of the day. Stock work should never be done in the presence of a customer, for it is disrespectful.

While stock work is sometimes assigned to other than salespeople, a reasonable amount should be welcomed by every salesperson. It acquaints him with his merchandise and with the location of each article. Customers become impatient and annoyed when a salesperson hunts for merchandise or asks another salesperson where to find it. If stock is shown promptly, handled carefully, and demonstrated expertly, the customer's confidence is gained and time is saved.

PREPARING DISPLAYS

Closely associated with stock work is the preparation of simple displays. For this work the salesperson should know something about color, line, and design. Displays should be attractive, should win attention, and should create desire on the part of the customer to possess the merchandise. A display showing the goods in practical use or in connection with related goods is always effective. The merchandise displayed should be fresh and clean and should be changed frequently. A further study of display will be found in Chapter 14.

MERCHANDISE CONTROL

While the introduction of electronic devices is providing detailed stock information automatically in some of the large stores, aiding the buyer to control his assortment is still an important duty of the salesperson. Each salesperson is assigned a portion of the stock and is responsible for the supply of all staple and regular lines. If the store has a reserve stockroom, each salesperson checks his section every night and orders from the reserve what is needed to replace the day's sales. Where there is no reserve, inventories are taken by salespeople at regular intervals—usually once a week—and the buyer uses this information to determine what to buy. Between inventories, salespeople are expected to report any articles that are low in stock. Once a month salespeople may be given lists of slow-selling goods in their sections and asked to report on the quantity then on hand and the current selling prices.

Salespeople assist not only in keeping up a supply of previously stocked articles but also in the purchase of new ones. They turn in want slips which list articles that customers ask for but that are not in stock. The merchant or the buyer often asks salespeople for an opinion on articles that he is thinking about buying. Sometimes, too, salespeople are sent to competing stores to observe and to report on merchandise ideas that would be usable in their own departments.

PREVENTING WASTE AND LOSS

An important duty in the interest of both the store and the customer is to prevent waste and loss. Illus. 11-4 shows ways to do this.

How the Salesperson Can Prevent Waste and Loss

Handle goods carefully.
Keep goods in proper place.
Keep goods clean.
Avoid wasting supplies.
Be careful not to damage furniture and fixtures.
Avoid overselling, which leads to complaints and returns.
Avoid careless selling, which leads to complaints and returns.
Write all sales checks accurately.
Measure and weigh accurately.
Arrive on time and make effective use of time on the job.
Promote honesty among fellow workers and customers.

Illus. 11-4   How valuable a salesperson is to a store may be judged not only by the amount of sales he makes but also by his ability to keep store expenses down. Each salesperson has many opportunities to prevent waste and loss.

DIRECTING CUSTOMERS

Customers often enter a store without knowing exactly where to go to buy the things they wish. In a small store, directing customers is relatively simple, for each salesperson should be familiar with the entire stock. In a large store, however, the problem is much more difficult. Salespeople are frequently asked where something can be purchased, and the customer's goodwill depends upon a prompt and accurate answer. Nothing is more annoying to a customer than to be told to go first to one department, then to another, and finally to a third in a vain attempt to find something that the store probably has in stock but that poorly trained salespeople do not know about.

Directions to customers should be given courteously and accurately. A customer should never be directed unless the salesperson is sure he is right. Directions should be given clearly, so that the customer will understand every word.

HANDLING COMPLAINTS

In many stores the salesperson is required to handle complaints and to make adjustments. This requires tact, patience, and understanding. He should be thoroughly familiar with his merchandise and with store policies so that he will know what adjustments can be made. A kind word will often disarm an angry customer, and a courteous salesperson may not only make a satisfactory adjustment but an additional sale as well. If handled properly, customers with complaints may become regular satisfied customers. You will learn more about handling complaints in the next chapter.

A PROPER SELLING ATTITUDE

Essential to the efficient performance of a salesperson's duties is the development of a proper selling attitude. He must have a genuine liking for and sincere interest in other people. The salesperson must understand his customers and the motives that move them to purchase so that he will be able to present the right merchandise in the right way to each customer. He must understand himself and his abilities and find in his job a pride in the opportunity to be of service to people. Without a proper selling attitude, competence in other duties will still not result in effective selling.

CHECKING YOUR KNOWLEDGE

Vocabulary

1. product knowledge   2. stockkeeping

Review Questions

1. Why must a salesperson be well informed about his products in order to sell them?
2. What stockkeeping duties do salespeople often perform?
3. How do salespeople help in merchandise control?
4. How can the salesperson prevent waste and loss of merchandise?
5. Why is it important that salespeople be able to direct customers within the store?

Discussion Questions

1. Assume that as a salesperson you are expected to handle simple complaints and adjustments but are to refer others to your department manager. How would you handle each of the following situations? State exactly what you would say to the customer.
   (a) The customer bought the wrong size and wants to exchange the article for the right size. You are temporarily out of stock.
   (b) The customer has found a defect in an article bought a few days before and wants a refund instead of an exchange.
   (c) Another salesperson in your department promised delivery two days before, but the customer approaches you to complain bitterly that the goods have not arrived.
2. It has been suggested that special workers be hired to do stockkeeping, inventories, display, and to handle complaints thus permitting salespeople to devote all their time to selling. Would this be a workable plan?

Part C

Beginning of the Sale

From the viewpoint of the salesperson and what he must do, the selling process has the following eight steps:

1. Getting ready to meet the customer
2. Opening the sale
3. Determining customer wants
4. Presenting the goods
5. Answering objections
6. Obtaining a favorable customer decision
7. Performing the mechanics of closing
8. Taking leave of the customer

From the viewpoint of the customer and how she is affected by the sales talk, a sale has four steps:

1. Gaining the customer's favorable attention
2. Stimulating the customer's interest
3. Creating desire for the goods
4. Inducing action

These four steps make up what is sometimes called the *AIDA formula*—Attention, Interest, Desire, and Action.

When the two sets of steps are considered together, it is found that the customer's attention is gained during the opening of the sale and while the salesperson is determining the customer's wants. The customer's interest is stimulated while the salesperson is presenting the goods. The customer's desire for goods is also created while the salesperson is presenting the goods and answering the customer's questions and objections. And the customer is naturally induced to act when the salesperson closes the sale.

Courtesy of Federated Department Stores, Inc.

Illus. 11-5   An effective display can act as a silent selling tool in creating Attention, Interest, Desire, and Action.

THE PREAPPROACH

Even before the customer enters a store, the salesperson should prepare himself and his surroundings to make a favorable impression. This is the *preapproach*. Since all customers respond to neat and attractive surroundings, attention should be given to the physical appearance of the store and of the salespeople. The impression that the customer first receives of the surroundings and of the salesperson will have an important bearing on her mental attitude during the conduct of the sale. All the features of buildings, equipment, lighting, and layout discussed in Chapter 3 should be frequently checked; and the merchandise should be kept clean and neatly arranged.

As suggested in Part B, the salesperson must know his stock thoroughly so that he can select and produce promptly the merchandise best suited to the needs of his customers. He should know, without looking through his merchandise each time he is asked, which sizes are available in each style of merchandise that he stocks. He must know the price ranges and the relative attractiveness of the various grades of goods. He should know the general uses to which his merchandise may be put. If the features and facts about the merchandise are not known, this information should be requested from the buyer or the supplier.

Elements of a Successful Preapproach

Neat appearance of oneself and of the selling area

Appealing displays of merchandise

Knowledge of what is in stock and where it is

Product information, including characteristics and selling points of goods in stock

Knowledge of newspaper advertisements of the day

Memorization of names, backgrounds, and interests of specific customers

Five or six selling sentences prepared for most popular items

---

Illus. 11-6   If a salesperson includes in his preapproach all the elements given above, he will be almost certain to make a favorable impression upon his customers.

It is frequently possible to learn the names and the characteristics of many of the store's customers. If he can call the customer by name, the salesperson has made a good start. The salesperson should look at every sale as a preapproach for the next one. He should store away in his mind the name of the customer and any other facts that will help him in greeting and serving the customer when she comes in again. When time is available, it is a good plan to keep a notebook in which to write facts about each customer.

THE APPROACH

Just when to *approach* (actually meet) a customer who enters the store depends upon the type of store and the customer's attitude. In small stores and service stores handling convenience goods, the customer generally wants prompt attention. In large stores, especially those carrying shopping goods, she may wish to look around awhile before being approached. In self-service stores she may not expect to be approached at all. The time to approach the customer is when she seems to be ready to be shown merchandise or to be given information about it. Careful observation of every person who enters a store or a department, coupled with experience, will aid the salesperson in approaching at the right time.

People are usually willing to wait a reasonable length of time in a busy department in which all the salespeople are involved in taking care of customers. However, customers resent having to wait while employees arrange stock, balance their cash, fix their hair, visit with customers, carry on unnecessary telephone conversations, or gossip with other employees. The business of the store is to sell goods, and every other activity should give way at once to the serving of customers.

Almost as objectionable as keeping the customer waiting is forcing oneself on a customer when she is passing through a department. To rush after her calling, "Can I help you?" is inexcusable; yet it is frequently done. To pounce on a customer the moment she pauses before a display is equally irritating.

Qualities of a Good Approach

It is prompt.
It is friendly and courteous.
An interested tone of voice is used.
Varied phrasing is used.
It is appropriate.

Illus. 11-7   The salesperson who masters these qualities of a good approach is well on his way to making a successful sale.

The approach of the salesperson should always indicate to the customer that she is welcome, that she is not intruding or interrupting other duties, and that it is a pleasure for the salesperson to help her. The approach of the salesperson should definitely indicate to the customer: "I am at your service and am ready to help you solve your shopping problem."

THE GREETING

Approaching the customer generally requires a greeting. The salesperson should always give some thought to his greeting and should select that which seems most appropriate, rather than fall into the habit of greeting everyone in the same mechanical way.

The form of greeting that is probably used more than any other and that is acceptable if not overworked is, "May I help you?" or "May I be of assistance?" This type of greeting, called the *service greeting*, tends to put the customer at ease, shows the salesperson's attitude of helpfulness, and does not emphasize the desire of the salesperson to sell goods nor infer that the visitor is expected to buy.

Another greeting that receives the general approval of both skillful salespeople and customers is the simple, courteous, and cordial "Good morning," "Good afternoon," or a similar salutation. In discount stores, where the customer shops informally, the formal greetings, "May I help you?" or "Good morning," may be out of place. It is often better for the salesperson to make an immediate reference to the merchandise the customer may be examining. This is called the *merchandise approach* and may be used in any store if the customer already has her attention focused on a specific article. A majority of customers have either a definite want or a problem to be solved, and the salesperson can use his greeting as an invitation for the customer to make known her want or problem.

Several greetings that have been found to be unprofitable from the standpoint of producing favorable customer reaction are: "Was there something you wanted?" "Are you looking for something?" "Something in ties?" "Can I interest you in a blouse?" "May I show you some of our new shoes?" These may be classed as foolish questions since they are meaningless and overused.

A study of customer attitude toward the various steps in actual sales transactions reveals that the approach is the most important step in the sale. It has been found that if the approach is not right or if it does not attain its objectives, the chances for completing the sale are rather slim. There is a close correlation between the customer's overall impression of a transaction and her impression of the approach. First impressions set the tone of the sale. What is said and done in the first few seconds of the sale shows how well prepared the salesperson is.

DETERMINING CUSTOMER WANTS

An important aspect of opening the sale is determining customer wants. The variety of merchandise that is now available makes the task of decision making by the customer more difficult than ever before. The salesperson who develops skill in determining the wants of each customer saves time in the long run and builds customer confidence.

In determining the customer's wants, it is helpful to realize that she may be in one of three different moods at the time of purchase:

1. She may be decided, knowing exactly what she wants. She will probably ask for the merchandise without delay and will mention all the merchandise features she wants.
2. She may be undecided, knowing her need for an article of a general type but not having made up her mind about such details as price, material, or color.
3. She may be just looking, feeling no immediate need to buy but exhibiting an interest that the salesperson may be able to convert into desire for a product.

Studies of selling techniques reveal the importance of good questioning as a means of properly determining the customer's needs and readiness to buy. By asking questions about how the goods are to be used, by listening to the customer's ideas about her needs, the salesperson will be able to select and more effectively present the proper goods. Every customer is unique, and the salesperson should study customers as individuals by listening carefully to their questions and answers.

How to Determine What the Customer Wants	
Listen to her	She may tell you exactly what she wants. She may give hints about her problem. She may use expressions which will help you size up her needs.
Look at her	Study the clothes she wears. Study her manner.
Ask questions	"Is it for yourself?" "Where do you plan to use this?" "What colors do you now have?"
Show merchandise	Select a variety which you think suitable. Observe customer reaction.

Illus. 11-8 Determining what the customer wants is a part of opening the sale and is essential to making a sale.

CHECKING YOUR KNOWLEDGE

Vocabulary

1. AIDA formula
2. preapproach
3. approach

4. service greeting
5. merchandise approach

Review Questions

1. List the eight steps in the retail selling process from the viewpoint of the salesperson.
2. What should the salesperson do in the preapproach?
3. Why is the manner and timing of approach important in selling?
4. List at least four qualities of a good approach.
5. What are the three possible moods of a customer at the opening of a sale?

Discussion Questions

1. In stores or selling departments handling hundreds of merchandise items, is it reasonable to expect a salesperson to have a thorough knowledge of all aspects of the stock?
2. What can a salesperson do in order to learn the names and characteristics of many of his customers?
3. Some experts on selling modify the AIDA formula by inserting Conviction between Desire and Action and adding Satisfaction after Action. Discuss the significance of these two additional steps.

Part d

Heart of the Sale

The most important phase in the selling process—the heart of the sale—is the period in which the salesperson presents the merchandise to the potential customer, gains her interest, and converts that interest into a firm desire to buy.

There are five ways to present merchandise to a customer: (1) display it, (2) demonstrate it, (3) have the customer handle it, (4) talk about it, and (5) get the customer to talk about it. Of course, all these may be done in a single presentation. The purpose of the presentation is to turn the customer's interest into desire, that is, to help her decide which of the articles presented will best fit her needs.

DISPLAYING AND DEMONSTRATING THE GOODS

Goods should be displayed to the best advantage, in the best light, and in suitable surroundings. A piece of jewelry, for instance, should be handled carefully and could be placed on a piece of dark-colored velvet to express an appreciation of its value and to bring out its most attractive qualities.

Demonstrating is more than displaying. It means showing goods in action, as they would appear in use after the customer has acquired ownership. It involves showing what the goods will do for the customer or what she can do with them. A salesperson may demonstrate a vacuum cleaner by using it to clean a rug; a food preparation, by actually preparing it; a cosmetic preparation, by actually applying it; a necktie, by knotting it and holding it in front of a shirt; and a lamp, by placing it on a table similar to one the customer has at home.

CUSTOMER PARTICIPATION

Whenever possible, the presentation should involve more than a customer's passive observation of a salesperson's demonstration. The

Courtesy of Penney News, J. C. Penney Company, Inc.

Illus. 11-9   In selling clothing, a tailor or fitter may help the sales-man convince a customer that a jacket or suit will meet his requirements.

customer should be encouraged to handle the goods, to taste them, or to smell them—in fact, to act for the moment as their owner. Trying on a dress, sitting in an easy chair, operating a mechanical toy, putting a drop of perfume on one's wrist, or tasting a piece of cheese—these activities change interest into desire more effectively than can displays or demonstrations.

SALES CONVERSATION

During display, demonstration, and participation, neither the salesperson nor the customer remains silent. The salesperson calls attention to certain features of the merchandise. He volunteers information about durability, usefulness, and care that do not appear on the surface; and he answers questions raised by the customer. He appeals both to the reason and to the emotions of his customer. He gives facts and figures about the product itself, and he points out the satisfaction the customer will gain from owning it. He selects from his fund of information about each article those points that make it particularly desirable to customers. These are called *selling points*. Thus, the chief selling points of a certain blanket may be its warmth, its light weight, and its large size. The selling points of an article should reach the customer's mind through as many of the five senses as possible.

An effective selling conversation requires that the salesperson have specialized knowledge about all the following:

1. Uses of the product
2. How it will perform
3. What it is made of
4. How to use it
5. How to care for it
6. Background of interesting facts
7. Competing articles
8. Services available with the product

The key requirement in making use of features in a product is to relate them to the uses and benefits to be realized by the purchaser. For example, in presenting a pair of slacks made of woven two-way stretch material and treated for durable press, the salesperson may say, "The two-way stretch in these slacks will provide you maximum comfort in wear, and the finish assures that they will stay neat without pressing." Since, in retail selling, the statement that relates the features in the product to the consumer's need must be short, it is called a *selling sentence*.

GETTING THE CUSTOMER TO TALK

In addition to prevailing upon the customer to handle goods, a tactful attempt should always be made to draw the customer out and to get her talking. A customer is more likely to purchase if she has full opportunity to express herself, rather than if she is kept listening to the salesperson. Talking will bring into the open any objections she might have as well as any special needs that she might be trying to satisfy. Carefully worded questions will prompt the customer to talk about her needs and concerns.

Even if a customer voices strong objections, she should be allowed to complete all her statements. The salesperson should not break in to correct her. It is a psychological fact that once a person has had an opportunity to express a viewpoint fully, he is more likely to pay attention to another point of view.

ANSWERING OBJECTIONS

As the salesperson presents the merchandise, he may encounter customer objections. There are four kinds of legitimate customer objections. These are objections to price, to quality of merchandise, to store policies, and to buying immediately. The salesman should accept these objections as evidence of the customer's interest and as affording an opportunity to make clear the selling points of his merchandise. He should never permit himself to be annoyed by objections that are offered, and he should never argue or contradict.

An efficient salesman will be familiar with practically every objection to his product that can be offered and will be prepared to cope with each one. It is sometimes even wise to anticipate objections that persons are likely to raise when the customer takes the purchase home. For example, a man may have no objection to pleats in a skirt he is buying for his wife; but the salesperson may know that women sometimes object to pleats since they are difficult to iron. However, the pleats in the skirt under consideration may be permanent and thus present no difficulty in ironing. The intelligent salesperson will be sure to stress this point so that the customer may point this out to his wife.

Of course, there are also customer excuses that do not reveal the real reason for not wanting to buy. By careful probing, the salesperson can sometimes bring the real objection to the surface so as to be able to answer it. It is better to accept the excuse, however, than to offend by seeming overly insistent. It is much more important to leave the customer favorably disposed to the store.

Kinds of Objections

Objections to Price   "That's more than I want to pay."

"The price is too high."

"I can get it for less somewhere else."

An objection to price means that the customer is not convinced that the value of the merchandise justifies the price asked. The salesperson should *build up the value of the merchandise.*

Objections to Merchandise   "This is a poor quality of material."

"It looks too light."

"I'm afraid it won't hold up."

An objection to merchandise means that the customer is not sure about the point she raises. The salesperson should *give the facts* or show other goods.

Objections to Store Policy   "You don't deliver on time."

"Your credit department is too tough."

"I never heard of this brand."

An objection to store policy means that the customer has had an unpleasant experience with the store earlier. The salesperson should *reassure her.*

Objections to Buying Immediately   "I'll look around first."

"I didn't bring enough money."

"I'll have to talk it over with my husband."

An objection to buying immediately means that the customer cannot decide about whether or not to buy the merchandise. The salesperson should suggest the advantages of buying right away. Of course, this objection may be an excuse to get away and not reveal the true objection.

Illus. 11-10   Practically all customers make the same general kinds of statements when they are expressing objections to making a purchase. Above are some of these statements and the action a salesperson should take to answer each objection.

The salesperson should not attempt to close the sale until he has met all objections that the customer seems to have in mind. Asking the customer to buy before all objections have been met is high-pressure salesmanship. Such an approach will seldom achieve a satisfactory sale.

CHECKING YOUR KNOWLEDGE

Vocabulary

1. selling points

2. selling sentence

Review Questions

1. What is the heart of the sale?
2. List the five ways of presenting merchandise to a customer.
3. Distinguish between displaying goods and demonstrating goods.
4. What are the eight aspects of product information the salesperson must know in order to carry on an effective selling conversation?
5. What are the chief kinds of honest objections customers may raise? How do they differ from excuses?

Discussion Questions

1. Why is customer participation important in the selling process?
2. How can a salesperson determine a customer's real objection to an article of merchandise?
3. What should the salesperson do if he is asked a question about merchandise and he doesn't know the answer?
4. Under what conditions may the attempt of a salesperson to meet an objection simply strengthen the customer's resistence?

Part e

End of the Sale

The alert salesperson will be watching for signals that the customer is ready to buy. Signals may come as facial expressions, remarks about the merchandise, or actions such as handling the merchandise. When a signal is given, the salesperson should respond with a comment or question that attempts to bring the customer to a positive decision. These comments or questions are called *trial closes*. He may ask a definite question on a minor point requiring a decision and assume that the sale is closed. "How many would you like?" or "Would you like the yellow or the blue?" or "Would you like it gift wrapped?" are questions often used to help close the sale. By using a series of closing questions the salesperson can narrow the customer's choice to the article she wants at a price she is willing to pay.

Occasionally a salesperson encounters a person who simply has difficulty making up her mind. In this case, the salesperson must take an authoritarian attitude and make the decision for the customer. But he must be sure that this decision is truly in the long-range interest of the hesitant customer.

SUGGESTION SELLING

After the customer has made her major buying decision, there is an opportunity to suggest an additional purchase to her. This suggestion may be a larger quantity, a related item, or a timely special.

Much suggestion selling is best accomplished simply by displaying related and impulse items at attention points. At checkout counters in supermarkets are placed chewing gum, candy, razor blades, and other small articles that almost anyone can use. In clothing stores ties are usually displayed with shirts, so that customers will consider the purchase of a tie or two as they purchase the related item.

Suggestion selling undertaken by intelligent salespeople can add considerably to the size of the sale, if the following rules are observed:

1. Make the suggestion definite. Instead of "Something else?" say, "Do you need some flashbulbs to go with that film?"
2. Show the item as you suggest it; do not just talk about it.
3. Give a reason for making the suggestion. Point out how well the tie will enhance the new shirt or that the special is available today only.
4. Do not overdo your attempts at suggestion selling. Considerable ill will can be created if the salesperson is too persistent.

PERFORMING THE MECHANICS OF CLOSING

As soon as the sale has been closed, the salesperson must skillfully complete the mechanics of the transaction. For example, a salesperson in a retail store should know the store's procedures for writing sales checks, charges, ringing up sales on a register, handling cash, and wrapping packages. Procedures vary in different stores, and details are best learned after the salesperson is on the job.

Service Stores

Simple sales transactions in service stores are usually classified in the following manner:

1. *Cash take.* The customer pays cash and takes the merchandise with her.
2. *Cash send.* The customer pays cash and has the merchandise delivered by the store.
3. *Charge take.* The customer has the merchandise charged and takes it with her.
4. *Charge send.* The customer has the merchandise charged and has the store deliver it.
5. *COD.* The store collects the selling price when the merchandise is delivered to the customer.

In most large stores there are combinations of these transactions, such as a deposit on a COD sale or the layaway sale where the customer makes a number of cash payments on goods that are held for her until payments are completed. Each store gives its salespeople special instructions with regard to its methods of handling such complicated transactions. Small stores may use only *cash take* and possibly *charge take.*

Self-Service Stores

In self-service stores the mechanics of closing are not handled by salespeople but rather by cashiers and wrappers at a checkout point. Some departments may have an express lane where customers with only a few items may be checked out quickly. For discount stores and supermarkets good practice at checkout stations dictates that another checkout aisle should be opened if more than five customers are waiting in line. Both cash and charge sales may be handled at these checkout points, but the more complex COD's, part payments, and layaways should be handled at another desk.

When the customer in a self-service store selects from a sample, with the item itself located in reserve stock, a salesperson or "sales aide" must provide assistance. The customer signals one of these people who verifies the price and writes the serial number of the wanted item on a slip of paper which the customer takes to the department's checkout desk. A stock clerk brings the carton from the stockroom to the inspector-wrapper at the checkout counter. The customer then pays for and takes the goods.

The Sales Check

For complex sales and in departments selling furniture, rugs, jewelry and photographic equipment, where salespeople must be present to help the customer reach a decision, *sales checks* are still used. There are hundreds of variations in sales-check forms, but most of them provide the following information:

1. Date of purchase
2. Department or merchandise classification symbol
3. Salesperson's number
4. Name and address of purchaser
5. Kind of sale—cash, charge, or COD
6. Description and price of merchandise sold
7. Amount of money received from customer
8. Extra packages enclosed
9. Charge account identification and/or purchaser's signature

Generally a sales check consists of three distinct parts: (1) the *address label,* which is used in send and charge transactions; (2) the *body,* which gives all the information about the goods and the prices; and (3) the *voucher,* which is the salesperson's memorandum of the sale.

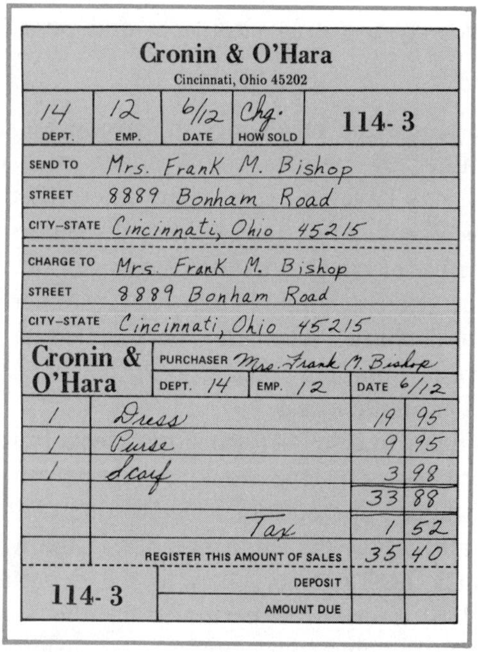
Cronin & O'Hara
Cincinnati, Ohio 45202

DEPT.	EMP.	DATE	HOW SOLD	
14	12	6/12	Chg.	114-3

SEND TO Mrs. Frank M. Bishop
STREET 8889 Bonham Road
CITY–STATE Cincinnati, Ohio 45215

CHARGE TO Mrs. Frank M. Bishop
STREET 8889 Bonham Road
CITY–STATE Cincinnati, Ohio 45215

Cronin & O'Hara — PURCHASER Mrs. Frank M. Bishop — DEPT. 14 — EMP. 12 — DATE 6/12

1	Dress	19	95
1	Purse	9	95
1	Scarf	3	98
		33	88
	Tax	1	52
	REGISTER THIS AMOUNT OF SALES	35	40
114-3	DEPOSIT		
	AMOUNT DUE		

Illus. 11-11 A typical sales check is shown above. Identify the address label, body, and voucher.

When a sales check is written in duplicate, the customer is given the duplicate voucher; the duplicate body is sent with the package; and the duplicate address label is pasted on the package of a "send" sale. If a sales check is prepared in triplicate, the triplicate copy, or tissue, is often used as an office copy in case the original is damaged or lost.

It should not be assumed that when the sales check is used the sales register is not. Many stores use a register for all cash-take transactions and use it with sales checks for almost all other transactions. When the register and sales check are used together, the sales check is slipped into a slot on the register and is imprinted with the same information that appears on the register receipt. Today new point-of-sales electronic registers are replacing conventional registers and will be discussed in a later chapter.

Building Goodwill

To have customers think favorably of a store and its goods and services is a major aim of every retailer. Without this favorable attitude of its customers, a store would have great difficulty in succeeding. The

Courtesy of Federated Department Stores, Inc.

Illus. 11-12   Some stores use push bells to request the attention of a salesperson to help the customer complete the purchase.

prestige that a company earns from the approval and support of its customers is called *goodwill*. Goodwill is so important to retailing that it is considered an intangible asset (see Chapter 4).

Up to the close of the sale, many salespeople do exactly the right things to build goodwill. Then, in writing the sales check, handling the cash, or wrapping the purchase they will do or say something foolish or tactless. The customer may say, "Never mind," and walk out of the store or leave with his purchase but with irritation. Slow and inefficient sales check writing, change making, and packaging are particular customer irritants. Advertising, word-of-mouth recommendations, appearance of the store, and its reputation tend to create goodwill. These practices do not result in establishing lasting goodwill unless they are backed up by the salesperson who sells merchandise that satisfies the customer in every way and who offers accompanying services and courteous treatment.

TAKING LEAVE OF THE CUSTOMER

Earlier you learned that the approach to the customer depends on the conditions existing in the department where the salesperson is stationed. Similarly, taking leave of the customer must vary with the kind of merchandise sold, the length of time spent with the customer, and the number of customers waiting for service. In some cases all that the salesperson or cashier can do is to say "Thank you" as he makes the change. In other cases, he may accompany the customer to the door of the store or limits of the department.

Such pleasantries as "I'm sure you will enjoy your purchase," or "We shall be glad to see you again," or "It was a pleasure to serve you; have a pleasant weekend," or "Have a good day" do much to retain customer goodwill. Those who fail to buy should also be provided the same courteous leave-taking.

CHECKING YOUR KNOWLEDGE

Vocabulary

1. trial close
2. cash take
3. cash send
4. charge take
5. charge send
6. COD

7. sales check
8. address label
9. body
10. voucher
11. goodwill

Review Questions

1. How can a salesperson determine the right time to close a sale?

2. List four rules that should be observed in suggestion selling.
3. Name the five classifications of sales transactions found in retail stores.
4. What information is provided on most sales-check forms?
5. What are some ways in which the salesperson may favorably take leave of the customer?

Discussion Questions

1. Some salespeople believe that there is a psychological moment when the sale should be closed. Do you agree or disagree. Why?
2. Should suggested items always be related to the major purchase? Why or why not?
3. Should suggested items always be of lesser dollar value than the major purchase? Why or why not?
4. What actions of a salesperson create customer ill will during the closing of a sale? What actions create goodwill?

BUILDING YOUR SKILLS

Improving Communications Skills

Each of the following sentences contains two verbs in parentheses. On a separate sheet of paper, write the number of each sentence and the correct verb to be used in that sentence.

1. You (can, may) take either the elevator or the escalator to the furniture department.
2. If it (was, were) you, would you have used a merchandise approach?
3. He (was, were) faced with two tough objections at the beginning of the sale.
4. You (can, may) meet your sales quota if you try hard enough.
5. Terry and Marge (was, were) on duty when the customer came in.
6. (Was, Were) you certain the vending machine gave the right change?
7. (Can, May) I come to your house to see the damaged furniture?
8. Everyone (can, may) do some suggestion selling.
9. Neither Rich nor Rob (was, were) successful in satisfying the customer.
10. Craig (was, were) given two turns to wait on customers.

Improving Arithmetic Skills

Calculate the percentages in the exercises below. On a separate sheet of paper, write the number of each exercise and your answer for each.

1. During one day a salesperson contacted a total of 80 customers. Sales were made to 56 of these customers. To what percentage of the customers did the salesperson make sales?
2. A salesman earned a commission of $617.60. What percentage is his commission if his sales for the period were $7,720?
3. As a means of sales promotion, Fox's Drug Store carried discount coupons in its printed advertising. Discount coupons were presented at the store from each media as follows: *Weekly Shopper*—27; morning paper—117; evening paper—123; store handout—43. What percentage redemption came from each media?

4. The gross sales from the August anniversary sale of Gibson's Men's Store amounted to $27,540. Gross sales for the previous year's sale had been $24,260. What was the percentage of increase in sales?

5. Nadine estimated that her suggestion selling resulted in sales of $981. If her total sales for the period were $6,540, what percentage was the result of suggestion selling?

6. A customer comes to your lumber and building supplies store. He asks for 30 meters of chain-link fencing. How many feet of fencing does he want? If the retail price of the fencing is $3.95 a yard and there is a 4% sales tax, how much will the 30 meters of fencing cost the customer? (See Appendix on page 622.)

Improving Research Skills

1. Clip from a newspaper two advertisements, each giving three or more selling points for the article advertised. On a separate sheet of paper, list the selling points used.

2. Develop a selling sentence for five of the following: a solid state TV set, a bone china plate, a pair of skis, a bicycle, an electric clock, a desk, indoor-outdoor carpeting, hedge clippers, health bread.

3. Your instructor will appoint you a member of a small committee to interview a salesperson in or a manager of one of the following stores: (a) drugstore, (b) men's furnishings store, (c) shoe store, (d) furniture store, (e) cosmetic and perfume shop, (f) hardware store. Ask the person you are interviewing about the customer objections he or she most frequently encounters. Make a report to the class.

4. Select an item in which you are interested and present a sales demonstration of that item in class. A classmate will act as a difficult customer. Members of the class should rate the demonstration by using a form similar to that on page 369.

Improving Decision-Making Skills

1. A mother and her teenage daughter have been in the sweater department on three previous occasions. On each previous visit you were able to get the daughter to choose a sweater she liked, but her mother raised an objection to buying. In this, the fourth sales conversation with them, you learn that the daughter is using her own money to buy the sweater. You also learn that the daughter wants the sweater to wear to a party this coming weekend. What trial closes would you attempt, knowing these additional facts? Write what you would say to both—to the daughter or to the mother.

2. The one regular salesman in the garden shop of a small department store was so busy bedding down evergreens that he did not want to be bothered answering customers' questions. He referred all customers to two high school students who had just been assigned to the shop as part-time workers. The regular salesman told the customers that the students knew all the answers. Of course, this was not the case; and the students were very much embarrassed.

If you were one of these students, how would you handle the situation? Would you complain to the regular salesman? Would you tell the customers that the salesman was playing a joke on you? Would you pretend to know, even if you gave misinformation? Or just what would you do?

SCORE SHEET FOR DEMONSTRATION SALES
(On each line, check one column)

Student Salesperson Rated _____

		Poor	Fair	Good	Excel-lent
Advance Preparation:	Merchandise & Displays	0	1	2	3
The Salesperson:	Good Health	0	1	2	2
	Suitable Dress	0	1	2	3
	Suitable Grooming	0	1	2	3
	Correct Posture	0	1	2	2
	Pleasant Voice	0	1	2	3
	Absence of Mannerisms	0	1	2	2
The Approach:	Right Timing	0	1	3	4
	Correct Greeting	0	1	2	3
	Interested Manner	0	2	4	6
Determination of Customer Wants:	Clear Comprehension	0	1	3	5
	Ready Location of Mdse.	0	1	3	5
Presentation:	Effective Display	0	1	2	3
	Smooth Demonstration	0	1	2	3
	Customer Activity Secured	0	1	3	4
	Right Opening Remarks About Merchandise	0	2	3	5
Knowledge of Merchandise:	As Exhibited Throughout Sales Talk	0	2	4	6
Meeting of Objections:	Right Attitude Toward Objections	0	2	3	5
	Convincing Answers	0	2	3	5
Close:	Attempt Well Timed	0	1	3	4
	Phrasing Impelling	0	1	3	5
Plus Selling:	Intelligent Suggestions Made	0	2	3	5
	Inviting Leave-Taking	0	2	3	5
Mechanical Closing:	Quick, Accurate, Smooth	0	1	2	3
Sustained Attitude:	Helpful, Genuine Interest	0	2	4	6
TOTAL OF SCORE: _____		0	(33)	(67)	(100)

Remarks: _____

Rater: _____

APPLYING YOUR KNOWLEDGE

Chapter Project

Collect information about the duties of a manufacturer's sales representative. You may do this by locating a library book or article that discusses this subject or by interviewing such a sales representative. Compare these duties with those of the retail salesperson, as discussed in this chapter. Put your information in report form.

Continuing Project

Perform the following activities for your manual:

1. Prepare a list of the nonpersonal selling aids that you will utilize in your store, and list the departments in which you will use salespeople.
2. Explain in a composition of not less than 500 words how you will handle the mechanics of closing a sale in each department of your store. Explain what training the salespeople, cashiers, wrappers, and other store employees will need to perform the mechanics of closing.
3. List the special ways in which you would endeavor to create goodwill in your store.

Special Skills in Selling

a. The almost universal way of recording sales was, until recently, by the use of a cash register. This is now being replaced by the new electronic point-of-sale terminal.

b. Merchandise is wrapped so that it can be carried or delivered easily and safely. Wrapping quickly and economically is a skill a salesperson must have.

c. The telephone is an important medium for selling to both old and new customers. Proper telephone selling techniques can be helpful to both the salesperson and the customer.

d. Receiving customer complaints is inevitable in retailing; and to retain customer goodwill, the salesperson must handle complaints tactfully.

e. The organization of the selling function differs from store to store. No matter how selling is organized, all persons in selling must work together as a team.

Part a

Recording Sales Information

Each time a sale of merchandise is made the retail store must have a record of that sale, and the customer must be given a receipt of her payment or charge. The recording must be done rapidly and accurately and yet provide the information about the sale that the merchant and the customer need. The customer wants the mechanics of the sale handled quickly and properly by the store's staff.

THE SALES REGISTER

The almost universal instrument for providing receipts and records of sales has been the cash register or, as it is being referred to more frequently, the sales register. The register with its record of sales serves as an information-collection center. It records information for each transaction by department, merchandise classification, salesperson, amount of sale, number of items, kind of sale, and computes the amount of change due the customer. When sales checks are needed, they can be stamped by the register.

Electronic Registers

Numerous attachments are available to permit sales registers to be used with electronic data processing equipment. Sales information placed in the register may be punched at the same time on paper tape or printed on magnetic tape. The tape is then fed into a computer; and the retailer receives a daily, weekly, or monthly sales analysis which aids in all his merchandising activities.

The newest entry to the sales register field is the *electronic point-of-sale terminal* system. Complete data about each sale is recorded immediately in a minicomputer. The newest device for picking up the information from price tickets or labels is an electronic wand or scanner. As it passes over special price tickets it reads and reports the information to the terminal.

This system can verify credit, calculate the entire sale, and compute any applicable taxes or discounts. The register units visually provide the amounts being recorded and print a customer receipt, sales check, and an audit tape.

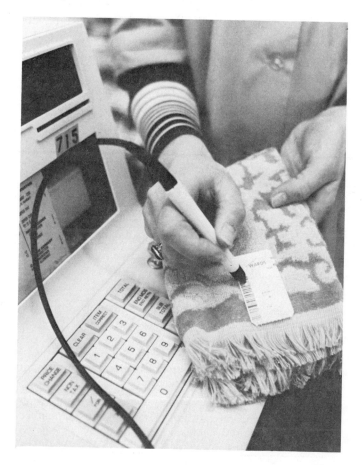

Courtesy of Montgomery Ward

Illus. 12-1   An electronic sales register linked to a minicomputer reads merchandise information directly from a coded price tag by means of an electronic wand or scanner. This speeds service to the customer and provides the retailer with more—and "fresher"—point-of-sales data.

The Sales Register Operator

The operator of a register, whether the sales register or the new electronic point-of-sale terminal, is often the salesperson but also may be a floor cashier. A cashier is essential in self-service operations. Even in stores where there are salespeople, floor cashiers are sometimes provided to relieve salespeople of the mechanical aspects of the sale and the problem of handling cash. The floor cashiers receive all sales checks and cash from salespeople and make change.

Sales registers provide fast and efficient recording of sales only if the operator is properly trained. Cashiering is more than making change accurately and giving courteous service. It means working under pressure, especially when long lines of customers are waiting to be checked out. It requires a thorough understanding of the kinds of sales and the specific information demanded by the store system, and it requires manual skill. The operator must also have a complete knowledge of the register and its capabilities and must know how to operate it with speed and accuracy.

Advantages of the Electronic Point-of-Sale Terminal

Speeds up checkout since essential data is picked up automatically from the price tickets and does not have to be recorded by punching keys

Virtually eliminates arithmetic errors in calculating rates, figuring sales taxes, finding totals, etc.

Cuts credit losses since status of each customer's account can be determined almost instantaneously

Simplifies bookkeeping since customers' accounts are charged at time of purchase and the entry made on the customer's bill automatically

Provides essential dollar and unit sales data for merchandise control, automatically including the adjustment of the inventory records and sometimes the automatic writing of reorders

Assists in personnel management since sales of each salesperson in both dollars and transactions can be determined automatically and as frequently as required

---

Illus. 12-2   The electronic sales register performs a wide variety of record-keeping tasks. Which of these advantages would be most important to a fashion store?

CASH TRANSACTIONS

When a cash-take sale is made, no sales check is needed, except for the receipt that the register usually issues. Many customers will pay cash for a purchase just to speed progress through the sales checkout. It is important that in cash transactions the mechanics of the procedure be carried out quickly and accurately.

Cash Sale Procedures

For cash sales the amount of the sale, plus any applicable tax, is entered in the register. If the register has departmental keys, each item purchased is recorded under the proper key. Payment is taken from the customer and change returned, if necessary. For some items, particularly in apparel stores, a portion of the price tag is removed to serve as the store's record of the sale. The body of the price ticket provides data that is used for stock control purposes. If the goods are to be sent, a sales check is necessary to provide the name and address for the delivery-man. If the new electronic register is used, the price tag data is punched into the register or picked up by a scanning device and stored in a computer.

Making Change

The salesperson or cashier needs considerable practice in the procedure to be followed in making change. The total amount of the sale should be announced to the customer. When the customer offers payment, the amount of the bill or check should also be announced. When money is received from a customer, the money should be placed on the shelf above the cash drawer. This eliminates the possibility of a dispute as to how much money the customer gave the salesperson.

Change should be made with as few coins as possible—for example, a dime should be given rather than two nickels. The change should be

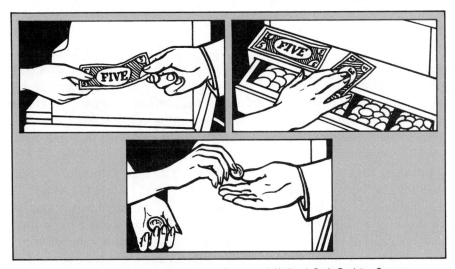

Courtesy of National Cash Register Company

Illus. 12-3   In making change, the amount of money received from the customer should be named. The money and the printed receipt should be left in sight while change is being made. The cashier or salesperson should count up from the purchase price to the amount of the payment, making change with as few coins and bills as possible and giving coins and bills to the customer one at a time. The change-making process should be ended with a "Thank you."

counted in a definite way. The usual plan is to count up from the purchase price, giving change of the smallest denomination first. Thus, if a sale amounts to $3.15 and the customer gives a five-dollar bill, the salesperson should count back aloud as follows: $3.15 out of $5. $3.25 (giving the customer a dime), $3.50 (giving a quarter), $4 (giving a half dollar), $5 (giving a dollar bill)." When more than one bill is given in change, each should be counted separately and placed one by one in the customer's hand.

If a customer is shortchanged, efforts to build goodwill usually fail. Some customers who are shortchanged never come back at all, and the store loses these customers. On the other hand, giving too much change means a direct loss to the store.

CHARGE TRANSACTIONS

If a purchase is to be charged, a sales check traditionally has been needed, even though the customer may take the goods with her. The sales check has been needed to charge the amount of sale to the customer's account and to assure that a designated store authority has approved the credit transaction. However, as indicated below, new procedures are now being introduced.

Identifying the Customer

As the sales check is written, all that is needed before ringing up the sale on the sales register is to be sure that the customer is properly identified (that the person shows evidence that he is the person he claims to be) and that the charge sales is authorized (that the purchase is within the customer's credit limit). In small stores the owner or manager sometimes knows the customer by sight and can perform both identificatiton and authorization. In large stores the customer makes application to the store's credit department. After the customer's credit standing has been investigated and approved by the credit department, the customer is supplied with a *credit card*. As indicated in Chapter 5 some stores accept other credit cards such as those issued by banks. The card will have the customer's name, address, account number, and, in some cases, a colored photograph of the customer. At the time of a charge transaction the card is given to the salesperson. The card is placed in an embossing device that imprints the information from the charge card onto the sales check.

Authorizing Credit

In many stores the salesperson is allowed to release goods to an identified customer if the purchase is less than a certain amount—

Courtesy of Federated Department Stores, Inc.

Illus. 12-4   A credit card is placed in an embossing device that imprints the information from the charge card on to the sales check.

the *floor limit*. For sales of a larger amount, the sale may be referred to the office or to a central credit department for authorization. This may be done by direct telephone connection, especially when the sale is a "take with." The same procedure can be used for cards issued by an outside credit agency, which may also provide the cooperating stores with updated lists of delinquent accounts, as explained in Chapter 5.

More and more stores are using electronic credit authorizers. Credit authorization is obtained by inserting the customer's credit card in a telephone-like device usually located near the sales register station. As the card is inserted the account number is transmitted and then the amount of the credit sale is entered. In seconds the cashier or salesperson is given an audio, a light, or a printed response indicating that credit is authorized or that a check with the credit department should be made.

These authorizers are incorporated in the new electronic point-of-sale systems so that data from the price ticket, from the customer's credit card, and from the salesperson's identification number are all recorded at once. Not only is the authorization performed but, if it is satisfactory, the customer's account is automatically billed. The sales-person and the department are automatically credited for the sale, and the stock records are automatically adjusted to reflect the sale of the item.

CHECKING YOUR KNOWLEDGE

Vocabulary

1. electronic point-of-sale terminal   3. floor limit
2. credit card

Review Questions

1. What kinds of information are recorded by a sales register?
2. What are the qualifications of an efficient sales register operator?
3. What are the advantages of electronic register systems?
4. Describe the correct procedure for making change.
5. What is the difference between identification and authorization in a credit transaction?

Discussion Questions

1. What can stores do to speed sales register checkout procedures?
2. What are the most common mistakes a person is likely to make when learning to operate a sales register?
3. In what kinds of stores are electronic point-of-sale terminals likely to replace traditional cash registers?
4. What are the pros and cons of authorizing credit transactions by electronic means?

Part b

Wrapping Packages

When a customer decides to take the merchandise with her, the salesperson is usually responsible for wrapping the package. In many large stores, however, there may be a person called the *inspector-wrapper* who compares the sales check with the price ticket on the merchandise and then wraps the merchandise. In supermarkets and some discount stores a *bagger* or *carry-out boy* is responsible for putting the customer's purchases in bags or wrapping them.

Merchandise is wrapped so that it can be easily carried, so that the customer is saved the embarrassment of having her purchase exposed to the public, and so that the goods are protected. In addition, many stores use the package wrapping as a means of advertising by imprinting

Courtesy of International Business Machines Corporation

Illus. 12-5   In this supermarket a computerized display, keyboard, cash drawer, and printer make checking out easier and faster for the checker and the consumer. A bagger stands by ready to assist the checkout girl so that customers may be moved through the lines as quickly as possible.

the store name on boxes, paper, wrapping tape, and bags. Wrapping protects the customer from the suspicion that may fall on one who leaves the store carrying unwrapped merchandise. Gift wrapping also improves the appearance of the package.

Wrapping can be either wasteful or economical. Many stores have made careful studies to determine the weight of paper, size of bag or box, and strength of cord that is best suited for each purpose. Sales-people and wrappers need careful training regarding the size of paper, box, or bag to be used for different articles and the most economical use of twine, gummed tape, and rubber bands.

PACKING AND WRAPPING MERCHANDISE

Where a bag is used for packing small items, the salesperson must simply select the proper size for the goods. Using too large a bag is wasteful and makes the package bulky. If too small a bag is used, the merchandise will be exposed. Customers like neatly wrapped packages that will not come apart.

In supermarkets the packer, or the cashier, is responsible for packaging or sacking the customer's order. The packer must be sure to make a solid base (with canned goods or cartons) in the proper size bag and then place light and perishable merchandise on top. Wet or frozen goods should be put in a special bag before being placed in the sack; otherwise the sack becomes weakened by the moisture and may break.

If a customer is carrying several packages, even though not all of them were bought in the store, the salesperson should offer to wrap them together for her. The customer will be grateful for this service. When a customer asks to have a package gift wrapped, the salesperson should be careful not to enclose the sales check, price ticket, or cus-tomer's receipt. Some stores use tissue paper and white wrapping paper for gift packages and enclose gift cards.

If it is the job of the salesperson to wrap and tie bundles, and if he is not taught, he should observe how experienced salespeople do the work and then practice wrapping and tying until he can do it neatly and quickly. A customer often measures a salesperson's efficiency by the manner in which he performs this duty. All that is needed for a compact, strong package is suitable wrapping paper or a cardboard box and twine or tape. These materials should be on hand before the day's work begins. A sufficient number of wrapping stations should be provided so that it is not necessary for salespeople to make long trips to wrap packages every time a sale is made.

PREPARING PACKAGES FOR DELIVERY AND MAILING

When merchandise is to be delivered by truck or by common carrier, it is often necessary to pack the goods to withstand rough handling. A knot should be tied at each intersection of the cord when tying the package to prevent it from falling apart if the twine breaks. With a little practice a retail employee can become expert at this skill. It is also necessary to make sure that the customer's name and address are correct and clearly legible and that the store's return address is clearly marked.

In some large stores goods to be delivered are not wrapped and packed by salespeople but are sent in bags, with the sales checks attached, to a *central wrap*. Breakable articles are commonly sent to the packing department where expert wrappers and packers prepare the merchandise for delivery. Then the packages are sent to the delivery department where they are sorted according to the deliverymen's routes and are *sheet-written* or *stubbed*. When sales are sheet-written, the name and address of each customer are entered on a list upon which are recorded all packages turned over to a driver. When sales are stubbed, the stub of each sales check is removed from the package as it is turned over to the deliveryman. The stubs are then filed to provide a list of the customers' names and addresses. The lists or stub file may be used to fix responsibility when a customer fails to get a package.

Formerly it was thought necessary that all goods to be delivered by the store should be packed in such a way, regardless of the expense involved, as to allow for rough handling. In recent years, however, there has been a great change in thinking about this matter. If the customer plans to take the goods with her in her car, it is often best to give her the goods unwrapped, with simply a tag or a cash register receipt attached. Even if the goods are to be delivered by truck, it may be best to leave them exposed. For example, in packing a lamp, it would be very difficult to avoid breakage if the package were dropped or thrown onto the customer's porch. But if the deliveryman is given the lamp unwrapped and is provided with protective material, he can place the lamp in his truck so as to prevent breakage in transit. He will then be sure to handle it carefully when removing it and turning it over to the customer.

PREPACKING

Prepacking merchandise in advance of sale—in *unit prepacks* (individual packages) ready for delivery to the customer—is becoming standard practice. This prepacking is generally done by the manufacturer in consultation with the retailer. In supermarkets, however, the store usually prepacks its own produce and meats. In some chains meats are prepacked in the warehouse, and each manager orders the particular assortment of cuts he requires for sale.

Courtesy of Clark Equipment Company

Illus. 12-6   Some chain supermarkets prepack meats in the warehouse, and each manager orders the particular assortment of cuts he requires for sale.

Many manufacturers are constantly improving the packaging of their products, and the developments in packaging have been phenomenal. But there is still room for improvement in the packaging of handbags, china and glassware, children's wear, and toys. Nevertheless, both retailers and manufacturers have realized the power of the prepackaged item as a means of reducing time and expense. Merchandise unit-packed by the manufacturer and suitable for delivery to customers is finding favor among retail buyers and consumers.

A great deal of research has been undertaken in connection with both prepacking and packing in the store of items not packed by the manufacturer. The objective is to find the best packing method and the best materials that will provide the lightest and most economical packages and still give excellent protection. In many instances the use of excelsior or wastepaper stuffed around a small article in a bulky container is giving way to the use of corrugated cardboard or plastic foam notched to support the article and protect it from shock.

PACKING IN A PLASTIC BUBBLE

Goods that are breakable—particularly chinaware—are usually packed today by laying the pieces ordered by the customer on a large, heavy piece of cardboard and then covering them with a plastic film that is applied by heat in such a way that every article is firmly sealed to the base. With each piece immobilized, breakage is virtually eliminated.

Manufacturers of small hardware items use a similar device for goods that are to be sold on a self-service basis. The articles are retained in a *plastic bubble* attached to the card. This assures that every article carries with it information on its use and that thieves will be restrained from stealing small articles if they have to shoplift a bulky card at the same time.

Courtesy of Federated Department Stores, Inc.

Illus. 12-7   Gift package bows are protected from damage by means of a plastic bubble packing.

CHECKING YOUR KNOWLEDGE

Vocabulary

1. inspector-wrapper
2. bagger
3. carry-out boy
4. central wrap

5. sheet-written
6. stubbed
7. unit prepacks
8. plastic bubble

Review Questions

1. Why is merchandise wrapped?
2. What is the difference between wrapping and packing?
3. What materials are necessary for a strong package?
4. What precautions should be taken in wrapping merchandise for delivery and mailing?
5. Why is prepacked merchandise gaining favor among retailers?

Discussion Questions

1. As a customer is leaving the store the cord on a package of her purchases breaks and some items are broken. Is the store responsible? What would you do if the customer asks for replacement of the broken goods?
2. A customer calls and says that when she reached home some of the purchases she made at your store were not in the package. What questions would you ask, and what action could you take?
3. Explain the instructions that you would give a merchandise wrapper on how to prepare for mailing each of the following items: (a) a man's suit; (b) a china figurine which is not prepacked; (c) auto parts—including brake shoes, spark plugs, and headlights.

Part C

Telephone Selling

The use of the telephone in retail selling is increasing, and the salesperson is often called upon to sell by telephone. This is a special skill which requires study and practice. More and more customers are finding it convenient to do their shopping by telephone, especially if they are shopping for food, staple clothing, or items advertised in the newspaper or in a mail-order catalog. When a customer finds it difficult to go to the store because of transportation problems or family commitments, she can generally purchase her daily needs by telephone. Many specialty shops find it profitable to telephone customers when new goods are received, and grocery stores sometimes telephone customers on rainy days. Salespeople develop lists of customers whom they know personally and telephone them when interesting offers are available. If such solicitations are tactfully made and are made at reasonable hours, they can bring in much additional business.

Alert retailers who realize the potential of telephone selling for increasing their sales and profits advertise this customer service and provide telephone order departments with special clerks to handle the orders. Some stores, even though closed on Sundays, keep their order departments open. A store that caters to telephone selling must make arrangements for delivery, offer customer credit in most cases, and provide intelligent and helpful telephone-order salespersons. Higher markups, lower selling costs, and greater use of the existing facilities can be realized by an efficiently managed telephone-order department.

Not all retailers are convinced of the merits of telephone selling. Some believe that telephone selling keeps customers from coming to the store, increases merchandise returns, increases operating expenses, and creates ill will. These merchants generally are the cash-and-carry businessmen. Such objections can be overcome by proper planning, adequate training of employees, and effective promotion of this important sales-producing method of customer contact.

GUIDELINES TO SELLING BY TELEPHONE

Selling by telephone presents some problems that differ from those of selling over the counter. When a customer makes a personal trip to the store, the salesperson has an opportunity to greet her pleasantly, to show her the goods, to observe her reaction, and to get her to take part in the sales presentation. The telephone salesperson, however, has only the customer's voice to guide him through the sales presentation. He must be able to tell from the tone of the customer's voice whether she is interested, whether desire has been created, and whether he should attempt to close the sale. Since he cannot show the customer the goods, he must be able to paint a word picture of his merchandise. He must create desire by the enthusiasm of his own voice; and he must know about the sizes, colors, prices, and quantities of the goods he has on hand in order to tell the customer whether the order can be filled promptly. When the order is actually given, great care must be taken to obtain the following necessary facts:

1. Name of person telephoning
2. Name and address of person to whom goods are to be charged
3. Address to which goods are to be. sent
4. Any special delivery instructions
5. Exact description of each article, including quantity, price, brand, size, quality, and special preparation

The salesperson must be particularly careful not to leave the customer on the phone for more than a few moments while he gets needed information. Telephone customers resent any indication that they have been forgotten.

Tact is needed when the telephone connection is not clear and hearing is difficult. The customer should not be required to repeat an order too often. Polite apologies, such as "Pardon me" and "I'm sorry," help to keep the customer in a pleasant frame of mind if it is necessary to have her repeat what she has said. Should there be a poor connection, it may be wise to ask the customer for her phone number and to say, "Let me try to get a better connection. I'll call you right back."

One should not confuse order taking by telephone with telephone selling. Although the instrument is used for both activities, selling over the telephone requires unusual ability, whereas taking orders by telephone is a rather simple procedure after the technique has been learned. Salespeople who are most successful in telephone selling have a complete knowledge of their merchandise, have a "voice with a smile," and have an ability to understand voices over the telephone. They know the technique of selling. They answer the telephone promptly, giving the firm's name and the department. They are courteous throughout the conversation, they are quick and accurate in taking orders, and at the end of the sale they may suggest related merchandise. Above all, they never forget to thank the customer.

SUGGESTION SELLING BY TELEPHONE

A customer who has made a special effort to telephone for goods is particularly susceptible to suggestion selling. Additional merchandise and even substitute goods can be readily suggested by the trained salesperson. The salesperson must learn to analyze his telephone customer quickly. If she is fast-talking, cold, distant, or reserved; if she seems to be reading from a prepared order or statement; if she is decided on the quantity, color, size, and price of the goods she is ordering, she is probably a person who will not readily accept or act upon suggestions regarding additional merchandise. In this case, the salesperson should make suggestions sparingly, with caution, or not at all. On the other

---

Pointers for Telephone Selling

Answer the telephone promptly.
Pay close attention so as to prevent repetition.
Make your voice pleasant and cheerful.
Use suggestion selling.
Paint word pictures to describe the merchandise.
Take down details of the order correctly.
Thank the customer.

Illus. 12-8   The salesperson who puts into practice these telephone selling pointers can soon become expert in using the telephone to persuade customers to buy his store's merchandise.

hand, if the telephone customer is less decided in her manner, more cordial and gracious, she is likely to react more kindly to the salesperson's suggestions of additional goods.

FILLING ORDERS

When the salesperson receives a telephone order, he may also be expected to fill the order for delivery to the customer. If he has performed his telephone selling properly and has all the information at hand, this job is not difficult. All that is needed is a knowledge of where the goods are located within the store or stockroom. Many stores that do a brisk telephone-order business set aside a definite place in the store or stockroom for order filling. Here the orders may be given to special employees, called *order fillers*. These workers, guided by the information on orders written by salespeople and telephone-order clerks, assemble the goods asked for by the customer. The order filler must be careful to see that correct quantities, colors, and sizes are sent. Items for an order are placed in a container and are given to a wrapper for packaging for delivery. High school students sometimes are introduced to the world of retailing by this type of job.

Large mail-order houses, which do business by mail and telephone orders, set up elaborate systems of processing the orders. The customers' orders are opened by an order clerk or recorded by a telephone operator, sorted, and checked for cash remittance or credit authorization; requisitions are prepared for the merchandise; and the goods are picked, assembled, wrapped, and finally shipped to the customer. All this is done according to a time schedule so that it is possible to know at what time a certain order will be in the shipping room after it has been received in the mail-order room.

CHECKING YOUR KNOWLEDGE

Vocabulary

order filler

Review Questions

1. Why is the use of telephone selling increasing?
2. List five items of information that should be recorded when accepting an order by telephone.
3. Name four items of merchandise information that should be possessed by a telephone salesperson.
4. Give seven pointers for telephone selling.
5. What duties are involved in the job of order filler?

Discussion Questions

1. What kinds of goods are best suited for telephone selling? Are there some kinds of goods that should never be sold by phone?
2. Cash-and-carry retailers do not use telephone selling to any great extent. Discuss the pros and cons of this policy.
3. Do you think it is better for a city customer to shop for home furnishings in the stores or to shop for them at home from a mail-order catalog and phone in her order?

Part d

Handling Complaints

"The first time I washed it all the color came out." "It was broke when I opened the package." "It says size 10, but it is much too big." "This isn't what I ordered." Such complaints by customers are certain to be heard by the retailer. No matter how carefully a store develops and implements its merchandising policies and procedures, customers are going to have reason for dissatisfaction sometimes. Many things can cause a customer to complain, and the realistic retailer expects to receive some complaints each day.

In most stores the assignment of listening to the customer and making certain adjustments, such as merchandise exchanges, is delegated to the salesperson. Since the adjustment must satisfy both the customer and the store, it is essential that the salesperson develop a special skill in handling customer complaints.

SYSTEMS FOR HANDLING CUSTOMER COMPLAINTS

A store may use one of three systems for handling customer complaints. The first type is a centralized system in which all complaints are handled by a single person or a single office. Small stores generally use a centralized system, with complaints handled by the owner-manager. Sometimes large stores also use a centralized system, and all customers with complaints are referred to an *adjustment office.*

The second system is a decentralized one. Under this system all complaints are handled on the selling floor by the salespeople, buyers, and department managers. The third system is really a combination of the centralized and decentralized systems. Certain types of complaints

—such as complaints involving merchandise—are handled on the selling floor. Other types of complaints—such as those received by mail and telephone and those requiring a check of store records—are handled by an adjustment office. This combination system is most frequently used in large stores.

MAINTAINING THE PROPER ATTITUDE TOWARD COMPLAINTS

The majority of retailers feel that it is most desirable for the salesperson or his superior, rather than an adjuster in a central office, to handle complaints whenever possible. The salesperson is more familiar with his customers and their needs and is more knowledgeable about the merchandise involved than is the adjuster. A salesperson with the right attitude toward customer complaints can earn much goodwill for the store, but a salesperson with a poor attitude can cost the store many customers.

Too many salespeople and department managers become defensive when a customer comes to them with a complaint. They feel that the complaint reflects badly on the store and on them, even though they may not have made the original sale to the customer. Often salespeople become angry with the customer and resist making the adjustment even before they have heard the customer's explanation. Such an attitude will almost certainly lead to loss of the customer's goodwill and future patronage. What is more important, additional customers can be lost. A dissatisfied customer is certain to tell her friends and acquaintances about the shabby treatment she received, and these persons are likely to stop buying at the store.

The salesperson—or anyone else who handles complaints—should always assume that the customer has a legitimate complaint. He should listen to the customer's explanation before making a suggestion concerning settlement, and he should maintain an open mind about the complaint. He should recognize that complaints are bound to occur—through the fault of the customer, through the fault of the store, and even through the fault of a third party such as a transportation company or a manufacturer. The most important thing to remember is that the way a complaint is handled is the best opportunity to create customer goodwill. A fair adjustment, quickly made, often makes a more favorable and lasting impression upon a customer than does an efficient sale.

Many stores have a rule that no one on the selling floor may ever say no to a customer. Whenever a customer makes what seems to be an unreasonable demand and balks at a suggested compromise, she must be referred to the general manager's office or to a central adjustment office. There, only a store executive may deny a customer's demands. Usually these executives tend to be lenient and agree to most demands. Nevertheless, it is a good plan to take potentially costly decision making out of the hands of salespeople and other personnel on the selling floor. This plan protects them and acts as a deterrent to many customers who are willing to test the salesperson but who hesitate to make unfair demands of an experienced adjustment employee.

PROCEDURES IN HANDLING COMPLAINTS

There are three major kinds of complaints: (1) complaints about merchandise, (2) complaints about service, and (3) complaints about billing. A merchandise complaint may be about a gift article of clothing

Courtesy of Penney News, J. C. Penney Company, Inc.

Illus. 12-9   Merchandise complaint. A fair adjustment, quickly made, often makes a more favorable and lasting impression upon a customer than does an efficient sale.

that did not fit properly or about a defective appliance in the home. A service complaint may be about late delivery. A billing complaint may concern an incorrect merchandise price recorded on the customer's charge account. Such complaints may be caused by poor quality merchandise, carelessness or inefficiency on the part of store personnel, inefficiency in store procedures, or poor supervision of merchandising activities.

The complaints a salesperson will most often encounter involve merchandise. As you have learned, customers commonly go to an adjustment office or to another department, such as the credit department, with complaints about other matters. Thus, in discussing the

Courtesy of Montgomery Ward

Illus. 12-10   Service complaint. Repair service technicians provide a variety of in-home repairs and adjustments—including checking to see if the appliance is plugged in! This is one of the questions repair service switchboard operators are trained to ask—much to the annoyance of some customers.

Illus. 12-11   Billing complaint. These customer service representatives are problem-solvers. They are trained to handle telephone complaints—many of which require a check of store records. They must make certain that each transaction is completely satisfactory to the customer.

procedures a salesperson should follow in handling a complaint, we shall assume that he is handling a complaint about merchandise.

Determining the Facts

A salesperson should first try to determine the facts surrounding a complaint. Most customers will have a just complaint because of defective merchandise or a store error, but the salesperson can expect to meet some customers who are sincere in their complaints but whose ignorance or inexperience about the product in question or the store's policies make the complaints unfair. Unfortunately, the salesperson will also encounter customers who make unreasonable claims in an effort to take advantage of the store's policy of trying to please all customers. The salesperson should always assume that the claim is a just one until all the facts have been obtained.

The customer should be allowed to explain her reasons for making the complaint, and the salesperson should listen attentively. He should then ask questions to uncover any facts that seem to be missing. If the merchandise item in question is defective, he should examine it in front of the customer. The salesperson should, of course, express regret that the customer has been inconvenienced; and he should reassure her that the store wishes to make a fair adjustment. Then he should take action to see that the problem is settled.

Making an Adjustment

The adjustment that a salesperson makes will be influenced by several factors: (1) the cost of the item in question; (2) the value of the customer to the store; (3) how often the customer makes complaints; and (4) the responsibility for the complaint.

Let us see how the salesperson might use each of these factors in a given situation. Suppose a customer complains that a paper stapler, which cost $2.69, broke the second time it was used. The salesperson might examine the stapler quickly to see if it showed any signs of unusual abuse, but he would almost certainly give the customer a new one. The price of a new stapler, $2.69, is too small to risk losing the customer's goodwill by refusing to make the replacement.

How valuable the customer is to the store is an important factor in making an adjustment. Suppose a customer complained that she just noticed a hole in the upholstery of an occasional chair that she purchased a few days earlier. The salesperson may have a doubt as to whether the hole was in the chair before it was delivered or whether one of the customer's children accidentally tore the upholstery. If the customer has just placed an order with that salesperson for two rooms of new furniture, the store will be wise to replace the chair or offer to repair it rather than risk cancellation of the large order.

How often a customer makes complaints is also important in making an adjustment. There are customers who shop carelessly with the attitude that "I can always take it back"; and there are customers who are chronic complainers. Perhaps a salesperson in a home furnishings department has come to recognize a woman who often returns used goods with the complaint that they do not meet advertised standards for wear. Replacing these goods obviously represents a direct loss to the store. If a number of adjustments have already been made and if, upon examination, the goods do not seem to be in such condition as to warrant a complaint, the salesperson should refer the customer to a superior or to the adjustment department where future adjustments may be refused. The store may lose the woman's patronage, but the cost of making the adjustments she demands is probably greater than the loss of her business.

If a store delivers red shoes when a customer ordered black shoes, the adjustment would be made without question; the cause of the complaint was the store's error. Suppose, though, that a customer complains that a dress does not fit properly nor look attractive since she laundered it and that she wishes the dress replaced. The salesperson might know that the manufacturer's directions state that the dress must be dry cleaned. If she can prove this by showing the customer an identical dress with the directions attached, she can explain to the customer that she has no authority to make a replacement. She should, however, express sympathy with the customer's predicament and perhaps consult with her superior, who may agree to grant the customer a partial refund or credit so that she may replace the dress.

No matter what adjustment is made, the salesperson should explain carefully to the customer why it is being made or is not being made. The customer wants a quick solution, and she also wants a fair one.

RETURNED GOODS

Returned goods present a serious retailing problem to almost all stores. In such merchandise lines as dresses, millinery, rugs, and decorative housewares, returns commonly exceed 10 percent of the gross sales. This does not mean, however, that 10 percent of all such items purchased are returned. Expensive merchandise is generally returned more often than is inexpensive merchandise. When a large investment is involved, customers are particularly demanding.

The cost of handling returned goods triples the usual cost of handling a sale. It costs as much to put goods back into stock as it costs to sell them in the first place, and they must still be sold a second time. Furthermore, returned goods frequently cannot be sold at the original price. The return may be soiled or damaged or may be going out of fashion and must be resold at a lower price.

There are four ways to reduce returns:

1. *Set general rules in regard to returns.* Rules often are communicated in the form of a statement on sales checks, price tickets, or store signs. Typical rules are that any returns must be made within a certain number of days after the sale and that the sales check must accom-

pany the return. Some goods are sold with no return privilege for sanitary reasons or because the goods are sold "as is," with the store assuming no responsibility for their condition or quality.

2. *Maintain high standards of merchandise quality, so that defects will not appear in use.* This involves choosing reliable resources, testing samples before purchase, inspecting goods very carefully when they are received at the store, and again just before they are delivered.

3. *Train salespeople to fill all orders with utmost care.* You have already learned about this topic in connection with telephone selling.

4. *Insist that salespeople do a complete selling job while the customer is in the store.* The salesperson should seldom, if ever, encourage the customer to take several merchandise items home with her to make a decision. If the salesperson provides intelligent aid in helping customers make a good selection, it is unnecessary for the customer to look upon the sale as "on approval," and then bring or send the goods back because they are unsuited to her needs. Defects in merchandise should be noted by the salesperson before the sale; and suitable color, style, price, and size should be assured.

CHECKING YOUR KNOWLEDGE

Vocabulary

adjustment office

Review Questions

1. What are the three systems that a store may use to handle complaints?
2. Why do many retailers believe that complaints should be handled by salespeople or their immediate supervisors?
3. Describe the three major kinds of complaints.
4. What should the salesperson do when a complaint is received?
5. Name four ways of reducing returns to the store.

Discussion Questions

1. An apparel shop requires that any returned merchandise be accompanied by the sales slip and that the return be made within 15 days of date of purchase. Is this a good policy? Why or why not?
2. Some stores maintain a liberal attitude toward customer complaints. Even when there is a doubt about the validity of the complaint, they will make the adjustment to the customer's satisfaction. What do you think of such a policy?
3. Is it better to handle customer complaints under a centralized system, decentralized system, or combination system? Explain your answer with a particular type of store in mind.

Part **e**

Organizing the Selling Function

The successful accomplishment of the selling function in a retail store involves salespeople, advertising, display, special events, and other nonpersonal selling devices. The combination of these selling tools for any given period or for a selling event is referred to as the *promotional mix*.

How the selling function is organized tends to differ with the kind of store. But no matter how it is organized, it should be remembered that retail salespeople seldom work alone. They are members of a team, and cooperation is essential if the individuals are to be in a frame of mind that leads to good service of customers. Development of team spirit depends largely upon the qualities of leadership possessed by the store or department manager. If he is genuinely interested in his salespeople and gives them every opportunity to live up to their abilities, they will probably give him their enthusiastic support and will cooperate with one another.

SELLING IN SMALL STORES

The selling function in a small store is divided among all its employees. The small-store merchant who employs two or more salespeople would find it advantageous to place one of them in charge of selling and to hold him responsible for the displays, advertising, and sales promotion of the store. One of the reasons that a small store remains a small store could be that no one is definitely appointed to originate sales campaigns and to plan a promotional mix designed to increase sales volume. Organizing the selling function would mean that better attention would be paid to the proper sales training of new sales personnel, to window and interior displays, to advertising, and to sales promotional events.

SELLING IN CHAIN STORES

Selling is a separate division in most chain-store organizations. The head of this division is the sales director, who supervises all the store units in the chain and arranges for the fast sale of goods to consumers by deciding on the selling tools to use. To help him in this central function of retailing, the sales director organizes a staff of specialists.

The central staff—consisting of advertising, display, and training special-ists—plans all sales campaigns, initiates and develops window and interior displays, and plans the organization of the training programs for sales personnel. The regional supervisors and the unit store managers under them then carry out the plans in the stores of the chain.

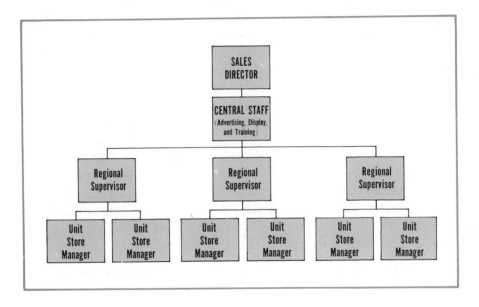

Illus. 12-12   This chart shows the organization of the selling division for a chain of stores. What are the advantages and disadvantages of such an organization as compared with a separate organization for each unit of the chain?

SELLING IN DEPARTMENT STORES

As indicated earlier, personal selling is often combined with the buying function in the merchandising division of the department store. But nonpersonal selling, or publicity, is commonly made a separate division because large stores in downtown locations or in regional shopping centers have to depend to a great extent upon advertising to attract trade. Furthermore, if publicity is conducted on the large scale required, it demands specialized talent that can be obtained best when a separate publicity division is maintained. The talent needed to write and prepare advertisements is very different from that required to supervise salespeople.

The work of the publicity division is to bring people into the store to buy the goods that the merchandising division has purchased. A store must have customers as well as merchandise. Stores, therefore, often rank the publicity director on an equal basis with the merchandise manager. The publicity director supervises all forms of advertising, display, and special features that attract customers. He prepares the plans and the expense budgets of his division. Advertising and display managers are directly responsible to him.

The advertising manager directs the preparation of the advertising copy, the drawing of the illustrations, and the planning of the layout of the advertisements. He approves each advertisement before it is released. The display manager plans and schedules window and interior displays, sign writing, and store decorating. The director of feature publicity obtains free publicity for the store in the news columns of publications, stages fashion shows, and often edits a fashion magazine.

Clearly, the publicity division handles only the nonpersonal selling activities of a department store, even though a few large stores have experimented with the chain-store concept of combining both personal and nonpersonal selling under a single sales promotion manager. But in most department stores, salespeople are not in the publicity division; they are either (1) in the merchandising division under the buyer, (2) in the store management division under a service manager, or

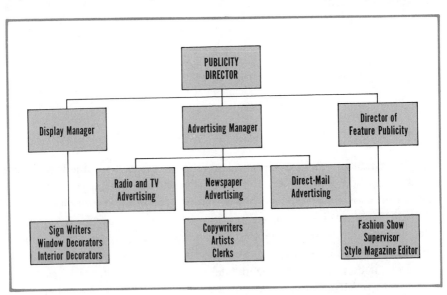

Illus. 12-13   Study carefully this organization chart of the publicity division in a department store. You will find it helpful to have this chart in mind as you read Chapters 13 and 14, and you may wish to refer again to this illustration as you read those chapters.

(3) in the case of branches, under *departmental sales managers* who report to the branch manager. These sales managers are responsible for keeping up their basic stocks and must cooperate with the buyers of the branch system and with the central advertising manager in carrying out sales promotion plans.

Publicity and merchandising take many forms. Illus. 12-14 shows scenes of the numerous activities that may occur in one retail store in one day. Notice the calendar of events—placed at the escalator on each floor—informing customers of what is going on, and where, in the store. A business women's luncheon and fashion show are being held, with two orchestra seats to a popular theatrical production offered as a door prize to those in attendance. In the household goods department a cooking demonstration with free samples of blueberry cake is featured. Holiday money, for which the customer will be billed later, is available at exchange desks in various parts of the store. The teen fashion board is in session. Free classes on hairdressing are being held. A decorator do-it-yourself display is available to customers. All these events are the result of the combined efforts of the publicity director, the advertising manager, the display manager, and the director of feature publicity.

COORDINATING SELLING EFFORTS

In most department stores the buyer of each department—in conjunction with his superior, the merchandise manager—makes initial plans with regard to what and when he wants to promote, what advertising he would like to have undertaken, what displays arranged, what signs prepared, what additions made to the sales force, and what special training provided. Once these plans are approved at the merchandising level, requests are submitted to the publicity director for advertising and display. The publicity director usually has the final word in regard to the proposed ads or window displays. His responsibilities may include (1) seeing that space available is used for those departmental offerings that will bring the best public response, (2) seeing that the store uses a predetermined amount of space every day or every week in those media found most effective, and (3) maintaining well-balanced window and interior displays.

Advertising and display are likely to be ineffective unless they are carefully coordinated with personal selling. Nothing does more damage to a store's promotional plans than to have salespeople uninformed as to what has been advertised or what is on display in the windows. It is a major duty of either the buyer or the departmental sales manager

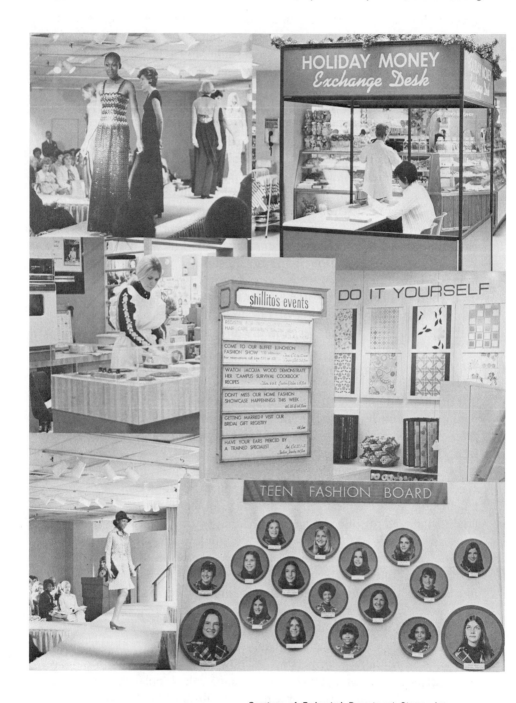

Courtesy of Federated Department Stores, Inc.

Illus. 12-14 A few activities in one day in a large department store.

to keep the salespeople fully informed and to give them special instructions about how to present the featured merchandise. Regular weekly department meetings should be held to explain the features of new goods, to review the best ways to present slow sellers, and to discuss immediate selling problems.

CHECKING YOUR KNOWLEDGE

Vocabulary

1. promotional mix

2. departmental sales manager

Review Questions

1. What factors are involved in the accomplishment of the selling function?
2. How does the organization of the selling function in the chain store differ from the organization of the selling function in the department store?
3. What are the activities carried on by the publicity division?
4. Explain the duties of these persons: (a) publicity director, (b) advertising manager, (c) display manager, (d) director of feature publicity.
5. How may selling efforts be coordinated?

Discussion Questions

1. What can the individual salesperson do to contribute to the team approach in selling?
2. Discuss the problems of organizing the selling function where branch stores are involved.
3. What information should salespeople have about merchandise that is advertised and displayed?

BUILDING YOUR SKILLS

Improving Communications Skills

On a separate sheet of paper, complete each of the following sentences by writing the correct tense of the irregular verb given in parentheses after each sentence.

1. Five of the prepackaged china sets were _____ in the transfer to the branch store. (break)
2. Have you _____ the sales check for the sale? (write)
3. Several of the cashiers _____ their lunches in the advertising office last Friday. (eat)
4. For years I _____ trying to improve my selling technique. (to be)
5. After the customer left, the salesperson wondered if she had _____ the right things about the merchandise. (say)

6. She has always _____ the proper clothes for selling. (wear)
7. Unfortunately several of the telephone orders had been _____ away. (throw)
8. I have _____ an unusual day in the sportswear department. (have)
9. The cashier _____ all she could to speed customers through her line. (do)
10. Yesterday he _____ to the bank for his employer. (go)

Improving Arithmetic Skills

On a separate sheet of paper, write the number of each exercise, your answer, and explain your calculation.

1. Janice sold 16 meters of drapery material at $1.99 a yard. What was the amount of her sale? (See Appendix on page 622.)
2. Frank ran 1,600 lines of advertising at $12.50 for 100 lines. What was the cost of this advertising?
3. Find the amount of the annual commission on sales of $72,000 if the rate of commission is 8 1/3%.
4. If 33 1/3% of the 1,260 employees of a large store are nonselling workers, how many employees are engaged in selling?
5. If 11 1/9% of gross sales of $81,900 are returned, what is the value of the net sales?
6. If there is a total of 2,400 square feet of space in a store building and 65% of it is used for selling space, how many square meters of space would this be? (See Appendix on page 622.)
7. Ten liters of oil is equivalent to how many gallons? (See Appendix on page 622.)

Improving Research Skills

1. Visit several different types of retail stores and observe the kinds of sales registers used. What differences did you notice in the registers used?
2. Collect sales register receipts from several stores and explain the printing found on the tickets.
3. Collect several sales checks from different stores in your community. In what ways are the sales checks alike, and in what ways are they different?
4. Visit several stores and learn the methods used for identification and authorization of charge transactions. Be prepared to report your findings to the class.
5. If there is an electronic point-of-sale system in operation in your area, investigate it in detail and report to your class.

Improving Decision-Making Skills

1. You operate a small store with just one sales register station. Your register is many years old but does provide a record of dollar sales, number of transactions, and a sale-by-sale record on a detail tape. You have been considering buying a new sales register. Investigation shows that the new machines have a wide range of features including totally electronic systems having instantaneous inventory and re-

ceivable control. Before making a decision as to which type register to get, what factors should you consider? Which of these factors would be most important for your store?

2. You are a salesperson in a women's ready-to-wear department. A shabbily dressed women brings you a lightweight coat in a box. She says she bought it a year ago but never wore it. The coat and the box indicate it is from your store, and all tags are still attached. She has the sales slip and would like a refund. The garment is out of style, and you no longer buy from that coat manufacturer. What would you do?

APPLYING YOUR KNOWLEDGE

Chapter Project

The concept of a *cashless society* has been discussed and forecast for some time. As a chapter project, your class will determine the extent of use and growth in use of credit cards in your area. Contact at least three retail firms in each of several categories (variety store, drugstore, department store, service station, specialty store, etc.) and ask the following two questions. Add others of your own if you wish.

Question 1.   What percentage of your sales are charged using your own credit cards? using outside credit cards?

Question 2.   How much have these percentages changed in the last five years?

When you have collected the data, put your findings into charts or tables and prepare a written interpretation of what you have learned.

Continuing Project

Prepare an outline of the chief facts that you would want to impress upon your employees with regard to:

1. Operating sales registers
2. Making change
3. Filling orders
4. Wrapping packages
5. Telephone selling
6. Handling complaints

chapter 13

Advertising

a. Advertising provides a systematic means of communicating with potential customers. The major aim of retail advertising is to encourage customers to come into the store and personally examine merchandise offered for sale.

b. The major advertising medium for retail stores is the newspaper. Other media, such as magazines, radio, television, direct mail, and supplementary aids, are used for promotions and for special advertising needs.

c. Since only a small portion of a store's stock can be advertised, care must be taken in selecting the goods to be promoted.

d. The printed advertisement usually has four parts: headline, illustration, copy, and signature plate. These elements must be coordinated to provide an effective selling instrument.

e. Certain government regulations control portions of the advertising effort. However, the accuracy of advertising generally depends upon the ethics and truthfulness of the individual advertisers.

Part a

Psychology of Advertising

Advertising provides the retailer with a means of communicating messages to the public. As stated in Chapter 11, advertising is any paid presentation of a message about goods and services carried by a medium such as a newspaper. Advertising directly supports the personal selling efforts of the store staff. Through advertising a consumer is made aware of a product, a brand, or a company. The effectiveness of advertising can be judged by the number of people who become interested and the number of people who actually buy the product or brand or buy at a given company.

COMMUNICATION THROUGH ADVERTISING

One of the major tasks of the retail advertiser is to determine which combination of words, pictures, and, in some cases, sounds will communicate most effectively to certain individuals or groups.

There are certain barriers to communicating with potential customers through advertising. In printed advertising the reading ability of the consumer can be a barrier. In broadcast advertising the listening ability, or span of attention, can be a barrier. The individual's personality or taste can be a barrier to accepting an advertising message. For example, if an individual does not enjoy country-western music, any advertising on a radio station featuring country-western programming will probably not reach that person.

OBJECTIVES OF ADVERTISING

Advertising by the retailer can be classified as either promotional or institutional advertising. *Promotional advertising* focuses on merchandise with the intent of drawing immediate traffic and creating a volume of sales. *Institutional advertising* focuses on the firm with the intent of building store prestige and store acceptance over a long period of time. There are several goals which retailers hope to achieve using either promotional or institutional advertising or both.

1. To bring customers into the store to inspect merchandise offerings and to use services
2. To introduce new goods, styles, and services
3. To stimulate demand for a product

Illus. 13-1   This contemporary scene is designed to attract youth. Nostalgia is achieved by a poster of a popular movie star of the 30's, but the beat of background rock music emphasizes the present and the need for clothing for today's casual living. Words, pictures, and sound are used to draw traffic and create sales.

4. To teach new uses of a product
5. To prepare the way for the salesperson in selling
6. To keep the company name or slogan before the public
7. To keep the customer satisfied with previous purchases
8. To create goodwill, leading to decisions to shop in the store when in search of the types of goods carried by the store

REQUIREMENTS OF SUCCESSFUL ADVERTISEMENTS

Psychological studies show that people act on three levels: (1) on the conscious level when they deliberately do certain things, (2) on the subconscious level when they act on the basis of emotional urges but do not admit the real reason for their actions, and (3) on the unconscious level when they act a certain way but do not know the reason for their actions. These studies have also determined that advertising appeals to the subconscious and unconscious levels are more effective than those appeals aimed at reason alone.

the   disbelievers

"I read one of your little ads the other day. It was a letter from some guy about what good service you gave him. Tell me, are those letters real or do you make them up?"

Can anyone seriously think that a reputable store would fake a testimonial? Some people obviously can since the question is asked not infrequently.

In the course of a year we print many letters from Wallachs customers, complaints as well as compliments. We don't use names and addresses unless given permission. But, within a reasonable period of time, any of the originals are available for inspection if anyone is that skeptical.

Maybe there are still some New Yorkers who don't even believe that Wallachs will replace a missing button, free of charge, for anyone, any time. Some people will disbelieve anything.

Courtesy of Wallachs, New York City

Illus. 13-2   Stores frequently use institutional advertising to build goodwill or to create in customers' minds images which will eventually result in increased sales. Study this institutional advertisement. What do you think the store wished to accomplish?

A successful advertisement contains the same elements as the psychological steps of a sale. These are to attract attention, develop interest, create desire, and induce favorable action. In fact, the favorable action induced by an advertisement is a visit to the store or a phone call to purchase the advertised merchandise.

Attracting Attention

To possess value, an advertisement must be seen or heard, or both. Consequently, the problems of attracting the eye and the ear should receive serious thought when an advertisement is prepared. Psychologists tell us that attention must be caught and held before a message can be impressed upon the mind. Speakers have found that they get attention by means of contrast. If the audience is noisy, the speaker suddenly stops. Attention is immediately focused upon him.

The advertisement cannot perform its function unless it attracts the attention of the customer. In written and printed advertisements, various methods are used to catch and to hold the reader's attention. Illustrations, vivid colors, decorations, preferred positions, unusual let-

tering, clever spacing, strong headlines, and short, forcible sentences at
the beginning are some of the devices used to attract attention. Some
advertisers even scent their advertising messages so as to attract attention by means of a pleasant fragrance.

Developing Interest

Attention is momentary. When it is held for any length of time we
call it interest. The initial attention to the advertisement must, therefore,
be prolonged in order to develop interest. People are always interested
in matters that relate to themselves; hence, they are interested in
merchandise and services that satisfy their needs and desires. Descriptions of merchandise should, generally speaking, be in terms that everyone understands. Long, wordy explanations and technical descriptions
should be avoided.

Creating Desire

Successful advertisers, like successful salespeople, are students of
human nature. They try to create a desire for their merchandise by
appealing to their customers' emotions as well as to their reason. Among
the buying motives appealed to are hunger; curiosity; imitation; com-
panionship; pride; ambition; a desire for good health; a desire for comfort; and a desire for pleasure, fun, and even excitement.

Just which buying motive or motives should be appealed to depends
upon the kinds of goods advertised and the kinds of customers to be
reached. If an appeal is to create a desire for the goods, it must have
the *you* approach; that is, it must answer the questions that are always
in the customer's mind: What will the goods do for me? Why should
I buy them? How shall I benefit from their possession?

Inducing Favorable Action

If all the preparatory steps of an advertisement have been carefully
planned, the desired action should result. The action suggested should
be easy to perform. It may involve making a trip to the store, filling out
a simple order coupon, or making a telephone call. In many instances
advertisers induce action by calling attention to the fact that there is a
limited supply of an article or that the goods must be ordered at once
for a holiday. A gift discount coupon sometimes is a stimulus to action.
Institutional advertising is less intense in its appeal for immediate action
than promotional advertising. Nevertheless, the institutional advertisement should induce the customer to visit the store for the kinds of goods
or services that the store sells.

HOW MUCH MONEY IS SPENT ON ADVERTISING?

Expenditures on advertising of all kinds in the United States in a recent year were $21 billion. National advertising, that is, advertising on a nationwide basis, accounted for approximately $12 billion. Local advertising, that is, advertising within a local market area, accounted for about $9 billion. Advertising by retail stores is usually directed toward a local market area and is primarily local advertising.

Some people believe that expenditures for advertising are an economic waste. It should be noted, however, that advertising contributes immensely to converting purchasing power into actual sales. Actually both the retailer and the consumer benefit by an adequate level of communication about available goods and services.

Total expenditures for newspaper advertising account for the greatest percentage of the advertising dollar. Television is the next greatest followed by direct mail, magazines, radio, farm and business papers, and then outdoor advertising. Local retail advertising follows a similar pattern with the greatest amount of advertising money spent for newspaper advertising.

CHECKING YOUR KNOWLEDGE

Vocabulary

1. promotional advertising   **2.** institutional advertising

Review Questions

1. What are some of the barriers to advertising communications with potential customers?
2. Name at least six goals which retailers hope to achieve through advertising.
3. According to psychological studies on what three levels do people act?
4. Through what four steps does an advertisement attempt to lead a customer?
5. Approximately how much is spent on advertising? How much of this is for national advertising, and how much is for local advertising?

Discussion Questions

1. Which of the eight goals listed on pages 405 and 406 would best be accomplished by promotional advertising? by institutional advertising? Why?
2. How can an advertisement create desire that will prompt a customer to act on the unconscious level?

3. What might be the consequences of a federal law eliminating all advertising?
4. Could any other device take the place of advertising to inform customers of merchandise and price and to educate them toward a higher standard of living by showing them how to satisfy their wants?

Part b

Advertising Media

There are numerous ways that a retailer can communicate information about his store and merchandise to potential customers. He or his employees can talk with individuals in or out of the store. Satisfied customers can tell their friends about the store or its merchandise. This person-to-person communication is called word-of-mouth publicity. Word-of-mouth publicity is not considered advertising since it involves an unpaid form of communication. However, the retailer can pay to have his message distributed. He can have it printed in a newspaper, in a magazine, on a sign, or on a slip of paper to be mailed to customers. He can have the message read over the radio or presented on television. Any means by which advertising can be presented is known as a *medium*. Collectively these means of advertising are called *advertising media*.

COMMUNICATION CHANNELS

Obviously not all people listen to the same radio station or read the same newspaper. The retailer must determine which route or channel will result in reaching potential customers. If a communication channel can be identified as one that has a high probability of reaching a given type of consumer, the next step is making sure that the message is properly coded. By *coding* is meant the language and illustrations used—also voice and music if radio is involved. It is important to the retail advertiser that he have feedback from receivers of his advertising message, so that he can properly evaluate the communication channel used. For example, if a men's store has a new line of sportcoats, it may present its advertising through a particular radio station to reach the intended young audience. If the same store has another line of sportcoats for older men, it may take another communication channel, perhaps a newspaper, to bring the sportcoat line to their attention. Sales revenue from the radio and newspaper advertising will provide the retailer the feedback he needs to determine the merits of each medium and choose which will best carry his message to the appropriate public.

Dividing the consumer market into relatively small segments that have similar characteristics and selecting the medium that is most likely to appeal to each segment is called *market segmentation.* It is recognized that few merchandise offerings appeal to everybody and that it is wasteful to broadcast a message to everybody if only a few will be interested.

Do you work in the World Trade Center?

If your home-away-from home is way downtown, you're closer than you may realize to the World's Largest Store. The Broadway IRT will take you right to our door in a matter of minutes. Ditto the PATH. And when you get here . . . well, there's no other store like it.

Macy*s is never far from home

According to the MTA schedule, the subway riding time from the Trade Center to Macy's Herald Square is 11 minutes.

Courtesy of Macy*s

Illus. 13-3   This institutional advertisement is aimed at a specific segment of the buying public—those who work in the World Trade Center.

However, for merchandise of very wide appeal, television is appropriate; whereas direct mail is preferred to reach a special market, such as nurses or the people living in a new apartment house development.

Newspapers

Even though it is true that the newspaper is the chief medium for the retail store, a careful study of the character and the circulation of the paper is made by large stores before they place their advertisements in it. They want to know how many and what class of people read that newspaper. They want information as to which parts of the city the newspaper serves best, which parts it serves least, and why.

The best newspaper is the one that best reaches at a reasonable cost the groups to whom the store caters. Stores that are located in the downtown section of a city draw their customers from all parts of the trading area. They find that newspaper advertisements attract customers to the store in sufficient numbers to insure adequate sales and to yield a satisfactory net profit. Neighborhood stores, however, which have a small trading area, do not use the general newspaper because all the circulation outside the immediate area of the neighborhood is wasted; and the newspaper advertising rates are determined on the basis of the entire circulation. In some large cities there are weekly newspapers and special editions of daily newspapers that cover just part of the city, and these are valuable advertising media for neighborhood stores.

In comparing the relative cost of space in competing newspapers, the merchant should compare the milline rates of each. The *milline rate* is the cost of a single agate line of space adjusted to a newspaper circulation of one million. An *agate line* of space is 1/14th of an inch deep by one column in width. For example, if a newspaper charges 25 cents a line and has a circulation of 100,000, its milline rate is 10 times 25 cents, or $2.50. As a formula:

$$\text{Milline rate} = \text{line rate} \times \frac{1,000,000}{\text{actual circulation}}$$

The newspaper with the lowest milline rate is not necessarily the best, however, for it may not reach the consumers who are the best prospects for the particular store or for the particular goods being advertised.

Magazines

Since the circulation of magazines is usually national rather than local, magazines would seem to be a poor advertising medium for most retail stores. There are times, however, when retail advertising in magazines is desirable. Chain stores and some associations of independent stores have units all over the country. The national circulation of magazines is not wasted in such cases because nearly any reader of the magazine has access to one of the chain's or the association's outlets.

Many national magazines have developed regional advertising programs which permit retailers to buy space in just those magazines circulated in their area. Some magazines are concerned with only a single city and its environs—for example, *New York* magazine in New York City.

Direct Mail

Direct-mail advertising—letters, postcards, and other mailable matter sent directly to prospective customers—is favored by many merchants. For one thing, it can offer merchandise to the public without informing competitors about it. Some stores like direct-mail advertising because small, distinct classes of people can be addressed in a personal manner. Results of direct-mail advertising can be easily determined, and expenditures for this medium can be controlled accordingly. Some stores make direct mail their major advertising medium. Closed-door discounters, for example, rely almost entirely on direct mailings to their members. It is important in any direct-mail advertising effort that the mailing list used by the store be up to date. It is important also that letters and other enclosures attract attenion, develop interest, create desire, and induce favorable action.

Catalogs

While catalogs mailed to customers may be thought of as direct mail, they deserve special mention as an advertising medium. In addition to one or two annual catalogs, many retail stores find it worthwhile to prepare special catalogs, particularly for Christmas selling. Items so advertised vary from novelty items for about a dollar to "his and her mummy cases, gratefully vacant, that are 2,000 years old." Catalogs not only sell merchandise directly but they also prompt many customers to come to the retail store to examine goods.

Radio

Radio is used as an advertising medium by many retail stores. Some sponsor a definite program at scheduled times. When specific goods are promoted by radio, the radio advertisement must contain all the elements of the written advertisement and generally some form of entertainment. Word pictures, drawn by the expressive voice of the announcer, take the place of illustrations. The time of broadcasting is important. Some stores like to advertise immediately after a very popular radio program in order to capture the attention of the audience that has been listening to the program.

Small retail stores frequently think radio advertising is too expensive. Some, however, select a local station and use short spot advertisements that can be given between programs. These spot announcements take the form of a message about goods or services, with emphasis on the store and its location. Several retail stores in a business area or shopping center may arrange to share the cost of a program with each store having a message broadcast.

Television

Television is becoming an increasingly important medium for many retailers. Among the stores using television—regional chains, furniture, and other specialty stores—the outlay seldom exceeds 15 percent of the promotion budget. Most retail advertising on TV is over local stations, but the national networks are used by some big chains.

Most retailers find that the best time to advertise, cost considered, is in the afternoon, to attract the homemaker who has finished her chores. The second best time is in the early evening when children are watching. Virtually all the ads are short spot announcements, usually of a 30-second duration. Ten-second spots are in second place.

There are great differences in the variety of television offerings. A few stores use television for institutional advertising, but most concentrate on specific merchandise or a related assortment in order to reach a large audience.

Supplementary Media

Outdoor advertising—consisting chiefly of billboards, posters, painted signs, electrical displays, and exhibits—is used by retailers primarily for gaining recognition rather than for advertising special merchandise. Promotional stores and discount houses often include banners, floats, and advertising placards on motor vehicles as part of their outdoor advertising media.

Car-card advertising—consisting primarily of small posters in public transportation vehicles—is read daily by people of every class. Car-card advertising may be used by stores wishing to advertise for prestige purposes or to advertise a special line of goods or a special sale. On the whole, car cards are best suited to the advertising of national brand convenience goods and widely used services.

Script for a Television Advertisement

30 seconds—The Dining Room

VIDEO (Suggested technique: film, tape)	AUDIO
Completely furnished dining room, decorated with appropriate accessories. Drapes, carpeting, accent pieces should all be included. Table should be set for guests, centerpiece and candles also. Camera should move and pick up various furniture details and focus on overall impression of an elegant room.	Since furniture is something you live with for a long time, it should always bring you pleasure and comfort. Your dining room, for instance. It's more than just a place to eat. It's an elegant room, yet practical. It's where you entertain and share many memorable moments with guests. The dining set, designed by (designer name) , is crafted for good looks, long wear, and easy care. The rich grained oak table and buffet piece combined with six strikingly patterned chairs for a contemporary, luxurious look. This dining set, available with accompanying pieces, and sensibly priced is available at (store name). For a complete selection of fine, beautiful furniture at reasonable prices, come to (store name) , located at (address) .
Close with exterior shot of store.	

Courtesy of Television Bureau of Advertising, New York City

Illus. 13-4 Television spots for commercials are generally prepared by listing the scenes and the action at the left of a page and the words spoken at the right. It is not necessary to have high-priced performers.

Handbills are single sheets of printed advertisements which are distributed to each house in a neighborhood. To get the best results from this type of advertisement, the retailer should advertise only one or two leaders to get the customer to come to the store. The remainder of the handbill should be used to promote regular merchandise of good value. Care must be taken not to create ill will by littering doorways and lawns with this type of advertising. Some stores distribute handbills in the store, calling attention to unadvertised specials.

Shopping news is a paper devoted entirely to advertising and is distributed directly to customers' homes. Advertisements in a shopping news are less likely to be seen than are those appearing in a newspaper because the reader's interest is not called to different pages in the shopping news by news items such as those appearing in newspapers.

Inside posters are placed near entrances, on elevators, near escalators, and at other key points in large stores. They attract attention to special offerings in various departments and to special services such as fur storage.

Novelty advertising takes many forms, such as printed advertisements on calendars, pencils, or matchbook covers. The distribution of gifts is also a form of novelty advertising. One retail carpet and linoleum store issued to every person who came to the store a pocketknife with a linoleum cover, on which was printed the store's name and address.

Program Sponsorship

Many stores pay for announcements in programs of educational institutions and civic organizations. Some may sponsor athletic teams or cultural events. Such announcements or sponsorship usually represent a donation by the store to local events rather than a serious attempt to get results through advertising.

ADVERTISING COSTS RELATIVE TO SALES

Retailers spend a large amount of money for advertising. Illus. 13-5 shows that the advertising expenses of the different lines range from 0.50 to 4.62 percent of sales. The average is about 1.50 percent. The amount spent on advertising by a retailer will depend upon the advertising policy and size of his store, the amount of competition that he faces, and the distance from which he wishes to attract customers. Small neighborhood stores spend very little—occasionally using a handbill or a small advertisement in a neighborhood weekly newspaper. On the other hand, a large department store located in the midst of competing department stores and specialty shops will have a policy of consistently advertising in most of the media that will reach its widely scattered customers.

Large stores draw a distinction between the cost of advertising and the cost of publicity. The former includes the cost of space and of engravings or mats paid for in a medium such as a newspaper, or for time on television or radio. The cost of publicity includes all the expenses of advertising. display, and other promotional activities, including salaries and supplies. Total publicity expense sometimes runs as high as 6 percent of sales.

Advertising Expenses in Different Kinds of Stores	
Kind of Store	Percentage of Net Sales
Appliance, Radio and TV (Sales $250,000 to $500,000)	2.10
Automobile Dealers	1.36
Convenience Food Stores	.84
Department Stores	3.51
Feed and Seed Stores	.50
Florists (Sales $25,000 to $50,000)	2.14
Furniture Stores (Sales $250,000 to $500,000)	4.62
Gift Shops (Sales $25,000 to $50,000)	1.60
Hardware Stores	1.50
Jewelry Stores (Sales $100,000 to $300,000)	3.00
Lumber and Building Materials	.51
Mass Merchandising	2.31
Music Stores	1.74
Office Products (Sales under $250,000)	.97
Service Stations	.77
Shoe Stores (Sales $150,000 to $250,000)	2.30
Specialty Stores (Sales $1,000,000 to $5,000,000)	4.19
Variety Stores	1.51

Illus. 13-5 The amount of money a retailer spends on advertising is dependent upon many factors, including the size of his store and amount of competition. The figures above give only average amounts spent on advertising by different types of stores, but they can serve as general guides to suggest to the retailer whether he is spending too much or too little on advertising.

CHECKING YOUR KNOWLEDGE

Vocabulary

1. medium
2. advertising media
3. coding
4. market segmentation
5. milline rate
6. agate line
7. direct-mail advertising
8. outdoor advertising
9. car-card advertising
10. handbill
11. shopping news
12. inside posters
13. novelty advertising

Review Questions

1. What factors must be considered in selecting the newspaper in which to advertise?
2. Name several different kinds of direct-mail advertising used by stores.
3. Name several forms of supplementary kinds of advertising used by stores.
4. According to the table on page 417 which type of store spends the most for advertising? Which type of store spends the least?
5. What is the difference between advertising and publicity?

Discussion Questions

1. What information would a retailer need about a media in order to determine if it would be appropriate for his store and merchandise?
2. Why do most retailers spend much of their advertising money in local newspapers?
3. Why do most retailers use more than one medium to carry out their advertising?
4. What is your opinion of the practice of offering gifts, or the opportunity to enter a prize contest, as bait to join a club that offers customers a new selection of goods each month?

Part C

Selecting Goods for Promotion

The selection of the right goods to advertise is the most important single factor in sales promotion. Experienced advertisers know that even good advertising will not sell unwanted merchandise. Thousands of dollars have been lost in advertising goods for which there was no demand. No amount of advertising will sell outmoded goods to people —the merchandise is simply not wanted. On the other hand, wanted merchandise can be, and often is, sold by poor advertising. A combination of the two—good merchandise and good advertising—will, of course, give the best results.

FACTORS AFFECTING MERCHANDISE SELECTION

Stores cannot advertise all the merchandise they have in stock, because to do so would mean a large rise in advertising expense without proportional sales increases. Accordingly, retailers must choose representative items that will bring to the stores the largest number of possible buyers and build the most goodwill. Which goods in the store will win the approval of a significant segment of the public? Which goods will bring customers to the store? The retailer must answer these questions. However, in order to answer them from the proper viewpoint, he must put himself in the customer's place.

Current Demand

Advertising fast-selling, popular items will bring customers into the store and will increase sales. Stores that sell moderately priced merchandise generally feature articles that are in current demand. The advertising of these goods shows customers that the store is up to date and that it will sell them goods they want at prices they are willing to pay. A fast-selling item is usually one that has won the approval of many customers. It is generally merchandise in fashion or for which there is a steady demand.

Fashion

The store with a policy of fashion leadership does not advertise the accepted best-seller but advertises instead the new styles that the store believes will become the fashion. Its customers watch its advertisements for new and unusual merchandise, not established items. The customer who knows the policy of this type of store and is interested in wearing the latest fashions is sure that she is getting up-to-the-minute fashion merchandise when she buys what the store has advertised.

In most stores, however, new styles should be put before the public cautiously. Many stores test the sales possibilities of new goods by a small advertisement or a small display to get the customers' reactions. Should the item take hold and the demand become brisk, it may be stocked in larger quantities and aggressive advertising employed.

Distinctiveness

Many people not only desire new things but also want exclusive merchandise. In the case of clothing, they desire something different in detail from what others are wearing. Distinctive merchandise is usually an excellent selection for advertising, provided the media used reaches the appropriate customers.

Special Events

Merchandise connected with a special occasion is also available for advertising. Thus, toys and gifts have high news value at Christmas time, spring clothes at Easter, flags before the Fourth of July, and children's clothing prior to the opening date of school.

Special Promotional Events	
Store Opening	Manager's Day
Store Anniversaries	Sports Events
Back-to-School	School and College Events
Suppliers' Special	Civic Functions
Wholesaler's Promotion	Holidays
Remodeling	Seasons
Expansion	Outdoor Activities
Founder's Sale	Home and Garden Improvement

Illus. 13-6   Advertising merchandise for special events is usually very successful. Above are special events which can influence a store's selection of merchandise to be promoted. What merchandise might be advertised in connection with each event?

Price

Retail stores generally advertise merchandise that has a distinct price appeal. This is because many people must economize, and almost everyone is looking for a bargain. Discount houses, for instance, use the drawing power of reduced prices and feature merchandise that has already won customer favor. For standard merchandise, they attract even affluent customers who buy most of their clothing and decorative home furnishings in high-class department stores and specialty shops.

Single and Multiple Items

Discount houses seldom advertise single items. Rather, they use *omnibus* (relating to many things at once) *advertisements* that feature 15 or more bargains of various sorts, all on the same page. The price endings are usually in odd cents—such as 1¢, 3¢, and 7¢—which are not the customary price endings for traditional stores.

There is room in large promotional stores, however, for the major promotion of single items that are of interest to a great many people who might read the newspaper or hear a broadcast. Examples of such single items are TV sets, women's hosiery, and men's shirts. But the store must be reasonably sure that the probable sales results will warrant the purchase of considerable advertising space for the item. For example, a scarf advertised at $2.89 may cost the store $1.95, thus providing a margin of 94 cents on each scarf. If the ad costs the store $188, it would be necessary to sell 200 scarves, simply to cover the cost of the ad without any allowance for other expenses ($188 ÷ $.94). Results would have to be much better than this to make the advertising directly profitable. Occasionally a high-class store will promote a very expensive item such as a $50,000 diamond, which few persons in the community could possibly afford. This is a form of institutional advertising rather than a merchandise offering. It is a dramatic attempt to impress the public that this store carries the best products that money can buy.

Food and household goods that are bought regularly should be consistently advertised to insure steady repeat patronage. Supermarkets advertise weekly, but they make sure that enough variety is included in their advertising to break the monotony of customers' reading about the same items all the time.

Private Brands

When a retailer is building a market for his private brands, he should consistently advertise the merits of his products. One large department store ran a series of advertisements comparing national brands with the store's private brands and pointing out the difference in prices for comparable items. This advertising approach gave the items a selling role; the products almost sold themselves. People could easily see why it was advantageous for them to buy the store's private brands. The story of the private brands was a consistent, continuing central theme of that store's advertising.

MERCHANDISE THAT SHOULD NOT BE ADVERTISED

Many advertisers make the mistake of regularly featuring leftovers, slow-selling goods, and old stock. They do this in the hope of covering up buying mistakes. Such goods will fail to attract customers unless there is a big price concession. Even salespeople do not like to sell old and overstocked merchandise.

One retailer advertised a good quality woolen blanket for sale at $14.95. The advertisement brought many buyers to the store. The retailer failed, however, to state in the advertisement that he had a limited quantity on hand. He was soon sold out and when customers asked for the blanket, he tried to sell a substitute. Many people suspected a trick and left the store without making a purchase. This retailer made the mistake of advertising merchandise of a very limited quantity. He lost many customers through this advertising blunder. Merchandise that is so limited in quantity as to be insufficient for the demand created by the advertising is better sold through display or through direct-mail advertising.

Similarly, merchandise that cannot be quickly reordered may not prove good for advertising purposes. The advertising may create a demand that the store will not be able to meet, and the result will be a lowering of the store's prestige.

It is often a great temptation to insert an advertisement for goods before they arrive at the store. A delay in shipping may, however, result in the goods not being on hand when customers call for them. To maintain their customers' goodwill, stores have been forced to sacrifice high-grade merchandise at low prices. The problem is particularly difficult in chain operations, where the goods have to be ready in each store, marked at the special advertised price, because the ad has to be released in advance.

Goods that have not been moved by previous advertising should not be advertised again unless there is a change in the situation that makes the goods more salable; otherwise the second advertisement will be wasted.

Finally, no goods should be advertised without salespeople being informed. Few situations are more annoying to a customer than to have salespeople show ignorance about the goods advertised.

Goods That Should Not Be Advertised

Leftover merchandise offered at regular prices or available in a quantity insufficient to justify the advertising expense

Quantities of desirable merchandise that may prove too small to fill the demand created by the advertising or quantities of merchandise for which prompt refills by the manufacturer are not possible

Goods that may not be in the store, properly priced, on the day the advertising appears

Goods that have not been moved by previous advertising and that do not give any indication of becoming more salable

Goods that have not been "advertised" to the salespeople

Illus. 13-7 From a practical standpoint and from an ethical standpoint, some kinds of goods should never be advertised. Listed above are some of these goods.

PLANNING ADVERTISING

For most retailers, advertising is their second or third largest expense outlay, less than payroll but often equal to rent. Accordingly, advertising expenditures must be planned with the utmost care. It is necessary to develop a seasonal plan which, in its simplest form, involves five steps:

1. Set a sales goal that challenges the whole store and yet is realistic, considering last month's and last year's sales figures.
2. Decide how much advertising will be needed to meet that sales goal, in view of what was spent last month and last year and what the competition is likely to do.
3. Decide which items or services to promote according to the sales contribution made by each department.
4. Prepare a month-to-month schedule of advertising expenditures and then a day-to-day schedule within each month. Take advantage of the payroll days of large, important firms; days of the week when traffic is heaviest; local night openings; national and local merchandising events offering tie-in possibilities; current prices; and stock on hand.
5. Check actual performance against sales results.

FACTORS AFFECTING THE PROMOTIONAL MIX

The promotional mix of a store, as was mentioned in Chapter 12, is the combination of selling tools used in promotion. The retailer should be alert to external changes which may affect the choice of media and merchandise to be promoted. Changes in the population of a market area, changes in income status, and changes in competition are each potentially significant factors that may prompt advertising adjustments.

CHECKING YOUR KNOWLEDGE

Vocabulary

omnibus advertisements

Review Questions

1. Why is the selection of the right goods so important in advertising?
2. Name the characteristics of goods that may be successfully advertised.
3. List the characteristics of goods that should not be advertised.
4. Outline the steps for developing a seasonal advertising plan.
5. What changes may affect goods advertised or media used?

1. Can the retailer create customer demand by good advertising?
2. Is there any justification for advertising a sale in which the markup on the goods is no more than the cost of the advertising?
3. Under what circumstances might a retailer advertise goods that are in limited supply?

Part d

Preparing the Advertisement

To prepare an effective advertisement, the retailer must have clearly defined objectives in mind. In small stores the owner or manager may make some rough notes of what he wants and call upon the advertising department of the newspaper or radio for help. In large stores the buyer or head of the department indicates to the store advertising department —consisting of artists and copywriters—just what is wanted in the advertisement. The preparation of the advertisement then proceeds through the steps of attracting attention, arousing interest, creating desire, and inducing action.

ELEMENTS OF A PRINTED ADVERTISEMENT

Advertisers use the four major elements of an advertisement—headline, illustration, copy, and signature plate—to accomplish the objectives of printed advertising.

Headline

The headline in an advertisement must accomplish three functions:

1. It must attract the attention of potential customers.
2. It must arouse interest.
3. It must lead the observer into reading the copy.

Probably the most common and easiest way to attract attention to an advertisement is to use large type in the headline. Contrast in size of type is the mechanical means of drawing the reader's eye to the headline. In one glance the headline should be able to sift potential customers from those who have no interest in the product. This sifting process is performed by the content of the headline. For instance, most men would not notice the headline *FUR SALE,* yet most women would read the headline.

To hold the attention of potential customers beyond the glance stage and make them want to know more about the product advertised is the second function of the headline. The advertisement must not only be noted, it must also be read. The reader's interest is aroused if the headline relates to his needs or wants and states outstanding selling points about the item advertised. If the reader's interest is aroused by the headline, he can be led into reading the remainder of the copy.

It is easier to read an advertisement that is broken up by contrasting type sizes. Several headlines of different type sizes, all larger than the copy type, are often used by advertisers to make it easy for the reader to develop an interest in and an understanding of the copy.

The best kind of headline is that which gives use or benefit information and gives the key facts about the item. An effective headline is also short, clear, and specifically related to a particular product.

Illustration

It is a well-established fact that more inquiries and more sales will result from an advertisement which contains a picture than from one which is merely a block of copy. Many people are "eye minded"; that is, they are most readily impressed by what they see. Pictures can make a definite appeal to people's instincts and emotions.

A picture that is related to the product advertised and is tied in with the copy will attract attention to the whole advertisement as well as begin to develop an interest and a desire for the product. Like the headline, the illustration must connect the reader's experiences to the product advertised. The illustration should usually appeal to human interest. A picture of a smiling, contented, and happy man, wearing the advertised shirt, is more effective than a picture of the shirt alone.

Illustrations—photos and drawings—are often used by advertisers for the purpose of directing the reader's eyes to the copy or to the name of the product advertised. They are also used to show the selling points of a product rather than to employ many words to tell about them.

Today, with the increased use of television as an advertising medium, illustrations and pictures are more important than ever. With the use of color, both in printed media and in television advertising, the attention-getting value of pictures has increased.

Copy

Advertising is talking to many people, one at a time. The "talking" of advertising is the copy that gives the reader information about the goods. It creates desire to own the goods and leads to action.

A successful copywriter once said, "I write as though one customer is standing in front of me and I am talking to her, trying to convince her that she should have the merchandise. I write from her viewpoint—how she looks at the goods, what they will do for her."

Since the customer is almost always interested in details about goods she plans to buy, complete and specific merchandise facts should be included. The language used should be simple, not complicated.

Rules for Writing Headlines and Copy

Write from the customer's point of view.

Write in a conversational language.

Write as though talking to the customer.

Express ideas in new and vigorous ways.

Give product information in the headline.

Develop one outstanding idea to be carried through headline and copy.

Be accurate in making product statements.

Use good advertising English—short words, sentences, and paragraphs written in a simple style—so that ideas may be grasped easily.

Include an urge to action.

Illus. 13-8   The beginning copywriter will find these rules helpful in composing headlines and copy for an advertisement. Can you think of any other rules that might be added?

Signature Plate

Information necessary to secure the favorable action of the reader should be included in the store's *signature plate* (sometimes called the *logotype*). Within the signature plate there usually appears a distinctive type face, trademark, emblem, or symbol which immediately identifies the store for the reader. The signature plate is placed in the advertisement near the top or bottom. Close to the store name and usually in smaller type are the address of the store and the store's slogan.

Other items of information that are commonly considered part of the signature plate are: what hours the store is open for business, whether mail or telephone orders will be accepted for the product advertised, and branches where the same product is available.

COMBINING THE ELEMENTS

A successful layout has a definite starting point; that is, there is one spot in the headline or illustration that attracts one's attention first. The layout should then be so arranged as to lead the eye of the reader in regular sequence to the other parts of the advertisement in order to take him through the psychological steps of developing interest, creating desire, and inducing action.

In order to obtain the maximum psychological reaction, the advertiser who is planning the layout has several elements to consider. He

Courtesy of Federated Department Stores, Inc.

Illus. 13-9   These are examples of well-known signature plates. In a printed advertisement, the signature plate helps to identify the store immediately.

must determine the exact size and arrangement of the headlines, illustrations, copy, and signature plate. In addition, he is concerned with the backgrounds and borders of his advertisement, as well as the selection of the type sizes and type faces to be used.

The person who prepares an ad imagines how he thinks the ad should look in order to attract public attention, and he draws a rough sketch of this image. This reveals the general layout and may even include a specific headline. In a large store, this sketch may be prepared by the advertising manager and turned over to an artist, a copywriter, and a layout man who work out the details and then submit a dummy to their supervisor. When approved, the dummy is worked out in detail and submitted to the newspaper for reproduction and printing. In a small store, as indicated earlier, the ad may be prepared by the newspaper's staff.

HELPS FOR ADVERTISERS

The beginner in advertising should seek the help of his local newspaper's advertising experts. They will, in most instances, be glad to suggest illustrations, copy, and layout for the small-store advertiser. The Retail Advertising Bureau of the American Newspaper Publishers Association provides an excellent monthly service for small retailers that is available through the space salesmen of the local newspaper members.

Sometimes the wholesaler and manufacturer will offer advertising aid to the retailer. Many wholesalers and manufacturers supply *mats*—advertisements on sheets of specially prepared paper that are suitable for making metal molds of the advertisement. On the mat, space is left for insertion of the store name or the store signature plate.

Courtesy of Federated Department Stores, Inc.

Illus. 13-10   A department store artist working on sketches for newspaper advertisements.

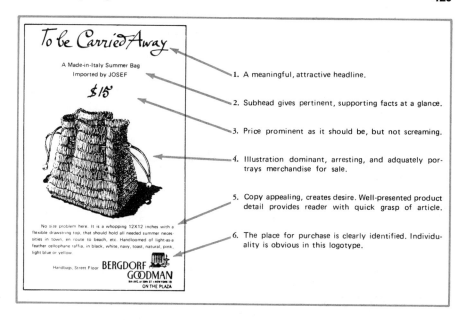

To be Carried Away

A Made-in-Italy Summer Bag
Imported by JOSEF

$15

No size problem here. It is a whopping 12X12 inches with a
flexible drawstring top, that should hold all needed summer necessities in town, en route to beach, etc. Handloomed of light-as-a
feather cellophane raffia, in black, white, navy, toast, natural, pink,
light blue or yellow

Handbags, Street Floor   **BERGDORF GOODMAN**
                          5th AVE. at 58th ST • NEW YORK 19
                                 ON THE PLAZA

1. A meaningful, attractive headline.

2. Subhead gives pertinent, supporting facts at a glance.

3. Price prominent as it should be, but not screaming.

4. Illustration dominant, arresting, and adquately por-
   trays merchandise for sale.

5. Copy appealing, creates desire. Well-presented product
   detail provides reader with quick grasp of article.

6. The place for purchase is clearly identified. Individuality is obvious in this logotype.

Illus. 13-11   Good advertising principles are exemplified in this
neat, orderly ad. The eye follows naturally from headline to logotype,
the type face is well selected, and the entire ad reflects the character
of the merchandise and of the store.

In general, retail advertisers do not make use of advertising agencies
in the same way that most national advertisers do because (1) retail
advertisements must be planned and executed with speed and at short
notice and (2) most newspapers make available to local stores a local
rate that is considerably below their national rates. Stores that depend
largely on institutional advertising, which can be prepared far ahead of
scheduled insertion dates, make effective use of advertising agencies.

ELEMENTS OF BROADCAST ADVERTISEMENTS

Advertisements presented over radio or television contain the same
four elements as printed advertisements. The functions of each element
are also the same although, because of the medium, they may be presented in a different way. For example, headline and signature plate may
be accompanied by a musical theme that is used every time a certain store
has an advertisement. Soon listeners or viewers associate that theme with
a certain store. The illustration on a radio advertisement may be communicated by sound effects and on television the product can actually
be shown in use.

CHECKING YOUR KNOWLEDGE

Vocabulary

1. signature plate, or logotype   **2.** mats

Review Questions

1. What are the three functions of a headline?
2. What purposes are served by pictures, illustrations, or drawings in an advertisement?
3. Give at least six rules for writing copy.
4. List the items of information usually contained in a signature plate.
5. Where can the beginner in advertising obtain help?

Discussion Questions

1. Should an advertisement headline or illustration be used to attract attention if the headline or illustration has nothing to do with the product being advertised?
2. In preparing copy for a retail advertisement for a dishwasher, would you use a factual appeal or an emotional appeal? Why?
3. Should radio and television advertisements be scattered throughout programs as they are now or presented in half-hour segments four or five times a day?

Part e

Advertising Standards

Much has been written about the importance of advertising in the development of our country. It has been said that advertising is in a large measure responsible for mass production, lower prices, higher standards of living, and many of the other benefits of our modern age. Without a doubt, advertising has been a contributing factor to our progress. At its best, it is a tool to educate and inform customers about the great variety of merchandise and services available to them so that they may make intelligent purchase decisions. It also channels demand toward specific items which can then be produced in quantity at lower cost. But advertising is not the miracle worker that some writers have called it. It has been proved again and again that advertising cannot sell goods that people do not want, that it is not the cure-all for economic and business ills. This in no way belittles the importance of and the need for advertising but merely helps us to look at advertising in the proper perspective.

This multibillion dollar business, advertising, has been subjected to much criticism; and it is necessary that retailers understand its strengths and weaknesses before using it. In order to build and hold the confidence of the buying public, it is necessary that advertising maintain certain standards of truthfulness and ethics.

TRUTHFUL ADVERTISING

It is natural to expect that an advertiser will tend to state only the good points about his product. Suppose that you wanted to sell a used car. If it contained a radio and heater, you would want to mention that. You would probably not advertise that the car needed painting or that the tires were old. You would advertise the best features of the car. So it is with store advertising. The retailer advertises the qualities that make a particular product a good value for the price. He does not usually make public the shortcomings of his products. If the reader understands this limitation, he will soon realize that the great bulk of twentieth-century advertising is accurate. It should be observed, however, that some stores have held successful clearance sales by deliberately mentioning the shortcomings of the merchandise.

ETHICS IN ADVERTISING

Even the truth can sometimes be misleading. For example, "English Leather Watch Strap"[1] gives the impression that the leather and the strap were made in England. If the strap were made here in the United States, the description should read "Watch Strap of English Leather— Made in U. S. A." in order that the advertising be ethical. A manufacturer who cuts the leather for the manufacture of gloves in New York and then ships the pieces to Japan to be sewn has a difficult problem in advertising the finished glove to his customers. To be ethical, the manufacturer should insert a statement such as "Sewn in Japan" in his presentation of the gloves.

One of the most flagrant misuses of advertising is in the promotion of false leaders, discussed in Chapter 10, Part D. To advertise an item at a fictitious list price marked down to the customary price is clearly an attempt to deceive the public. Another unethical practice is to advertise an article at a remarkably low price but make every effort to sell profitable substitutes to those customers attracted by the ad.

---

[1] *A Guide to Retail Advertising and Selling,* Association of Better Business Bureaus, Inc.

Trade associations, both national and local, together with the Better Business Bureaus, have contributed much to improving the ethics of advertising. Through their efforts, legislation that prevents the use of misleading, fraudulent, and untruthful advertising has been passed. Most states now have so-called *Printers' Ink statutes* that make deceptive advertising unlawful. Every retail advertiser should have for constant reference a copy of the publication of the Association of Better Business Bureaus, Inc., called *A Guide to Retail Advertising and Selling*. It consolidates the various standards and recommendations adopted by leading retail advertisers with the objective of improving the relations between retailers and the public. Government regulations pertaining to claims that may or may not be made and the correct terminology to use in advertising are included.

Printers' Ink Model Statute

Any person, firm, corporation or association who, with intent to sell or in any wise dispose of merchandise, securities, service, or anything offered by such person, firm, corporation or association, directly or indirectly, to the public for sale or distribution, or with intent to increase the consumption thereof, or to induce the public in any manner to enter into any obligation relating thereto, or to acquire title thereto, or an interest therein, makes, publishes, disseminates, circulates or places before the public, or causes, directly, or indirectly, to be made, published, disseminated, circulated, or placed before the public, in this State, in a newspaper or other publication, or in the form of a book, notice, handbill, poster, bill, circular, pamphlet, or letter, or in any other way, an advertisement of any sort regarding merchandise, securities, service, or anything so offered to the public, which advertisement contains any assertion, representation or statement of fact which is untrue, deceptive or misleading, shall be guilty of a misdemeanor.

Illus. 13-12   This model statute was developed by *Printers' Ink* magazine as a means of legally preventing the use of untruthful advertising. Most states have adopted the statute as law.

GOVERNMENT REGULATION OF ADVERTISING

Statements made by retailers in regard to their goods are regulated by law, although other agencies—such as Better Business Bureaus—are doing much to raise the ethical standards of advertising by voluntary action. Better Business Bureaus have been organized in leading cities by newspapers and businessmen to stamp out unethical selling practices and misleading advertisements.

Advertising of mixed fiber products

| CORRECT | INCORRECT |

Sheerest

CURTAINS

for sunny rooms

$5.00

~~~~~~~~

~~~~In a silk, rayon and acetate blend.

☞ *Fibers disclosed in proper order and same size type.*

Silk and Linen

ROBES

$12

~~~~~~~~

☞ *Fibers disclosed in proper order and same size type.*

Men's

S-T-R-E-T-C-H

SOCKS

$1.59

~~~~~~~~

~~~~nylon, cotton and other fibers.

☞ *Remaining fiber 5% or less.*

---

famous DRESS designer

uses a blend of

SILK and cotton

~~~~~~~~

☞ *Incorrect since only disclosure of fibers is not in proper order and same size type.*

Cotton, silk, rayon and nylon

DRESSES

~~~~~~~~

☞ *Even if the order by weight is correct the "nylon" listing is improper, since in this instance it is 3% and must not be listed by generic name but should be listed as "other fiber."*

TROPICAL SUITS

wool, nylon & rayon

~~~~~~~~

☞ *Incorrect as the constituent fibers are not given in the order of their predominance by weight. In the above instance the fibers were 65% Rayon, 25% Wool and 10% Nylon.*

Courtesy of Better Business Bureau, Metropolitan New York

Illus. 13-13   Under the Textile Fiber Products Identification Act, the fiber content of textile products must be disclosed to the customer in advertising. The advertising statements on the left conform to the Act, but the statements on the right do not.

Many states and municipalities have passed statutes that make false advertising a misdemeanor. For example, in New York City an ordinance regulates fire sales and going-out-of-business sales. A permit must be obtained, and inspectors must check to see that additional goods are not brought into the store especially for the sale event.

The federal government, through the FTC (Federal Trade Commission), has set up trade-practice rules for advertising and selling the products of many industries. These rules have the force of law. The Textile Fiber Products Identification Act requires that the fiber content of most textile products be disclosed to the potential buyer on labels and in advertising. There are also federal laws governing the labeling of wool products, furs, foods, and drugs.

In recent years a great many governmental agencies have increased their activities to assure that consumers are properly protected from harmful and hazardous merchandise and that they are properly informed through labels, packages, and advertising about the products they buy. More information on government regulations will be provided in Chapter 18.

CHECKING YOUR KNOWLEDGE

Vocabulary

Printers' Ink statute

Review Questions

1. Why must advertising maintain standards of truthfulness and ethics?
2. What organizations have helped raise the standards of advertising?
3. What is the purpose of the *Printers' Ink* statutes?
4. How do Better Business Bureaus help raise the ethical standards of advertising?
5. What government agencies are involved in assuring consumers of accurate product information?

Discussion Questions

1. Many people say that they do not believe advertisements. Why is this true? What can be done to make advertising more believable?
2. What tests should be applied to advertisements to make sure that the advertising is truthful and ethical?

3. What do you think of the propriety of the following advertised statements?

In a newspaper ad: Buy now or lose the chance to take advantage of the greatest offer in our history.

In a direct-mail piece: You have been especially selected to receive this special offer of a Brand X TV at 20% below its regular price of $125.

BUILDING YOUR SKILLS

Improving Communication Skills

A. Each of the following sentences contains two pronouns in parentheses. On a separate sheet of paper, write the number of each sentence and the correct pronoun to be used in each sentence.

1. Neither Bill Block in menswear nor Tom Stafford in children's wear adequately planned (his, their) spring advertising budget.
2. Department managers must study the market for (his, their) products before an advertising medium is selected.
3. Both the copywriter and the artist presented (his, their) work to the advertising director.
4. Hal Jones and Alan Carson thought (his, their) ad should be illustrated.
5. With the help of local advertising, the sales team in the branch store believes that (it, they) will exceed (its, their) quota.

B. A retail advertising manager received the following complaint from a customer:

Dear Sir:

On a recent morning I was looking through the city newspaper and noticed that you had advertised a popcorn popper that butters popcorn automatically. I immediately picked up the phone and called long distance. The salesperson I reached told me they were all out of the poppers. I had just gotten my paper off the front porch. She said she didn't even know they were advertised. I wasted a phone call on your false advertising.

Mrs. W. M.,
Livonia, Mich.

The manager found that the newspaper had omitted a line that stated that poppers were on sale in only two of the chain's four stores in that city. The store to which the customer placed the call did not have the popcorn poppers on sale.

Write a letter of apology to the customer, including a statement of any adjustment you think desirable.

Improving Arithmetic Skills

Perform the exercises given below involving finding interest by the 6%, 60-day method.

1. Interest on $500 at 6% for 60 days = (Move the decimal point two places to the left in the principal.)

2. Interest on $850 at 6% for 6 days = (Move the decimal point three places to the left in the principal.)
3. Interest on $1,250 at 6% for 30 days =
4. Interest on $3,600 at 6% for 90 days =
5. Interest on $5,700 at 3% for 30 days =

Improving Research Skills

1. Assume that you are the manager of an appliance store. You have an excellent line of humidifiers and wish to send prospective customers letters advertising them. For your community, list the sources you might use to obtain the names for a mailing list.
2. Select two local radio or television stations that serve your community. Listen to each station for one hour (try to listen for the same time period—that is, Station A from 8 to 9 one night and then Station B from 8 to 9 another night). Keep a record of the advertising sponsors, what was advertised, and the type of radio or TV program presented. From this information make a judgment of the listening audience that each radio or TV station was probably attempting to reach.
3. Examine the newspaper advertisements of three stores. List any items that you consider unwise to advertise. Compare your lists with those of others in the class who may have examined the same advertisements. Discuss reasons for the selection of the different articles listed.

Improving Decision-Making Skills

1. If you were the manager of a women's specialty store located in a major shopping center, which of the radio or TV stations selected for Question 2 in "Improving Research Skills" would you use? List the factors that influenced your decision.
2. The managers of the various selling units of a great retailing chain have disagreed as to whether it is better to advertise a special of 4 shirts for $10 or a special of one shirt for $2.50. Which would you vote for? Defend your position. Under what conditions would the other alternative perhaps prove better?
3. An investigation of a supermarket chain in a large city revealed that 35% of over 500 items advertised over a five-month period were either not available when the advertisement appeared or were marked higher than the advertised price. The company's excuse was that the goods had failed to arrive at the stores when scheduled or that the local managers had not had time to reprice the goods to coincide with the ads. Among the suggestions made were (1) to give the customer rain checks, (2) to not release the ad until the goods are reported to be in stock at all the stores.

Are either of these suggestions practical? Have you a better one?

APPLYING YOUR KNOWLEDGE

Chapter Projects

1. As a class or club project prepare a list of the advertising media available to retailers in your community. Indicate the nature of the

media, the address and telephone number, estimated circulation or audience, and basic advertising rates. If you are in a major metropolitan area you may do the above for the chief media for the retailers in your school area.
2. Prepare a television 60-second spot advertisement for a product of your choice, using the video and audio arrangements suggested in the illustration on page 415.

Continuing Project

Perform the following activities in your manual:

1. Prepare a six-month calendar of sales promotion and advertising events for your store.
2. Select five items that you would advertise for your store opening. Explain why you selected these items for promotion, pointing out the human interest appeal of each item.
3. Prepare a rough sketch of an advertisement for one or a related group of items you selected. Try to sketch the illustration, or clip from a magazine or newspaper an illustration which closely resembles the items you want to advertise. Give careful consideration to the suggestions in the text.

Display

a. If a customer sees a merchandise object on display, greater desire to buy it will be induced than if she simply hears or reads about the object.

b. An effective window display is an artistic composition that incorporates proven principles of selling and presents wisely selected goods.

c. Interior displays should be coordinated with window displays and should carry on inside the store the favorable impression made by the windows.

d. Color increases the attention-getting value of a display and also creates moods that can induce customers to buy more readily.

e. Effective displays are achieved through careful planning, careful preparation of the display area, wise selection of merchandise and props, and constant evaluation of display results.

Part a

Psychology of Display

To *display* means to show or exhibit goods or ideas. Such activity has been a part of retailing since the early days of trading. When stalls and marketplaces existed instead of stores, the merchant who had the largest array of goods on his tables or cart attracted the largest crowds. The early American trader with the best display of axes, blankets, and yard goods also attracted the greatest number of trappers and hunters. The pulling power of displayed goods worked in primitive times and continues to do so presently. It has been only recently, however, that retailers have given attention to the psychological principles of display.

Today's customers wish to inspect and compare a variety of items before deciding which will best satisfy their wants. The alert retailer knows that customers are curious, that they like to see new and useful items, and that they often buy on impulse. Also, he knows that customers are attracted by effective combinations of color and design. The store that makes a careful study of display and implements its display knowledge is rendering an extra service to the customer. A good display will save a customer time and money and will give desirable merchandise information.

VISUAL MERCHANDISING

Visual merchandising is everything that is planned to meet the customer's eye as she enters and tours the store. Displays may be prepared for the exterior windows of a store, or they may be located in each selling department. Visual merchandising includes displays as well as many other elements of the store. Numerous merchandise aids form the visual impression that a customer receives of a store:

Department layout	Furniture
Selling fixtures	Fitting rooms
Display fixtures	Wrappings (bags and boxes)
Wall colors	Color and arrangement of background stock
Lighting	Grooming and appearance of store staff
Signs	(uniform or conservative attire)
Floor coverings	Color of telephones
Arrangement of aisles	Shape and visibility of cash registers

The term *visual merchandising* signifies that the display function is not simply to show goods to the public but rather to arrange attractively both the merchandise and the store so as to achieve eye appeal.

OBJECTIVES OF DISPLAY

One practical retailer says that display has only one purpose: to sell goods. Although this statement sums up in three words the objectives of display, it is somewhat oversimplified. It is true that, in the long run, every retailer hopes to sell more goods through his displays; otherwise the displays would not be created. However, a display may be directed toward the immediate sale of specific goods, or it may be designed to call attention to certain benefits the customer will receive from purchasing at the store. For instance, a hardware store used its best window to show, with pictures and actual materials, the manufacturing process for paint. The objective was not only to sell paint but also to build customer confidence in the store by informing the public that the store looked carefully into the manufacturing processes of all goods it bought for resale. Window signs explained the importance of high quality and explained that store buyers must check the manufacturing processes of the goods offered to customers.

Here are the most important objectives of display:

1. To sell goods
2. To show new uses for merchandise
3. To introduce new goods
4. To build prestige and goodwill
5. To show proper care of merchandise
6. To suggest merchandise combinations

REQUIREMENTS OF SUCCESSFUL DISPLAY

A display that is successful is pleasing to the eye, tells a story, and leads the customer to the place where the product can be purchased. The requirements for a successful display are the same as those of a successful advertisement. A display should stop people by getting their attention. Next, it should develop interest by its timeliness and its appeal to customer needs and wants. Third, the display should make customers desire to own the merchandise displayed. Finally, it should prevail upon them to act. In the case of window display, action involves entering the store to examine the goods more closely. In the case of interior display, action involves either contacting a salesperson or—in the case of self-service—handling the goods and making the purchase decision unaided by a salesperson.

Displays and advertisements should actually work together to sell goods. For example, when a woman visits a store in response to a dress advertisement, she should see the featured item in a display which leads her straight to the merchandise. Attractive displays of impulse and semi-demand items may be placed along the path that the woman will follow. The merchant thus makes it easy for the customer to find the advertised item and also presents additional merchandise that may be desired. In this way the merchant coordinates advertising and display through carefully located displays along store traffic routes.

Courtesy of Federated Department Stores, Inc.

Illus. 14-1   This display serves a triple purpose: it is a leader, an end display, and on a store traffic route. Also, the product is such a bargain that it will be a good impulse purchase.

DISPLAY AND THE CUSTOMER

Our knowledge of the world about us is obtained by using our various physical senses. It is generally agreed that, of the physical senses, sight influences our actions most. Sight is the chief means for a person to keep in touch with the outside world and is a major factor in merchandise selection. For example, baby foods packaged in glass jars generally sell better than those packaged in cans because mothers feel they can better judge the food's quality if they can see it.

The customers' use of physical senses can be encouraged by artful display of goods. Proper combinations of color, light, and arrangement can help the customer visualize the product in her home (such as a painting). An invitation to smell or taste the product (such as perfume or cheese), or to touch and handle the material (such as a utensil or fabric) or to hear the merchandise (such as a record or a radio) stimulates interest, creates a desire for its possession, and induces action to purchase it.

Display people are using new visual and audio technology to deliver literally hundreds of messages in space that would otherwise accommodate only one display. As display appeals extend beyond the visual sense, the impact upon the customer must be given careful consideration. Display may entertain and intrigue, but it must primarily serve as an aid to merchandising.

CHECKING YOUR KNOWLEDGE

Vocabulary

1. display   **2.** visual merchandising

Review Questions

1. How can displays be helpful to customers?
2. List at least twelve items that are included in visual merchandising.
3. What are the most important objectives of display?
4. List the four requirements of a successful display.
5. What effect can displays have on customers?

Discussion Questions

1. What are some of the similarities in display, advertising, and personal selling?
2. Will persons of different ages and backgrounds react in the same manner to a given display? Why or why not?
3. What are some of the detractors from effective display?

Part b

Window Displays

The first impression customers get of the character of a store and of the kinds of goods it carries is from the window displays. Persons are more interested in seeing things for themselves than in reading or hearing about them. It is not surprising, therefore, that window displays are the most important means of attracting new customers into neighborhood stores and that for downtown stores window displays are almost as important as advertising.

PRINCIPLES OF WINDOW DISPLAY

If a window display is to be successful, it must follow certain well-defined principles. These principles are discussed in the next paragraphs.

Customer Uses and Benefits

The window must be trimmed from the customer's point of view. It should have human interest and should dramatize the goods. The display will have human interest if it suggests the use to which the goods are to be put rather than merely shows them. Thus, a daytime dress is more likely to interest a customer if it is displayed on a mannequin than if it is merely hung on a stand. The use of an article or the occasion for which it might be used can sometimes be pointed out by using a sign.

Maintain Timely Merchandise Selection

An effective window display must have timely merchandise and a timely setting. There should be a special reason for displaying the goods at that particular time. For example, a display of school supplies in late August or early September would be considered timely. The window background should also reflect the special display reason. In October a display of men's topcoats might be accentuated by a background suggesting a football game. A topcoat displayed in December might have as its background the suggestion of a wet or snowy day.

For certain kinds of merchandise, any display is timely. For example, London has many silver shops, some of which specialize in exquisite antique silver of the Georgian period. To potential customers, displays of such merchandise are always timely. Many sales are made

Courtesy of <u>Penney News</u>, J. C. Penney Company, Inc.

Illus. 14-2   This window specialist carefully examines and puts finishing touches on a department store window display.

from items displayed in the windows, and these items are replaced with similar objects selected from the continually changing collections of wholesale dealers.

Keep Central Idea for Display

Window displays must have a *central theme* or idea. The average customer does not stop to study a window but rather grasps the display idea in passing. The entire display, therefore, should be built around a single idea; and just enough merchandise should be displayed to bring out the proper effect.

Some stores display many different merchandise items in their windows. As a result, the windows look like stockrooms with plate glass in front of them. These stores believe that *mass display* (the piling together of great quantities of merchandise) gives an impression of low prices and brings immediate sales. If such displays are used, they may be improved by dividing the windows into sections and grouping related merchandise around one theme.

A central theme for a drugstore window display might be the contents of a medicine chest, and the window might be trimmed to show the different items that should be purchased for the home medicine chest. In a clothing store, groups of related merchandise might be displayed. The window might feature blouses, skirts, and sweaters for one week; and the next week, emphasis might be placed on boys' pajamas, underwear, and socks.

Maintain Cleanliness

The window must be clean. It should be carefully prepared for display by a thorough cleaning; and all dust, dirt, and grime should be removed from the glass, floor, background, and fixtures. Preparing a display in a dirty window is as undesirable as putting a new suit on a man who has dirty hands and a dirty face. The merchandise in the display should also be clean and neat.

Use Backgrounds and Lights Effectively

The backgrounds and lights must attract attention and accent the merchandise. Backgrounds give atmosphere to windows and frequently mean the success or failure of an entire display. In large stores the backgrounds are changed with the displays. In small stores, where time and budgets do not permit a new background to be built for each display, permanent backgrounds frequently are used.

Care must be taken to see that backgrounds do not detract from the merchandise. One merchant who used movable panels for his background put a hanging mirror in the center of each panel. When customers stopped to look at the window, their attention was immediately drawn to one of the mirrors. They adjusted their hats and ties, perhaps glanced quickly at the display, and passed on. In this case, the background received more attention than the merchandise.

Some stores have no backgrounds for their windows. The window is simply a means of letting customers look into the store. This type of window is effective for a small specialty shop in which the store interior has considerable display value. Strangers often hesitate to enter an exclusive shop if they cannot easily see the interior from the street. If, however, they can see other customers inside the store, they are also likely to enter. A food store window without a background will attract more customers if the interior has a pleasing appearance.

Lighting Tips for Specific Merchandise

1. Use large area lighting fixtures plus incandescent downlighting to avoid heavy shadows when displaying major appliances and furniture.

2. Use general diffuse lighting, accented with point-type spotlights to emphasize the beauty of china, glass, home accessories, and giftware.

3. Bring out the sparkle and luster of hardware, toys, auto accessories, highly polished silver, and other metalware by using a blend of general light and concentrated light sources—spotlights.

4. Use concentrated beams of high brightness incandescent sources to add brilliant highlights to jewelry, gold and silver or cut glass.

5. Highlight the colors, patterns, and textures of rugs, carpets, upholstery, heavy drapes, and bedspreads by using oblique directional lighting plus general low-intensity overhead lighting.

6. Heighten the appeal of menswear by using a cool blend of fluorescent and incandescent— with fluorescent predominating.

7. Highlight women's wear—especially the bright, cheerful colors and patterns—by using natural white fluorescents.

8. Bring out the tempting colors of meats, fruits, and vegetables by using fluorescent lamps rich in red energy, including the deluxe cool white type. Cool reflector incandescent lamps may also be used for direct-type lighting.

Illus. 14-3   As you read the above tips notice that the type of lighting recommended for each kind of merchandise has but one purpose: to present the product so attractively that the customer will buy it.

Light has the power to attract customers' attention; it draws customers to windows and gives the impression of a bright, clean store. Windows should be well lighted, but lights should not shine into the eyes of passersby and should not make shadows on the merchandise. Concealed lights are excellent for window displays.

Use Good Principles of Color and Design

The window display should exemplify the rules of good design. A successful display is largely a matter of design. Color should also be used to attract attention and to create interest. The study of color and design is so important in window display that Part D is devoted to it.

Reflect Character of Store

The window display should reflect the character of the store. An artistic display featuring the newest fashions is not appropriate for a

Courtesy of Flah & Co.

Illus. 14-4   This exclusive gift shop uses simplicity in its window display. Notice that only a three-shelf fixture with a low display table on each side is used. The passerby has an uncluttered view of expensive merchandise in the interior of the store.

discount store. Nor is a window showing a mass display of merchandise suitable for an exclusive specialty shop. The customer who is misled by a window display is not likely to purchase after entering and discovering the real nature of the store.

Show Merchandise in Action

The merchandise should be displayed as it might be used. This can make a display dramatic and can create desire for the merchandise. Special characteristics of the items can be emphasized by putting the merchandise into action. For example, china might be shown in a table setting with silver, glassware, linen, and centerpieces. Fall and winter sport clothes may be shown in a college football or winter resort background. How many young women have chosen their wedding gowns from beautiful bridal displays?

Change Displays Often

In many shopping districts the same people pass a store window every day. They become tired of looking at the same merchandise. They like to see something new and different, and they look forward to new displays. The rapidity of change in displays should vary with the location of the store. A neighborhood store may find it necessary to change its window displays every other day if it wants to hold the interest of its potential customers. Downtown stores, however, may change windows only once a week since most customers do not go to the central shopping district more often than that.

SELECTING MERCHANDISE FOR DISPLAY

The selection of specific merchandise items for display must be done with understanding and awareness of the overall display objectives. In most small retail stores and specialty shops, the procedure is not too complicated; the number of items that can be displayed is usually limited. The season of the year, displays recently used, and special advertising plans reduce the selection to even fewer items. Inquiries by customers or comments by friends may prompt the small retailer to prepare a display of a certain kind of merchandise. The store manager can also draw on a multitude of local events—even a change in weather —to help decide on merchandise. In the small store the time between selection of merchandise and execution of a display can be very short.

Large stores must follow different procedures in merchandise selection. The amount of merchandise from which they can select is much greater, and there are more display areas to be used and coordinated. Because of the more elaborate displays, more time is needed between merchandise selection and the actual creation of the display. In a large store, buyers, department heads, the merchandise manager, the display manager, and the display staff are all involved in each display. The communications among all these people must be carefully organized.

Whether the selection of merchandise is being made by the owner-manager in a small store or by the department head or display director in a large store, these points should be observed:

1. The merchandise selected for display should fairly represent the entire line of merchandise from which it was taken.
2. The merchandise should be stocked in sufficient quantities to meet the demand created by the display.
3. It should create a desire to come into the store and examine the goods more closely.
4. It should suggest other items to the passing customer.

CHECKING YOUR KNOWLEDGE

Vocabulary

1. central theme   **2.** mass display

Review Questions

1. List the principles of window display.
2. Why should window displays be built around a single idea?
3. When can a window without a background be effective?
4. Why should displays be changed often?
5. How should merchandise be selected for display?

Discussion Questions

1. Should merchandise in window displays always be marked with the price? Why or why not?
2. Would large stores find it wise to obtain window display suggestions from salespeople?
3. For what reasons should stores use backgrounds for their window displays?

Part C

Interior Displays

In spite of the importance of window displays, some modern stores have almost eliminated them in favor of interior displays. In supermarkets and in many suburban stores where customers are welcome to browse, the windows have no backgrounds; and customers look directly into the store interiors. This plan makes the entire store interior a part of the window display and is especially suitable for mass selling where privacy in the store is not required. Many large stores whose locations do not lend themselves to window shopping have almost eliminated window displays. Branches of large department stores frequently provide merchandise displays only at the store entrances and give the rest of their display attention to the interior.

When both window and interior displays are used, the displays should be coordinated. Interior displays should harmonize with what customers see in the windows, and the favorable impression made by the windows and entrances should be carried on inside the store.

FACTORS INFLUENCING INTERIOR DISPLAYS

The following factors must be considered in developing interior displays:

1. *Layout*—placement of various departments or groups of merchandise
2. *Decor and appearance of the store*—walls, ceiling, lights, floors and fixtures
3. *Merchandise displays*—counter, showcase, floor, and shelf displays

Layout and store decor require permanent planning, while merchandise displays change constantly. A good layout provides an easy flow of customer traffic through the store and speeds the sale of goods. Special decorations are desirable for selling events such as Christmas and Easter. Trees, paper decorations, special lights, flowers, decorative posters, and flags are some devices that may be used to give the entire store a gala effect. In discount houses overall store decorations such as bunting, balloons, flags, and giant-sized posters give a permanent carnival atmosphere to the store. Certain customers are stimulated by such an atmosphere and spend freely.

THE BOUTIQUE

A relatively new concept in store layout and merchandise arrangement is the *boutique*. Instead of grouping merchandise into traditional departments, such as dresses, suits, coats, shoes, bags, and millinery, the merchandise is so grouped as to have in one place the articles of apparel that are likely to be of interest to a particular segment of the store's customers. Thus, a teenage girls' boutique contains various articles of clothing, all at coordinated prices, that appeal to the teenager. There may also be a "His and Hers" shop for young married couples. Boutiques are not limited to groups classified by age and sex. They include special interest groups. An Italian boutique features small leather and silk objects and exclusive clothing. A Scandinavian boutique specializes in home accessories from Sweden and Denmark. An Idonesian shop contains merchandise from the Southeast Asian islands.

Assemblying goods of different types that are likely to be of interest to customers tends to increase their purchases and also gives them a feeling of personal attention.

On the other hand, the assortment of any one type of merchandise carried in a boutique is limited. The customer may feel that she must visit other shops before making her selection of an article. Care in the construction of boutiques may make possible frequent internal appearance changes in the store at a low cost.

INTERIOR DISPLAY IN SUPERMARKETS AND DISCOUNT STORES

The supermarket and the discount store have given interior merchandise display a new role. These stores depend heavily upon displays to sell the goods. Normally every different article stocked is displayed and usually is displayed in such a manner that the customer can handle it. The merchandise facts that most customers want to know can be presented by means of signs and labels.

Pegboard displays and pin-ups are frequently used to highlight advertised items. Displays of items with human interest or a newsworthy theme are used more and more to sell to the impulse buyer.

ASSIGNING INTERIOR DISPLAY SPACE

It is always a problem to decide how much space to allot to certain interior displays. Chain stores have developed the technique of allotting display space to merchandise in proportion to its sales. Best-selling articles yielding a reasonable profit are given the preferred space and the most space on counters.

Care is always taken to avoid placing impulse items in blind spots. For example, if fancy olives (generally an impulse item) are placed across the aisle from coffee (which most customers buy), the customers will have their backs to the olives and will seldom notice them. Displays located at eye level are considered to be in the best position to attract the most attention.

KINDS OF MERCHANDISE DISPLAYS

The most common kinds of interior merchandise displays are open displays, end displays, closed displays, architectural displays, platform displays, and ledge and wall displays.

Open Displays

Open displays, whether of an assortment or of a specific item, allow customers to handle the merchandise. Goods may be placed in an orderly fashion on tables, racks, or gondolas. The *basket,* or *dump, display* is also a form of open display. Merchandise is piled into wire baskets or onto bargain tables in a helter-skelter fashion to give the impression of a great volume of merchandise being offered at low prices.

End Displays

Stores use *end displays* (displays placed at the ends of merchandise aisles) primarily to feature advertised merchandise. End displays with

Illus. 14-5   This open display of a power tool enables the customer to examine the product, learn how to operate it, and decide on its application for his purposes. With not a salesperson in sight, the AIDA formula is used successfully to sell this company's merchandise.

arches or canopies seem to do a better job of focusing attention upon the featured merchandise than do other open displays. The larger an end display and the more prominent its location, the greater are the chances of a sales increase. Manufacturers and wholesalers, convinced of the sales value of end displays, employ special display people to erect displays in those stores that wish them to do so.

Closed Displays

Closed displays allow customers to view the merchandise but do not permit them to handle it. Examples of closed displays are glassed-in showcases, wall shelves, interior windows, and niches (often near elevators and escalators). Closed displays protect goods from physical damage and theft and are easy to keep in order.

Architectural Displays

Architectural displays show goods in a realistic, decorative setting, such as a model bedroom or a completely equipped kitchen. Some stores

Courtesy of Federated Department Stores, Inc.

Illus. 14-6   Many edible goods require closed displays for health reasons and also to keep the food fresh.

use seasonal architectural displays for sportswear, keeping the same store space for each season but varying the background and accessories. A yearly schedule for these seasonal architectural displays might be:

Cruise Shop	December 31-February 28
Beach Shop	March 25-July 30
College Shop	August 15-September 15
Spectator Tweed Shop	September 25-November 1
Winter Sports Shop	November 10-December 30

Platform Displays

Platform displays may consist of one or two clothed mannequins placed on a small platform. Such displays are usually found beside elevators and escalators and near store entrances.

Ledge and Wall Displays

Ledge and wall displays utilize space which would otherwise be left empty. Signs and pictures directing customers to advertised merchandise or informing them of special store services may comprise a ledge or wall display. Certain types of merchandise, such as pictures, may also be displayed in this manner.

SELLING MESSAGES

Since more and more customers want to know facts about what they are buying as well as to see the goods, a great deal of attention is being given to preparing signs and labels that will state the distinctive features of the merchandise in addition to the price. As in the case of advertising headlines, a label or sign which contains a statement of the key facts about an item is much more useful than a label or sign which contains only the name and price of the article. For many products—particularly packaged goods, drugs, textiles, and fur products —the federal government requires labels that provide information about the composition of the product. Today customers must be provided with the important facts about merchandise—its material or ingredients, its uses, its performance, and its price.

CHECKING YOUR KNOWLEDGE

Vocabulary

1. boutique
2. open display
3. basket, or dump, display
4. end display

5. closed display
6. architectural display
7. platform display
8. ledge and wall display

Review Questions

1. What factors must be considered in developing interior displays?
2. How do discount stores depend upon interior displays to sell their merchandise?
3. Describe the technique followed by chain stores for assigning interior display space to merchandise.
4. What are the kinds of interior displays which a store might use?
5. Why are display selling messages increasing in importance?

Discussion Questions

1. Under what conditions would a dump display be more effective than a neat, orderly display?
2. What procedures would you follow in determining how much display space to assign to certain merchandise?
3. Some merchants believe that goods in an interior display should be displayed only in the department where sold. Other merchants think that any goods can be featured in interior displays even if the department where goods can be purchased is in another part of the store. Which of these views is correct? Which circumstances would favor one or the other of these points of view?

Part d

Color and Design

You have already learned that, even to the small store, display is so important that some stores hire display specialists to trim their windows and set up interior displays. It is better, however, if a member of the staff who has the interest and ability in display work can take over the display job along with his other duties. Then there is likely to be more coordination between window displays and personal selling efforts.

The person who plans and executes displays must have a specialized knowledge of color and design. This knowledge is of importance to the store buyers and sellers of fashion merchandise as well as to the ultimate consumer.

FUNDAMENTALS OF COLOR

Today color is recognized as one of the major factors in consumer choice and in attracting consumer attention. Color plays an important role in the packaging of the goods and in exterior and interior displays. In fact, the principles of color should be mastered by all who wish to improve the images of their stores. The retailer should know the terminology of color, which colors harmonize, and how to use lights most effectively with color.

Terminology of Color

Color is described by three terms; hue, value, and intensity. *Hue* refers to a particular point in the spectrum of colors, such as yellow. Thus, hue is actually the name of the color. *Value* is the degree of lightness or darkness of a color. *Intensity,* or *chroma,* is the degree of saturation, or the freedom of a color from black or white. Colors such as yellow, red, and blue-violet are sometimes called *chromatic colors.* Black, white, and gray are called *achromatic colors.*

A chromatic color may be either a primary color or a secondary color. *Primary colors* are yellow, red, and blue; they cannot be produced by mixing other colors. *Secondary colors* are orange, purple, and green; these colors may be obtained by mixing two of the primary colors. Yellow and red produce orange; yellow and blue produce green; and blue and red produce purple.

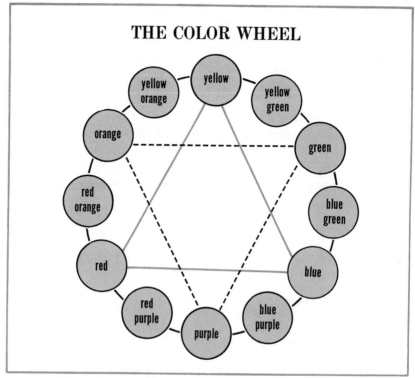

THE COLOR WHEEL

Illus. 14-7   Knowledge of the color wheel is essential in all aspects of display planning and execution. Study the wheel carefully before reading any further in this part. As you read the remainder of Part D, you will probably want to refer to this illustration. Notice that the colors connected by the solid line triangle are the primary colors (yellow, blue, and red). Colors connected by the dotted line triangle are secondary colors (green, purple, and orange).

Any color resulting from a mixture of white and a hue is called a *tint* or a pastel color. Any color resulting from a mixture of black and a hue is called a *shade*. Any color resulting from a mixture of black, white, and a hue is called a *tone*.

Harmony in Color

Perhaps the most important rule for creating harmony with color in displays is that the colors used must be related to one another in some way. Color relationships involve analogous colors, monochromatic colors, complementary colors, split complementary colors, double split complementary colors, and triadic colors.

Analogous colors are those colors adjacent to each other on the color wheel. Thus, red harmonizes with red-orange and red-purple;

and green harmonizes with yellow-green and blue-green. The safest color relationship for an inexperienced display specialist to use is a *monochromatic* one. This relationship is based on one hue and uses different tints or shades of that hue.

Complementary colors are those directly opposite each other on the color wheel. Secondary colors and primary colors are always complements. Thus, orange complements blue, purple complements yellow, and green complements red. Complementary colors provide strong but pleasing contrasts and thus have great attention-getting value in display.

The display specialist who is planning to use a split complementary color relationship first selects a hue from the color wheel. The *split complements* of this hue will be the colors on either side of its complement. Thus, the split complements of yellow are red-purple and blue-purple. The *double split complements* of a hue are its two neighboring colors and the two neighboring colors of its complement. The double split complements of yellow are yellow-orange, yellow-green, red-purple, and blue-purple.

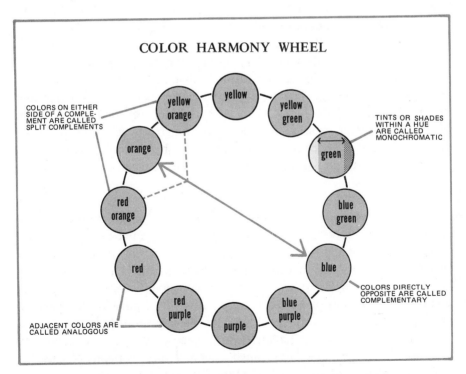

Illus. 14-8   The color harmony wheel above shows the relationships among analogous colors, monochromatic colors, complementary colors, and split complementary colors.

Some Psychological Color Associations

Red Orange Yellow	Warmth, excitement, fire, sunny (especially yellow), fall and winter, confined
Green	Cool, relaxed, spring, trees
Blue	Distant, cool, expansive, night (dark blue)
Purple	Royalty, rich
White	Cleanliness, purity

Illus. 14-9   Some psychological color associations are shown above. Do you react to these colors as indicated in the right-hand column? Which season of the year do you associate with a combination of green and red?

Triadic colors are those which form an equilateral triangle on the color wheel Yellow, red, and blue are triadic colors; and an effective display might be built around them.

Red, orange, yellow, and their intermediate hues are *warm,* or *advancing, colors.* They tend to excite and can be seen from a distance. Warm colors are preferred for displays in cold weather and for suggesting compactness. They tend to make the space look smaller and the merchandise look larger. Greens and blue are *cool,* or *receding, colors.* They tend to seem farther away than they actually are. They tend to make the space look larger and the objects look smaller. Cool colors are preferred for summer displays and for suggesting spaciousness.

Color and Lighting

The type of electric lamp used in store displays has a great deal to do with color effect. Basically, a lamp must be rated on (1) its light output or efficiency—the most light per dollar of cost; (2) *color rendition*—the degree to which the lamp lights all colors so that they look their best while still preserving the proper relationships among them; (3) the atmosphere the lamp creates—its contribution to a feeling of coolness or warmth; and (4) the heat output of the lamp.

As you learned in Chapter 3, stores may use both filament and fluorescent lamps. The latter have become very popular because of the soft, cool, and diffused light and greater illumination per watt. The general use of fluorescent lamps often makes a store interior too bright. So, today, stores use a combination of both types. The filament lamps help to spotlight the merchandise and to produce pleasing color effects on walls and ceilings.

Self-service stores usually prefer to have a great deal of light. This suggests efficiency and gives the customer an opportunity to take in a great deal of merchandise at a glance. On the other hand, specialty shops prefer soft lights, such as those used in a living room. The color of light a store chooses helps define its image. Promotional stores use cool lights, often called standard cool white lights; prestige stores frequently have standard warm white lamps. When color rendition of merchandise is important, deluxe cool white or deluxe warm white lamps are used. A wise merchant will use cool white to display such items as appliances and warm white to display furniture.

FUNDAMENTALS OF DESIGN

Design is the arranging of various elements into a display so as to achieve desired visual effects. The elements of design are line, direction, shape, size, and texture.

Elements of Design

Lines in displays may be either straight or curved. A straight display line—such as a row of shoes—gives the impression of precision, rigidity, and a positive direction. A curved line, such as a half-circle grouping of luggage, gives the impression of flexibility, action, and continuity.

A sense of direction can be created in a display with one of three types of arrangements. The horizontal arrangement suggests quiet, and restfulness and in clothing adds width. The vertical arrangement has poise, balance, dignity, and can give the impression of height. Vertical arrangements must be handled with care, for they can visually divide displays in half and can make an unattractive appearance. The diagonal arrangement suggests action and can be used to guide eye movement to a particular merchandise object. A right (high) to left (low) diagonal should be avoided, however, since it leads the eye in an unnatural movement.

When lines are joined, they create shapes. Straight lines may form squares, triangles, or rectangles. Curved lines may create a variety of circular shapes. Careful combination of straight and curved lines can produce an unlimited range of shapes for visual merchandising.

Size is an important element of display, especially when the merchandise and the display area are not entirely compatible. The distance between items of merchandise and between merchandise and observer may cause one item to dominate a display. Changing the distances can reduce an item's dominance and change the entire display effect.

Texture refers to the surface appearance of objects—the smoothness or roughness, dullness or sheen of an object. The texture of merchandise and the texture of backgrounds can suggest informality or sophistication in a display.

Principles of Design

Combining the elements of design into harmonious relationships is done according to certain principles. These principles involve repetition, contrast, emphasis, balance, and proportion.

Repetition is a design principle frequently used, because it is almost certain to result in a harmonious display. When a merchandise item is repeated in the same size, color, style, and spacing throughout a display, the display is using *exact repetition*. With *alternate repetition* the same general merchandise item is displayed, but it may appear in different colors or sizes and in different, irregular positions throughout the display. When *repetition by progression* is used, the same item appears throughout the display, but an apparent growth or reduction of merchandise lines and shapes is present. An example is a display of teflon-lined pans arranged from the smallest to the largest size. Displays using alternate repetition and repetition by progression are more interesting than displays using exact repetition.

When the display specialist groups together various objects purposely to call attention to their differences, he is using the principle of contrast. This can create an interesting display, but it is more difficult to use because of the possibility of creating a displeasing appearance.

If one wants to call attention to a particular item in a display, the principle of emphasis is employed. Every display should have at least one center of emphasis, although more than one item may be singled out for emphasis. A simple device for emphasizing a particular object is a show card directing the customer's attention to the desired object.

Balance is an important design principle. With *formal balance* both sides of a given display are identical in composition, and a line drawn through the display's center gives two equal sides. *Informal balance* maintains a harmonious appearance but achieves this appearance by placing different objects on each side in relation to the center. Thus, an informal balance might consist of two small mannequins on one side of a display and a large mannequin on the other side. Informal balance is more interesting and more likely to attract attention than is formal balance.

If all objects in a display bear a pleasing size and shape relationship to one another and to the display space available, that display has good proportion. *Proportion* refers to what is generally accepted as being a proper relationship between objects and spaces. For example, if a display consisted of three electric can openers placed beside a refrigerator, that display would be considered out of proportion because the size difference is too great to be visually pleasing.

CHECKING YOUR KNOWLEDGE

Vocabulary

1. hue
2. value
3. intensity
4. chroma
5. chromatic colors
6. achromatic colors
7. primary colors
8. secondary colors
9. tint
10. shade
11. tone
12. analogous colors
13. monochromatic
14. complementary colors

15. split complements
16. double split complements
17. triadic colors
18. warm, or advancing, colors
19. cool, or receding, colors
20. color rendition
21. design
22. exact repetition
23. alternate repetition
24. repetition by progression
25. formal balance
26. informal balance
27. proportion

Review Questions

1. What is the most important rule to remember in creating harmony with color?
2. Which color harmonies are easiest to obtain by the beginner in display work?
3. List four factors that are considered in rating an electric lamp for display.
4. Name and explain the five elements of design.
5. Name and explain the five principles of design.

Discussion Questions

1. How may unpleasant color combinations be avoided?
2. What color or colors would you use for background and accessories in a display featuring women's sport outfits in a new color called *jade* (a shade somewhat darker than the basic color wheel green).
3. Which of the design elements should receive first attention in a display? Explain your answer.
4. How would you apply the information in this chapter to the purchase of clothing?

Part e

Creating Effective Displays

An effective display does not just *happen*—it is the result of careful planning and of skill in trimming. Display work is more than just the occasional creation of a display; it requires a level of excellence that must be maintained week after week and requires meeting deadlines for unveiling displays that can defeat many persons not suited for display work. Effective displays are competitive; each store tries to create visual selling devices that attract more passersby, sell more merchandise, and —in general—please more people.

There are certain procedures in the creation of effective displays which are common to all stores. An understanding of these basic procedures will permit the potential display worker to advance quickly to more involved display work and to learn faster under the guidance of the experienced display specialist.

THE DISPLAY REQUISITION

The process of creating a display begins, as you have already learned, with the selection of merchandise to be displayed. For example, in a large department store, a buyer of children's wear may advise the department head that she has purchased a new style of playsuit in several attractive colors. The department head feels that the price and quality of the merchandise are excellent and that the merchandise, if promoted, would stimulate sales for the department. The department head would like to feature the playsuits in a newspaper advertisement and in a window display.

To get the window display space, the department head must complete a *display requisition*. The display manager checks the completed requisition to determine whether the merchandise offered for display will blend properly with other displays for that period of time, whether the display department can carry out the display at the time requested, and whether the necessary props and other display materials are available. If all aspects of the display order can be acted upon favorably, the display manager and the department head will confer on the display design and upon color, size, and accessories to be featured.

The display director will have even greater influence over merchandise selected for display if the store is building a central theme for a

---

ENGLEWOOD'S

DISPLAY REQUISITION

DEPARTMENT___Children's Wear____ DATE REQUESTED___10/12___ DATE OF DISPLAY___11/9-18___

NUMBER OF DISPLAYS NEEDED___3___   WINDOW(S)___1___   INTERIOR(S)___2___

MERCHANDISE
TO BE FEATURED Children's playsuits with mittens, caps, and boots as accessories.
Playsuits are of new style in five colors for either boys or girls, sizes 2 to
6x. Fabric is polyester, ankle and wrist cuffs of cotton rib-knit, elasticized
back for better fit, ankle zippers, front zipper with large ring, and two snap-
close side pockets.

DEPTH OF STOCK More than adequate for anticipated customer response. Item will
be carried as regular stock for remainder of season. Additional shipments of
goods already ordered.

LOCATION DESIRED Prefer Window 3 be used and that one of each color be shown (red,
blue, yellow, rust, and lime). Small platform display with three items near
center escalator. Large architectural display in center of children's wear
department.

RELATED PROMOTION Newspaper advertising on 11/8 (Sunday) 1/2 page and on 11/12
(Thursday) 1/4 page; 30-second spots on "Noontime" TV show.

REQUESTED BY___*Peg Barwarski*___   APPROVED___*Tom Shaw*___

Illus. 14-10   Here is a typical display requisition that might be used
in a department store. Study the form and note the kinds of information
which are required before the display materials can be obtained and
the display can be executed.

storewide promotion. He may ask each merchandise department head
to submit a list of items which will contribute to the promotion. The
display director will then select those items that can be developed into a
related and attractive series of displays.

PLANNING THE DISPLAY

In the large department store the display director receives many
requests from department heads for window displays. With recommendations from the publicity manager or the merchandise manager, he must
select what he feels are the most important items to present to the public.
He looks at the total display effort of the store and from this viewpoint
will decide what space to assign to the merchandise selected. Once a
specific display area has been determined, the location of each item to
be included in that area is decided. Next, a theme or selling story is
developed which will appeal to the window shopper. A sketch of the

display is made, and a list of props and display materials is prepared. The sketch gives the general layout of the display and position of the merchandise and gives notes on any special effects such as lighting or color. All the important information on the merchandise to be displayed is sent to the advertising department where a professional copywriter creates a message for the window show cards.

Routine displays may take only a few weeks to prepare, but major themes or seasonal promotions may take many months to plan and develop. To help guide the display department in its work, a display calendar is maintained. This calendar shows what display is to be in each display area every week. Such a calendar aids in budgeting space to

Courtesy of Federated Department Stores, Inc.

Illus. 14-11   Of all display preparations, a grand opening requires the most time and effort. Here a young man attaches a sign to a mobile ceiling fixture. Notice the theme of a cracked egg hatching the new store and the store emblem emerging.

various departments. Also, by planning well in advance, the display department can avoid having to prepare a heavy load of new displays within a short period of time.

Many stores set up both window and interior displays prepared by the manufacturers of the goods to be displayed. These save the store considerable effort and cost, but there is a danger that they will not reflect the store image or will put too much emphasis on a single brand.

PREPARING THE DISPLAY AREA

In the normal cycle of display work, there is always one display to dismantle before another can be installed. To reduce the time a display area is barred from carrying a selling message, late evening and early morning hours are often used for dismantling and installing displays.

Care should be taken that dismantling is done with as little interference as possible with other work areas. A curtain is usually drawn across the window to prevent customers from viewing a messy and unattractive setting. The first step in dismantling a display is removing the accessories. These are placed in plastic bags or appropriate wrappers or cartons. The merchandise is then removed from the props, neatly folded or placed on hangers, and returned along with the accessories to the respective departments to be placed back in stock for selling. The props are then removed and loaded on a stock truck for return to the display department. If a mannequin has been used, special care must be taken to protect it from damage. The next steps are to wash the window glass, replace lights if necessary, and clean the floor and backdrop, removing any evidence of the previous display.

BUILDING THE DISPLAY

The preliminary sketch prepared by the display manager is given to one of the trimmers as soon as the details of the display have been approved. The trimmer selects the functional props and decorative props from the display department or makes up the needed items in the display workroom. *Functional props* are those items used to hold the merchandise to be displayed or used to support some part of the display material. *Decorative props* are the decorative items which indicate the season or the motif to attract the eye of the customer.

Background items and bulky props are placed according to the plan provided. Then merchandise is placed on the props. If clothing is to be shown on mannequins, the fitting of dresses or suits to the form is often done prior to bringing the form into the display area. The skill of properly fitting clothing to a mannequin is one that should be learned early and thoroughly by the display worker.

After the feature items have been trimmed, the accessories are arranged. The decorative props are placed, then the selling message is added for the finishing touch. The lighting effect is checked, and shadows are eliminated or arranged as needed. The display worker makes a final inspection, checking details and viewing the display from all angles to make certain it is pleasing to the customer's eye. The display director is called in to give his approval; then a new visual selling message is offered to the passing shopper.

EVALUATING THE DISPLAY

The real payoff in display work is the number of customers brought into the store or department for a closer examination and purchase of the merchandise. Many retailers keep a record of the traffic, inquiries, and sales in the department having a display. Recording the average daily sales of merchandise prior to appearance of the display and then during the time a display is visible will provide an indication of the pulling power of the display. If other advertising media have been used during the same period, a judgment must be made as to the contribution of each toward any increase in sales.

Displays featuring merchandise for sale—called *promotional displays* —can usually be evaluated through tangible sales results. Displays designed to create goodwill—called *institutional displays*—can be evaluated through customer expressions of appreciation or approval of the store's efforts.

The display department is constantly evaluating its own efforts as indicated in Illus. 14-12. Display people often pose as passing customers and listen to customers comment on the display being observed. The selling personnel of a department are also frequently asked for their reactions to displays.

ORGANIZING THE DISPLAY FUNCTION

In a very small store or service establishment the owner or a salesperson does the display work. The slightly larger specialty shop probably will require the services of a part-time display worker. This could be a person on the regular staff or a free-lance display specialist who trims windows for a fee. The display budget will probably be small, and each dollar's worth of material must go a long way.

ENGLEWOOD'S
DISPLAY RECORD

DEPARTMENT Children's Wear   DATE OF DISPLAY 11/9-18   COST $75

WINDOW   1   INTERIOR   2   INSTALLED BY   William Ruitt

LOCATION   Window 3; platform near center escalator; Children's Wear Department.

SALES $2,800 (nine selling days)

MERCHANDISE Children's playsuits with related accessories (mittens, caps, and boots). Window display showed five different colors in various sizes--2 to 6x. Platform display featured two suits with show-card message "weather or not" and departmental location. Architectural display showed same colors and sizes and accessories as in window.

SETTING   Window--background of playground scene done in water colors; foreground covered with grass turf and scattered colored leaves; merchandise and accessories on child mannequins placed randomly as if at play. Platform--floor covering of gold burlap; two suits French wired with large card message. Architectural--four sided, merchandise and accessories on child mannequins playing on jungle gym. See attached photos of displays.

SIGN COPY   See attached sign requisitions and photos.

REMARKS   Customer response highest to architectural display. Few stopped at platform display. Window drew some response, especially first three days. Reaction to merchandise very favorable, although some customers questioned the wearing quality of material in suits.

Illus. 14-12   Records of displays should give the date, setting, and background, merchandise, sketches or photographs of the signs, direct cost, sales of the merchandise during the display period, and any pertinent remarks. Such records provide a basis for analyzing past activities to insure improvement in the future and act as idea stimulators when preparing future display activities.

In the medium-sized store there may be a display staff consisting of a display specialist with one assistant or a very few assistants. There will be facilities for sign painting and a workroom where displays may be constructed and remodeled and where display equipment may be stored.

In the big-volume store, display is an important operation. Here a display director operates at the executive level—often directly under the sales promotion manager or publicity director. There may be from ten to thirty people working on display activities. The display director serves as liaison man between general management and the buyers and department heads to plan promotions, schedule displays, and assign space for display areas. Workers are specialized for greater efficiency. Assistant display directors may be designated for window display, interior display, or special promotions. There may be ready-to-wear trimmers, home furnishings trimmers, menswear trimmers, stylists, and helpers in each area.

CHECKING YOUR KNOWLEDGE

Vocabulary

1. display requisition
2. functional props
3. decorative props
4. promotional displays
5. institutional displays

Review Questions

1. What information is asked for on a display requisition?
2. What must be done to plan a display?
3. Describe the steps that are taken to prepare the display area.
4. How may the effectiveness of a display be evaluated?
5. How is the display function organized in large department stores? in specialty shops?

Discussion Questions

1. Assume that you are the display director of a department store. Several department heads have requested window display space for the same time period. On what basis might you decide which request should be honored?
2. What advantages does a display calendar have for the small retail store?
3. Should the store always have on hand a stock of everything displayed in the window, or is it sometimes permissible to have other similar goods on hand?

BUILDING YOUR SKILLS

Improving Communication Skills

Complete each of the following sentences by writing on a separate sheet of paper the correct form of the adjective given in the parentheses.

1. The color combination in Craig's display looked _____ in the workroom than in the display window. (good)
2. The platform display with motion attracted _____ viewers that a similar display without motion. (much)
3. Because Scott's display possessed no central theme, it was _____ than Candy's. (bad)
4. The lettering on Barbara's show card was _____ neater than any of the others. (much)
5. The mass display sold _____ goods than the end display. (few)
6. Mary placed the large objects _____ from the center of the display area than the small ones. (far)
7. The _____ of the six displays was awarded a prize. (good)

8. The pulling power of the window display was _____ than that of the interior display. (little)
9. Julie's display was the _____ beautiful in the group of china displays. (much)
10. Based on gross sales the sports window was the _____ of the six featured this month. (bad)

Improving Arithmetic Skills

Perform the exercises given below. For each of the problems determine (a) the amount of trade discount; (b) the net amount of the invoice if no cash discount is taken; (c) the date by which the net amount must be paid if no cash discount is taken; (d) the amount of cash discount; (e) the date by which the invoice must be paid in order to take advantage of the cash discount. Refer to Chapter 8, Parts B and C, for guidance in performing these calculations. Remember that cash discounts are deducted from the amount remaining after trade discounts have been deducted.

1. Invoice amount, $1,100; trade discount, 10%, 5%; date of invoice, June 5; terms, 2/10, n/30.
2. Invoice amount, $3,550; trade discount, 20%; date of invoice, March 16; terms, 2/10, n/30, EOM.
3. Invoice amount, $5,000; trade discount, 10%, 10%; date of invoice, August 21; terms 1/30, n/60—60 extra.
4. Invoice amount, $4,800; trade discount, 10%, 5%; date of invoice, September 18; terms, 2/10, n/60—90 extra.
5. Invoice amount, $2,275; trade discount, 10%, 5%, 5%; date of invoice, November 11; terms, 2/10, n/30, FOB destination. (In this case the merchant paid the transportation charges amounting to $7.55. Since the terms indicate that the shipment was to be prepaid, the merchant should deduct the transportation charges from his remittance.)

Improving Research Skills

1. Determine for each of the following retail establishments appropriate display ideas for each of the four major seasons: (a) men's clothing store, (b) hardware store, (c) variety store, and (d) women's specialty store.
2. Your instructor may appoint one or more committees from the class to talk with local merchants whose stores have especially attractive window and interior displays. Each committee should report on the procedures each store follows in the designing and building of the displays.
3. Select a merchandise line or item to be displayed; then draw a sketch of a proposed window display with a complete list of props and materials needed to prepare the display.
4. Inspect an attractive store window or interior display and report on the following factors: (a) cleanliness, (b) background, (c) lighting, (d) color scheme, (e) central theme, (f) probable pulling power.

Improving Decision-Making Skills

1. Assume that you are the display manager for a five-unit chain of variety stores. You are responsible for planning and developing

materials for the display of the entire chain. Your staff takes care of all window displays, and the individual store managers are expected to use the materials you provide to change all interior displays as scheduled. One store manager consistently ignores this responsibility, and often his interior displays are weeks or months behind the advertising and window promotions. What action could you take that would encourage his cooperation in carrying out the display plans of the chain?

2. Assume that you are working in a small store with a salesperson who has charge of preparing all window and interior displays for the store. You know from your study of color and design that the displays are not attractive and pleasing. You believe that you could make much better sales-producing displays, yet you hesitate to criticize the other salesperson's efforts. How would you go about putting your display ideas into operation?

APPLYING YOUR KNOWLEDGE

Chapter Project

It is possible to practice the principles of display work by creating interior displays and window displays in miniature. These miniature displays are called *dioramas*. Build a diorama using a large cardboard box, open at one side. The display may depict either a window display or an architectural interior display. The display should have an attractive background and floor covering. If desired, it may be illuminated by a small electric light. The class may be divided into teams with each team building a diorama. A local display manager may be selected to act as judge and make awards.

Continuing Project

Perform the following activities in your manual:

1. Prepare several sketches of window displays for your store.
2. Write and illustrate, by sketches or pictures, three interior displays that you would use in the largest department in your store.
3. Set up a schedule for changing displays.
4. Describe the procedures you would establish to be sure that all selling activities in your store are coordinated.

UNIT 5

Controlling the Store

Retailers must be alert to new opportunities as well as to potential pitfalls as they continue their business operations. Incomplete notes and mental impressions do not provide a reliable picture of what happened last year, last week, or even yesterday. There are too many details in the operation of a modern retail enterprise to expect that a casual approach will be successful. The merchant must develop a record system that will provide him with the necessary data for planning and controlling his business activities. Numerous government regulations also require keeping records of certain data on business operations. With an adequate record system covering all aspects of his company's activities, the retailer has an assurance of achieving profitable growth.

chapter 15

Fundamental Records

CHAPTER PREVIEW

a. Records essential to business planning and control include those on purchases, inventory, expenses, sales, and financial standing.

b. Purchase orders and invoices are the two essential purchase records needed by every business. Inventory records are necessary for planning future buying, promotional efforts, and profit determination.

c. Classification of expenses permits identification and analysis of areas in which costs may be reduced or in which additional outlays may be needed.

d. The sales transaction is a key event in the merchandising cycle. Transactions are recorded on sales registers which are frequently linked with a data processing system to give quick analysis of sales data.

e. The income statement and the balance sheet are prepared using information from the company's records. These statements give the retailer a comprehensive picture of his company's financial status.

Part a

Record Systems

Some retailers seem to always know what is going on in their companies and in each department. They make decisions quickly and respond to requests for information without delay. Other retailers seem to be unsure of how things are going. When decisions are needed, they often make *guesses* rather than take positive action. The probable difference between the two is that one has a record or accounting system that provides the up-to-date quantitative facts needed to plan and control business operations.

A good system of business records is necessary to keep pace with a fast-moving merchandising operation. Records are also needed to determine federal, state, and local taxes, to serve as a basis for loans, and to establish credit ratings. Successful stores consider record systems so important that they will invest considerable money—even purchase sophisticated electronic equipment—to assure that they have the data needed for planning and control.

WHAT IS A RECORD SYSTEM?

A *system* is a combination of procedures, processes, or techniques maintained by a human or mechanical means to accomplish a given purpose. In a record system the purpose is to provide answers to a retailer's questions about his business. The system may be large or small, may be formal or informal, and may be designed for a specific business purpose. Under normal business conditions the proprietor of a small store does not need extensive records. A simple system of accounting with an understanding of what the records mean in terms of business decisions may be adequate. As businesses become larger, with greater varieties and amounts of stock, more personnel, and variations in expenses, questions become more complicated and more difficult to answer. Thus, the record system must be expanded or modified to provide answers to more complex questions.

The details of a record system vary, but retailers usually want a system that will pinpoint planning and control effort. If a merchant has four stores, an overall set of records obviously will not be sufficient. He will want to know the performance of each store. Likewise, within a store, the merchant will want a further breakdown of information by department or merchandise lines. The mechanics of a record system also will vary. For a very small store a manual (one kept by hand) record system may be sufficient. For stores of considerable size, however, the use of electronic data processing (EDP) equipment, either owned by the store or rented, is fast becoming standard practice. The larger the store the greater the value of having fast, accurate, and comprehensive analyses of records.

ESSENTIALS OF A RECORD SYSTEM

There are certain records that are essential to a business of any size. By looking at the basic activities of a business, we can identify these essential records. First, all businesses must have capital with which to operate. Using part of the capital, the businessman purchases merchandise and creates an inventory. A record of purchases and a record of inventory must be kept. To sell the merchandise, the store must create a place to display it; and fixtures, furniture, and similar items must be obtained. The business must advertise, employ sales-people, provide for wrapping and delivery, and incur certain other expenses in the process of selling the merchandise. A record of these expenses is necessary. The sale of merchandise results in a receipt of cash or accounts receivable; such transactions must be recorded. At the end of the selling cycle, business statements can be prepared using the information from the other records. These statements give a comprehensive picture of the company's financial standing and show whether or not the business has made a profit. If a profit has been made, there will be more capital in the business at the end of the cycle than at the beginning, unless withdrawals have been made during the period. With the new capital, the business can begin the selling cycle again.

In summary, then, the essential records that a business must maintain are:

1. Purchases
2. Inventory
3. Expenses
4. Sales
5. Financial standing

With these basic records, a businessman can answer such questions as the following:

1. What is the investment in merchandise?
2. How much gross margin was earned last month?
3. What were last month's losses from delinquent credit accounts?

4. What were the expenses, including those not requiring a cash outlay?
5. Are sales increasing or decreasing?
6. Which merchandise lines or departments are making a profit, breaking even, or losing money?

RECORD SYSTEMS FOR SMALL STORES

There are many systems for record keeping that can be used by small stores. Manufacturers and wholesalers in certain lines of trade make available to their dealer-customers record systems specifically designed for the customers' kinds of businesses or for general use in any small business.

Many small retailers use the services of public accountants who specialize in working for small businesses. The merchant submits his records to the accountant and then receives periodical financial statements and interpretations. The service may also include the preparation of tax returns and other reports for governmental agencies and technical services such as preparation of payrolls and accounts payable.

The retailer who is now using mechanical means—such as sales registers—to keep some records but whose enterprise is not large enough to afford its own electronic data processing (EDP) equipment will find that he can procure a prompt and detailed analysis of his transactions from an EDP center at a moderate service charge. These analyses are most helpful in merchandising management.

RECORD SYSTEMS FOR LARGE STORES

The small retail establishment may have only a few salespeople and may sell only one general type of merchandise, but the large retail establishment has many workers and sells a wide variety of merchandise. As the merchandise categories and sales volume increase, the scope of the accounting system must be enlarged. The same information must be maintained as for a small store, except that additional records must be maintained for the large store.

In large stores, an important use of records is in planning merchandising budgets. Budgets may be drawn for divisions, departments, or merchandise classifications; they reflect estimated sales, income, and expenses. Budgets for a given period are compared to what had been planned and what had been experienced in the previous accounting period. Budgets for most large retail stores are planned in considerable detail for three to six months ahead. More general plans are made in rounded dollar or unit amounts for six to twelve months ahead. Forecasts are also made for as far as three, five, or ten years ahead to permit planning for adequate facilities and trained personnel. Only through the continuous maintenance of sound records can such planning be made with any degree of accuracy.

EVALUATING THE RECORD SYSTEM

Most merchants appreciate the value of a good system, but many wonder how to determine the effectiveness of their current system. There are five factors which can be used to evaluate a record system:

1. *Information.* A good record system should furnish all the quantitative information that is needed to control the business properly. It should keep the businessman informed of the firm's economic condition by giving totals of cash sales, credit sales, money received on account, money paid out, and outstanding credit business. It should give information on each salesperson and on each charge customer, and it should give cumulative figures on the overall operation of the business.

2. *Protection.* The record system should be thorough enough to protect the businessman against losses due to human factors—carelessness, forgetfulness, or theft. The system should be able to report at any given time the condition of any aspect of the company's operation.

3. *Service.* The system should provide for good service to the customer and the supplier. Sales should be handled and recorded quickly. Payments to suppliers and billing of customers should be efficient. The system should minimize the possibility of oversight or duplication of billing or payment.

4. *Convenience.* The record system should be convenient to maintain. The maintenance procedures should be simple, workable, and practical. The time required to maintain the system should not be so great as to disrupt the main selling function of the store.

5. *Economy.* All functions of a good record system should be performed with a minimum of time and work. The cost of record-keeping supplies and equipment must be as low as possible without sacrificing the efficiency of the system.

CHECKING YOUR KNOWLEDGE

Vocabulary

system

Review Questions

1. Why is a good system of records necessary to a business?

2. What are the essential records that a business should maintain?
3. With good records what questions should a businessman be able to answer?
4. How far in advance do large stores develop detailed merchandising budgets?
5. List five factors that can be used to evaluate a record system.

Discussion Questions

1. What problems might a new business encounter if a poor record system were set up?
2. Describe the major differences in record systems of a small store and of a large store.
3. Which is most important to a record system—that it is convenient or that it is economical?

Part b

Purchase and Inventory Records

The merchant who orders merchandise that he does not need or who fails to reorder goods before they are out of stock should check his purchase and inventory record system. Maintaining control over stock and purchases is important in all kinds and sizes of retail operations. To have records that quickly show which merchandise has been ordered, which has been received, and the amounts in inventory can save both time and money for the retailer.

PURCHASE RECORDS

For staple merchandise lines, many merchants develop a *basic stock list* which gives the amount of each different article, size, color, and price that they wish to have in stock at all times. A similar guide for shopping and fashion lines is the model stock plan which is used to determine purchases prior to a selling season. The *model stock plan* names by classification, size, color, and price the stock which should be maintained for maximum selling potential. Another guide to purchases is the want list, or out-of-stock sheet. As you have learned, this record is kept by salespeople and serves to notify the store owner or buyer that certain items must be ordered. Items in low supply should be listed early enough to allow time for delivery before the stock is exhausted.

MODEL STOCK PLAN: MEN'S PAJAMAS, FALL

	Dollars	Units
Total planned stock	$5000	
Reserve for specials and clearance	750	
Available for model stock	$4250	476
Price Lines: $7	$1064	152
$9	2106	234
$12	1080	90

DISTRIBUTION TO CLASS, MATERIAL, COLOR, AND SIZE

Class	Material	Price	Units	Navy & Blue				Brown & Gold				Green & Olive				Prints			
				S	M	L	XL	S	M	L	XL	S	M	L	XL	S	M	L	XL
Button-down	Cotton broadcloth	$7	36	2	2	2	2	2	2	2	2	1	1	1	1	4	5	4	3
		$9	58	2	4	3	3	3	4	3	2	1	2	2	1	6	8	8	6
		$12	25	1	2	1	1	1	1	1	1	1	2	2	1	2	3	3	2
	Dacron polyester	$7	43	1	2	2	1	1	2	1	1	1	2	1	2	6	8	8	4
		$9	60	1	2	2	1	1	3	2	2	2	3	3	2	9	11	10	6
		$12	35	1	1	1	1	1	3	1	1	1	2	2	1	4	5	5	5
	Cotton flannel	$7	22		1	1	1	1	1	1	1	1	1	1		2	4	4	2
		$9	32	1	2	2	2	2	3	3	2	1	2	2	1	2	3	3	1
		$12	30	1	2	2	2	1	2	2	1	1	3	3	1	2	3	2	2
Pullover	Cotton broadcloth	$7	12	1	1	1	1					1	1	1	1	1	1	1	1
		$9	20	1	1	1	1	1	1	1	1	1	1	1	1	2	3	2	1
	Dacron polyester	$7	12		1	1		1	1	1	1	1	1			1	1	1	1
		$9	26	1	2	2	1	1	2	2	1	1	2	2	1	2	3	2	1
	Cotton flannel	$7	27	1	2	1	2	2	3	3	1	1	1	2	1	1	3	2	1
		$9	38	2	3	3	2	2	3	3	1	2	3	3	2	2	3	2	2
TOTAL			476	16	28	25	21	20	31	26	18	17	27	26	16	46	64	57	38

S = Small   M = Medium   L = Large   XL = Extra Large

Illus. 15-1   Preparation of the model stock plan requires careful thought and knowledge of past experiences and future trends. What do you think is the starting point in preparing a model stock plan?

The records of merchandise ordered and received center around two forms. The first form is the purchase order. The merchant usually maintains a purchase order file which shows what has been ordered, where the merchandise is coming from, how it is to be shipped, and the date it is expected to arrive. Some firms keep this file current by making a carbon copy of each purchase order, on which they may enter the retail price to be marked on the merchandise and may note any changes agreed upon with the supplier.

After the merchandise has been received, it is checked and prepared for the selling floor as described in Chapter 9. The invoice from the supplier is matched with the corresponding purchase order. Invoices—the other important form relating to purchases—show the cost of purchases. Invoices are usually calculated at both cost and retail prices. The cost prices are recorded by the vendors, and the merchant marks the retail prices on each invoice opposite the cost prices. Thus, the record of purchases is kept at both cost and retail prices.

When an invoice is paid, it is removed from the "unpaid invoice" file and placed in a "paid invoice" file. The total remaining in the "unpaid invoice" file is the amount due creditors. So that records of assets and expenses can be more easily and quickly prepared, purchases of fixtures and other items necessary in store operation are separated from the invoices that represent merchandise purchases.

Merchants who want a more complete record of purchases enter the amount of the invoices in a *purchase book,* which is a record of all invoices received. In a department store, the purchases of each department are separated in the purchase book. From this book they transfer, or post, the information to a *vendor's ledger,* or *accounts payable ledger.* In this ledger each creditor's account is kept on a separate page, and payments made are deducted from each account.

INVENTORY RECORDS

The retailer is flirting with loss when he lets his inventory become unbalanced or when he does not know the exact state of his inventory. The two major means of maintaining inventory records are through physical inventory and through book, or perpetual inventory.

Physical Inventory

To determine the financial standing of his business and to determine profit for a period, a retailer must know the total value of the stock on hand. This value may be found by actually counting the goods on hand, a process known as taking a *physical inventory.* Most stores take two inventories a year, generally at the end of January and at the end of July. Some stores take only one, and there are still a few small stores that take no complete inventory but merely guess at the value of the stock on hand. These merchants lose the opportunity of determining just what is in stock, of analyzing it to control buying and promotion, and of familiarizing personnel with the goods on hand.

Wide-awake merchants reduce their stocks on hand to a low point between seasons before taking inventory. This practice accounts for the many preinventory sales in stores. Goods are pulled out of dark corners and bins, reduced in price, and sold before inventory taking begins.

Procedures in Taking a Physical Inventory. After stock has been reduced as much as possible through clearance sales, the merchandise is sorted and put back into its proper place. Missing price tickets and labels are replaced. Then the merchandise is counted, usually at retail value. One of three listing methods may be employed. With one method, tags numbered is sequence are attached to every different style or lot number of merchandise; the merchandise is counted; and the count is entered on each tag. With a second method, sheets are used rather than tags; and many lot numbers are listed on each sheet. The third method involves two people—a counter and another person to record the data on punched cards or tape. As the counter calls out the item and number, the data are recorded on the cards or tape by pressing keys. In some operations, the counter dictates the data directly into a tape recorder or into a mini-computer.

Courtesy of Monarch Marking Systems
A Subsidiary of Pitney Bowes

Illus. 15-2   This data transmitter and recorder system makes it possible to take inventory by pressing the keys of the hand-held unit.

Identifying Slow Sellers. In taking the physical inventory, it is good practice to record the age of each item on hand, measured from the date of receipt. Subtotals may then be calculated to show how much merchandise on hand is new (perhaps less than three months old), how much is three to six months old, and so on. If the proportion of old stock is increasing, markdowns and other promotional steps should be taken to get it moving.

Book, or Perpetual Inventory

The book inventory of merchandise is the amount of merchandise that should be on hand based on the store records. The book records may be maintained either in dollar figures for the value of the goods or in actual count of units or items. With either method, what the retailer has to begin with is called his *opening inventory*. What is added he calls his *purchases*. What is taken out he calls his *sales*. What should be left is his *closing book inventory*. What he actually has by count is his physical inventory.

Inventory is usually calculated in terms of retail values. Here is the procedure for calculating a book inventory at retail for one three-month period.

Physical inventory as of May 1		$ 6,000
Purchases May through July		10,500
Total merchandise handled		$16,500
Sales May through July	$9,500	
Markdowns May through July	500	
Total		10,000
Book inventory		$ 6,500
Physical inventory as of July 31		6,400
Merchandise shortage		$ 100

Note that price changes—particularly markdowns—must be included in the calculation of retail inventories.

Advantages of Perpetual Inventories. The book inventory—if computed at regular intervals—may be called a *perpetual inventory* because the value of the goods on hand can be determined at any time without the labor of counting the goods. An accurate record of stock on hand every week or month is one of the most important guides to successful merchandising. In order to have ample stock to meet customer demand and yet keep the investment as low as possible, an up-to-date record of the stock on hand is needed. This record is also a great aid in case of fire loss. Without such a record a store has no way of telling the exact value of the goods destroyed by fire.

Shortage and Overage. If the physical inventory is smaller than the book inventory—which is the usual case—there is a *shortage,* which may indicate that there has been an actual loss of merchandise in the department. If the physical inventory is larger than the book inventory, there is an *overage,* which often indicates an error in the physical count.

In many stores today merchandise shortages exceed 2 percent of the store's sales, and in some it is much higher. While some of the reported shortage represents clerical errors in keeping the records or in taking the physical inventory, a considerable proportion represents theft. The problem has become so serious that an entire part in Chapter 17 is devoted to this subject.

Major Reasons for Shortages

Clerical Errors

Failure to record all markdowns taken

Charging goods to wrong departments

Errors in handling records of sales and customer returns

Failure to count part of physical stock

Physical Loss

Shoplifting by outsiders

Pilfering by employees

Breakage and damage

Giving customers more goods than they are charged for

Undetected shortage in receipts from vendors

Physical shrinkage in weight or bulk of certain goods

Illus. 15-3   The reasons for shortages in the retail value of an inventory are classified above as clerical errors and physical loss.

Inventory at Current Market Value

Merchants usually take inventory at the current retail prices and, for profit figuring purposes, translate the total retail value to cost, or *current market value.* This is done by determining the markup percentage on the purchase and then applying this percentage to the retail inventory. For example, if the current retail inventory is $10,000 and the markup on the goods handled to date is 40 percent, the closing market value is $6,000.

Some merchants, however, take inventory at cost prices by referring to codes on price tickets or to another source of cost data. Since some of the merchandise on hand will be shopworn and some will be out of style, it will have depreciated. Thus, this merchandise should be evaluated at the current market value. For example, if the actual cost of a lot of goods was $1,000 but the merchant estimates that goods of the same style and type in the same physical condition can be obtained today for $700, he will value the merchandise accordingly. However, if the replacement value is $1,100, that is, $100 more than the cost, the goods will be valued at cost ($1,000 in the example). The accepted rule is to value merchandise at "cost or market, whichever is lower."

CHECKING YOUR KNOWLEDGE

Vocabulary

1. basic stock list
2. model stock plan
3. purchase book
4. vendor's ledger,
   or accounts payable ledger
5. physical inventory
6. opening inventory
7. purchases
8. sales
9. closing book inventory
10. perpetual inventory
11. shortage
12. overage
13. current market value

Review Questions

1. What is the difference between a basic stock list and a model stock plan?
2. Name the two major means of maintaining inventory records.
3. Explain procedures that might be used in taking a physical inventory.
4. What are the chief reasons for merchandise shortages?
5. How is the current market value of an inventory determined?

Discussion Questions

1. In a store with several buyers why is it important that every purchase order be filed in the purchase order file?
2. Why is it necessary to determine closing inventory at cost rather than at retail only?
3. If a physical inventory is being taken while the store is open and customers are buying merchandise, how can an accurate count be obtained?

Part C

Expense Records

Certain costs will be incurred in the operation of a retail business. Those cash outlays and debts which come about because of the operation of the business are referred to as *expenses*. The outlay for merchandise is called cost of goods; and money spent for assets, such as fixtures and equipment, is considered part of fixed capital. Certain expenses such as rent, utilities, and insurance are regular and recurring. Other expenses such as office supplies, bad debt losses, and advertising may vary considerably in amounts from month to month. For planning purposes these expenses can, however, be estimated on the basis of past experience.

CLASSIFYING EXPENSES

Numerous expenditures for a wide variety of services and supplies are made during a business year. These expenditures should be classified to assist the businessman in the analysis of his expenses. The owner of a small store can keep a simple record of expenses and can pay them by check when they are due. By classifying and analyzing entries in his expense record, he can periodically get a total of his expenses and a breakdown by expense categories. In the large store detailed classification of expenses is necessary for efficient operation.

There are several ways of classifying expenses. No matter which system is used, it should provide a sound basis for analyzing the company's expenses, should provide guidance to management in making future business decisions, and should permit comparison with expense records of other similar stores. Often a store will use several means of classification at the same time.

Natural Expense Categories

One way to classify expenses for frequent analysis is to set up so-called natural expense categories. Stores of different sizes will use different kinds and numbers of expense categories. A small store may need only six or nine categories; a large chain may classify its expenses using twenty or more categories. Here are the categories standardized for department and specialty stores:

1. Payroll—salaries, wages, commissions, and bonuses
2. Fringe benefits
3. Advertising—all payments for media used
4. Taxes—all local, state, and federal taxes, except income taxes
5. Supplies—wrapping, delivery, office, and for repairs
6. Services purchased—cleaning, repair, delivery, trash collection, light, heat, and power
7. Unclassified—cash shortages, meal money, etc.
8. Traveling—transportation and hotel bills
9. Communications—postage, telephone, and telegrams
10. Pensions—retirement allowance
11. Insurance—fire, public liability, etc.
12. Depreciation—building, equipment, and fixtures

13. Professional services—legal, public accounting, resident buying office, etc.
14. Donations—charitable, welfare, educational
15. Losses from bad debts—including bad checks
16. Equipment rentals—cash registers, delivery trucks, etc.
17. Real property rentals

Functional Expense Categories

Large stores classify their expenses also by the major functions of the business, such as Merchandising, Direct Selling, Sales Promotion, and Control and Accounting. Under these headings, they include the natural divisions that are applicable. Almost all functional divisions have payroll, supplies, services purchased, and depreciation. The need for other natural divisions varies with the function.

Fixed, Semivariable, and Variable Expenses

Another means of classifying expenses is to consider them as fixed, semivariable, or variable expenses. *Fixed expenses* include rent, insurance premiums, taxes, and other expenses that do not change with the sales volume. *Semivariable expenses* are those, such as advertising expenditures and charitable donations, which vary somewhat according to sales volume but which are usually more or less controlled as a matter of management policy. *Variable expenses* fluctuate in almost direct relation to sales volume. Commissions to salespeople and expenditures for supplies are examples of variable expenses.

Direct and Indirect Expenses

Some stores are not large enough to have distinct selling departments; but when such departments exist, each must bear its share of the expenses. Expenses then may be classified as either direct or indirect expenses. Expenses that are paid out solely for the benefit of one department and are charged against that department's income are called *direct expenses*. Direct expenses include salaries for employees, advertising, selling supplies, and some traveling and communication expenses.

Included in *indirect expenses* are outlays that serve the whole store. Examples are rent, heat and light, taxes, insurance, and payroll of nonselling departments. Thus, if a department's sales are $10,000, the cost of the goods it sells is $7,000, and its direct expenses are $2,000, the department is contributing $1,000 to the store as a whole to help cover indirect expenses and to help yield a profit for the store. Some stores allocate indirect expenses among the departments, but it is not necessary to do so.

ANALYZING EXPENSE RECORDS

After expenses have been properly classified, they can be analyzed either by comparing the dollar figures in each classification with figures from past experience or by translating the dollar figures into percentages of sales. The latter method of analysis is preferred. Simply comparing the dollar figures does not always give an accurate picture of the relation of expenses to other aspects of the company's operation. Suppose, for example, that payroll expense was $16,800 last year and $17,500 this year. Comparing these two figures indicates that payroll expense is increasing, and this knowledge might cause the businessperson concern. However, suppose that last year's sales amounted to $210,000, and this year's sales amounted to $250,000. The payroll expense last year was 8 percent of sales; this year it was 7 percent of sales. Thus, the dollars-and-cents increase in payroll expense should cause the businessperson no alarm.

Merchants know that, through the reduction of expenses, they can earn a greater net profit for themselves. There are some expenses which cannot be reduced from week to week, while there are others that can. For instance, the amount of insurance expenses and the depreciation on assets do not rise and fall with the amount of sales. Rent, too, is usually the same each month. On the other hand, the retailer may be able to reduce the amount of certain variable expenses—such as his payroll, advertising, or delivery expense—through better management.

Sometimes it is wise to increase the amount of expenses in order to increase business. For instance, a businessperson thinks he will be able to increase his sales $1,000 a month by distributing a weekly advertising circular in the neighborhood. The cost of printing and distributing such a circular will be about $20 a week or about $87 a month. He also plans to pay $120 a month for a part-time employee to handle the increased amount of business. Thus, his monthly expenses will be increased approximately $232 ($87 for circular plus $120 for part-time salary plus $25 for wrapping, delivery, and other items). If the sales of $1,000 involve goods costing $650 he will have a margin of $350. Thus, the increase in sales will justify the increase of $232 in expenses.

SPECIAL EXPENSE RECORDS NEEDED IN SMALL BUSINESS

Three types of expenses that are frequently carelessly handled by the small business owner are petty cash expenses, delayed expenses such as depreciation and interest, and the expense of his personal salary. It is easy to fail to record these expenses, but every small businessperson should make a special effort not to overlook them in record-keeping procedures.

Petty Cash Fund

Small expenditures, such as those for electric bulbs, pencils, and postage, are paid from the *petty cash fund*. The merchant may write a check for $25 and keep the cash in a box from which he pays out these small amounts. When the fund becomes low, he cashes another check to restore the amount of the fund to $25. A record of the amounts spent and of the different purposes for which the petty cash was spent should be maintained so that periodically the merchant can classify these expenses along with his other expenses.

	PETTY CASH RECORD					
Date	For	Paid To	Cash in Fund		Cash Paid	
Jan 3	Cash	Petty Cash	25	00		
Jan 6	Pencils-Felt Pens	Green's Variety			3	17
Jan 11	Order Forms	B&D Printing			5	60
Jan 17	Stamps	U.S. Postal Service			4	80
Jan 21	Newspaper	Craig Winn			2	60
Jan 29	Display Signs	Graphics Limited			8	32
			25	00	24	49
Jan 31	Balance			51		
Jan 31	Cash	Petty Cash	24	49		
Jan 31	New Balance		25	00		

Illus. 15-4   Since small expenditures are often poorly recorded in the small business, it is wise for the owner-manager to set up a petty cash record.

Delayed Expenses

In all stores the merchant keeps records of the expenses that involve cash outlays, but these records do not give information about all the expenses. Some expenses do not involve any immediate cash payment. For example, a delivery truck for which $5,000 was paid may wear out in five years. When first purchased, the amount paid is treated as an asset, not as an expense. Every year, however, the truck is worth $1,000 less. This amount should be included in expenses under the heading Depreciation Expense. Likewise, any taxes due during the year are expenses, even though not paid. Again, a store may spend $100 during a period for supplies, but at the end of the year $25 worth of supplies may still be on hand. The expense figure for supplies would be the cost of supplies used—$75. The $25 worth of supplies left would be an asset.

Personal Salary

The merchant may include in his expenses a reasonable salary for himself. If he draws this out regularly, it will appear with other expenses in his cash payments record. If he does not draw it out, he may include the undrawn salary in expense and treat the amount as a store liability—an amount owed him by his store. Although such a salary deduction is not allowed for income tax purposes, it does help the merchant to determine whether he is earning from the business anything in addition to a reasonable salary. If he ultimately incorporates his store, he will be able to include a salary for himself in his store expenses. He may do this for tax and analysis purposes.

CHECKING YOUR KNOWLEDGE

Vocabulary

1. expenses
2. fixed expenses
3. semivariable expenses
4. variable expenses
5. direct expenses
6. indirect expenses
7. petty cash fund

Review Questions

1. List at least eight natural expense categories.
2. What is the difference between fixed and variable expenses?
3. Describe two ways of analyzing expenses after they have been classified.
4. Which kinds of expenses can usually be reduced by careful management?
5. List the three special expense records that may be carelessly handled by the small businessperson.

1. Which of the natural expense categories would be most directly affected by a substantial change in sales volume?
2. Why would a merchant want to classify as many expenses as possible in the direct category?
3. Would it be helpful to express expenses in each classification as a percentage of total expense?
4. If you wish to determine all your sales promotion expenses (advertising, display, publicity, and others), which of the 17 natural divisions will you have to include?

Part d

Sales Records

The sales transaction is a key event in the merchandising cycle. The retailer is keenly interested in not only the dollar volume of sales but also what is sold. Each store or department is trying to sell more than in the same period a year ago or is striving for a certain level of sales. The merchant may take hourly sales readings to determine if promotions are working or if quotas are being reached. Analyses of both success and failure and planning for the future require that adequate sales records be maintained.

RECORDING CASH SALES

A sales register is the major means of recording sales data. In a small business, it is usually the sole source of sales records. When the small merchant makes a sale, he rings it up on the register. The register contains a small adding machine that adds each sale as it is made. If the numbers on the machine are turned back to zero at the beginning of the day, the amount shown at the end of the day represents the total amount of cash sales. Therefore, if the register adding machine reads $60, the merchant knows that he has sold $60 worth of merchandise for cash that day.

In stores with more than one register, the total daily sales are the sum of the readings of all the registers. Some merchants do not turn the registers back to zero at the beginning of each day. The last reading of the register becomes the starting number for the next day. For instance, if the merchant did not turn the register back to zero, the $60 would be the start of the second day's sales. If at the end of the second day, the register reads $135, he would have to subtract $60 from it to get the second day's sales, which would be $75. The register should contain $75 in cash plus the cash fund used to start the second day. For a busy Saturday, some supermarket managers start each register with about $75 in change to handle customers' bills. The starting amount is added to the sales reading of the register to determine the amount that the register drawer should contain for the period being checked.

RECORDING CREDIT SALES

If a customer charges a purchase, the sales record of the transaction must show that it was a charge sale and provide the information necessary for billing the customer for the purchase. In small stores the salesperson may complete a sales slip, mark it as a charge, and have the customer sign the slip. At the end of the day a total is made of all credit sales, and the slips are filed in customer folders. At the end of the month bills are prepared using the slips in each folder. Customer payments are recorded in a similar manner. In stores with modern sales registers and accounting machines it is possible to enter the charge sales in the sales register and record charge purchases daily on each customer's bill.

With electronic equipment it is even possible to record the sales and bill the customer at the same time. When a charge sale is made, two cards—the customer's charge plate and the price ticket for the merchandise—may be inserted by the salesperson in a floor recording unit. The floor unit transmits the information to a central computer. The computer totals the charge sales automatically by department and merchandise classification and stores them by customer name. At the end of the billing period, the computer prints out a bill for each customer which shows the department, merchandise classification, and price of goods purchased on various days, the amount paid on account, and the balance due. Carrying charges, if any, are also figured and included in the amount due.

DETERMINING TOTAL SALES

All businesses must determine total sales for a given period. Without this figure, no other data from the store records can be interpreted and utilized for store control. In small businesses using old cash registers, it may not be possible to ring up credit sales. Thus, the total sales for the day are determined by taking the cash register reading and adding the total of the credit sales slips. If the register reading is $60 and the total of the credit sales slips is $25, the merchant knows that the total sales for the day were $85. With the new sales registers which permit

Courtesy of Federated Department Stores, Inc.

Illus. 15-5   A checkout clerk approves a customer's charge plate before processing purchased merchandise through a computerized sales register.

the ringing up of charge sales as well as cash sales, the merchant has only to take the register reading to determine the total sales. If any merchandise is returned by customers, the value of the returned goods is subtracted from the day's gross sales to obtain the amount of net sales.

In some specialty stores a sales slip is made out for every sale, even if it is a cash sale. In such cases, obtaining the total sales is a simple matter. At the end of the day, the amounts on all the sales slips are added. The total is the amount sold that day. When sales slips are used to record sales, it is important that control be exercised over every sales slip, for a missing sales slip may cause the sales figures to be incorrect. Therefore, sales slips are numbered; and a sales audit is made to determine whether any sales slips are missing.

In large stores in which there are many departments and many salespeople, the total store sales must be analyzed by breaking them down into the amount of sales for each department or for each salesperson. In supermarkets, for instance, the sales register will record sales figures for the grocery, meat, produce, dairy, and drug departments and for any other department which has a separate register key. In determining total sales using the register reading, it is necessary that the cash drawer be checked to see that the amount of cash there agrees with the register reading and that the amount is neither short nor over. Some sales registers have a separate drawer for each salesperson who uses the register, and the register records the sales figures for each drawer separately. The procedure for checking the amount of cash against the register reading (*proof of cash*) is shown below.

Proof of Cash

Last register reading	$4,657.00	
Former register reading	3,124.00	
Sales for the period		$1,533.00
Beginning cash		65.00
Drawer must account for		$1,598.00
Vouchers and Receipts in Drawer		
Refunds (vouchers necessary for all items)	$ 45.00	
Removal for deposit (receipts necessary)	500.00	
	$ 545.00	
Cash in Drawer		
Checks	$625.00	
Bills	392.00	
Coins	35.45	
Total cash	$1,052.45	
Total cash, vouchers, and receipts		$1,597.45
Short		.55
		$1,598.00

Illus. 15-6   Study this illustration carefully. Retail personnel are frequently called upon to make proofs of cash.

COLLECTING SALES DATA

There is a variety of sales registers used in retail stores that have the capacity for accumulating considerable sales data. On some registers the detail tape is printed with optical font type which can be read by an optical scanner. Other registers record data on punched paper tape which can also be interpreted by a computer. The newest is a wand that "reads" price tickets, computes the total sale, and transmits the data to a computer. Electronic point-of-sale systems store data magnetically either in a floor unit or in a central computer. In each case the sales data can be periodically sorted, calculated, and tabulated into a sales report.

The electronic systems are proving a boon to fast-moving sales operations, such as discount houses. They reduce the training time required, since many operations such as figuring taxes are handled automatically. Errors are dramatically reduced, and lines at the sales registers move faster. There is a saving in people, time, and money. The detailed records that become available on each item also tend to make smaller stocks possible.

CHECKING YOUR KNOWLEDGE

Vocabulary

proof of cash

Review Questions

1. How can daily sales totals be obtained from sales registers without turning the counters back to zero?
2. How is it possible with electronic sales registers to record credit sales and bill customers at the same time?
3. How do merchandise returns by customers affect the daily sales total?
4. How are total sales determined in retail stores which have several sales registers?
5. Describe the procedure involved in proof of cash.

Discussion Questions

1. What potential problems exist in a store where sales records are based entirely on sales slips?
2. What effect would a power failure have on the selling activities of a large department store? If you were a salesperson what could you do?
3. With greater use of sophisticated record-keeping equipment it is not necessary that the owner-manager know much about fundamental record keeping. Why is this statement false?

Part e

Business Statements

Business statements can take various forms, depending on the nature of the business and the type of system used. Their purpose is to document the significant facts of the business for current and future use. With records of purchases, inventories, expenses, and sales, the businessperson can prepare a statement reflecting the total picture of his operation. The arrangement of the information on these records into an income statement and a balance sheet provides the businessperson with a measure of his business success.

THE INCOME STATEMENT

The *income statement*—also known as the *profit-and-loss statement*—shows the progress of a business during a certain period of time. To explain how an income statement is prepared let us return to Marilyn Marsh who opened a card, book, and gift shop. She prepares an income statement so that she can calculate her net income for each month. From her sales records, Miss Marsh determines that net sales for a month were $2,410. She then examines the inventory record and finds that the month's opening inventory at cost was $4,790. Next she checks the purchase records to find the amount of merchandise purchased at cost during the month. The sum of the opening inventory and net purchases during the month is the total cost of merchandise available for sale. Marilyn's net purchases were $1,640, so the total cost of merchandise handled is $6,430.

Marilyn must now determine how much merchandise is left at the end of the month; so she calculates the book inventory at retail and converts this figure to a cost figure. With a book inventory of $7,400 at retail and cost prices averaging 65 percent of retail, the ending inventory at cost is $4,810. Now Marilyn subtracts the amount of the ending or closing inventory from the total cost of merchandise handled and determines that the cost of the goods sold was $1,620. This figure is subtracted from the net sales figure to give the amount of *gross margin*—$790.

Marilyn still does not know how much profit she has made. She knows that the $790 gross margin is not all profit, for during the month she had to pay certain expenses of operation. Her expense record shows that the total expenses amounted to $330. The final step in preparing the income statement is to subtract the total expense figure from the gross margin figure. The resulting figure—$460—is Marilyn's *net income* and represents her earnings for operating her own business and assuming the risks involved.

The income statement for Marilyn's Gift Shop is shown in detail in Illus. 15-7.

Importance of Figuring Net Income

An accurate calculation of net income is important in many ways. It enables the merchant to determine how much income tax he must

```
                         Marilyn's Gift Shop
                          Income Statement
                    For Month Ended March 31, 19--


                                                                      %

Revenue from sales:

   Gross sales.......................      $2,460

     Returns and allowances.............        50       2.0*

     Net sales.........................          $2,410  100.0

Cost of merchandise sold:

   Opening inventory, March 1.........      $4,790

   Purchases (including transportation)$1,680

   Returns to vendors.................      40

   Net purchases......................       1,640

   Total merchandise handled..........      $6,430

   Closing inventory, March 31........       4,810

     Cost of merchandise sold...........          1,620  67.2**

Gross margin.........................          $  790  32.8**

Operating expenses...................             330  13.7**

Net income (Operating profit).........          $  460  19.1**

   *Percentage of gross sales
  **Percentage of net sales
```

Illus. 15-7   Marilyn Marsh prepares an income statement like this each month. Some firms prepare such statements weekly, and others do so only on a quarterly basis. Notice that in order to make month-by-month comparisons easier the cost of merchandise sold, gross margin, operating expenses, and net income are expressed as percentages of net sales.

pay. It indicates whether he is making a success of his business or is heading toward bankruptcy. It helps him decide how much money he can afford to draw out of the business without impairing the operation and profit-making potential.

Perhaps the chief value of the income statement is in showing how net income may be increased in the future. There are three basic ways of increasing net income:

1. To increase sales with only a proportionate increase in cost of merchandise sold and little or no increase in expenses

2. To decrease cost of merchandise sold without decreasing sales—this is equivalent to realizing a larger gross margin or markup

3. To reduce expenses

Elements in Profit

The small retailer should look at the question of profit from an objective point of view. He should consider himself first as manager of the store. For his management, he should draw a weekly salary. Then, if he owns the store, he should consider the amount of money he has invested in it. This money is used to buy merchandise in suitable quantity and assortment to satisfy customer needs and to buy fixtures such as counters, registers, floor coverings, and window and interior display models. On the total amount of his investment the small retailer should receive a fair rate of interest, just as if he were to deposit the money in a bank and earn interest on it. This amount of money, called *interest on the investment,* is not the retailer's pure profit but is simply the amount due him for having "lent" money to his business to operate it.

In addition to earning a salary for his managerial services and receiving interest on his investment, the merchant is entitled to a reward for the risks he assumes in organizing and owning a business. He runs the risk of losing all or part of his investment. When he is fortunate and able enough to earn more than salary and interest, this excess is what the economist calls *pure profit,* or the return for risks assumed. Pure profit is not assured, for the merchant may earn less than salary and interest and thus suffer a loss. In the long run, his pure profit generally does not average more than 1 to 3 percent of his sales.

THE BALANCE SHEET

At the time an income statement is prepared, a balance sheet is also usually prepared. The *balance sheet* shows (1) the value of the assets that a merchant owns, (2) the liabilities he owes, and (3) the merchant's interest in the business. This third element, called *equity*, is the difference between assets and liabilities. On the ordinary balance sheet, it appears under Proprietorship. For a corporation it may appear under Capital or Stockholders' Equity.

Assets

The assets of a store are determined as follows: Cash includes the cash in the bank and the cash in the store, which may be in a petty cash fund. Government Securities are those owned by the store that can be turned into cash in a short time. Accounts Receivable—the amount due from customers—is determined from the records. Merchandise Inventory is determined by the actual count already discussed and is valued at cost not retail. Some assets, such as supplies, will be used up as expenses in the operation of the business. Likewise, insurance may be paid for several years ahead; and it represents an asset until the year in which the insurance is provided, when it then becomes an expense. The sum of these items—cash, securities held in place of cash, accounts receivable, supplies, and prepaid insurance—is called Current Assets.

Land, buildings, furniture, and fixtures are called Fixed Assets. The value of these assets is determined from a record of the original amount paid for them, and depreciation is figured on them (except land) in accordance with the number of years it is estimated they will last. They are included as assets at the present-day estimated value, with the depreciation being treated as an expense. Any long-term investments are included in fixed assets.

Liabilities

After the assets have all been determined, the merchant lists his liabilities. The chief ones generally are Accounts Payable—obtained from a record of merchandise purchases still unpaid—and short-term Notes Payable, which have to be repaid within a year. Accrued Expenses are expenses incurred but not yet paid, such as salaries that have been earned by salespeople but not yet paid by the store. These items comprise the Current Liabilities, those that will be due within a relatively short time, usually within a year. To these are added Fixed Liabilities, such as a mortgage or a long-term promissory note on which money was borrowed. Fixed liabilities are those that are paid over a number of years in the normal operation of the business.

Proprietorship or Equity

The difference between the total assets and the total liabilities is the amount of the merchant's interest or equity in the business. In the balance sheet (Illus. 15-8), Pat Baxter's interest, or equity, consists of his original investment plus accumulated profits, less withdrawals.

Importance of the Balance Sheet

The balance sheet supplements the income statement in that it shows the value of the business at a specific time rather than its income and outgo over a period of time. A balance sheet is generally required by a bank from which the merchant desires to borrow money because it

```
                      Pat Baxter's Adobe Shop
                           Balance Sheet
                        December 31, 19--


                              Assets

Current assets:
   Cash..............................................$ 1,000
   Government securities..............................    500
   Accounts receivable................................  3,800
   Merchandise inventory.............................. 14,000
   Supply inventory...................................    800
   Prepaid insurance..................................    300
         Total current assets.............................      $20,400

Fixed assets:
   Building (less depreciation)......................$27,000
   Furniture and fixtures (less depreciation)...........  3,000
   Delivery equipment (less depreciation)...............  1,200
         Total fixed assets...............................       31,200

Total assets..........................................          $51,600

                           Liabilities

Current liabilities:
   Accounts payable...................................$ 4,500
   Notes payable (short term).........................  2,000
   Accrued expenses...................................    800

Total current liabilities.............................          $ 7,300

Fixed liabilities:
   Mortgage payable...................................           25,000

Total liabilities.....................................          $32,300

                         Proprietorship

Pat Baxter, Capital...................................           19,300

Total liabilities and proprietorship..................          $51,600
```

Illus. 15-8   Compare this balance sheet for Pat Baxter with the income statement of Marilyn's Gift Shop. How does the balance sheet differ from the income statement? What effect would there be on this balance sheet if Pat Baxter rented the building instead of owning it?

shows even better than the income statement whether a store will be able to repay borrowed money when it is due.

CHECKING YOUR KNOWLEDGE

Vocabulary

1. income statement, or
   profit and loss statement
2. gross margin
3. net income
4. interest on the investment
5. pure profit
6. balance sheet
7. equity

Review Questions

1. What is the purpose of having business statements?
2. Why is it important for a businessperson to calculate net income?
3. Outline the three basic ways of increasing net income.
4. Name the three major elements or sections of a balance sheet.
5. What is the difference between current and fixed liabilities?

Discussion Questions

1. How often should a retail business prepare an income statement? Should a new business such as Marilyn's Gift Shop prepare such a statement more frequently than a well-established firm? Why or why not?
2. Some people say that no business should be allowed to make pure profit. Do you think that pure profit is justified? Why or why not?
3. If a business has an increasing amount of sales and a sizable increase in cash, does this mean that the business has increased in financial strength? How could this situation occur and the firm still experience a decrease in profits?

BUILDING YOUR SKILLS

Improving Communication Skills

Each of the following sentences contains adjectives and adverbs in parentheses. Only one of them may be used correctly in each sentence. On a separate sheet of paper, write the number of each sentence and the correct word to be used in the sentence.

1. Store records must be kept (careful, carefully).
2. Classifying expenses is not (near, nearly) so difficult as one might imagine.
3. With good records slow-selling items can be spotted (real, very) quickly.
4. One (sure, surely) cannot waste time and be a success.
5. The merchant must organize his records (good, well) in order to understand his business.
6. The busy retailer can (hardly, not hardly) keep complete records.
7. Simplifying sales records will (sure, surely) make your work easier.
8. Selling furniture is the (harder hardest) of the three selling jobs.
9. (Most, Almost) every record written by Jane is easy to read.
10. The Oak Street store is the (more, most) promising of the two on the south side.

Improving Arithmetic Skills

Perform the exercises given below involving the income statement and the balance sheet.

1. Give the formula for finding (a) net sales, (b) cost of goods sold, (c) gross margin, (d) net income, (e) net income as a percentage of net sales.

2. Compute the net income from the following information and express it as a percentage of net sales:

Sales	$57,000
Opening inventory	20,000
Closing inventory	22,000
Purchases	40,000
Expenses	15,000

3. Recalculate the problem above, making allowance for the following adjustments:

Returns from customers	$300
Returns to vendors	200
Transportation charges	100

4. Prepare an income statement using these figures:

Gross sales	$ 95,000
Returns from customers	500
Opening inventory	100,000
Purchases	50,000
Returned purchases	1,000
Transportation costs	700
Closing inventory	83,000
Expenses	17,000

5. Assume that at the end of the accounting period your business has these figures in addition to those given in Problem 4:

Cash	$10,000
Accounts Receivable	17,000
Fixed Assets	40,000
Accounts Payable	20,000
Notes Payable	5,000

   Assume that the beginning capital was $114,200. Prepare a balance sheet for the accounting period just past.

Improving Research Skills

1. Visit several retail stores in your neighborhood and observe the type of sales register used by each. From what you observe, which types of data are collected on each sales transaction?

2. Select one of the retail store pairs listed below and develop a list of the kinds of records each store in that pair must keep. Which records are needed by both? Which records are unique to each?

Variety Store	Pet Shop
Service Station	Shoe Store

Supermarket .... Sporting Goods Store
Women's Ready to Wear .... Book Store
Men's Clothing Store .... Florist

3. Using your school or public library as a resource, determine how businesses may depreciate business equipment such as fixtures, sales registers, and marking equipment. Develop, as an example, how a store might go about the depreciation of a mannequin which cost $375.

Improving Decision-Making Skills

1. One of your friends has plans to open a small children's wear store. He asks you to help him set up a record system for the store. He expects to carry an inventory at retail of about $15,000 and attain annual sales of about $50,000. Outline the basic records you would recommend he have and describe the relationship among these records.
2. You are the manager of a medium-sized hardware store. You are bothered by discrepancies between your book inventory record and physical inventories. Sometimes there are overages and other times shortages in almost every department. List a series of steps that could be taken to locate the cause of these overages and shortages. What would have to be checked?

APPLYING YOUR KNOWLEDGE

Chapter Project

Individually or with a small group of your classmates investigate the inventory procedures used by three local retail businesses. Determine how physical inventory counts are made and how frequently they are taken. Based on your findings what suggestions for improvement would you make to each firm?

Continuing Project

Perform the following activities in your manual:

1. Explain and illustrate your system for keeping purchase and expense records.
2. Describe or outline how sales data are collected in your store.
3. Prepare an income statement and a balance sheet for your first year in business. Use realistic goal figures and explain any variations from the financing plan made in Chapter 4.

chapter 16

Processing Store Records

CHAPTER PREVIEW

a. The transaction is the origin of each separate piece of data that is accumulated into a flow of information that results in necessary store records. The recording of this data can be done manually, mechanically, or electronically.

b. Automatic data processing involves procedures whereby recorded information about transactions is arranged into meaningful reports by mechanical means.

c. The electronic computer can perform arithmetic calculations with amazing speed. It can collect and store vast amounts of information, and can be programmed to perform a great variety of successive operations.

d. Electronic data processing is most suitable for handling great numbers of repetitive transactions. Retailers do not need to own their own computers. Arrangements can be made with suppliers and data processing centers for preparation of reports that are most helpful.

e. In addition to using the computer for standard merchandising and accounting reports, retailers use it for planning, control, ordering, credit authorization, handling telephone mail orders, and a variety of major retail decisions.

Part a

Data Acquisition

As you have seen, there are several reasons for having accurate and complete store records. There is the need to account for the money that is received and spent. There is the need to know the profit or loss and the amount of taxes that must be paid. Records are needed also to guide the retailer in merchandising and management decisions. A sudden increase in the sale of a particular style, color, or model should be known to the retail buyer immediately so that reorders can be placed and goods received while the demand is still active. To collect information on the thousands of items in the typical store and then to arrange this data quickly into useful reports have been major problems for retailers.

THE TRANSACTION

The *transaction* is the origin of each separate piece of data that is accumulated into a flow of information that eventually results in the necessary store records. Transactions take many forms. A transaction may be a sale to a particular customer, a customer return, a purchase order sent to a supplier, a return to a supplier, a price change, a payment made to an employee for hours worked, or a payment on account. Even a small store will have thousands of business transactions in a year.

Facts recorded about transactions are of two kinds: (1) *identification facts* that reveal the nature of the transaction and its pertinent characteristics and (2) *quantitative facts* that report the number of items and values involved in the transaction. For example, the identification facts for hosiery may include the brand, type, material, color, and size. The quantitative facts may include the number of pairs sold and the price.

Some facts about certain transactions may be unimportant for future managerial decision making and may require no analysis. However, most transactions are worthy of classification and study since they can provide guidance for future decisions. The sale of a particular style and size of slacks may not seem worthy of study; but the style sold may have certain characteristics common to other styles sold, such as material, cut, or color. If the sales of slacks are analyzed by these characteristics, important trends in customer demand may become apparent; and profitable changes in buying and selling plans may result.

RECORDING TRANSACTIONS

There are three different approaches to recording the data needed for a given transaction. The data can be recorded manually, that is, by having a worker write out all the details of a transaction and hand sort the desired information. Data can be recorded and analyzed with the use of mechanical recorders such as punch card equipment. The third approach is to use electronic computers and associated equipment. An example of a sales transaction under each approach follows.

Manual Recording

Sara Goldberg bought two gift candles and a greeting card at Marilyn Marsh's store. The amount of the sale was $2.60 including tax. If this is all the information recorded Marilyn will not know what has been sold at the end of each day and each week. Therefore, Marilyn makes out a handwritten sales slip for each sale. The sales slip for this sale lists 2 candles (714) at $1.00 each—$2.00; 1 card (W-89) at 50 cents; and 10 cents tax. The sale is rung up on the cash register. The original of the sales slip is kept by the store, and the copy of the slip is given to Sara Goldberg. Every week Marilyn must record the information from each sales slip onto summary sheets so that she can develop the store records she needs. Because her store is small and she has limited resources, the manual approach to recording data is feasible.

Mechanical Recording

In Burke's Hardware store all merchandise is classified by department. Whenever an item is sold the amount of that sale is recorded on the sales register by that department number. For example, Dennis Scholl sold two paint brushes and a package of light bulbs to Mike Lagoni. The paint brushes ($2.98 each) were rung up under Department 3 which is the paint department. The package of light bulbs ($1.49) was rung up under Department 6 which is the electrical department. The sales register will provide Dennis with the amount sold in each department of the store and a total of all sales. If Mike Lagoni should return one of the paint brushes Dennis would refund the amount by ringing a "paid out" from Department 3. If Dennis wanted detailed information about merchandise within a department he would have to use other means such as a punched ticket which could be tabulated and sorted by punch card equipment.

Electronic Recording

As Pat Baxter increased his business in the Adobe Shop he found need for more and faster information on his merchandise. By adopting an electronic sales register system he was able to get detailed data on each sale and frequent comprehensive reports on sales and stock. When Pat sold Mr. Dobbins a sportcoat he recorded on the sales register the following information: color, size, style, vendor, price, and salesperson number. This information, along with similar information from all other sales, was stored in the sales register. Once each week the stored information was transferred to a computer center where the various reports on sales and merchandise needed by Pat Baxter were prepared. What would have required many hours of manual or mechanical work was done electronically in a few minutes.

Combination Systems

Even within one store there are various needs for transaction data. Because of this, most stores tend to use combinations of manual, mechanical, and electronic recording. The means will vary primarily with size, volume, merchandise, and store operation needs.

EMERGENCE OF DATA PROCESSING EQUIPMENT

Until the 1930's most retail stores sorted and tabulated manually the information needed for store reports. Store personnel hand sorted sales checks, price ticket stubs, expense vouchers, and all other transaction records.

The first major improvement of retail information processing was in the development of mechanical equipment to assist in these laborious tasks. The use of mechanical means of processing data is called *automatic data processing* (ADP). The fundamentals of ADP were developed by Dr. Herman Hollerith. He developed a system for automatically processing the 1890 census data. His system, with refinements, was soon introduced in business, primarily through the efforts of the International Business Machines Corporation (IBM) and the Remington Rand Division of Sperry Rand. The larger retail firms began using the automatic or mechanical means of processing data for store records in the 1930's.

The next significant development for information processing came with the electronic computer. The first workable computer was developed at the University of Pennsylvania in 1946. With the advancement of technology, computers for business application were produced in 1953 by Remington Rand and IBM. The expansion of computer development since that time has been phenomenal. The use of *electronic data processing* (EDP) has been extended to nearly every aspect of government, business, and education. Data processing with ADP will be discussed in Part B. Electronic computers and EDP will be discussed in Part C.

CHECKING YOUR KNOWLEDGE

Vocabulary

1. transaction
2. identification facts
3. quantitative facts

4. automatic data processing
5. electronic data processing

Review Questions

1. List the different forms of transactions.
2. What two kinds of facts are recorded about a transaction?
3. What three approaches can be taken in recording transactions?
4. Who developed the fundamentals of ADP?
5. When were the first computers for business application produced?

Discussion Questions

1. What factors must be considered when deciding which information about a transaction should be recorded?
2. What can Dennis Scholl do if he wants more detail on sales in the Sporting Goods Department?
3. What information is needed on each sales transaction in a home appliance store? in a women's ready-to-wear store?

Part b

Automatic Data Processing

As it relates to business and the retailer, *data processing* is a procedure or combination of procedures whereby recorded information about transactions is arranged into meaningful reports. As indicated in the previous part, when this data processing is done by mechanical means it is called automatic data processing.

ELEMENTS OF THE AUTOMATIC SYSTEM

Processing data with an automatic system involves four basic procedures: (1) punching the information about transactions into a standard card, (2) verifying the accuracy of each card punched, (3) sorting the punched cards into predetermined groupings, and (4) calculating and tabulating the information contained in the sorted punched cards.

Punching the Information into a Card

Punched cards are flexible cards of identical dimension and thickness. They may be of various colors to facilitate visual identification. Depending upon the type of equipment being used the card will be 3¼ inches wide by 7⅜ inches long or 2⅝ inches wide by 3¼ inches long; have 80 or 96 columns for data; and be punched with rectangular or circular holes. Examples of these cards are shown in Illus. 16-1 and Illus. 16-2.

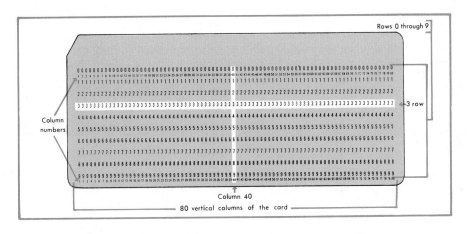

Illus. 16-1   This is an 80-column card. It has 12 rows in each column. Ten rows are for digits 0-9. The two top rows, along with the zero row, provide instructions to the system.

A card punch machine, with a keyboard similar to that of a standard typewriter, is used to punch holes in each card. The pattern of placement of these punches is the symbol form representing the data. The data recorded in each card are referred to as *input*. Although the punched card is the most common input for ADP other forms of input can be used and are described at the end of this part.

Verifying the Accuracy of the Punched Card

Several methods may be used to verify the accuracy of punched data. With one method, a special machine called a *verifier* is used to check

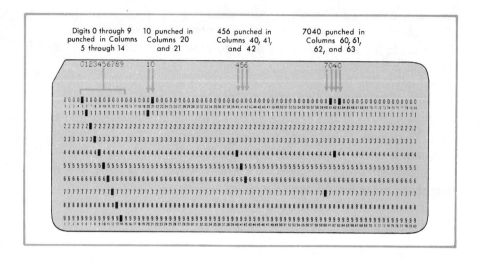

Illus. 16-2   Numeric data have been punched into this card. At the far left you can see how punching records the digits 0-9. Then you can see how the numbers 10, 456, and 7,040 are punched into the card. Note that to record a given number the digits comprising that number must be punched in different columns. No more than one digit can be punched in a column.

the accuracy of each column of the card after key punching. The operator activates the verifier to compare the holes in the punched card with the same keys depressed on the verifier machine. This is an essential step in the process, because it is easy to make errors in punching.

Sorting the Punched Cards

A mechanical *sorter* arranges the cards in any grouping desired. Brushes moving over the punched cards motivate a mechanism to drop each card into a *bin*—a long tray that holds punched cards in neat stacks—that accumulates all the cards with holes punched at a specific location on the card. As the cards are sorted, a card file in each bin results. It is often necessary to merge two or more card files into one new file by using a machine known as a *collator*. For example, a customer's name and account balance may be recorded on one card and the customer's charge sales on other cards. These two files are merged so that the card with the account balance and the charge sales cards are brought together for each customer. It is necessary that the cards for each customer be arranged in this order so that the tabulating machine can print the correct total in proper sequence for each customer. Each sorting of the cards arranges a group by one field only, such as

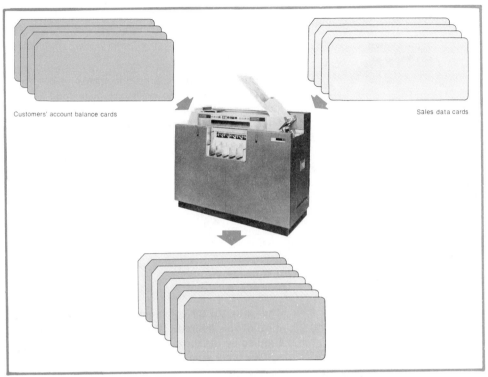

Customers' account balance cards

Sales data cards

Illus. 16-3   The collator combines two or more card files into a single file of punched cards which the tabulating machine uses to provide information to the retailer.

merchandise classification. Cards can be run through the machine again to sort them another way or to sort them into the price lines within each class.

Calculating and Tabulating the Sorted Punched Cards

Calculating and tabulating of cards is usually done by a tabulating machine that is activated by the punched holes in the cards to perform one or a number of the following operations: add, subtract, subtotal, total, print, and space the printed form. The machine can also handle summary cards to be used for balances that are to be brought forward. The information that is produced as a result of these manipulations is called *output*. Sales reports, stock reports, and payroll listings are examples of media used to report this information. Current information can be invaluable to the retailer when trying to dispose of unsold merchandise and in keeping stock up to date.

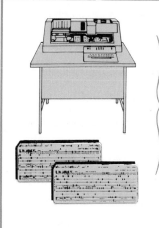

Input

Information on the source documents to be processed is punched into cards or tape in code form. Common office machines with card-punch or tape-punch attachments or a card-punch machine may be used. Ordinarily, a verifier is used to check the accuracy of the punched cards before they are processed.

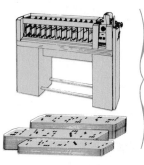

Processing and Storage

The cards are sorted and grouped according to the information desired. This is an automatic process handled by the sorter. The cards are then ready for further processing.

Output

The grouped cards are run through the tabulator. The tabulator selects the data desired from the punched cards and prints the information on output media such as sales reports, statements, and checks.

Illus. 16-4   This illustration summarizes the procedures involved in processing data by the automatic system. You will gain valuable experience and insight if you can arrange to see these machines in operation.

COLLECTING INPUT DATA WITH ADP

With ADP it is time consuming to punch cards from price tickets or from sales checks, and errors in transferring the information are frequent. Accordingly, ADP systems have been developed to streamline the input of data, particularly of sales data. One method is to prepare price tickets in the form of punched cards that can be fed directly into the sorting unit. Since this requires awkwardly large price tickets, another more practical plan is to use relatively small price tickets with tiny pinholes arranged to show price, merchandise classification, and so on. These price tickets are processed by a unit that prepares regular full-size punched cards for every pinhole ticket. The punched cards are then sorted and tabulated.

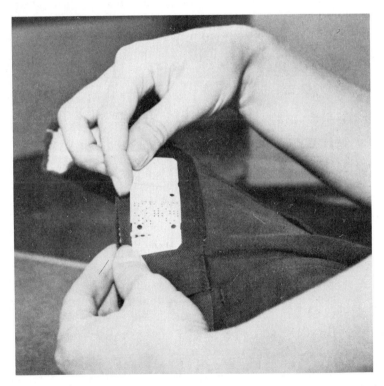

Courtesy of Penney News, J. C. Penney Company, Inc.

Illus. 16-5   When the punched ticket is used as a source for data input, the salesperson must carefully remove a portion of it when an item is sold. Data punched into the ticket are placed in the computer or converted to a regular size punched card which can then be sorted and tabulated.

Instead of pinhole price tickets, *mark-sensed cards* that employ electrically conductive pencil marks in code may be used. The code is marked with the electrically conductive pencil when the price tickets are prepared. A special unit interprets the recorded pencil marks and punches cards that duplicate the recorded information. The punched cards are then processed in the usual manner. This method is not commonly used with price tickets requiring much information since it requires considerable space on the ticket to record the data.

Punched paper tape is also used to record input. The tape is usually prepared automatically by an attachment to the sales register or business machine as each transaction is recorded. The punched paper tape is later processed by a tape reading machine, and punched cards are automatically prepared. Transactions may be also recorded on magnetic tape which can be processed directly to punched cards. Using tape to record data at the sales register or business machine eliminates having a card punch operator transfer data from a source document to a punched card. This saves time and usually lessens the chance of error.

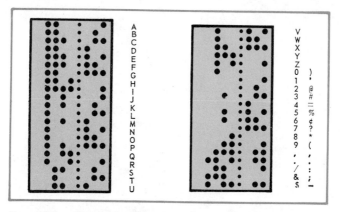

Illus. 16-6   Punched paper tape is a frequently used means of recording input data. In this strip of tape, the letters of the alphabet, the numbers 0-9, and several symbols have been punched.

CHECKING YOUR KNOWLEDGE

Vocabulary

1. data processing
2. punched cards
3. input
4. verifier
5. sorter

6. bin
7. collator
8. output
9. mark-sensed cards

Review Questions

1. What four procedures are necessary when processing data with an automatic system?
2. How are data recorded on punched cards?
3. How can the accuracy of punched data be determined?
4. How may two card files be automatically combined into one file?
5. What are some of the alternative means of collecting input data for automatic data processing?

Discussion Questions

1. What would be some of the major advantages of using mark-sensed cards, punched paper tapes, or punched price tickets for ADP input rather than having a card punch machine operator recording data from hand-written sales slips?
2. If a furniture store maintains a punched card on each item of merchandise received into stock, what sorts of tabulations might the retailer want at the end of each week or month?
3. What effect would an error in recording, either on a sales slip or on a sales register, by a salesperson have on the ultimate ADP output?

Part C

Electronic Data Processing

The use of ADP provided many retailers with much needed assistance in developing needed store records. However, as retail firms increased in size, expanded into new merchandise areas, and attempted to find laborsaving techniques, the need for an improved system of data processing became apparent. The development of the electronic computer provided the retailer with a means of handling the masses of data that were beyond the capacity of ADP. This part will discuss the electronic computer and the components necessary for electronic data processing.

TYPES OF COMPUTERS

There are three types of computers—the digital, the analog, and the hybrid. The operation of the *digital computer* is based on numbers—adding, subtracting, multiplying, dividing, and comparing figures. The *analog computer,* used primarily in engineering, manipulates physical quantities and typically gives out its information in curves rather than in numbers. It functions by changes in the voltage of electric current. The *hybrid computer* combines features of both the digital and analog. We shall center our discussion on the digital computer as this type is most frequently used in business.

Computers are, of course, made in different sizes and for different purposes. Some computers are general purpose computers and are capable of performing a wide variety of tasks. Other computers are special purpose computers and are designed to perform only certain types of data processing. The new minicomputers are good examples of special purpose computers. Nearly 40,000 of these minicomputers were made in 1973 for use by industry and business for special and limited range computation work.

COMPONENTS OF THE COMPUTER

The typical general purpose digital computer has five essential components: (1) input unit, (2) memory unit, (3) arithmetic unit, (4) output unit, and (5) control unit. The relationship of these units is shown in Illus. 16-7.

Input Unit

The *input unit* feeds data into the computer in the form of electronic or magnetic impulses. These impulses are arranged into numbers by means of the *binary system*—a system of numbers that uses only two digits (0 and 1). In the binary system a digit, either the 0 or the 1, is called a *bit*, which is the contraction of *binary digit*. The various input devices or media may be punched cards, magnetized disks, special typewriters, wand readers (discussed in Chapter 12, Part A), voice or sound, and various forms of tape. Three major kinds of tape used as input media are punched paper tape, *magnetic tape* on which there are magnetized spots instead of holes or sound patterns, and *optical font tape* with printed characters that can be read by an optical scanning device.

Memory Unit

The *memory unit* stores data in the form of electronic impulses that are fed into it from the input or arithmetic unit. The piece of equipment called the memory unit is actually made up of several subcomponents that store data. These storage subcomponents might be magnetic cores, disks, tapes, or newer developments such as crystalline film or silicon

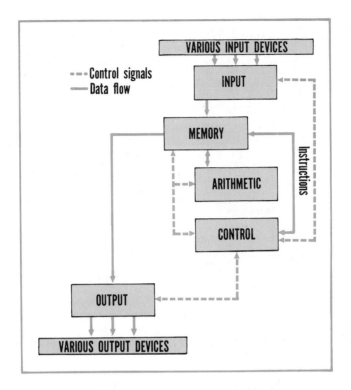

Illus. 16-7   In this illustration you can see the components of the computer. By studying the arrows indicating data flow and control signals, you can also see the relationships of these components to each other.

chips. The cost and bulk of magnetic cores, disks, and tapes have led to these newer devices which take up much less space and store greater amounts of data. The crystalline film stores bits in the form of magnetic bubbles that are polorized in the opposite direction from the film. A bubble on the film represents a 1 and its absence a 0. These bubbles are microscopic, measuring only 330 atoms and store one billion bits in one square inch of space. Still another device already in use is the tiny silicon chip, about ⅛ of an inch in diameter, that contains 2,048 microscopically small storage circuits. When requested, the memory unit can go to the appropriate subcomponent and recall or report the data stored there.

Arithmetic Unit

The *arithmetic unit* performs the calculating functions in the computer. Data from the computer's memory (either internal or external) are fed into the arithmetic unit in the form of electronic impulses. The

Binary Positions				Binary Number	Value of the Binary Number
8 (4+4=8)	4 (2+2=4)	2 (1+1=2)	1 (1)		
0	0	0	1	0001	1
0	0	1	0	0010	2
0	0	1	1	0011	3
0	1	0	0	0100	4
0	1	0	1	0101	5
0	1	1	0	0110	6
0	1	1	1	0111	7
1	0	0	0	1000	8
1	0	0	1	1001	9
1	0	1	0	1010	10

Illus. 16-8   Computers use the binary number system as a code for numeric and alphabetic data. This table gives some examples of numbers written in binary code form. Note that as the binary digit is moved one place to the left and a zero placed after it, the resulting number is two times the original number.

arithmetic unit then adds, subtracts, multiplies, and divides using these data. It may accumulate results of an arithmetic operation until it is directed to store these results in the memory. If instructed to do so, it will communicate these results to an output unit which will reproduce the data in the form of a tabulated report. This report may give such information as the cost, markup, selling price, markdown, sales returns, and certain percentage analyses of these merchandising data.

Output Unit

Many different media may be used to produce the output data. An *on-line printer*—it prints an entire line of data in one stroke—is capable of printing 1,200 lines or more a minute. It is one of the most rapid ways of providing output in permanent legible form. It would take a typist about eight hours to complete the 1,200 lines of average length copy produced in one minute by the on-line printer. The electric typewriter, often used for input, may also be used for output.

Visual output can be made on television type monitor screens. Such output devices are frequently used as desk or remote terminals where the retailer or buyer wishes to have up-to-the-minute information on sales and inventory.

Control and Programming

The *control unit* which is a part of the central processing unit or CPU directs the operation of the other four units. It instructs the input devices concerning the information to be stored in the memory. It tells the memory where to store the information being received. It directs the arithmetic unit regarding the operation it is to perform, where to find the data in the memory, and where to store the results of the calculations. It also controls the form and nature of the output.

Programming is the direction given the control unit by a human being. Every step to be performed in an operation is meticulously spelled out. The person—known as a *programmer*—who prepares these detailed procedures must organize instructions in language that is machine-readable; the instructions are actually translated into electrical impulses. Assume that the memory unit has stored in one place information on the number of hours Employee A worked this week. In another place it may have stored information on the hourly rate of pay. The programmer must instruct the computer to find the data on A's hours, move these data to the arithmetic unit, locate the information on the rate of pay, and move it to the arithmetic unit. The arithmetic unit must then be instructed to multiply. Next, the product must be printed on a check, and A's name must be filled in. The instructions must then call for the computer to repeat the sequence with Employee B, and so on. When there are payroll deductions, the instructions are much more complicated. For some elaborate operations, as many as 60,000 instructions are required.

CHECKING YOUR KNOWLEDGE

Vocabulary

1. digital computer
2. analog computer
3. hybrid computer
4. input unit
5. binary system
6. bit
7. binary digit
8. magnetic tape
9. optical font tape
10. memory unit
11. arithmetic unit
12. on-line printer
13. visual output
14. control unit
15. programming
16. programmer

Review Questions

1. What are the three types of computers?
2. What are the five components of the digital computer?

3. What are the three kinds of tape used as computer input media?
4. What types of storage components might be found in a memory unit?
5. How does the programmer affect the operation of a computer?

Discussion Questions

1. What is a "word" insofar as an electronic computer is concerned?
2. How does a computer know when to print out information through a printer or present information on a visual display and when to store accumulated information?
3. How do electronic data processing and automatic data processing differ?

Part d

Data Output Reports

With the adoption of electronic data processing many retail stores have found it possible to prepare more reports and with greater frequency. They have also found it possible to ask for data in different forms such as ratios, percentages, frequencies, and comparisons with store or industry averages. It must be remembered however, that the computer does only what it is instructed to do. Successful reports result only because the retailer and others have put in long hours of careful planning on the activities to be performed.

PLANNING THE PROCESSING OF REPORTS

Before any data is processed, it is necessary to determine (1) what data must be collected, (2) what classifications and comparisons of data are needed, and (3) how quickly the data reports must be available for use. The answers to these three questions establish some of the major guidelines for whatever form of data processing the retailer will use for his store records. The answer to the first question will influence the nature of the source document or original transaction. The answer to the second question will depend upon how the information is to be used by retail management, buyers, and other store workers. The answer to the third question will have implications for the equipment and procedures used in data processing.

The actual processing of data, whether done manually, mechanically, or electronically, involves four basic steps:

1. Recording the data about the transactions in an orderly and standardized way
2. Transmitting the data to processing equipment where they may be sorted and analyzed

3. Manipulating the data by arranging them, combining them, and relating them to data already on hand
4. Reporting data, usually in tabular form, for use by management

KINDS OF RETAIL DATA PROCESSED

Modern data processing methods are well suited for handling large numbers of repetitive transactions. Five types of repetitive retailing transactions which occur in large numbers each day in most stores are (1) daily sales and their audit; (2) purchases by credit customers, recorded in accounts receivable; (3) data for merchandise and inventory control (sales, purchases by the store, and inventories by classifications); (4) store personnel performance; and (5) payroll computations.

Sales Audit

Every store audits its sales. If the store is departmentalized, it sorts out by department sales checks and other records of sale, such as sales register readings, and totals the sales for each department. An accuracy comparison is then made of the totals by checking against the salesperson's tallies or sales register readings and against charges to customers' accounts. Returns from customers and allowances to customers are also included in this analysis. A data processing system into which such data can be received as soon as the transaction occurs or shortly afterward greatly reduces the cost of making the audit.

Accounts Receivable Posting

As indicated in Chapter 5, when a store sells on credit it charges each customer's account for each purchase made and credits the account for payments made or goods returned. If this recording is done manually, an extra copy of a sales check must be prepared to use in posting the customer's account. A copy of the current customer account becomes the store's record of the status of each account. Charges to customer accounts are checked daily against the sales audit figures compiled by each department to determine any errors in recording.

With electronic data processing the transaction data are sent to the computer immediately or periodically during the week. These data are entered automatically in each customer's account card at the same time that the store's record of charge sales is reported.

Merchandise Inventory Control

Probably the greatest value that stores realize from automatic or electronic data processing is the computation of sales and inventory information by units of analysis smaller than the totals of each selling department. Stores that formerly felt it was too much work to analyze sales for groupings less than a selling department can now procure sales and purchase data for each merchandise classification within each department and even for each price line within each classification. The computer is especially well suited for this purpose. The computer's storage of previous inventory figures can be drawn upon, and book inventory figures can be calculated automatically for each classification as frequently as desired, usually once each week. With such current knowledge of sales and inventories in each of many classifications, merchants can adjust their purchases to maintain a better balance between sales and stock. This leads to fewer markdowns and to the more efficient use of capital available for merchandise investment.

Store Personnel Performance

Most large stores sort out records of sales transactions by salesperson as a basis for evaluating performance. This includes determining a monthly or weekly selling cost for each salesperson, which is the ratio of his salary and commissions to his net sales. In the past this procedure was done manually, and many smaller stores did not bother to do it. With ADP and EDP the job can be done quickly and efficiently. Much information can be prepared that was never available with the use of manual methods. Sales by each salesperson in each merchandise classification and within each price line are reported easily. Customer returns can also be analyzed for each salesperson. The cumulative sales of each salesperson for a week, a month, or a season can be obtained quickly. The weekly earnings of each salesperson can be reported, and cumulative selling costs for each can be determined.

Nonselling employees' production can be measured in terms of such factors as number of records handled, number of price tickets attached, and number of packages wrapped or delivered. With such a wealth of information, retail managers are able to see objectively the performance of each individual. Analysis by the computer thus serves as a measure of performance for store personnel and as a basis for allocation of the workload.

Payroll Preparation

The preparation of a large weekly and monthly payroll is an operation particularly well suited to EDP techniques. With a computer each person's base pay can be fed into the computer's memory along with the rate of commission the person is to earn, his overtime rate, and the amounts to be withheld for taxes, social security, and health insurance. Purchases made by each employee and charged against his salary, overtime hours worked, sales made, goods returned from customers, and rate of commission (in the case of salespeople working on a commission basis) can be fed into the computer. The computer will then calculate each person's take-home pay and print on pay envelopes the details of the calculation. If employees are paid by check, the check can be prepared automatically.

DATA PROCESSING CENTERS

Many retailers, especially those with small stores, may find that they cannot afford to have their own computer equipment. By subscribing for service with a *data processing service center,* even the smaller stores can have access to modern data processing. These service centers are operated by computer manufacturers, independent firms, and as a sideline by banks or other firms.

Subscribers use a data processing center largely for merchandise analysis. The stores periodically submit data that permits two kinds of reports: (1) a weekly sales report and (2) a monthly sales and inventory report.

The illustration on page 522 is an example of the weekly sales report. The computer arranges the sales data by code number and reports the units sold each week within each code. The sales figures are totaled for groups of codes comprising classifications, departments, and divisions. Price lines are multiplied by units sold to give dollar as well as unit sales. Sales from previous weeks are added to current sales, thereby providing cumulative data for each month.

The illustration on page 523 is a monthly sales and inventory report in dollars instead of units. The input consists of data on purchases, price changes, opening balances, sales, and markdowns for the current month, and past sales and purchases that are stored in the computer's memory. The closing balance for each coded classification or subclass is automatically calculated by adding the purchases to the beginning inventory (BOM) and subtracting sales and markdowns.

Stores may obtain additional reports if they care to pay an increased service fee. For example, the center will process the reports of physical inventories requested, compare the physical inventory figures in each coded class with the book inventory, and note the shortages in each. It will also prepare a report of planned purchases, which is part of the six-month merchandising plan that you will study in Chapter 17.

SALES REPORT

CLIENT NO. 10-002-051

WEEK JAN. 24-31, 19—
REPORT = 1

CODE	PRICE RANGE	DEPT.—CASUAL DRESSES	WEEK UNITS	WEEK $	MONTH TO DATE UNITS	MONTH TO DATE $
700	8.98	DRESSES—MISSY	17	153.00	61	549.00
702	10.98	DRESSES—MISSY	20	220.00	40	440.00
704	13.98	DRESSES—MISSY	25	350.00	56	784.00
706	19.98	DRESSES—MISSY	20	400.00	78	1,560.00
707	26.98	DRESSES—MISSY	8	216.00	34	918.00
708	36.98	DRESSES—MISSY	4	148.00	17	629.00
		TOTAL—MISSY	94	1,487.00	286	4,880.00
710	8.98	DRESSES—JUNIOR	22	198.00	76	684.00
712	10.98	DRESSES—JUNIOR	27	297.00	95	1,045.00
714	13.98	DRESSES—JUNIOR	21	294.00	81	1,134.00
716	19.98	DRESSES—JUNIOR	10	200.00	42	840.00
		TOTAL JUNIOR	80	989.00	294	3,703.00
		TOTAL CASUAL DRESSES	174	2,476.00	580	8,583.00

National Retail Merchants Association

Illus. 16-9   This is an example of a weekly sales report that a store might receive from a computer center. Such a report can be created from point-of-sale recording of data on punched paper tape or can be created by office personnel recording the data into tape after the sale. The record of sales can be in dollars, units, or dollars and units.

SALES AND INVENTORY REPORT

CLIENT NO. 10-002-051

MONTH ENDING JAN. 31, 19__
REPORT #2

CODE	PRICE RANGE	DEPT.—CASUAL DRESSES	B.O.M. BALANCE 1/1/—	PURCHASES $	SALES $	MARKUP/ DOWNS $	MARKUP/ DOWNS % TO SALES	E.O.M. BALANCE 1/31/—	PURCHASES TO DATE	SALES TO DATE	MARKUP/ DOWNS TO DATE
700	8.98	DRESSES-MISSY	742.00	608.00	549.00	30.00	5.4	771.00	3,120.00	2,760.00	146.00
702	10.98	DRESSES-MISSY	616.00	430.00	440.00	35.00	8.0	621.00	2,390.00	3,307.00	175.00
704	13.98	DRESSES-MISSY	1,320.00	925.00	784.00	49.00	6.3	1,412.00	4,625.00	3,820.00	250.00
706	19.98	DRESSES-MISSY	3,214.00	1,726.00	1,560.00	179.00	11.5	3,201.00	8,630.00	7,800.00	898.00
707	26.98	DRESSES-MISSY	2,037.00	1,100.00	918.00	149.00	16.2	2,120.00	5,420.00	4,582.00	750.00
708	36.98	DRESSES-MISSY	1,485.00	610.00	629.00	57.00	9.00	1,409.00	3,080.00	3,050.00-	294.00
		TOTAL—MISSY	9,464.00	5,449.00	4,880.00	499.00	10.2	9,534.00	27,265.00	24,319.00	2,513.00
710	8.98	DRESSES-JUNIOR	700.00	520.00	684.00	42.00	6.1	494.00	2,600.00	3,542.00	210.00
712	10.98	DRESSES-JUNIOR	1,493.00	1,100.00	1,045.00	84.00	8.0	1,464.00	3,625.00	5,225.00	418.00
714	13.98	DRESSES-JUNIOR	1,970.00	1,320.00	1,134.00	130.00	11.4	2,026.00	6,700.00	5,570.00	647.00
716	19.98	DRESSES-JUNIOR'	2,143.00	1,008.00	840.00	60.00	8.1	2,251.00	5,030.00	4,100.00	301.00
		TOTAL JUNIOR	6,306.00	3,948.00	3,703.00	316.00	8.5	6,235.00	19,955.00	18,437.00	1,576.00
		TOTAL CASUAL DRESSES	15,770.00	9,397.00	8,583.00	815.00		15,769.00	47,220.00	42,756.00	4,089.00

National Retail Merchants Association

Illus. 16-10   The sales and inventory report is invaluable in keeping stock in each classification balanced to sales. Note the extremely large closing stock that is on hand in Code 716. In Code 710, however, the closing stock seems to be quite small in relation to sales. This knowledge would enable the buyer to adjust his planned purchases to fit the needs of these two classes.

ADVANTAGES OF DATA PROCESSING CENTERS

The use of a data processing center by a business firm has the following advantages:

1. The businessman, particularly in the small business, obtains the efficiencies of EDP without having to buy or lease a computer.
2. Use of a data processing center provides specialized programming without having to employ specialized personnel. For many businesses, standardized programs have already been developed.
3. By using a center, the businessman can switch to another kind of data processing or drop data processing altogether without suffering financial loss on capital expenditures.
4. Use of a center provides protection against obsolescence of purchased computer equipment.
5. Data processing services are available on short notice, since centers are always operative and have adequate equipment.

CHECKING YOUR KNOWLEDGE

Vocabulary

data processing service center

Review Questions

1. What three things must be determined before processing data?
2. Describe the four basic steps in processing data.
3. List five repetitive transactions that occur in most retail stores.
4. Why is EDP well suited to payroll preparation?
5. What are the advantages of a data processing center to a business?

Discussion Questions

1. Why is it so important to carefully identify the data to be collected and how it will be sorted and analyzed before beginning to process data? Why can't changes be made if different treatments are desired?
2. Even with the latest electronic equipment much of the original transaction information is recorded in written form. What should a person with a hard-to-read writing style do to make sure his information is correctly converted on EDP input?
3. If you were in charge of data processing for a large store what would you do if you found that many of the reports you were producing were not being used by management or buyers?
4. What would be some of the important considerations to a retailer who is planning to subscribe to a data processing center for EDP services?

Part e

Computer Applications in Retailing

In addition to the uses of EDP already presented in this chapter the retailers have found many other significant ways of using this technology. New applications of electronic data processing are being developed all the time. The following six applications will be presented in this part: (1) in planning and control, (2) in retailer-wholesaler programs, (3) in electronic ordering, (4) in credit authorization, (5) in mail orders, and (6) in major retail decisions.

USING THE COMPUTER IN PLANNING AND CONTROL

With information on sales, stock, and outstanding orders for each separate item, the computer can use a formula to plan sales for the future, calculate stock-sales ratios, compute planned purchases, subtract outstanding orders, and determine the open-to-buy. In many cases the computer is used to calculate reorder quantities for staples and is used to write out and follow up orders. Fashion goods, too, are being analyzed by characteristics such as color, fabric, style, and trim to determine changes in customer demand that should be promptly reflected in the merchandise inventory. It is also possible to have the computer choose the most desirable suppliers from whom to purchase. Factors to consider in the choice and the weight assigned to each factor can be programmed, and the facts known about each supplier can be matched with the standards fed into the computer. The computer can then choose the best resource.

The greatest step forward in the application of EDP to store control has been *classification analysis* as described in Part D. Stores that formerly kept records and controlled purchases and sales by means of only a few departments are now using hundreds of merchandise classifications. The result is that inventories are being much better balanced to sales; purchases are being directed into the classifications needing replenishing; and markdowns are being taken at more opportune times. When the department was the basis for control, maladjustments in the various subsections of the departments frequently never came to light; and the open-to-buy figures for the departments did not indicate how they should be alloted to classifications.

Courtesy of General Telephone
& Electronics Corporation

Illus. 16-11   Computerized record keeping provides services of all kinds. Detailed printouts are available to the retailer to help him make decisions and to plan for the future.

RETAILER-WHOLESALER PROGRAMS

As various wholesalers and suppliers have adopted computerized services, they have influenced the many retailers with whom they do business. The coordination of data processing programs between wholesaler and retailer has meant that even small retailers have gained some of the advantages of computerized record keeping. In some cases a retail association will include computer services as part of the association's service to members.

For example, one association offers the retailers either a general ledger or an accounts receivable program, or the two together. The general ledger program includes monthly profit-and-loss statements, balance sheets, departmental operating statements, a general ledger, and other related information. In the accounts receivable program, the retailer receives duplicate monthly statements for each customer account and a complete printout of each account's status.

Some retailer-wholesaler programs involve an *inventory maintenance plan.* Data from sales transactions are analyzed on a regular basis (most often weekly). As the inventory on certain staple goods reaches a pre-determined point, the computer automatically writes an order for the needed amount of replacement units. The retailer can set whatever stock levels he believes appropriate and can instruct the computer to change levels on any item to reflect changes in business activity.

A limitation to the retailer-wholesaler or association plan is that it works for only certain types of business. The retailer who buys most of his merchandise from a single wholesaler will find such a coordinated program of value. For the retailer who buys from many manufacturers and wholesalers such a plan is not feasible.

ELECTRONIC ORDERING

Some suppliers have worked out supplementary computer systems that simplify the ordering process for the retailer. The retailer uses a portable electronic unit consisting of a magnetic cassette tape recorder connected to an input device the size of a hand calculator. The retail buyer can punch in the order number, descriptive data (color, size, weight), and the amount desired. The information is recorded on the tape. When the order is finished, the data on the tape can be trans-mitted over the telephone to the supplier or to the warehouse.

Some stores have data processing programs which serve as reorder systems. These stores feed unit sales and purchase data into their computers which will calculate recommended reorder quantities and transfer the information onto optical font tape. The buyer will scan the tape and make any desired adjustments, then the tape will be sent to the manufacturer as the store order. The tape will be processed by the manufacturer's EDP system, which will prepare the required price tickets and perform all other necessary paper work. The price tickets will be attached by the vendor as a part of his assembly process, and the goods will be shipped to the store very soon after the order is received. These procedures, like so many others associated with computers, eliminate the often inaccurate handwritten records and reduces the amount of human labor to accomplish necessary tasks.

CREDIT AUTHORIZATION

Another important use of the computer is the authorization of credit purchases. When the customer presents her charge card, the salesperson records the customer's number on the sales register or inserts the card in a machine. In either case the information is transmitted to the computer. The computer has in its memory an up-to-date list of all *referral accounts*—those which should be given special attention before additional sales to the account are authorized. If the account number is not found in the computer's memory as a referral account, the computer will activate an audio or visual authorization of the transaction.

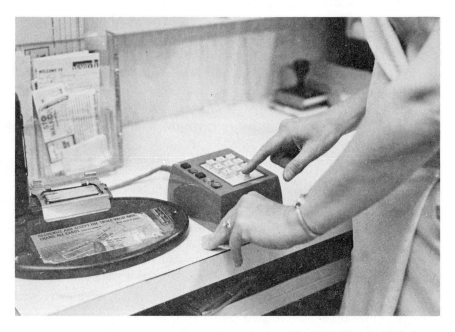

Courtesy of Montgomery Ward

Illus. 16-12   Instant credit authorization is made possible by linking a computerized credit center with each cashier. Here information is transmitted to the computer when the charge card number is punched into this terminal.

MAIL ORDERS

With the growing number of customers using telephone mail ordering for goods they wish, it is not surprising that mail order firms are beginning to use extensive computer communication systems. In one firm the catalog customer calls a national number by phone—at no charge—and gives her name, address, charge account number, and the style number, color, and quantity of the items she wishes to purchase. The oral request is translated into machine language and fed into a central computer that is connected to all the chain's regional distribution points. The central computer relays the order to the distribution center that serves the particular customer's area. Here the order is filled, sometimes within minutes, and started on its way to the customer. The laborious manual steps of writing down the order in a local office, sending it to the proper distribution point, checking the customer's credit, and preparing shipping documents are eliminated. The personnel formerly required to perform these manual operations can now be used for other jobs in the store. Many of these jobs were created because of increased sales resulting from this streamlined method of ordering.

MAJOR RETAIL DECISIONS

Major decisions made by retail management include forecasts of future business conditions and trends. These forecasts often include combinations of estimates which must be considered in several different ways. The mathematical power of the computer permits management to calculate the effect of different decisions. Some of these decisions may be whether to establish a new store, build a new warehouse, change brand policy, purchase certain real estate, set different markup goals, or add new lines of merchandise. It may never be possible to include and correctly weigh all the factors that might mold the future of a retail firm into a program for a computer. Computer analysis will, however, provide information that will help management in more rational decisions.

CHECKING YOUR KNOWLEDGE

Vocabulary

1. classification analysis

2. inventory maintenance plan

3. referral accounts

Review Questions

1. How is the computer used in store planning and control?
2. What are some of the advantages of classification analysis?
3. How have retailers and wholesalers cooperated in computer services?
4. How is the computer used in the authorization of credit purchases?
5. Explain how telephone mail orders are handled by computers.

Discussion Questions

1. Do you think that suppliers who knew their performance was being checked by computers would make any extra effort to meet their obligations to the retailer?
2. A divisional merchandise manager finds that the computerized planned purchases for the boys' department call for purchase of 96 sweat shirts in various sizes. The buyer for that department is planning to order only 24 sweat shirts. Should the merchandise manager go with the computer decision or the buyer's decision?
3. One retail authority predicts that customers will soon have a computer terminal and a television screen in their homes. By use of a keyboard they can call up for viewing on the TV screen products they may wish to buy. If they want what they see they can use the keyboard to send their order to the supplier of the product. What impact would this use of electronic computers have on traditional retailing?

BUILDING YOUR SKILLS

Improving Communication Skills

Each of the following sentences contains two words in parentheses. Only one of the words may be used correctly in the sentence. On a separate sheet of paper, write the number of each sentence and the correct word to be used in each sentence.

1. If I (were, was) you, I would ask for a weekly sales audit report.
2. The manager called upon Sue and (I, me) to take the inventory.
3. The programmer and his assistant (has, have) come back for the card files.
4. Sears just issued (their, its) spring and summer catalog.
5. The controller (saw, seen) a demonstration of the new computer.
6. After looking at the printout it was obvious that the input data (was, were) in error.
7. The store management attempts to handle data processing the best way (it, they) can.
8. Every person in the department should give (his, their) attention to slow-moving stock.
9. The computer center people announced (their, its) new schedule of charges.
10. It was up to Russ and (I, me) to decide how the merchandise in the new department was to be classified.

Improving Arithmetic Skills

Perform the exercises at the top of page 531. On a separate sheet of paper, write the number of each exercise and the answer to each.

1. The accounting records for a hobby shop show total merchandise handled for the year at cost as $73,600. The total merchandise handled at retail was $124,000. The ending inventory at retail is $27,000. What is the ending inventory at cost?

2. Gross sales for a gift import shop amounted to $217,000, of which $7,000 was returned. Salaries for the same period amounted to $22,000. What percentage of net sales is the amount paid for salaries?

3. At the beginning of one month a fashion apparel store had an inventory of $14,000 at retail. During the month purchases amounted to $6,400 at retail, and net sales were $8,700, with markdowns of $600. What should be the book inventory at retail at the end of the month?

4. If a customer asks for two lengths of chain, one 6 meters long and the other 8.5 meters long, what should be the length of each piece in feet and inches?

5. (a) What are the numbers in our decimal system that correspond to the following binary numbers: 0111, 1110, 101010?
   (b) What are the binary equivalents of 16, 50, 100?

Improving Research Skills

1. For a period of one week keep a list of all the ways you are affected by or have contact with any aspect of electronic data processing. In what ways did EDP most frequently influence or affect you as a person?

2. Read three current articles on new developments in connection with the computer. Summarize these articles and state what application, if any, these developments may have in retailing.

3. Using the yellow pages of your local telephone book and/or the city directory for your area, develop a list of firms that offer computer services, computer programming services, or other electronic data processing services that might be used by retailers.

Improving Decision-Making Skills

1. Suppose that you operate a men's apparel store with a sales volume of $1 million a year. You are convinced that you have much to gain from EDP. What are the various possibilities open to you, and how would you evaluate them? What are the first analyses you would want the computer to perform for you?

2. You are the manager of a large paint and wallpaper store. Presently you use a computer service which provides monthly sales and inventory reports. The cost of this service is $110 a month. Your average inventory at cost is $24,000. You believe that with weekly sales and inventory reports, and with more detailed classification of data, you could reduce your average inventory at cost to about $20,000 and maintain a better balanced stock. The weekly cost of the computer service is $30.
   (a) Should you switch to weekly computer service on sales and inventory reports? Why or why not?
   (b) What is the logic in hoping for a one-sixth reduction in inventory by obtaining more frequent and detailed records?

APPLYING YOUR KNOWLEDGE

Chapter Project

Develop an information flow chart that shows the various records and reports that would be affected by a single sales transaction in a retail store. Your completed chart should show the sequence in which the transaction data would be used as they are incorporated into each record and report.

Continuing Project

In your manual, illustrate and explain the kinds of EDP reports that will be required for the retail store you have chosen. You may find it necessary to consult the school library as well as local business firms when preparing your illustrations.

Planning for Profit

CHAPTER PREVIEW

a. Careful retail planning should lead to a healthy and profitable business. Good planning starts with a specific statement of purpose and includes programs of action to realize goals decided upon.

b. The six-month plan is actually a budget with dollar figure goals for sales, reductions, stocks, purchases, expenses, and markups.

c. Systematic stock control can be accomplished with either dollar control or unit control. The use of systematic stock control can help prevent problems such as slow selling merchandise accumulation.

d. Merchandise shortages are caused by a variety of recording errors but most often by pilferage or shoplifting. Shoplifting, especially by teenagers, has been an increasing problem for retailers all over the country.

e. Control of operations is concerned with comparing actual business results with planned figures. The control function is highly organized in large retail stores and in chain organizations.

Part a

Fundamentals of Planning

Planning is that activity which establishes policies and assigns responsibilities for procedures to accomplish these policies. It also involves reviewing past accomplishments and projecting future action.

For the small retail firm the planning and direction of action in each area of the business can be done by the owner. In large retail firms specialization of personnel is necessary. Large-store executives deal primarily with policy, with the direction of needed action being done by middle management. As indicated in Chapter 4, in a small store activities can be grouped into four areas: buying, selling, operating, and control. In large retail stores eight or more areas can be identified. Specialized personnel must be employed to work in each of these areas. For example, customer service is a part of operating a small store. In a large store, however, it is usually considered so important that it is a separate area of activity with trained personnel assigned to that function.

Courtesy of Gamble-Skogmo

Illus. 17-1   This all-purpose convenience center takes care of credit applications, layaway purchases, refunds, and gift wrapping. It serves as a notary public; accepts mail deposits; issues insurance policies and travelers' checks. Customers can pay utility bills, cash checks, and purchase money orders at this counter.

THE PLANNING PROCESS

The very nature of a retail firm is the buying and selling of merchandise. The other aspects of a firm's operation serve to make the buying and selling of goods as efficient as possible. The material that follows shall be limited largely to planning as it applies to merchandising activities.

The basic planning that must be done is the development of a *merchandise plan,* or *budget.* This plan provides a means of analyzing the different aspects of merchandising (buying and selling) activity in terms of amounts of money. Store personnel are more likely to do their best when they have definite goals to reach. Advertising is wasteful unless there is a carefully thought out promotional campaign to build customer goodwill and repeat trade. Markup cannot be increased simply by wishful thinking. A definite markup goal should be set for each season. Every time an article is marked up to less than the goal plans must be made to sell other articles with more than the average markup to compensate for the difference.

The following program of merchandise planning, if carefully carried out, should result in a profitable business:

1. Set a central merchandise policy for your store. Decide the type of customer you wish to attract. Give your store an image by emphasizing one or two, but not all, of the following: fashion leadership, exclusive lines, high quality, large assortments, low prices, personal service, convenience.

2. Prior to each six-month season, lay out a detailed plan of what you will do to make your policy effective. Keep your focus on the type of customer you have decided to serve.

3. Formulate your program in terms of dollars and cents by setting figure goals for sales, stocks, purchases, markdowns, markups, and expenses. The goals should be realistic, attainable, and made known to all. Goals should be set for each department and determined with the knowledge of past performance records, changes in the competitive situation, and local and national economic conditions.

4. At regular intervals, compare with the budgeted goals the actual sales obtained, the purchases made, the markups realized, the amount of stock carried, and the expenses incurred. Determine which departments, which activities, and which factors need adjusting. Generally it is easier to correct unfavorable variations between planned and actual performance if the time period between comparisons is short. Encourage key personnel or department managers to set and check their own goals and budgets. It is important to know what each department is doing early enough in the planning period so that constructive action may be taken, if necessary.

SETTING FIGURE GOALS

A store that has been in business for some years will use the records of its past sales, stocks, markups, and expenses as a guide in translating current plans into dollars and cents. If previous policies and methods continue unchanged, the plans need deviate only insofar as outside conditions are changed; but if policies or methods of realizing results are to be radically altered, it will not be necessary to give a great deal of attention to past figures.

Outside conditions that influence the retailer's dollar figure goals can be gathered from a variety of sources. One of the best and easiest methods to determine the trend of general business conditions is to subscribe to qualified business and economic services offered to merchants. These services employ expert economists who forecast business conditions. They consider such business indicators as employment trends; incomes; prices and price levels; cost-of-living indexes; financial information, such as consumer borrowing and spending, government spending, and business spending for plant and equipment; the gross national product; and disposable personal income.

Illus. 17-2   Economists consider many indicators before they forecast the trend of general business conditions.

In addition, the retailer should consider local conditions that may influence the setting of his dollar figure goals. Such conditions as shifts in the population to or from the store trading area, probable changes in customer purchasing power, or changes in the competitive situation are important elements that will influence his judgment in setting the figure goals.

LEVELS OF MERCHANDISE PLANNING

In a large store, such as a department store, the planning is done by specific levels. These levels usually are (1) the entire store, (2) major store divisions, (3) departments within each division, and (4) classifications within each department.

Store Level Planning

A store owner will consider the factors previously discussed in setting figure goals and in arriving at an overall store plan. The plan may call for a 10 percent increase in certain expenses, a 16 percent increase in net sales, and an 8 percent increase in profits. If the store is part of a chain, central planning may call for the store to improve its stock turn rate and improve the maintained markup. For the single unit retail business, the store is the first level of planning. For the multiple unit retail business, the overall company is the first level of planning.

Division Level Planning

Once the overall plan has been made it is then necessary that allocations be made to each of the store's merchandising divisions. If the store expects to have $980,000 in sales during the period planned and there are four merchandising divisions the question is: How much is each division expected to sell? The planners may conclude from the projected conditions that a certain division will do well just to maintain a previous level of sales. Another division may be expected to show sizable increases in sales.

Department Level Planning

Sales opportunities differ among departments as well as among divisions; therefore, it is unrealistic to expect the departments within a division to have the same amount of sales. The costume jewelry department will not have the same level of sales as the suit and dress department. The department is a critical level for planning, where the results of decisions become readily apparent. Here the performance of individual buyers and managers is easily measured. The effect of advertising can be judged more precisely. Even at the department level, however, the plan, for say $36,000 in sales, still must be divided into merchandise categories.

Classification Level Planning

Where many kinds of merchandise are carried in a department, it is desirable to make plans for each class of merchandise. To plan just for the entire stock of a department might lead to serious omissions or imbalances in needed merchandise. In Chapter 16 it was pointed out how the development of the computer and EDP made it possible for the retailer to keep track of many different classifications of merchandise. The grouping of merchandise by classification can be done several different ways. Classifications can be by kinds of merchandise, materials, price, color, size, and supplier. Two examples of planning purchases by classification are shown in Illustration 17-3. Note the variation among the different classes. Obviously if only the totals were used for planning, the possibility of error would be much greater.

Some retailers advocate planning for each specific item within a classification. This means planning for each unit of stock or *SKU* (stock-keeping unit). This additional level of planning can be justified where knowledge of each SKU is essential to the success of the store's merchandise planning.

TOP-DOWN VERSUS BOTTOM-UP PLANNING

The sequence of planning just described could be called *top-down planning*. With a top-down type of planning the overall stock, sales, expense, and other figures are established and then subdivided to the lower levels of planning.

The reverse of this sequence would be called *bottom-up planning*. This starts with estimates of sales by classification and then data are accumulated upward through department and division to the overall store level. This approach may result in different goals from the top-down approach. The salespeople who sell certain classes of merchandise may see merchandise trends not known to top management. Their supervisors thus may be more optimistic or more pessimistic than high levels of management.

A blending of the top-down and the bottom-up systems tends to give salespeople and department level managers substantial input into the store plan. Management, of course, will exercise its responsibility of final decision making.

CLASSIFICATION CONTROL PLAN

Class	Planned Season Sales	Opening Stock	Planned Closing Stock	Planned Season Purchases
A	$20,000	$ 4,500	$ 4,000	$19,500
B	12,000	3,400	2,500	11,100
C	10,000	2,600	2,000	9,400
D	5,000	1,500	1,000	4,500
E	3,000	1,000	500	2,500
Total	$50,000	$13,000	$10,000	$47,000

BREAKDOWN OF PLANNED SEASON PURCHASES

Class	February Purchases Planned	February Purchases Actual	March Purchases Planned	March Purchases Actual	April Purchases Planned	April Purchases Actual	May Purchases Planned	May Purchases Actual	June Purchases Planned	June Purchases Actual	July Purchases Planned	July Purchases Actual
A	$4,000		$ 5,000		$ 5,000		$ 3,000		$ 1,500		$ 1,000	
B	4,000		3,000		3,000		1,000		100		---	
C	900		1,000		1,000		2,000		2,500		2,000	
D	2,100		1,000		500		500		400		---	
E	---		500		500		500		500		500	
Total	$11,000		$10,500		$10,000		$ 7,000		$ 5,000		$ 3,500	

Illus. 17-3   Planning purchases by classification is more precise than planning by department. Here are two classification plans for a department of a store. The first plan states how much to buy in each classification during a season, and the second plan states how much to buy in each classification in each month during the season.

CHECKING YOUR KNOWLEDGE

Vocabulary

1. planning
2. merchandise plan, or budget
3. SKU
4. top-down planning
5. bottom-up planning

Review Questions

1. Describe the four steps in developing a program of merchandise planning.
2. What factors should the retailer consider as he sets his sales figure goals?
3. List the four levels of merchandise planning or budgeting.
4. At what level of planning can the performance of individual buyers and managers best be measured?
5. What are some of the ways in which merchandise can be classified?

Discussion Questions

1. Is planning equally important to both the small store and the large store?
2. Is planning by classification needed in a small store where the merchant can visually check almost all the merchandise in the store?
3. Why do past figures have less meaning to the store if there has been a change of policies or procedures in the store?
4. What effect will a strict top-down type of planning have on the ambitious department manager or buyer?

Part b

Preparing the Six-Month Plan

The retailer can plan his merchandising activities for any given period of time. However, most retailers find that planning for six months at a time works quite well. The six-month plan serves as a guide for fairly definite action and can be adjusted to actual performance during the period.

The six-month plan is actually a budget in the form of dollar figure goals. For the well-organized small store the budget items may consist of sales, stocks, purchases, and expenses. The large-scale retailer's six-month plan may contain, in addition to those mentioned, reductions (including markdowns, employee discounts, and stock shortages), stock turn, merchandise returns, amount of average sales, gross margin, and profit.

PLANNING GOALS

Let us suppose it has been decided that $3,000 is a reasonable profit for Department M in the six-month period just ahead. This figure was determined after taking into consideration the profits of similar departments, profits realized by the department in the past, store policies, and trends of business conditions.

The next step is to set realistic figure goals for sales, reductions, stocks, purchases, expenses, and markups so that the department will reach the established goals and yield a profit of about $3,000. The following procedures are used to fill out the merchandise plan so as to reach this profit goal.

PLANNING SALES AND REDUCTIONS

The manager of the department plans total sales of $57,500 for the six-month period. This total is based on past sales adjusted to the planned profit goal, to changes in policy, and to changes in the general business situation that may make customers more or less willing to buy. The six-month sales plan is then broken down into monthly plans on the basis of past experience. Sales are planned first because they depend so much on outside conditions. It is easier to adjust stocks, markups, and expenses to sales possibilities than it is to plan these factors and then try to reach a sales goal consistent with them.

Markdowns, merchandise shortages, and employee discounts are collectively called *reductions*. They represent the inability to sell goods at original retail prices. Reductions are commonly planned for the season and sometimes for each month. In our example, they are planned at $5,000 for the six-month season and, as we shall see, are a factor in planning the initial markup for the department.

PLANNING STOCKS

After sales are planned by months, the next step is to plan the amount of stock to have on hand at the first of each month. The model stock plan gives a guide to the average stock to carry, and increases and decreases may be planned in line with the anticipated monthly variations in sales.

Attention should be given to stock turn. Every retailer should understand stock turn in order to make better use of his investment capital, to control his inventories, and to realize the maximum profits. If a retailer buys $100 worth of goods and prices them to sell for $150,

SIX-MONTH MERCHANDISE PLAN

DEPARTMENT M: Season's Profit Goal: $3,000
                  Season's Reduction Goal: $5,000

	Feb.	March	April	May	June	July	Aug.	TOTAL
Sales last year	$ 6,700	$10,100	$11,700	$ 9,500	$ 8,900	$ 6,500		$53,400
Planned sales	7,700	10,100	13,000	10,500	9,500	6,700		57,500
Actual								
Stocks last year-- First of month	12,000	17,000	20,000	16,000	13,000	11,000	9,000	14,000 (av.)
Planned stocks-- first of month	13,000	16,500	18,000	15,500	14,000	12,000	10,000	14,150 (av.)
Actual								
Purchases last year	11,700	13,100	7,700	6,500	6,900	4,500		50,400
Planned purchases	11,200	11,600	10,500	9,000	7,500	4,700		54,500
Actual								
Selling salaries last year	630	720	780	710	600	560		4,000
Planned salaries	700	900	1100	900	800	600		5,000
Actual								
Advertising last year	310	340	400	340	270	240		1,900
Planned advertising	350	370	430	370	310	270		2,100
Actual								
Other expenses last year								4,800
Planned other expenses				`				5,900
Actual								
Markup last year	33.0%	33.1%	33.2%	33.0%	33.1%	32.9%		
Planned markup	33.6%	33.6%	33.6%	33.6%	33.6%	33.6%		
Actual								

Illus. 17-4   A step-by-step explanation of this six-month merchandise plan is given on the following pages. Refer to this illustration frequently to better understand the relationships among the factors discussed.

he will have a $50 margin when the goods are sold. At this price it may take a whole year for the goods to be sold. If, however, he prices the $100 worth of goods at $135 and is able to sell the goods in six months, or two lots of goods during the year, he will have attained a $70 margin for his $100 investment.

The number of times the average stock is sold during the year is called the *rate of stock turn*. Suppose a retailer stocks an average inventory worth $5,000 at retail price. From that $5,000 worth of stock, he has sales for the year of $30,000. His rate of stock turn is 6. It is possible to achieve a sales total of $30,000 with an average inventory of $5,000 because, as the goods are sold, the merchant orders more goods, so that his stock level is always kept at about $5,000.

Computing Stock Turn

Stock turn is usually computed by one of the following equations:

1. Stock turn $= \dfrac{\text{Net sales}}{\text{Average stock at retail price}}$ (Retail basis)

2. Stock turn $= \dfrac{\text{Cost of merchandise sold}}{\text{Average cost of stock}}$ (Cost basis)

3. Stock turn $= \dfrac{\text{Number of units sold}}{\text{Average number of units in stock}}$ (Unit basis)

The retail basis for computing stock turnover is preferred when stores keep records of the retail value of their stock. When information about stock is available only in terms of cost, however, the cost basis of computing stock turnover is satisfactory. The unit basis is useful in studying the number of items carried in relation to the number sold. For example, a store may stock 60 pairs of shoes in a certain style to provide a size assortment and may sell 30 pairs in a month. The stock turn is one half, or at the rate of 6 a year.

Stock turn may be computed for any convenient period, such as a year, a month, or a week. When stock turn is computed for a shorter term, the yearly rate may be found by multiplying the turn figure by the number of such periods in a year.

Finding Average Inventory

The chief problem in computing stock turn is to determine the average stock carried during the period. The average stock figure may be found by adding the stocks on the first of every month, plus the ending stock, and dividing this sum by 13 as shown on page 544:

Stock on hand at retail   Jan.   1, $ 21,000
                                    Feb.   1,   23,000

Jan.	1,	$ 21,000
Feb.	1,	23,000
Mar.	1,	26,000
Apr.	1,	27,000
May	1,	25,000
June	1,	20,500
July	1,	18,000
Aug.	1,	21,000
Sept.	1,	25,000
Oct.	1,	26,000
Nov.	1,	28,500
Dec.	1,	25,500
Dec.	31,	19,000

$$13\,)\overline{\$305,500} = \$23,500$$

For a given amount of sales the rate of stock turn will increase as the average stock figure is reduced.

Stock Turn Rates

Different lines of merchandise have different rates of stock turn. For instance, the rate for food stores is greater than the rate for furniture stores. Many food items must be sold quickly or they will spoil. Food is also purchased frequently by customers. The food retailer must buy in limited quantities and sell quickly. Consequently, the average number of stock turns a year for grocery stores is about 19. A furniture store, however, must have a large assortment of merchandise, and customers buy infrequently. The stock turn for many furniture stores is less than 2. The retailer's constant effort is to keep stock large enough to meet customer demand but small enough to reduce the risk of his goods going out of style, spoiling, or tying up funds unnecessarily.

Methods of Reducing Stock Levels

Reducing the number of price lines carried

Eliminating odd lots of unsalable goods

Reducing the number of brands and duplicate styles

Buying frequently in small quantities

Reducing reserve stocks

Preparing carefully buying plans to avoid unsalable goods

Illus. 17-5   Stock turn often can be increased without affecting sales by reducing the amount of average inventory. The methods above can be used to reduce stock levels.

Advantages of Increasing Stock Turn

Decreases markdowns and depreciation

Increases sales because of steady incoming flow of new goods

Reduces interest expense on merchandise investment

Frees capital for investment in additional lines of goods

Reduces insurance and taxes on merchandise

Reduces rent for storage space

Reduces selling effort and expenses, since fresh goods sell with less effort

---

Illus. 17-6   The retailer should make every effort to increase stock turn. Many advantages and few disadvantages result from increasing stock turn.

PLANNING PURCHASES

Once sales and stocks have been planned, it is fairly easy to plan the amount to receive into stock each month. The planned purchases may be calculated by using this formula:

Planned Purchases = Planned Sales + Increase (or − Decrease) in Inventory

In the merchandise plan for Department M, the planned sales for February are $7,700. The planned retail stock on February 1 is $13,000, and the planned retail stock on March 1 is $16,500. The desired increase in inventory, therefore, is $3,500. By inserting these figures into the formula, we find that planned purchases for February are $11,200.

Planned Purchases = $7,700 + $3,500 or $11,200

Actual purchases are kept in line with planned purchases by using the open-to-buy. As was explained in Chapter 6, the open-to-buy is the order limit for delivery during a particular period. It is the difference between the planned purchases for a period and the merchandise orders already placed for that period. The open-to-buy may be calculated by using this formula:

Planned Purchases − Orders = Open-to-Buy

We know that the planned purchases for Department M for February amount to $11,200. Assume that orders for $1,200 worth of merchandise have already been placed. By using the above formula, we find that the open-to-buy for February is $10,000 at retail value.

PLANNING EXPENSES

Expenses include all outlays made or incurred to operate the business during the period. Based on past experience and outside comparisons, a percentage allowance for each category of expense can be made for the six-month plan. Salaries for store employees are often the largest expense of the retail store running from 5 percent to 20 percent depending on the type of store—lowest in self-service stores and highest in service types of retail businesses. In the merchandise plan shown in Illus. 17-4, the planned selling salaries for the season are about 8.7 percent of the season's planned sales of $57,500.

How advertising is planned for a season was discussed in Chapter 13 and should be reviewed. In the merchandise plan shown planned advertising is estimated at about 3.6 percent of sales.

In the preparation of a complete expense budget, a list of all expense categories may be drawn up. For each, an estimate of the minimum outlay necessary for providing the service may be planned.

PLANNING MARKUP

In Chapter 10 you learned how the initial markup is planned. Turn back to that chapter and reread Parts A and B. The planned markup is usually set for the entire season rather than separately for each month. Using the planning formula given in Chapter 10, the planned markup for Department M is calculated as follows:

$$\text{Planned Markup} = \frac{\$3,000 \text{ (profit)} + \$13,000 \text{ (expenses)} + \$5,000 \text{ (reductions)}}{\$57,500 \text{ (sales)} + \$5,000 \text{ (reductions)}}$$

$$= \frac{\$21,000}{\$62,500} = 33.6\%$$

While there may be monthly variations in markups the important goal is the markup for the entire season.

CHECKING YOUR KNOWLEDGE

Vocabulary

1. reductions

2. rate of stock turn

Review Questions

1. In making a merchandise plan, why should sales be planned first?
2. What are the three formulas for computing stock turn?
3. What are six ways to reduce stock levels? six advantages of increasing stock turn?
4. What is the difference between planned purchases and open-to-buy?
5. At the department level which expenses need detailed planning by months?

Discussion Questions

1. How may the stock turn rate be affected by the way in which a store operates?
2. Under what circumstances might it be wise to buy more than the open-to-buy figure indicates?
3. Can a small store apply the merchandise planning procedures outlined in this part as successfully as a large store? Why?
4. What effect will an overestimate of expenses have on a six-month plan? an underestimate of expenses?

Part **C**

Stock Control

Stock control consists of a systematic plan for recording and reporting types and quantities of merchandise on hand and on order. A good stock control system makes possible efficient management of a model merchandise assortment and proper inventory level. So many factors depend on the proper stock balance that stock must be frequently and accurately checked. There are two methods for controlling stock—the dollar-control method and the unit-control method.

METHODS OF STOCK CONTROL

With the *dollar-control method,* retailers calculate book inventories or take physical inventories at frequent intervals and then check the stock count obtained against the planned stock figure. This general check discloses whether the stock is too high or too low in relation to the planned stock figure. However, the dollar-control method does not give any specific information on items in or out of stock or information on slow-selling items. Many merchants using the dollar-control method keep no record of the number of units of each kind of goods in stock. They must depend upon observation and memory—which are sometimes faulty—as sales are made and as goods are ordered and received.

Because the dollar-control method has proved unsatisfactory for many retailing enterprises, the unit-control method is commonly used in place of or in connection with it. With the *unit-control method*, an organized procedure for recording the stock by units of merchandise is set up. A complete record by merchandise classification, style number, size, color, material, or any other merchandise characteristic is maintained for the entire stock. As we noted in Part A, each unit so controlled is called an SKU (stockkeeping unit). Thus, the retailer can tell exactly which items and how many of each are on hand at any time.

Stock Control Goals

1. To maintain correct quantities within merchandise assortments
2. To guide the purchase of new merchandise in each classification
3. To determine price ranges that will serve the store's clientele
4. To simplify merchandise ordering
5. To identify appropriate items for sales promotion
6. To point out slow-selling merchandise items
7. To increase the return on the investment realized from each item handled

---

Illus. 17-7   The goals of a stock control system serve the interest of the retail store in many ways. To meet these goals information must be supplied quickly to the buyers and store management.

The merchant may be losing up to 10 percent because he does not have adequate merchandise in stock. Without unit stock records, he may carry too few of the best-selling items and too many of the slow-selling items. Moreover, the annoyance and ill will he creates by telling a customer that he is out of an item will cut down on future sales and profits. Progressive merchants are now comparing the dollar markup realized on the quantity of each SKU sold with the size of the merchandise investment in that item. Except for staples, they are concentrating on those items that not only sell well at a substantial markup but also have a high stock turn.

KINDS OF UNIT STOCK CONTROL SYSTEMS

There are a number of types of unit stock control systems in operation today. The paragraphs that follow discuss several of the most commonly used systems. Each store must determine the best type of system for the merchandise it handles.

Checklist System

For convenience goods and many shopping goods that are not subject to quick change in fashion, the simplest unit stock control system is the *checklist* or *never-out list system.* On the checklist are listed all the regular items and the amount of each item to be carried normally. Once a week—or at other regular intervals—the list is checked against actual stock to see if there is an adequate quantity of each item on hand. If there is not, an order is placed. This system is particularly satisfactory for such goods as staple groceries, drugs, hardware, stationery supplies, and household textiles. Usually the buyer indicates a maximum (or model) stock level for each item, and an order is placed for the difference between this maximum and the actual stock count.

Dept._____		**NEVER-OUT LIST**					Section_____	
Firm	Style No.	DESCRIPTION	Price	Size	Color	Model Stock	Date Checked	

Illus. 17-8   On a never-out list staple items are listed and checked at regular intervals.

Perpetual Inventory System

For fashion goods, such as women's dresses, a fairly elaborate control system is necessary. Sudden changes in demand for some styles make it necessary for the buyer to know his stock condition every day. For such merchandise, lists of what is sold are made at the end of each day. If a computer is not used, these lists may be prepared from copies of the sales checks or from stubs of price tickets that are torn off when a sale is made. Where the space to store merchandise on the selling floor is strictly limited, incoming goods may be stored in a reserve stockroom and the control system limited to the stock received into and disbursed to forward stock from the reserve. Requisitions by salespeople to fill in forward stock are checked and filled by stock clerks, and the items and quantities appearing on the requisitions are regarded as sales. When the forward stocks are low, the requisitions provide a fairly accurate picture of what has been sold to customers since the last requisition was made. This is called a *reserve requisition system.*

Illus. 17-9   Unit control is most effective when it provides a picture of inventory performance. Here the buyer is using a system which shows the current money-making value of each item in her stock.

In addition to accumulating and analyzing customer sales (or reserve requisitions) daily, a perpetual inventory of each unit is maintained. A card may be made out for each style, and the number of that style sold each day may be recorded on it. Entries may also be made on the card of the number ordered and of the number received. Thus, it is possible to keep a perpetual inventory for each style. For example, one card is made out for 12 dresses ordered in style No. 72 on June 6. On June 16, 10 of these dresses arrive and are recorded on the card as a receipt. The next day, June 17, 1 dress is sold and is entered on the card as a sale. The balance of 9 is then recorded in the "On Hand" column. If 3 were sold on June 19, the balance on hand would be reduced to 6, but the other 2 on order may arrive on the same date, (June 19), giving an "On Hand" of 8. Computers can perform these operations more rapidly than by manual entry, and their use is discussed below.

From time to time the "On Hand" figures appearing on the cards or issued by a computer are checked against the actual stock. If only 7 are found in stock when the perpetual inventory figure indicates 8, the one missing is a shortage. An effort is made to find it, and the card is checked over to make sure that no error was made in the records. If the difference cannot be accounted for, the garment may have been stolen; and action must be taken to safeguard stock better in the future.

The perpetual type of unit control system is more expensive to maintain than that based on periodic counts, for every sale has to be recorded. This form of control is desirable under the following conditions:

1. When shortages must be watched carefully
2. When styles change rapidly
3. When it is very difficult to count stock frequently

"Warehouse" Control System

When the physical stock cannot be readily inspected—as when the stock is in a warehouse or in one of the units of a chain—the *"warehouse" control system* may be used. This system is also used for items of high unit value, such as expensive ready-to-wear clothing, jewelry, furniture, and bulk goods controlled by the case as the unit. A control card is prepared for each separate unit of merchandise. Thus, if 12 items of one style are received, 12 control cards are made out. On each card the history of the piece is revealed: when it was received, the cost, the original retail price, any markdowns taken, and when it was sold. As the articles are sold, these cards are removed from a visible index file. Thus, the file presents a picture of the stock at all times. At a glance, it may be observed whether the stock in any classification, size, or color is getting low.

A variation of this plan is to attach to a price ticket a number of stickers, one for each item in the warehouse or reserve stockroom. The price ticket, in turn, is attached to a sample item on the selling floor. As a sale is made, one sticker is removed from the ticket and attached to the sales check. Thus, there is little danger of taking an order for something which is not in stock.

Computerized Unit Control Systems

When a retail store reaches a certain size, say $5 million in sales or has more than three store units, there is probably need for a computerized stock management system. This system provides detailed information on the activity of every classification, or each SKU can be regularly reported to the merchant.

The conversion from a manual or a manual-mechanical system to a computerized reporting system is not always easy. Careful consideration must be given to the following:

1. What effect will the new system have on the present staff and assignment of duties?
2. What goals should the reporting system achieve?
3. How can the reports be made easy for the executive staff to analyze
   for decision making?
4. Who will determine the nature and number of the reports, and who
   is to have access to them?

Obviously a computerized unit control system must be tailored to
the individual retail organization in which it is to be used.

THE PROBLEM OF SLOW-SELLING MERCHANDISE

Unit stock control systems are invaluable in pointing out slow-
selling merchandise items. For a stock assortment to yield a profit, old
stock must be moved out quickly to make room for new stock. *Slow-
selling merchandise* may be defined as merchandise that has been in
stock a longer period than experience indicates is desirable. Department stores set the limit for much of their merchandise at six months,
for it has been found that goods that fail to sell before that time are
likely to fail to sell at all unless they are given special attention. The
time limit for fashion merchandise is generally much shorter—in some
cases, only four weeks. Rugs, furniture, and some other house furnishings may be allowed a year because there will be little depreciation in
that time. To force the sale of such merchandise in less time by means
of markdowns would mean that it would have to be replaced in order
to maintain assortments. This would lead to unnecessary loss.

Slow-selling merchandise presents a serious problem to the merchant. Money tied up in slow sellers could be used more profitably if
it were invested in fast-selling merchandise. Often the merchant is
prevented from buying desirable goods because he cannot recover the
money he has invested in the slow sellers. Even if he has the necessary
funds with which to purchase needed merchandise, the slow sellers may
be tying up all his storage space.

The usual way to dispose of slow-selling stock is to take drastic
markdowns; but sometimes goods may be moved by promotional efforts,
such as advertising and special bonuses to salespeople. Frequently all
that is needed is for the buyer to "talk up" the slow-selling goods to
salespeople; if they can be convinced that there is nothing wrong with
the goods, they can generally sell them without a markdown. In fact,
if slow-selling goods are still in fashion, it is sometimes wise to round
out the size and color assortment by buying more goods.

Methods of Moving Slow Sellers

Take large markdowns. One large markdown will move out merchandise faster than will three or four small markdowns. Markdowns should make it worthwhile for the customer to buy.

Offer P.M.'s (premium money) to salespeople. It should be pointed out that the merchandise represents a good value for the price and that all that is needed to sell it is a little extra effort.

Give extra attention to the merchandise. Since odds and ends of merchandise are hard to sell, perhaps the retailer might fill in sizes, round out assortments, or complete missing parts.

Advertising. Special promotional effort can be given to slow sellers if the quantities, styles, and colors are worthy of being advertised. If the merchant believes that he has merchandise that is wanted or needed, it might be wise to invest in advertising those items.

Display. A display might be set up in a noticeable spot to attract attention and create desire.

Special selling idea. Perhaps a new idea for selling the merchandise could be developed. Tie-in sales, a free gift offer, special service, and extra time to pay are possible special selling ideas.

Illus. 17-10   Retailers must move out old stock as rapidly as possible to make room for new stock. Here are some methods of moving slow-selling merchandise.

CHECKING YOUR KNOWLEDGE

Vocabulary

1. stock control
2. dollar-control method
3. unit-control method
4. checklist or never-out list system
5. reserve requisition system
6. "warehouse" control system
7. slow-selling merchandise

Review Questions

1. What are the advantages and disadvantages of the dollar-control method of stock control? of the unit-control method?
2. Explain the operation of a perpetual inventory system of stock control.
3. For what merchandise items is the "warehouse" control system used?
4. Why is slow-selling merchandise a problem to the retailer?
5. Name six ways in which slow-selling items may be moved.

Discussion Questions

1. Which systems of unit stock control would you recommend for (a) a hardware store, (b) a sports goods store, (c) a supermarket? Explain your answers.
2. What might cause a merchandise item to sell rapidly in one store and slowly in another store?
3. What impact has EDP had on the control and management of stock?
4. If a store uses computerized stock control, is it assured that there will be no slow-moving stock or shortages? Why?

Part d

Control of Merchandise Shortages

Most retailers will agree that merchandise shortage is one of the leading profit-killers today. With merchandise shortages increasing as a percentage of sales, prevention and control has become a major problem for merchants. Some shortages are caused by clerical errors, but many more are the result of shoplifting or pilferage.

CAUSES OF SHORTAGES

When shortages were typically under one percent of sales, it was estimated that half may have been due to errors in book or physical inventory. The rest were attributed to pilferage by employees and shoplifting by outsiders. Some were caused by employees and outsiders working together. It is now estimated that such theft accounts for well over three fourths of the shortage figure. The National Retail Merchants Association estimates that retail shortages run over $8 million each day. This is forcing merchants to seek higher markups to offset the heavy loss.

KINDS OF SHOPLIFTERS

There are many reasons given for shoplifting. Those who do shoplift can be one of these three kinds:

1. *Professional thieves,* who make a living by stealing and who know all the tricks of the trade.
2. *Opportunists,* who see an opportunity to steal, without being detected so they think, and do so as a lark. Some of these may be *kleptomaniacs*—persons who have an abnormal and persistent impulse to steal.
3. *Juveniles,* who steal for kicks, to gain admiration of their peers, or to feed a drug habit. Over 50 percent of all shoplifters caught are juveniles.

TRICKS USED BY PROFESSIONALS

Professionals use many devices to steal goods, and these devices are often resorted to by opportunists and juveniles as well. Goods may be slipped into large handbags, records are slipped into large notebooks, garments are put on in dressing rooms and worn out under street clothes.

Some shoplifters use a more elaborate device called a *booster box*. This looks like a securely gift-wrapped package but has a flap making it possible to whisk goods inside in an instant. Other thieves wear garments with false pockets or carry brief cases or purses with hidden spaces for goods.

Theft does not always occur on the selling floor. It occurs where goods are received into the store, in warehouses and stockrooms, and while goods are being moved about for delivery. One danger point is the receiving station. A truck driver, who may be conspiring with a receiving clerk, may deliver 9 out of 10 cartons in a shipment and have the clerk sign for 10. The stolen goods are sold through a *fence*, a specialist in disposing of stolen goods.

PROTECTIVE MEASURES

Most large stores employ security officers or contract for protection services from private agencies. These people are trained to observe any questionable conduct on the selling floor or other store areas. They know how to approach suspicious-looking customers without running the risk of making a false arrest. Since security officers cannot be everywhere at once, they often make use of in-store television sets with cameras directed at various parts of the store. Thus, one security officer can, from one spot, watch a group of screens that reveal activities in many parts of the store.

To supplement the work of security officers, many other devices are used. Several leading stores have installed the *Sensormatic System*. Special tags are attached either to all merchandise or to selected articles of the type likely to be stolen. Scanners are placed at each side of the entrances to the store or department. If any tagged article is moved between the scanners, an alarm is sounded electronically. Illus. 17-11 shows a control tag, and Illus. 17-12 shows how the system works. If a customer purchases a tagged article the salesperson will deactivate or remove the special tag. Thieves who take a tagged item and set off the alarm often drop the concealed goods making it easier for security officers to catch them. Potential thieves soon learn that the system is in operation and avoid taking the chance of being caught.

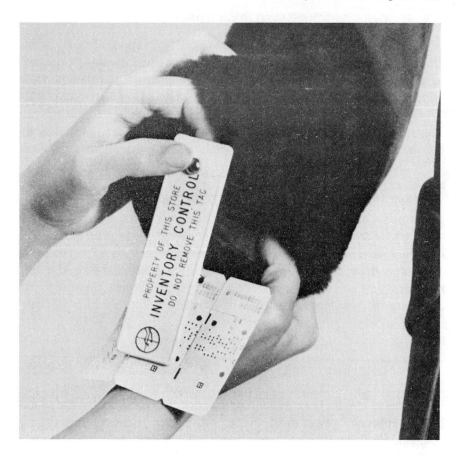

Illus. 17-11   The control tag used in the Sensormatic System is
easily attached to the merchandise for which control is desired.

Some stores have cameras set up over the sales register. Every time
a sale is rung, a picture is snapped automatically that shows the amount
rung up, the goods, and the customer. Examination of these photos will
reveal failure of the goods to compare with the amount rung up. Since
thieves sometimes hide in stores overnight to steal valuables at their
leisure, a few big stores use trained dogs to roam the building at night
sniffing for concealed prowlers.

Store personnel are trained to keep a watchful eye on all customers
in their section. The use of cleverly arranged mirrors helps salespeople
watch several areas of their department. Salespeople are taught not to
leave valuable goods with a customer while going to a stock area for
something else to show the customer.

Alarm alerts store personnel.

Sensormatic TAGS are attached to all items to be protected.

Remote alarms and lights can be located at other points in the store.

TAG removed at point of purchase.

Scanners create a "field of protection" at customer exits.

All shoplifters are detected at this point.

Illus. 17-12   To apprehend shoplifters customers must pass through protected areas which set off alarms if the inventory control tag has not been removed from the merchandise.

EDUCATION OF PUBLIC

The loss to retailers from shoplifting has more than doubled as a percentage of sales in the past few years. One store in the East was forced to close, partly because of the raids by young people on their way home from school. To offset the notion among so many young people that shoplifting is a lark and a sign of self-reliance, merchants are undertaking educational campaigns. Efforts are made through parent-teacher groups, through special lectures in schools, and through city-wide advertising campaigns. The theme of these efforts is basically to warn young people that to be caught stealing endangers their entire lives. It often makes admission to college impossible; it makes it difficult to get a job, and to qualify for advancement. Merchants have been forced to become tough and prosecute the great majority of those caught. While state laws vary, the penalty for any theft under $100 may be 60 days in jail and as much as a $500 fine.

Recently the Philadelphia Merchants Association conducted a major campaign called STEM—"Shoplifters Take Everybody's Money." The target was the teenage shoplifter who often comes from a middle-class suburban home.

Television and radio stations ran hundreds of free public service "spots" during prime time. Before the campaign these spot announcements were seen and heard only late in the evening and did not reach young people. Two messages were emphasized:

1. Shoplifting is no joke; it is a very serious crime.
2. Shoplifters Take Everybody's Money (STEM), since they raise retail prices.

Some of the statements made in the announcements were the following:

Ken swapped a college education for a $6 pair of jeans.
Meg just traded her engagement ring for a $6 blouse.

Courtesy of Federated Department Stores, Inc.

Illus. 17-13   Another protective measure to prevent shoplifting is an alarm system that activates if a garment is removed from a rack without assistance from a salesperson. A distinct sign warns the customer that she cannot remove merchandise without assistance.

Karen exchanged a $2,500 scholarship for a $9.95 pullover.
Carol just traded a $100-a-week job for a $3 belt.

As a result of this campaign, Philadelphia stores have reported a downward trend in shoplifting. Other cities, such as Minneapolis, have undertaken similar campaigns.

THE PILFERAGE PROBLEM

There is growing concern over the fact that a great deal of the present merchandise shortage is caused by employee pilferage sometimes made easy by a partner who poses as a customer. Some employees seem to regard helping themselves to merchandise as a right-benefit, and many new employees also have this attitude. The situation is difficult to control.

One technique is to rule that all employees must enter and leave the store at special entrances. Any packages an employee has with him on arrival are checked, and any purchases he makes in the store are delivered to the checkout point. No unauthorized packages may be taken out.

Watchfulness on the part of honest employees, willingness to reprove dishonest fellow-workers and, as a last resort, to report them—all are required.

CHECKING YOUR KNOWLEDGE

Vocabulary

1. kleptomaniac
2. booster box
3. fence
4. Sensormatic System

Review Questions

1. What are the causes of merchandise shortages?
2. Name three kinds of shoplifters.
3. Describe three protective measures that retailers are using against shoplifters.
4. What group was the focus of the Philadelphia Merchants educational campaign?
5. How can pilferage be controlled?

Discussion Questions

1. Some people believe that shoplifting can be controlled by greater enforcement and stiffer penalties. Other persons think that chronic shoplifters are

suffering from a disease and, if arrested, should receive medical treatment. Are either of these views correct? What other alternatives exist?

2. A recent survey shows that most of the shortages in the supermarket occur in the dairy, meat, bread, and produce departments. Why are losses in these areas greater than in the grocery department?

3. Do you think educational promotions such as those described in this part will have a major impact on young people, leading to a sharp decrease in theft? Should every major city undertake such campaigns?

Part e

Control of Operations

The merchant who has made all the necessary plans for the operation of his business must make sure that those plans are accomplished. Whenever results are not following plans the retailer has to take corrective action. Prompt attention to differences between goals and results will keep the business headed toward the profit goals desired.

PHASES OF STORE CONTROL

The activity of comparing actual results with planned figures and taking corrective action is called *control*. In the paragraphs that follow, you will learn how sales, purchases, expenses, and markup can be controlled and will learn how the control function is organized in stores.

Controlling Sales

If the sales figure is less than that planned, an experienced retailer looks for (1) merchandise that is priced too high—not meeting competition, (2) ineffective advertising—not bringing customers into the store, (3) poor buying—assortments are not what the customer wants, and (4) poor personal selling. The corrective measures seem obvious and should, of course, be taken. Sales personnel should be stimulated by additional rewards (which may be simply full recognition for their accomplishments); or quotas should be set and a system worked out by which performance can be measured. It is possible that the sales staff may need retraining or should be reminded of the sales goals set in the merchandise budget.

If external business conditions are affecting sales so that they do not meet the planned figure, the sales figure should be revised downward and the rest of the merchandise plan should be revised accordingly.

Controlling Purchases

Purchases may be made to conform to the planned figure in the budget by adjusting the open-to-buy figure. This adjustment will be downward if sales fail to meet the planned sales figure or if stock accumulation is greater than planned. The adjustment will be upward if sales exceed the planned sales figure.

Controlling Expenses

If expenses exceed the planned figure, the profit goal is in danger even if sales are up. It is clear that the gross margin must be greater than expenses in order that a net profit be realized. As you learned in Chapter 15, there are three major methods by which a healthy balance between gross margin and expenses can be maintained: (1) by increasing sales, (2) by increasing the gross margin percentage by means of higher markups and lower markdowns, and (3) by reducing the expense figure itself.

Control of advertising expenses is an especially important part of controlling expenses. Failure to adjust the monthly advertising expenditures to monthly sales is common in many retail stores. Money for advertising is often spent when sales do not warrant the expenditure, and inadequate advertising is therefore the result in high sales periods. Of all indexes available for planning, the monthly variation in sales is one of the most regular. Every store manager should be able to tell within very close limits what percentage of his yearly volume is to be realized in any month. There is little excuse for not keeping advertising expenditures in line with anticipated monthly sales.

Controlling Markup

Markup may be controlled by comparing every week or every month the actual markup realized on purchases with the planned markup as it appears on the merchandise plan. Many buyers place the retail price of each item on the manufacturer's invoice next to the cost, so that the markup on each item can be calculated. If the buyer's actual markup is substantially lower than planned, he should be challenged to obtain a higher markup on subsequent purchases.

CONTROLLING BY MEANS OF STANDARDS

For purposes of controlling the various merchandising activities, retailers often set up standards or yardsticks for various aspects of their businesses. For instance, a women's shoes' chain set a standard of

8 percent of planned sales for its selling costs; a supermarket set 55 percent of its sales for groceries and 45 percent foods, meats, produce, and dairy products; a furniture dealer set his stock turn at 1.9. A business can set up a standard for almost every important retailing activity. This can include even such things as the number of packages a wrapper should be able to wrap in a day or the number of transactions a salesperson can handle each day.

Standards must be carefully determined if they are to be of value to the retailer. To set an arbitrary standard because the retailer believes such a standard is reasonable is not the way to manage an efficient business. Past records and past experiences of the business must be studied; these should be compared with the operating results of comparable retailers; and then a standard for the store may be set. Standards should be put down on paper and compared with actual performance at frequent intervals. Many small retailers arbitrarily set standards and carry the figures in their heads. This is of little value from the viewpoint of efficient management. In such cases, if the standards are not met, the retailer often rationalizes the point by telling himself that his standards were not really accurate in the first place.

Information on how comparable retail businesses are managed is available to the retailer from such sources as the United States Depart-

Average Loss from Bad Debts (In Percentage of Net Sales)	
Appliance and Radio-TV Dealers	0.1-0.60%
Bookstores	.10
Children's and Infants' Wear	.02
Department Stores	0.1-0.25
Drug Stores	0.1-0.30
Florists	.07
Furniture Stores	.60
Grocery Stores	.02-.03
Hardware Stores	.15
Menswear Stores	.02
Office Supply and Equipment Dealers	.11-.28
Restaurants	.02
Service Stations	.02
Specialty Stores—Women's	.03
Sports Goods	.30

Illus. 17-14   Average loss from bad debts for various kinds of businesses is a standard used by retail managers to evaluate the adequacy of their store's control of credit and accounts receivable. Can you see any logic in the differences?

ment of Commerce, Dun and Bradstreet, the Merchants' Service Division of the National Cash Register Company, the national trade association for his type of store, research bureaus of universities, and some of the Federal Reserve Banks.

ORGANIZING THE CONTROL FUNCTION

Since the control function involves the checking of actual results against plans and standards and making adjustments accordingly, the keeping of business records becomes the first task of a store's control division. In the very small store, the merchant may attempt to keep the records himself; but as the store grows, he may turn the record-keeping job over to a bookkeeper. A part-time accountant may also be retained to prepare financial statements and other analyses that the merchant may want in order to obtain a detailed picture of his sales, inventories, markups, and expenses. Stores that are corporations must retain a certified public accountant to audit the books. He comes in at least once a year to check the reports that must be made to public authorities, and to certify that the statements correctly reflect the true condition of the business.

The Control Division

The function of the control division is to act as the watchdog over profits. The control division converts every operation into a figure fact that is to be reflected in the income statement or balance sheet. In a large store the head of the control division is called the *controller*. He is responsible for all accounting records and reports. The controller has the responsibility for the preparation of merchandise and expense budgets.

The decision on budgetary goals is the responsibility of the merchandise manager, the publicity director, and the operations director. The merchandise manager, for example, works with each of his buyers to develop a merchandise plan for each department, and he controls these plans by means of the open-to-buy. But it is the controller who assembles all the figures about past performance to be used in planning the budget, and it is he who insists that the budgets be prepared. He, or an assistant, may act as an "expense controller" and check the requisitions of department managers for the expenditure of funds.

Control in Chain Stores

The control division in a chain-store organization is even more highly organized than that just described. In a chain-store organization the controller and his staff handle all the financial records and the bookkeeping connected with credit and collections, accounts payable, cash receipts and expenditures, payroll, and budgets. Legal matters and real estate problems are also cleared through this office.

With the increase in government regulations and the expansion of business, it has become necessary for many chain-store organizations to modernize their control function with EDP. In national chain operations controllership may be assigned to regional offices to permit closer control of stores.

Control in Department Stores

Like the control division in chain stores, the organization of the control division in department stores is composed chiefly of highly skilled personnel trained in finance and accounting. The controller safeguards the net profit by checking the other divisions of the business to see that they keep their expenditures in line with their budgets. He sees to it that the merchandise division keeps up its sales volume. He checks on inventories and tries to impress upon the buyers the importance of rapid stock turn. The illustration below shows the organization of this division.

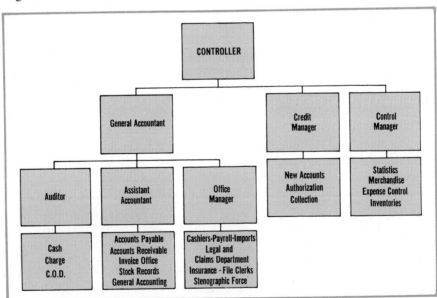

Illus. 17-15   This illustration shows the typical organization of the control division in a department store. Would you make any changes in this organization that might achieve a more effective operation for the division?

CHECKING YOUR KNOWLEDGE

Vocabulary

1. control   **2.** controller

Review Questions

1. What are some of the reasons why sales do not reach the planned figure?
2. How can actual purchases be made to conform to the planned purchases figure?
3. How can a business set up standards for controlling the efficiency of various phases of its operation?
4. From what sources can a retailer obtain information about the operation of similar retail businesses?
5. Briefly describe the organization of the control division in a department store.

Discussion Questions

1. In the control of merchandising operations which is more important: to compare current results with planned goals or with last year's results?
2. What standards might a retailer use year after year? What standards would have to be changed almost every year?
3. Should the controller be permitted to set sales, expense, and profit standards for the various merchandising divisions of a store? Why?

BUILDING YOUR SKILLS

Improving Communication Skills

Each of the following sentences contains one word that makes the sentence incorrect. On a separate sheet of paper, write the number of the sentence, the word that is used incorrectly, and the word that should be used.

1. I don't want no overstock; so I check open-to-buy frequently.
2. I didn't see nobody taking inventory in the stockroom.
3. I have sent them six-month plans to the divisional manager.
4. Have you heared that we are getting new sales registers?
5. He tried for three days to learn him the stock turn equations.
6. The controller said he ain't concerned about high planned purchases.
7. Sarah obviously don't know how to set up a classification plan.
8. Neither Ralph or I have had a chance to make our six-month plans.
9. The punched cards fell off of the table and onto the floor.
10. Being that you are going down anyway, how about taking this box, too?

Improving Arithmetic Skills

Perform the exercises involving calculation of stock turn and open-to-buy. You will have to know the formulas shown below:

$$\text{Stock turn} = \frac{\text{Net sales}}{\text{Average stock at retail price}}$$

$$\text{Open-to-buy} = \text{Planned purchases} - \text{Commitments}$$

1. On a separate sheet of paper, provide the missing items.

Sales	Average Stock	Rate of Turn
(a) $60,000	$10,000	. . .
(b) $18,000	. . . . . .	4.5
(c)	$20,000	7.3

2. A certain SKU costs $6 and sells for $10. During the month 36 units are sold with an investment of 72 units. What is the percentage return on the investment in this SKU measured at the markup level?
3. Assume that in your store, planned sales for June are $12,000; planned stock on June 1 is $30,000; and planned stock on July 1 is $25,000.
   (a) What are the planned purchases for June at retail?
   (b) If the planned markup is 30% of retail and $3,000 worth of goods at cost have already been ordered for June delivery, what is the open-to-buy at cost?
4. Assume that in your store, planned sales for September are $5,000; actual retail stock on September 1 is $20,000; planned retail stock on October 1 is $24,000. Assume also that orders placed in July and August for delivery in September amount to $1,500 at cost and that the markup is 40% of retail.
   (a) Find the open-to-buy on September 1.
   (b) If additional orders of $3,000 at cost are placed between September 1 and 15, what is the open-to-buy on September 15?

Improving Research Skills

1. Select one basic clothing item such as—but not limited to—gloves, hats, shoes, or shirts. Develop as many subclassifications of that item as you can. At what point does the subclassification no longer have value to merchandising planning?
2. Draw up a table of stock turn for five different businesses in your community. Give explanations as to why you believe some particular businesses have a high turn or a low turn.
3. Review the newspaper stories and other reports on shoplifting in your community. Try to determine to what extent shoplifting is a problem, what action is taken after arresting shoplifters, and what individual merchants have done to control shoplifting.

Improving Decision-Making Skills

1. Redway Furniture is a low-margin, high-volume furniture store that has shown sales increases of over 15% each of the last five years.

Mr. Redway, owner and manager, is primarily concerned with getting the merchandise in and out. He insists on keeping the dollar sales volume high and each week better than the comparable week of a year ago. Mr. Lajos has been hired as the controller for Redway Furniture. He finds that no one in the firm knows how many beds, end tables, lamps, or anything else is in stock. The entire operation has been on strictly a dollar basis. If you were Mr. Lajos, what action would you take? Why?

2. You are employed in a variety store which has yearly gross sales of about $200,000. There is no merchandise planning and no information on sales or stock by classification or unit. Your employer is discouraged because old stock is accumulating, expenses are increasing, and profits are dwindling. What reasons would you give him for introducing a system of merchandise planning? How would you go about setting up a merchandise plan?

APPLYING YOUR KNOWLEDGE

Chapter Projects

1. Obtain from city officials, police department, chamber of commerce, or other sources in your community information on the level of shoplifting in your community's retail stores. Try to learn which types of merchandise are most frequently stolen, characteristics of the shoplifters, and the penalties imposed on those caught. Develop your findings into a report that could be used as a basis for a news story or feature article.
2. Determine trends in local population, economic level, consumer purchasing power, and other factors important to retailers in your community. Based on your research develop a statement of expected retail conditions for the next five years.

Continuing Project

Perform the following activities in your manual:

1. Set up a merchandise plan for your store for a six months' period.
2. Describe the merchandise classifications you would set up for your store.
3. Tell whether or not you would maintain a unit stock control system; and, if you decide to use such a system, explain how the chosen system would operate.

chapter 18

Government and Retailing

a. Federal, state, and local governments regulate certain business practices to make sure that businesses operate in a manner that is fair to employees, customers, and competitors.

b. Federal and state regulations on pricing and selling practices have been created to prevent price-cutting, and price discrimination, to assure full disclosure on extension of credit, and to protect the consumer.

c. There are numerous federal regulations on the processing, packaging, and labeling of merchandise. These have been provided to inform and protect the consumer.

d. An employer has many legal responsibilities for his employees. Most labor regulations are administered by the states, but the federal government enforces wage and hour laws, the Social Security Act, and the Occupational Safety and Health Act.

e. All businesses pay different kinds of taxes. Taxes paid by retailers include income, property, sales, payroll, and special local taxes.

Part **a**

Government Regulation of Business

The operation of a retail store within certain local, state, and federal regulations is an accepted part of the retailer's tasks. During the past ten years the number of federal controls on business operations, merchandise, and personnel has increased dramatically. Hardly a hundred years ago the retail businessman had considerable freedom in how he advertised, in setting the prices he charged, and in employing workers and fixing their salaries. Taxes were paid and some responsibility was required for injuries to workers or customers on the store premises. Basically, though, at the beginning of this century, retailers were almost free from government regulation.

REASONS FOR GOVERNMENT REGULATION

Some of the 18th and 19th Century businessmen took advantage of their freedom and were guilty of unethical treatment of their employees, competitors, and customers. Merchandise sometimes did not live up to the overenthusiastic claims of advertisements. Sometimes employees worked long hours under uncomfortable and even dangerous conditions. Because business as a whole was reluctant to police the actions of individual businessmen, consumer and employee organizations pressed for government regulation of certain aspects of business. Using authority granted in the Constitution, federal, state, and local governments passed laws and formed agencies to administer the laws to insure that fair business practices would be provided to all businesspeople, employees, and consumers. During the 20th Century more and more government regulations have appeared.

There have been many reasons for the trend toward increased government regulation. Some of the most important reasons are:

1. To protect citizens against hazards arising from business buildings and equipment
2. To protect the interests of employees
3. To protect competitors against the unfair prices and practices of some businesses that might tend toward monopoly
4. To protect consumers against the sale of harmful goods, against misrepresentation in advertising and selling, and against high prices caused by conspiracies among sellers
5. To tax business to help pay for increased governmental services

Perhaps the most important point that can be made about reasons for government regulations is that they are designed as much for the protection of ethical business practice as for the protection of the consumer. However, the current trend has been to emphasize consumer protection.

ATTITUDES TOWARD GOVERNMENT REGULATION

It has been argued that the interests of society are best served when business has freedom of action and an unrestricted opportunity to make profits. Even today, some people feel that a free market with its aggressive competition is the consumer's best protection and that the retailer should have the right to decide to whom he shall sell and at what price. They believe that business, freed from the hand of government, would provide a larger flow of goods and services to consumers and would offer more prosperity for everyone.

In the past, businesspeople have often been opposed to additional government regulation. Today, however, a partnership between business and government is emerging. Business owners recognize that high standards must be set and maintained in their dealings with customers and employees. As business has grown, it has recognized that it has a social responsibility that goes beyond just buying, selling, and making a profit for the owners. Today most businesspeople feel that this responsibility can best be achieved by some governmental regulation, though there is not always agreement on the amount and kind of regulation that is necessary.

AREAS OF GOVERNMENT REGULATION

The most important government regulations affect commerce, competition, public health and safety, and labor. All government regulations are not aimed at and do not directly affect the retailer. However, because some of these regulations indirectly affect the retailer or affect the general economic atmosphere, it is important that you be familiar with them. The retailer is generally most concerned with the regulations on competition (particularly concerning pricing and advertising), public health and safety (particularly concerning merchandise), and labor.

Regulation of Commerce

The Constitution gives the federal government the authority to regulate *interstate commerce*—commerce among states. The states are given the authority to regulate *intrastate commerce*—commerce carried on within a state's boundaries. The federal government agencies responsible for enforcing interstate commerce regulations are the Interstate Commerce Commission (ICC) and the Civil Aeronautics Board (CAB). The regulations of these agencies affect the retailer's transportation costs on incoming goods.

Regulation of Competition

Government regulations do not attempt to stifle competition; rather, they are intended to promote fair competition. *Monopoly*—the control of the price or production of a good or service—is the greatest threat to competition. In the late 19th Century, many powerful monopolies existed; and the Sherman Antitrust Act was passed to dissolve these monopolies. This law provided that "every person who shall monopolize . . . or combine or conspire to monopolize . . . shall be guilty of a misdemeanor." In 1914 the passage of the Clayton Act strengthened the Sherman Antitrust Act by outlawing price discrimination. There are some intentional monopolies in certain fields, such as power companies, but these are strictly regulated by the government.

Regulation of competition may be broadly defined to include the protection of the consumer from false and misleading advertising and selling practices. Many laws have been passed to insure fair competition and consumer protection. The Federal Trade Commission is the government agency responsible for supervising many of these laws. A discussion of competitive practices, particularly in the fields of pricing and advertising, will be presented in Part B of this chapter.

Regulations for Public Health and Safety

Many federal, state, and local laws exist to protect the health and safety of this country's citizens. These laws range from laws on the correct labeling of drugs to laws on building construction. A retailer is most affected by the laws concerning merchandise—its processing, its packaging, and its labeling; and Part C will discuss these laws.

Labor Regulations

One of the most important federal laws regarding labor is the Social Security Act. Under the portion known as Old-Age, Survivors, and Disability Insurance, it provides pensions to retired employees and their families, benefits to survivors of employees who have died, and benefits to disabled employees. The money to provide the benefits comes from taxes paid by the employee and his employer. This and other laws regarding labor are discussed in Part D.

Local Regulations

Most of the major regulations affecting retail businesses are established by either the federal or the state government. There are additional regulations, however, that are established by the county, city, or town in which the business is located. Local regulations specify where the business can be located; the type and construction of the business building; the various services which are to be provided customers; and whether Sunday opening is permitted and, if permitted, restrictions on the merchandise that may be sold.

The purpose of local regulations is largely to limit or control those who plan to operate certain types of businesses. When a retailer applies for a permit or license he will have to provide certain details of his operation and pay an annual fee or tax associated with the permit or license. The business may be inspected to determine if it meets the requirements established. If the business does not operate under the conditions or regulations established, it may lose the right to do business in that locality.

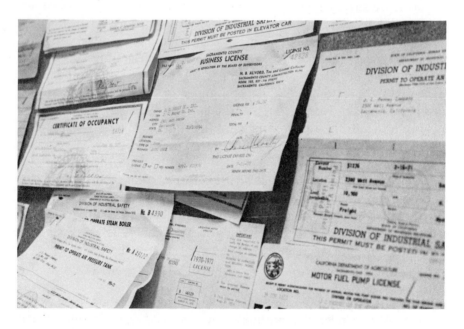

Courtesy of Penney News, J. C. Penney Company, Inc.

Illus. 18-1   Every community requires that stores obtain special licenses to sell certain merchandise, such as prescription medicines and optical goods. Certificates or permits to do business and to occupy the premises are also required. Some stores must have several dozen licenses which must be displayed prominently.

CHECKING YOUR KNOWLEDGE

Vocabulary

1. interstate commerce
2. intrastate commerce
3. monopoly

Review Questions

1. What are five reasons for increased government regulation?
2. Which government agencies are most responsible for regulating interstate commerce?
3. Name two federal laws enacted to combat monopolies.
4. What are the basic provisions of the Social Security Act?
5. List at least four local regulations that may affect a retail business.

Discussion Questions

1. Discuss the pros and cons of government regulation of business, particularly retailing.
2. Do you believe that there will be more or less regulation by government in the future? Why?
3. If the federal, state, and local governments each have a different regulation on the same matter, which agency's regulation should be followed by the retailer? Why?

Part b

Pricing and Selling Regulations

Government pricing and selling regulations have been created to promote competition by preventing monopoly and restraint of trade. Regulations on prices are an important part of this attempt to prevent unfair competition. Without laws the prices a business charges for its goods could be unfair either to competitors or to customers. Competitors are injured (1) when a seller charges prices at which he is really losing money, (2) when a seller's low prices are made possible by his having received unfair purchasing concessions from his suppliers, and (3) when a supplier's low prices are made available only to certain favored customers. Consumers are injured (1) when groups of sellers agree to sell at prices so high that the least efficient of them makes a profit and (2) when a merchant takes advantage of his customer's lack of mobility —that is, the inability to shop in another locality at a store whose prices are lower.

In recent years a great many federal and state laws have been passed which affect the pricing policies of retailers and suppliers of consumer goods. The major pricing laws of concern to the retailer are those dealing with resale price maintenance, unfair practices, price discrimination, and retail credit.

RESALE PRICE MAINTENANCE

Many manufacturers want to set the prices at which their merchandise is sold to the consumer. These manufacturers believe that to have the prices of their products vary by individual retailer may cause customers to question the quality of the product and the honesty of the company. *Fair-trade laws* permit manufacturers or distributors of trademarked or brand name goods to fix by contract with wholesalers and retailers the prices at which these goods will be resold. The setting of resale prices is called *price fixing,* and the article whose price is set by the manufacturer or distributor is called a *fair-traded item*. The only legal kind of price fixing is *vertical price fixing*—such as the setting of retail prices between manufacturer and retailer. *Horizontal price fixing*— the setting of prices among retailers—is prohibited. Setting uniform discounts, markups, and delivery charges is also illegal.

Fair-trade laws permitting resale price maintenance are enacted by the individual states. At the height of fair-trade popularity 45 of the then 48 states had such laws. Enforcement of the laws is not done by governmental agencies. If a manufacturer believes that his agreement with a retailer has been violated, he must take legal action himself and bear all the expenses involved. As cases have been brought before the courts many fair-trade laws, or some provisions of the law, have been held to be unconstitutional. As a result many states have abandoned, partially or wholly, their fair-trade laws.

UNFAIR-PRACTICES LAWS

A majority of states have *unfair-practices laws*. These laws prohibit dealers from selling merchandise below cost and are designed specifically to prevent the use of loss leaders.

The principal provision in unfair-practices laws is that it is illegal for any person to sell an article below the cost he incurs (cost of the article plus, perhaps, the costs involved in procuring it) or to give away any article with the intent of eliminating competition. However, items may be sold below cost if they are closeouts of a product line or of seasonal goods, if they are sold upon court order, or if they are damaged or perishable goods. Cost of the item to the retailer is generally measured by the invoice price or by the replacement cost of the article, whichever is lower. Some states have set a certain percentage above invoice price to arrive at the minimum resale price.

PRICE DISCRIMINATION

Price discrimination laws attempt to keep sellers, particularly manufacturers, from giving some buyers an unfair price advantage. The laws provide that any difference in prices to buyers must be justified on a quantity or method-of-sale basis. This means that the manufacturer may pass on to his customer any saving in his manufacturing, selling, or delivery costs, but that he may not charge a smaller proportion of his overhead to the big buyer than he does to the small one. These laws give some protection to small retailers who may have been paying a great deal more than a favored competitor.

The Clayton Act made a start toward preventing price discrimination; but its amendment, the Robinson-Patman Act, is the federal law primarily responsible for prohibiting price discrimination. Some states have similar laws of their own. This Act outlaws price discrimination on goods of like grade and quantity, but it does provide that there are certain justifications for differences in prices quoted to different buyers for the same kind of merchandise. A price difference is justified

1. If it does not exceed the saving in manufacturing, selling, and delivery costs resulting from different selling or delivery methods or from the sale and delivery of different quantities of merchandise
2. If it is due to changes in the salability of the goods, such as the offering of a lower price on fashion goods that are going out of style
3. If it is the result of an offer made in good faith by the seller to meet competition

A price difference that does not come under one of these justifications is not allowed. It should be noted that the Robinson-Patman Act does permit *functional discounts* (discounts at different levels of distribution). Thus, a wholesaler may be charged less than a retailer (even though the quantity bought by each is the same) on the theory that since the wholesaler will perform a special marketing function (resale to the retailer), he is entitled to a discount not given to the retailer.

Besides outlawing discriminatory prices, the Robinson-Patman Act also prohibits certain practices that may indirectly constitute price discrimination. Thus, the Act provides that

1. An employee of a buyer may not call himself a broker and thus receive from the manufacturer a brokerage fee not available to other buyers.

2. A manufacturer may not pay a store for special services, such as displaying or advertising, unless he makes payments to all buyers on proportionally equal terms.

3. A manufacturer may not provide the retailer with any special services, such as demonstrators or dealer helps, unless these services are made available to all buyers on proportionally equal terms.

The Robinson-Patman Act is enforced by the Federal Trade Commission. When the FTC finds that a business is violating a law, it can issue a *cease and desist order,* which instructs the business to stop the practice prohibited by law.

Commercial bribery is a subtle form of price discrimination. The common law recognizes bribery as unfair by holding that a store is not bound to a contract if its buyer or agent accepts a bribe for signing the contract. Many states also make it a misdemeanor for a seller to give or to offer a commission or a gift with the intent of influencing the action of any agent or employee of the buyer. The agent, too, who accepts a bribe is subject to criminal action by his employer. Bribery may take the form of a cash payment or a gift or appear as a commission to the store buyer for promoting the resale of the seller's product.

UNIT PRICING

The laws in a number of states and in New York City require that packaged goods, especially food products, be priced not only with the package price, but also with the price for an ounce, pound, or other appropriate unit of measure. For example, an 8-ounce container of instant coffee marked at 96 cents would also have to be priced at 12 cents an ounce. The reason is to make it easy for the customer to compare prices of different brands and different sized packages. This practice does help value-conscious customers who have little brand preference. But it is of little interest to customers who insist on particular brands. For fresh meats, not usually bought by brand, unit pricing has long been practiced and is helpful. Its wider application, however, adds considerably to the costs, particularly of the small merchant, who does not have access to appropriate calculating equipment to do the figuring.

RETAIL CREDIT REGULATIONS

One of the major retail store chains has about 15 million active charge accounts. Most other large retail firms also have their own credit operations. In addition, bank-based retail credit accounts have grown to where they service well over a million of the two million retail outlets in the United States. This rapid expansion of credit buying by consumers has often led to abuses involving extremely high service charges and severe penalties to customers who did not fully understand their obligations.

The Truth-in-Lending Act, or as it is officially known, the Consumer Credit Protection Act, became effective July 1, 1969. The stated purpose of this legislation is "to assure a meaningful disclosure of credit terms so that the consumer will be able to compare more readily the various credit terms available to him and to avoid the uninformed use of credit." Every retailer who makes a sale and does not collect the full amount of the sale in cash is extending a loan to the buyer of those goods. The objective of the Truth-in-Lending Act is to put consumer credit on a more competitive basis.

The Truth-in-Lending Act is a *disclosure law*. It does not set any minimum or maximum interest rates, nor does it require drastic changes in a retailer's operating policies. It merely requires that all disclosures on credit and credit charges be made in writing, typed or printed; be clear and conspicuous; and be in standard terminology. The most important disclosures to customers buying on credit are (1) the finance charge and (2) the annual percentage rate. These two figures (finance charge and annual percentage rate) must be shown on credit applications and on the periodic statements sent to credit customers by the store. The annual percentage rate is the credit charge expressed on an annual basis divided by the average amount owed by the customer.

ADVERTISING AND SELLING PRACTICES

The Federal Trade Commission Act and related legislation gives the FTC authority not only to protect competitors against unfair competition, but also to protect consumers against false and misleading advertising and selling practices. Some of these regulations have already been discussed in Chapter 10, Part D, and in Chapter 13, Part E; you should reread these parts.

One advertising practice particularly frowned on by the FTC, and also by Better Business Bureaus all over the country, is to make use of misleading comparative prices. For example, the advertisement, "Special $9.95—Elsewhere $15," is permissible only if the item is actually selling in other stores in the area in substantial volume at $15 or more. To say "Special $9.95—Manufacturer's List Price $15" is permissible only if stores in the area that do not engage in discounting are actually charging $15 or more for the product.

To say "Special $9.95—Regularly $15" is permissible only if $15 was the price at which the product was offered to the public just before the price reduction.

CHECKING YOUR KNOWLEDGE

Vocabulary

1. fair-trade laws
2. price fixing
3. fair-traded item
4. vertical price fixing
5. horizontal price fixing

6. unfair-practices law
7. price discrimination laws
8. functional discounts
9. cease and desist order
10. disclosure law

Review Questions

1. How are competitors injured when a businessman charges unjustly low prices for his merchandise? How are consumers injured by unjustly high prices?
2. Why do some manufacturers want to control the prices at which their products are sold?
3. Under what conditions may merchandise be sold below cost in a state having unfair-practices laws?
4. What are the legal justifications for quoting different prices on the same merchandise to different buyers?
5. What two disclosures must a retailer make to a customer buying on credit?

Discussion Questions

1. If a retailer operates stores in several locations should he be required to carry the same price on the same article in each of the stores? Why?
2. Do you think it is proper for a manufacturer to give to certain retailers who buy from him pairs of 50-yard line professional football season tickets? Should the retailers accept them?
3. Is it proper to think of retail credit costs as part of the price that consumers pay for merchandise? Why?

Part C

Merchandise Regulations

Almost all government legislation enacted to regulate the processing, packaging, and labeling of merchandise is designed to protect the consumer. In our country's history there are many stories about unscrupulous manufacturers and retailers who knowingly processed and sold inferior or even harmful merchandise or merchandise which was falsely represented. Perhaps the best example of unethical distribution of merchandise was the manufacture and sale of patent medicines. Such medicines, in spite of the enthusiastic claims of their sellers, almost invariably turned out to be overpriced and of no medicinal value.

As you have learned, consumers eventually became tired of being taken in by sellers of such products, and they pressed for government regulation of merchandise—its processing, its packaging, and its labeling. Although the manufacturer is most concerned with merchandise regulations, the retailer should also be familiar with them. No ethical retailer should stock or sell goods that fail to comply with government standards and regulations.

FOOD AND DRUG LEGISLATION

More laws have been passed regulating the processing and sale of foods and drugs than have been passed in any other merchandise area. The most important of these laws is the federal Food, Drug, and Cosmetic Act. It was passed in 1938 to replace the weaker federal Food and Drug Act of 1906. The 1938 Act, striving to promote honesty and fair dealing in the consumer's interest, set up minimum standards for manufacture and required accurate and detailed labeling of products. The three principal purposes of this Act are:

1. To prohibit the manufacture, sale, and transportation of adulterated or misbranded food, drugs, cosmetics, and therapeutic (medical) devices
2. To regulate the processing of foods to prevent contamination
3. To regulate the manufacture of new drugs so that no drug injurious to human health or inadequately tested is put on the market

The Act sets forth detailed descriptions of what constitutes adulteration and misbranding. A product which is not pure is said to be *adulterated*. For example, food may be considered to be adulterated if it contains any elements which are injurious to human health. A drug is adulterated if any substance has been packed with it which reduces the drug's strength or quality. A cosmetic is adulterated if it contains any color additives not allowed by law.

Any product which is not properly packaged or labeled is said to be *misbranded*. For example, under federal law a food is misbranded if it is an imitation of another food and is not so labeled. A drug is misbranded if the printing on its label is not conspicuous and readable. A cosmetic is misbranded if its container is so made, formed, or filled as to be misleading.

The Food, Drug, and Cosmetic Act is administered by the Food and Drug Administration. This agency carefully and regularly inspects food and drug processing establishments to make certain they are complying with the law.

REGULATIONS ON NONFOOD ITEMS

There are many important federal and state government regulations on merchandise other than food and drugs. For example, some states regulate the sale of bedding, allowing only the use of new materials and inspecting returned goods carefully before they can be resold. The Flammable Fabrics Act prohibits the sale in interstate commerce of clothing materials that are fire hazards. The federal Hazardous Substance Act of 1960 regulates the contents and labeling of household supplies, such as cleaners, which may be harmful to humans or animals.

PACKAGING AND LABELING REGULATIONS

Packaging is a function not normally performed by retailers, but all retailers who sell under private labels or who design their own packages and set packaging specifications must make sure they comply with government regulations. Most packaging regulations are included in food and drug legislation. For example, the food and drug laws require that the container used to hold a product must not be made of any substance which could contaminate the contents. Also, no substances may be added to a product in packaging to make it appear that the customer is getting more for his money.

The Fair Packaging and Labeling Act, usually referred to as the Truth-in-Packaging Act, is an important piece of legislation. It has five general provisions:

1. Containers must be labeled so that shoppers can easily see the weight or volume of the contents.
2. Meaningless or misleading designations such as "jumbo pound" or "giant half quart" cannot be used.
3. When a package promises to give a certain number of servings, it must state the weight per serving.
4. A certain ratio of air space between the top of the box and its contents must be maintained.
5. The use of "cents off" labels that indicate an item is being sold at a bargain price are regulated but not prohibited.

A reduction in the number of different sizes of packages is also recommended but not required.

Retailers have long recognized the importance of complete and accurate labeling of the products they handle. Some of the value of proper labeling is to assist the retailer in his management of the goods. A large part of the value of labeling is to inform the consumer about the product and to encourage its use. The first national attempt to regulate the labeling of merchandise was made in the Food, Drug, and Cosmetic Act. The federal Wool Products Labeling Act was a strong attempt to secure accurate merchandise labeling. This Act required that a label on woolen merchandise indicate the percentage of the wool, its condition (new, processed, or reclaimed), the percentage of any other nonwool materials in the cloth, and the name of the manufacturer. Subsequent legislation such as the Fur Labeling Act of 1951, the Textile Fiber Products Identification Act of 1958, and the Hazardous Substance Act of 1960 added several labeling requirements that affected retailers and suppliers.

Since the passage of the Fair Packaging and Labeling Act the Federal Trade Commission has made many important interpretations and issued numerous advisory guides and Trade Practice Rules relative to consumer goods labeling. Most of the labeling regulations center on such matters as source of goods, composition of goods, quality or nutrition of goods, construction of goods, quantity of goods (weight, length, coverage, or other dimension), and proper use and care of the product. For many consumer products the label must be permanently attached. This is particularly true of goods that require care and use information for consumer safety and satisfaction.

New FTC regulations suggest and may require that certain packaged foods labels must reveal the number of calories, and the amount of protein, fats, and carbohydrates of each serving. The previous listing of ingredients by quantity and vitamin content is still required.

In some localities, as an added protection for the consumer, perishable packaged goods, such as milk, certain other dairy products, breadstuffs, and fresh meats, must be labeled with the date the package must be removed from sale as fresh or the date it was processed.

CONSUMER PRODUCT SAFETY ACT

The Consumer Product Safety Act was passed by Congress in 1972 because it was believed that too many consumer products presented unreasonable risks of injury. Risks associated with products often could not be anticipated by consumers, nor could consumers protect themselves adequately against them. The definition of a consumer product under this Act is very broad and covers almost every product sold by retailers other than exempt products covered under other federal regulations, such as tobacco or automobiles.

Under this Act a Consumer Product Safety Commission has been set up to protect the public against unsafe goods. Regulations and standards —of performance, composition, contents, design, construction, finish, packaging, and labeling—are used to prevent or reduce "unreasonable risk of injury." If standards will not protect the public from danger, the Commission may ban the product. Retailers, distributors, or manufacturers who detect a product hazard are obligated to immediately inform the Consumer Safety Commission. Regulatory functions previously handled by other federal agencies—such matters as hazardous substances, poison prevention, toy safety, and flammable fabrics—are included in the responsibilities of the Consumer Product Safety Commission.

MAINTENANCE OF STANDARDS

All government regulation of the processing, packaging, labeling, and safety of goods is dependent upon standards. Standards of quality must be set up against which merchandise items can be measured. The government agencies responsible for setting up standards and seeing that they are met are the National Bureau of Standards, the Department of Agriculture, and the Food and Drug Administration.

The Bureau of Standards makes tests, establishes standards, and controls weights and measures. Any manufacturer who wishes to produce a certain product can get the necessary information on standards from this organization.

The Department of Agriculture conducts all inspections of meat, butter, and eggs sold in interstate commerce. States must conduct inspections of meat which is locally produced and must maintain federal standards. The Department of Agriculture also sets up standards and makes sure that other foods are graded and inspected to insure their wholesomeness and quality. Four grades have been established: Grade A, Grade B, Grade C, and Off Grade. Products designated as Off Grade are wholesome foods but do not meet the standards of the other grades in certain respects. Standards have not been established for all foods, but more and more foods are being covered by standards all the time.

CHECKING YOUR KNOWLEDGE

Vocabulary

1. adulterated
2. misbranded

Review Questions

1. What are the three principal purposes of the federal Food, Drug, and Cosmetic Act?
2. What are the five general provisions of the Truth-in-Packaging Act?
3. List the types of merchandise information that may be required under the labeling regulations.
4. What is the purpose of the Consumer Product Safety Act?
5. Name the three government agencies that are responsible for setting merchandise standards.

Discussion Questions

1. In what ways has government regulation of merchandise processing, packaging, and labeling affected the economy? the individual consumer?
2. Should any special restrictions be placed on a manufacturer that frequently produces a product that is unsafe for the consumer to use? Why?
3. Is it important for an American consumer to know that a product is made or assembled in a foreign country?
4. How much attention do you believe people pay to the great quantity of information that must by law appear on so many packages and other containers? Does the value of this information for the consumer justify the cost of providing it?

Part d

Labor Regulations

A rapidly expanding labor force working in an increasingly complex society has been a concern of the government. The well-being of workers has prompted the creation of regulations designed to protect the welfare of employees. The conditions of earning a living, even in a progressive retail business, represent a concern for workers, management, and government. From the employee's point of view, the chief reasons for government labor regulations are:

1. Pleasant, safe, and clean working conditions
2. Increased leisure time
3. Regularity of employment free from the extremes of seasonal changes or economic fluctuations
4. A minimum wage that provides an acceptable standard of living
5. Equal pay for the performance of equal work

6. Consideration of employers for employees
7. Security in case of illness and in old age

The principal labor regulations deal with employee welfare and with labor union and management relationships.

REGULATIONS FOR EMPLOYEE WELFARE

In general, federal and state labor regulations are designed to protect the welfare of employees. The principal regulations for employee welfare concern wages and hours of work, social security benefits, workmen's compensation, and working conditions.

Wage and Hour Laws

Some states have set minimum wages and maximum working hours, particularly for minors. There are also some federal laws which establish minimum wages and maximum hours. When state and federal laws cover the same subject, the more stringent law takes precedence.

The Fair Labor Standards Act, passed in 1938, set a minimum wage of 25 cents an hour, a 44-hour maximum work week, and provided for time and a half pay for overtime work. This law has been amended a number of times since its passage; but while the hourly wage and the length of the work week have changed, it remains the basic law regulating wages and hours. It is often called the Wage and Hour Act.

All employees in this country are not covered by the provisions of this law. Retailing personnel are covered only if they work for stores whose sales volume exceeds a certain amount set by law. Persons who hold certain jobs in retailing, such as executives, are not covered.

The Equal Employment Opportunities Act, passed in 1963, is another important law regulating wages. It applies to employers who are subject to the Fair Labor Standards Act and requires that employers pay the same wages to employees of both sexes, if these employees are performing jobs requiring equal skill and responsibility and if the jobs are performed under the same working conditions. The extension of equal pay provisions was made to professional, executive, and administrative employees under the Education Act of 1972.

Social Security Benefits

The Social Security Act, passed by Congress in 1935 and amended many times since then, has three important programs: (1) Old-Age, Survivors, and Disability Insurance, (2) health insurance, and (3) unemployment insurance.

Old-Age, Survivors, and Disability Insurance (OASDI). Almost every employee in this country is covered by OASDI. This program provides pensions to retired employees, death benefits to survivors of employees, and benefits to disabled employees. The money to provide these benefits comes from taxes paid by the employee and his employer. The employee pays a certain amount of tax prescribed by law while he is working, and the employer pays an equal amount.

Our social security laws also provide old-age benefits to self-employed persons. Benefits are paid to the self-employed retailer, as for all others, based on the amount of money he has contributed to his social security account.

Health Insurance. The Social Security Act has been amended to provide health insurance for people 65 and older. This program is called *Medicare*. Hospital insurance provided under this program covers certain expenses of a worker who is hospitalized. Medical insurance is also offered under this health insurance program. Persons pay a small monthly charge for the medical insurance, and the federal government pays an equal amount.

Unemployment Insurance. The federal Social Security Act provides for federal grants to the states to aid in the administration of unemployment compensation systems. All states have set up their own unemployment insurance plans, which have been accepted by the federal Social Security Board. Weekly benefits are paid to each qualified individual who is totally or partially unemployed. The employer of four or more persons (except employers of exempted classes) is required to pay a state and a federal tax on his payrolls.

Workmen's Compensation

All states provide for the compensation of injured employees in case of occupational accidents. State laws do differ, however, so each employer should be familiar with the laws of his particular state. Some types of workers are not covered by workmen's compensation legislation, but almost all business employees are covered. The employee has the right to compensation even if the employer has not been negligent.

Working Conditions

States commonly regulate the working conditions of businesses so that employees can work in a safe and pleasant environment. For example, state laws usually require that store premises be kept sanitary and well ventilated, that an adequate supply of pure drinking water be available, and that adequate rest room facilities be provided. Many states also have regulations to insure employees' safety on their jobs.

The inadequacy of some state regulations and weak enforcement prompted the federal government to pass legislation on working conditions. The Occupational Safety and Health Act (OSHA), passed by Congress in 1970, requires that an employer furnish his employees a place of employment free from recognized hazards that might cause serious injury or death. The employer is obligated to inspect his place of business and to make sure that it meets federal standards.

LABOR UNION-MANAGEMENT LEGISLATION

As you learned in an earlier chapter, many retailers do not have as much contact with labor unions as do employers in other areas of business and industry. Some retail employees are members of unions, however; and retailers—particularly large-scale retailers—should be familiar with the regulations governing what unions and management legally can and cannot do in their relationships.

There are three laws of major importance in regulating the union-management relationship. These laws are the Wagner Act, the Taft-Hartley Act, and the Landrum-Griffin Act.

The Wagner Act is the basic labor law. It provides workers with the right to organize unions and assures the right of these unions to bargain collectively with employers. It also sets down certain *unfair labor practices* in which management cannot engage.

The Taft-Hartley Act supplements the Wagner Act and adds certain *unfair union practices* to the unfair labor practices of the Wagner Act. An example of an unfair union practice is the refusal to enter into collective bargaining with an employer. An outgrowth of this Act is the passage by many states of *right-to-work laws*. These laws specify that a person does not have to join a union to get and keep a job.

The Landrum-Griffin Act is perhaps of more concern to unions and union members than to management. This law provides new protection for members of unions and places more restrictions on union activities.

CHECKING YOUR KNOWLEDGE

Vocabulary

1. Medicare
2. unfair labor practice

3. unfair union practice
4. right-to-work laws

1. List six reasons for government regulations for the protection of workers.
2. Which federal law regulates wages and hours of employees? Are all workers covered by its provisions?
3. Describe briefly the provisions of the OASDI, health insurance, and unemployment insurance provisions in the Social Security Act.
4. Who sets up and administers unemployment insurance plans?
5. Name the three most important laws in the regulation of the union-management relationship.

1. Discuss the advantages and disadvantages of minimum wage laws.
2. Is it better for a person to provide for his old age by voluntary saving or for the government to force both him and his employer to contribute to an old-age pension fund?
3. Would excessive noise or temperature fluctuations be a hazard to a worker? How could these be controlled by a retailer?

Part e

Taxation

Every person going into business for himself finds that he is subject to a variety of federal, state, and local taxes. The individual should have a clear and complete idea of his tax liabilities in advance. He should plan for taxes liberally in estimating his expenses; otherwise, he is likely to find that he is losing money.

Some taxes are levied for purposes of regulation. For example, a special tax is placed on chain stores in some states to equalize competition between these large-volume stores and small retailers. Most taxes, however, are levied to collect revenue. The revenue collected from these taxes is used to run government agencies and provide many benefits, such as highways, to citizens.

TAX POLICIES

All taxes are levied according to one of two basic tax policies: proportional taxation and progressive taxation. With *proportional taxation,* the tax rate is the same regardless of the base on which it is levied. Real estate tax is an example of proportional taxation; the tax per thousand dollars of valuation is the same no matter how much real estate a person owns. The sales tax is another example. With *progressive taxation,* the tax rate increases as a person's income increases. A progressive tax is based upon the individual's ability to pay. The federal income tax is an example of progressive taxation. State and city income taxes are also examples of progressive taxation.

KINDS OF TAXES

The determination of tax payments and the interpretation of tax regulations are so complicated that merchants are wise to secure the help of a tax expert, either an accountant or a lawyer. Large businesses employ full-time tax experts whose sole job is to handle the computation and payment of taxes and the record keeping involved. Small businesses should engage the services of an outside accounting firm to help them with their tax problems. Regardless of who handles the company's tax affairs, it is necessary that detailed, accurate records be maintained.

A retailer pays a number of different kinds of taxes: income taxes, property taxes, sales taxes, payroll taxes, special taxes.

These taxes will be discussed briefly in the paragraphs that follow. Because tax laws and tax rates vary from state to state and even from city to city within a state, the retailer should contact the proper authorities to learn the tax laws for his state.

Income Tax

Businesses—like individuals—must pay a federal income tax based upon their profits. In a majority of states, the owners must pay a state income tax as well; and in recent years a number of cities have also established local income taxes. State and local tax rates are considerably lower than federal rates.

Owners of corporations are actually taxed twice. The corporation's profits are taxed; then the stockholders pay personal income taxes on dividends they receive. Persons owning partnerships and sole proprietorships are not taxed in this way. They pay no taxes on their business earnings, but rather pay personal income tax on the money they receive from the business.

Property Taxes

The real estate, tangible personal property, and intangible property owned by a businessperson are cover by property taxes. A *real property tax* is one levied on real estate, such as land and buildings. Local government units get most of their operating funds from real property taxes. A *personal property tax* often is levied on such items as furniture, merchandise, and equipment. An *intangible property tax* is levied on the stocks, cash, and securities a business has. Property taxes are stated in terms of mills or of dollars for each thousand dollars of valuation.

Review Questions

Sales Taxes

The sales tax is the largest single source of revenue for state governments. The *general sales tax* is paid by the consumer when she purchases almost any good or service at retail, and the retailer is responsible for collecting these sales taxes and remitting them to the government. Most states have a general sales tax, ranging from two to six percent of retail prices. Some items, such as food not consumed on the store's premises, may be exempt from the tax. There may also be a general city or county sales tax, usually one to two percent of retail prices.

There are, however, certain *selective sales taxes* which apply only to such items as liquor, cigarettes, and gasoline in all states.

The *excise tax* is similar to the sales tax. It is usually a federally imposed tax on manufacturers, wholesalers, or retailers. These persons pay the tax as a percentage of the value of certain items sold, such as jewelry and luggage. The amount that the manufacturer, wholesaler, or retailer pays is eventually passed on to the consumer.

Payroll Taxes

As you have learned, employers pay taxes to provide employee benefits under the provisions of OASDI and the unemployment insurance programs. In some states the employer purchases insurance to provide for workmen's compensation, but in other states he pays a tax—a certain percentage of his payroll—to the state to form a workmen's compensation fund from which payments can be made.

The employer is also responsible for withholding from his employees' wages the amounts they must pay toward federal, state, and local income taxes and social security benefits.

Special Taxes

Depending upon the city in which they are located, some businesses must pay an *occupational tax*. This is a tax paid for the privilege of occupying a certain location within the city. The *license tax* is similar to the occupational tax. As you have learned, certain businesses must obtain licenses before they can operate; and they must pay a tax when they obtain the license. There are certain other taxes which vary with a retailer's location.

RECORDS RETENTION

Every business has a variety of business records which must be kept for legal reasons. Some must be kept only a short period of time simply for purposes of immediate operations. Other records are required by law to be retained for a minimum time period for possible inspection by government agents. For example, information on employee wages and hours must be retained for three years to comply with the Fair Labor Standards Act. Payroll records which include wage payments and deductions for federal income tax and social security must be retained for at least four years after the tax becomes due or is paid. Some state and local regulations require that payroll records be kept longer than four years. State and federal income tax returns and the records which confirm the figures on the returns should be kept at least six years. Because of the importance of records the retailer should obtain legal help in establishing a schedule of record retention that will meet local, state, and federal requirements for his business. Records should also be protected to withstand any disaster that might strike the business.

CHECKING YOUR KNOWLEDGE

Vocabulary

1. proportional taxation
2. progressive taxation
3. real property tax
4. personal property tax
5. intangible property tax
6. general sales tax
7. selective sales tax
8. excise tax
9. occupational tax
10. license tax

Review Questions

1. What are the two reasons for levying taxes?
2. Give two examples of proportional taxation and two examples of progressive taxation.
3. How do owners of corporations pay income tax twice?
4. What is the largest source of revenue for state governments?
5. Name the payroll taxes that an employer must pay.

Discussion Questions

1. Do you think that a proportional tax policy or a progressive tax policy is fairer? Why?
2. What would happen if businesses paid no taxes?
3. Do you think businesses pay too many taxes? If so, which taxes should they be exempt from paying?
4. Would it be possible to use just the income tax for all consumer taxation? Why?

BUILDING YOUR SKILLS

Improving Communication Skills

Only one of the three principal parts of each irregular verb is given below. On a separate sheet of paper, copy the form below and insert the missing parts.

	Present	Past	Past Participle
1.	. . . .	. . . .	lain
2.	. . . .	laid	. . . .
3.	let	. . . .	. . . .
4.	. . . .	. . . .	left
5.	. . . .	sat	. . . .
6.	. . . .	raised	. . . .
7.	set	. . . .	. . . .
8.	rise	. . . .	. . . .
9.	. . . .	. . . .	gone
10.	see	. . . .	. . . .

Improving Arithmetic Skills

On a separate sheet of paper, write your answers to each of the tax computation problems given below.

1. If a store employee earns $117.00 and the social security deduction is 5.85%, how many dollars and cents should be withheld?
2. A city mercantile tax of 1¾% is based on the net sales volume of businesses. If a merchant sells $262,000 a year, what does he pay in mercantile tax?
3. Real estate taxes on a store's property are 4.15% of the assessed value. If the property is assessed for $700,000, what is the real estate tax?
4. In selling an item that retails for $29.95, a merchant must add a 3½% sales tax. How much should he ask the customer to pay?
5. If the accumulated records for a business average one pound per week, how many weeks will it take before 220 kilograms of records have been accumulated?

Improving Research Skills

1. Develop a list of the licenses and permits that might be required of the various retail businesses in your community. Describe each in terms of where and how it can be obtained and the cost involved. (This information can usually be obtained from the office of the city clerk.)
2. Determine which state and federal laws and regulations govern employment in retail firms in your area. List the wage regulations and the hours and conditions of work on two separate sheets. Explain any exceptions that are permitted either on wages or on hours and conditions of work.
3. Determine the causes of accidents to workers in your community. Use as your source newspaper reports or reports from the state agency in charge of workmen's compensation. Which type of

accidents are most frequent? What percentage of the accidents reported are from retail businesses?

Improving Decision-Making Skills

1. Marilyn Huber manages the Sand Hill Variety Store. The store carries an exceptionally broad stock, as it is the only variety store in the community. A salesman for Complete Wholesalers, Inc., has called on Marilyn several times trying to have her add a line of ceramic pottery. The salesman has said that no other store in the area carries the line, and it will be profitable for Marilyn to sell it. The salesman also has said that he will give Marilyn an extra 15% discount if her order is at least $1,900. What are some of the factors Marilyn should consider before dealing with Complete Wholesalers, Inc., or placing an order for pottery?

2. Irv Cottin manages the Southside Supermarket. He hires both young men and young women for general store work. The women work most often as checkout cashiers. The men are employed for the most part as stock clerks or on carryout work. Frequently, however, both women and men do the same type of work. Cottin pays beginning women $2.00 an hour and beginning men $2.20. A government representative has informed Cottin that he must pay his beginning female and male employees the same salary. Cottin maintains that they are not doing the same work; therefore, different salaries may be paid. Do you think the salary differential is just? What should the retailer do?

APPLYING YOUR KNOWLEDGE

Chapter Project

Your class should be divided into committees with each committee taking one of the following topics for study. Obtain as much additional information as possible on the topic and then present your findings to the class in a panel type presentation.

1. Retail pricing regulations
2. Merchandise labeling regulations
3. Occupational safety
4. Consumer credit regulations
5. Wage and hour regulations

Continuing Project

Prepare and add the following materials to your manual.

1. Determine, by checking local, state, and federal laws, what minimum wage you will have to pay employees of your business.
2. Make a list of the taxes which will affect your business.
3. Make a list of the permits or licenses that you will need to operate your business.

UNIT 6
Your Career in Retailing

Alert young men and women who enjoy dealing with consumers, have the ability to work with others, and who possess imagination and boldness can have successful careers in retailing. The care and study put into selecting a retail job and gaining successful employment may serve as a basis for career development and continued employability. Sound work habits and a commitment to continuous self-improvement are essential ingredients of success.

chapter 19

Planning a Career in Retailing

CHAPTER PREVIEW

a. There are many different career opportunities in retailing. The young person who wants to go into retailing should understand his own interests and abilities before going to sources of retail job information.

b. The personal data sheet summarizes significant information about a person's objectives and personal, educational, and occupational background.

c. Application letters must be carefully prepared. They are really sales letters, designed to sell an applicant's services to an employer.

d. Interviews are an important part of the job-seeking process. Applicants should be prepared for interviews, because the impression they make during an interview can determine whether they are hired.

e. To achieve success the individual must accept responsibility, be loyal to his employer, be resourceful, show initiative, and practice good human relations. Each person should develop a personal long-range plan.

Part a

Deciding on a Retail Career

In Chapter 1 it was pointed out that one of your freedoms as an American is your right to choose the type of work you want to do. As you have studied merchandising, you probably have noticed that the jobs vary considerably as do the abilities needed by the individuals who perform them. One of the great merits of retailing as a career is that there are jobs for individuals with almost any interest or talent. Also, retail jobs are found in communities of all sizes and in all parts of the country. This part will discuss the nature of potential retail careers, the importance of understanding yourself, and the sources of information about retail jobs.

NATURE OF RETAIL JOBS

When people talk about a *career* they usually mean a job or a sequence of jobs held over a period of time. A career in retailing may begin with a part-time job in which you perform routine tasks within a certain area of work. With experience or with additional training you may advance to jobs involving more responsibilities. To help describe various jobs or occupations in retailing, they will be divided into two broad classes of possible employment.

Nonexecutive Positions

The *nonexecutive positions* in retailing are those that do not involve supervising the work of other people. The greatest number and variety of jobs in retailing are in the nonexecutive category. The nonexecutive jobs are at two levels—the junior nonexecutive level and the senior nonexecutive level.

Junior Nonexecutive Level. The inexperienced employee frequently is assigned a job such as stock clerk, order filler, messenger, marker, driver's helper, or mail-order clerk. A beginning job offers the opportunity to become acquainted with the merchandise and the store system. A junior level job is a stepping-stone to selling and other senior positions.

Senior Nonexecutive Level. The salesperson is the typical senior nonexecutive worker. There are many others, of course, such as head of stock, receiving clerk, merchandise checker, and comparison shopper. There are senior nonexecutive jobs in all four divisions of a store—merchandising, publicity, management, and control. The person who prefers to sell merchandise rather than assume responsibility over others may develop a career as a professional salesperson at the senior nonexecutive level.

Extras. Both junior and senior nonexecutive jobs may sometimes be filled by *extras*—people who are employed for a few hours a day or a few days each week. Stores hire three classes of extra workers: (1) regular part-time workers who work during just a few busy hours each day or week; (2) occasional part-time workers who work during special sales or when full-time workers are absent because of illness or vacation; and (3) seasonal extras who work, often full time, during the Christmas, Easter, and other rush seasons. Employment as an extra provides an excellent opportunity for a beginner. There are usually more openings for extras than for regular full-time employees, and the best of the extras are frequently offered jobs as *regulars* when openings occur.

Executive Positions

Executive positions involve responsibility for the planning and direction of the work of others. With the expansion of shopping centers and the creation of large store units, opportunities for executive level employment continue to be good. Like nonexecutive positions, executive positions are divided into two levels—junior and senior.

Junior Executive Positions. The salesperson eager to become an executive usually aspires to become an assistant buyer, a section manager, or, in the case of a chain or a small store, an assistant store or department manager. Other junior executives include assistant managers of the various nonselling departments of the store. Not every salesperson who produces a large quota of sales is qualified to perform the work required in these jobs, however. As already pointed out, some persons are better suited to be professional salespeople.

Senior Executive Positions. The senior executives of a store are the buyers and managers for different selling departments, the heads of the nonselling departments, the managers of the store units of a chain, supervisors, and the heads of the firm.

In small stores it is not possible to draw a distinct line between the four classes of jobs described here. So few people are employed that every employee must to some extent perform all jobs. The owner, who is the main executive, may even sweep the floor, wrap packages, or substitute for the cashier. The chief duty of practically everyone in a small store is selling, and the progress of any employee will depend largely on how well he performs this duty.

UNDERSTANDING YOURSELF

Before deciding which job to pursue, you should make sure that you understand yourself. Your work should be a reflection of your interests, abilities, and values. Your career should be personally satisfying and socially useful. What interests do you have? What abilities do you have or can you develop? What values are important to you? What life-style do you want? Your career should complement what you want to be as a person and contribute to the life-style that you want to have.

Guidance counselors can provide considerable help in understanding yourself. "Interest tests" provide insight into your interests. The results of these tests, along with conversation with a counselor, often reveal interests you didn't know you had. Listing twenty things you like most to do and twenty things you like least to do may prove a helpful self-analysis. The retail job you select should involve several activities that you like.

Most people do certain things well. As with interests, there are ways of learning your abilities, strengths, and potentials. A few tests and a talk with a counselor often reveal potential ability in unknown areas. Many retail positions require an ability to get along well with many different people. There are other positions, however, where ability to perform physical tasks or detailed tasks are more important.

Values are beliefs held by individuals concerning what they consider good, important, or desirable. Each individual should attempt to analyze his or her own value structure. The person planning a career in retailing should try to learn the values of the firm and the people with whom he may become associated. The values of a potential employee and the values needed for a particular position may conflict.

Your interests, abilities, and values establish a base for what is called a life-style. *Life-style* includes the various dimensions of how an individual lives. As you develop life-style preferences, you should consider

Courtesy of Dayton Hudson Corporation

Illus. 19-1   Courtesy and the ability to understand telephone instructions are necessary for these employees who handle orders in this retail store sign shop.

your goals two, five, or ten years from now. What you want to be as a person and what life-style you wish to have should become major considerations in selecting a type of work.

SOURCES OF JOB INFORMATION

There are several sources of information for retail jobs. The prospective employee should contact several of these sources to learn the requirements and opportunities of available jobs. The advantages of each job possibility should be weighed carefully. Application should be made to those firms in which the job seeker has a sincere interest.

Friends and Acquaintances

When you are looking for employment you should tell your friends and acquaintances that you are interested in a particular kind of job. They may know or learn of an opening or suggest an employer who may be interested. Many retail firms urge their employees to recommend friends who are well qualified. If you let it be known that you are looking for a job, perhaps your friends can suggest your name to their personnel directors.

Classified Advertisements

The help wanted columns of newspapers and trade magazines regularly carry job openings in selling and nonselling areas. Advertisements may call for a letter of application but usually ask for a direct interview. Beginners can often locate positions in the help wanted columns of newspapers. Experienced workers may find what they are looking for in the classified columns of trade magazines or papers.

Employment Agencies

Retailing positions are often filled through private and public employment agencies. In every large city there are private agencies that, for a fee (sometimes paid by the employing company), place experienced store workers as well as beginners. Some agencies specialize in retail personnel, especially senior executive positions.

The best known public employment agency is the state employment service. Trained interviewers help individuals find the most appropriate types of employment and schedule them for interviews with firms that have reported job vacancies. This is a free service to job seekers.

School Placement Bureaus

For young people in school or recent graduates the placement bureaus of schools or colleges are perhaps better than employment agencies. Employers regularly list with school placement offices their needs for new personnel. Schools having Distributive Education or Cooperative Retailing Programs generally have a coordinator who is well acquainted with the retail employment needs of the community. A card of introduction from the coordinator to a retail employment manager will assure a prompt and cordial interview.

CHECKING YOUR KNOWLEDGE

Vocabulary

1. career
2. nonexecutive position
3. extra
4. regular
5. executive position
6. values
7. life style

Review Questions

1. What is one of the merits of retailing as a career?
2. Name two examples of nonexecutive positions. Which are jobs for beginners?

3. Why is it difficult to make distinctions among the four classes of jobs in small stores?
4. How can you find out what interests and abilities you may have?
5. List four sources of information for retail jobs and potential employment.

Discussion Questions

1. Under what circumstances is it possible for a person not previously employed to begin as a senior nonexecutive worker?
2. What can a person do to better assure that a job and potential career will be personally satisfying?
3. What are some of the more successful ways to obtain part-time retail employment?

Part

Preparing a Personal Data Sheet

A summary of important personal, educational, and occupational facts about a person is called a *personal data sheet*. Such a summary is also referred to as a *résumé* or a *vita sheet*. The personal data sheet is an important and useful document for the prospective retail worker. It is usually mailed to potential employers along with a letter of application. It may also be used when making personal contacts with potential employers. A personal data sheet provides a comprehensive summary of an individual's background and experience. Whether or not a person is hired for a particular job, the personal data sheet usually becomes a permanent part of a business file. When a job vacancy occurs, businesses many times check their files for possible candidates. Thus, a person who has a personal data sheet on file may be contacted and possibly hired.

INFORMATION FOR THE PERSONAL DATA SHEET

The information contained in a data sheet can be fairly detailed. There is no reason, however, for including unnecessary information in which an employer would not be interested. The information included in a data sheet concerns the applicant's career objective, education, experience, and personal details. Employers like to know the kind of job the applicant is seeking as well as the career objective. To recognize one's immediate readiness for a job and also to have a business goal are signs of maturity that are most appreciated by employers.

In giving information about education, the applicant should always start with the most recent schooling and work backward. It is usually

Courtesy of Dayton Hudson Corporation

Illus. 19-2 Ability, training, interest, and a little experience open the door of a retail store to the young man who wants to pursue a merchandising career.

unnecessary to go further back than high schools attended. Any diplomas or degrees earned should be mentioned. Applicants may wish to enumerate specific courses they have taken, especially if these courses would be helpful in the job in question. If the applicant earned high grades, this fact might also be mentioned. Most employers are also interested in extracurricular activities in which the applicant has participated, particularly if leadership duties were involved.

When giving information about work experience, the applicant should also start with the most recent job and work backward. A general rule of thumb is that if the applicant has held more than five different jobs, only the five most recent or the most important should be listed. Descriptions of work experiences should be as brief and concise as possible, but they must give the employer a picture of the responsibilities and activities of the applicant.

There is difference of opinion as to whether references should appear in the data sheet. If it is to be sent to a considerable number of potential employers, references should not be included. A statement that references will be provided on request is sufficient. To include references may result in a premature investigation of the applicant, of which the latter may have no knowledge. When a data sheet is sent or given to someone who has shown interest, however, the references may be included.

Three or four references are generally sufficient. Businesspeople prefer that these references be taken from different professions—that is, one person could give the employer information about your work in school, one could describe your work on the job, and another could give information about your character. No person's name should be used as a reference without permission. It is important that complete addresses and titles of references be given so that the employer can contact them easily.

A mistake frequently made in preparing personal data sheets is the inclusion of too much personal information. It is usually necessary to state only age, height, weight, and general health. If the applicant has hobbies or special interests relating to the job in question, this information should also be included.

APPEARANCE OF THE PERSONAL DATA SHEET

There is no standard form for setting up a data sheet. Almost any style is acceptable as long as it appears well balanced, uncrowded, and neat. However, the amount of information an applicant wishes to give will determine the style used.

It is preferable that a data sheet be one page long, since this makes it easier for the employer to handle it. However, it is better to use two pages for the résumé than to have a crowded appearance. There should be at least one inch of white space in the top, bottom, and side margins. The topics of education, experience, references, and personal details are generally set up as headings. They may be underlined or typed in all capital letters to set them apart from other material. The résumé may be single spaced, with double or triple spacing between topics.

The sheet should be titled *Personal Data Sheet,* and the title should be centered at the top of the page. Beneath the title the applicant's name, address, and telephone number are centered. Most persons prefer to use short statements rather than complete sentences in composing their résumés. Complete sentences may be used if space permits, but one should be consistent in using either complete sentences or brief statements.

PERSONAL DATA SHEET
William C. Schroeder
223 Meadowlark Drive
St. Charles, Missouri 63301
(314/671-8242)

OBJECTIVE

Copywriter leading to assistant advertising manager for a
growing store that handles menswear and other general merchandise. Goal: A career as sales promotion or marketing
director either in a retail store or with a manufacturer.

EDUCATION

1972-74   McGill College. Received Associate of Applied
          Science degree, majoring in Advertising, June, 1974.

          Major Courses Studied:

                Principles of Marketing   Psychology
                Principles of Retailing   Advertising Layout
                                                and Design
                Principles of Advertising   Copywriting

          Activities:

                Advertising staff of campus paper--two years
                Tennis team--two years
                Debating team--two years

          Scholastic Record:

                Graduated in upper 20 percent of class while
                earning 60 percent of college expenses through
                cooperative work program.

1968-72   St. Charles High School, St. Charles, Missouri.
          Graduated June, 1972.

EXPERIENCE

July, 1974   Advertising copywriter and artist with Globe-
   to   Dispatch. Consult with advertising manager in
Present   selection of sales promotion ideas. Prepare
             advertising layouts. Write copy. Supervise
             two cooperative students.

1972-74   Advertising copywriter on staff of Globe-Dispatch.
(Part-time)

1970, 1971   Salesman in Overton's Men's Store, St. Charles,
(Summers)   Missouri. Assumed some managerial duties in
             addition to selling duties and learned almost
             every aspect of retail store operation.

PERSONAL

             Age, 22; height, 6 feet; weight, 160 pounds;
             health, excellent; hobbies: writing, painting,
             photography.

REFERENCES

             Will be provided upon request.

Illus. 19-3   Personal Data Sheet

Data sheets should be typed. Persons who are applying to a number of firms sometimes have their data sheets printed. Employers do not object to this practice, but it can be expensive for the beginning job seeker.

CHECKING YOUR KNOWLEDGE

Vocabulary

1. personal data sheet   **3.** vita sheet
2. résumé

Review Questions

1. What is the purpose of a personal data sheet?
2. What information is included in a personal data sheet?
3. What information about education should the applicant provide in a personal data sheet?
4. Who should be asked to serve as references?
5. Describe how you would set up a data sheet.

Discussion Questions

1. Should an individual include every work experience in the personal data sheet?
2. Some businesspeople think there is little point in checking references in a personal data sheet because the individual lists only those who will give a good reference. Do you think it is wise for the potential employer to contact references?
3. Review the personal data sheet in Illus. 19-3. Is any information unnecessary? Is significant information omitted?

Part C

Writing the Application Letter

An application letter is one of the most important letters a person writes, because the letter is presenting the individual to a prospective employer. The letter of application is really a sales letter; its object is to sell the applicant's services. Since it is a sales letter, it should include all the steps in a sale. Thus, it must first attract favorable attention through its physical appearance. The contents of the letter should be planned not only to gain favorable attention but also to develop interest in the applicant and to create a desire for his services. Finally, the letter should induce action on the part of the employer.

WHEN TO WRITE AN APPLICATION LETTER

Application letters are generally written in response to help wanted advertisements that specify a reply by letter only. However, application letters may also be written in certain other situations. When a person is interested in a position described in a *blind advertisement,* the individual should write an application letter. A blind advertisement is one that directs applicants' letters to a post office box number; it does not name the company placing the advertisement. Blind advertising is used so that a company may review an applicant's job ability before contacting him.

Application letters should also be written whenever the job applicant is applying for an out-of-town position. Sometimes, too, a prospective employer may ask for a letter of application even after the job seeker has been interviewed. This permits the employer to further judge the applicant's ability to express himself.

Courtesy of Penney News, J. C. Penney Company, Inc.

Illus. 19-4   Product knowledge and ability to express himself are the necessary qualities for the salesperson who is consulted by sports enthusiasts in the selection of equipment.

HOW TO WRITE AN APPLICATION LETTER

Whether or not an applicant gets the job can depend upon how well the application letter is written. If a potential employer receives a poorly written, unattractive letter, it is doubtful that he will ever contact the applicant for an interview. Thus, great care should be taken in preparing the application letter.

Gaining the Employer's Attention

The letter's physical appearance is important in gaining the prospective employer's attention. Most businesspeople prefer that letters be kept to one page in length. They must often read hundreds of letters written in response to an ad, and frequently they will not finish a long, boring letter. Keeping the letter to a one-page length is not as difficult as it sounds. Since most application letters are accompanied by a data sheet, a lengthy description of one's abilities is not necessary in the letter.

It is necessary that the letter be neatly prepared, preferably typed, and set up in an attractive manner on the page. Correct letter placement and punctuation should be used. The letter should always be an original, never a duplicated or a carbon copy.

An important way of gaining the employer's attention is to address the letter to a specific person in the firm rather than addressing it to "Gentlemen." It is possible to learn the name of the proper person by calling the firm in question or by contacting someone who works for the firm. Before writing the letter, it would also be wise to learn more about the firm's operations. Information can be obtained from annual reports, company house organs, or by questioning someone who works for the firm. Such information is helpful in deciding whether the job is really what the applicant wants, is helpful in writing the application letter, and is helpful in the interview.

Application letters are typically three or four paragraphs long. The first paragraph, like the letter's physical appearance, is designed to attract the employer's attention. Too many job applicants feel they must make their letters unique, and they try to be too clever. They may use anecdotes, questions, or breezy language in an effort to attract interest. Letters using such an approach are seldom successful; few businesspeople finish reading them. Most employers are more impressed with a straightforward letter that tells them what the applicant can do for the firm.

In the first paragraph the applicant should try to make a personal contact with the reader—that is, if he is answering a newspaper advertisement, he should say so. If he is applying at the suggestion of a person whom the reader knows, he should mention that person's name.

223 Meadowlark Drive
St. Charles, MO 63301
December 12, 1975

Mr. Lawrence C. Graves
Personnel Manager
Simpson's
6789 Lindbergh Boulevard
St. Louis, MO 63126

Dear Mr. Graves

Because of my educational background in advertising and my
work experience as a copywriter and as a salesman, I believe
that I qualify for the position of advertising copywriter
you described in Monday's Globe-Dispatch.

In 1974, I received an Associate of Applied Science degree,
majoring in Advertising, from McGill College. While in
college I received cooperative training as a copywriter on
the staff of the Globe-Dispatch and also worked on the advertising staff of the campus newspaper. For two summers,
while in high school, I was employed as a salesman in Overton's Men's Store and received practical training in almost
every aspect of a retail store operation. I am currently
employed as an advertising artist and copywriter with the
Globe-Dispatch.

Attached is a personal data sheet which gives detailed information on my qualifications for the position your advertisement
described. I think that you can better evaluate these qualifications if you can see samples of advertisements I have
prepared. I will be happy to show you my portfolio at a time
convenient to you.

May I have an interview to answer any questions you may have?
You may reach me by telephone at 242-7666 between 8:30 a.m.
and 5:00 p.m. or at 671-8242 after 5:30 p.m.

Sincerely yours

William C. Schroeder

William C. Schroeder

Enclosure

Illus. 19-5   Letter of Application

If he is not certain that a vacancy is available, he should describe the position in which he is interested. In the first paragraph—and in the whole letter, for that matter—the applicant should use the *you approach*. He should tell the employer what he can do for the firm.

Stimulating Interest and Creating Desire

The middle paragraphs of the application letter should stimulate the reader's interest and should create desire to know more about the applicant. In these paragraphs the applicant should tell how his abilities and experiences equip him for the job. Since the résumé will give rather detailed information about the applicant, he should single out only his most important qualifications for inclusion in the application letter. He should refer to the résumé, of course. No high-pressure tactics should be used in any portion of the letter. A natural, conversational writing style is most effective.

The next-to-closing paragraph may present the strongest selling point. Here the applicant may give references. A copy of a letter of recommendation may also be sent. If the applicant is confident that he can best show his talents by presenting samples, he should mention that he has samples of his artwork or advertising copy available and will be happy to show them.

Inducing Action

The action that most applicants want employers to take is to contact them for an interview. The last paragraph should be brief and should tactfully request that an interview be granted. Telephone numbers at which the applicant can be reached should be given.

CHECKING YOUR KNOWLEDGE

Vocabulary

1. blind advertisement   **2.** you approach

Review Questions

1. Under what circumstances might a person write a letter of application?
2. Describe several ways of gaining the employer's attention with an application letter.
3. What is a desirable length for an application letter? Why?
4. What should the middle paragraphs of an application letter attempt to do?
5. What action should application letters induce employers to take?

Discussion Questions

1. What sort of responses do you think a student would receive to a hand-written letter of application and a personal data sheet on a bright yellow paper?
2. A growing practice in job hunting is to prepare a number of copies of a personal data sheet and mail these to 30 or 40 possible employers. Would you recommend this method to a high school graduate seeking a career in retailing? Why?
3. Should a job seeker include in his letter or personal data sheet the telephone number of the firm where he may be presently working?
4. Should a personal data sheet ever be sent to a potential employer without a letter of application?

Part d

Going on an Employment Interview

Employers generally require a personal interview with prospective employees. From the employer's point of view, the purpose of the interview is to learn or confirm basic information about the applicant. During the interview the principles of personal salesmanship must be used if the applicant is to be successful. Personal appearance, posture, grammar, voice, and manner—all play an important part in getting the job. Preparation for a personal interview should be as careful as preparing to meet a customer.

THE INTERVIEW

The personal interview should be used as a test of selling skill. The failure to land a job should be analyzed just as the failure to make a sale is analyzed. This will enable the job seeker to eliminate the weak spots in his job-getting techniques. Since practice is the best way to improve an applicant's skill in the interview, many teachers of retailing and distributive education conduct a series of practice interviews with their students, as suggested in the project at the end of this chapter.

Preparation

First of all, the applicant should be careful about his appearance. Lack of personal cleanliness or carelessness in dress will kill all chances for employment of the applicant. The applicant should find out as much as possible about the prospective employer and his business. He should, by all means, know the employer's name and be able to pronounce it correctly. Finally, the applicant should be prepared to show how he can fit into the business.

Approach

When the time comes to be interviewed, the applicant should walk in with a businesslike manner. He should try to avoid signs of nervousness. He should remember that, after all, the employer is a human being who is interested in hiring ambitious and conscientious people, not in turning them away. The applicant should be neither too friendly nor too reserved. If courtesy and good manners are habitual, conduct will take care of itself.

Conduct of the Interview

Sometimes the interview is simply a casual conversation, but it is a conversation with a purpose. It must give the employer information he wants. Shown in Illus. 19-7 are typical questions the interviewer may ask an applicant. Every applicant should have a short, clear answer for each question.

Courtesy of Federated Department Stores, Inc.

Illus. 19-6   Good health, self-discipline, and stamina are the qualities of a model. Large department stores hold frequent fashion shows, and it is not unusual for a model to require five or six complete changes of outfits during a one-hour fashion show.

Questions You Should Be Prepared to Answer

What work have you done?

Did you use any special tools or equipment?

How much did you earn?

Have you done any volunteer work—work without pay—at church, school, or home?

Do you have any hobbies or special interests?

What education have you had?

What is your goal for the future?

Why do you want to work for us?

What kind of work do you want?

How much salary do you expect to earn?

Illus. 19-7   The employer is especially interested in the experience and training which qualify you for the job. So be prepared to answer questions such as those above.

In answering such questions or in giving a personal history, the applicant should speak clearly and to the point. Elaborate details should always be avoided and care should be taken not to air personal troubles. The applicant should realize that more important than the questions and answers themselves is the impression he makes.

An interview is not just a one-way flow of information. The applicant should feel free to ask questions of the employer.

When You Have an Interview

Whenever possible, acquaint yourself with the facts about the company beforehand.

Check your appearance. Be neat and clean.

Arrive for the interview a few minutes early.

Avoid having others along, since an employer is interested in the way you present yourself.

Look alert, watch your posture, and listen to what is being said and asked.

Respond politely, honestly, and naturally.

Be ready to ask questions about any aspects of the work that may not be clear to you.

Illus. 19-8   The above list contains basic tips for the person who is going to have a job interview.

Closing

The personal interview may end with the applicant's getting the position. In that case he should be sure that he knows where and when to report and, of course, he should thank the interviewer in a businesslike manner and leave promptly. On the other hand, the interviewer may close with a promise to "let you know." If this is the result, the applicant should leave promptly, in a pleasant manner, thanking the interviewer for his attention. Remember that very often jobs are not obtained on the first interview. A gracious leave-taking may eventually land the job. It is often a good policy not to wait for the employer to "let you know." The fact that the applicant is persistent and at the same time courteous and tactful is likely to make a good impression on an employer. Return visits by the applicant help to keep him in mind so that he may be the first one to be thought of when an appropriate job is open.

APPLICATION BLANK

Most employers and employment agencies require that applicants fill out an application blank. In some stores, a brief preliminary interview is held before the blank is filled out. This preliminary interview enables the employer to note the appearance and the physical characteristics of the applicant and to determine the kind of work sought. Well-qualified applicants are then asked to fill in the application blanks; the others are dismissed. A person may be interviewed on the same day on which he fills out an application blank or may be called back when there is need of someone with his qualifications.

Illus. 19-9 is a typical application blank. Notice that there are questions about education, experience, references, and personal information. Each question should be answered fully and in neat and legible handwriting. The interviewer later will form part of his impression of the applicant from the way the application blank has been filled out. Misstatements of any kind, whether regarding the applicant's age, education, health, or any other matter, are dangerous. Such falsehoods are generally discovered upon writing to references, and the applicant will probably be given no further consideration.

TESTS

Many stores supplement the employment interview with a test or a battery of tests. These tests are designed to determine the aptitudes and the proficiency of the applicants.

APPLICATION FOR EMPLOYMENT
WITH
SIMPSON'S

PERSONAL INFORMATION   DATE Dec. 12, 1975   SOCIAL SECURITY NUMBER 302-35-2601

NAME   Schroeder, William   Charles
        LAST   FIRST   MIDDLE

PRESENT ADDRESS   223 Meadowlark Drive,   St. Charles,   Missouri   63301
        STREET   CITY   STATE   ZIP CODE

PERMANENT ADDRESS   Same
        STREET   CITY   STATE   ZIP CODE

PHONE NO. 671-8242   OWN HOME   RENT X   BOARD

DATE OF BIRTH Oct.6, 1953 HEIGHT 6'   WEIGHT 160 lbs.   COLOR OF HAIR Brown   COLOR OF EYES Brown

IF RELATED TO ANYONE IN OUR EMPLOY, STATE NAME AND DEPARTMENT - - -   REFERRED BY - - -

EMPLOYMENT DESIRED

POSITION Advertising Copywriter   DATE YOU CAN START Jan. 2, 1976   SALARY DESIRED Standard rate for position

ARE YOU EMPLOYED NOW? Yes   IF SO, MAY WE INQUIRE OF YOUR PRESENT EMPLOYER? If necessary

EVER APPLIED TO THIS COMPANY BEFORE? No   WHERE   WHEN

EDUCATION	NAME AND LOCATION OF SCHOOL	YEARS ATTENDED	DATE GRADUATED	SUBJECTS STUDIED
HIGH SCHOOL	St. Charles High School St. Charles, Missouri	1968-72	1972	Distributive Education
COLLEGE	McGill College St. Charles, Missouri	1972-74	1974	Advertising
TRADE, BUSINESS OR CORRESPONDENCE SCHOOL				

FORMER EMPLOYERS   (LIST BELOW LAST FOUR EMPLOYERS, LAST ONE FIRST)

DATE MONTH AND YEAR	NAME AND ADDRESS OF EMPLOYER	POSITION	REASON FOR LEAVING
FROM July, 1974 TO Present	Globe-Dispatch 8415 Carpenter Ave. St. Charles, Mo.	Advertising Copywriter	
FROM 1970-71 TO (Summers)	Overton's Men's Store 723 Springer St. St. Charles, Mo.	Salesman	Went to College
FROM TO			

REFERENCES

NAME	ADDRESS	OCCUPATION
Mrs. Margaret Jacobs	St. Charles High School	Teacher
Mr. David Karl	Globe-Dispatch 8514 Carpenter Ave.,St.Charles	Editor
Mr. Edgar Overton	Overton's Men's Store 723 Springer St., St. Charles	Retailer

SIGNATURE OF APPLICANT *William C. Schroeder*

Illus. 19-9   An Application Blank

A satisfactory battery of tests to determine whether an applicant will make a good salesperson is still in the experimental stage. One reason for this is that the qualities needed for selling vary somewhat with the line of merchandise to be sold and with the policies of the store. For example, a person selling hosiery has to be quick, forceful, and positive, whereas a furniture salesman has to be deliberative and highly social. The tests help to indicate applicants who have little or no chance of succeeding, but they are not so effective in spotting those who may later prove to be outstanding.

In some stores no employment is final until the applicant has passed a physical examination. Stores try to avoid employing people who may be unable to endure the strain of standing long hours and of working indoors. Such care protects both the store and the employee.

CHECKING YOUR KNOWLEDGE

Review Questions

1. How would you go about preparing for a personal interview?
2. What are the elements of a good approach at the time of an interview?
3. List six questions an employer may ask during an interview.
4. What information is generally requested on an application blank?
5. What is the significance of tests as part of the interview process?

Discussion Questions

1. An important part of interviewing is knowing the proper clothes to wear to make the best impression. How do you think these persons should be dressed for an interview: (a) a girl applying for a job as a jewelry sales-woman in a downtown department store and (b) a boy applying for a job as a shoe salesman in a suburban store?
2. An accepted practice today is for a job applicant to write a follow-up letter to the prospective employer after an interview. What could be said in such a letter? Do you think it is a wise practice to write such a letter?

Part e

Moving Ahead in Retailing

Once he has obtained a retail position, the new employee is faced with the need to do his job satisfactorily. If he does his work well, is accepted by his co-workers, and is ambitious, he will soon be recognized as an outstanding employee. This good performance, along with a program of additional education, will prepare the way for advancement and increases in pay.

GUIDELINES TO ACHIEVE SUCCESS

For the young person eager to achieve success in retailing, several guidelines must be kept in mind. Many of these relate to the worker's relationships with superiors or co-workers. The new employee must learn to develop good work habits and to adjust to each work situation.

Accept Responsibility

Willingness to accept responsibilities and to fulfill them successfully is a measure of the value of an employee. It is an employee's duty, therefore—as well as a real opportunity—to accept all responsibilities given him. The person who constantly complains "that is not my job" is not in line for promotion and is probably marked for an early dismissal from the organization.

It is the duty of the ambitious person to be helpful to fellow employees with whom he comes in contact and especially to new employees who are assigned to the department or store. Older workers sometimes fail to give newcomers a fair chance to succeed. A willingness to help other employees, even those holding minor positions, will create goodwill among all concerned.

Be Loyal

Loyalty is something that the worker owes the firm that pays his salary. Sometimes questions arise regarding conflicting loyalties, when loyalty to one person results in apparent disloyalty to another. Such questions are especially likely to arise when an employee receives orders from two different persons over him in the organization. Just what constitutes proper conduct under such circumstances is difficult to decide. In general, however, the immediate superior should assume the responsibility for giving an order, and the employee who carries out his immediate superior's instructions should be considered in the right.

Be Resourceful

The employee should do every job assigned to him to the best of his ability. He should not ask the supervisor for detailed instruction at every step. In school, students are accustomed to having teachers plan work for them in detail; and they often expect store supervisors to do the same. The supervisor has many duties, and when he gives general instructions, he expects the employee to carry them out. Nothing exasperates a supervisor more than to be bothered again and again by a person to whom a job has been assigned.

Show Initiative

The retail employee should never hesitate to do a needed extra job. An ambitious salesperson, for example, might visit competing stores in his free time to compare their appearances, services, assortments, and values with those of his store. Frequently this will make him a better salesperson by giving him greater confidence in his own store or department. Moreover, he may acquire ideas that he can tactfully pass on to his supervisor.

In every store there are ways in which store methods and systems of operation can be improved. Store executives may have been too close to the operations to realize the need or may have been too busy to attend to it. Any employee who takes the trouble to study and report on possible improvements will usually find that his ideas receive sympathetic consideration. Some stores have a suggestion system. Store employees are urged to make suggestions, and monthly prizes are awarded for the best suggestions or for all that are put into operation.

Courtesy of Federated Department Stores, Inc.

Illus. 19-10   An ability to please and a sincere effort to help the customer are obvious in this young salesman. What other outstanding qualities do you see in this retail menswear employee?

HABITS TO AVOID

Certain personal habits can quickly lead to conflict among co-workers and concern among superiors. Persons building a career in retailing should be alert to these problem-creating habits and eliminate them from their own behavior pattern.

1. Tardiness and absence. Consistent tardiness or excessive absenteeism places a burden on co-workers and reflects poor character.

2. Disagreements. Differences of opinion do occur, but these should never be discussed in the presence of customers.

3. Sales grabbing. Eagerness to serve customers is commendable, but it should not be done at the expense of other salespeople.

4. Loafing. Failure to do one's share of the duties necessary in a department soon finds the offender receiving little cooperation from co-workers.

5. Dependence. Constantly asking co-workers to repeat information and to do favors are indicative of laziness and not appreciated in a busy retail operation.

DEVELOPING A PERSONAL PLAN

The person aspiring to success in retailing can do a great deal to make sure that progress toward the desired goal is as rapid and direct as possible. Once the first retail job is obtained the individual should identify the next stepping-stones that can be used to move ahead. The individual should carefully set forth a plan for the next year or two as well as develop a long-range career plan. Considering both immediate and long-range goals the aspiring retailer should determine which skills and abilities he will need and make arrangements to acquire them. With such a personal plan the immediate work in retailing becomes more exciting and a career more challenging.

IMPORTANCE OF CONTINUING EDUCATION

The predicted rate of change in society and business over the next forty years makes continuation of education essential for survival. It is a mistake to assume that major retail career opportunities await high school graduates who do not continue their education through periodical full-time or part-time study. A few highly talented high school graduates do succeed in retailing without higher education. However, most who lack additional education do not progress beyond minor executive positions. It is true that some experienced executives are not college trained. The same is not true, however, of young executives in large retail organizations. Today, a higher percentage of college-prepared people are in retailing than ever before. Chain stores, department stores, low-margin stores, and franchised businesses are competing for the best personnel that higher education can produce.

In order to forge ahead, then, an outstanding young retailer should plan for additional education and training. Besides subscribing to the various publications that will keep him abreast of his particular line in retailing, individual courses such as buying, management, salesmanship, marketing, merchandise information, store control, and computer operation are available to him in practically every large university. A detailed study of up-to-the-minute methods of various retailing operations can provide the difference between just getting along and becoming outstanding.

CHECKING YOUR KNOWLEDGE

Review Questions

1. List the four guidelines to achieve success.
2. How can a worker show initiative while working in a store?
3. What are five problem-creating habits to be avoided by the retail worker?
4. Why should you develop a personal long-range plan?
5. Why is it important to develop a continuing education plan?

Discussion Questions

1. Should an employee be so loyal to his firm that he will perform activities which he knows are wrong or illegal?
2. Besides those listed in Part E, what are some additional problems that should be avoided by retail workers?
3. What methods, other than those suggested in this part, would be helpful in achieving retailing success?

BUILDING YOUR SKILLS

Improving Communication Skills

Only one of the pronouns given in parentheses in each sentence below may be used to make the sentence correct. On a separate sheet of paper, write the number of the sentence and the pronoun you would use for each of the sentences.

1. Neither John nor (he, him) checked the sales figures.
2. Mr. Jones asked Hank and (I, me) for the reports.
3. Sue will work with (her, she) and (I, me).

4. (He, Him) and (they, them) are responsible for calling the sales meeting.
5. It must be (he, him), since the manager invited the entire department.
6. Was it (them, they) who purchased the new equipment?
7. The discussions are being held for (we, us) and (them, they).
8. It was (I, me) who prepared the display.
9. John asked (she, her) and (I, me) to act as representatives.
10. These products were designed for (we, us) merchants.

Improving Arithmetic Skills

Perform the review exercises given below.

1. A retailer paid $192 for one dozen pairs of shoes; markup is to be 40% of retail. Find (a) the selling price for each pair of shoes and (b) the total retail sales value of the shoes.
2. Compute the interest on $900 at 8% for 60 days using the 6% 60-day method.
3. If hardware sales of $1,176 represent 14% of a retailer's total monthly sales volume, what was the total volume for that month?
4. Compute the net amount of an invoice for $500 which was dated June 1 with terms of 2/10, n/30 and was paid (a) June 11, (b) June 18.
5. The Big Sound Stereo Shop uses 20% of its selling space for tapes and records. If the selling space measures 9 meters by 21 meters how many square feet is used for tapes and records?

Improving Research Skills

1. From an interview with the proprietor or manager of a local store, get enough information to prepare a report describing (a) the jobs available in the store, (b) where the store finds most of its job applicants, (c) the store's employee selection procedure.
2. There are numerous articles published in magazines on such topics as "How to Succeed." "How to Improve Yourself," or "Getting Ahead in Business." Locate and read two such articles and summarize the recommendations made by the authors of these articles.
3. Investigate the opportunities for continuing your retail and business education in your community. Develop two lists. Make one list of the opportunities to continue your education by full-time attendance in school. Develop another list of courses or programs that can be taken on a part-time basis. Determine the approximate cost of each opportunity.
4. Carry out the suggestion on page 597 to list twenty things you like to do and twenty things you don't like to do. In view of this research of your own interests, for which careers in retailing do you seem best fitted. Which should you avoid?

Improving Decision-Making Skills

1. Suppose that you are an employer interviewing an applicant for a job opening in your store. The applicant is a young person who is interested in retailing but who speaks poorly and is inaccurate in arithmetic. The appearance of the applicant is satisfactory, and you can

tell by his sincerity that he is of good character and is interested in retail work. What would you do?

2. You have been seeking employment in a retail store. Two stores offer you employment opportunities that are very attractive and almost equal in terms of salary, hours, and other factors important to you. One store is a local independent firm, and the other is a unit of a successful national chain organization. What other factors would you consider when making your choice between these two stores?

3. You are the supervisor of four workers in a nonselling department. One regularly comes to work in soiled clothing, with dirty fingernails, straggly and unkempt hair, often not shaved, and frequently with an offensive body odor. On three previous occasions you have mentioned the need for good grooming. Each time the employee has improved for a day or two but soon drops back to old habits. The problem is again obvious. Write a paragraph on what you would do to correct this problem.

APPLYING YOUR KNOWLEDGE

Chapter Project

1. The box below gives ten major qualities important for success in retailing. Study it; then supply the information requested.

    (a) List any of the ten qualities that you believe you now possess to a marked degree. Try to be very honest with yourself.

    (b) List the qualities that you think you have developed consistently during the past year.

    (c) List the qualities in which you are now weak, and in a paragraph describe a plan you intend to follow to develop and strengthen each weak quality.

Do You Have the Necessary Qualities for Success in Retailing?

1. Cooperation—ability to get along with others
2. Genuine interest in the buying problems of customers
3. A commercial interest in goods—that is, a desire to buy them, not for personal use, but for resale
4. Confidence in your own ability
5. Initiative and drive—ability to keep working industriously and without direction from others
6. Stability and emotional control
7. A sense of responsibility
8. Honesty and loyalty
9. Ability to comprehend and use figures
10. Language facility

2. With the aid of your classmates, dramatize several personal job interviews. Compose a checklist of what you will want to observe in the interviews: appearance, posture, voice, manners, and ability to answer questions. After several demonstrations have been given, select the student who would have been hired on the basis of the interview and explain why he would have been hired. You may wish to invite an employer or a personnel director to your class to demonstrate a typical job interview.

Continuing Project

Perform the following activities in your manual:

1. Make a list of the types of positions that would be available in your business.
2. Prepare an application blank that you would want prospective employees to fill out.
3. List the questions you would ask a job applicant during an interview.
4. Write a description of how you would determine promotions and salary increases for your employees.
5. Since you are now finishing this activity, assemble all the material you have prepared for your continuing project. Prepare a table of contents and a title page and enclose it in an attractive cover. Submit it to your teacher for review and evaluation.

Comparing
the Most Common
Measurement
Units

(Approximate Conversions)

	When you know the	You can find the	If you multiply by
LENGTH	inches	millimeters	25
	feet	centimeters	30
	yards	meters	0.9
	miles	kilometers	1.6
	millimeters	inches	0.04
	centimeters	inches	0.4
	meters	yards	1.1
	kilometers	miles	0.6
AREA	square inches	square centimeters	6.5
	square feet	square meters	0.09
	square yards	square meters	0.8
	square miles	square kilometers	2.6
	acres	square hectometers (hectares)	0.4
	square centimeters	square inches	0.16
	square meters	square yards	1.2
	square kilometers	square miles	0.4
	square hectometers (hectares)	acres	2.5
MASS	ounces	grams	28
	pounds	kilograms	0.45
	short tons	megagrams (metric tons)	0.9
	grams	ounces	0.035
	kilograms	pounds	2.2
	megagrams (metric tons)	short tons	1.1
LIQUID VOLUME	ounces	milliliters	30
	pints	liters	0.47
	quarts	liters	0.95
	gallons	liters	3.8
	milliliters	ounces	0.034
	liters	pints	2.1
	liters	quarts	1.06
	liters	gallons	0.26
TEMPERA-TURE	degrees Fahrenheit	degrees Celsius	5/9 (after substracting 32)
	degrees Celsius	degrees Fahrenheit	9/5 (then add 32)

Career Information Index

A